EUROPE'S WONDERFUL LITTLE HOTELS & INNS, 1992

Great Britain & Ireland

EUROPE'S WONDERFUL LITTLE HOTELS & INNS, 1992

Great Britain & Ireland

Edited by Hilary Rubinstein

Managing Editor: Caroline Raphael

Contributing Editor: John Edington

Published in London as part of
THE GOOD HOTEL GUIDE, 1992

St. Martin's Press • *New York*

Cover illustration by Garnet Henderson

Editorial assistants: Katinka Ardagh, Philippa Carlile, Susan Carlile, Mari Roberts

ISBN 0-312-06346-6

First U.S. Edition
10 9 8 7 6 5 4 3 2 1

Published in Great Britain as part of *The Good Hotel Guide, 1992,* by Macmillan London Ltd.

Contents

A note for new readers	vii
Introduction	ix
The César Awards 1992	xv
Special hotels	xviii
How to read the entries	xxii
England	1
Wales	209
Scotland	229
Channel Islands	277
Northern Ireland	283
Republic of Ireland	287
Alphabetical list of hotels	311
Maps	316
Hotel reports	327
Hotel report forms	

A note for new readers

This is an annual guide to hotels, guest houses and inns in the British Isles and Ireland that are of unusual character and quality. There's a companion guide to hotels on the Continent (including Turkey and Morocco). If you prefer the two books together, the one-volume work is available in the UK where it is published under the title *The Good Hotel Guide.*

The entries are based on reports from readers who write to us when they come across an establishment which has given them out-of-the-ordinary satisfaction, and who also send us their comments, critical or appreciative, when they visit places already included in the guide. Our task is to collate these reports, check and verify them, making inspections where necessary, and select those which we consider make the grade. No cash changes hands at any point: contributors are not rewarded for writing to us; hotels do not pay for their entries; the Editor and his staff accept no free hospitality.

We do not attempt to be comprehensive. There are many blank areas on our maps, including many major cities that lack a single entry. We see no point in lowering our standards in order to recommend an indifferent establishment as "the best available." But of course we are always particularly glad to receive nominations for hotels in a town or a region that is poorly represented. If you can help to plug our gaps, please do so.

Most of our entries are for small establishments in the hands of resident owners. We don't have any prima-facie objection to large hotels or those run by managers, except that, in our experience, they normally fail to provide the welcome and care for guests' comforts that can be found in the best of the small individually owned hostelries. And this failure is particularly evident in the case of hotels owned by a chain, which explains why there are few such entries in these pages.

The entries in this book cover a wide range. People want different things from a hotel according to whether they are making a single-night stop or spending a whole holiday in one place, whether they have young children with them, whether they are visiting a city or staying in the remote countryside, and according to their age and means. We make no claims of universal compatibility, but we hope that our descriptions will help you to find hotels that suit your tastes, needs and purse. If an entry has misled you, we beg you to use one of the report forms at the back of the book and tell us, in order that we can do better next time; and we hope that you will also write to us if you have found the guide useful and a hotel has fulfilled your expectations: endorsement and criticism are both essential if the guide is to achieve its purpose. A hotel is dropped unless we get a positive feedback.

We should emphasise that this is a thoroughly personal work. We started the guide fifteen years ago because we wanted a book that would really tell us what to expect when we make a reservation. Brochures are an aid, but are often deceptive. It's not the fault of the copywriters that most of their products sound alike: they mostly are alike. Travel agents can sometimes be helpful if they specialise in particular localities, but they often know at recent first-hand only a fraction of the hotels on their books, and may be tempted to push a hotel or a chain that offers them a higher commission. Thus many hotels in these pages would never be recommended by an agent as they don't offer commissions. *Michelin* is an invaluable touring companion, but all those conventional signs, useful though they are, can tell us almost nothing about the feel of a place. For many, the most reliable way to choose a hotel is by word-of-mouth recommendation. One way to describe this work is to say that it is the word of mouth in print.

The book's aim is to reflect the discriminating taste of its readers. From the first edition, we have depended on the generosity of those who write to us about the places where they stay. We could not function without this continuous blood transfusion. We are greatly in the debt of all who take the trouble to write; we appreciate even the briefest endorsement or comment; but it is of course the stylish, witty, perceptive reports that help to give the guide its special character. We are always grateful, too, for suggestions as to how to make the guide more useful.

Inevitably, the book is full of personal prejudices and preferences, including the Editor's. We loathe big anonymous hotels where we might as well be in Los Angeles or Lisbon as in London. We avoid, if we can, those boring establishments which lack any individuality in their decor or any warmth in their welcome. We care a lot about good food, but decry pretentiousness in cooking. We cherish the dedicated hotelier who, like a monk, has taken a solemn vow of hospitality.

Introduction

It has been the worst of times.

At the start of 1991, with the recession showing no sign of easing and with the Gulf War causing a virtual cessation of travel, the hotel industry was seriously haemorrhaging. Hotels that relied largely on business travellers and package tourism were hit worst of all, but any hotel with a heavy overdraft at a time when interest rates were so high was almost equally vulnerable. Everywhere hoteliers were confessing that they had never had it so bad.

Six months later, many patients are still looking sick. The rapid end of the war was expected to boost tourism again, but these hopes were frustrated by the deepening recession. Bad weather in the spring and early summer of 1991 has made matters worse. As we go to press, it is still the bleakest of seasons. Many hotels have lost their entry this year because there has been a change of ownership or because they have had to close their doors. Often it is the hotels owned by international corporations that are able to survive a downturn of trade; the small, personally run establishments – those at the heart of what this guide is about – find it harder to keep going when the barometer turns stormy.

What can hoteliers do when conditions are as adverse as they have been this past year? They can lay off staff, delay improvements, practise discreet economies of one sort or another hoping the customer won't notice. (A common piece of husbandry is to turn on the heating only when the weather gets really cold or when the traveller actually books in – "The room was icy when we arrived" is a perennial complaint.) They can covertly pile on a host of extra charges that won't show up till the customer settles the account (*Don't worry, sir. We'll put it on the bill* – page xi). They can endeavour to fill their rooms by organising special weekend or week-long events, but the number of those who want to spend their spare time tasting wine or learning hang-gliding is limited. And of course they can hope to attract more business by cutting their rates or being more flexible about one-night bookings at weekends.

In the early months of 1991, we heard a lot about the drastic discounting that was going on in the big cities. London offered the most dramatic special offers. Country hotels have been much more reluctant to change their tariffs, fearful that once they started offering bargains they would be stuck with them. The more a hotel seeks to simulate a staying-with-friends attitude the more uncomfortable they are at the notion of having to bargain with strangers over the phone, though loyal regulars might well be given some favours on the quiet. One owner of a country house hotel told us in confidence that, during the bleakest part of the 1990/91 winter, he had invited his most faithful regulars to a free weekend. He had no difficulty in filling all his rooms, but reckoned that the goodwill of the exercise was worth it, and he intends to repeat the invitation this year too.

One hotelier told us huffily: "We are not in the habit of negotiating room rates." Most though, when pressed, accepted with varying degrees of diffidence that their rates were open to discussion. One hotel manager said that a customer wanting to make a reservation would normally be quoted the rack rate, but that if he were to ask for better terms the desk clerk would have discretion to quote a lower price, perhaps the weekend-break rate even if it was a weekday or for one night when the break rate normally required a two-day stay. Another, to my surprise, said that he would ask the traveller what he was prepared to pay. The message was clear: you should not feel embarrassed to probe and bargain. You may get a frosty reception, however, if you push your luck too far.

Without exception, all the innkeepers I talked to told me that they automatically upgrade a customer's room at no extra cost if they have the accommodation available. They claim that this has always been their policy, but I doubt it. Upgrading is a cheap painless way to earn a traveller's gratitude, but in my experience only too often neglected. It's certainly worth asking hotels, when you make your reservation, to confirm that they will be game to upgrade you if they can.

Why, I wonder, don't hotels have a regular stand-by arrangement like the airlines or like theatres? If you are prepared to take the risk of there being no room at the inn, and turn up on the night and the hotel has vacancies, you would be able to claim the empty bed at the stand-by rate, perhaps half-price, with no need to haggle.

I've tried the idea out on a number of hoteliers. I was delighted to discover that one famous country house hotel, not in the UK but in *Åkerblads* in Tällberg, Sweden (q.v.), has been operating just such a scheme for years, charging virtually a half-price rate for last-minute bookings after 6 pm, and finding the discounting well worth their while. But some hoteliers I talked to seemed wary of inaugurating a policy that they might find hard to cancel when times are better. I think they are being short-sighted. Airlines don't have any compunction about withdrawing stand-by facilities when it suits them. Theatres only offer stand-by discounts when they know they are going to have empty seats. Stand-bys don't demean airlines or theatre managers; they aren't in any sense trading down. I hope hoteliers will think seriously about adopting such a policy – not just for 1991/2 but as part of their overall strategy for attracting more guests. It could be an obvious boon both to cash-hungry hotels and to the not-so-well-off traveller. And it could enfranchise many who at the moment find hotel prices beyond their means.

"Don't worry, sir. We'll put it on the bill"

Last year, we commented on the growing profusion of freebies being offered by some hotels – though of course the customer always pays in the end. This year, more correspondents than ever before have been telling us of their astonishment at the number of items that turn up on the account at the end of their stay. "We paid extra for *everything* – nothing was included in the price. Our nerves were jangled by the amazing prices," wrote one reader, herself the owner of a smart London hotel, who was horrified to find, after a visit to a luxury country house hotel, that the final charge was approximately four times the basic room rate. Another was delighted to be offered tea on arrival, especially as there were no tea-making facilities in the room, but less amused to find a charge of £6.50 (about $11) on the bill for what had in any case only been teabags in the pot. The same hotel charged £3.80 for a plate of vegetables to supplement their £30 main course, £3.60 for the freely offered Perrier, and a further £3.80 per head for coffee. At another luxury country house where the tariff is quoted for the room only, a charge of £9 per head had been levied for the continental breakfast. We also heard of 75p being put on the bill for filling a bedroom vacuum jug with cold water and of £1.50 being added for a bowl of cereal with the continental breakfast.

In the light of these eye-popping extortions, it seemed positively considerate of a hotel manager to tell a honeymoon couple who had booked a double room (£199, not including breakfast) and who were arriving at midnight, that he had taken the liberty of arranging for a bottle of champagne to be in their room and that the cost would be £29.50. Many hotels, we know, make a point of giving a bottle of champagne to honeymooners gratis – but, when it comes to this sort of generous gesture, or offering tea to guests turning up after a long journey, it often appears that the generosity of the establishment is in inverse proportion to the cost: more means meaner.

Hotels pile on these extras hoping the customer won't scrutinise the bill too closely on departure, or will be reluctant to make a fuss, or couldn't care less if the company is picking up the tab. It is of course true that the clientele of smart hotels – and most of these complaints refer to hotels at the top end of the market – rarely challenge the account whatever the charges. But in the long run it will surely put these places out of business, and the practice inevitably discredits the catering industry itself and rubs off unfairly on the many establishments who are striving to give better value for money in these difficult times rather than the reverse.

Recession may be only a temporary blip in the upward curve of western economies – it would be pleasant to think so – but we sense a growing resistance among our readers to the more swagger kind of hotel even if its cuisine is an out-of-this-world experience. The charade of obsequiousness, the parade of flunkeys, the multiplicity of freebies in the bedroom and toiletries in the bathroom, the rituals of wining and dining, all those *amuse-gueules* before and after the meal, the pushing of brand-named products which so often come in the wake of a rosette or two – this display of conspicuous extravagance is beginning to appear not just over the top (it's been that for a long time), but no longer quite decent in the age we live in. And the way the extras add up when the moment of reckoning comes is, for many, a final straw.

We'd be glad to have your comments on this issue, and if you come across flagrant instances of extortionate charges, do please tell us.

Little angels and little horrors

For the past two years, ever since we took issue with the many British hotels in the Guide – and the many more not included – that refused to accept families with young children, there has been much discussion of the topic not just in our correspondence but in countless articles and TV programmes. We are delighted that the matter is being so thoroughly aired, while being disturbed by the vehemence of the opposition. "You wax poetic about hotels which cater for children," writes one reader. "I say 'Bunk!' The world was not created as a gigantic playpen. Those of us whose children are now grown, and who have paid our dues, resent the intrusion of juveniles while we are relaxing. Family hotels are truly necessary, but adult-only establishments are even more desirable. Unfortunately, they seem to be vanishing before the onslaught of the 'ain't kids wonderful' brigade."

We do understand the point of view represented by this Disgruntled from Cincinnati and the dilemma expressed by another correspondent: "How on earth is the poor hotelier to know if parents want to bring little angels or little horrors? How much easier for them to say 'no children'." If hotels are to welcome children more generously than they have done in the past, there must be an unwritten obligation on the part of parents not to abuse that hospitality.

Fortunately, we see plenty of signs of a shift in attitudes. Working parents these days want to spend more leisure time with their young offspring than the previous generation. Many of them have no enthusiasm for the wholly child-centred establishments – all peanut-butter sandwiches and kiddy games – and are looking for hotels that are hospitable to all age groups. Those places that fail to provide a genuine welcome are given a wide berth. And hoteliers, for their part, are coming to appreciate the importance of cultivating the clientele of tomorrow.

And hoteliers can do something to minimise the risk of young children upsetting fellow-guests or the staff. We liked the leaflet which the *Porth Tocyn*, Abersoch, sends to families when they make their booking. It goes into considerable detail about what parents can and can't expect: such matters as the nature of the accommodation, the amenities available, the prospects for child-minding (not guaranteed), the activities in the area and suchlike. There's quite a lot about meals: breakfast ("usually no problem, but there's a cosy room next door to the restaurant if parents feel the din is too terrible for other guests to handle and blood pressures are rising"); lunches ("casually indoors or out between 12.30 and 2 pm"); high teas which can be served in the children's sitting room, in bedrooms or outside between 5 and 6.15 ("a nightmare because no two children ever want the same thing"); and finally, dinner: "Children are welcome at dinner over the age of seven, though if a six-year-old is having a special treat and can handle the situation – OK. But our wish is to keep this end of the day as one largely for adults."

Nick Fletcher-Brewer, the owner of the hotel and himself a father with small children, says that his simple guidelines have saved hours of explanation and cut down much friction and stress for staff and prospective guests. Perhaps his strategy can help other hoteliers to be less child-shy than at present.

Reservation hassles

Among the many grievances that surface year after year, the matter of reservations not honoured has cropped up with greater frequency than ever these past twelve months irrespective of whether deposits have been paid or not. Problems arise most often with bookings for just a night or two which have to be made a long time in advance. It obviously makes sense to confirm any booking by fax, since you then have clear evidence that the message has been received. But fax machines are no remedy if the hotel chooses to turn you away.

We imagine that cash-flow anxieties have much to do with these defaultings. One honeymoon couple told us that, despite a written confirmation of their booking, they had been required to leave the hotel early to make room for a larger, longer, more profitable booking, and the innkeeper seemed to regard that as a normal business practice. Another reader reported no less than four instances of reservation difficulties that he had experienced within the space of two years.

We don't automatically disenfranchise a hotel that slips up over a booking, but we regret that so many hoteliers, who naturally deplore no-shows that can cause them grievous loss of revenue, are less than punctilious in keeping their side of the bargain. We would be glad if readers would tell us when they experience this problem – and how apologetically or cavalierly the hotels dealt with it.

What gets our goat

An editor asked us recently to list ten things about hotels which annoyed us most. Many of the plaints that fill our postbag are of course hardy perennials: things like heating, ventilation, insulation, plumbing, privacy, security, lousy breakfasts after decent dinners, the unfairness of charging people on their own a supplement for occupying a double room, not to mention the resentment that many of us feel over the whole business of adding 10–15% to the bill as an obligatory service charge – and often leaving open the bottom line of the credit card voucher as well. But perhaps we have banged on enough about that subject already, and we notice that bad habits like nudging for tips are slowly abating, at least in hotels – restaurants are another story.

Anyway, here, in no special order, is our 1992 list of what gets our goat most:

1. Sloppy housekeeping: poor standards of cleaning, defects not rectified when reported.
2. Inadequate or ill-placed bedside lighting.
3. Geriatric beds.
4. Kitchen or smoking smells in bedrooms or public spaces.
5. Lack of intimacy in the restaurant: tables too close together, too much noise, intrusive muzak.
6. Pretentious menus.
7. Pretentious cooking.
8. Obsequiousness or offhandedness from staff or owner.
9. Hidden extras when you come to pay the bill.
10. Loud, offensive, boring, boorish fellow-guests.

We would be delighted to hear from readers about their own pet hates. And at the same time do please continue to send us contributions to *Traveller's Tales* – the more eye-popping or hair-raising the better.

HILARY RUBINSTEIN

Exemplary country home guest house

Chilvester Hill House, Calne

Every year for the past decade more and more country house owners have been opening their doors to paying guests. The popularity of these sophisticated guest houses has been growing too, even though communal meals aren't for everyone. The Dilleys have been dispensing their own special, more personal kind of cosseting for the past seven years. Only three bedrooms – but those who have been lucky enough to be their guests have had an experience to savour.

For resurrecting a fitting home for one of the grandest hotel views in Britain

The Cottage in the Wood, Malvern Wells

For many years past, this eyrie high up in the Malvern Hills has been a so-so hotel. We salute the Pattin family for bringing this far-from-cottagey hotel back to its former state, providing a decent life-support system for those who cherish a room with a view.

Best budget B&B

Jeake's House, Rye

The Hadfields' beautiful listed house on one of Rye's cobbled streets is an exemplary bed-and-breakfast. Beds, bathrooms, books, pictures, furnishings, are all of a piece. And the splendid breakfasts served in the old Quaker meeting house next door cater for vegetarians as well as bacon-eaters. That the prices are exceedingly reasonable is an added bonus.

For utterly acceptable mild eccentricity

The Old Rectory, Campsea Ashe

Stewart Bassett is an original. His restaurant-with-rooms home is full of good books and pictures, but don't expect conventional fixtures, like TV in your bedroom. Upkeep and service can be wayward. No-choice menu; you eat what the good Bassett provides – which is often wonderful. The wine list is a marvel – and marvellously reasonable. For those bored with lookalike board and lodgings, *The Old Rectory* can give you a less predictable, more piquant experience.

Special hotels

City hotels with luxury and grandeur

England
Queensberry, Bath; Connaught, London; Athenaeum, London; Capital, London; Middlethorpe Hall, York
Scotland
One Devonshire Gardens, Glasgow

Town hotels of character and/or value

England
Angel, Bury St Edmunds; Cotswold House, Chipping Campden; Evesham, Evesham; Marlborough, Ipswich; At the Sign of the Angel, Lacock; Lansdowne, Leamington Spa; D'Isney Place, Lincoln; Basil Street, London; Beaufort, London; Blake's, London; Durrants, London; Hazlitt's, London; L'Hotel, London; Portobello, London; Old Parsonage, Oxford; Abbey, Penzance; Jeake's House, Rye; Swan, Southwold; George, Stamford; Castle, Taunton; Mount Royale, York
Scotland
Mansion House, Elgin; Clifton, Nairn

Rural charm and character in the luxury class

England
Elms, Abberley; Hartwell House, Aylesbury; Mallory Court, Bishop's Tachbrook; Gidleigh Park, Chagford; Charingworth Manor, Charingworth; Gravetye Manor, East Grinstead; Whatley Manor, Easton Grey; Manoir aux Quat'Saisons, Great Milton; Hambleton Hall, Hambleton; Hintlesham Hall, Hintlesham; Chewton Glen, New Milton; Stapleford Park, Stapleford; Ston Easton Park, Ston Easton; Cliveden, Taplow; Thornbury Castle, Thornbury; Sharrow Bay, Ullswater
Wales
Bodysgallen, Llandudno; Llangoed Hall, Llyswen
Scotland
Inverlochy Castle, Fort William; Cromlix House, Kinbuck
Channel Islands
Longueville Manor, St Saviour
Ireland
Park Hotel Kenmare, Kenmare

Rural charm and character at medium price

England
Rothay Manor, Ambleside; Wateredge, Ambleside; Little Barwick House, Barwick; Cavendish, Baslow; Netherfield Place, Battle; Farlam Hall, Brampton; Collin House, Broadway; Grafton Manor, Bromsgrove; Danescombe Valley, Calstock; Aynsome Manor, Cartmel; Uplands, Cartmel; Brockencote Hall, Chaddesley Corbett; Chedington Court, Chedington; Highbullen, Chittlehamholt; Summer Lodge, Evershot; Stock Hill House, Gillingham; Congham Hall, Grimston; Tarr Steps, Hawkridge; Bel Alp, Haytor; Heddon's Gate, Heddon's Mouth; Langley House, Langley Marsh;

Lastingham Grange, Lastingham; Hope End, Ledbury; Arundell Arms, Lifton; Maiden Newton House, Maiden Newton; Cottage in the Wood, Malvern Wells; Brookdale House, North Huish; Whitechapel Manor, South Molton; Oaklands House, South Petherton; Bridgefield House, Spark Bridge; Stonor Arms, Stonor; Plumber Manor, Sturminster Newton; Calcot Manor, Tetbury; Priory, Wareham; Hurstone, Waterrow; Old Vicarage, Witherslack

Wales

Gliffaes, Crickhowell; Tyddyn Llan, Llandrillo; Lake Vyrnwy, Llanwyddn; Portmeirion, Portmeirion; Maes-y-Neuadd, Talsarnau; Minffordd, Talyllyn

Scotland

Summer Isles, Achiltibuie; Invery House, Banchory; Kinloch House, Blairgowrie; Polmaily House, Drumnadrochit; Factor's House, Fort William; Dunain Park, Inverness; Cringletie House, Peebles; Airds, Port Appin; Knockinaam Lodge, Portpatrick; Tiroran House, Tiroran

Channel Islands

Château La Chaire, Rozel Bay

Ireland

Gurthalougha House, Ballinderry; Rathsallagh House, Dunlavin; Marlfield House, Gorey; Assolas, Kanturk; Roundwood House, Mountrath; Currarevagh House, Oughterard; Coopershill, Riverstown; Ballymaloe, Shanagarry

Rural charm, simple style

England

Frog Street Farm, Beercrocombe; Tanyard, Boughton Monchelsea; Old Cloth Hall, Cranbrook; Glebe Farm, Diddlebury; Woodmans Arms Auberge, Hastingleigh; Parrock Head, Slaidburn; Manor Farm Barn, Taynton; Upper Green Farm, Towersey; Howtown, Ullswater

Wales

Cnapan, Newport

Scotland

Riverside, Canonbie; Glencripesdale House, Glencripesdale; Argyll, Iona

Ireland

Coopershill, Riverstown

Hotels by the sea, luxury style

England

Marine, Salcombe; Island, Tresco

Scotland

Knockinaam Lodge, Portpatrick

Hotels by the sea, medium-priced or simple

England

Winterbourne, Bonchurch; Look Out, Branscombe; Hell Bay, Bryher; Treglos, Constantine Bay; Crantock Bay, Crantock; Whiteleaf, Croyde; Penmere Manor, Falmouth; Marina, Fowey; Tregildry, Gillan; Meudon, Mawnan Smith; Port Gaverne, Port Gaverne; Garrack, St Ives; St Martin's, St Martin's; Seaview, Seaview; Soar Mill Cove, Soar Mill Cove; Talland Bay, Talland-by-Looe; New Inn, Tresco

Wales

Porth Tocyn, Abersoch; St Tudno, Llandudno

Scotland

Summer Isles, Achiltibuie; Isle of Colonsay, Colonsay; Enmore, Dunoon; Kinloch Castle, Rhum; Isle of Barra, Tangusdale Beach; Baile-na-Cille, Timsgarry

Channel Islands

White House, Herm

Skiing, walking or mountain hotels

England
Seatoller, Borrowdale; Lodore Swiss, Keswick; Mill, Mungrisdale; Hazel Bank, Rosthwaite; Howtown, Ullswater; Wasdale Head, Wasdale Head
Wales
Pen-y-Gwryd, Nantgwynant; Minffordd, Talyllyn
Scotland
Summer Isles, Achiltibuie

Small hotels and inns with outstanding cuisine

England
Bell, Aston Clinton; Belle Alliance, Blandford Forum; Lower Pitt, East Buckland; Stock Hill House, Gillingham; White Moss, Grasmere; Hope End, Ledbury; Brookdale House, North Huish; Seafood Restaurant, Padstow; Pool Court, Pool-in-Wharfedale; Well House, St Keyne; McCoys, Staddlebridge; Calcot Manor, Tetbury; White House, Williton; Feathers, Woodstock
Wales
Plas Bodegroes, Pwllheli; Crown, Whitebrook
Scotland
Farleyer House, Aberfeldy; Crinan, Crinan; Peat Inn, Peat Inn; Knockinaam Lodge, Portpatrick; Altnaharrie, Ullapool
Ireland
Doyle's Townhouse, Dingle; Ballymaloe House, Shannagarry

Friendly informality/hotel run like a private house

England
Chapel House, Atherstone; Frog Street Farm, Beercrocombe; Little Hodgeham, Bethersden; Chilvester Hill House, Calne; Thornworthy House, Chagford; Old Cloth Hall, Cranbrook; Woodmans Arms, Hastingleigh; Huntsham Court, Huntsham; Fallowfields, Kingston Bagpuize; Otley House, Otley; Reeds, Poughill; Howe Villa, Richmond; Sugarswell Farm, Shenington; Downhayes, Spreyton; Old Millfloor, Trebarwith Strand
Wales
Old Rectory, Llansanffraid Glan Conwy
Scotland
Glenfeochan, Kilmore; Ard-na-Coille, Newtonmore; Baile-na-Cille, Timsgarry

Hotels that welcome children

England
Cavendish, Baslow; Eagle House, Bathford; Woolley Grange, Bradford-on-Avon; Bulstone, Branscombe; Hell Bay, Bryher; Crantock Bay, Crantock; Evesham, Evesham; Penmere Manor, Falmouth; Highfield House, Hawkshead; Huntsham Court, Huntsham; Lodore Swiss, Keswick; Lastingham Grange, Lastingham; Polurrian, Mullion; Port Gaverne, Port Isaac; Boscundle Manor, St Austell; Garrack, St Ives; St Martin's, St Martin's; Star Castle, St Mary's; Seaview, Seaview; Soar Mill Cove, Soar Mill Cove; Bridgefield House, Spark Bridge; Cliveden, Taplow; Old Millfloor, Trebarwith Strand; New Inn, Tresco; Island, Tresco; Nare, Veryan; Hurstone, Waterrow; Walletts Court, West Cliffe

Wales
Porth Tocyn, Abersoch; Riverside, Abersoch; St Tudno, Llandudno; Lake Vyrnwy, Llanwddyn; Cnapan, Newport
Scotland
Loch Melfort, Arduaine; Isle of Colonsay, Colonsay; Isle of Eriska, Eriska; Enmore, Dunoon; Glencripesdale House, Glencripesdale; Ard-na-Coille, Newtonmore; Cringletie House, Peebles; Philipburn House, Selkirk; Baile-na-Cille, Timsgarry
Ireland
Coopershill, Riverstown; Ballymaloe, Shanagarry
Channel Islands
White House, Herm

No-smoking hotels

England
Audley House, Bath; Haydon House, Bath; Somerset House, Bath; Sydney Gardens, Bath; Old Windmill, Bradford-on-Avon; Woodmans Arms, Hastingleigh; Northleigh House, Hatton; Cotswold House, Oxford; Nanscawen House, St Blazey; Sugarswell, Shenington; Upper Green Farm, Towersey; Archway, Windermere
Wales
Old Rectory, Llansaffraid Glan Conwy
Scotland
Brook Linn, Callander; Altnaharrie, Ullapool

How to read the entries

The Long and the Short of it Entries vary in length. A long entry does not imply an especially good hotel nor a short one a marginal case. Sometimes we need a lot of space to convey a hotel's special flavour and sometimes we can't resist quoting at length from a well-written lively report. Our aim is to be entertaining as well as informative. In general, city hotels get less space than country ones because the atmosphere of a hotel matters less in towns, and also because it is often helpful, when a hotel is in a relatively remote or little-known area, for the entry to say something about the location.

Names The names in a citation are of those people who have nominated that hotel or endorsed the entry that appeared in a previous edition. We do not give the names of those who have sent us adverse reports – though their contributions are every bit as important as the laudatory ones.

Italic entries We put an entry in italics when we feel a hotel is worth considering, but which for various reasons – inadequate information, lack of feedback, ambivalent reports – does not at the moment justify a full entry. We are particularly keen to get more reports in these cases, and hope that, with the help of such feedback, many will rate full entries next year.

Symbols We are against providing, as some other guide books do, a lot of potted information in complicated, hard-to-decipher hieroglyphic form. But, as last year, we have used a "Budget" label alongside the name of hotels offering dinner, bed and breakfast at up to around £40 (about $70) per person, B&B about £25 and dinner around £15. Days and months are abbreviated, but virtually the only other shorthand we use is "B&B" for bed and breakfast and "alc" for à la carte; the "full alc" price is the hotel's estimate per person for a three-course meal and a half-bottle of modest wine, including service and taxes. "Alc meals" indicates the price excluding the wine.

Disabled We try to give as much information as possible (ground-floor rooms, lifts, etc) so that disabled people can judge whether or not a hotel might be suitable for them. If a hotel tells us it has special facilities for the disabled we give details; if we know it is not suitable we say so, using the disabled sign. But we do often lack precise information; disabled people should always check with the hotel.

Tariffs Terms are regrettably complicated. A few hotels have a standard rate for all rooms regardless of season and length of stay, but most operate a highly complicated system which varies from low season to high (and some have a medium-high season as well), according to length of stay, whether there is a bathroom *en suite* and, in the case of most British hotels, whether a room is in single or double occupancy. And, on top of all that, most British hotels offer breaks of one kind or another, but rarely of the same kind. When figures are given without mention of single or double rooms they indicate the range of tariffs per person; otherwise we give a room rate. Lowest rates are what you pay for the simplest room, or out of season, or both; highest rates are for the "best" rooms – and in high season if the hotel has one. Meal prices are per person; value added tax (VAT) and service are included unless we state otherwise.

There is one crucial point that must be emphasised with regard to the tariffs: their relative unreliability. We ask hotels when they complete our questionnaire in the spring of one year to make an informed guess at their tariffs the following year. There are many reasons why this is a difficult exercise. If hotels are unable to give next year's rates we print the 1991 tariffs, making it clear that these are last year's terms. *Please don't rely on the figures printed. You should always check at the time of booking and not blame the hotel or the guide if the prices are different from those printed.*

Special offers If you are going for two days or more to a hotel in the British Isles, it's worth asking about the exact terms of any special offers available. Sometimes these bargain terms are an amazing value, and can apply throughout the year, not just in the winter, but they may call for some adjustment in your holiday plans in order to qualify.

We end with our customary exhortation: we implore readers to tell us of any errors of omission or commission in both the descriptive and informative parts of the entries. We make constant efforts to improve our information under "Location," especially with the more out-of-the-way places, but would be very grateful if readers would let us know of any cases where they have found our directions inadequate. We recognise what an imposition it is to be asking readers to write us letters or fill in report forms, but it is essential that people do let us know their views if the guide is to meet consumer needs as well as it can.

England

Brookdale House, North Huish

ABBERLEY Hereford and Worcester **Map 2**

The Elms
Stockton Road, Abberley
Nr Worcester WR6 6AT

Tel Great Witley (0299) 896666
Fax (0299) 896804

Last year, under new (corporate) owners, *The Elms* resumed its place as first entry in the Guide and regulars this year warmly endorse it: "We have known the hotel for years through its ups and downs. It always had a very relaxed atmosphere, and the new owners have improved it no end; the manageress is first class. The chef, Michael Gaunt, is very competent; we had two extremely good dinners." *The Elms* is a beautiful and grand Queen Anne mansion, in a peaceful setting in well-kept grounds with lovely views. "Inside are lofty reception rooms with antique furniture, plenty of flowers, and – *most important* – excellent lighting. The food is light and delicious, and service, by young and mostly English staff, quick, friendly and professional. Bedrooms are very comfortable and well lit, and supplied with the usual extras. At night a chambermaid comes in specially from a nearby village to turn down beds and provide yet more fluffy white towels. There's a pleasantly relaxed and friendly atmosphere, backed up by high standards of housekeeping." "The new owners have extensively redecorated and the hotel offers the highest standards of comfort, food and service. The new manager, the Swedish Cecilia Rydstrom, is able to combine efficiency with a warm welcome – and to achieve a consistent standard." (*Mrs GM Allwright, D Whittington, Mr and Mrs JM Pashley*) Fairly formal: jacket and tie for men are required in the restaurant; jeans are out.

Open All year.
Rooms 5 suites, 18 double, 2 single – all with bath (23 also have shower), telephone, radio, TV, baby-listening. 9 in adjoining Coach House.
Facilities 2 lounges, library, bar, restaurant; conference/functions facilities. 10-acre gardens with tennis, putting, croquet, helipad.
Location Off A443, 13 m NW of Worcester. 2 m after Great Witley, not in Abberley village.
Restrictions Only restaurant suitable for ♿. No dogs.
Credit cards All major cards accepted.
Terms [1991 rates] B&B: single £82–£105, double £97–£128, suite £128–£150. Set lunch £14.95, dinner £22; full alc £33. Weekend breaks.
Service/tipping: "Service at guests' discretion."

ALDEBURGH Suffolk **Map 3**

Austins
243 The High Street
Aldeburgh IP15 5DN

Tel Aldeburgh (0728) 453932
Fax (0728) 453668

"A bijou hotel," writes our inspector, introducing this new entry. "Welcoming and attractive. Charming and attentive hosts; very theatrical. Cooking mildly innovative, but menu doesn't change much." Robert Selbie, a former actor, and Julian Alexander-Worster, who does the cooking, are keen collectors, and their small hotel/restaurant, formerly three 18th-century cottages, is filled with antiques and good pictures. The elegant bar is hung with theatrical memorabilia – posters, programmes, signed photographs. Bedrooms are on the small side, but well lit, with good furniture and fabrics though not a lot of storage space; tea-making equipment is provided, but not "extras". Some of the bath or shower rooms have been quite awkwardly put in. In the restaurant the accent is on fresh fish. Our inspector had a slightly mixed meal, and was surprised that breakfast orange juice was not freshly squeezed, and that toast was made from commercial sliced bread, but her verdict is positive: "Not for children or the disabled," she writes, "but definitely a Guide entry." Aldeburgh is a delightful seaside town, popular with yachtsmen; and is a good centre for exploring Suffolk. It is busy during the internationally famous music festival in June, but otherwise unspoilt. More reports please.

Open All year except 2 weeks late Jan/early Feb.
Rooms 5 double, 2 single – all with bath and/or shower, telephone, radio, TV, tea-making facilities.
Facilities 2 lounges, bar, restaurant. 1 min's walk from shingle beach.
Location At end of high street, 5 mins' walk from centre.
Restrictions Not suitable for ♿. No children under 12. No dogs in public rooms.
Credit cards Access, Amex, Visa.

Terms B&B £37.65–£47.75. Set lunch (Wed and Sat) £11.50; full alc dinner £24.65. 3-day off-season breaks. New Year and Easter packages.
Service/tipping: "Tips at guests' discretion. Distributed proportionately among the staff."

ALSTON Cumbria — Map 4

Lovelady Shield
Nenthead Road
Alston CA9 3LF

Tel Alston (0434) 381203
Fax (0434) 381515

Returning to the Guide under new owners, *Lovelady Shield* enjoys "a stunning position" in the High Pennines, in "beautiful, wild and untouched countryside, beside a river at the foot of majestic fells". It is an attractive 19th-century country house, and the "friendly but unobtrusive" owners, Kenneth and Margaret Lyons, have made many improvements to the accommodation and decor since their arrival two years ago. "Good value for money. Room large and well appointed. Food excellent, with adventurous starters at dinner and kedgeree on offer for breakfast." "Food slightly *nouvelle* and well presented. Large, airy dining room with views of lawns, ducks and rhododendrons." "Warm welcome; open fires in public rooms. Staff exceedingly pleasant." (*Philip W Runchman, Mrs K Evans, Captain JRC Johnston, and others*) "We are very quiet," say the Lyons. "The house is up a long tree-lined drive. No piped music, no organised entertainment. Guests can get away from it all and relax." Some of the rooms are quite small; best discuss when booking.

Open 1 Mar–2 Jan.
Rooms 10 double, 2 single – all with bath and/or shower, telephone, radio, TV, baby-listening.
Facilities 2 lounges, bar, restaurant. 4-acre grounds with croquet and tennis. Golf, fishing, riding nearby.
Location 2¼ m NE of Alston; take A689 to Stanhope.
Restrictions Not suitable for ♿. No smoking in restaurant and 1 lounge. No dogs in public rooms.
Credit cards All major cards accepted.
Terms B&B £37.50–£48.50; dinner, B&B £59.50–£69. Set lunch £11.50, dinner £22.50. 3-day breaks; Christmas and New Year breaks. Reduced rates and special meals for children.
Service/tipping: "No service charge. We do not expect or seek tips; if anything is left it is distributed among all staff according to hours worked."

AMBLESIDE Cumbria — Map 4

Rothay Manor
Rothay Bridge
Ambleside LA22 0EH

Tel Ambleside (053 94) 33605
Fax (053 94) 33607

César award: For maintaining traditional hotel virtues

"This comfortable hotel exudes the enveloping warmth of hoteliers whose successful formula has satisfied countless guests for 25 years. Spotless rooms, glowing brassware, deep carpets, lovely flower arrangements, efficient heating, books to read, magazines to leaf through, comfortable and smart lounges. Cheerful, well-trained staff, who wear Victorian dress to serve dinner, and are unobtrusively directed by the owners. The gardens are lovingly tended. Cooking is "the best of

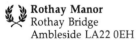

English"; uncomplicated dishes beautifully cooked and served in sufficient portions to satisfy starving walkers. Dinner included classics like lamb, roast beef, poached salmon. Starters tend to be spicy or garlicky. Cheese is a good selection of cow and goat, soft and hard. Excellent wine list, but you cannot beat the recommended bottles by the main dishes, some as cheap as £7.50 each. Help yourself to as much coffee and exquisite petits fours and chocolates as you like after dinner. Copious and excellent breakfast." (*Francine Walsh; also Mattye B Silverman, Alan Greenwood*)

The Nixon brothers' handsome Georgian house, with some original features still intact, is half a mile from Lake Windermere in two acres of garden in a valley surrounded by fine Lakeland mountain scenery. There are comfortable lounges with antiques and flowers; bedrooms are bright and clean, with bathrooms filled with innumerable extras. The dining room, decorated in browns and golds with deep-pile carpets, velvety curtains, polished candle-lit tables, heavy glass and tableware, overlooks the gardens. Weekend dinner menus offer a two-course and a five-course option. Weekday lunch is a generous buffet. Children and the disabled are welcome at *Rothay Manor*. There's a busy one-way traffic system close by but rooms have effective double-glazing. In winter the Nixons offer music and gourmet weekends, and house parties for Christmas and the New Year.

Open All year except Jan, 1st week Feb.
Rooms 3 suites (1 honeymoon, 2 family) in annexe, 13 double, 2 single – all with bath, shower, telephone, radio, TV, baby-listening. 2 adapted for ♿.
Facilities 3 lounges (1 with bar), 2 dining rooms. 2-acre garden with croquet. Near river Rothay and Lake Windermere (¼ m). Sailing, water-skiing, fishing, riding, golf.
Location On A593 SW of Ambleside towards Coniston. Garden-facing rooms quietest.
Restrictions No smoking in dining room and 1 lounge. No dogs.
Credit cards All major cards accepted.
Terms B&B: single £63–£69, double £90–£108, suite £125–£140; dinner, B&B: single £78–£92, double £122–£154, suite £156–£186. Lunch: weekdays about £8, Sun £13.25. Dinner £19 (2-course) and £25 (5-course). Off-season breaks; music courses, French regional dinners. 4-day Christmas house party, 3-day New Year programme. 2-night min booking at weekend. Reduced rates for children sharing parents' room; special meals.
Service/tipping: "No service charge. Service at guests' discretion."

Wateredge Hotel *Tel* Ambleside (053 94) 32332
Borrans Road, Waterhead *Fax* (053 94) 32332
Ambleside LA22 0EP

"Everything just right. Rooms delicately decorated with a feminine touch, and excellently equipped. Limited choice of food but beautifully cooked and served, with something to please everyone. Staff friendly and helpful." "Maintains its high standards of civilised comfort. Plenty of comfortable chairs in the two small, beamed lounges and the large lounge with picture-windows overlooking the lake. Bathwater always very hot, lots of fluffy towels. Good breakfasts, including home-made granary bread and croissants." Warm words from two visitors already planning a return visit to the appropriately named *Wateredge*, which enjoys a choice position at the head of Windermere looking down the length of the lake with views of Loughrigg fells and other landmarks. Owned and run by

Mr and Mrs Cowap, it consists of a pair of 17th-century fisherman's cottages with some modern additions and retains much period charm. Bedrooms in the original part are beamed and traditionally furnished; the newer ones are larger, with pine furniture. There are five spacious suites, with patio and balcony, in an annexe. All have numerous extras – hair-drier, fresh fruit and so on. Meals, interesting without being pretentious, and using good local meat and fish, are served in the two dining rooms in the old part of the building, with low-beamed ceilings and painted old stone walls. There is a choice of starter, followed by soup, then a sorbet, then two alternative main courses, generally a roast and a fish dish. The dessert, which "provoked the appreciative and greedy attention of guests on their way into dinner", is followed with a large selection of British cheeses. (*David RW Jervois, Margaret H Box; also Mr and Mrs DP Whittaker, Carolyn Davies*) The only problem is that there can be noise from the main road behind; lakeside traffic, heavy at weekends, passes close by the hotel.

Open Early Feb–mid-Dec.
Rooms 5 suites (across a small courtyard), 15 double, 3 single – all with bath and/or shower, telephone, radio, TV, tea-making facilities.
Facilities 3 lounges, TV room, bar, restaurant. 1-acre grounds with patio, lake frontage, private jetty, boats available to guests free of charge; fishing, bathing.
Location ½ m S of town; just off A591 at Waterhead on Kendal–Keswick road (rooms on road can be noisy).
Restrictions Not suitable for ♿. No smoking in dining room. No children under 7. Dogs by prior arrangement, not in suites or public rooms.
Credit cards Access, Amex, Visa.
Terms [1991 rates] B&B £34–£62; dinner, B&B £42–£70. Set dinner £21.50. Winter breaks. 1-night bookings sometimes refused for Sat. Reduced rates for children sharing parents' room.
Service/tipping: "No service charge. All tips are distributed equally to all staff."

ARNCLIFFE North Yorkshire — Map 4

Amerdale House
Arncliffe, Littondale
Skipton BD23 5QE

Tel Arncliffe (075 677) 250
from Jan 1992 (0756) 770250

Nigel and Paula Crapper's manor house on the edge of a pretty, unspoilt Dales village in lovely, open country is said to have Elizabethan origins, but was extended and converted in 1871 and is substantially Victorian. Since they came here four years ago the Crappers have continued to redecorate and refurbish; there are now ten bedrooms in the main house and one in the converted stables, all well equipped with masses of toiletries in the bathrooms. Public rooms are large, warm and comfortable. "It is on a human scale," was a comment last year. "The rooms are pleasant, if not outstanding." Recent visitors have enjoyed the peaceful atmosphere, the "stunning" location, the "excellent service from friendly staff" and the four-course dinners. "Thank goodness we were walking; it was the only way to justify the amount we ate, though the portions were just right. Superb value for money." "Food ambitious and innovative; vegetables nicely crisp, all well presented." "Mr Crapper could not have been more helpful and relaxed. Wine list interesting and fairly priced." (*FL Douglas, Brian Beedham, and others*) Not all the bedrooms have central heating and one visitor found the convector heaters supplied were inadequate in very cold weather, "and it would have been pleasant if the (very small) towels had been changed after the third night without our having to ask".

Open Mid-Mar–mid-Nov.
Rooms 2 suites, 9 double – all with bath and/or shower, TV, tea-making facilities. 1 on ground floor in converted stables.
Facilities Lounge, bar, restaurant. 2-acre grounds.
Location 17 m N of Skipton; take left fork off B6160 to Arncliffe.
Restrictions Not suitable for ♿. No smoking in dining room. No dogs.
Credit cards Access, Visa.
Terms [1991 rates] Dinner, B&B £48.50–£50.50. Set dinner £17. 1-night bookings refused for bank holidays and high-season weekends. Reduced rates for children sharing parents' room; special meals.
Service/tipping: "No mention of a service charge is made in our literature, nor are tips expected by staff. If guests wish to give tips they are gratefully received and shared equally."

ASHBOURNE Derbyshire — Map 4

Callow Hall
Mappleton Road
Ashbourne DE6 2AA

Tel Ashbourne (0335) 43403
Fax (0335) 43624

"Must be one of the best hotels of its type in the country." "Friendly, relaxing and informal. Competent staff." "Very comfortable stay. Owners accommodating. Food excellent." Just a few of the tributes this year to David and Dorothy Spencer's impressive 19th-century Derbyshire house (with many original features still intact) up a long drive through large grounds with lovely trees. It is in attractive countryside, quietly located not far from the centre of the small market town. Bedrooms vary in size; some are "beautiful, large and comfortable", with "high ceiling, deep bay windows with shutters (which worked!) and glorious fabrics", others smaller but still well furnished and equipped with "an immaculate bathroom". Old-fashioned service is the order of the day: shoes are cleaned and early morning tea brought to the room if desired (not everyone finds the tea-making equipment easy to use). The Spencer family have been bakers in Ashbourne for the last five generations and *Callow Hall* has its own bakery and patisserie. *Patron*/chef David Spencer buys meat by the carcass and all hanging and butchery is done on the premises. Food is "very good, not too fussy" and well presented. "At breakfast the orange juice was freshly squeezed. Home-made sausages were an unexpected treat." (*Mike Bowman, BA Orman, Carol Jackson, CG, JEM Ruffer; also RCJ Gordon, CWM, and others*) There is private fishing for trout and grayling, with tuition available. The restaurant is popular locally and the hotel is sometimes taken over for local functions, which can diminish the pleasure of residents, particularly as the lounge and bar are not very large. One reader this year found the lighting in his bedroom badly positioned.

Open All year except 25/26 Dec and possibly 2 weeks Jan or Feb. Restaurant closed for lunch except Sun, for dinner Sun.
Rooms 12 double – all with bath, shower, telephone, radio, TV, tea-making facilities, baby-listening.
Facilities Lounge, bar, 2 restaurants; functions/conference facilities. 42-acre grounds with garden, woodland, farmland, stables; fishing (tuition available).

Location ¾ m from Ashbourne; take A515 to Buxton; sharp left at top of first hill by *Bowling Green* pub, first right to Mappleton; cross bridge – drive is on right.
Restrictions Not suitable for ♿. No smoking in restaurants. Dogs by arrangement; not in public rooms.
Credit cards All major cards accepted.
Terms B&B: single £63–£78, double £85–£115; dinner, B&B: single £86–£101, double £131–£161. Set Sun lunch £12.50, dinner £23.50; full alc £27.50. Weekend and midweek breaks. Reduced rates and special meals for children by arrangement.
Service/tipping: "Tipping is neither encouraged nor necessary."

ASHBURTON Devon — Map 1

Holne Chase
Ashburton
Nr Newton Abbot TQ13 7NS

Tel Poundsgate (036 43) 471
Fax (036 43) 453

"Most comfortable and restful hotel" owned and run by Bromage family for many years in "delightful old house" W of Ashburton. Large grounds with river (with fishing rights) on lower slopes of S Dartmoor; surrounded by woods to which residents have free access. Warmly recommended for spacious, well-furnished public rooms, decent-sized, well-equipped bedrooms, tranquil atmosphere, discreet, professional service, good food – and welcome to dogs. 15 rooms, all with bath/shower, 3 in stable cottage. No smoking in restaurant. All major credit cards accepted. 1991 rates: B&B £41–£59; dinner, B&B (min 2 nights) £52–£75.50. Set lunch £14.25, dinner £23. Was in earlier editions. Now has new chef. More reports please.

ASTON CLINTON Buckinghamshire — Map 1

The Bell Inn
Aston Clinton HP22 5HP

Tel Aylesbury (0296) 630252
Fax (0296) 631250

"Very comfortable, well-furnished room in stable annexe. Nice antiques. Staff friendly, but 'correct'. Plus point: breakfast available from 7 am, even on Sunday. Good value (for a chauvinist Northerner) for near London." At the foot of the Chilterns, on what is still a busy main road, this has been an inn since 1650 and was once a staging post for the Duke of Buckingham between his seat at Stowe and his palace on the Mall. But the term "inn" is quite inappropriate to today's sophisticated establishment which has been owned and run, along with a wine business, by the Harris family since 1939; Michael Harris, son of the founding father, and his wife Patsy are much in evidence. It has comfortable bedrooms, half a dozen of them in the original inn with antiques (some have four-posters), and fifteen, spacious and more modern, and perhaps quieter, in converted stables, grouped around a cobblestoned flower-filled courtyard. There's a pavilion across the road for weddings and conferences. But the *raison d'être* of the *Bell* is its popular restaurant with pretty murals where cooking by Kevin Cape is "classical French with a modern touch". The set menu is extremely good value; the à la carte more adventurous; there's a continually changing vegetarian menu and a "long and tempting" wine list; but also a recommended wine which changes weekly – "the one on our night was remarkably reasonable". There are generous extras in the bedrooms, but it is more a restaurant-with-rooms than a hotel, and "the feeling of a tradition, of the caring of the owner, of keen and cheerful staff, nearly all French, creates a most welcoming impression". (*Dr Peter Aston, HR*) There is some difference of opinion on the service in the restaurant. One reader found it "unnecessarily intrusive"; others consider it "exemplary; extraordinarily attentive". More reports please.

Open All year.
Rooms 8 suites, 13 double – all with bath, shower, telephone, radio, TV, baby-listening. 15 in annexe round courtyard.
Facilities Ramps. Drawing room, smoking room, bar, restaurant. Garden with croquet.
Location On A41, 4 m SE of Aylesbury. Road-facing rooms double-glazed; quieter rooms at rear.
Restrictions No smoking in restaurant (smoking room available). Dogs by arrangement.
Credit cards Access, Amex, Visa.
Terms B&B: single £97.50, double £118, suite £144. Set lunch £18.50, dinner £22; full alc from £35. "English weekend" breaks Jan–Mar. Reduced rates for children sharing parents' room; special meals.

ATHERSTONE Warwickshire — Map 1

Chapel House BUDGET — *Tel* Atherstone (0827) 718949
Friars' Gate, Atherstone CV9 1EY

David and Pat Roberts's small guest house, predominantly Georgian, stands in a pretty walled garden just off the square of this old market town which is only two miles from the A5. "It is typical of what is best in the Guide," wrote readers last year, "small, personal, individual, welcoming, comfortable, good value, and run with love. Bedroom small but comfortable with lots of extras such as pot-pourri, dried flowers and shoe-cleaning materials. Downstairs was extremely comfortable and spacious." "Furnishings mainly antique, with nice pieces of china. It's really too attractive and smart to be called a guest house." And this year's crop of reports on balance supports this verdict, though one reader had a single, which, "though clean and quiet, was tiny, with knick-knacks covering every surface". Another found her room "rather brown – brown sheets, brown carpet, etc – but it was very comfortable". Things can get hectic at times in the popular restaurant ("charming, if slightly over-decorated"), which offers residents a no-choice menu at 7 pm – but they can take the non-residents' dinner if they prefer. Meals continue to be appreciated, especially breakfast: "One of the few times I've had good scrambled eggs." "We liked the large platter with eight choices of jam, marmalade and honey – nothing packaged." When the owners are away the welcome can be variable.

Open All year except Christmas.
Rooms 7 double, 6 single – most with shower (1 also has bath), all with telephone, radio, TV, baby-listening.
Facilities Lounge, dispense bar, 2 restaurants, conservatory. ½-acre garden.
Location In market square. Public parking in cul-de-sac in front of hotel.
Restrictions Not suitable for ♿. No children under 10 in restaurant after 8 pm. No dogs.
Credit cards Access, Diners, Visa.
Terms B&B: single £29.50–£42, double £50–£55; dinner, B&B single £40–£52.50, double £71–£75. Set dinner £10.50; full alc £27.50. Weekend discounts for 2 nights.

Service/tipping: "We do not make a service charge. Tips are optional, and shared among all staff."

AYLESBURY Buckinghamshire — Map 1

Hartwell House
Oxford Road
Aylesbury HP17 8NL

Tel Aylesbury (0296) 747444
Fax (0296) 747450

This mellow and serene country seat with Jacobean and Georgian facades stands in lush parkland designed by a pupil of Capability Brown, with a lake, a ruined church and lots of noble statuary. Louis XVIII, the exiled King of France, lived here for five years from 1809. The house has been brought to its present luxurious state by Historic House Hotels Ltd, an organisation dedicated to the resuscitation of noble British houses which has already done lavish conversions on *Bodysgallen Hall*, Llandudno, and *Middlethorpe Hall*, York (qq.v.). The interior is equally impressive, with an exotic Gothic central staircase, a spectacular 18th-century great hall, a fine library, and much else of opulent splendour. One of Britain's best designers, Janey Compton, has given the decor a luxurious but harmonious style. There are fine paintings and antiques. Bedrooms are spacious – some huge – and well equipped; some have magnificent panelling, original oil paintings and four-posters; extras include current magazines and "real" books. The restaurant, under Aidan McCormack, won a *Michelin* rosette in 1991; it offers a long à la carte menu and short set-price ones for every meal. The emphasis, as with the other houses in the group, is on modern British country house cooking, "with dishes not contrived or over-decorated, nor too obviously following a fashion". Readers in mid-1990, connoisseurs of rosetted establishments, were disappointed with their meal on several counts and complained of hectic and impersonal service – "like high-speed robots". They also regretted the absence of a ban on cigarettes in the restaurant. Men are expected to wear jacket and tie for dinner.

By the end of 1991 there will be sixteen more bedrooms and suites in a converted stable block, to be known as Hartwell Court, and a Hartwell Spa in a new building built like an orangery, with a large indoor swimming pool, whirlpool bath, beauty salon and café. New facilities in a restored coach house, the Hartwell Rooms, will separate conference trade from private visitors in the hotel. We would be glad of reports on the developing Hartwell complex.

Open All year.
Rooms 3 suites, 25 double, 4 single – all with bath, shower, telephone, radio, TV. 10 suites, 6 doubles in converted stables due to open in Nov 1991.
Facilities Ramp. Lift. Great hall, morning room, drawing room, library, bar, restaurant; conference facilities. Spa with indoor swimming pool, whirlpool, beauty salon, café to open in Nov 1991. 80-acre grounds with trout lake, woodlands, croquet.
Location 2 m S of Aylesbury on the A418 to Thame, outside the village of Stone.
Restrictions No children under 8. Dogs in grounds only.
Credit cards All major cards accepted.
Terms [Until April 1992] B&B: single £98.50, double £153–£216, suite £216–£316. Set lunch £19, dinner £32.50; full alc £48.60. 2-night summer breaks; winter champagne breaks.
Service/tipping: "Service included. Should a guest wish to tip it is up to him or her; the money is distributed to all staff."

BAKEWELL Derbyshire Map 4

Milford House BUDGET *Tel* Bakewell (0629) 812130
Mill Street, Bakewell DE4 1DA

This unsophisticated hotel, "peaceful, spotless, a delightful oasis of comfort", is in a quiet part of Bakewell, close to the river Wye. It has been owned by the Hunt family for over three decades. The decor is simple; bedrooms are "rather 1950s with comfortable beds, good sheets and good quality blankets"; all have bath or shower with plenty of hot water and decent towels. The Hunts and their staff are friendly and helpful. A gong announces dinner and breakfast. The latter is English, good and generous. During breakfast you are asked which main course you would like for dinner (which is at 7 pm); there are three choices, including chicken and a roast. Sunday supper is a cold meal for residents only. Bar snacks are available Monday to Saturday. "Food not wonderful but hot, plentiful and well cooked. There are many excellent walks from the hotel, including the best way of seeing nearby Chatsworth. First-class value for money." (*H Patterson, Brenda Morris; also SPW Browne*)

Open 1 Apr–31 Oct.
Rooms 10 double, 2 single – all with bath and/or shower, TV, tea-making facilities.
Facilities Hall with bar, lounge, dining room. 1½-acre grounds with croquet.
Location 300 yds from town centre; right turn off A6 to Buxton. Parking.
Restrictions Not suitable for ♿. No children under 10. No dogs.
Credit cards None accepted.
Terms [1991 rates] B&B £28–£34; dinner, B&B £40–£46. Set Sun lunch £12.50, dinner £15. Bar snacks available to residents Mon–Sat; packed lunches on request. Weekly rates.
Service/tipping: "No service charge included. If guests wish to tip they give directly to staff."

BARWICK Somerset Map 2

Little Barwick House *Tel* Yeovil (0935) 23902
Barwick, Yeovil BA22 9TD

"This was our second visit. As before we were most comfortable and appreciated the informal but thoughtful and attentive hospitality. Mrs Colley's cooking continues to be very good indeed and her choice of dishes interesting. Super breakfast. Agree with the Guide that this is an excellent, unpretentious place of high quality to spend a night or two – and very reasonably priced." (*KGM*, warmly endorsed by *LM, PE Carter*)

Christopher and Veronica Colley's Georgian dower house, "lovingly cared for", is in a beautiful garden in a secluded corner of the attractive, minuscule village of Barwick, two miles from Yeovil. It looks out across the valley towards the village with its church and outlying obelisks on the skyline. Essentially it's a restaurant-with-rooms, and none of the six bedrooms is particularly large, nor luxuriously furnished, but each is comfortable, with firm beds, very good linen, good lighting, and individually controlled central heating as well as fresh flowers, mineral water, etc; telephones and radios have been added this year. The restaurant is popular with non-residents; there's a four-course set menu with choices at each stage. Food is "carefully cooked and not too messed about", game is particularly good, and the desserts varied and not all highly calorific. Vegetarian and special diets are catered for. The friendly, "unassuming but efficient" Colleys, the "attentive, smiling and unobtrusive" girls who serve dinner, the "sensible and unfussy" atmosphere all continue to be warmly appreciated. The Colleys write to tell us that the elder of their two Doberman bitches has died, "and her daughter is being kept out of the kitchen!"

Open All year except Christmas, New Year, 2 weeks Jan. Closed to non-residents on Sun.
Rooms 6 double – all with bath (2 also have shower), telephone, radio, TV, tea-making facilities, baby-listening.
Facilities 2 lounges, dining room, breakfast room. 3½-acre garden.
Location Follow signs from Yeovil to Dorchester (A37). Turn left off A37 at the *Red House* pub. Hotel is ¼ m on left.
Restrictions Not suitable for ♿. No smoking in dining room. Dogs by arrangement only; not in public rooms.
Credit cards Access, Amex, Visa.
Terms Dinner, B&B: single £63, double £80–£103. Reductions for 2 nights or more. Winter breaks. 1-night bookings sometimes refused on Sun off-season. Reduced rates for children sharing parents' room.
Service/tipping: "Service is included, but any money left is divided among the staff."

BASLOW Derbyshire — Map 4

The Cavendish
Baslow DE4 1SP
Tel Baslow (0246) 582311
Fax (0246) 582312

"Eric Marsh is the perfect host, supported by an excellent staff, many of whom have been there for years." "The great asset is the location, with a stunning view over Chatsworth Park, enormously enjoyable on a summer evening." "Dinner each night a real treat: interesting dishes, good home-made rolls. We were delighted to be able to have breakfast as late as we wanted."

The *Cavendish* is one of the few luxurious hotels in the Peak District. It is on the edge of Chatsworth Park, which all the bedrooms overlook, and has been run with style since 1975 by Eric Marsh. Public rooms have log fires, antiques, fine paintings (some of which come from Chatsworth House) and exceptional flower arrangements. Bedrooms, though comfortable, clean and quiet, and well equipped with mini-bar, hair-drier, etc, can be less distinguished, and variable in size; some, we are told this year, are in need of redecoration. It is worth discussing your accommodation when booking. In the restaurant Nick Buckingham's cooking is *nouvelle*, with smallish portions; some readers have found it "over done-up", but the menu states that food can be plainly cooked on request. For £35 you can eat at a table in the "spotless and extremely efficient" kitchen and watch the chef at work. More casual meals are served in the Garden Room between 11 am and 11 pm. Winter weekend rates are good value – if you book for Friday and Saturday nights you can stay for Sunday night at no extra charge. (*Erica Wallace, Sir Timothy Harford, D and J Allom*) One reader was allotted a room under the staff quarters which he found noisy. Another complained of inadequate heating and a dismal breakfast. And an unusual niggle: "The free newspaper offered was the *Financial Times*; I asked for the *Daily Telegraph* and was made to pay."

Open All year.

Rooms 1 suite, 23 double – all with bath, shower, telephone, radio, TV, tea-making facilities, mini-bar, baby-listening. 2 on ground floor.
Facilities Hall/reception, lounge, bar, garden room, 2 restaurants; private dining room, conference room. 2-acre grounds with putting green; fishing in rivers Derwent and Wye.
Location On A619 in Chatsworth grounds (leave M1 at exit 29).
Restrictions No smoking in main restaurant. No dogs.
Credit cards All major cards accepted.
Terms [Until Mar 1992] Rooms: single £65–£75, double £85–£95, suite £110–£125. Breakfast: continental £4.60, English £8.65. Set lunch/dinner £25; full alc £35. Winter bonus weekends. Cots/extra beds available for children (£7.50); special meals by request.
Service/tipping: "No service charge. If a client wishes to leave a tip it is gratefully accepted and shared among all staff."

Fischer's at Baslow Hall *Tel* Baslow (0246) 583259
Calver Road, Baslow DE4 1RR

In 1988 Max and Susan Fischer, well known to gourmets from *Fischer's*, the restaurant they ran in nearby Bakewell, bought this imposing building which, though built in 1907, looks considerably older, and opened it as a restaurant-with-rooms. It entered the Guide last year following an inspector's report: "The Fischers are a charming couple, their staff without exception well mannered and efficient. Max Fischer is a compulsive collector of antiques and the house is crammed with furniture, primarily Victorian and country pine; the walls are bedecked with prints and pictures. The wallpapers and fabrics are at times rather hectic but are of high quality. Fresh flowers, plants, immense bowls of pot-pourri abound. The dining room is light and airy, with well-spaced tables; dinner (four courses with choices for every course) was excellent, everything beautifully presented and uncluttered, properly hot and competently served. The bread rolls were home-baked. There's a separate, welcoming room for breakfast which was probably the nicest I have ever had. Bedrooms, with lots of blue and pink, are up a carved oak staircase. Ours was spacious, dominated by a half-tester bed; it was comfortable and cosy but could have done with a bit less furniture. Bathrooms vary in size and style, some of the loos and showers are almost historic in themselves; there was plenty of hot water at all times." The bedrooms have antique pine furniture and lace bedcovers, and extras such as fruit, mineral water and bathrobes. Some are quite small – and cheaper than the others. One dissident reported limited hanging space for clothes, slow breakfast service, neglected grounds, "and the menu did not change during our three-day stay".

Open All year except Christmas. Restaurant closed to non-residents Sun evening and Mon lunch.
Rooms 1 suite, 5 double – all with bath and/or shower, telephone, radio, TV, baby-listening.
Facilities Lounge, 2 dining rooms; breakfast room. 4½-acre grounds.
Location Take A623 Calver–Stockport through Baslow. Last entrance on right within village boundary.
Restrictions Only restaurant suitable for ♿. No smoking in restaurant. No children under 10 at dinner. No dogs.
Credit cards Access, Amex, Visa.
Terms [1991 rates] B&B: single £62.50–£77.50, double £87.50–£107.50. Set lunch £19, dinner £31.50. Weekend breaks. Reductions for children's meals.
Service/tipping: "No service charge. Tipping optional; shared by a tronc *system."*

BASSENTHWAITE LAKE Cumbria — Map 4

The Pheasant Inn
Bassenthwaite Lake
Cockermouth CA13 9YE

Tel Bassenthwaite Lake (076 87) 76234
Fax (076 87) 76002

This popular low, white-washed inn, just out of sight of the lake, has been run by Mr and Mrs Barrington Wilson for many years. It nestles at the bottom of a dip with wooded slopes rising steeply on three sides. The other side borders the A66; one cannot see the road, but traffic can be heard with a north wind. It has a very pretty woodland garden with a stream frequented by ducks. Inside there are spacious drawing rooms and lounges, all agreeably furnished – good rugs on polished oak floors, a great many easy chairs and sofas, prints and paintings, magazines, and flower arrangements; also beamed ceilings, sparkling copper and brassware, and crackling fires in winter. "The bar," say the owners, "has not changed character in living memory." Bedrooms vary in style and size; some are attractively decorated and well equipped (though none has TV, radio or telephone); but one this year was found "sparse and inadequate". And as in previous years the verdict on breakfast and dinner (both traditionally English) is that they do not come up to the standards set elsewhere in the inn. Staff are "friendly, if a bit inexperienced". More reports please.

Open All year except 24/25 Dec.
Rooms 15 double, 5 single – 18 with bath, 2 with shower. 3 in bungalow annexe – 1 suitable for ♿.
Facilities 3 lounges (2 for residents), bar, dining room; private party/small conference facilities. 1½-acre grounds. Sailing, fishing, pony trekking, golf nearby.
Location 7 m NW of Keswick just off A66 (on W side of Bassenthwaite Lake).
Restrictions No smoking in dining room and 1 lounge. No dogs in bedrooms.
Credit cards None accepted.
Terms B&B: single £48, double £88; dinner, B&B (min 3 days): single £65, double £124. Set Sun lunch £10; set dinner £22. Bar snacks. Weekly rates; winter breaks. 1-night bookings for Sat sometimes refused. Reduced rates for children sharing parents' room; supper at 6 pm.
Service/tipping: "A 10% service charge is included in rates and distributed on a points system to all staff."

BATH Avon — Map 2

Audley House
Park Gardens
Bath BA1 2XP

Tel Bath (0225) 333110
Fax (0225) 482879

Warm endorsements for Gordon and Sheila Talbot's three-roomed 19th-century house, in large grounds west of Victoria Park, but a short walk to the Royal Crescent, the Circle, and other attractions. "Very good in all departments. Bedroom large and well furnished, with good bathroom and separate loo. Generous and delicious breakfast – and no hassle in giving our salmon overnight accommodation in their deep freeze." "The house has been renovated and decorated with loving care and attention. Our room was enormous and filled with antiques, chintz drapes, matching headboard, lace coverlet and all modern amenities. The Talbots were always there when you needed them, and had well-thought-out recommendations for dining and activities." "Hosts warm and friendly.

Good quality everything – bed linen, loo paper, soap; decent hangers in wardrobe. Breakfasts very good. All in all, a place to recommend for those wanting a quiet, civilised stay." (*Judith Swinger, Cathryn Bryck, Ms P Jefferies*) An evening meal is available by arrangement; bring your own wine. There's ample parking.

Open All year.
Rooms 3 double – 2 with bath, 1 with shower, telephone, radio, TV, tea-making facilities.
Facilities Lounge, dining room. 1¼-acre grounds with croquet.
Location 1 m NW of centre. From Upper Bristol road, turn into Park Lane. At end turn left. Park Gardens 100 yds on left.
Restrictions No children under 12. No smoking. No dogs.
Credit cards Access, Visa.
Terms B&B: single £40, double £60. Evening meal by arrangement £16; bring your own wine.
Service/tipping: "No service charge. I advise guests not to tip, and decline it if they do."

Haydon House **BUDGET**
9 Bloomfield Park
Bath BA2 2BY

Tel Bath (0225) 427351
and 444919
Fax (0225) 469020

Magdalene Ashman's sophisticated no-smoking B&B in a spacious Edwardian semi-detached house a stiff walk up from the centre of Bath is a favourite with American visitors. It has a pretty garden, a terrace for summer drinks, and a comfortable chintzy lounge, with a fine Victorian fireplace, family photos and dried flowers. Bedrooms with Laura Ashley wallpapers and fabrics include many cosseting extras. Standards of decor and housekeeping are high. Cooked breakfast, communally served at flexible times, includes a fresh fruit platter, porridge with whiskey or rum and the usual variety of eggs; marmalade and croissants are home-made. For those who do not enjoy "the fellowship around the breakfast table" a generous continental breakfast can be served in the bedrooms. There is ample street parking and garages are available. The Ashmans are happy to advise on local eating places and make reservations for guests. More reports please.

Open All year.
Rooms 4 double – 1 with bath, 3 with shower, all with telephone, radio, TV, tea-making facilities.
Facilities Sitting room, breakfast room. ½-acre garden with sun terrace. Sports and leisure centre nearby.
Location From Bath take A367 (Exeter) up Wells Road about 1 m. Turn right into shopping area with *Bear* pub on right. At end of short dual carriageway fork right into Bloomfield Road, then take 2nd right turn into Bloomfield Park. Street parking, garages.
Restrictions Not really suitable for ♿. No smoking. Children "by arrangement". No dogs.
Credit cards Access, Visa.
Terms B&B: single £32–£38, double £48–£55. Reduced rates for longer stays; 3 days for the price of 2 mid-Nov–mid-Mar except Christmas and New Year. Reduced rates for children sharing parents' room. (No restaurant.)
Service/tipping: "No service charge. Since we are effectively welcoming guests into our home the question of tipping does not arise."

The length of an entry need not reflect the merit of a hotel. The more interesting the report or the more unusual or controversial the hotel, the longer the entry.

Paradise House Hotel *Tel* Bath (0225) 317723
88 Holloway *Fax* (0225) 482005
Bath BA2 4PX

"Bath has always been a favourite place, and was made even more enjoyable by this cosy, welcoming hotel. Our room (No 4) was beautifully decorated and clean and had a marvellous view of the city." "We loved it. The temperature hit 100 the day we arrived and the hosts bundled us right into one of their whirlpool baths!" (*Kathleen Byrnes Touart, Mrs George F McEvoy*) This civilised B&B run by David and Janet Cutting is seven minutes by foot down to the Roman Baths, the Pump Room and the Abbey – and rather longer and a steep uphill slog on the return journey. It is in a quiet cul-de-sac, almost traffic-free, formerly part of the old Roman Fosse Way. There are three lock-up garages. The house is early 18th-century and has been carefully restored by the Cuttings; decor is in Laura Ashley/Designers Guild style, with period features restored. It has fine views of the Georgian city, and a secluded walled garden. The rates include an English breakfast.

Open All year except Christmas.
Rooms 9 double – 6 with bath, 1 with shower, all with telephone, radio, TV, tea-making facilities. 1 on ground floor.
Facilities Sitting room, breakfast room. ½-acre garden with patios and croquet.
Location From A4 turn left at first main traffic lights on to A36, A367 Wells and Exeter ring road. At large roundabout (bisected by railway viaduct) take first left (A367 Exeter road). Continue up hill, the Wellsway, about ¾ m; turn left at small shopping area near Dewhurst butcher; continue left down hill into cul-de-sac. Hotel is 200 yds on left. 3 garages (£1 a night) and parking.
Restrictions Not really suitable for ♿. No smoking in breakfast room. No children under 3. No dogs.
Credit cards Access, Amex, Visa.
Terms B&B: single £37–£55, double £44–£65. Reduced rates for 5 nights or more. 1-night bookings refused for Sat. Children sharing parents' room £10. (No restaurant; dinner reservations made in local restaurants.)

The Queensberry Hotel *Tel* Bath (0225) 447928
Russel Street *Fax* (0225) 446065
Bath BA1 2QF

Stephen and Penny Ross's unashamedly upmarket B&B (now managed by David Brooks) is in a small townhouse which was designed by John Wood for the Marquis of Queensberry in 1772. It is in a residential street not far from the Assembly Rooms; parking can be awkward. The interior has been decorated to complement its 18th-century stucco ceilings and cornices. There is a comfortable, elegant drawing room, a bar where light meals are available, and a small paved garden. Bedrooms are warm, comfortable and well furnished. Some are large, others, at the top, are quite small, but are priced accordingly. A good continental breakfast is served in the bedrooms, and there is a 24-hour room service for cold snacks. Service is helpful and friendly. (*Dr Alec Frank, ID Hunter-Craig, JC Ford*) One complaint: "The bathroom arrangements could be improved by having some shelving at the same height as the wash basin; the eye-level shelf was awkward."

Open All year except 2 weeks over Christmas and New Year.

Rooms 24 double – all with bath, shower, telephone, radio, TV; baby-listening by arrangement.
Facilities Drawing room, bar. Private meeting room. Small patio garden.
Location Off Lansdown Road, above Assembly Rooms.
Restrictions Not suitable for ♿. No dogs.
Credit cards Access, Amex, Visa.
Terms B&B: single occupancy £75–£85, double £85–£140. 2-night winter breaks. (No restaurant but 24-hour light-meal service.)
Service/tipping: "Service charge incorporated in room rate but not at a fixed percentage. This is to discourage tipping unless guests wish to give something extra."

Somerset House *Tel* Bath (0225) 466451
35 Bathwick Hill
Bath BA2 6LD

The Seymours' no-smoking hotel in a handsome Regency mansion is a short drive or bus-ride or a stiffish walk uphill from the city centre. A parrot greets you as you enter; there are two dogs and a cat, a model railway in the garden, and a distinctive style, irksome to some, and wholly congenial to others. "Our sixth visit. We continue to be enthusiastic supporters. We enjoy the professional service of the Seymours and their staff and particularly applaud their policy of concentrating their skills on providing a modest range of dishes all of high quality. Accommodation is comfortable, attractive and immaculate." "Wouldn't stay anywhere else in Bath. Friendly owners, a mine of information on local activities. Excellent food. Always a vegetarian dish offered. Unusual dishes, sometimes with local connections. We like no TV in rooms." "Breakfasts particularly good." (*Harry Robinson, and others*) Bedrooms are well maintained, and have private facilities, but one double and the single are said to be very small. The basement dining room, where the Seymours' son Jonathan is chef, also caters for non-residents; much home-grown or local produce is used, ice-cream, yoghurt, soups etc are home-made. The plentiful meals are described by those in favour as "real food"; "home-cooking not gourmet", but critics find them "dull" or "amateurish". They also react against "the unfunny advice notes and general air of self-satisfaction" and not everyone appreciates the decor of the public rooms – "but perhaps the older clients prefer it to be like a set for the local dramatic society doing an Agatha Christie". Dinner is generally served at about 7 pm, though the Seymours also do an earlier theatre plate by prior arrangement. Credit cards are not accepted for special breaks.

Open All year. Dining room closed Sun evening.
Rooms 9 double, 1 single – all with bath and/or shower, telephone, radio, tea-making facilities, baby-listening. 2 on ground floor.
Facilities 2 lounges (1 with bar, 1 with TV), dining room. 1½-acre garden with 7¼-inch gauge model railway. 5 mins from Kennet and Avon canal – angling for temporary members at Bathampton Angling Club; canal boat trips. 15 mins' walk from centre.
Location Junction of Bathwick Hill (which leads to Bath University) and Cleveland Walk. Carpark.
Restrictions Not suitable for ♿. No smoking. No children under 10 except babies. Small dogs only, not in public rooms.
Credit cards Access, Amex, Visa.
Terms B&B £21.45–£29.20; dinner, B&B £38.95–£46.45. Set Sun lunch £8.65, dinner £17.50. Midweek breaks; special interest weekends, e.g. Georgian Bath, Roman Bath, Brunel. 5-day Christmas house party. Reduced rates for children

sharing parents' room; special meals.
Service/tipping: "No service charge. If we are forced to take a tip it goes into a tin for the staff."

Sydney Gardens Hotel
Sydney Road
Bath BA2 6NT

Tel Bath (0225) 464818 and 445362

Stanley and Diane Smithson's handsome Italianate Victorian villa in a pretty garden is ten minutes from the city centre – just far enough to be peaceful, yet a short walk to Bridge Street. You can park your car in the grounds. The garden is "a haven in this busy city". The Kennet and Avon canal is adjacent; there are good walks along the towpath. The hotel is B&B only, and no-smoking. Visitors appreciate the prettily decorated and comfortable bedrooms, mostly quite large, and the elegant drawing room with lovely views. "Very interesting art throughout the house, much of it by Mr Smithson"; original clocks also add interest to the house. The rates include a generous English breakfast. (*Elizabeth Ring; also Dr RA Mayou*) Only snag – the hotel is close to a railway line which is said to be busy till midnight and after 6 am.

Open All year except 19–27 Dec, 1–24 Jan.
Rooms 6 double – all with bath (5 also have shower), telephone, radio, TV, tea-making facilities.
Facilities Lounge, breakfast room. $\frac{1}{3}$-acre garden; private gateway to park with tennis and walk along adjacent Kennet and Avon canal.
Location From A4 turn left on to A36 ring road towards Exeter and Wells. Cross Avon; turn right, pass Holburne Museum on left, then turn left. Hotel is 200 yds up slope on left. From S, approach road (A36) takes you past hotel door. Parking.
Restrictions Not suitable for ♿. No smoking. No children under 4. Small dogs by arrangement, not in public rooms.
Credit cards Access, Visa.
Terms B&B: single £50–£62, double £59–£69. Extra bed £15. 15% discount for 3-night midweek bookings mid-Nov–end Mar. 1-night bookings sometimes refused at weekend. (No restaurant.)
Service/tipping: "As we run the business ourselves, we do not expect tips. If anything is kindly left it is shared among staff."

BATHFORD Avon — Map 2

Eagle House
Church Street
Bathford BA1 7RS

Tel Bath (0225) 859946

Bathford is a pretty conservation village three miles east of Bath. It's a pleasant alternative to staying in Bath itself; you can avoid the problems of parking in the city by taking a bus. Its quite busy main road climbs a hill; on a small road off to the right, just near the church where Nelson's sister Ann is buried, is this B&B in an imposing listed Georgian building by John Wood the Elder. It is set in one and a half acres of garden, and has a large, handsome drawing room with plenty of well-spaced chairs and sofas, tables with magazines and a fine marble fireplace; there's a large landing upstairs with sofas, chests of drawers, etc. Bedrooms are mostly spacious with a comfortable bed and a scrupulously clean bathroom, though one of the oldest ones has been described to us as "poky". Two are in a walled garden cottage with a sitting room and kitchen. John and Rosamund Napier are "exceptionally warm and hospitable" and pride themselves on the informality of their approach, for example the flexible breakfast times. As they wrote last year: "*Eagle House* is one of the very small number of establishments in the Bath area which has found it possible to welcome guests who smoke, guests who drink, guests with dogs and guests with children. We are anti-embargo and pro-hospitality." No dinner is served, but there are plenty of small restaurants and pubs nearby, and, of course, in Bath. (*Ted Rothstein; also Graham Gilly*)

Open 5 Jan–23 Dec.
Rooms 1 suite, 6 double, 1 single – all with bath and/or shower, telephone, TV, tea-making facilities, baby-listening. Also 2 doubles in cottage with sitting room, kitchen.
Facilities Drawing room, sitting room, breakfast room. 1½-acre garden with croquet, sandpit, swings.
Location 3 m E of Bath on A363. At roundabout immediately after Batheaston follow sign to Bathford; fork left after railway bridge; after 300 yds take Church Street (first on right). Hotel is 200 yds on right behind high stone wall and wrought-iron gates. Conservation area, so hotel sign not permitted. Ample parking.
Restrictions Not suitable for ♿. No dogs in public rooms.
Credit cards None accepted.
Terms B&B: single £28–£36, double £39–£56, suite £60–£75. Winter breaks. 1-night bookings sometimes refused for Sat and bank holidays. Children free in parents' room. (No restaurant.)
Service/tipping: "Service is included. Tipping is permitted but not expected."

The Orchard *Tel* Bath (0225) 858765
80 High Street
Bathford BA1 7TG

John and Olga London's listed Georgian house is set well back from the hill which is the main road of this pretty village, in an immaculate one-and-a-half-acre garden. It has a pretty sitting room with books, deep, comfortable chairs and antique or period furniture, and attractive unfussy bedrooms with pastel decor, deep-pile carpet, and large windows overlooking the garden. A particularly quiet bedroom is the Folly at the back of the house, with its own entrance, which is agreeable in summer, having its own patio with a bench. There are no telephones in the bedrooms, but you can use the payphone under the staircase. On arrival guests are offered tea by the helpful but unobtrusive Londons. Breakfast, in a pretty dining room, is taken round one large table. It is very good, with lots on offer: fresh orange juice, cereal, eggs and bacon, local 'live' yoghurt, croissants and good wholemeal toast. There's no portion control, nothing is wrapped or packaged. For local meals the Londons recommend the *Crown*, a well-run pub at the bottom of the hill. (*CR*)

Open Mar–Oct.
Rooms 4 double, all with bath, shower, TV. 1, with separate entrance, adjoins house.
Facilities Lounge, dining room. 1½-acre grounds.
Location Under railway bridge; first left at *Crown Inn*, up hill; past village store on left. *Orchard* is 100 yds on right.
Restrictions Not suitable for ♿. No smoking in bedrooms and breakfast room. No children under 11. No dogs.
Credit cards None accepted.

Terms B&B double £42.50–£60. 1-night bookings sometimes refused weekends. (No restaurant.)
Service/tipping: "We make it clear that our prices are totally inclusive."

BATTLE East Sussex — Map 3

Little Hemingfold Farmhouse *Tel* Battle (042 46) 4338
Telham, Battle TN33 0TT

This "higgledy-piggledy" early Victorian farmhouse in "bucolic" surroundings in large grounds up a bumpy track re-entered the Guide last year in an italicised entry under new owners (since 1988), Paul and Allison Slater. It is warmly endorsed: "A gem if you want to get away from it all. Everything you could possibly need in your bedroom, but no frills. Marvellously relaxed and informal. It's very pretty, with wild countryside around." "Its most charming feature is having place cards for guests at dinner, and moving the cards each evening so that everyone becomes acquainted." "We had a room in the coach house with a four-poster and, bliss, a wood-burning stove. Generous quantities of uncomplicated but excellent food cooked by the hardworking owners who are inconspicuous unless called upon for something." The set dinner is at 7.30; you choose your starter and dessert before 6; no choice of main course, but special diets can be catered for; many ingredients come straight from the garden. For those who can't face communal dining separate tables can be arranged. Generous English breakfasts are cooked to order. A few bedrooms are in the main house, others are in an old coach house. "No starchy formality here," adds our inspector. "You feel like privileged guests in a simply but attractively furnished private home, and are given the run of two comfortable living rooms complete with games for children, books and a piano. The bedrooms vary in size and decor, furnishings in the rooms and bathrooms are fairly basic, but all have telephone, TV and electric blanket. Paul Slater is only too keen to challenge his guests to a game of tennis, rods are available for fishing on *Little Hemingfold*'s own lake, and maps are provided outlining walks on the property. What it lacks in luxury it makes up for in hospitality." (*Mary Cantacuzene, Elizabeth D Lawson, Deborah Kalinke, and others*) The whole place can be taken for house parties of up to 24.

Open All year.
Rooms 13 double – 11 with bath, all with telephone, radio, TV, tea-making facilities, baby-listening. 9 in adjoining coach house (6 on ground floor).
Facilities 2 lounges, bar, restaurant. 40-acre grounds, lake with fishing and bathing, tennis court, wood.
Location 1½ m SE of Battle; lane is on A2100 after road sign on left indicating bend. From S this is about 1 m past Beauport Park.
Restrictions Not suitable for ♿. No smoking in restaurant and 1 lounge. No dogs in public rooms.
Credit cards Access, Visa.
Terms B&B: single £30–£35, double £55–£65; dinner, B&B: single £40–£48, double £80–£96. Set lunch £15, dinner £18. Special breaks of 2, 4, 7 days; 2-day house parties; Christmas and New Year packages. Children under 4 free in parents' room; 25% discount for under-14s.
Service/tipping: "Service at guests' discretion; tips distributed to all staff according to hours worked."

Give the Guide positive support. Don't just leave feedback to others.

Netherfield Place
Battle TN33 9PP

Tel Battle (042 46) 4455
Fax (042 46) 4024

Michael and Helen Collier's redbrick, Georgian-style 1920s country house is peacefully situated in large well-kept grounds. The decor is of a high standard, and traditional; the pretty lounge has comfortable chairs, fresh flowers, and a log fire in winter. Bedrooms, in light colours, vary in size; the doubles on the first floor are said to be particularly attractive. All have flowers, fresh fruit, chocolates and so on, and well-equipped carpeted bathrooms with bathrobes and capacious towels. The panelled restaurant is popular locally – lunch is good value. "It's not the kind of place where you are made to feel one of the family," a reader said last year, "but more a small and welcoming hotel with an upmarket restaurant – and the residents are at no disadvantage as the table d'hôte menus offer plenty of choice and good value." The food is modern, not *haute cuisine*, but freshly prepared and cooked, using ingredients from the large kitchen garden, and "served with style"; there is a vegetarian menu. There's plenty to do in the extensive grounds (see below).

Open All year except last 2 weeks Dec, first 2 weeks Jan.
Rooms 10 double, 4 single – all with bath (8 also have shower), telephone, radio, TV, baby-listening.
Facilities Lounge, sun lounge, bar, restaurant; conference facilities. 30-acre grounds with gardens, tennis, putting, croquet, clay-pigeon shooting, woodland walks. Golf, fishing, riding nearby.
Location 2 m S of Battle on A2100; turn left towards Netherfield. Hotel is 1½ m on.
Restrictions Not suitable for ♿. No dogs in public rooms.
Credit cards All major cards accepted.
Terms B&B: single £48, double £85–£110. Set lunch £14.50, dinner £18.50; full alc £28. 2-night breaks. 1-night weekend bookings generally refused Mar–Oct. Children £5 in parents' room; special meals by arrangement.
Service/tipping: "Left to guests' discretion. Any tips are divided among all the staff."

BEER Devon — Map 1

Bovey House BUDGET
Beer, Seaton EX12 3AD

Tel Branscombe (029 780) 241

Historic, architecturally interesting stone manor quietly situated in 2½-acre walled garden off B3174 NW of Beer. Run by Mr and Mrs Cole and their daughter and husband, the Gosdens. Fine panelled dining room, large drawing room with Adam ceiling, inglenook bar; one bedroom ceiling depicts Charles I hiding in oak tree. Reasonably priced meals in restaurant and wine bar; impressive wine list, Devon cider a speciality. "Quiet, relaxed and friendly; atmosphere of an ancient and comfortable home." "Impeccable" bedrooms vary in size (not all have private facilities). Open mid-Feb–end Dec. 11 doubles, 6 with bath, 3 with shower. Not suitable for ♿. Access, Visa accepted. Double room: B&B £36.50–£57; dinner, B&B £64.50–£85. New nomination. More reports please, especially on the food.

> Most hotels have reduced rates out of season and for children, and more and more British hotels offer "mini-break" rates throughout the year. If you are staying more than one night, it is always worth asking about special terms.

BEERCROCOMBE Somerset — Map 1

Frog Street Farm BUDGET — *Tel* Hatch Beauchamp (0823) 480430
Beercrocombe, Taunton TA3 6AF

⊞ *César award in 1988: For outstanding farmhouse hospitality*

Veronica Cole's large, airy, well-kept and reasonably priced 15th-century farmhouse/guest house, "a clean, comfortable home from home" with "a happy, tranquil atmosphere", is on a large working farm, deep in rural Somerset, about 21 miles from the north and south coasts. It has fields and woods on one side, orchards on the other, and a heated pool under the cherry trees. Mrs Cole lets only three bedrooms, so there are no more than six guests at any time. Meals are by arrangement: guests are consulted about their preferences on booking. She is a good straight-forward cook; the no-choice menus include roast lamb, roast chicken, pheasant casserole, and "wicked" desserts; most produce is from the farm. No licence, you bring your own wine. Again this year visitors are enthusiastic: "Most hospitable hostess, real English farmhouse atmosphere. Excellent bed, linen, etc. Our meal was generous and delicious. Mrs Cole went out of her way to include asparagus when she heard that I love it." "We entirely support the entry; we thoroughly enjoyed our stay. English breakfast very good indeed – and what a pleasure to have good cafetière coffee with both meals." (*GG Adcock, AD Parsons; also G Ditchfield, and others*)

Open Mar–Nov.
Rooms 3 suites – 2 with bath, 1 with shower, all with tea-making facilities, radio.
Facilities 3 sitting rooms (1 with TV), dining room. Garden with heated swimming pool. On 160-acre working farm with trout stream.
Location 7 m SE of Taunton. Leave M5 at exit 25; take A358 to Ilminster, then the turning to Hatch Beauchamp. Turn at *Hatch Inn*, down Station Rd. Then left all way down no-through road. Signposted.
Restrictions Not suitable for ♿. No smoking. No children under 11. No dogs.
Credit cards None accepted.
Terms B&B £25; dinner, B&B £40 (unlicensed – bring your own wine). Weekly rates.

BETHERSDEN Kent — Map 3

Little Hodgeham BUDGET — *Tel* High Halden (0233) 850323
Smarden Road, Bethersden
TN26 3HE

"Hospitality, quality and kindness." "Comfortable beds, delicious food. Each room different, decorated with care by the owner, Erica Wallace, not 'decorator' decorated." "Warm welcome. A very special place providing wonderful value for money." Australian-born Miss Wallace's 500-year-old half-timbered Tudor cottage in the tiny village of Bethersden in Kent is "typical chocolate box", with roses, honeysuckle, ancient beams, antiques, fresh flowers from the garden, log fires in cold weather. It is set in a flower-filled garden, with a swimming pool, a pond stocked with carp and tench, and a water garden. There are three double bedrooms with comfortable beds and lace-trimmed duvets. In the dining room Miss Wallace presides over "delicious" communally eaten meals elegantly served with fine bone china and crystal. Guests are consulted in advance about their likes and dislikes. The private house-party atmosphere of *Little Hodgeham* is appreciated by those who enjoy socialising with their hostess and meeting their fellow guests. Full hotel amenities are not on offer. (*Mr and Mrs P Gemoets, Margaret Garner, V Alexander*)

Open Easter–1 Sep.
Rooms 3 double – all with bath and/or shower, radio, tea-making facilities, baby-listening.
Facilities Drawing room, TV room, dining room, conservatory. ½-acre garden with unheated swimming pool, fishing pond, water garden. Tennis, golf nearby.
Location 10 m W of Ashford. From Bethersden, at *Bull* pub, take Smarden road for 2 m.
Restrictions Not suitable for ♿. Children by arrangement. Small dogs by prior arrangement, not in public rooms.
Credit cards None accepted.
Terms [1991 rates] Dinner, B&B £44.50 (£39.50 for 4 nights or more). Reduced rates for children sharing parents' room, depending on age; special meals with advance warning.
Service/tipping: "No service charge. Staff are told never to tout for tips."

BIBURY Gloucestershire — Map 2

Bibury Court Hotel
Bibury
Nr Cirencester GL7 5NT

Tel Bibury (028 574) 337
Fax (028 574) 660

"Our fourth visit, but the sheer beauty of the garden and its landscape setting still took us by surprise. Once inside there is little evidence that you are in a hotel; everything contributes to the impression of a private house and one relaxes accordingly. The food was excellent, particularly the meat and vegetables; we would have appreciated smaller, more delicate desserts." "Exactly what I was looking for. Large bedroom, four-poster, huge stone windowseat and leaded windows overlooking garden, churchyard and stream. Made me feel like a country squire. Be sure to go during the trout-fishing season; the hotel can provide tackle." (*George and Betty Dunton, Margaret Brocato*)

This imposing mansion, Tudor with later additions, housing panelled rooms, four-posters and much fine antique furniture, is owned and run "on country-house lines" by Jane Collier with her sister and brother-in-law Anne and Andrew Johnston, and makes a tranquil base for touring the Cotswolds. The Coln river forms the boundary of the six-acre grounds. Behind the grand facade it is elegant, but lived in. The public areas are well furnished; there's a huge open fireplace in the main lounge. Bedrooms vary considerably in style and decor; some have splendidly old-fashioned bathrooms. The converted coach house restaurant has now closed, and meals are again served in the house; there are good bar lunches. *Bibury Court* does not claim to be smooth and professional; informality is the keynote – occasionally readers find the casualness excessive. One cry of pain: "Cigars are permitted and sold in the dining room; a crying shame to ruin good food."

Open All year except Christmas.
Rooms 1 suite, 16 double, 3 single – all with bath, telephone, TV, tea-making facilities, baby-listening; radio on request.
Facilities Lounge, bar, breakfast room, dining room, conference room. 6-acre grounds with croquet and fishing. Golf nearby.

Location Behind church on edge of village on B4425 (formerly A443) Burford–Cirencester.
Restrictions Not suitable for severely ♿. No dogs in dining room.
Credit cards All major cards accepted.
Terms [1991 rates] B&B: single £41–£52, double £62–£68, suite £88. Cot/extra bed £18. Set lunch £15, dinner £20; full alc £25. 2-day breaks out of season except Cheltenham Gold Cup week. Special meals for children.
Service/tipping: "We do not pretend to give service and therefore make no charge."

BIGBURY-ON-SEA Devon — Map 1

Burgh Island Hotel
Bigbury-on-Sea TQ7 4AU

Tel Bigbury-on-Sea (0548) 810514
Fax (0548) 810243

Art Deco extravaganza, on 26-acre private island in Bigbury Bay: "One of the joys is getting there at high tide by giant sea tractor (at low tide you can walk across the sand)." Lovingly restored to former glory by Beatrice and Tony Porter – Palm Court with Peacock Dome; Twenties Bar serving exotic cocktails; sun lounge for cream teas; "magnificent" ballroom where dinner ("good cooking, nouvelle *in style but not portion, local fish and meat, nicely crisp vegetables") is served (on Sat to live 1930s music). Very good service by young locals. Natural rock pool for swimming; water sports, tennis, cliff walks. 14 suites, all with sitting room and bath (with handshower). Not suitable for ♿. No dogs. Dinner, B&B £74–£125. Warm new nomination: "Highly romantic." More reports please.*

BISHOP'S TACHBROOK Warwickshire — Map 2

Mallory Court Hotel
Harbury Lane
Bishop's Tachbrook
Leamington Spa CV33 9QB

Tel Leamington Spa (0926) 330214
Fax (0926) 451714

Jeremy Mort and Allan Holland have been fourteen years at their luxurious country house in the Lutyens manner. It enjoys a rural setting, but is only nine miles from Stratford-on-Avon, and a little more from the National Exhibition Centre outside Birmingham. The large grounds with formal gardens, unheated swimming pool, tennis and squash courts, are carefully maintained. There are several immaculate sitting rooms and a small veranda. Bedrooms, with a floral theme, are comfortable and mostly spacious; all are differently decorated with fine fabrics and period furnishings and are sumptuously equipped. The Blenheim suite, with its spectacular art deco bath and *trompe l'œil* painting on the ceiling, is particularly noteworthy. *Michelin* awards a rosette for the "accomplished meals, pleasantly served" in the oak-panelled dining room under the direction of Allan Holland; there is an extensive wine list. The atmosphere is formal – male guests are expected to wear a jacket and tie at dinner. Lavish teas are served, on a sunny terrace in fine weather. One reader, noting a few weaknesses in her bathroom (limited shelf space, inconvenient mirror) would have liked a little less chi-chi and rather more practicality. And two reports this year find the atmosphere impersonal, for example: "Staff are well-trained and efficient, but they change frequently. You feel you are one of a succession of affluent tourists who must be processed, albeit in a very satisfactory way." Trips to the Royal

Shakespeare Theatre at Stratford on Avon are arranged by the hotel, and also hot-air ballooning.

Open All year.
Rooms 1 suite, 10 double – all with bath, shower, telephone, radio, TV.
Facilities Lounge, drawing room, garden room, dining room. 10-acre gardens with unheated swimming pool, tennis, squash, croquet. Balloon trips, golf nearby.
Location 2 m S of Leamington Spa off B4087. Take left turning to Harbury.
Restrictions Not suitable for ♿. No children under 9. No dogs (kennels nearby).
Credit cards Access, Visa.
Terms B&B: single from £105, double from £120, suite £350. Dinner, B&B from £102.50 per person. English breakfast £10.25. Set lunch £24.50, dinner £42.50. Min 2-night stay at weekend. 3-day winter breaks.
Service/tipping: "We actively discourage tipping. It is stated on all our literature that all prices include VAT and service."

BLAKENEY Norfolk — Map 3

The Blakeney Hotel — *Tel* Cley (0263) 740797
The Quay, Blakeney NR25 7NE — *Fax* (0263) 740795

Overlooking National Trust harbour, with lovely estuary views, quietly situated traditional family hotel with "decent sized" heated indoor swimming pool, saunas, ¼-acre grounds. Bedrooms vary in size; most are quite simple, but well and comfortably furnished. Staff "well trained and exceptionally nice". Dinners mostly liked, but some criticisms of breakfast. Children welcome "provided they do not spoil the enjoyment of others"; high teas. 52 rooms, all with bath and/or shower. All major credit cards accepted. 1991 rates: B&B £53–£63. Light lunch on weekdays from £6, set Sun lunch £12.50, set dinner £15. Readmitted last year; entry endorsed, but we'd like more reports please.

BLANCHLAND Durham — Map 4

The Lord Crewe Arms — *Tel* Blanchland (0434) 675251
Blanchland, Nr Consett — *Fax* (0434) 675337
DH8 9SP

Blanchland is on the river Derwent, about thirty miles south-west of Newcastle upon Tyne, surrounded by moors, fields, forests and a lake – some of the loneliest scenery in Britain. The village is named for the white robes of the monks who inhabited Blanchland Abbey from its founding in the 12th century until its dissolution in the 16th. The hotel was once the abbot's lodgings, guest house and kitchen, and later a manor house. It has a priest's hole in what is now a lounge, a crypt, now a bar and, it is said, a ghost. The hotel, under previous owners, had an entry in earlier editions of the Guide and is brought back by two enthusiastic reports: "A must. There is nowhere quite like it in Britain; and it hasn't changed, except possibly for the better. One enters to the warmth and comfort of huge wood fires and well-upholstered settles and chairs. Everything shines with elbow grease. The ancient stone-flagged floors are spotless, and the whole atmosphere – at least in February – is peaceful. In summer there are lots of visitors, and in autumn there are shooting parties; the hotel also caters for conferences. Messrs Todd and Gingell have been owners for three years and have almost finished a complete refurbishment of the place. The public rooms were filled with bowls of *pot pourri* and hyacinths. The bars were warm and comfortable with a vast choice of beers, including real ale. We had an excellent bar lunch; Ian Press's dinner menu was interesting and well balanced. The staff were happy and smiling." "Food of a high standard, carefully cooked. Service charming and efficient. Bedrooms light and well appointed, clean and comfortable." (*Stephanie Sowerby, KH Rich*) Some of the best bedrooms are in *The Angel*, an old inn used as an annexe near the main building.

Open All year except 1 week Feb.
Rooms 18 double – all with bath and/or shower, telephone, radio, TV, tea-making facilities, baby-listening. Some in *The Angel*, 30 yds away. 3 on ground floor.
Facilities Lounge, bar, restaurant; conference facilities. 1-acre grounds with walled garden.
Location On B6306, 10 m S of Hexham.
Restrictions Not really suitable for ♿. No dogs in public rooms.
Credit cards All major cards accepted.
Terms B&B: single £70, double £97. Full alc £29. Half-board rates for 2 nights or more £58–£63 per person. Children under 14 sharing parents' room charged for meals only.
Service/tipping "We do not encourage tipping, but it is general in the restaurant."

BLANDFORD FORUM Dorset — Map 2

La Belle Alliance
White Cliff Mill Street
Blandford Forum DT11 7BP

Tel Blandford (0258) 452842
Fax (0258) 480053

"Warm welcome; fresh tea immediately provided. Bed very comfortable." "The outstanding quality was the service; the owners and staff struck just the right note of warm hospitality combined with formal discretion that made us feel comfortable and well cared for. (We have often failed to find this quality and tone in far more expensive and smart hotels.)" "Makes no pretence to be a hotel and is all the better for that. The bedrooms have been redecorated and furnished with flair. Food excellent and well presented; the menu provides a sufficient range of choice to suit everyone and Philip Davison frequently makes unscheduled additions depending on materials available locally. The wine list, though not large, has been selected with care and provides a variety and quality which can match larger establishments." (*HD Astley, Marion and David Fanthorpe, Peter J Shaw; also GR Murray*)

With the odd dissenting note about the accommodation, the majority is firmly in favour of this restaurant-with-rooms run by Lauren and Philip Davison (he the chef) in a spacious Victorian house on the quiet outskirts of a pleasant market town in the heart of Hardy country. Meals, in the quite formal dining room, are the centre of things. There is a set-price dinner menu, changing almost daily, with five or six choices at each course, much use of local produce, and excellent home-made ice-creams. There is an intimate lounge for aperitifs. Bedrooms, which were redecorated in early 1990, all have designer fabrics and a canopy over the beds. They vary in size from "very spacious" to one which last year was described to us as "cramped". The Davisons tell us this has now been redesigned, with built-in furniture and an especially good bathroom.

Open Feb–Dec. Restaurant closed Sun and Mon evening except bank holidays; lunch served Sun, other days by arrangement only.

Rooms 6 double – all with bath, shower, telephone, TV, tea-making facilities, baby-listening.
Facilities Lounge, restaurant. Small garden. Riding stables opposite.
Location Go through town (1-way system); bear left on to Shaftesbury (Warminster) road; restaurant is 300 yds on right. Parking for 13 cars.
Restrictions Not suitable for ♿. No smoking in dining room. Children under 7 by arrangement. No dogs in public rooms.
Credit cards Access, Amex, Visa.
Terms B&B: single £48–£52, double £59–£74. Set Sun lunch £12.50, dinner £16 and £22. 3-day gourmet breaks. 1-night bookings sometimes refused at bank holidays. Reduced rates and special meals for children sharing parents' room. *Service/tipping: "We do not expect tips as we believe we pay our staff a fair wage for the good service they offer."*

BLOCKLEY Gloucestershire **Map 2**

The Crown
High Street, Blockley
Nr Moreton-in-Marsh GL56 9EX
Tel Blockley (0386) 700245
Fax (0386) 700247

Civilised conversion of "gem" of an old inn run by Champion family on high street of exceptionally pretty, unspoiled Cotswold village off A44 between Moreton-in-Marsh and Broadway. Mellow stone and old beams alongside modern comforts; small garden. 2 bars, 2 restaurants (à la carte and grill – fish a speciality). Recommended for pleasant atmosphere and good fresh food. 21 rooms, all with bath and shower. Access, Amex, Visa accepted. 1991 rates: B&B £36–£58. Set menus £18 and £27. New nomination. More reports please.

BOLTON ABBEY North Yorkshire **Map 4**

The Devonshire Arms
Bolton Abbey, Nr Skipton
BD23 6AJ
Tel Bolton Abbey (075 671) 441
Fax (075 671) 564

Former traditional coaching inn owned, like the Cavendish, *Baslow (q.v.), by the Duke and Duchess of Devonshire, who brought it upmarket and added a modern wing. Antiques and paintings from Chatsworth. 4-acre grounds in Yorkshire Dales National Park, 5 miles E of Skipton. Was in earlier editions but dropped after warmth of welcome and quality of food were queried by the editor. Now reinstatement is urged: "Welcoming reception, comfortable, attractive public rooms, quiet bedroom with view of cattle and sheep in field opposite. Food excellent and interesting. Service very good. Dogs welcome for no extra charge." Good fishing nearby. 40 rooms, all with bath and shower. All major credit cards accepted. B&B double £98–£112. Set lunch £14.50, dinner £24. 2-day breaks. More reports please.*

BOLTON-BY-BOWLAND Lancashire **Map 4**

Harrop Fold
Bolton-by-Bowland
Clitheroe BB7 4PJ
Tel Bolton-by-Bowland (020 07) 600

Farmhouse, "an oasis of tranquillity", in remote location in heart of Pennines, run as a hotel by "hospitable and delightful" Wood family for over 20 years.

Recommended for comfortable bedrooms with large beds and numerous amenities including TV, *and home-cooked meals "with wide variety of interesting choices", served at flexible times. 8 double rooms all with bath. Not suitable for ♿. No dogs. Access, Visa accepted. Dinner, B&B: double £89. Reinstated last year. More reports please.*

BONCHURCH Isle of Wight — Map 2

Winterbourne
Bonchurch, Nr Ventnor PO38 1RQ
Tel Isle of Wight (0983) 852535
Fax (0983) 853056

A hotel with strong Dickensian associations (he stayed there while writing David Copperfield and bedrooms are named after characters in his books) re-enters the Guide after an absence of some years: "We spent a sunny, enchanting weekend. We arrived on Saturday afternoon, unannounced. A wedding reception was going on, some of the guests were walking in the lovely grounds, others were in or around the swimming pool. The atmosphere was of happiness, elegance and charm. The hotel was fully booked but the receptionist organised an improvised double room – Steerforth, actually a single, a sort of attic, with its own bathroom just down the corridor, and a spectacular view of sea and gardens. We took a pre-dinner drink by a huge fireplace in the elegant Copperfield Room and dined in the Regency Room, also furnished with taste and style. Service was pleasant and easy-going, mostly by trendy-looking young women. Good quality English breakfast next morning – but they should have changed the tablecloth, we recognised ours from the night before." (*Gabriele Berneck and Christine Herxheimer*) Other readers also tell of minor housekeeping niggles. A new chef has arrived since that report was written; more reports would be welcome; the six-course table d'hôte menu, with plenty of choice, changes daily.

Dickens wrote of *Winterbourne*, "It is the prettiest place I ever saw in my life, at home or abroad." Our report in 1984 backed him up: "The hotel's location is delightful. It is next to the tiny old church in a quiet cul-de-sac and, behind the buildings, enchanting gardens slope down the hillside in interlocking terraces of beautiful lawns, gravel paths, herbaceous and rose borders. Hidden away are sheltered areas for sunbathing and a secluded 40-foot swimming pool. A stream and waterfall gurgle away downhill and one can go down to the beach through a gate at the bottom of the garden opening on to a footpath which meanders down to the shore." In addition to the rooms in the main house, there are five in a converted coach house, less characterful perhaps, but larger.

Open Early Mar–mid-Nov.
Rooms 1 suite, 14 double, 4 single – 18 with bath, 1 with shower, all with telephone, radio, TV, baby-listening; tea-making facilities on request. 5 in adjacent coach house.
Facilities 2 lounges, restaurant. 4½-acre grounds with heated swimming pool.
Location 1½ m NE of centre of Ventnor, off A3055 to Shanklin; 100 yds from Duck Pond in Bonchurch.
Restrictions Not suitable for ♿. No smoking in restaurant. No children under 3 in dining room at dinner (room-service meals). Dogs in public rooms by arrangement only.
Credit cards All major cards accepted.
Terms B&B: single £45–£49, double £90–£116, suite £108–£116; dinner, B&B: single £50–£55, double £100–£128. Light lunch available. Set dinner £16.50.

Service/tipping: "Credit card forms are not *left blank to encourage tipping. Any tips are distributed equally to all staff."*

BORROWDALE Cumbria **Map 4**

Seatoller House BUDGET *Tel* Borrowdale (076 87) 77218
Borrowdale, Keswick CA12 5XN

César award in 1984: Most sympathetic guest house

"It's hard to think of new ways of expressing one's appreciation without going over the top. It's still the same, even to Margaret, the live-in help. David Pepper still enjoys a game of bridge and there were lively games of Scrabble and much interesting conversation. Though no special concessions are made to children (high tea, games room etc), they fit in very well and respond to the civilised atmosphere." "*Seatoller*'s hard core of regular visitors enjoys admirable cooking, a well-chosen wine list, warm bedrooms and excellent drying facilities. The conversation at the two long dining tables ranges far and wide. The atmosphere is delightfully informal. A very special place." "We have stayed five times in the past five years and plan to continue this annual visit as long as we can walk the fells. David Pepper combines an easy manner and real friendliness with an unobtrusive efficiency, which ensures that his guests feel at home in a perfectly run house."

Seatoller is over 300 years old, and has been a guest house for more than a century. It enjoys a breathtaking setting at the head of the Borrowdale valley, near the Honister Pass, close to the starting point of many spectacular fell walks. Run by David and Ann Pepper, it is remarkably inexpensive, and has long been a favourite of Guide readers in search of homely comfort, and good value rather than lavish decor, *haute cuisine* and hotel-type facilities. Meals – breakfast at 8.30 am and dinner (no choice) at 7 pm – are communal. Bedrooms, some of them quite large, are "spotless and sympathetically decorated"; they all now have a private bathroom, "with large and fluffy towels, but not all are *en suite* so you need a dressing gown". (*Abigail Kirby Harris, Col and Mrs Geoffrey Powell, LRB Elton*)

Open Mar–Nov. Dining room closed Tue evening.
Rooms 9 double – all with bath and shower. 1 in converted bakehouse. 2 on ground floor.
Facilities Lounge, library, dining room, self-service tea-bar; small conference facilities; drying room. 2-acre grounds.
Location 8 m S of Keswick on B5289. Regular bus service from Keswick.
Restrictions No smoking in dining room, sitting room and bedrooms. Not suitable for severely ♿. No children under 5. No dogs in public rooms.
Credit cards None accepted.
Terms (No service charge) Dinner, B&B £30.50–£32. Packed lunches available. Weekly rates; special rates for parties of 18 or more. 1-night bookings sometimes refused. Reduced rates for children under 12 sharing parents' room.

****

Traveller's tale *The waiter dropped my hard-boiled egg on the floor, disappeared behind the floral arrangement and then brought it to me with a flourish, as though nothing had happened.*

****

BOSHAM West Sussex — Map 1

The Millstream
Bosham Lane, Bosham
Nr Chichester PO18 8HL

Tel Bosham (0243) 573234
Fax (0243) 573459

In main street of delightful old fishing and sailing village (featured in Bayeux Tapestry), 4 m W of Chichester, this hotel, popular for lunch and drinks in season, is composed of small manor house and surrounding malthouse and cottages. 1½-acre peaceful grounds with stream and ducks. Comfortable public rooms and bedrooms; quite simple decor with period furniture. "Perhaps a certain lack of polish at reception, but no lack of desire to help; food of consistently high standard, excellent dining-room service." 29 bedrooms, most of good size, all with bath and shower. Not suitable for ♿. No smoking in dining room. All major credit cards accepted. B&B double £87–£97. Set menus (changed daily) £16.25. Bridge breaks, Christmas package. Dropped from earlier editions due to critical reports, now warmly re-nominated. More reports please.

BOUGHTON MONCHELSEA Kent — Map 3

Tanyard
Wierton Hill,
Boughton Monchelsea
Maidstone ME17 4JT

Tel Maidstone (0622) 744705

"We try to go every year. On each visit it has, if anything, improved. It seems as fresh and immaculately clean as the day we first saw it. The standards of care, attention and hospitality are exceptional. The atmosphere is informal and one finds oneself dropping into easy communication with fellow guests gathering in the front room before an enormous log fire for pre-dinner drinks." "What a delightful place. My room looked over duck pond and cornfields. The whole place seemed recently done up, with designer pastels, chintzes and antiques. Very friendly all-female staff. Excellent set dinner. Very peaceful except for quacking."

This lovingly restored medieval yeoman's house, later a tannery, is now a very small hotel – "a brilliant combination of mod cons with the ancient" – owned and run by Jan Davies. It has an attractive garden with a pond, and enjoys a secluded position on the edge of the Weald of Kent, looking out over orchards and cottages. Leeds Castle and Sissinghurst, Folkestone, Dover and Gatwick are all within an hour's drive. There are only six bedrooms: heavily beamed, furnished with good antique pieces, comfortable and well provided with "extras". Some are small, but a magnificent suite with far-reaching views and a bathroom with a spa bath occupies the whole of the top floor. Food, cooked by Ms Davies, is "imaginative, without being bizarre, and served in satisfying portions, everything bursting with freshness". There is no choice of the four courses at dinner except for dessert, but guests are asked if they would like alternatives. There is a reasonably priced wine list. Due to its historic nature this house is not for the elderly or disabled. (*Jeremy and Anthea Larken, Mr and Mrs E Vesely, and others*) One niggle this year: "Pity about the packet orange juice at breakfast."

Open Early Mar–mid-Dec. Restaurant closed for lunch.

Rooms 1 suite, 4 double, 1 single – all with bath and/or shower, telephone, radio, TV, tea-making facilities.
Facilities Hall/reception, lounge, restaurant. 1-acre garden; 9-acre farmland.
Location 5 m S of Maidstone. From B2163 at Boughton, turn down Park Lane opposite *Cock* pub. First right down Wierton Lane. Fork right; *Tanyard* is on left at bottom of hill.
Restrictions Not suitable for ♿. No children under 6. No dogs.
Credit cards All major cards accepted.
Terms [1991 rates] (Excluding VAT) B&B: single £42–£48, double £60, suite from £75; dinner, B&B: single £58–£64, double £92, suite from £107. Set dinner £16. 1-night bookings refused at weekend.
Service/tipping: "Tips are not expected, but if given are distributed to all staff according to hours worked."

BOURNE Lincolnshire **Map 4**

Bourne Eau House *Tel* Bourne (0778) 423621
South Street, Bourne PE10 9LY

Not a hotel, but "the home of a very interesting English family" in "magical" setting in conservation area of small market town. 1-acre grounds separated by the Bourne Eau, complete with geese and swans, from 12th-century abbey; ruins of Hereward the Wake's castle across the road. George and Dawn Bishop's listed country house – Elizabethan/Georgian, with inglenooks and oak beams, is recommended for comfortable accommodation, civilised ambience, very good (no-choice) meals – English home-cooking. Closed Christmas, New Year. 3 rooms, all with bath/shower. Not suitable for ♿. Credit cards not accepted. B&B £25–£45; dinner, B&B £37–£62. New nomination. More reports please.

BOWNESS-ON-WINDERMERE Cumbria **Map 4**

Lindeth Fell *Tel* Windermere (096 62) 3286
Bowness-on-Windermere
LA23 3JP

"What a beautiful and quiet setting. The Kennedys are welcoming hosts. The food suited us best of all the hotel food we ate on our trip. Our bedroom was very comfortable. We were directed on memorable walks." "Good choice of fish on menu, and delicate herby soups." (*Betsy Wilhelm, Jennifer Hubbard*)

This solid, well-built Lakeland-stone house stands in a tranquil setting above the bustle and activity of Bowness in extensive grounds (open to the public once a year) with rhododendrons and azaleas, tennis and croquet, and a small tarn with trout. It is owned and run by Pat Kennedy, ex-RAF, and his wife Diana, who does most of the cooking assisted by Sarah Churchward. There are two lounges, one of which has a beautiful Adam-style plaster ceiling and tall, wide windows looking over the treetops to Windermere, and lots of books which you are encouraged to borrow. Most bedrooms overlook the lake; they are clean and comfortable, with crisply laundered sheets, well-placed lights and lamps, and good towels. The three best, which are large, cost slightly more than the others. Food is good traditional English cooking with some choice on each menu. The wine list is extensive and reasonably priced. The "warm, outgoing" Kennedys are a mine of information on local walks, climbs and gardens.

Open 6 Mar–9 Nov.
Rooms 12 double, 2 single – all with bath and/or shower, telephone, radio, TV, tea-making facilities, baby-listening. 1 ground-floor room.
Facilities Ramp. Hall, 2 lounges, dispense bar, dining room. 7-acre grounds with gardens, tennis, croquet, putting, tarn with fishing. Windermere $\frac{3}{4}$ m.
Location 1 m S of Bowness on A5074.
Restrictions Smoking in dining room discouraged. "More suitable for children over 7." Dogs in grounds only.
Credit cards Access, Visa.
Terms [1991 rates] Dinner, B&B £44–£49.50. Set lunch £7.50, dinner £21.50. 1-night bookings sometimes refused over bank holidays. Children sharing parents' room half price; special meals.
Service/tipping: "I disagree with arbitrary service charges. Here it is optional."

BOX Wiltshire — Map 2

Clos du Roy
Box House, Box SN14 9NR

Tel Bath (0225) 744447
Fax (0225) 743971

In 1989 Philippe Roy, formerly a Bath restaurateur, opened a restaurant in this fine Georgian house, once a vicarage in a lovely Wiltshire village 5½ miles north-east of Bath on the A4 (and within earshot of the trains which use Brunel's Box tunnel nearby). 7-acre grounds with swimming pool in walled garden back on to the village church. Now there are 9 immaculate and pretty bedrooms, all with bath and shower. The Roy style of cooking pleases some, is too fancy for others, and the atmosphere can be impersonal. Daytime nanny, special children's meals, baby-listening, baby-sitting. Only restaurant suitable for ♿. All major credit cards accepted. 1991 rates: B&B double £110–£130. Set lunch £15.50, dinner £29.50. New nomination. More reports please.

BRADFORD-ON-AVON Wiltshire — Map 2

Bradford Old Windmill
Masons Lane
Bradford-on-Avon BA15 1QN

Tel Bradford-on-Avon (0225) 866842

"Very friendly owners, comfortable hotel, interesting building, wonderful position. Good value for money," writes *Jenny Tozer,* succinctly endorsing the entry for this mill run by Peter and Priscilla Roberts, founders of the Distinctly Different Association of granaries, chapels, oast houses, railway carriages and the like, turned into inexpensive guest accommodation. Quietly set in a small garden on a steepish hill overlooking Bradford, it has lovely views and is furnished throughout with old pine and decorated with an eclectic collection of *objets trouvés* acquired during the proprietors' travels round the world. Rooms "come in all shapes and sizes"; the Round Room has a round bed, the Tower Room a water bed. Priscilla Roberts is a vegetarian and her husband an omnivore, so they compromise in the catering. At breakfast (which is communally taken) there's a wide range of alternatives "to suit carnivores, vegetarians, vegans, healthy and unhealthy eaters". Evening meals are exclusively vegetarian, usually with an international flavour; visitors should check on their availability as Mrs Roberts likes to take the occasional night off. "Our aim," she writes, "is to make our guests feel part of the household –

We depend on detailed fresh reports to keep our entries up to date.

with all the advantages and disadvantages that this entails." The mill is a no-smoking establishment; it is unlicensed, so bring your own wine.

Open All year. Dinner sometimes not served (check with owners).
Rooms 3 double, 1 single – 1 with bath, 2 with shower; all with radio, TV, tea-making facilities.
Facilities Lounge, dining room. Small garden. River Avon 5 mins' walk.
Location In Bradford on A363 find *Castle* pub. Go down hill towards centre. After 100 yds turn left into private drive immediately before first roadside house.
Restrictions Not suitable for ♿. No smoking. No children under 6. No dogs.
Credit cards None accepted.
Terms B&B: single £30–£50, double £39–£59. Set dinner £16–£18. Min 2-night stay for advance bookings. Reductions for 3-night stays; winter breaks, honeymoon packages. Reduced rates for children sharing parents' room.
Service/tipping: "Service included in the price. As proprietors we do not expect to be tipped for being nice to our guests. Our payment is in their return visits."

Woolley Grange
Woolley Green
Bradford-on-Avon BA15 1TX

Tel Bradford-on-Avon (022 16) 4705
Fax (022 16) 4059

César award: For offering families the best of both worlds

"To long-term hedonists but relatively recent parents this hotel was a find, if a rather expensive one. *Woolley Grange* is geared to sybaritic yuppies with children; the nursery meals and nanny-run crèche are a boon. The four resident Chapman children mean that real parental concern has gone into the planning. For grown-ups there is cheerful service, beautiful surroundings and facilities. Large grounds and good thick walls mean that the other children are not too obtrusive, but if I was there on a break from kids or preferred their absence I would breakfast in my bedroom." "My room was rather small but quiet, well furnished, comfortable, not unreasonably priced. Service attentive and pleasant, though at dinner rather bucolic." (*Sara Nathan, TM Wilson*)

This mainly Jacobean manor house, multi-chimneyed and mullion-windowed, with an oak-panelled drawing room and a bright conservatory, stands in large grounds with a fishpond, fountain, large walled kitchen garden, designed by Geraldene Holt, swimming pool and grass tennis courts. It has been carefully restored by the Chapman family, and decorated with flair, "the bedrooms cleverly fitting into the old structure, lots of beams, windows in odd places, hand-picked old pieces of furniture, amusing pictures"; there are brass beds and gas fires in many bedrooms. A few are attic rooms and tiny. In the large dining room much local produce is used, some of it organic; pastries and breads are baked on the premises; English cheeses are a special feature. In July 1990 Ian Mansfield was promoted to chef, and an inspector in November enjoyed his meal after initial problems in attempting to order. "And the Chapmans have put a lot of thought into attracting families with young children without putting off childless visitors." There is a nursery with a trained nanny and a large playroom in a converted coach house. One reader felt the nursery arrangements were not adequately organised. Nursery tea is served at 5 pm. There's plenty to amuse older children as well. There is no extra charge for these facilities or for cots; prices are per room, so that parents can have as many children in their room as they wish or can tolerate without paying extra.

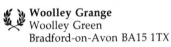

To keep their hotel full, the enterprising Chapmans, now in their third year, also run off-season breaks and honeymoon packages, and arrange cycling, riding, golf, hot-air ballooning and many other activities locally. "What we offer," writes Nigel Chapman, "is a relaxed but stylish atmosphere for adults while meeting the needs of children on a completely different level, ensuring that neither party 'at play' is especially aware of the other, unless they wish. We do not 'flunky' our guests. Once they realise that visiting us is a little like staying in a friend's (rather large) house they generally relax and enjoy themselves." Bedrooms vary in size, as do bathrooms – some are large and lavishly done up, but one "was so tiny I was grateful not to be fatter or pregnant; and it had a shower so lacking power that hair-washing was impossible".

Open All year.
Rooms 2 suites, 17 double, 1 single – all with bath and/or shower, telephone, radio, TV, baby-listening. 6 in converted dairy.
Facilities Lounges, conservatory, dining room. 14-acre grounds with dining terrace, gardens, heated swimming pool, tennis and croquet. Boating and fishing in the Avon 1 m.
Location 1 m NE of Bradford-on-Avon off B3109.
Restriction No dogs in restaurant.
Credit cards All major cards accepted.
Terms B&B: single £80, double £90–£125, suite £160. Set lunch £10–£16, dinner £24.50–£32; full alc £40. Off-season packages; Christmas/New Year packages. 1-night bookings at weekends generally refused. Reduced rates and special menus for children (if sharing parents' room charged for meals only).
Service/tipping: "We do not make a service charge. If a guest feels disposed to tip, the staff share this among themselves."

BRAITHWAITE Cumbria — Map 4

Ivy House — *Tel* Braithwaite (076 87) 78338
Braithwaite, Keswick CA12 5SY — *Fax* (076 87) 78338

In the centre of a small village two miles from Keswick, recently extensively redecorated and refurbished by Nick and Wendy Shill, *Ivy House* has a comfortable lounge with beams, and log fires at each end in winter, a pretty staircase, and mostly well-appointed bedrooms; decor is traditional, with some nice old furniture. The friendly Shills run the hotel with a "talented and efficient small staff". Readers appreciate the relaxed atmosphere, and the dinners, "reasonably priced, and first-rate, combining the traditional with the imaginative", cooked by Mrs Shill and "elegantly served on fine linen, with silver, crystal and china", in a first-floor restaurant, "oak-beamed, candle-lit and soothing in character". There is ample choice on the menu, with vegetarian tastes considered; portions are generous. The hotel has no grounds, but there are good walks from the doorstep – and the Shills keep a walkers' book in which guests enter their planned route in case anyone should get lost. (*Mr and Mrs BN Turvey; also Michael Firth, Michael Pinto, Mrs CJ Wormald*) There are three more rooms this year – a double and two singles. One couple reported a sub-standard room on the ground floor.

Open All year except first 2 weeks Dec, all Jan.
Rooms 10 double, 2 single – all with bath and/or shower, telephone, TV, tea-making facilities, baby-listening.
Facilities Lounge, bar, dining room. Lakes, fishing, walking nearby.

Location In centre of village 2 m W of Keswick.
Restrictions Not suitable for ♿. No smoking in dining room. Dogs by arrangement; not in public rooms.
Credit cards All major cards accepted.
Terms B&B £30–£36.50; dinner, B&B £42.50–£49 (£10 supplement for single occupancy). Set dinner £18.75. Reductions for long stays. Off-season midweek rates; Christmas and New Year breaks. Reduced rates for children sharing parents' room.
Service/tipping: "We have no policy about tipping. If guests have enjoyed their stay and wish to reward staff we are delighted."

BRAMPTON Cumbria — Map 4

Farlam Hall
Brampton CA8 2NG

Tel Hallbankgate (069 77) 46234
Fax (069 77) 46683

A long-established country house hotel, at the smarter end of that spectrum, run by the "courteous and professional" Quinion and Stevenson families – parents, son, daughter and son-in-law, with "a well-drilled, attentive staff". It lies in unspoilt countryside near Hadrian's Wall in lovely gardens with mature trees and an ornamental lake. The house dates from the 17th century but was considerably enlarged in the 19th. Inside it is "visually delightful, with charming *objets d'art*, fine fabrics and paintings everywhere"; in cold weather there are "real fires, warm and friendly". Bedrooms, "clean, bright and well cared for", vary considerably in size and shape; they are "very comfortable, with 'give-aways' in abundance, and readable bedside books". Dinner is somewhat formal, served punctually at 8 pm, with jacket and tie expected of male diners. The meal, based on local produce, is generally considered "excellent, well cooked and presented"; the house wine is good value. Breakfast is said to include "some interesting non-run-of-the-mill choices". The restaurant is closed for lunch, but light meals are provided for residents by prior arrangement. One reader found the bedroom decor "a touch ornate".

Open Mar–Jan. Closed Christmas. Restaurant closed for lunch.
Rooms 12 double, 1 single – 12 with bath and shower, 1 with shower, all with telephone, radio, TV. 1 in converted stable block. 2 on ground floor.
Facilities 2 lounges, bar, dining room. 5-acre grounds with croquet. Golf nearby.
Location On A689, 2½ m SE of Brampton (*not* in Farlam village).
Restrictions Not suitable for ♿. No children under 5. Dogs by arrangement only; not unattended in bedrooms or public rooms.
Credit cards Access, Visa.
Terms Dinner, B&B £77–£97. Set dinner £25.50. Winter and spring breaks.
Service/tipping: "No service charge. Tips optional. Guests who wish to thank the staff should be allowed to do so. Tips are divided among the staff at the end of the season according to the amount of work done."

BRANSCOMBE Devon — Map 1

The Bulstone BUDGET
Higher Bulstone
Branscombe EX12 3BL

Tel Branscombe (029 780) 446

Peter and Barbara Freeman's small hotel caters specially for families with small children: ten bedrooms have been designed to be practical and safe for children. There is an efficient laundry and many thoughtful touches to lighten the load of parents. Children under five are free, and there are generous reductions, varying according to season, for under-12s. *The Bulstone* is on the edge of the pretty village of Branscombe, scattered along a valley, much of which belongs to the National Trust. It entered the Guide last year, warmly nominated by *Jane Curley:* "We demand a certain standard of accommodation and food, and have a toddler whose requirements are very different. We like to take frequent holidays so our budget is fairly limited. *The Bulstone* satisfied us all. We occupied a family suite. The decor, with pine furniture, Laura Ashley fabrics, and a plain-coloured, good quality carpet made a welcome change from the usual clashing colours often found in 'family' hotels. The children's rooms have a bunk bed and a cot, dimmer switches and night-lights. Our daughter's one had a window, but four of the six suites have internal bedrooms for the children – an advantage for most mums as the children don't argue about its being light at bedtime! Everything was provided for children – high chairs, changing mats, nappy buckets, baby-listening. Children's high tea at 4.45 pm was plentiful and nutritious. There was an unspoken agreement that parents would endeavour to have the children in bed by dinner; children were not allowed in the coffee lounge after dinner. The four-course meal, with locally produced vegetables and a good range of choices, including a vegetarian dish, was very good. The hotel has a playroom, a well-equipped outdoor play area, and a paddock with goats, a pig, a pony and chickens. Children were encouraged to feed the animals and collect the eggs. It's brilliant! But pity any unsuspecting guest who arrives without children." More reports please.

Open Feb–Nov inclusive.
Rooms 10 suites, 2 double – 6 with bath and shower, all with tea-making facilities, baby-listening. Some on ground floor.
Facilities Lounge, TV lounge, bar, restaurant; mothers' room, playroom, laundry. 3½-acre grounds with children's play area. Near sea and beaches; fishing and water sports.
Location A3052 from Sidmouth. Take turning on right marked Bulstone ¾ m. Ignore all other turnings to Branscombe.
Restriction No smoking in bedrooms, TV lounge, playroom, dining room. No dogs in bedrooms; in public access at other guests' discretion.
Credit cards None accepted.
Terms B&B £17.50–£29; dinner, B&B £30.50–£42. Set dinner £13.50. Packed lunches, snacks available. Spring and autumn breaks. Children under 5 free; reductions according to season for under-12s; high teas.
Service/tipping: "Service is included. We do not suggest that tips are given. If customers do give tips, they are distributed among the staff."

The Look Out *Tel* Branscombe (029 780) 262
Branscombe EX12 3DP

"Most rewarding. To start with they have the great advantage of a splendid position. In addition the owner, Peter Leach, is still an active antique dealer and the hotel is furnished with some quite delightful pieces. The bedrooms are extremely comfortable with superb views. Food was exceptional, and the choice of wines excellent, at a price which did not bring tears to my eyes. The welcome is quite understated but nevertheless genuine." (*MJ Hutton; also Mr and Mrs K Pearlman*)

Peter and Dodie Leach's small hotel in attractively converted coast-guard cottages, "delightful, comfortable, with peaceful atmosphere and friendly service", is quietly situated on a cliff on the edge of the village in a pretty garden, with views over Lyme Bay and easy access to magnificent National Trust cliff walks and Branscombe's vast shingle and sand beach. Inside are flagstones, oak beams, antique and period furniture. The bedrooms, all with sea view, some quite large, are comfortable and pretty; all have bath and/or shower but they are not all *en suite*. There is a new chef this year, Steven Hart. Dinner is at about 8 pm; guests are asked to be down at 7.30 to choose from the table d'hôte menu. A vegetarian dish is always available. In reply to last year's criticisms the Leachs write: "We now serve only freshly squeezed orange juice; only one of our bathrooms can be considered small."

Open All year except Christmas/New Year. Restaurant closed Mon eve and for lunch except bank holidays.
Rooms 1 family suite, 5 double – all with bath and/or shower, TV, tea-making facilities, mini-bar; cordless phone available.
Facilities Lounge/bar, restaurant. 1-acre garden. Direct access to beach; fishing, boating, golf nearby.
Location ½ m beyond village centre; follow signs to beach.
Restrictions No children under 6. No dogs in public rooms.
Credit cards None accepted.
Terms B&B: single £45–£55, double £75–£85; dinner, B&B: single £65–£80, double £115–£135. Set dinner £23–£25. Discount on 7-night stays all year and on 2-night stays in low season. Reduced rates for children in family suite; special meals on request.
Service/tipping: "No service charge. Tips given at guests' discretion if they are entirely happy with the service; divided among all staff."

BRAY-ON-THAMES Berkshire **Map 1**

Monkey Island Hotel
Bray-on-Thames
Nr Maidenhead SL6 2EE

Tel Maidenhead (0628) 23400
Fax (0628) 784732

A hotel full of character and history on an island in the Thames not far from Maidenhead (once known as Monks Eyot because it was used by monks who had a fishery there) makes its Guide debut. In the early 18th century the third Duke of Marlborough built a "fishing lodge" and "fishing temple" on the island and these buildings, now called the Pavilion and the Temple, and Grade I listed, are the origins of the present hotel. By 1840 it had become a popular inn and at the turn of the century King Edward VII and Queen Alexandra enjoyed taking tea on the lawn; HG Wells and Rebecca West were later well-known visitors. The present hotel consists of two stately white buildings, spruce and well maintained. One houses the Regency-style restaurant, with lovely views upstream, the terrace bar which overlooks the well-tended lawns, and the Monkey Room or lounge, with a delightful early 18th-century painted ceiling depicting monkeys, dressed in the fashion of the day, in sporting scenes – fishing, boating, shooting, etc. The Temple houses the bedrooms, some of which were added in sympathetic extensions in 1963 and 1970, and the Wedgwood and Temple rooms (the former has a fine plaster ceiling), both of which are used for private functions. On weekdays much of the hotel's business consists of conferences, and it is popular on Saturdays for weddings, but it is also a highly agreeable place to stay at least at weekends when it offers good value packages. Dinner (for which men are expected to wear jacket and tie) is traditional English, so is breakfast which is generous and of the non-packaged variety, and is served at the weekend until 11 am.

Open 10 Jan–25 Dec. Restaurant closed for lunch Sat.
Rooms 2 suites, 21 double, 2 single – all with bath, shower, telephone, TV, tea-making facilities, baby-listening. Some on ground floor.
Facilities Lounge, bar, restaurant; conference, functions and banqueting facilities. On 4½-acre island; fishing by prior arrangement.
Location 2 m SE of Maidenhead. From A308 turn to Bray village. Hotel is signposted.
Restrictions Not suitable for ♿. No dogs.
Credit cards All major cards accepted.
Terms [Until Apr 1992] B&B: single £89.50, double £118.50, suite £170. Bar lunches available. Set lunch £17, dinner £24.65; full alc £40. Weekend half board from £60 per person per night.
Service/tipping: "No service charge. Tips generally welcome; shared among staff by tronc *system."*

BRIGHTON East Sussex — Map 3

The Dove
18 Regency Square
Brighton BN1 2FG
Tel Brighton (0273) 779222
Fax (0273) 746912

Peter and Deborah Kalinke's "clean, friendly, well-run" small hotel in the heart of Brighton – in a listed house in a seafront Regency Square next door to *Topps*, below – entered the Guide in an italicised entry last year and is now promoted: "For a total bill of £75 [1990] we had a spacious first-floor front room, with a box of toys as well as a truckle bed set out for our daughter, drinks on arrival, a light but very pleasant, well-prepared supper, and breakfast from an imaginative menu." There's no lift; rooms vary in size and position and are priced accordingly; the decor is simple with bright clear colours. There's plenty of choice on the breakfast menu and it is served until 10.30 am. If you want the cooked variety in your bedroom it is brought in two stages to avoid the food getting cold. The hotel has a residential licence. (*Pauline Asher, and others*) Mrs Kalinke says, "We are very flexible about the light meal we provide. We always offer fresh vegetables and salad with what is on our menu, and we always consult beforehand. One house party wanted traditional food and we made them steak and kidney puddings, roasts, jam roly-polys, etc. Architecturally our house is not ideal for children but we very much welcome families and endeavour to give both parents and children the chance to relax and enjoy themselves."

Open All year except Christmas.
Rooms 7 double, 1 single – all with bath, shower, telephone, radio, TV, tea-making facilities, baby-listening.
Facilities Lounge/bar, dining room.
Location 200 yds from centre, opposite West Pier, but quiet. NCP carpark nearby.
Restrictions Not suitable for ♿. No smoking in dining room. No dogs.
Credit cards Access, Amex, Visa.
Terms B&B: single £32.80, double £56.25–£79.95. Light meal £10.50. Weekend and long-stay reductions; house parties. 1-night bookings sometimes refused in conference season. Reduced rates and special meals for children.
Service/tipping: "Our charges include service. We do not expect or encourage tipping, but any gratuities left are shared among staff."

Topps Hotel
17 Regency Square
Brighton BN1 2FG

Tel Brighton (0273) 729334
Fax (0273) 203679

"We were most impressed – especially by the helpfulness and generosity of spirit of the place. Our room, 175, was large, comfortable, a pleasure to be in. Exceptionally good value for the area." "A haven. I wouldn't stay anywhere else." "Really a Topps hotel. Mr and Mrs Collins go out of their way to fill every need. Special vegetarian meals, meals served in the bedroom when the restaurant is closed, laundry beautifully done." (*Mr and Mrs RB Fairweather, Braham Murray, Mrs MD Prodgers; also Ted Rothstein, Ivor Hall*)

Paul and Pauline Collins's conversion of two terraced houses next door to *The Dove* is eclectically furnished, and decorated in soft colours. There's only one public room, which acts as reception, library and meeting place, "inhabited by a wonderful, enormous old dresser, other antiques, and an elderly dog". Bedrooms, some spacious, are warm, well lit, furnished and equipped, with special touches like fresh flowers and fully stocked drinks fridge. Five have a gas fire, two have a four-poster and balcony. Bathrooms, too, are well appointed, with lots of huge towels, dressing gowns, toiletries and medicaments. In the pretty basement restaurant, *Bottoms*, bistro-type dinners are cooked by Mrs Collins. Breakfasts, "with quantities of grapefruit juice, freshly made bread, smoked haddock", are also liked. But one reader this year is less enthusiastic: "There was a slight but unmistakable smell of drain in the bathroom, some of the flowers were fading badly, no half-bottles of wine as promised in your entry. Good, but not seeking perfection, and shows it."

Open All year except Christmas. Restaurant closed Jan, and Sun and Wed.
Rooms 13 double, 1 single – 10 with bath and shower, 3 with bath, all with telephone, radio, TV, tea-making facilities.
Facilities Lift. Reception lounge/bar, restaurant. 100 yds from sea, safe bathing.
Location 200 yds from centre, opposite West Pier, but quietly situated. NCP carpark nearby.
Restrictions Not suitable for ♿. No dogs.
Credit cards Access, Amex, Visa.
Terms B&B double £59–£100. Set dinner £19.50; full alc £26. 20% reduction for any two nights Fri/Sat/Sun except bank holidays. Reduced rates for children sharing parents' room; special meals.
Service/tipping: "Service is free."

BROADWAY Hereford and Worcester — Map 2

Collin House
Collin Lane
Broadway WR12 7PB

Tel Broadway (0386) 858354

"We have stayed several times and have always had the most personal service. Every comfort is provided in the bedrooms; meals are excellent." "It was refreshing to find friendly service in old-style surroundings." John and Judith Mills's pretty old Cotswold house is built of golden stone, with mullioned windows and leaded lights, and stands in large grounds in a lovely location outside Broadway. The bar has oak beams and a huge inglenook fireplace; in the lounge there's a carved stone fireplace. Bedrooms, all different, are furnished "with care and taste, warm and spacious, with plenty of books, magazines and local information, and a large bathroom, well supplied with toiletries. Beds very comfortable; the only sound at night was an owl. No telephone or radio in the bedrooms, but this is essentially a quiet country hotel with pleasant staff and proprietors who look after you well. Breakfast was enjoyable, with a good choice. Dinner in the restaurant, beamed, mullion-windowed and candle-lit, was traditional English with old-style puddings." The wine list, too, is recommended, also the snacks. (*Mr and Mrs Wheatley, TW Judd, Joan A Powell*) In addition to the menu, extra dishes are offered each day, such as fresh fish and local specialities.

Open All year except 5 days from 24 Dec.
Rooms 6 double, 1 single – 5 with bath, 2 with shower, all with tea-making facilities; TV on request.
Facilities Lounge, lounge bar, restaurant. 4-acre grounds with unheated swimming pool, croquet, badminton. Horse riding, golf nearby.
Location 1 m W of Broadway on A44. Turn right at Collin Lane (signposted Willersey).
Restrictions Children under 7 by arrangement only. No dogs.
Credit cards Access, Visa.
Terms B&B: single £44, double £85–£98; dinner, B&B £50–£61. Set lunch £14.50, dinner £17.50–£21. Winter breaks Nov–Mar, midweek breaks Apr–Oct. 1-night bookings occasionally refused at bank holidays. Reduced rates for children sharing parents' room; special meals.
Service/tipping: "Tips are not solicited, but staff are allowed to accept them if offered."

BROMSGROVE Hereford and Worcester — Map 2

Grafton Manor
Grafton Lane
Bromsgrove B61 7HA

Tel Bromsgrove (0527) 579007
Fax (0527) 575221

A "beautiful old house, very *Horse and Hound*", owned and run by the Morris family, supported by a young team ("service friendly rather than expert"). *David Morris* (no relation) reports: "Food excellent, with full use of fresh herbs. Stephen Morris is developing as a good host, which this type of hotel needs, but doesn't always have." "The family has none of the overbearing county image one might expect from the owners of such a property," adds another visitor.

Grafton Manor is an architecturally splendid, early 18th-century mansion built in stone and pink brick. It is not far from Birmingham, down an isolated lane, but close to the M5; some rooms facing the motorway have secondary glazing which keeps the traffic out of earshot if not out of sight. Bedrooms vary considerably; the better ones are traditionally decorated, and some have a gas coal-fire. One is an outsize suite occupying half of one wing on the first floor. The hotel has lovely grounds with a lake, water gardens and a herb garden which provides herbs for extensive use in the traditional and modern British dishes served in the magnificent and fairly formal dining room; there is a four-course vegetarian menu as well as the normal table d'hôte. At times the public rooms can be dominated by business visitors, and the cooking, though generally appreciated, can be uneven. One visitor this year reported general disappointment: "Small standard room, rather gloomy, with oddly assorted bits of furniture; nowhere to put things in the bathroom; casual housekeeping. We could both see and hear the motorway."

Another was put out by being offered coffee-making facilities rather than fresh coffee for a 7 am departure. More reports please.

Open All year.
Rooms 2 suites, 6 double, 1 single – all with bath, shower, telephone, radio, TV, teletext. 1 suite on ground floor.
Facilities Lounge, lounge/bar, restaurant. 11-acre grounds with gardens, lake, chapel. 2 golf courses nearby.
Location 1½ m S of Bromsgrove off B4091, opposite Stoke turning.
Restriction Dogs in kennels only.
Credit cards All major cards accepted.
Terms [1991 rates] B&B: single £85–£95, double £105–£125, suite £150. Set lunch £14.95 and £20.50, dinner £28.50.
Service/tipping: "Service included. Tipping is not encouraged."

BRYHER Isles of Scilly — Map 1

Hell Bay Hotel
Bryher, Isles of Scilly
Cornwall TR23 0PR

Tel Scillonia (0720) 22947
Fax (0720) 23004

The only hotel on the tiny and peaceful island of Bryher, where there are no made-up roads and no public transport, is owned by Sorrel Atkinson who is steadily upgrading it, and stands by Bryher Pool, across the island from the landing point where you can be met off the boat from Tresco or St Mary's. It is a converted farmhouse in large grounds with accommodation in warm and comfortable suites built round a sheltered lawn in subtropical gardens. Each suite has a sitting room; some have a second bedroom with bunk beds; a few have cooking facilities and are let on a weekly self-catering basis. The hotel is particularly suitable for and welcoming to children. Readers recommend it for the friendly management and staff, and the high standard of traditional cooking; fresh seafood – lobsters, crabs, oysters – is always available. More reports badly needed.

Open End Mar–mid-Oct.
Rooms 14 apartments – all with shower (3 also have bath), TV, tea-making facilities, some with kitchen; portable baby-listening device available.
Facilities Lounge/reception, bar, dining room. 10-acre grounds with pitch and putt golf. Adjacent to sandy beaches.
Location 3 mins by boat from Tresco, 20 mins from St Mary's, then taxi.
Restrictions Not suitable for ♿. No smoking in dining room. No children under 5 in dining room in evening.
Credit cards Access, Visa.
Terms [1991 rates] Dinner, B&B £45–£61. Bar lunches. Set dinner £17. Full à la carte £23. Spring breaks. 1-night bookings sometimes refused in high season. Reduced rates for children sharing parents' room; high teas.
Service/tipping: "It is indicated to guests that tipping is not necessary. Anything given is shared among staff."

****

Traveller's tale *Dinner was served by one young and rather dim girl who had to trot back to the kitchen to seek answers to: "Roasted artichokes – are they fresh?" (the starred veggie dish I fancied). Answer: "That's not a very popular dish and No they're tinned." "How is the duck cooked?" Answer: "I think it's put in the oven."*

****

BUDOCK VEAN Cornwall — Map 1

Budock Vean Hotel
Budock Vean, Nr Falmouth
TR11 5LG
Tel Falmouth (0326) 250288
Fax (0326) 250892

"How refreshing to find a 'country house hotel' which doesn't pretend to be a private house with all the attendant inhibitions. *Budock Vean* is a first-rate hotel and proud of the fact, with plenty of braid and smart uniforms to prove it. From the moment one arrives at the canopied entrance one is made to feel welcome by the very pleasant staff. New bedrooms and old – we have stayed in both – are comfortable, airy, quiet and well equipped. Fluffy towels, white for the bathroom and yellow for the swimming pool, turned-down beds, carefully polished shoes and a cheerfully brought early morning tea tray spoil one further. Elegant public rooms are spacious, yet cosy. Food and drink are tempting and attractive. Breakfasts are some of the best around. Our evening started with a drink from the long-serving Sicilian barman, who has the biggest smile in the business. The five-course dinners were delectable, with food carefully cooked and full of flavour, and ending with a wide range of puddings and an excellent cheeseboard. We are not golfers but felt perfectly at ease with those who were. The superb swimming pool with log fire burning in the corner was our territory. The extensive grounds offer pleasant walking, with a private waterfront on Helford Passage a few minutes away. The surrounding area offers plenty of attractions, from Truro Cathedral and the Barbara Hepworth museum at St Ives, to the delightful Cornish Seal Sanctuary at nearby Gweek. An excellent hotel." (*Mary Woods*)

This resort-style hotel, half owned by the Barlows of *Treglos*, Constantine Bay (q.v.), enjoys a fine position in large grounds with sub-tropical gardens. There's no extra charge to residents for the use of the nine-hole golf-course (there's a resident professional, David Short), two all-weather tennis courts and the large, covered swimming pool – open in summer, with a log fire in winter. It re-entered the Guide last year in an italicised entry after a change of ownership and extensive renovation. The new wing has roomy if rather functional bedrooms; those in the original building are prettier but smaller. One reader, however, was less euphoric: "Boring for the non-golfer, and one evening the dining room was excruciatingly loud thanks to a table of twenty celebrating male golfers. We felt the management should have given them separate quarters."

Open Feb–Dec.
Rooms 5 suites, 43 double, 10 single – all with bath, shower, telephone, radio, TV, baby-listening; tea-making facilities on request.
Facilities 3 lounges (1 non-smoking), 2 bars, dining room. 68-acre grounds with 9-hole golf course, 2 tennis courts, river frontage.
Location 4 m S of Falmouth. From Truro take A39 towards Falmouth, then A394 to Helston. Follow signs to Mawnan Smith; in village fork right at *Red Lion*; after about 1 m bear right, signposted Budock Vean.
Restrictions Not suitable for severely ♿. No children under 5 in restaurant or lounge after 8 pm. Dogs by prior arrangement; not in public rooms.
Credit cards All major cards accepted.
Terms [1991 rates] Dinner, B&B £52–£80.50. Set dinner £20. 10% discount given to guests booking next visit on departure. Golf schools at certain times of year. Christmas and New Year packages. Reduced rates for children in parents' room; high tea at 5.30 pm.

BURY ST EDMUNDS Suffolk **Map 3**

The Angel
Angel Hill
Bury St Edmunds IP33 1LT

Tel Bury St Edmunds (0284) 753926
Fax (0284) 750092

César award in 1985: Best country town hotel

Owned by the Gough family, who have been hoteliers for over a quarter of a century, and managed by Mary Gough, this hotel is 15th century in origin with an 18th-century classical facade, now softened by creepers. It is on the main square opposite the great abbey gate, one of Bury's glories, and is very much part of the life of the market town. The comfortable public rooms bustle with activity, particularly on market day (Wednesday). Teas, sometimes accompanied by harp or piano, are popular. Charles Dickens stayed here, and literary dinners are an annual feature. Bedrooms are furnished with chintz and mahogany, fresh flowers, magazines, books, etc; they vary greatly in size and shape, as in all old buildings, so it is important to discuss your requirements when booking; the best ones are spacious and elegant; others, while smaller, are "clean and bright", and also comfortable. Front rooms, which overlook the square, can be noisy, but are double-glazed; back ones are generally quietest. Staff, mostly quite young, are "cheerful, polite and attentive". The hotel has two dining rooms; the main one is fairly formal, the other, in the vaults (which were refurbished in early 1991), cosier and more modern in style. The cooking (apart from breakfast) has previously been criticised, but the new general manager, John Robson, has brought in a new chef, Graham Mallia, so we'd be glad of more reports, particularly on the food.

Last year we reported problems experienced by one couple; there is a happy sequel. The Guide took the matter up with Mrs Gough, and they were offered a free weekend at the *Angel*'s sister, the *Marlborough* at Ipswich – which as a result returns to our pages this year.

Open All year.
Rooms 1 suite, 25 double, 14 single – 39 with bath, 1 with shower, all with telephone, radio, TV, baby-listening; tea-making facilities on request.
Facilities Lounge, bar, 2 restaurants; conference facilities. Parking for 50 cars. Abbey gardens opposite.
Location Central, near Information Centre (front rooms double-glazed). Parking.
Restrictions Not suitable for ♿. No smoking in main restaurant and some bedrooms. No dogs in restaurants.
Credit cards All major cards accepted.
Terms [1991 rates] Rooms: single £70, double £100, suite £150. Breakfast: continental £6.50, English £9.75. Set dinner (restaurant) £19.95; full alc £30. 2-day breaks; weekend rates. Christmas programme.
Service/tipping: "Service included. Tipping at guests' discretion."

Ounce House
Northgate Street
Bury St Edmunds IP33 1HP

Tel Bury St Edmunds (0284) 761779

Victorian merchant's house in fine residential street just north of Abbey Gardens, run by Simon and Jenny Pott. Ample parking. Quietest rooms overlook walled garden. Antiques, good pictures, fresh flowers; grand piano in lounge.

Large beds in comfortable bedrooms with plenty of storage space. Good breakfasts served at one large table. Restaurant ("serving food with a touch of verve and a dash of humour") open for lunch and dinner but closed Sun/Mon. 3 double rooms, 1 single, all with bath/shower. Smoking in 1 drawing room only. Access, Visa accepted. Rates until April 1992: B&B £32.35–£35. Set lunch £8–£12, dinner £15.20; full alc £20. New nomination. More reports please.

CALNE Wiltshire **Map 2**

Chilvester Hill House *Tel* Calne (0249) 813981
Calne SN11 0LP *Fax* (0249) 814217

César award: Exemplary country home guest house

Dr and Mrs Dilley's spacious Victorian mansion, run in a relaxed but thoroughly cosseting way, is in large grounds with fine views close to, but out of earshot of, the A4. Two and a half acres, with a small, well-cared-for swimming pool, heated in summer, are available to guests; Mrs Dilley breeds cattle on the rest. This is not a hotel, but "the private house of a professional family" to which paying visitors are welcomed. The Dilleys do not have a brochure; enquirers get a friendly letter describing the accommodation and the area, and discussing individual requirements. The house, built of Bath stone, has large and airy rooms, warm colours and books everywhere; "everything is beautifully decorated and in good condition". Bedrooms are "traditional, with fresh flowers and every modern convenience". The Dilleys join their guests for pre-dinner drinks or coffee, and occasionally for dinner which is served in the family dining room round one "magnificently set" table (couples may find themselves split up). "Good, plain, real food" is served; vegetables are from the garden. There's no choice of menu, but likes and dislikes are discussed in advance, and Mrs Dilley keeps records of meals served "so that I do not duplicate unless guests want to eat the same as last time". But there's no obligation to dine in, and the Dilleys are happy to advise about local eating places and make reservations for guests. "Wonderful cooked-to-order breakfasts" are served at flexible times. "The big plus," a reader wrote last year, "is the quality of the food preparation. The unique qualities are Gill Dilley's personality and John Dilley's inexhaustible local knowledge. The imponderable is who you sit with at dinner. We were lucky!"

Open All year, except a week off-season (autumn or spring).
Rooms 3 double – all with bath, handshower, radio, TV, tea-making facilities.
Facilities Drawing room, sitting room with TV, dining room. 2½-acre grounds with swimming pool; also 5 acres used for cattle; golf and riding locally.
Location ½ m W of Calne; A4 towards Chippenham, after ½ m right turn to Bremhill; immediately turn right into drive with gateposts with stone lions.
Restrictions Not suitable for severely ♿. No smoking in dining room. Generally no children under 12. No dogs.
Credit cards All major cards accepted.
Terms B&B: single £40–£50, double £60–£75. Set dinner £18–£22; packed or snack lunches. Reductions for stays of a week or more.
Service/tipping: "No service charge. Tips not expected; but if anything is left 'for the girls' it is put in a 'kitty' and shared."

We are particularly keen to have reports on italicised entries.

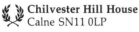

CALSTOCK Cornwall — Map 1

Danescombe Valley Hotel
Lower Kelly
Calstock PL18 9RY

Tel Tavistock (0822) 832414

"A happy mix of old-world charm and modern comfort. The setting is delightful. The simple meal was well prepared and interesting and they have a good nose for wine." "Comfortable room with considerate touches. Quiet and wonderfully relaxing atmosphere." This friendly hotel has a tranquil setting on the steep wooded slopes of the river Tamar with lovely views. It adjoins the grounds of Cotehele House, an exceptionally rewarding National Trust property, 15 minutes' walk away. Martin Smith and his half-Italian wife, Anna, have extensively renovated the house with Laura Ashley fabrics and antique and traditional furniture. There are deep carpets, well-placed lighting, flowers, plants, magazines and books, and generally a light, airy feeling about the place. Bedrooms are well equipped with pretty duvets and huge pillows. There are big fluffy towels and many extras – including wind-up bath toys – in the bathrooms. *Danescombe Valley* dispenses with many of the things that are expected of hotels these days – no telephones in bedrooms, no TV, for example. Guests are treated more like friends than fee-paying visitors and first names tend to be used all round. Dinner is "at 7.30 for 8"; Anna Smith cooks "delicious, well-balanced and very fresh" no-choice meals (but you are consulted about likes and dislikes in advance); vegetables are properly cooked, local cheeses are a special feature; wines are reasonably priced. No cooked breakfasts; but a generous choice including fresh orange juice, poached fruit, yoghurt. (*Mr and Mrs FD Santilhano, Joan Taylor*)
Credit cards are now accepted.

Open 3 Apr–31 Oct, and Christmas. Closed Wed and Thu.
Rooms 5 double – all with bath; tea-making facilities on request.
Facilities Lounge, bar, restaurant. 4 acres of steep woodland; steps down to river Tamar. Fishing, walking, golf and riding nearby.
Location ½ m W of Calstock village; under viaduct, past Methodist church, turn sharp right; follow road parallel to river Tamar for ½ m.
Restrictions Not suitable for ♿. No smoking in dining room. No children under 12. No dogs in house.
Credit cards Access, Diners, Visa.
Terms Dinner, B&B: double £175, single by arrangement. Set dinner £27.50. 1-night bookings sometimes refused Fri or Sat.
Service/tipping: "Tips refused unless our refusal gives offence."

CAMBRIDGE Cambridgeshire — Map 3

Gonville Hotel
Gonville Place
Cambridge CB1 1LY

Tel Cambridge (0223) 66611
Fax (0223) 66611 ex 301

Well-positioned dependable hotel overlooking Parker's Piece, not far from station and an easy walk from most university buildings. Ample parking. Large, comfortable lounge, pleasant patio garden, well-run restaurant serving good food. "Managed with great efficiency by elegant Mrs Hooper who has been here for years. It may lack old-world charm, but offers excellent accommodation, courteous and friendly service, comfortable, well-equipped bedrooms and good value." Closed 23–29 Dec. 62 rooms, all with bath and shower. Bedrooms not suitable for ♿. Access, Amex, Visa accepted. 1991 rates: B&B: single £61.50, double £77. Set lunch £11.50, dinner £13.95. Our only entry for Cambridge, newly nominated. More reports please.

CAMPSEA ASHE Suffolk — Map 3

The Old Rectory BUDGET
Campsea Ashe
Nr Woodbridge IP13 0PU

Tel Wickham Market (0728) 746524

César award: For utterly acceptable mild eccentricity

Stewart Bassett's individualistic restaurant-with-rooms is in a spacious Georgian rectory with high ceilings and grandiose antiques. It enjoys a peaceful setting in a large garden with statuary. (There are jets at a nearby airbase, but they are seldom heard.) It's a "comfortable, unpretentious establishment run with idiosyncratic flair". "It may have a seedy gentry air, the pictures, paintings, prints and photographs may be askew (it is a picture straightener's paradise), and the leg of a table in the dining room was held up by a piece of cardboard to stop it wobbling, but the place has character. My bedroom was quiet, clean, spacious and comfortable; so too was the *en suite* bathroom. It didn't have a radio, TV or phone, but so what? The lounge is large, with a log fire, comfortable armchairs and lots of glossy books. There was no choice of food but it was excellent. The wine list is amazing – one of the best I have seen – and very reasonable, with lots of half-bottles." "Tremendous value. Optional, and I mean optional, service of which there was not too much from a foreign 'student' serving breakfast and dinner." Other readers have reported "a great feeling of tranquillity; we felt like guests at a private house party of the inter-war years". Atmosphere and service are extremely laid-back, which doesn't suit all comers, but it's a wine buff's dream. Regular customers telephone a day or so before to place their order; to many it is a relief not to have to choose the food as well. (*BRA Blaxall, Brian Wicks, Ivor Hall, Gwen and Peter Andrews*) "We have heard that when Stewart Bassett does produce a disaster, it can be on a grand scale," writes a regular, "but we have never experienced one." A reader this year, however, does report a very disappointing meal.

Open All year except Christmas, 3 weeks Feb/Mar, 1 week Nov. Restaurant closed to non-residents on Sun.
Rooms 5 double, 1 single – all with bath, tea-making facilities.
Facilities Drawing room with TV, conservatory restaurant, breakfast room, private dining room. 4-acre garden with croquet.
Location 1½ m E of A12 on B1078. Next to church.
Restrictions Not suitable for ♿. No smoking in restaurant or bedrooms. No dogs.
Credit cards All major cards accepted.
Terms B&B: single £30, double £46; dinner, B&B: single £45.50, double £77. Set dinner: residents £14.50, non-residents £19. Special meals for children on request. *Service/tipping: "No service charge. Tipping is left to customers' discretion. Tips are distributed evenly among all staff."*

Our italicised entries indicate hotels which are worth considering, but which, for various reasons – inadequate information, lack of feedback, ambivalent reports – do not at the moment warrant a full entry. We should particularly welcome comments on these hotels.

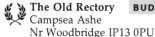

CANTERBURY Kent — Map 3

Thruxted Oast — *Tel* Canterbury (0227) 730080
Mystole, Chartham
Canterbury CT4 7BX

A welcome return of an unusual and comfortable guest house, owned by Tim and Hilary Derouet, which was dropped from the Guide a few years back for no other reason than lack of feedback – hardly surprising, perhaps, since it has only three bedrooms. It's a converted oast barn, built in 1791, in picturesque grounds with a handsome garden. Its bedrooms still retain evidence of their original use, but are attractively decorated with stripped pine furniture and patchwork quilts and equipped with remote control TV, towelling bathrobes and other comforts. Breakfast, served in the large farmhouse kitchen, includes home-laid eggs. "We were welcomed like family friends and enjoyed extremely high standards of comfort in the heart of the Kent countryside." (*BA Hepple, also Elizabeth Ring*) The oast also houses the owners' picture-framing workshop.

Open All year except Christmas.
Rooms 3 double – all with shower, telephone, radio, TV, tea-making facilities.
Facilities Lounge, breakfast room/kitchen. ¾-acre grounds with croquet.
Location 4 m SW of Canterbury. A28 towards Ashford; 100 yds after 1st major traffic lights turn left into St Nicholas Road; go 3 m. After *Fagge Arms* pub go over crossroads, then down hill; oast is 300 yds on right.
Restrictions Not suitable for ♿. No children under 8. Smoking forbidden in breakfast room and bedrooms; discouraged in lounge. No dogs.
Credit cards All major cards accepted.
Terms B&B double £68. (No restaurant.)
Service/tipping: "No service charge. No tipping."

CARTMEL Cumbria — Map 4

Aynsome Manor — *Tel* Cartmel (053 95) 36653
Cartmel, Grange-over-Sands
LA11 6HH

"I stay here two or three times a year, either on holiday or as a stop-over on a long journey. It is unfailingly friendly and stylish (most hotels are one or the other, and some manage to be neither), and restful too. The welcome has been the same whether it has been full or I have been the only guest. The restaurant attracts many locals, and the wine list is long, and should suit most pockets." "Menu varied and interesting, food well served and in good quantity." (*Robert Ribeiro, and others*)

The picturesque village of Cartmel is eight miles south of Windermere and a couple of miles inland of Grange-over-Sands (on the sea, but poor beaches). It is a good base for fell walking (though you need a car). The *Manor*, dating back to the 16th century, is a handsome building with a cobbled courtyard, small garden and lovely views of streams and meadows to the fine 12th-century priory church. It has been restored by the resident proprietors, Tony and Margaret Varley, who run it with their son Christopher and his wife Andrea. Bedrooms (apart from minor grumbles about the single room) are comfortable and traditional; some are in Aynsome Cottage, across the courtyard, which has its own sitting room. There's an upstairs lounge of fine proportions with a splendid marble fireplace, and an oak-panelled dining room with a moulded plaster ceiling, decent paintings, good silver and crystal; formal dress is required for male diners. The five-course dinner is generally served at 7 pm; you should advise the hotel if you need to eat later. Lunch is served only on Sunday, followed by a "good" supper (soup, cold buffet, etc).

Open All year except 2–27 Jan. Lunch served Sun only.
Rooms 12 double, 1 single – 11 with bath, 1 with shower, all with telephone, radio, TV, tea-making facilities, baby-listening. 2 in cottage annexe.
Facilities 3 lounges, cocktail bar, dining room. ¾-acre garden. Outdoor swimming pool 2 m, Windermere 7 m.
Location ¼ m NE of Cartmel village.
Restrictions Not suitable for ♿. No smoking in dining room. No children under 5 in dining room for dinner.
Credit cards Access, Amex, Visa.
Terms Dinner, B&B £45–£50. Set Sun lunch £10, dinner £18. Winter breaks. Christmas programme. 1-night bookings refused for bank holidays. Reduced rates for children; high tea 5–6 pm.
Service/tipping: "Guests don't like to be told what to do with their money. We leave the matter optional. The staff do not expect gratuities."

Uplands *Tel* Cartmel (053 95) 36248
Haggs Lane, Cartmel
Grange-over-Sands LA11 6HD

"High standards sustained." "Service faultless, food superb, accommodation extremely comfortable." This year's endorsements for *Uplands*, co-owned with John Tovey of the *Miller Howe*, Windermere, by Tom and Diana Peter (he in the kitchen, she front of house). It's less theatrical in style than the parent house, less pricy and offers fewer choices on the four-course fixed-price dinner menu, but mealtimes are more flexible. Earlier comments: "We were delighted with the food, welcome and generosity of the Peters." "The food never disappointed – flavours are robust and vegetables never boring. Sweets first-class, with judicious use of seasonal and imported fruit." "Service quiet and efficient." "Excellent, generous breakfasts" – each table has its own toaster with a choice of breads. The hotel is on a hillside in two acres of garden with views over Morecambe Bay, in the uncrowded southern end of the Lake District. It is attractively decorated and furnished: the lounge and dining room are "elegant, in restful pastel greys and pinks"; tables in the dining room are well spaced. Bedrooms, though not spacious, are comfortable and well equipped; two have a lovely estuary view. (*William Rankin, Elizabeth Wilcox, and others*) The Peters no longer add a service charge for either accommodation or food.

Open 24 Feb–1 Jan. Restaurant closed Mon.
Rooms 5 double – all with bath and/or shower, telephone, TV.
Facilities Lounge, dining room. 2-acre garden. Golf nearby.
Location 1 m from centre of Cartmel: with *Pig & Whistle* on right, take road opposite to Grange for 1 m; hotel is on left.
Restrictions Not suitable for ♿. No smoking in dining room. No children under 8. No dogs in public rooms.
Credit cards Access, Amex, Visa.
Terms Dinner, B&B: single £64–£74, double £108–£128. Set lunch £14.50, dinner £24.50. Midweek breaks 5 Nov–end Apr. 4-day Christmas package. 1-night bookings refused for Sat. Reduced rates for children sharing parents' room; special meals on request.
Service/tipping: "We do not now make a service charge, either on rooms or on food."

CASTLE CARY Somerset — Map 2

Bond's Hotel and Restaurant — *Tel* Castle Cary (0963) 50464
Ansford Hill, Castle Cary BA7 7JP

Kevin and Yvonne Bond's "gem of a small hotel", a listed Georgian house on A371 near station in agreeable mid-Somerset town, is comfortably but stylishly furnished, welcoming and warm. Informality is the key-note. "Imaginative, well-cooked food, quiet and attentive service; good range of wines at reasonable prices." Open fires. 1-acre grounds; hot-air ballooning. Not suitable for ♿. No children under 8. No dogs. Closed Christmas. 7 bedrooms, all with bath/shower. Access, Visa accepted. 1991 rates: Dinner, B&B £43–£65. Set meals from £12.50. New nomination. More reports please.

CHADDESLEY CORBETT Hereford and Worcester — Map 2

Brockencote Hall — *Tel* Kidderminster (0562) 777876
Chaddesley Corbett — *Fax* (0562) 777872
Nr Kidderminster DY10 4PY

This turn-of-the-century "rich man's domestic pile" in 70-acre grounds not far from Birmingham, with Anglo-French owners, Joseph and Alison Petitjean, has pale stone walls, and is a little austere from a distance. "Inside, however, the overriding impression is of warm honey-coloured wood, elegant furnishings and a light, cheerful atmosphere." Public rooms are large, light and high-ceilinged, furnishing "agreeable and not too designerish". Bedrooms vary in size. "Our split-level room over-looked the front pastureland," wrote a visitor last year. "It was quite large, pleasantly furnished in a restrained country-house style and well equipped, with plenty of storage space. Furniture was reproduction with much dark wood; carpet and wallpaper were suitably discreet. Restaurant service is impeccable. Breakfast is reasonable. The owners are charming and professional; the staff particularly well trained and accommodating."

There's a new conservatory-style restaurant and a new chef arrived in January 1991. Three three-course menus are offered (all with a French accent); coffee and service are included so no nasty surprises arrive with the bill. We'd be grateful for more reports, especially on the gastronomic front.

Open Mid-Jan–end Dec. Closed New Year and 1 week Aug. Restaurant closed for lunch on Sat, for dinner on Sun, also bank holiday Mon.
Rooms 7 double, 1 single – all with bath and/or shower, telephone, radio, TV, baby-listening.
Facilities Bar, lounge, 2 restaurants, 2 functions/conference rooms. 70-acre grounds with lake.
Location On A448 from Kidderminster to Bromsgrove, just S of village.
Restrictions Only restaurants suitable for ♿. No dogs.
Credit cards All major cards accepted.
Terms B&B £63. Set lunch from £16.50, dinner from £21.50. Weekend breaks, Christmas package. Regional French meals; musical evenings.
Service/tipping: "Service included. Tips at customers' discretion."

> Important reminder: terms printed must be regarded as a rough guide only to the size of the bill to be expected at the end of your stay. For latest tariffs, check when booking.

CHAGFORD Devon — Map 1

Gidleigh Park
Chagford TQ13 8HH

Tel Chagford (0647) 432367
Fax (0647) 432574

César award in 1989: Most sumptuous traditional country house hotel

"Truly a most sumptuous hotel. Staff courteous, welcoming and genuinely friendly. Meals superb and not too heavy." "We have been visiting *Gidleigh Park* for ten years. Many friends accuse us of being in a rut, but we like the position, we like the staff, we thoroughly enjoy the food and wine, and to us it is the ultimate in rural cosseting. Service is that rare and perfect balance between respect and friendliness. Shaun Hill is a chef with acute visual sense and sets trends in cooking rather than wait for new ideas to arrive from London. Even when he is away his fine team maintain a high standard. The hotel *is* very expensive but I still consider it good value for money; there is a generous spirit; rooms are sublimely comfortable, portions of food are generous, afternoon tea is a glutton's delight, good wines have a low mark-up. You feel as comfortable coming in off the moor cold, wet and muddy and sitting round the fire for tea as you do when dressed for dinner in the evening. A totally unstuffy hotel." "Deserves a *César* as a dog's paradise – lovely walks through woods and by a stream, with squirrels to chase adding to the fun." (*Jean Taylor, Padi Howard, Mrs C Smith; also Pat and Jeremy Temple*)

Gidleigh Park, now in its fourteenth year, is a country house hotel *de grand luxe*; the aim of American owners Paul and Kay Henderson with their managing director and head chef, Shaun Hill, is to provide total comfort in a private-house atmosphere for "affluent connoisseurs". It is set far down a single-track lane in an exceptionally peaceful and beautiful position on the edge of Dartmoor and the banks of the North Teign river. Inside it is immaculate and sophisticated. The drawing room is spacious and comfortable, with log fires and a "superb collection of watercolours"; a bar conservatory overlooks the lovely grounds. Bedrooms are luxuriously furnished, with equally luxurious bathrooms, and filled with fresh flowers, fruit, books and many other extras; this year the three smallest ones have been rebuilt and expanded. Prices – inevitably high – are according to the size of the room and its view; courtyard-facing ones are the least expensive. Croquet is taken seriously here: there are four good quality lawns.

A few niggles, mainly arising from the high prices: not everyone agrees about the warmth of the welcome; several readers this year report that the menu hardly changed during their visit; and one felt that afternoon tea should have been included, "and I had to ask for more vegetables, as they were almost non-existent". In the past there have been moans that cooked breakfast was extra but a new breakfast menu has been introduced, and cooked breakfast is now included in the rates as well as morning tea or coffee and mineral water and coffee at dinner.

In 1990 *Michelin* withdrew its rosette which it had first awarded nine years earlier. Paul Henderson took issue with the *Michelin* inspectorate, claiming (and he's not the only one) that it is too narrowly French in its rating criteria. *Gidleigh* has no entry in the 1991 edition. A mini Star War?

Hardly. We guess that they'll be back in 1992, rosetted or not.

Open All year.
Rooms 2 suites, 12 double – all with bath (12 also have shower), telephone, radio, TV. 2 in north wing 75 yds from front door; 2 in pavilion 350 yds away.
Facilities Hall, lounge, bar, loggia, 2 dining rooms. 45-acre grounds with gardens, croquet and tennis. Fishing, golf, riding, walking nearby.
Location Approach from Chagford, *not* Gidleigh. From main square, facing Webbers with Lloyds Bank on right, turn right into Mill Street. After 150 yds fork right; go downhill to Factory Crossroad. Go straight across into Holy Street; follow lane 1½ m to end.
Restrictions Not suitable for ♿. No smoking in restaurant. Children by arrangement. No dogs in public rooms.
Credit cards Access, Visa.
Terms Dinner, B&B: double £215–£325, suite £285–£350. Set lunch £33 and £43, dinner £43 and £50. Winter walking holidays. 1-night bookings sometimes refused.
Service/tipping: "We discourage tipping."

Thornworthy House *Tel* Chagford (0647) 433297
Chagford TQ13 8EY

"Lovely situation, very comfortable bedrooms; interesting 'old-world' atmosphere, friendly welcome." "Pleasant and informal. Visitors are trusted in that they are lodged in rooms with countless small knick-knacks, some of them fairly valuable. Food rather better than good – basic English cooking with an imaginative use of sauces and herbs. Wine and bar prices very modest." (*Mr and Mrs FD Santilhano, WE Parker*)

This rambling Victorian house is, despite its address, three miles out of Chagford, down twisting lanes to the very edge of Dartmoor, and 1,200 feet up, with lovely views ("the narrow access road is quite difficult to follow at night"). It stands tranquilly in a country garden, with a tennis court. Philip and Vicky Jevons have given it the atmosphere of a comfortable family house, with soft colours, thick carpets, good quality fabrics, pictures and family photographs. There are comfortable reception rooms with log fires; bedrooms are spacious, with lovely views; some have private facilities. The "very nice, hospitable" Jevonses ("who have ten children between them, his, hers and theirs, so they are used to catering for numbers"), run *Thornworthy* as their private home – so do not be surprised if you find toys or children's clothes in your bedroom. Normally there are not more than six or eight guests at one time. Dinners, served at about 8 pm, offer three choices for each course. Not everyone agrees about the food: "They fall down in presentation." "Can be inconsistent." About the knick-knacks one correspondent noted sadly: "Our son quickly wiped out a few and we had to replace them."

Open All year.
Rooms 6 double, 2 single – 4 with bath and shower; TV and tea-making facilities on request. Some in studio conversion.
Facilities Lounge, TV lounge, dining room. 2½-acre grounds with tennis and clock golf. Riding, golf, fishing, windsurfing nearby.
Location 3 m SW of Chagford. Turn right at top of square. After 150 yds fork left to Fernworthy. At top of hill take second turning on right to Thornworthy. Follow signs to *Thornworthy House*.
Restrictions No smoking in dining room. No dogs in public rooms.
Credit cards None accepted.

Terms B&B £36.50; dinner, B&B £55. Set dinner £18.50. Reduced rates and special meals for children.
Service/tipping: "Tips not solicited, but accepted if given."

CHARINGWORTH Gloucestershire — Map 2

Charingworth Manor
Charingworth
Nr Chipping Campden GL55 6NS

Tel Paxford (038 678) 555
Fax (038 678) 353

This beautiful house, in a secluded setting up a long winding drive, with huge grounds, agreeable gardens and lovely views, "is just what a Cotswold manor should be". It is early 14th century, with Jacobean additions; the sitting room has mullioned windows, oak beams, log fires and antique furniture; bedrooms in the main building, some also beamed, some with four-poster, have a period feel; the attractive modern ones in converted stables are cheaper. Last year its entry was in italics. "We recommend a full entry," write visitors in late 1990. "The front door opened when our tyres scrunched on the gravel, and our bags were carried to a delightful bedroom overlooking the garden. It was one of their less expensive ones, but had a stone fireplace, low, oak-beamed ceiling and a comfortable, firm bed. There was complimentary sherry and all the other extras; the bathroom, equally luxurious, was spotless, with white bath and china and gold taps. The manor has been refurbished in a muted and sympathetic way with plain walls, polished floors, Indian rugs and good period furniture in the public rooms. Dinner is superbly presented and unveiled with a flourish. The emphasis is on quality rather than quantity; it's served by friendly and courteous staff, and unpolluted by any kind of canned music. It is expensive, but we felt that we received value for money." "There is no formal bar, which makes one feel like a house guest. The gardens are a pleasure to walk in. The food is very good, modern with a choice of table d'hôte or à la carte. If there are any faults, we didn't find them." (*Jennifer and Nigel Jee, Norman and Marian Windsor*) Men are expected to wear jacket and tie for dinner.

Open All year.
Rooms 3 suites, 22 double – all with bath, shower, telephone, radio, TV, baby-listening.
Facilities 3 lounges, restaurant; conference facilities. 50-acre grounds.
Location 2½ m E of Chipping Campden, just N of B4035.
Restrictions Not suitable for ♿. No dogs in public rooms.
Credit cards All major cards accepted.
Terms B&B: single from £85, double from £105, suite from £200; dinner, B&B: single from £110, double from £155, suite from £250. Set lunch from £12.50, dinner £25; full alc £35. Short breaks (min 2 nights). 1-night bookings occasionally refused. Reduced rates and special meals for children.
Service/tipping: "No service charge is included, or expected."

****

Traveller's tale *We had been recommended the –* Hotel. *There was no one around when we arrived. Eventually we found a man who said that there were rooms available and asked if we were going to have dinner. "Yes, presuming that it will be excellent." "No, it is crap," was the answer. There didn't seem much point in staying.*

****

CHEDINGTON Dorset — Map 2

Chedington Court
Chedington
Nr Beaminster DT8 3HY

Tel Corscombe (0935) 891265
Fax (0935) 891442

"A party of ten of us celebrated grandmother's 80th birthday here – the youngest was four years old. It was not easy to find a hotel with the necessary qualifications: comfort and a view for the grandparents, good food for the parents, some entertainment for the elder grandchildren, and a welcome for the tiny one. *Chedington Court* succeeded triumphantly in all departments. Mr Chapman was self-effacing but he and his wife could not have been more kind. The dinners and breakfasts were superb; teas were equally memorable." "It's hard to define the atmosphere of the house; we felt very much at home. Our bedroom was cosy and warm; dinner was well thought out and beautifully presented. Mr Chapman did a number of small things to make our stay pleasant." (*David Ing, Sandra E Garrick; also RCJ Gordon*)

Philip and Hilary Chapman's splendid, 1840s country house hotel in the Jacobean style, with curved gables and mullioned windows, is spectacularly positioned high up in the Dorset hills with panoramic views across Dorset, Devon and Somerset. It is quietly set in ten acres of parkland, which matches the grandeur of the building: balustraded and terraced gardens, lots of yews, a croquet lawn and a lake down below. This year a nine-hole golf course has been added. Public rooms are "well furnished with lovely curtains and masses of books", but not extravagantly decorated. There is a pretty conservatory and a billiard room. The hotel is informally run, with no reception procedure and not much room service; guests tend to be left to their own devices. There is limited choice on the five-course dinner menu cooked by Hilary Chapman, but a vegetarian alternative is offered to the main meat dish. The wine list is "remarkable for content and value"; with a good selection of half-bottles. Some visitors find the lack of hotel-style facilities and effusive reception disconcerting, not everyone is enthusiastic about the food, and some would like more choice, but the majority are much in favour.

Open Feb–early Jan. Closed Christmas.
Rooms 10 double – all with bath and/or shower, telephone, radio, TV, tea-making facilities, baby-listening. 1 with 4-poster and double jacuzzi.
Facilities Drawing room, library, billiard room, dining room; conservatory. 10-acre garden with croquet, putting. Golf, fishing nearby; coast 10 m.
Location 4½ m SE of Crewkerne, just off A356 at Winyard's Gap.
Restrictions Only restaurant suitable for ♿. No dogs in public rooms or unattended in bedrooms.
Credit cards Access, Amex, Visa.
Terms Dinner, B&B: single £87–£104, double £154–£188; B&B only, 20% less. Set dinner £28.50. Reductions for stays of more than 1 night. 1-night bookings often refused weekends. Reduced rates for children sharing parents' room; special meals.
Service/tipping: "Service is already paid for so no extra is added or expected."

> "Set meals" refers to fixed-price meals, which may have ample, limited or no choice on the menu. "Full alc" is the hotel's own estimated price per person of a three-course meal taken à la carte, with a half-bottle of house wine. "Alc meals" are as full alc but do not include the cost of wine.

CHELWOOD Avon — Map 2

Chelwood House Hotel
Chelwood
Nr Bristol BS18 4NH

Tel Compton Dando (0761) 490730
Telex (0761) 490730

"I enjoyed every minute of my stay. Rooms a delight, friendly atmosphere, very high standards, lovely views from every room." This dower house, built in 1681, is now a small hotel, run by Jill and Rudolf Birk. It is on the A37 (windows are double-glazed, back rooms are quietest), almost equidistant from Bath, Bristol and Wells, in a small village with fine views of open countryside. There is angling in Chew Valley Lake nearby, and there are numerous golf courses in the area. Public rooms are well proportioned, with period furniture and fresh flowers. Bedrooms (three have a four-poster) are comfortable, with spacious and well-planned bathrooms. Breakfasts are "excellent, with first-class croissants". Last year one visitor considered the food over-elaborate; Mr Birk, whose "good, straightforward" cooking has been praised in the past, has taken over the kitchen again; dishes from his native Bavaria tend to feature in the conservatory-style restaurant (there's a "Taste of Bavaria" menu on Friday). We'd be grateful for reports from the gastronomic front. Several readers find the decor a bit fussy.

Open All year except Christmas and New Year.
Rooms 9 double, 2 single – all with bath and/or shower, telephone, radio, TV, tea-making facilities.
Facilities 2 lounges, dining room. 1½-acre grounds with croquet. Fishing and golf nearby.
Location On A37 8 m S of Bristol (front rooms double-glazed).
Restrictions No smoking in dining room. No children under 10. No dogs.
Credit cards All major cards accepted.
Terms [1991 rates] B&B: single £59.50, double £75–£94. Set menu £14.50; full alc £28. Weekend breaks and midweek breaks.
Service/tipping: "No service charge. We do not encourage tipping but do not discourage guests from showing appreciation if they choose; tips are shared by all staff."

CHICHESTER West Sussex — Map 1

Crouchers Bottom
Birdham Road, Apuldram
Chichester PO20 7EH

Tel Chichester (0243) 784995
Fax (0243) 539797

A recent venture – owners Ron and Pam Foden, he a dental surgeon, she a former French teacher, with no previous hotel experience, came here in 1988. "Yes," writes its nominator, "there really is a hotel of that name, and its proprietors have heard all the jokes before but appear to be bearing up under the strain. I was introduced to it in October 1989 when, as an actress on tour, I gratefully took refuge after staying in a Worthing hotel apparently run by the Munsters. It is well placed for both the city and the sea. Pam Foden is a friendly, attractive person who makes you welcome without being at all intrusive. She runs a tight ship but the atmosphere is easy and relaxed. The house possesses a very personal sense of design and decor; each room has furnishings and co-ordinated colour schemes that have been lovingly chosen and there is fine attention to detail right down to flasks of fresh milk for the coffee-making facilities. This extends to the food; Mrs Foden is no amateur. Desserts are a pièce de résistance. Outside, *Crouchers Bottom* enjoys the privacy of its own grounds; they are not overlooked, so seem larger than they are. On my last visit I enjoyed getting stuck into watering the livestock; and the geese, bantams and various fancy breeds are amusing to watch." (*Ruth Moore*) The six bedrooms are in a converted coach house; one is specially adapted for disabled guests. Eggs for the English breakfast are laid by the Foden's free-range hens. Pre-theatre dinners and light meals in the bedroom are available in addition to the short dinner menu. When possible, Mr Foden skippers evening supper charters in Chichester Harbour on his 31-foot yacht. More reports please.

Open All year except 23 Dec–15 Jan. Dining room closed for lunch.
Rooms 6 double – 5 with bath and shower, 1 with shower only, all with telephone, radio, TV, tea-making facilities, baby-listening. All in coach house. 1 adapted for ♿.
Facilities Ramps. Lounge, dining room. ¾-acre garden with pond.
Location 2 m S of centre, off A286 to the Witterings. Hotel is on left after *Black Horse* pub on right.
Restrictions No smoking in dining room or bedrooms. No dogs.
Credit cards Access, Visa.
Terms B&B: single £45–£55, double £58–£85. Set dinner £17.50. 3-day breaks all year, 2-day breaks Nov–Apr. Activity breaks; bicycling holidays. Reduced rates and special meals for children.
Service/tipping: "All our prices include service; tipping is not encouraged."

Suffolk House Hotel *Tel* Chichester (0243) 778899
3 East Row, Chichester PO19 1PD *Fax* (0243) 787282

This 18th-century townhouse, once owned by the Dukes of Richmond, had an entry in earlier editions of the Guide but was omitted last year because the illness of its proprietor, Serge Paris, made its future uncertain. It was taken over by Michael and Rosemary Page in April 1990 – Mrs Page was chef under Mr Paris, and continues in that role. "They carry on the excellent service and cuisine for which the hotel was renowned. In the very hot weather Mrs Page produced the most excellent salads. Full marks for presentation and taste. Service is attentive. Our room was spotless and tastefully furnished." "No falling off of standards. Mr Page works extremely hard to ensure one's comfort." "It is quietly situated but very central; the atmosphere is informal and friendly. Our double room was spacious, airy and comfortable. The dining room is very pleasant and leads on to a garden. Mrs Page was quite willing to depart from the menu, given notice, when we wanted a light meal. The rate was very reasonable for the service received." (*David and Ruth Angwin, Peter Reynolds, Eileen Wood*)

A reader in early 1990 wrote to us about the extreme kindness shown towards small children during the regime of Mr Paris; the Pages tell us that two of their double rooms can be converted to family rooms, with minimal charges for children. One snag: "There are no public rooms to speak of."

Open All year.
Rooms 1 suite, 7 double, 4 single – 6 with bath and shower, 6 with shower, all with telephone, radio, TV, tea-making facilities, baby-listening.
Facilities Lounge/bar, restaurant; small conference facilities. Small garden with patio.

Location Central. Enter city at east end of East Street, take 2nd turning right (Little London), turn right at top. Hotel is on left (Union Flag flying).
Restriction No dogs in public rooms.
Credit cards Access, Amex.
Terms [1991 rates] B&B: single from £56.50, double from £79, suite from £97. Full alc from £22. Reduced rates and special meals for children.
Service/tipping: "No tipping."

CHIPPING CAMPDEN Gloucestershire — Map 2

Cotswold House
The Square
Chipping Campden GL55 6AN

Tel Evesham (0386) 840330
Fax (0386) 840310

A fine Regency building in the heart of a small Cotswold town, extensively restored and refurbished by the owners of the last five years, Robert and Gill Greenstock. It has a particularly noble central staircase; well-selected antiques sit comfortably next to modern upholstery; "real pictures" hang on the walls; the flower arrangements are "beyond criticism". Comfortable bedrooms, decorated with the same flair, have impeccable bathrooms. The better proportioned bedrooms face the street and are sound-proofed. The quietest ones, at the back, overlook the walled garden, as does the no-smoking dining room with ceiling-high French windows, agreeably light and airy, and fairly formal; jacket and tie are *de rigueur* for male diners. A resident pianist plays four nights a week. Last year's entry is endorsed by *Dr FP Woodford*: "The key element is charm. The whole ensemble, from the embroidered cushion covers, to the black mourning ribbons on the Regency silhouettes, the froth of peach tulle on the mock four-poster, the *tromp l'oeil* view at the entrance to the dining room of an imaginary garden that echoes the view of the real garden from the other end of the room – all is put together with such wit and taste that one is constantly delighted. And the comfort and the excellence of the food are real. Service was rustic, far from perfect, but so willing, apologetic and open to correction that it mattered little if at all." As before, however, comments on the kitchen under Raymond Boreham are mixed, and one reader felt that the food, "though competently cooked, was unimaginative and not as good as the price and pretensions of the restaurant led one to expect". In addition to the restaurant, there is an "eatery" offering less expensive meals throughout the day.

Open All year except 25/26 Dec.
Rooms 12 double, 3 single – all with bath and/or shower, telephone, radio, TV.
Facilities Reception lounge, sitting room, bar, dining room, coffee house; private dining room. Courtyard/patio, 1½-acre grounds with croquet.
Location Central (front rooms sound-proofed). Parking.
Restrictions Not suitable for ♿. No smoking in restaurant. No children under 8. No dogs.
Credit cards All major cards accepted.
Terms [1991 rates] B&B £41.50–£67.50; dinner, B&B £64–£90. Set dinner £22.50. Set Sun lunch £16.95. Special breaks all year except bank holidays. 1-night bookings generally refused at weekends. Special meals for children by arrangement.
Service/tipping: "We are against any form of tipping. But if we have done our job properly our guests will, if they are customary tippers, show appreciation. All tips are given to staff with instructions that everyone receives a share."

Please make a habit of sending a report if you stay at a Guide hotel.

CHITTLEHAMHOLT Devon — Map 1

Highbullen
Chittlehamholt
Umberleigh EX37 9HD

Tel Chittlehamholt (0769) 540561
Fax (0769) 540492

César award in 1991: Utterly acceptable mild eccentricity

"Our favourite hotel," write two readers this year of this wholly individual hotel. "The delight of the place," continues one, "is its wonderful sporting facilities combined with very comfortable surroundings, beautiful scenery, peacefulness, and the ability to mix relaxed informality, where you are left to your own devices much of the time, with good service when it is needed. Since the Neils' daughter Colette took charge in the kitchen, the menu has been revamped and refreshed while retaining many of the old favourites. The general standard of food was extremely high. Facilities continue to be improved. Our room was well decorated, well maintained and clean. But don't expect the sort of formal service and lackeys on call that you would get at most hotels in this class. And the Neils still keep a tight rein on the place even though their son and daughter are now playing a bigger part." "Food consistently good," says the other, "and the general efficiency highly commendable – all without the tendency to ostentation which seems to be creeping in to so many hotels." Other views: "Slightly disconcerting on arrival to find no reception area and to have to hunt for someone. But we got used to this and to the absence of room keys; they became part of *Highbullen*'s charm." "Breakfasts and bar lunches good. Vegetables have improved. Drinks fairly priced. Overall good value." (*Dave Watts, TS Stephens, Jane Bailey, Richard Townend*) The hotel has lovely views across a Devon valley and many facilities for the sporting and unsporting (listed below) – though the golf course is said to be "not to be taken too seriously". Bedrooms in the main house, a Victorian Gothic mansion, are traditional; those in the outbuildings are modern, many are spacious. A visitor in early 1991 felt that the sitting room and some bedrooms in the main house needed a facelift, "and we could get only scalding water from our shower, which made it unusable. But we had a very happy week." Children are now accepted over eight years old (formerly over ten): a small victory for the child lobby.

Open All year.
Rooms 34 double, 1 single – all with bath, shower, telephone, TV, tea-making facilities. 23 in converted farmhouses and cottages. Some on ground floor.
Facilities Drawing room with conservatory, library, bar with small dance-floor, dining room, cellar restaurant, billiard room; hairdressing and massage facilities; indoor tennis court and swimming pool, sauna, steam room, spa bath, sunbed, exercise room, table-tennis room, squash court. 60-acre grounds with 6-acre garden, 9-hole golf course, tennis, croquet lawn, putting green, outdoor heated swimming pool. Golf and tennis tuition. Fishing in river Mole ½ m.
Location Leave M5 at exit 27; on A361 at South Molton take B3226 for 5 m, turn right up hill to Chittlehamholt; go through village ½ m to hotel.
Restrictions Not suitable for ♿. No smoking in restaurant. No children under 8. No dogs.
Credit cards None accepted.
Terms Dinner, B&B: single £60–£70, double £100–£130. Set lunch £10.50–£12.50, snack lunches. Set dinner £17.50. Midweek reductions. 1-night bookings sometimes refused for Fri and Sat. Reduced rates for children sharing parents' room.

Service/tipping: "We make it quite clear that service is included and no tips are expected. Some people insist on leaving tips; they are distributed in proportion to individual staff earnings."

CONSTANTINE BAY Cornwall — Map 1

Treglos Hotel
Padstow PL28 8JH

Tel Padstow (0841) 520727
Fax (0841) 521163

A traditional seaside hotel, excellent for a family holiday, in a choice position overlooking Constantine Bay, 400 yards from a sandy beach (recently declared one of Britain's few Good Beaches) with rock pools at low tide. It has a sheltered sunken garden for sunbathing, and an indoor heated pool. The National Trust coastal footpath is nearby; maps of walks are provided by the hotel. *Treglos* has been run for 26 years by Ted and Barbara Barlow – who now also own a half share in the *Budock Vean Hotel* (q.v.); the restaurant manager has been there for twenty years and the chef for sixteen. The hotel goes in for old-fashioned courtesies such as cleaning shoes, carrying luggage, room service, tidying rooms during dinner; it has many devoted regular visitors. The disabled and children are welcome; in low season it is a favourite of retired people. Its decor – brick fireplaces, with log fires in cool weather, chintzy furniture and patterned carpets – is conventionally English. Bedrooms, many with sea views, have light colour-schemes and white fitted furniture; some have a balcony. Staff are friendly and extremely helpful. The food is "basically very good", with a surprisingly ambitious five-course dinner menu – over-ambitious some say. Men are expected to wear a jacket and tie for dinner. "I know," writes Ted Barlow, "that this irritates a minority, but most of our guests prefer it – and meals can be served in the bedroom if required. Our aim is to provide a peaceful and quiet holiday – no canned music, no entertainment, log fires in early and late season." There are special weekly rates for Thursday-to-Thursday bookings, and there's a bridge tournament week in late October. More reports please.

Open 12 Mar–7 Nov.
Rooms 4 suites, 32 double, 8 single – all with bath, shower, telephone, radio, TV, baby-listening; tea-making facilities on request. 1 suite on ground floor. 4 self-catering flats in grounds.
Facilities Lift, ramps. 4 lounges, cocktail bar, bridge room, restaurant; children's den, snooker room; indoor heated swimming pool, whirlpool bath. 3-acre grounds. Sandy beach 400 yds. Golf, tennis, riding nearby.
Location 4 m W of Padstow. Avoid Bodmin and Wadebridge. From crossroads at St Merryn take B3276.
Restrictions Smoking in dining room discouraged. No children under 7 in dining room after 7.45 pm. Dogs at management's discretion; not in public rooms.
Credit cards Access, Visa (restaurant only).
Terms B&B £40.50–£56; dinner, B&B £48.50–£64. Bar lunches. Set Sun lunch £11, dinner £19; full alc £30. Weekly rates. Bridge week.
Service/tipping: "No service charge; tips at guests' discretion."

> Hotels often book you into their most expensive rooms or suites unless you specify otherwise. Even if all room prices are the same, hotels may give you a less good room in the hope of selling their better rooms to late customers. It always pays to discuss accommodation in detail when making a reservation and to ask for a free upgrade on arrival if the hotel isn't full.

CRANBROOK Kent
Map 3

The Old Cloth Hall
Cranbrook TN17 3NR
Tel Cranbrook (0580) 712220

This Elizabethan house with later extensions enjoys a lovely setting deep in the country in large grounds with gardens noted for rhododendrons and azaleas; there's also an unheated swimming pool and a tennis court. "Furniture from various periods sits on highly polished floors in the low-ceilinged, panelled public rooms," wrote a reporter last year. "There are books, magazines and flower arrangements everywhere, and a miscellany of relics from a lifetime of journeys, sitting next to mellow antiques, family portraits and personal whimsy objects, all reflecting the originality and strong artistic sense of the owner, Katherine Morgan, who emphasises that this is her home, not a hotel." The three guest bedrooms "are scattered among those of Mrs Morgan and her absent family"; the best has a splendid four-poster. Guests have drinks with her before dinner and dine with her at a large, highly polished table by candle-light. Many are regulars who enjoy the cooking – "simple dinner party stuff; desserts are the strongest point; second helpings are offered", the "absence of the anonymity of an ordinary hotel", and the fact that there are no extras on the bill. (*Francine Walsh, Mrs R Wilkinson*) The reverse side, a correspondent points out, is that "you feel slightly guilty about asking for another glass of claret to go with your cheese as you don't know if you are paying for it", and you won't necessarily find a virgin cake of soap in your bathroom.

Open All year except Christmas.
Rooms 3 double – all with bath and/or shower, radio, TV.
Facilities Drawing room, dining room. 13-acre grounds with unheated swimming pool, tennis, croquet.
Location 1 m SE of Cranbrook on the Golford Road to Tenterden. Private road immediately before cemetery.
Restrictions Not suitable for ♿. No children under 10. No dogs.
Credit cards None accepted.
Terms (No service charge) B&B: single £45, double £65–£90. Set dinner £18–£20.

CRANTOCK Cornwall
Map 1

Crantock Bay Hotel BUDGET
Crantock, Newquay TR8 5SE
Tel Crantock (0637) 830229
Fax (0637) 831111

Traditional seaside hotel in lovely setting on Cornish coast near old village on West Pentire headland, 5 m SW of Newquay. Run for many years by David and Brenda Eyles. 200 yds from sandy beach with rock pools and safe bathing. Excellent leisure facilities: indoor swimming pool, spa bath, toddlers' pool; six golf courses nearby. Many regulars – mainly families with young children (entertainments organised in season) and retired people. Excellent, friendly service. Food, conventionally English, strongly criticised this year, "but excellent wine list"; decor and service also come under fire – "perhaps they have become complacent". And few facilities for under-5s, apart from toddlers' pool. Open Mar–Nov. 36 rooms, all with bath and shower. All major credit cards accepted. 1991 rates: Dinner, B&B £33.50–£45. Bar lunch from £4, set dinner £14. 5-day packages; bargain breaks in spring and autumn; half-term rates. More reports please.

CROSBY-ON-EDEN Cumbria — Map 4

Crosby Lodge — *Tel* Crosby-on-Edden (0228) 573618
High Crosby, Crosby-on-Eden — *Fax* (0228) 573428
CA6 4Q2

Michael and Patricia Sedgwick's castellated 18th-century country house, 4½ m NE of Carlisle, is a popular local restaurant, serving straightforward food, continental and British, in generous portions; sweets a speciality. Staff "pleasant but not intrusive". 9 comfortable bedrooms reached by carved staircase in main house, with period furniture and good fabrics; 2 simpler ones in stable block; all with bath/shower. 3½-acre grounds; good walking nearby; river Eden ¼ m. Closed first 3 weeks Jan. Access, Amex, Visa accepted. 1991 rates: B&B double £82–£95. Set lunch £15, dinner £23. Weekend breaks. New nomination. More reports please.

CROYDE Devon — Map 1

The Whiteleaf at Croyde — *Tel* Croyde (0271) 890266
Croyde, Nr Braunton EX33 1PN

Croyde is an attractive seaside village with thatched, colour-washed cottages. The North Devon coastal path and the Exmoor National Park are nearby. The *Whiteleaf* is on the outskirts, in a large garden surrounded by bungalows; the path down to the sweeping sandy beach is through 1930s-type wooden chalets. The house itself lacks charm, the decor is not particularly elegant, and the lounge not very large, but readers have been won over by the friendly atmosphere, the comfortable accommodation, the "devoted attention of the owners", and above all by David Wallington's cooking. His British-style menus (plenty of choice) show invention and imagination: the five-course dinners, served to everyone at about 8.15 pm, include five different vegetables with the main course, "all beautifully cooked, and every course carefully served by Mrs Wallington". There is a well-chosen, wide-ranging wine list with a good selection of half-bottles. The dining room is large, with well-spaced tables and a view of the garden; it is now open to non-residents for dinner. Bedrooms and bathrooms are on the small side, but clean and comfortable and equipped with "all we could think of, including a well-stocked fridge". Breakfasts, served until 10 am, include "fresh orange juice, baked eggs with smoked salmon on top, and vast quantities of toasted home-made bread and marmalade". (*B Dufton, and others*) A possible snag is that high teas are not provided for small children, and Croyde lacks eating places for them; and "the enforced intimacy with fellow guests" might not suit everyone.

Open All year except Jan, 2 weeks Apr/May and 2 weeks July/Aug.
Rooms 5 double – all with bath and/or shower, telephone, radio, TV, tea-making facilities, baby-listening.
Facilities Lounge, bar, dining room. ½-acre grounds. Footpath to Croyde beach with sand, rocks, surfing, bathing (lifeguard in season).
Location From Saunton, hotel is on left side before centre of village (400 yds before *Thatched Barn Inn*).
Restrictions Not suitable for ♿. No dogs in public rooms.
Credit cards Access, Amex, Visa.

Terms B&B £24–£32; dinner, B&B £40–£49. Set dinner £15–£21. Off-season breaks; 3- and 7-night rates. 1-night bookings occasionally refused in season. Reduced rates for children sharing parents' room.
Service/tipping: "We do not expect or solicit tips. Guests wishing to express appreciation will be so advised, but we will not embarrass them by refusing."

CRUDWELL Wiltshire — Map 2

Crudwell Court
Crudwell, Nr Malmesbury
SN16 9EP

Tel Crudwell (066 67) 7194
Fax (066 67) 7853

Brian and Susan Howe's pretty, grey stone, 17th-century vicarage, unusually large, is set back from the road in gardens adjoining the village church. There's an outdoor swimming pool tucked away in a walled garden. The entrance lounge is lemon yellow "and uplifting", the sitting room (with fire) is a warm peach. The Howes have built up a local restaurant trade which they are developing: recently a large conservatory extension, opening on to the garden, was added to the panelled dining room. A new chef, Chris Amor, previously at *The Close*, Tetbury, took over the kitchens in April 1991, and we'd be grateful for comments on the food. We are assured that the emphasis will still be on fresh ingredients and attractive presentation. There is plenty of choice on the menu; the price of the main course includes a starter and dessert. There is a fine wine list. The bedrooms are variable; those on the ground and first floors are large and high-ceilinged, those on the second, up a narrow staircase, are smaller (and cheaper), with good views over the surrounding trees and farmland. The best are quite elegant, with pastel colours and good fabrics; but some have furniture of "spare room quality", the decoration may be "rather kitsch", and insulation in the upper rooms can be poor. One light sleeper was disturbed during the night by the church clock sounding every half an hour, but the hotel assures us it is not very loud.

Open All year.
Rooms 15 double – all with bath, shower, telephone, radio, TV, tea-making facilities, baby-listening.
Facilities 2 lounges, dining room, conservatory. Functions facilities. 3-acre garden with heated swimming pool, croquet. River fishing, lake with water sports nearby.
Location On A429, 3 m N of Malmesbury. Front rooms double-glazed. Hotel is on green opposite *Plough* pub.
Restrictions Not suitable for ♿. No smoking in restaurant. No dogs in public rooms.
Credit cards All major cards accepted.
Terms [1991 rates] B&B: single £40–£65, double £77–£100. Set lunch/dinner £17.50 (snack lunch menu also available). Bargain breaks; Christmas and New Year packages. Reduced rates for children sharing parents' room; special meals.
Service/tipping: "No service charge. Tips are shared among all staff weekly according to hours worked."

****

Traveller's tale *Working in our hotel bedroom, the chambermaid was observed to give bidet and loo etc a final polish with the bath towel. Fair enough as it was destined for the laundry basket. But first it was used to dry the cups and saucers provided for DIY tea-making.*

****

DIDDLEBURY Shropshire — Map 1

The Glebe Farm BUDGET *Tel* Munslow (058 476) 221
Diddlebury
Craven Arms SY7 9DH

Michael and Eileen Wilkes's half-timbered Elizabethan house on a working farm is well endowed with oak beams, flagstones and inglenook fireplaces; they have run it for ten years as a modestly priced guest house. It stands in a garden with a stream, in the centre of a village near the Saxon church with its fortified tower (and bell which strikes throughout the night!), and is well situated for exploring Housman country and the Welsh Marches. There are only six bedrooms, three of which are in a garden cottage recently redecorated in Laura Ashley style; some have bath or shower fitted into the old structure. Some of the walls are very thin, and the private facilities in the garden cottage are rather cramped. But visitors write warmly about the "kind and welcoming" hosts, the "delightful" old house and garden, the comfortable beds and the efficient if minute "facilities", and the excellent value for money. A full English breakfast is served between 8.30 and 9 am and "simple but generous" evening meals at 7.45 pm. In the friendly atmosphere it is easy to get to know fellow guests. More reports please.

Open Mar–Nov. Closed 10 days in June. Dining room open 4 days a week.
Rooms 5 double, 1 single – 2 with bath and shower, 3 with shower, all with tea-making facilities, TV. 3 in cottage in garden.
Facilities Sitting room, bar with TV, dining room. 1-acre garden. Fishing, riding, walking nearby.
Location E of B4368, 4 m NE of Craven Arms.
Restrictions Not suitable for ♿. Smoking forbidden in dining room, discouraged in bedrooms. No children under 8. No dogs.
Credit cards None accepted.
Terms B&B £20–£24. Set dinner £13.50. Midweek breaks off-season. Reductions for children.
Service/tipping: "As owners we do not expect a tip. Any gratuities are divided equally among the staff."

DORCHESTER Dorset — Map 2

Casterbridge Hotel *Tel* Dorchester (0305) 264043
49 High East Street *Fax* (0305) 260884
Dorchester DT1 1HU

Old hotel in Hardy's "Casterbridge"; central, so front rooms can be noisy. Liked for the "sociable proprietors", Rita and Stuart Turner and their staff, and the "excellent and generous breakfasts". "Beautifully appointed", with traditional decor. Bedrooms vary in size; some are very small, ditto the bathrooms (6 are in modern annexe across small courtyard). 2 public rooms, conservatory with fountain. No restaurant. Closed 25/26 Dec. 15 rooms, all with private facilities. All major credit cards accepted. B&B: double £44–£60. Endorsed this year but more reports please.

Deadlines: nominations for the 1993 edition should reach us not later than 25 May 1992. Latest date for comments on existing entries: 5 June 1992.

DORCHESTER-UPON-THAMES Oxfordshire Map 2

The George Hotel
High Street
Dorchester-on-Thames OX10 7HH

Tel Oxford (0865) 340404
Fax (0865) 341620

An ancient coaching inn with a black-and-white facade in a showplace Thames-side village with an enormous abbey, once a 12th-century Augustinian priory, and also many antique shops. Wittenham Clumps – with their exhilarating views over the Thames Valley – are within walking distance. The hotel consists of a number of buildings lining the drive, some of them half-timbered. Bedrooms vary considerably, from large ones with four-poster, to "cosy" ones under oak beams; furniture is solid and old-fashioned. The restaurant is a cleverly converted barn with heavily beamed and raftered ceiling and brick walls, "stylish in the best Old English tradition", looking over a water garden. Cooking (despite a rather pretentious menu) is good – and on the traditional side, especially the Sunday lunch.

Open All year except Christmas.
Rooms 14 double, 4 single – all with bath (16 also have shower), telephone, radio, TV, tea-making facilities, baby-listening. 9 in 2 annexes.
Facilities Lounge, bar, restaurant. 2-acre grounds.
Location Off A423 Oxford–Reading road. Parking.
Restriction No dogs in public rooms.
Credit cards Access, Amex, Visa.
Terms B&B: single £62, double £76–£100. Set lunch £15, dinner £18; full alc £30. Weekend bargain breaks. Reduced rates and special meals for children by arrangement.
Service/tipping: "Service totally at guests' discretion. We wish the industry would adopt one system of collection and distribution as in Europe."

DREWSTEIGNTON Devon Map 1

Hunts Tor House BUDGET
Drewsteignton EX6 6QW

Tel Drewsteignton (0647) 21228

"This is a wonderful discovery. I enthusiastically confirm your entry. Our room was delightful, and cleverly contrived so that it had the effect of a mini-suite. Food far superior to the 'homely' you quote. The Harrisons are such a relaxed pair, yet so keen to get everything right; and very friendly. Not for those who need the posh or the pretentious." (*Peter Little*, warmly endorsed by *JA Vallance White and A Wheeler*)

Drewsteignton is a tiny picture-book village with a Norman church and thatched houses. *Hunts Tor* is extraordinary in that the original building, dating from about 1640, is enclosed within a large Edwardian house. At the heart of the building is a small, low-ceilinged, heavily beamed room, wood everywhere, which is one of the two dining rooms; a few steps away are the lounge and the larger dining room, which belong to the later part of the house. The four bedrooms, on the first floor, are stylish, but simple – no telephones, and only the suite has TV – but new, bright and clean, with an attractive, restrained colour scheme, plenty of storage space, good lights and private facilities. The house is full of Victorian and Edwardian furniture inherited from the previous owners, to which the present owner, Chris Harrison, who converted *Hunts Tor* into a guest house, has added Art Deco pottery and other collectors' items; the resulting decor is "very turn-of-the-century". The Harrisons have neither printed menu nor brochure; they do not take more than eight guests at one time, and dinner is for residents only. Guests eat at a communal table in the smaller dining room only if they are very few; there are four tables for separate dining in the other. The four-course, no-choice dinner is at 7.30, cooked by Sue Harrison who trained with Keith Floyd. Her style is "quite modern, with a tendency to the healthy". Guests should warn in advance of any allergies, etc. Breakfasts are "excellent, including freshly squeezed orange juice and home-made jam and marmalade".

Open Mid-Mar–end Oct. Dining room closed for lunch.
Rooms 1 suite, 3 double – all with bath; TV, tea-making facilities in suite.
Facilities Lounge, bar/dining room, dining room. River Teign nearby, with fishing.
Location In village which is 3 m N of Moretonhampstead.
Restrictions Not suitable for ♿. No smoking in dining room. No children under 14. No dogs in dining room.
Credit cards None accepted.
Terms [1991 rates] B&B (continental): single £28, double £40, suite £50. English breakfast £4. Set dinner £16.50. 1-night bookings sometimes refused bank holidays.
Service/tipping: "No tips expected."

DULVERTON Somerset — Map 1

Ashwick House — *Tel* Dulverton (0398) 23868
Dulverton TA22 9QD

"Your entry spot-on except that the lounge and library are no longer decorated in purple, but it does not stress the uniqueness of the ambience of this lovingly cared-for house." "Richard Sherwood maintains the excellent service and atmosphere created by his late parents and has improved the standard of food and presentation. Bedrooms most comfortable, and all needs supplied. I entertained guests to a snack lunch – only Richard would prepare a personalised menu for soup and sandwiches!" (*Valerie Yorke, Joy Glover*)

This small Edwardian country house is in a lovely peaceful setting, 900 feet up in the Exmoor National Park, in six-acre grounds with sweeping lawns, mature trees, water-gardens and lily ponds, overlooking the valley of the river Barle. The hall, with long broad gallery and log fire, still has the original William Morris wallpaper. Bedrooms, "quiet, with lovely views", are attractively decorated, with good lighting and more than the usual extras including TV with in-house films, changed every day, tape recorder, electronic scales "which announce your weight with malicious delight after the *Ashwick* dinner", magazines, mini-bar and fresh flowers. The bedroom called *Ash* is particularly recommended. Since the deaths of both his parents, Richard has run the hotel, continuing the *Ashwick* style of English home-cooking: a four-course meal with an emphasis on good local produce; each guest is given the menu in a scroll with their name written on it. There is no choice of main course, but you can express likes and dislikes when booking. Guests are expected to dine in. Generous breakfasts (served on a sunny terrace in summer) include freshly squeezed apple juice and good brown toast.

Open All year.
Rooms 6 double – all with bath, shower, radio, TV; telephone on request.

Facilities Hall, lounge, library, bar, dining room. 6-acre grounds, ponds, woodland, croquet.
Location 2½ m NW of Dulverton. Take B3223 Lynton road. Drive up to Winsford Hill and over cattle grid, then first left.
Restrictions Not suitable for ♿. No smoking in dining room. No children under 8. No dogs.
Credit cards None accepted.
Terms Dinner, B&B £56–£80. Set Sun lunch £12.95, dinner £18.95. Special rates for 2 or 5 nights. Christmas package.
Service/tipping: "No service charge added. Tips are not expected by staff, but if offered are gratefully accepted."

EASINGTON Cleveland — Map 4

Grinkle Park
Easington
Saltburn-by-the-Sea TS13 4UB

Tel Guisborough (0287) 640515
Fax (0287) 641278

Again warm endorsements for this fine stone Victorian house, owned by Bass PLC, in extensive grounds with lawns and a lake, approached by a long drive of rhododendrons. "Lovely old house, an efficient and welcoming hotel. Comfortable rooms, interesting menu and sensibly priced wine list. The grounds, with peaceful walks, are a great joy." "Welcome at reception included a glass of sherry. Good, inexpensive lunches and bar meals." The hotel has comfortable lounges and a fine staircase with a half-landing to a huge stained-glass window. Bedrooms are individually decorated: the most elegant, on the first floor, with four-posters, are named after flowers; those on the second floor are simpler and named after moorland birds. All are well appointed with good bathrooms. The dining room is formal in decor, with fresh posies of flowers, quality china, silver and glass, and tables set well apart. It serves "good sound Yorkshire fare at reasonable prices" with the emphasis on local supplies. Game comes from the estate, fish from the fishing village nearby. Mrs Atkinson, who lives on the estate, makes calorific desserts for the trolley. There is an English cheeseboard, plenty of coffee and an affordable house wine. Service, by local people, is good and friendly. Breakfast is "what you'd expect from a good Northern hotel – huge fry-up if you want it; kippers oak-smoked". (*Eileen Broadbent*) Only qualification: *Grinkle Park* has frequent conferences and functions, particularly weddings; holiday guests should discuss accommodation carefully.

Open All year.
Rooms 13 double, 7 single – 14 with bath and shower, 6 with shower only, all with telephone, TV, tea-making facilities; limited baby-listening.
Facilities 2 lounges, bar, billiard room, dining room; conference/functions facilities. 35-acre grounds with lake, tennis, croquet, clay-pigeon shooting. Sea 10 m with safe bathing; fishing, sailing, climbing, walking, shooting nearby.
Location 2 m E of Loftus. Turn N towards Grinkle off A171 Whitby road.
Restrictions Not suitable for ♿. No dogs in public rooms.
Credit cards All major cards accepted.
Terms [1991 rates] B&B: single £60, double £78–£85. Set lunch £10.50, dinner £15; full alc £18.50. Bar meals available. Weekend breaks; 5- and 7-day breaks.
Service/tipping: "Tips at guests' discretion; divided between all staff."

> Hotels are dropped if we lack positive feedback. If you can endorse an entry, we urge you to do so.

EAST BUCKLAND Devon **Map 1**

Lower Pitt Restaurant
East Buckland
Barnstaple EX32 0TD

Tel Filleigh (0598) 760243
Fax (0598) 760243

"At long last I have found somewhere I can boast about to my spoilt continental friends," writes a traveller from Munich. "Welcome was a lovely warm fire on a cold November evening and the Lyons were ever-smiling and friendly. The room was small but most thoughtfully appointed. Quiet, of course, and the bathwater always hot. Dinner was excellent; best were the vegetables. Residents have the clear run of the à la carte menu. It is most unusual to find such outstanding quality in such an out-of-the-way place. Breakfast was carefully prepared to order and as copious as you could wish." "Perhaps the best place of its small kind we have visited. Good wine list with plenty of half-bottles. Host and hostess charming. Admirable atmosphere. A real find." (*FW Daley, Brian Beedham*)

Suzanne and Jerome Lyons's Grade II listed 16th-century white-washed stone farmhouse is a popular restaurant-with-rooms. Tall visitors should mind their heads when passing through the doorways, a reminder of *Lower Pitt*'s cottage ancestry. It is in a peaceful hamlet in the fold of a hillside, surrounded by the walled fields of South Exmoor, "ideally situated for walking direct from the front door", yet only 45 minutes from junction 27 of the M5 thanks to the North Devon link road. The three small bedrooms are comfortable, with pine furniture, duvets, electric blankets and "nice touches such as fresh milk in a thermos for the tea". The Lyons recently added a conservatory dining room, creating a second sitting room. They offer very reasonable three-day midweek breaks. Residents are expected to take dinner.

Open All year except Christmas and New Year. Restaurant closed to non-residents Sun and Mon. Lunch by special arrangement.
Rooms 3 double – 1 with bath, 2 with shower, all with tea-making facilities.
Facilities 2 lounges, 2 dining rooms. 2-acre grounds with gardens and terrace. Sandy beaches and North Devon coast within easy reach.
Location 3 m NW of South Molton. Follow signs to East Buckland from new North Devon link road (A361).
Restrictions Not suitable for ♿. No smoking in dining rooms; smoking discouraged in bedrooms. No children under 12. No dogs.
Credit cards Access, Visa.
Terms Dinner, B&B £45–£50. Full alc £24. Midweek reductions (dinner, B&B £40 per person per night, 3 nights min).
Service/tipping: "No service charge; tips are at customers' discretion and are divided equally among all staff. As owners, we do not expect a tip."

EAST GRINSTEAD West Sussex **Map 3**

Gravetye Manor
East Grinstead RH19 4LJ

Tel Sharpthorne (0342) 810567
Fax (0342) 810080

César award in 1991: The epitome of the grand English country house hotel at its luxurious best

"An efficiently run hotel, serving impeccable food, which takes itself a little seriously. Our abiding memory is of *Gravetye*'s secret location amongst wooded hills, and the beauty of the old house viewed from its magnificent gardens on an unusually sunny summer's day. It has a more traditional feel than the country house hotels that started up in the late 1970s and early 1980s; having achieved eminence before this period it doesn't appear to have to run as hard to keep ahead of the pack. One might say it is looking slightly old-fashioned – the fabrics are subdued, the sitting rooms austere and formal rather than luxuriously padded in a chintzy way. The quality is there, however; furniture is antique rather than reproduction; the paintings are not a bought-in job lot; beautiful flower arrangements abound. In the bedrooms everything works. Our room was well stocked with information packs, books and magazines – but the cost per square foot was high. We had a large, comfortable bed with wall lights above for reading, but rather small side tables to accommodate telephone, radio, books, spectacles, teeth and other paraphernalia. The bathroom was small with limited shelf space and poor lighting, but otherwise well equipped. There was a hand basin in the bedroom in a curtained alcove, which probably dated from the period when private bathrooms were not *de rigueur* in such places. Both dinner and breakfast were excellent. Raw materials are first-class and handled well if without a great deal of innovation, though the food is modern in style. Waiters are efficient, mainly French, anxious to please, and showed equanimity in coping with a couple of health disciples at the next table. Full marks to the receptionists, also, for being remarkably pleasant and self-confident."

Other correspondents echo these sentiments; for many *Gravetye* devotees it is the "slightly old-fashioned" character that is its *genius loci.* Peter Herbert's immaculate Elizabethan manor house was once owned by William Robinson, pioneer of the English natural garden, who laid out the beautiful grounds which nowadays are maintained by six gardeners. It has spacious panelled public rooms and a renowned restaurant. Bedrooms, all named after trees, vary in size; the best have plenty of storage space and garden views. Bathrooms, too, are well equipped. The kitchen uses fruit, vegetables, herbs, spring water, free-range eggs from the estate, game obtained locally, and salmon, venison and duck breasts all smoked in the hotel's own smokehouse. (*David Wooff, Pat and Jeremy Temple, Betsy Wilhelm, and others*) Late news: chef Mark Raffan has left. Stephen Morey, former sous chef, assumes his *tocque*.

Peter Herbert quotes prices exclusive of VAT and breakfast which annoys some visitors (though he must be congratulating himself about the former this year); he accepts no credit cards. Another grumble: "The daft persistence in handing women, presumably only when accompanied by a man, unpriced menus." [Hear, hear – Ed.]

Open All year. Restaurant closed to non-residents on Christmas evening.
Rooms 16 double, 2 single – all with bath and shower, telephone, radio, TV, baby-listening; tea-making facilities on request.
Facilities 3 sitting rooms, bar, restaurant; private dining room. 30-acre grounds with gardens, croquet, lake with fishing.
Location 5 m SW of East Grinstead off B2110 at West Hoathly sign. Glyndebourne 40 mins' drive; Gatwick Airport 9 m.
Restrictions Not suitable for ♿. No smoking in restaurant. No children under 7 except babies. No dogs.
Credit cards None accepted.
Terms (Excluding VAT) Rooms: single £85–£100, double £110–£194. Breakfast: continental £6.50, English alc. Set lunch £19, dinner £22; full alc £40. 1-night bookings refused at weekends Apr–Sep.
Service/tipping: "Prices include service; our staff do not expect tips."

EASTON GREY Wiltshire **Map 2**

Whatley Manor
Easton Grey
Malmesbury SN16 0RB

Tel Malmesbury (0666) 822888
Fax (0666) 826120

This fine country manor house, parts of which date from the 18th century, underwent a massive reconstruction in the late 1920s and 1930s by Bertie Cox, then President of the Canada Life Assurance Company. He also lavished huge sums on the garden. After his death at the end of World War II it went into a decline, but in the 1970s it was rescued to enjoy a new lease of life as a country house hotel. The manor is spacious and beautiful but not intimidating, with antiques and fine rugs, an oak-panelled drawing room, a book-lined library bar, and a dining room enjoying views of the garden. Bedrooms, traditionally furnished, spacious and comfortable, are in the main house, a new connected terrace wing, and a secluded court house (where there is no room service). The grounds, with swimming pool, tennis and croquet, slope down to the river Avon. Other facilities are listed below. Children and dogs are welcomed; vegetarians are catered for. The hotel returned to the Guide last year in an italicised entry which is now endorsed: "As soon as we entered the hall, with its fresh flowers and fire, we felt totally relaxed. Our room had a lovely view and very adequate bathroom. The third member of our party had a room with a tub big enough for a football team. The food, particularly breakfast, was excellent. The management was not in evidence, but everything ran on fuss-free wheels." (*Peter and Lisa Simon*) There is easy access via the M4 and M5. The Christmas package is said to be particularly good value. More reports please.

Open All year.
Rooms 29 double – all with bath, shower, telephone, radio, TV, tea-making facilities, baby-listening. 11 in court house (no room service).
Facilities 2 lounges, bar, dining room; conference facilities. 20-acre grounds with tennis, croquet, river with trout fishing, outdoor heated swimming pool, sauna, solarium, jacuzzi, table tennis.
Location 3 m W of Malmesbury on B4040.
Restrictions Not suitable for ♿. No dogs in public rooms.
Credit cards All major cards accepted.
Terms [1991 rates] B&B: single £73.50–£84, double £101–£119.50. Set lunch £16.50, dinner £27.50. Weekend breaks. Christmas breaks.
Service/tipping: "We make no service charge. Tipping is left to guests' discretion. In my view we must be careful in telling them how to behave. But I would be delighted to see the industry adopt a common practice."

EVERSHOT Dorset **Map 2**

Summer Lodge
Evershot DT2 0JR

Tel Evershot (0935) 83424
Fax (0935) 83005

César award in 1985: Best country house hotel in the medium-price range

"When we arrived a white bunny was posing in a bunch of daffodils under the forsythia and a black one was walking down the lane. The atmosphere hasn't changed since our last visit, and the staff are as welcoming and charming as ever. All the bedrooms have been upgraded, with everything beautifully done; all now have TV. The dining room, too, has been enlarged and redecorated and is very sophisticated, in shades of blue, with lovely curtains, new hand-carved chairs, good linen and silver, and a garden view from almost every table. The food, under chef Roger Jones, is now excellent, with particularly good fish and sauces, and they still serve plenty of vegetables in dishes, not on silly little plates. There is a daily menu using the best of the market and a small *carte* which changes monthly." "Our room in the coach house had french windows opening on to a small private patio. No loss of personal touch; staff remembered our likes and dislikes. The walled garden is beautifully kept and the flower arrangements in the lounge and dining room were magnificent."

Nigel and Margaret Corbett, now backed by the "very helpful" manager, Michael Ash, constantly work to improve their country house hotel, the Earl of Ilchester's former dower house in a pretty Dorset village, "in all sorts of details most agreeable to regular guests", and it is hardly surprising that with the improvements noted above prices have gone up considerably since the days when it won its *César*. But there's still no shortage of praise from visitors, many of them regulars, for the "peace and dignity" of the establishment, for the afternoon teas ("what a spread"), for the "full and very English" breakfasts "with home-made marmalade and jam not in horrid little plastic tubs". Shoes left outside the room at night are polished, car windows are cleaned every morning; and there are no nasty surprises on the bill; newspapers, early morning and afternoon tea, and use of the tennis court are all included; only drinks are extra. (*Heather Sharland, Tom and Rosemary Rose, Charles Gorer, C Mackey, John and Carol Riddick, and many others*)

Open All year, except first 2 weeks Jan.
Rooms 14 double, 3 single – all with bath, shower, telephone, radio, TV, tea-making facilities. 6 in coach house annexe. 3 on ground floor.
Facilities Ramps. Drawing room, TV room, bar, dining room. 5-acre garden with heated swimming pool, croquet, tennis. Golf, fishing nearby. Sea 12 m.
Location 10 m S of Yeovil. (*Note*: The entrance on village street is for pedestrians only; cars must turn left on reaching village into Summer Lane and then right into drive to house.)
Restrictions No children under 8. Small dogs by prior arrangement (£2); not in public rooms.
Credit cards Access, Visa.
Terms B&B £50–£95; dinner, B&B £70–£125. Set lunch £17.50 (packed or light lunch also available), dinner £27.50; full alc £27.50. Reductions for stays of 2 days or more. 3-day breaks in low season; Christmas and New Year packages. 1-night bookings sometimes refused for Sat and bank holiday weekends. 40% reduction for children sharing parents' room.
Service/tipping: "Tipping left entirely *to our guests' discretion; not necessary as our staff are fully and properly paid."*

EVESHAM Hereford and Worcester — Map 2

The Evesham Hotel
Cooper's Lane
Evesham WR11 6DA

Tel Evesham (0386) 765566
Fax (0386) 765443

César award in 1990: Utterly acceptable mild eccentricity

An informal, friendly hotel run by the Jenkinson family, with jokey brochure, toy ducks and boats in the baths and resident teddy bears, which is genuinely welcoming to families with small children. It enjoys a secluded setting a short walk from the centre of town. Bedrooms and bathrooms are well equipped, clean and comfortable. The busy restaurant overlooks the large garden with a huge old cedar of Lebanon; chatty dinner menus offer exotic dishes from around the world as well as plain grills; lunch is a reasonably priced buffet or a choice of hot dishes; the extensive and informative wine list "encompasses Afrikanerdom to Zimbabwe". The Jenkinsons' determinedly jokey attitude may be a bit much for some – "rather self-conscious" says one correspondent. Last year we said "the cooking does not reach any gastronomic heights", and this has prompted some readers to rally to the defence: "Food well prepared, imaginative and delicious; superb buffet at lunch", and others to join the attack: "To say it's tolerable would be generous." One reader reports a muddle over breakfast for which no apology was made. But the staff are otherwise judged "courteous, competent, and helpful". (*Ann Saunders, Mattye B Silverman, and others*)

Open All year except 25/26 Dec.
Rooms 1 family, 33 double, 6 single – all with bath and/or shower, telephone, radio, TV, tea-making facilities, baby-listening.
Facilities Bar, lounge, restaurant; small indoor swimming pool. 2½-acre grounds.
Location 5 mins' walk from town centre, across river. Parking.
Restrictions Not really suitable for ♿. No dogs in public rooms.
Credit cards All major cards accepted.
Terms B&B: single £54–£66, double £84–£92, family £100–£110. Buffet lunch £6; full alc dinner £23. Off-season breaks. Reduced rates and special meals for children.
Service/tipping: "In a service industry, service is an intrinsic part of the product; to pay extra for it is like being asked to pay extra for the elastic when you buy a pair of knickers."

FALMOUTH Cornwall — Map 1

Penmere Manor
Mongleath Road
Falmouth TR11 4PN
Tel Falmouth (0326) 211411
Fax (0326) 317588

"As warm and welcoming as ever," writes a winter visitor. "The two new girls on reception are as pleasant as one could wish. The hotel must have a good system to ensure continuity of this standard. Bar and restaurant service excellent. One of the Popes is always in attendance. Never obtrusive, but available for help or a chat. The overall impression is of warmth, comfort and professionalism." "Very comfortable in every way." (*Geoff Barratt, Mrs C Stevenson*)

This unpretentious and dependable family hotel in a well-bred Georgian house has been run by the Pope family, five in all, for many years and has plenty of loyal regulars. Sandy beaches are a mile away. The hotel has five acres of sub-tropical gardens and woodland, a large walled garden sheltering a heated swimming pool, snooker and games rooms, and a well-equipped leisure centre. Visitors continue to appreciate the "superior" rooms in the new wing, added in 1989, "decorated in pastel colours and furnished with everything one might need including a folding ironing board". Food is not *haute cuisine*, but plentiful and well presented, with fresh fish and a vegetarian dish. Most visitors have enjoyed their meals but one reported overcooked vegetables and a greasy breakfast (and also a soulless atmosphere). Last year we reported one fly in the ointment: "There was a pianist during dinner, of the dozily and noisily romantic type, but we asked for a table in the far corner of the room and found it bearable." The Popes reply: "Our impression is that the vast majority enjoy Phil King's playing; he gets a great many requests." One of that vast majority writes: "Applause is generally recognised as approval . . . almost invariably accorded to Phil King for his rendering of diners' selections." (*Sir Alan Dalton*)

Open All year except Christmas.
Rooms 31 double, 8 single – all with bath and/or shower, telephone, radio, TV, tea-making facilities, baby-listening. 13 on ground floor.
Facilities Ramp. 2 lounges, restaurant, games room, snooker room, leisure centre. 5-acre grounds with heated swimming pool, adventure playground. Sandy beach, golf 1 m.
Location 1 m from Falmouth. In Penryn turn right towards Gweek and Constantine. Follow signs to Maenporth. Hotel sign on left into Mongleath road.
Restrictions No smoking in dining room. Dogs by arrangement; not in public rooms, must be accompanied in bedrooms.
Credit cards Access, Amex.
Terms B&B: single £52.50–£90.25, double £78–£106.50; dinner, B&B (2 nights min) £52.25–£70 per person. Set dinner £20; full alc £25. Reduced rates and special meals for children.
Service/tipping: "No service charge; staff are well remunerated for the services they give willingly. Anything left by guests is distributed among all staff including those behind the scenes."

FARNHAM Dorset — Map 2

The Museum BUDGET — *Tel* Tollard Royal (0725) 516261
Farnham
Nr Blandford Forum DT11 8DE

Village pub by church in "unprettified" village NE of Blandford Forum in heart of Hardy country, "an oasis in the bareness of Salisbury Plain". Coopers Bar has inglenook fireplace and original bread oven. Pub supper, or candle-lit dinner in attractive restaurant; reasonable wine list. Good English breakfast. "Excellent and simple, with no airs and graces." Only 4 bedrooms, all with bath/shower, in recently converted stable block: "Very comfortable with usual extras but no mirror in bedroom." Closed Christmas. No dogs. Access accepted. B&B double £55. Full alc £12–£18. New nomination. More reports please.

FLITWICK Bedfordshire — Map 1

Flitwick Manor — *Tel* Flitwick (0525) 712242
Church Road, Flitwick MK45 1AE — *Fax* (0525) 712242

Returning to the Guide under new (non-resident) owners, this epitome of a country house hotel is in a Grade II early 18th-century listed building, approached down an avenue of huge trees, set in a 50-acre park (though only seven acres of well-tended gardens belong to the hotel). Flitwick itself is not inspiring, but the *Manor* is well out of eyeshot of the village. "I was extremely impressed by the evidence that the management had tried to answer the question: 'How can a *real* service, of *real* quality, be delivered to our guests?' Postcards in the bedrooms were ready stamped. The guest information states, 'We pay a retainer to a local doctor and dentist. They are on call at all times on a private basis.' Wellies and tennis racquets are available on loan. Bedrooms are very good to excellent – only criticism: too many miniature bottles of less popular drinks, some looking rather ancient. You can ask to see the kitchens. We did, and rated them highly. Food was balanced, varied (with two thoughtful vegetarian dishes) and novel. There was no automatic service charge nor any aggressive messages to that effect. Service in all quarters was affable and efficient." (*GH Wheldon*) The manor has fine public rooms: a huge, high-ceilinged Gothic music room, with comfortable seats; a library with a moulded plaster cornice and frieze, and a Regency-style dining room. Bedrooms vary in shape and size and are well decorated, with good fabrics and antiques. Some have a four-poster, all have garden views. More reports please.

Open All year.
Rooms 2 suites, 9 double, 4 single – all with bath and/or shower, telephone, radio, TV, baby-listening. Some on ground floor.
Facilities Drawing room, library, morning room, restaurant; private dining room. 7-acre grounds with lake, tennis, croquet, 12th-century church and helipad; bicycles available. Set in 50-acre park (not hotel's).
Location Take exit 12 from M1, then A5120 towards Bedford. Hotel 2 m SW of Flitwick.
Restrictions Smoking forbidden in dining room, and discouraged in some bedrooms. Dogs allowed in bedrooms and public rooms with owners.
Credit cards Access, Amex, Visa.
Terms B&B: single £78, double £98, suite £165. Set lunch £21, dinner £35; full alc £40. Reduced rates for children sharing parents' room; special meals.
Service/tipping: "Tips optional; distributed by tronc *system."*

FOWEY Cornwall — Map 1

Marina Hotel — *Tel* Fowey (0726) 833315
The Esplanade, Fowey PL23 1HY

A reasonably priced hotel in a listed Georgian building, originally the summer retreat of the Bishops of Truro. It enjoys an outstanding setting in this charming town which tumbles down a hill to the water's edge. "It has minimal traffic as all vehicles must be left in the carparks on the edge of town. You can drive down the 1-in-6 hill to the hotel to unload your luggage but pre-arrival organisation with David Johns, the proprietor, is essential – unloading in front of the hotel blocks the Esplanade. And the altitude problem is not confined to the streets of Fowey; from the beach at the end of the *Marina*'s small and charming garden to the third and top floor there are 101 steps, 60 of them inside the hotel from the dining room to the top landing. The *Marina*, with a spacious entrance lobby, moulded ceilings and arches, a curved staircase lit from above by an overhead oval window, and an almost semi-circular first-floor landing, has the air of an elegant, well-maintained home rather than a hotel. Some bedrooms are quite small; those overlooking the estuary have lovely views, four of them have a balcony. Furnishing is simple but adequate, with flowery wallpaper and curtains. Beds are firm, with good linen. The dining room has a panoramic view and mealtimes are a picture show of riverscapes and boats. There is plenty of choice on the menu and fresh local fish is normally offered; the cooking is slightly variable but soups are good, and desserts good and abundant. Breakfasts nicely cooked; you get what you ordered." That description, written two years ago, is confirmed by this year's crop of reports: "Mr and Mrs Johns are most pleasant and helpful;

the situation is idyllic." "A most delightful establishment, sparkling clean throughout. David Johns could not have been more helpful." (*Meriel Packman, JH Smith; also Mr and Mrs JG Lustig, and others*) The hotel now provides a minibus service to the carpark each morning at 10.15. Only niggles: muzak in the bar, and "most rooms don't have a shower so hair-washing can be a problem".

Open Mar–Oct inclusive.
Rooms 11 double – 9 with bath, 2 with shower, all with telephone, radio, TV, tea-making facilities, baby-listening. 4 with balcony.
Facilities 2 lounges, bar lounge, dining room. Small walled garden with summerhouse, steps to water; moorings available to guests; fishing.
Location 1-way circuit, turn right at start of shops.
Restrictions Not suitable for ♿. No smoking in restaurant. No dogs in public rooms.
Credit cards All major cards accepted.
Terms B&B £25–£38. Single occupancy supplement 50%. Bar snacks £2–£3; packed lunches available. Set dinner £15; full alc £20. 2-day and weekly breaks. Reduced rates for children sharing parents' room; high tea.
Service/tipping: "No service charge. Tipping at guests' discretion at end of stay; shared by all staff."

GILLAN Cornwall — Map 1

Tregildry Hotel — *Tel* Manaccan (032 623) 378
Gillan, Manaccan TR12 6HG

The Norton family's white-painted, "relaxed and unpretentious" small seaside hotel is well off the beaten track in the middle of a field on a peninsula overlooking Gillan Bay. It's an easy ten-minute walk down to a quiet cove (good for fishing, bathing, windsurfing and boating), a tougher twenty minutes back. There are good walks nearby on the coastal path. "An excellent hotel, very reasonably priced, in a magnificent position with enviable views. Bedrooms are spotlessly clean and comfortable; beds are made while you breakfast – *that's* a sign of a good hotel. The staff are all unfailingly cheerful, polite and helpful. The food is excellent; not a lot of choice, but it doesn't matter when it is all so good. The wine list is short but obviously compiled by an enthusiast [Norton Senior was almost twenty years in the wine trade] and very reasonably priced." Bedrooms are "light and comfortable with exceptionally good bathrooms"; they are simply decorated and furnished, "without great individuality, but comfortable, efficient and pleasant. Good wholesome breakfast with home-made marmalade." The bar and lounge are "attractive and spacious enough to make even a really wet day enjoyable". Most bedrooms have fine views over the bay or creek. (*Brian Wicks, Carol Jackson; also RF Fernsby, BS Bourne, and others*) One tiny niggle: "Over-use of paper doilies."

Open Easter–mid-Oct.
Rooms 10 double – 9 with bath and shower, 1 with shower, all with TV, tea-making facilities.
Facilities 2 lounges, lounge bar, TV room. 4-acre grounds. Private path to beach – bathing, sailing, fishing, windsurfing.
Location 12 m E of Helston. From New Town St Martin, follow signs to Manaccan, then Gillan. Hotel sign at T-junction.
Restrictions Not suitable for ♿. No smoking in dining room and bedrooms. No dogs in public rooms.

Credit cards Access, Visa.
Terms [1991 rates] Dinner, B&B £38.50–£44. 30% surcharge for single occupancy. Bar lunch £1.60–£8, set dinner £16. 3-day breaks except in high season. 1-night bookings sometimes refused in high season.
Service/tipping: "Guests may tip if they want to. We hope our staff service is the same whether they do or not."

GILLINGHAM Dorset — Map 2

Stock Hill House
Wyke, Gillingham SP8 5NR
Tel Gillingham (0747) 823626/82
Fax (0747) 825628

César award in 1991: Dedicated hotelmanship

"One of the friendliest hotels I have ever visited, in a lovely part of the country. An oasis of peace and quiet, complemented by good honest cooking, fine wines and charming staff. At dinner the guests were actually enjoying themselves, not eating in solemn worship of the chef as so often happens nowadays. Nita Hauser is a natural hostess." "Gets better every visit. Meals have improved (they were pretty good before) and moved into a modern idiom, lighter, yet maintaining the Austrian influence. The whole house sparkles."

Peter and Nita Hauser's Victorian manor is quietly situated in ten acres of parkland, with stream, fountain, lawns, old and rare trees and lots of wildlife. They have spent much time and money refurbishing it since coming here six years ago and the result is colourful and opulent, with heavy drapes and elaborate chandeliers in the public rooms, and *objets d'art* collected over the years: "Indian horses, immense Siamese cats, Buddhas of various sizes squat in almost every recess; decorative plates, assorted pictures decorate the walls. All a little hectic perhaps but above all the atmosphere is warm and friendly and you really do feel welcome as a guest." Bedrooms are done up in similar style; they vary in size; the large four-poster room with sofa and armchair, huge bathroom, plenty of storage space, and many extras, is particularly commended. Beds, except the four-poster, have duvets, but you can ask for conventional bedding if you prefer it. Guests appreciate the "fresh, perfectly ripe fruit" and "excellent" bedside lights. Dinner is a leisurely affair. Peter Hauser's cooking concentrates on fresh, locally produced ingredients and home-grown herbs and vegetables; there is plenty of choice on the menu; wines are reasonably priced. Men are expected to wear jacket and tie at dinner. (*Padi and John Howard, Pat and Jeremy Temple; also Ian and Francine Walsh, Joan Taylor, Mrs A Cornall, John and Margaret Myring, and others*) Two niggles about breakfast: "Coffee is served a cup at a time; we had to keep asking to be topped up. We would rather have had a pot." "To make sure the toast was warm they brought it a slice at a time which sometimes meant long waits between slices." And one reader found the decor too exotic, and felt too many dishes contained cream and butter.

Open All year. Closed Sun evening and Mon except bank holidays.
Rooms 6 double, 2 single – all with bath and/or shower, telephone, radio, TV.
Facilities Foyer with small bar, lounge, breakfast room, restaurant. Indoor swimming pool heated May–Oct. 10 acres with stream, lake, croquet, tennis.
Location On B3081 1½ m W of Gillingham, just S of A303.
Restrictions Not suitable for ♿. No smoking in dining and breakfast rooms. No children under 7. No dogs.

Credit cards Access, Visa.
Terms Dinner, B&B £80–£90. Set lunch £19, dinner £28. Midweek reductions in winter. 1-night bookings refused over bank holidays. Reduced rates and special meals for children.
Service/tipping: "Tipping is between the guest and staff; we are very much against service charges."

GOATHLAND North Yorkshire — Map 4

Whitfield House BUDGET — *Tel* Whitby (0947) 86215
Darnholm, Goathland
Nr Whitby YO22 5LA

John and Pauline Lusher's old stone farmhouse in small grounds is in beautiful, peaceful setting, on fringe of hamlet ¾ m from Goathland, in heart of North York Moors National Park. Recommended for good, simple accommodation and country food (dinner at 7 pm, limited choice, using only fresh ingredients), and very reasonable prices. Closed 1 Nov–28 Feb. 9 rooms, all with bath/shower. No smoking in dining room and bedrooms. Credit cards not accepted. B&B £20. Set dinner £9.50. Recent nomination. More reports please.

GRASMERE Cumbria — Map 4

White Moss House — *Tel* Grasmere (096 65) 295
Rydal Water, Grasmere LA22 9SE

This small hotel and restaurant, formerly three 18th-century cottages belonging to Wordsworth's family – his descendants lived there until the 1930s – is owned and run by Susan and Peter Dixon. There are five rooms in the main house on the A591 (heavy lorries banned), and two up a steep footpath in Brockstone Cottage. They are smallish, with small bathrooms, but are extensively kitted out with cosseting extras – trouser press, sewing kit, hair-drier, bath essence, dried *White Moss* lavender, Crabtree and Evelyn soaps, and so forth. The lounge is not large, but comfortable, and conducive to after-dinner fraternising. Peter Dixon is the chef; dinners, served at "7.30 for 8", are five-course affairs: good local ingredients unpretentiously cooked with fresh herbs, lots of vegetables, no choice until dessert, a good selection of English cheeses, and a long and varied wine list. Recent comments: "Outstanding food." "Delightful room in main house." "Elegantly faultless cooking and service." But we'd like more reports please. The Dixons now have a boathouse on Rydal Water, with an old wooden rowing boat for guests' use.

Open Mar–Nov. Restaurant closed for lunch and on Sun.
Rooms 1 suite, 6 double – all with bath, shower, telephone, radio, TV. 2 in cottage on hillside (10 mins by car or direct footpath).
Facilities Lounge, bar, dining room. 2-acre garden with terrace. Near Rydal Water and river Rothay; swimming and fishing.
Location On A591 between Ambleside and Grasmere. Rooms double-glazed; cottage ones quietest.
Restrictions Not suitable for ♿. No smoking in dining room. No facilities for very young children. No dogs.
Credit cards Access, Visa.
Terms Dinner, B&B £60–£80. Set dinner £25. Reduced rates for some weekends Mar and Nov. 1-night bookings sometimes refused, especially Sat and bank holidays. 25% reductions July and Aug for children.

Service/tipping: "Tipping is not expected. Sometimes guests insist on leaving something, which we put in a staff box."

GRASSINGTON North Yorkshire — Map 4

Ashfield House BUDGET — *Tel* Grassington (0756) 752584
Grassington
Nr Skipton BD23 5AE

Creeper-covered 17th-century house in small garden, tucked away off main street of principal village in Upper Wharfedale, re-enters Guide, recommended for "friendly but not fussy new owners, Linda and Keith Harrison, cosy atmosphere, with log fires, clean and comfortable bedrooms, good food, good value". Informal atmosphere, limited facilities, home-cooked English food – generous breakfast, 4-course dinner at 7 pm (no choice of main course). Open mid-Mar–end Oct. Not suitable for ♿. No children under 5. No dogs. Smoking discouraged. 7 rooms, 5 with shower. Credit cards not accepted. Dinner, B&B £33.50–£37.50. Reductions for 2 or more nights. More reports please.

GREAT DUNMOW Essex — Map 3

The Starr — *Tel* Great Dunmow (0371) 874321
Market Place — *Fax* (0371) 876337
Great Dunmow CM6 1AX

"In a commanding peninsular position where two roads converge in the market place of Great Dunmow," writes our inspector, introducing to the Guide this "old inn, part Tudor and with much charm, which accurately describes itself as a restaurant-with-rooms; accommodation is in an old stable block, carefully converted to be in character by the use of dark stained slats. You park in bays under the rooms which are on an upper level. There are no grounds. All the rooms have names; ours, Poppy, was spotless, with modern furniture, fresh floral (poppy, of course) chintz bedcover and curtains, and bright green walls. Towels were acceptable if not sumptuous, radiator effective; hot water, oddly, came out of a tap marked 'F'. The only flaw was the lighting. Why cannot hotels appreciate the need for a good reading light? The menu in the agreeably beamed, softly lit restaurant is offered on a large blackboard and changes daily; every dish was patiently explained. Our meal was near flawless; the wines good value. Continental breakfast, served in the bedroom, arrived exactly on time but was unexceptional – limp toast, canned orange juice. But we were well and courteously looked after throughout." Stansted airport is only 15 minutes away.

Open All year except 1 week Jan. Closed Sat lunch, Sun dinner.
Rooms 8 double – all with bath, shower, telephone, radio, TV, tea-making facilities.
Facilities Restaurant; 2 private dining rooms.
Location In centre of small town on A120 between Braintree and Bishop's Stortford.
Restrictions Not suitable for ♿. No smoking in bedrooms. No dogs.
Credit cards Access, Amex, Visa.
Terms (Excluding 10% service charge) B&B: single £60, double £85; dinner, B&B: single £79, double £123. Set lunch £19 (light lunch menu also available), dinner £31.

Service/tipping: "Service charge distributed via a tronc system; all staff receive an equal share on a monthly basis."

GREAT LANGDALE Cumbria — Map 4

Long House BUDGET — *Tel* Langdale (096 67) 222
Great Langdale
Nr Ambleside LA22 9JS

17th-century Lakeland house in 2-acre grounds, 6 m W of Ambleside on B5343. Excellent base for climbing Langdale Pikes and exploring the valley. Low beamed ceilings, open fires; clean, comfortable. "Excellent cooking, in the best tradition of country farmhouses, well balanced and delicately seasoned, using fresh ingredients and local specialities"; bring your own wine. Unobtrusive but helpful hosts, the Wilkinsons. Recommended for a relaxed break in beautiful surroundings. Book well ahead. 3 rooms, all with bath. Closed 25 and 31 Dec, Jan; open weekends only (B&B) Nov–Mar. Not suitable for ♿. No children under 9. No dogs. Access, Visa accepted. B&B £19.50–£21.50. Set dinner £11.50. More reports please.

GREAT MILTON Oxfordshire — Map 1

Le Manoir aux Quat'Saisons — *Tel* Great Milton (0844) 278881
Great Milton OX9 7PD — *Fax* (0844) 278847

César award in 1985: Most brilliant newcomer

Raymond Blanc's celebrated 15th/16th-century manor house, its restaurant double-rosetted in *Michelin*, stands next to the church in a small and peaceful village near Oxford. There are 27 acres of parkland around, with lovely gardens, a heated pool and a well-laid-out *potager* which supplies the kitchens. The public rooms are decorated with fine fabrics, antique and period furniture and fresh flowers; bedrooms are lavish. But reports on the *Manoir* this year are very mixed, due in part, no doubt, to its "Himalayan" prices. Most readers continue to extol the food, with occasional murmurs about the *nouvelle*-sized portions, but comments on the accommodation, the welcome and the service vary wildly. On the plus side: "A delightful hotel. Our room in the newly converted stable block was large and beautifully furnished, with excellent bed linen, good bedside lighting and a huge and magnificent bathroom. Dinner was memorable; it was exquisitely presented and flavours were outstanding; M. Blanc was very much in evidence in his chef's whites. Continental breakfast in the conservatory was most enjoyable and so satisfying that we needed no lunch that day." "Our room was lovely and large; our children were welcomed and well treated." (*Kay and Neville Varley, Estelle Silverstein; also Mr and Mrs Donald Whitfield, Mr and Mrs Bågstam*) On the reverse side, however, there are reports of faulty plumbing, imperfect service and a plethora of extras on the bill: "You took your life in your hands if you sat on the bidet; the shower would only deliver very hot or very cold water." "We'd looked forward to using the jacuzzi but it didn't work." "We were hurried out of our room in the morning; waiting at breakfast inattentive and difficult because of poor English." "We sent up a tiny dessert to our children and were charged £21." Even the restaurant is not exempt: "Food exceptional only in price. Menu asked us not to smoke but M. Blanc was smoking non-stop a few tables away." "The sitting rooms reeked of cigarette smoke." When the *Manoir* won its *César* seven years ago it promised to provide a sublime experience – the hotel equivalent of Glyndebourne. No one doubts Blanc's brilliance as a chef, but whether he can achieve equal renown as a hotelier is still unproven.

Open All year except Christmas and New Year.
Rooms 3 suites, 16 double – all with bath, shower (some with whirlpool), telephone, radio, TV. 9 in converted stable block.
Facilities 2 sitting rooms, restaurant, conservatory restaurant; 2 functions rooms. 27-acre grounds with heated swimming pool, croquet, tennis.
Location 1 m W of M40/A40, 7 m SE of Oxford. From London take M40: exit 7, 1 mile, 2nd right. From Oxford, take A40, then A329 at Milton Common towards Wallingford, 2nd right.
Restrictions Not suitable for ♿. No smoking in conservatory. No dogs in building – free kennel facilities in grounds.
Credit cards All major cards accepted.
Terms [Until spring 1992] (No single rates) B&B: double £165–£275, suite £325–£375. Set lunch £26.50 (£29.50 on Sat), dinner £59.50; full alc £80. Midweek breaks; off-season breaks. 1-night bookings may be refused for Sat.
Service/tipping: "Service included. Tips are optional and distributed among staff."

GREAT SNORING Norfolk — Map 3

The Old Rectory
Barsham Road, Great Snoring
Fakenham NR21 0HP
Tel Fakenham (0328) 820597
Fax (0328) 820048

"'Idyllic' is a much abused word but this truly deserves the description. The building is a delight, the gardens lovely and the church next door worth a visit for the reminders of what happens if you feed the body and starve the spirit. The welcome is polite, friendly and unfussy. Our bedroom had a lovely view of the lawns and the huge copper beech which is floodlit. The 'no-choice menu' was somewhat misnamed: not liking pork, I was offered two alternatives. Dinners were very good – everything fresh, nothing over-elaborate – and the wine quite acceptable and not too expensive. Breakfast was superb. Service was extremely friendly. The place seemed to be staffed entirely by women. Perhaps this contributed to the general feeling that things were done properly and with no hint of snobbishness or competitiveness." This old building, Elizabethan in origin, developed and restored in Victorian days, and considerably grander than the average country parsonage, is tranquilly set in a large walled garden with a well-kept lawn and fine trees in an unspoilt village. Inside there are polished floor tiles, lots of dark wood furniture and flowers. Inevitably in such a venerable house the bedrooms vary in size; some can be cramped, others are "spacious with good antique furniture"; they are comfortable rather than luxurious. The dining room has mullioned windows, heavy oak beams and good quality silver, plate and glass. Food (in principle no choice of main course, but see above) is substantial, basic and well cooked, with plenty of vegetables, but not *haute cuisine*. (*Dr and Mrs A Winterbourne; also Gabriele Berneck and Dr C Herxheimer, Robert Hartford, and others*) A couple of complaints: prices a bit high given the limited choice of food, and an unheated bathroom.

One 1991 reader was very critical of the food.

Note: The hotel also owns five self-catering serviced cottages nearby – not an annexe but a quite separate operation.

Open All year except 24–27 Dec. Dining room closed for lunch.
Rooms 6 double – all with bath, telephone, TV.
Facilities Sitting room, dining room. 1½-acre walled garden.
Location Behind church on road to Barsham in village 3 m NE of Fakenham off A148.
Restrictions Not suitable for ♿. No smoking in dining room. Children under 12 not encouraged. No dogs.
Credit cards Amex, Diners.
Terms B&B: single £53–£60, double £75.50–£82. Set dinner £18.50.
Service/tipping: "No service charge. If a guest wishes to tip this is given to the staff concerned."

GRIMSTON Norfolk — Map 3

Congham Hall
Lynn Road, Grimston
King's Lynn PE32 1AH
Tel Hillington (0485) 600250
Fax (0485) 601191

"Expensive, but for a relaxing break in luxurious surroundings with excellent friendly service, it was just what we wanted. Our standard room was extremely comfortable; 'light' breakfast, brought on time each day, gave wide choice including freshly squeezed orange juice, cereals and eggs variously cooked." (*PM and M Tattersall, RM Everett; also AJM and AE Frank*)

Christine and Trevor Forecast's large and elegant Georgian manor stands in 40 acres of velvety lawn, country garden, paddocks, orchards and parkland, and has its own cricket pitch. Bedrooms vary in size but are well appointed; beds are turned down at night and fresh towels provided twice daily; new bedside lights have been added in response to Guide criticisms of the lighting. There's a beautiful drawing room and a dining room with a conservatory extension – male diners are expected to wear jacket and tie. Clive Jackson's cooking is modern with an emphasis on local produce, and much use is made of herbs grown on the premises. There are two dinner menus: a gourmet "Hobson's Choice" menu with seven light courses changing twice weekly, and a four-course menu offering six choices for each course. Last year a reader complained that there was no alternative at dinner to the two fixed-price menus, but Mr Forecast writes: "If only they had asked! We are always pleased to provide something lighter, and offer bar snacks and a room-service menu." At lunchtime on weekdays light meals are served – in the garden in summer, by the fire in winter – but some readers on weekend breaks have been disconcerted to find that not even a sandwich is available at lunchtime on Saturdays when the hotel is often busy with weddings.

Open All year.
Rooms 2 suites, 11 double, 1 single – 13 with bath and shower, 1 with shower, all with telephone, radio, TV.
Facilities Hall, lounge, bar, restaurant; boardroom for private parties and meetings. 40-acre grounds with heated swimming pool, jacuzzi, tennis, cricket pitch, parklands and orchards; stabling for visiting horses. Coast with sandy beaches 10 m; nature and bird sanctuaries, fishing, golf, riding nearby.
Location 6 m NE of King's Lynn. Turn right off A148 to Grimston; *Congham Hall* is 2½ m on left. Do not go to Congham.

Restrictions Only restaurant suitable for ♿. No smoking in restaurant. No children under 12. Dogs in kennels only.
Credit cards All major cards accepted.
Terms B&B: single £80, double £105, suite £165. Set lunch £15, dinner £28.50 and £35. Weekend breaks (Fri–Sun) all year; Christmas break.
Service/tipping: "Our tariffs state: 'No service charges are added for any facilities offered in the hotel.' If guests do leave a tip it is passed on to the staff who share it out."

GRITTLETON Wiltshire — Map 2

Church House BUDGET
Grittleton
Nr Chippenham SN14 6AP

Tel Castle Combe (0249) 782562
Fax (0249) 782562

Pretty Grade II listed Georgian rectory with 11-acre gardens and pasture in delightful village on edge of Cotswolds, just north of M4 (3½ m W of exit 17). Heated indoor swimming pool; good walking and riding locally. "House party atmosphere; meals served round large William IV table; excellent unpretentious cooking by Anna Moore" – organically home-grown vegetables, no choice, special requirements discussed in advance. Unlicensed; no corkage charge. 4 twin-bedded rooms, all with bath/shower, TV. *Not suitable for ♿. No children under 12. No credit cards. B&B double £45–£49.50. Set dinner £13; packed lunch £7. Low season midweek breaks. New nomination. More reports please.*

GULWORTHY Devon — Map 1

The Horn of Plenty
Tamar View House
Gulworthy, Tavistock PL19 8JD

Tel Tavistock (0822) 832528

Restaurant-with-rooms in a lovely setting 3 m W of Tavistock, with extensive grounds, trees and flowers, and views over Tamar valley. Most bedrooms in converted stables – spacious, simple, modern in style and furnishing, and well equipped. Famed for its food under Sonia Stevenson, it changed hands in late 1990. New owners, Elaine and Ian Gatehouse, have redecorated and refurbished and brought in new chef, Peter Gorton. A visitor in early 1991 speaks of "warm and genuine welcome", improved decor and facilities in main building – there is now a residents' lounge – good food, an extensive, interesting wine list and "excellent value for money". Open all year except Christmas. Restaurant closed Mon lunchtime. 7 rooms, all with bath and/or shower. No children under 13. Access, Amex, Visa accepted. 1991 rates: B&B (continental): single £51–£58, double £71–£78. English breakfast £8.50. Set lunch £18, dinner £25. More reports please.

HAMBLETON Leicestershire — Map 4

Hambleton Hall
Hambleton, Oakham LE15 8TH

Tel Oakham (0572) 756991
Fax (0572) 724721

César award in 1985: Comprehensive excellence in the luxury class

"Our third visit. Little changed. Room lovely, greetings warm. Everything exactly as we expected. We will return." "Staff always very pleasant. This time we had a larger room with a view of Rutland water, worth the extra cost. The food has improved enormously and is now among the best in the country. It is possible to chop and change from one menu to another which gives plenty of choice." "One of the nicest hotels we visited in England. Expensive but everything was top notch. Beautiful surroundings, outstanding floral arrangements." (*Stephen R Holman, Pat and Jeremy Temple, Clair and Jo Ann Kenaston*) This luxurious country house hotel, a stately Victorian mansion in manicured gardens with mature trees, enjoys a lovely setting overlooking Rutland Water, on what is almost an island. The proprietors, Tim and Stefa Hart, are dependably welcoming. The interior was decorated in 1980 by Nina Campbell who continues to supervise the redecoration each year. Bedrooms are comfortable and generally quiet. The restaurant, under chef Brian Baker, retains its *Michelin* rosette; the wine list, largely French, is of a piece with everything else. Though there is no age restriction on children, there are no facilities for entertaining the very young. Most visitors to *Hambleton Hall* continue to express their satisfaction, though one reader complained of inadequate heating and a shambles at breakfast, and another had a room over the front door "which was small and stuffy, and noisy when people left in the evening", and felt some of the decor was a little "tired". (Tim Hart tells us the drawing room and three bedrooms were redecorated in early 1991 which may answer that point.) Another gripe: "It would be nice to have a ban on cigarettes in the dining room." There are good walks and sporting activities in the area. In 1991 a heated swimming pool was built.

Open All year.
Rooms 15 double – all with bath, shower, telephone, radio, TV, baby-listening.
Facilities Lift, ramp. Drawing room, bar, dining room; small conference facilities, 2 private dining rooms. 17-acre grounds with swimming pool, tennis, lake with trout fishing, windsurfing, sailing. Riding, shooting by arrangement.
Location 1 m E of Oakham. Follow the Hambleton sign off A606 to Stamford.
Restriction Dogs by arrangement; not in public rooms, or alone in bedrooms.
Credit cards Access, Visa.
Terms [1991 rates] B&B: single £105, double £105–£225. Set lunch £29, dinner £40; full alc £50. Off-season discounts for 3 nights or more. Min 2-night stay Fri and Sat. Special meals for children on request.
Service/tipping: "Service included. No additional payment expected."

HAROME North Yorkshire — Map 4

Pheasant Hotel — *Tel* Helmsley (0439) 71241
Harome, Helmsley YO6 5JG

Once a smithy, two cottages and a shop in unspoilt small village 3 m SE of market town of Helmsley; spacious, well-equipped bedrooms overlook duck pond and millstream or courtyard and garden. Beams, oak furniture, rough stone walls. Dropped from earlier editions, when welcome and food were criticised. Regulars urge its reinstatement: "Food good, with lots of choice. The Binks family efficient and helpful behind an austere exterior. Very good value." 2 suites (across courtyard), 12 doubles, all with bath. No smoking in restaurant. No children under 12. Credit cards not accepted. 1991 rates: Dinner, B&B £42.90–£56.20. Bar lunches. Spring and autumn breaks. More reports please.

> If you find location details inadequate, please don't fail to let us know.

HARROGATE North Yorkshire — Map 4

The Ruskin — *Tel* Harrogate (0423) 502045
1 Swan Road
Harrogate HG1 2SS

This "very elegant establishment in a large Victorian house" in a conservation area of the town, but well placed for the Conference and Exhibitions Centre, is introduced to the Guide by a reader who stayed four times in a four-month period, occupying four of its six bedrooms. "I was pleased with them all. Bedrooms are decorated with antiques and Laura Ashley fabrics, and the public rooms are beautifully furnished yet homey. Full English breakfasts, cooked to order, are served in a pretty breakfast room overlooking the charming front garden. What distinguishes *The Ruskin* from Harrogate's many other hotels is its proprietors, Robert and Bryony Hebson. They provide a truly welcoming environment and are friendly but never overwhelming. In my case they provided service above and beyond the call of duty. I used the hotel as a base from which to find a flat as I was moving from Los Angeles to Harrogate; Bryony contacted estate agents on my behalf, Robert drove me around Harrogate to look at areas he thought might suit me. They generally smoothed my transition from America to England. Despite the hotel's elegance it welcomes children. The only possible drawback is the lack of a telephone in guests' bedrooms, but there is a payphone." The hotel recently opened the Gallery Restaurant, with a pre-Raphaelite theme, serving food with a somewhat French accent; it offers gourmet weekends. (*Alison Bracker*)

Open All year.
Rooms 4 double, 2 single – 2 with bath, 3 with shower, all with radio, TV, tea-making facilities, baby-listening; telephone available.
Facilities Lounge/bar, restaurant. Garden with terrace and croquet.
Location Just off A61; first hotel on left when turning left off Ripon Road into Swan Road. Carpark.
Restrictions Not suitable for ♿. Smoking restricted if guests object.
Credit cards Access, Amex, Visa.
Terms (Service at guests' discretion) B&B: single £35, double £60. Set lunch £8.95, dinner £14.95; full alc £25. Bargain breaks; gourmet weekends. Reduced rates and special meals for children.

HASSOP Derbyshire — Map 4

Hassop Hall — *Tel* Great Longstone (062 987) 488
Hassop — *Fax* (062 987) 577
Nr Bakewell DE4 1NS

Historic house 2½ m N of Bakewell in large grounds with tennis, croquet, helipad. Luxurious interior with impressive public rooms and pianist in the evening. Spacious, elegant country-style bedrooms with fresh fruit, flowers, sumptuous bathrooms. Recommended for welcoming proprietor, Mr Chapman, friendly and professional staff, good food with large choice on menu; vegetarians catered for. Closed 3 nights at Christmas; restaurant closed Sun dinner, Mon lunch. 12 rooms, all with bath and shower. All major credit cards accepted. 1991 rates: Rooms: single £59–£89, double £69–£99. Breakfast: continental £5.95,

English £8.95. Set dinner £20.95 (£24.50 on Sat). Re-entered the Guide last year, warmly re-nominated. More reports please.

HASTINGLEIGH Kent **Map 3**

The Woodmans Arms Auberge *Tel* Elmsted (023 375) 250
Hassell Street, Hastingleigh
Nr Ashford TN25 5JE

César award in 1988: Away-from-it-all delight in the doll's house class

"Wholeheartedly endorse your recommendation. The Campions are friendly and attentive without going over the top. Excellent breakfast with home-made croissants." "Exquisite bedroom and public rooms. Susan Campion is a most gifted cook. Thank you for finding this blissful place for us." "Room comfortable, quiet and attractive, food delicious, Campions charming. It is places like this, which we would never find on our own, which make your guide so valuable." (*Mr and Mrs R Dudley, Daisy Berger, Elizabeth Ring, and others*) As before, all the stops are pulled out by visitors to this 17th-century inn, now a very small and most unhotel-like *auberge*, with only three double rooms. It stands on a small lane leading to nowhere except the Downs, guaranteeing total peace and seclusion; without the owners' directions it can be difficult to find. Yet it is convenient for the Channel ports, and many showplaces, such as Leeds, Chilham and Dover castles, and Canterbury is only ten miles away. The house is attractively furnished, with every detail carefully thought out. The garden room has its own private garden with deckchairs. The *Auberge* has no staff, only the owners Gerald and Susan Campion, and is the kind of place where you are likely to end up on first-name terms with the proprietors. The restaurant can seat no more than ten and "is of a size that means conversation tends to flow freely between the tables". Dinner (four courses, no choice, but you are consulted about likes and dislikes) is at 7.30, *nouvelle cuisine* in style but not in quantity, with excellent fresh ingredients. Some ceilings are low (but beams over doorways have been thoughtfully padded), and tall guests might find the mirrors a bit low-hung. Commenting on last year's cautionary note, Gerald Campion writes: "Because we cannot soundproof the water tank, which is extremely noisy as it refills, there is a notice in two of the three bedrooms asking guests not to run a bath or flush the loo between 11.30 pm and 7.30 am."

Open All year except 18–24 Apr, 1 Sep–25 Oct. Restaurant often closed to non-residents.
Rooms 3 double – all with bath (2 also have shower), telephone, TV. 1 has private outside entrance and garden.
Facilities Lounge, dining room. Large grassed garden and paddock. Near sea at Sandgate and Hythe.
Location Off A28 Canterbury road. Hotel will send directions.
Restrictions Not suitable for ♿. No smoking. No children under 16. No dogs.
Credit cards None accepted.
Terms B&B: single £55, double £75; dinner, B&B: single £75, double £115. Set dinner (non-residents) £25. 1-night bookings often refused for Sat.
Service/tipping: "We do not expect tips."

Don't let old favourites down. Entries are dropped when there is no endorsement.

HATCH BEAUCHAMP Somerset — Map 1

Farthings
Hatch Beauchamp TA3 6SG
Tel Hatch Beauchamp (0823) 480664

Very mixed bag of comments this year on George and Claire Cooper's small Georgian house in secluded setting in quiet Somerset village 6 m SE of Taunton, well placed for exploring Somerset, Devon and Dorset. Some readers speak warmly of the welcome, the food and the accommodation – "not cheap, but one doesn't mind paying for quality". Others have arrived to find no one around and no help with luggage; one complained of a cold bedroom in winter, another suffered under a duvet in mid-summer. Value for money is called into question, especially by a reader paying a hefty single-room supplement, and comments on the food range from "some of the best we have ever eaten" to "very poor". Partly closed late Dec–early Jan. 5 double, 1 single, all with bath, shower, TV. *Not suitable for* ♿. *Access, Visa accepted. B&B: single £80–£95, double £100–£125. Full alc £27.50. More reports please.*

HATTON Warwickshire — Map 2

Northleigh House BUDGET
Five Ways Road
Hatton, Nr Warwick CV35 7HZ
Tel Warwick (0926) 484203

A small country house with a quiet setting in rural Warwickshire is warmly nominated: "A charming hotel with a marvellous hostess. After a terrifying car breakdown we arrived five hours late. Sylvia Fenwick greeted us with warmth and friendliness, showed us to a lovely blue room with a gorgeous soft bed in a blue-curtained alcove, pine furniture, blue couches and bamboo coffee table, tea-making facilities and fridge; and huge *en suite* bathroom with masses of hot water, big soft towels, shampoo etc. She produced a delicious midnight supper of omelettes, rolls, cheese, pâté, yoghurt, fruit and salad (she usually provides evening meals only by early arrangement). Hearty English breakfast was served to order in the pretty dining room overlooking the garden – there's a toaster on each table so none of those cold brown triangles. Next day she helped us find a garage to fix our car, arranged taxis for us to get around, offered to drive us to nearby restaurants if taxis were not immediately available, and treated us like family; she was always ready to help, but never pushy. We left rested and relaxed." (*Lisa Lamb*) No bar or restaurant, but there are many pubs and restaurants nearby. This is a no-smoking hotel.

Open Mid-Jan–mid-Dec. Evening meals by arrangement.
Rooms 5 double, 1 single – all with bath and/or shower, radio, TV, tea-making facilities.
Facilities Sitting room, dining room. Small garden and sheep farm.
Location 5 m NW of Warwick; S of Hatton. From A4177 at Five Ways Island take Shrewley turning for ½ m.
Restrictions Not suitable for ♿. No smoking. Dogs by arrangement, not in public rooms.
Credit cards None accepted.
Terms B&B: single £27–£36, double £40–£52. Hot or cold supper trays from £5.50; dinner by arrangement from £13.50.

In your own interest, always check latest tariffs with hotels when you make your bookings.

HAWES North Yorkshire **Map 4**

Simonstone Hall *Tel* Wensleydale (0969) 667255
Hawes DL8 3LY *Fax* (0969) 667741

The former home of the Earls of Wharncliffe, with "breathtaking" views of upper Wensleydale, is just over a mile from the popular resort town which can be uncomfortably crowded in summer. It was converted by John and Sheila Jeffryes, a former shipping consultant (known for his fund of anecdotes) and a kindergarten teacher respectively, into a comfortable country hotel. It has white-panelled drawing rooms with period furniture, a dining room, also panelled, hung with portraits, a bar with church pew seating, and spacious, comfortable bedrooms. Local produce is used in the kitchen, and meals, with some choice of each course, are carefully cooked, with good vegetables; local cheeses, including of course Wensleydale, are served. Also "wicked but gorgeous" desserts. "Relaxed, homey atmosphere. They also welcome dogs." "Nothing too posh, but a sense of taste and caring." (*Janice Pickup, HR*) "Many of our guests," write the proprietors, "are older, with time on their hands and they like our low-season break of three or four days including Sunday night when for Sunday they pay only £11 plus dinner per person. We offer vegetarian and 'healthy choice' menus." Walking holidays in the Dales are available at most times of year except high season. In May 1991 John and Sheila Jeffryes were named England's Warmest Hoteliers by the English Tourist Board.

Open All year except 2 weeks Jan.
Rooms 10 double – all with bath, shower, TV, tea-making facilities, baby-listening.
Facilities 2 lounges, bar, dining room. 3½-acre grounds with children's play area. Trout fishing ¾ m.
Location 1½ m N of Hawes. Follow signs for Muker then, at first junction, Simonstone.
Restrictions Not suitable for ♿. No smoking in dining room. No children under 8 in dining room at night (high tea at 5.30 pm).
Credit cards Access, Visa.
Terms Dinner, B&B £62–£79. £12 reduction for B&B. Set lunch from £12.50, dinner from £22; full alc £30–£35. Special breaks; weekly rates; walking holidays. 1-night bookings sometimes refused for bank holidays. Reduced rates and special meals for children.
Service/tipping: "No service charged or expected, but if it is given, it is distributed to all the staff."

HAWKRIDGE Somerset **Map 1**

Tarr Steps Hotel *Tel* Winsford (064 385) 293
Hawkridge, Dulverton TA22 9PY

This former Georgian rectory on Exmoor, twelve miles from the coast and 800 feet above sea level, is named for the rough stone cyclopean bridge, the Tarr Steps, owned by the National Trust and possibly of Bronze Age origin, which crosses the river Barle 200 yards away. It stands in eight acres of "slightly wild" grounds with lovely views down the river valley. Under the affable proprietor, Desmond Keane, it is a sporting hotel *par excellence*, and offers guests three miles of salmon and trout fly-fishing, stabling for their own horses, rough and formal shooting, and hunting.

Recently Mr Keane introduced three-day fly-fishing courses for beginners, and he arranges partridge and pheasant shooting in the autumn. Indoors the hotel is relaxed and comfortable, and homelike. There is no television, either in public rooms or bedrooms, no tea- or coffee-making facilities and only one telephone for guests. The food (traditional English, with some choice of each course) "is very good, well presented but unpretentious, entirely appropriate to the nature of this delightful country house hotel, and good value for money". Mr Keane also has some "very good wines". The hotel has been refurbished over the last three years, but its traditional character remains unchanged. Endorsed this year by *Susan Cadwallader*, but we'd like more reports please.

Open Mid-Mar–end Dec.
Rooms 11 double, 3 single – 11 with bath (1 also has shower). 3 in cottage annexe. 1 on ground floor with access for ♿.
Facilities Lounge, bar, dining room. 8-acre grounds with garden; rough and clay-pigeon shooting, fishing, fox and stag hunting; stables and kennels for guests' horses and dogs. River bathing 100 yds.
Location 7 m NW of Dulverton. From Hawkridge follow signs to Tarr Steps and hotel.
Restrictions No smoking in dining room. No dogs in public rooms.
Credit cards Access, Visa.
Terms [1991 rates] B&B £36; dinner, B&B £56. Set Sun lunch £16; dinner £20. Bar lunches available. Reductions for long stays; midweek breaks. 1-night bookings refused for bank holidays. Reduced rates and special meals for children.
Service/tipping: "No service charge. Anything left goes direct to staff and is shared equally."

HAWKSHEAD Cumbria — Map 4

Highfield House
Hawkshead Hill
Hawkshead LA22 0PN

Tel Hawkshead (096 66) 344
From Dec 1991 (053 94) 36344

Hawkshead is a pretty village with small squares linked by flagged or cobbled alleys and many unusual buildings. Pauline and Jim Bennett's traditional Lakeland stone building, a century old, is just outside the village on the road to Coniston. It stands on high ground in large gardens with fine trees and shrubs; from the public rooms there are lovely views of the valley and peaks. A visitor described it last year as "a splendid spot, properly equipped with daffodils, bluebells, wooden coat-hangers, good linen, inexpensive wine and plenty of good food. There's a warm welcome and a genuinely friendly atmosphere. It seems to have everything one could wish for – at a sensible price." This is now endorsed: "Well appointed, with high standards of cleanliness and comfort. Food imaginative and beautifully presented. Only those on a strict diet could resist the traditional puddings." "The Bennetts clearly enjoy visitors, but there is no forced bonhomie. English breakfast of a high standard." There are several choices on the dinner menu for each course, including a vegetarian dish; helpings are generous and you are always offered the opportunity of trying a second dessert. Children of all ages are welcomed; there are cots, baby seats and high teas, also the use of washing machine and drying facilities. (*C Hutchinson, ML Dalton; also DL Wigglesworth, and others*) Only niggles: The public rooms, though spacious, are not quite large enough to accommodate all guests at the same time, and heating could do with a control system, if only thermostat valves on radiators.

Open All year except Christmas.
Rooms 9 double, 2 single – 8 with bath and/or shower, all with radio, TV, tea-making facilities; baby-listening on request.
Facilities Lounge, bar, dining room; laundry facilities, drying room. 2½-acre garden. Fishing nearby.
Location ¾ m W of Hawkshead on road to Coniston and Tarn Hows.
Restrictions Not suitable for ♿. No smoking in dining room. No dogs in public rooms.
Credit cards Access, Visa.
Terms B&B £20–£31.20. Set dinner £13.75. Snacks and packed lunches available. Reduced rates for children sharing parents' room; special meals by arrangement. Off-season breaks.
Service/tipping: "Service included. Tips not expected but if offered are shared among all staff."

Rough Close BUDGET — *Tel* Hawkshead (096 66) 370
Hawkshead LA22 0QF — *From Dec 1991* (053 94) 36370

This small and simple but welcoming hotel in "beautifully kept" gardens, one mile south of Hawkshead, entered the Guide last year. It has lovely views across Esthwaite, and "is quiet and peaceful, clean and comfortable. The owners, Anthony and Marylin Gibson, are always helpful and charming, and the atmosphere warm and friendly." There is a lounge with TV and a log fire in cold weather, and a small bar. Breakfasts, served between 8.45 and 9.15 am, are of the filling English kind. "Extremely good" dinners (five courses and coffee with no choice except alternative desserts), cooked by the Gibsons, are served punctually at 7 pm; they start with home-made soups, and the main course is accompanied by plenty of fresh vegetables. Helpings are generous; nothing is over-elaborate. Mr Gibson serves and is the wine waiter (each menu suggests a wine to go with the meal). More reports please.

Open Mar–early Nov.
Rooms 5 double – 4 with bath and shower, 1 with shower, all with tea-making facilities.
Facilities Lounge with TV, bar, dining room. 1-acre grounds. Boating, fishing nearby.
Location 1 m S of Hawkshead on Newby Bridge road.
Restrictions Not suitable for ♿. No smoking in dining room and bedrooms. No children under 5. No dogs.
Credit cards Access, Visa.
Terms B&B £22.50; dinner, B&B £32.50. Reduced rates for long stays.
Service/tipping: "No service charge. We have a strong aversion to tipping. Clearly proprietors should not be tipped, nor, we believe, should staff, who are properly paid for the job they do."

HAWNBY North Yorkshire — Map 4

The Hawnby Hotel — *Tel* Bilsdale (043 96) 202
Hawnby, Nr Helmsley YO6 5QS

An engaging new entry, its brochure as pretty as a child's picture book. Formerly a drovers' inn, it was bought by the family of the Earl of Mexborough and has been decorated by the Countess with Laura Ashley fabrics. "A village pub but with six most comfortable and well-appointed bedrooms, all with bathroom *en suite*. Each room's name reveals its colour scheme – Rose, Buttercup, etc. Each has a wonderful view of Ryedale. The cooking is English and simple, with generous portions. The hotel is managed by Mrs Dorothy Allanson. It is a quiet retreat and represents excellent value for money. On the pub side it is popular with walkers, being famed for its bar lunches." (*Dr B Scaife*) The kitchen uses produce from the proprietors' farm and garden and game from their estate. Hawnby is a quiet and unspoilt village in the North Yorkshire Moors National Park; there's good walking nearby. More reports please.

Open Mar–Jan. Closed Christmas Day.
Rooms 6 double – all with bath, shower, telephone, radio, TV, tea-making facilities.
Facilities Lounge, bar, restaurant.
Location In small village 8 m N of Helmsley, off B1257 to Stokesley.
Restrictions Not suitable for ♿. Smoking discouraged. No children under 10. No dogs (kennels in village).
Credit cards Access, Visa.
Terms [1991 rates] B&B £30–£40; dinner, B&B £40–£50. Bar lunches. Set dinner £11. Reduced rates for 3 or more nights and in off-season.
Service/tipping: "Service charge not added. Tipping not encouraged; tips given are pooled among staff."

HAWORTH West Yorkshire — Map 4

Weaver's — *Tel* Haworth (0535) 643822
15 West Lane
Haworth BD22 8DU

Colin and Jane Rushworth's restaurant-with-rooms in cobbled main street of capital of Brönte-land, next to Parsonage Museum (use their carpark). Cleverly composed from three cottages to make a long, low building; decorated with antiques and bric-á-brac, "all in very good taste". "Excellent" northern cooking (desserts particularly praised), with reduced-price menu on weekdays if you order by 7.15 pm. "Atmosphere of good taste and competence; young staff, all working in harmony." Closed Sun. 4 pretty, well equipped if small bedrooms up a narrow staircase, all with bath/shower. Not suitable for ♿. No smoking in restaurant. No dogs. All major credit cards accepted. B&B: single £45, double £60. Set lunch/dinner from £13.50; full alc £30. Warm new nomination. More reports please.

HAYTOR Devon — Map 1

Bel Alp House — *Tel* Haytor (0364) 661217; *Fax* (0364) 661292
Haytor, Nr Bovey Tracey
TQ13 9XX

This imposing Edwardian house, once the home of tobacco millionairess Dame Violet Wills, is peacefully set in large grounds on the edge of Dartmoor, overlooking miles of pastoral scenery, and has been carefully restored. It had an italicised entry last year and is now promoted to a full one following warm reports. "It offers handsome accommodation, exceptional food and a beautiful setting, but most of all is distinguished by the sincere and warm hospitality of its owners, Roger and Sarah Curnock. Though our room did not have the dramatic view it was extremely comfortable, with everything one could want; the bathroom was enormous. All the rooms available to guests are comfortably appointed, never overstated. Paintings include some by and of the owners' relatives. In the dining room we were able to sit overlooking the hills and vales of South Devon stretching down to the sea. The food was tremendous. Furthermore, after leaving I discovered, on the eve of our return to Canada, that I had left a jacket with my passport in the hotel bedroom's wardrobe, and Captain Curnock's willingness to go beyond the call of duty to help endeared him to me forever." "We have renamed it 'The Jewel in the Crown of Haytor'. From the moment of our arrival, when Roger Curnock greeted us most warmly and by name, it had the feeling of a success story. Sarah Curnock's cooking is very professional; there's an extensive wine list." Rooms are large and airy, the decor is traditional, and there are attractive architectural features such as arches, an oak staircase and stained-glass windows. Some impressive bathtubs have survived. Dinner has five courses with a set main dish, but alternatives are available. (*Brian MacLeod Rogers, Paul and Christine Butler*)

Open Mar–Nov. Closed 1 week July.
Rooms 9 double – all with bath and/or shower, telephone, radio, TV, tea-making facilities, baby-listening. Some on ground floor.
Facilities Lift. Drawing room, bar/sitting room, dining room. 8½-acre grounds with croquet. Sea 15 m.
Location 2½ m SW of Bovey Tracey off B3387.
Restrictions No smoking in dining room. No dogs in public rooms.
Credit cards Access, Visa.
Terms B&B £60–£78; dinner, B&B £81–£111. Set lunch (3 courses) £22, dinner (5 courses) £33. Reduced rates and special meals for children.
Service/tipping: "We are against all service charges and tipping. We pay our staff very well and expect them to give excellent service without any extra payments. We feel that gratuities produce the wrong attitude in most staff."

HEDDON'S MOUTH Devon — Map 1

Heddon's Gate Hotel — *Tel* Parracombe (059 83) 313
Heddon's Mouth
Parracombe, Barnstaple EX31 4PZ

César award in 1990: For doing its own thing with verve

A "very comfortable" hotel in a turn-of-the-century Swiss/Victorian lodge with various extensions and steeply terraced gardens, providing lovely views over miles of moorland and wooded hills. The large grounds are surrounded by National Trust land and Exmoor National Park, and several private paths thread through the gardens – one directly on the South West Peninsula coastal path. "You can sit on the terrace overlooking the valley garden, and hear only birds and occasional sheep." Indoors are several sitting rooms, a "very good" library, and a "large, relaxing dining room, with good-sized tables". The decor has been described as "witty and sophisticated". The bedrooms vary enormously in size and style, and are priced accordingly. They are named for their original use – the Dressing Room, Grandmama's Room, the Servants' Quarters, etc. The Gardener's Cottage, in the grounds, has two bedrooms and a sitting room. The hotel has been under the same ownership for 24 years. Sadly, this year Robert Deville tells us that he and his wife Anne have divorced; he is running the hotel with the staff, many of whom have been there for years. Food was Mrs Deville's province in the past: "My biggest terror," he writes, "was whether I could tackle that, and train someone to do the presentation." Regular visitors report his success: "Food even better than before; interesting menus, well prepared, with very good ingredients. I particularly endorse the 1991 reference to the generosity of the hospitality: fresh fruit in the bedroom daily, plenty of freshly squeezed orange juice at breakfast, lots of hot water." "No slippage of standards whatever. The hotel continues to be the best of its kind that we know." "Service by a young and well-trained staff was quiet, courteous and deft." "The weekly rate was astonishing value." (*PE Carter, JP Berryman, Moira Jarrett, NA Taplin, and many others*) The full help-yourself afternoon tea is included in the rates.

Open 3 Apr–2 Nov.
Rooms 4 suites, 9 double, 1 single – all with bath and/or shower, telephone, radio, TV, tea-making facilities. 3 suites in terraced cottages with access for ♿ 70 yds from main building.
Facilities Sitting room, library, bar, card room, dining room. 20-acre grounds with terraced gardens. Access to sea (¾ m) and river (¼ m) by footpaths. Riding, pony trekking, fishing nearby.
Location 6 m W of Lynton; from A39 3 m W of Lynton take Martinhoe–Woody Bay road; turn left towards Hunter's Inn; hotel sign is at next crossroads.
Restrictions No children under 10. No smoking in dining room. Dogs by arrangement, not in dining room, not unattended in bedrooms.
Credit cards None accepted.
Terms Dinner, B&B £41.40–£59.60. Set dinner (at 8 pm) £18. Reductions for stays of 3 or more days; weekly rates. 1-night bookings occasionally refused. 50% reduction for children sharing parents' room.
Service/tipping: "We never make any service charge and staff do not solicit tips; any given are collected, taxed and shared out among staff on basis of hours worked."

HINTLESHAM Suffolk — Map 3

Hintlesham Hall — *Tel* Hintlesham (047 387) 334
Hintlesham, Ipswich IP8 3NS — *Fax* (047 387) 463

This grandly beautiful mansion was owned and run first as a restaurant by Robert Carrier, and then as a hotel by Ruth and David Watson; it won a César in 1988. Many readers were apprehensive when the Watsons sold it in mid-1990, and following our normal policy it was omitted from our 1991 edition. *Hintlesham* is now owned by David Allan, but key staff, notably manager Tim Sunderland and chef Alan Ford, have stayed on and we were delighted to hear this from a regular visitor: "A return visit after a change of ownership can be a sobering experience. Not so with HH! It was as good as, if not better than, before. I had a very large double room as a single for £60 including a light breakfast and a newspaper, and many lovely little touches – bathrobes, clothes brush, talcum, welcoming letter from GM etc. First-rate dinner. Excellent, attentive staff. Wonderful value. I could not fault anything." (*IC Dewey*)

The house dates from the 15th century but is mainly Georgian; it is sumptuously decorated in gentle pastels, mostly peach, white and grey, which set off the panelling and glorious plaster mouldings. Bedrooms have antique furniture, chintz curtains and covers and lots of ruching,

All our inspections are carried out anonymously.

magazines and books, excellent bathroom, and peaceful green views from the windows. They vary in size and grandeur, some are huge and exceedingly opulent; you should discuss options when booking. Chef Alan Ford trained at the *Dorchester*; his cooking has been described as "modern–classical, with a strong Mosimann influence". The hotel now has its own 18-hole championship golf course. Does it spoil the atmosphere? We'd welcome more reports.

Note: The normal single rates are somewhat higher than those enjoyed by Mr Dewey (see below).

Open All year.
Rooms 5 suites, 27 double – all with bath, shower, telephone, radio, TV. 11 in courtyard wing 20 yds away.
Facilities 4 lounges, 3 dining rooms; conference/functions room. 170-acre grounds with 18-hole golf course, tennis, riding, fishing, shooting.
Location 4 m W of Ipswich on the A1071 to Sudbury.
Restrictions No smoking in dining rooms. No children under 12 in restaurant. Dogs by arrangement, not in public rooms.
Credit cards All major cards accepted.
Terms [Until early 1992] B&B: single £85–£105, double £97–£160, suite £178–£300. Set lunch £17.50; dinner Sun–Thurs £27.50, Fri/Sat £37.50. Special breaks; Christmas package. 1-night bookings refused for Sat.
Service/tipping: "On our menus it is stated that they include, not only canapes, VAT and vegetables, but also service. Nothing more is expected. Service is our duty and pleasure."

HOCKLEY HEATH West Midlands — Map 2

Nuthurst Grange
Nuthurst Grange Lane
Hockley Heath B94 5NL

Tel Lapworth (0564) 783972
Fax (0564) 783919

"A really nice hotel; welcoming staff. Food excellent at dinner and breakfast," writes *David Crowe* of David and Daryll Randolph's Edwardian house which is approached by an immaculate drive through attractive English parkland. From outside its architectural merits are undistinguished but it commands superb views and is only five miles from Birmingham airport. There is some traffic noise from a new section of the M40 but it is half a mile away – "a real pity, but hardly detracts from the amenities of the hotel". Inside the hotel is furnished in traditional style, with lavish use of fabrics, plenty of comfortable sofas and stylish flower arrangements in public rooms. Bedrooms are different in colour scheme, light and spacious, and full of extras. There are set lunch and dinner menus, and you pay according to the number of courses taken; at dinner there is also a pricier alternative menu. Cooking is a blend of classical and modern, extravagantly presented, with desserts coming in for special praise. An extension with seven bedrooms was added in 1991, the former restaurant converted into a lounge, and the dining and functions facilities expanded. More reports please.

Open All year except 1 week over Christmas.
Rooms 15 double – all with bath (10 also have shower), telephone, radio, TV, safe, baby-listening; tea-making facilities on request. Some on ground floor.
Facilities Ramp; entrance for ♿. Reception, 2 lounges, restaurant; 2 private dining rooms; conference/meeting room. 7½-acre grounds with croquet, helipad. Riding, hunting, tennis, clay-pigeon shooting, golf, canal boating nearby.
Location ½ m S of Hockley Heath on A34. Turn right at noticeboard.

Restrictions Smoking in dining room discouraged. "Children must be well behaved." No dogs.
Credit cards All major cards accepted.
Terms B&B: single £85, double £99–£125. Set lunch £13.50 and £17.50, dinner £19.75–£35. Weekend breaks. Reduced rates and special meals for children.
Service/tipping: "I would prefer to see all service charges and tipping stopped immediately. My policy is to discourage the latter. However, if a customer does leave a tip it is divided among all staff who worked that day."

HOLBETON Devon — Map 1

Alston Hall
Alston Cross
Holbeton PL8 1HN

Tel Holbeton (075 530) 555 and 259
Fax (075 530) 494

Edwardian mansion S of Holbeton, 20 mins' drive from Plymouth, 3 m from sandy beach, quietly set in large grounds with extensive views. Recently extensively refurbished in traditional style by new owners. Fine oak-panelled lounge with stained-glass windows; pretty Peony dining room; well-appointed bedrooms. Conference facilities. Indoor and outdoor swimming pools, tennis, croquet. "Outstanding atmosphere, service, friendliness; splendid cooking; owners make you feel you are staying in a home they love." 20 rooms, all with bath/shower. Not suitable for ♿. Amex, Diners, Visa accepted. B&B: single £85, double from £125. Set lunch £15, dinner £25. New nomination. More reports please.

HOLDENBY Northamptonshire — Map 1

Lynton House
The Croft
Holdenby NN6 8DJ

Tel Holdenby (0604) 770777

This restaurant-with-rooms, new to the Guide last year, is in a Victorian former rectory in open country north of Northampton. The owner, Carlo Bertozzi, is Italian; his wife Carol does the cooking. Its exterior is red brick, and there's plenty of red and pink inside, and lots of pictures and fresh flowers in the entrance hall. The best bedroom, prettily decorated and adequately lit, has a splendid view over a patchwork of arable fields. There are no baths as Mr Bertozzi finds that his guests, many of them businessfolk, prefer showers. The attractive restaurant, with bay window and conservatory extension, is popular locally. "A delight," wrote our inspector last year. "There's plenty of choice, and it is not at all run-of-the-mill Italian cooking. Service was excellent throughout. We enjoyed the breakfast with perfectly cooked eggs and bacon. We did not meet Mrs Bertozzi who was in the kitchen; her husband is a charming and amusing host." There are good walks nearby and Holdenby House, with a fine garden, is worth a visit. More reports please.

Open All year except Christmas, 1 week in spring, 2 weeks Sep.
Rooms 1 suite, 2 double, 2 single – all with shower, telephone, radio, TV, tea-making facilities.
Facilities Lounge, cocktail bar, dining room, conservatory; conference/functions facilities. 2½-acre grounds.
Location 6 m NW of Northampton. Leave M1 at exit 18 or 16.
Restrictions Not suitable for ♿. No smoking in some bedrooms. No children under 6.

Credit cards Access, Visa.
Terms [1991 rates] B&B: single £60, double £70. Set meals (excluding VAT): lunch £13, dinner £19.75 and £23.50. Weekend rates.
Service/tipping: "No service charge; we discourage tipping."

HOLFORD Somerset — Map 1

Combe House — *Tel* Holford (027 874) 382
Holford
Nr Bridgwater TA5 1RZ

Richard Bjergfelt's hotel returned to the Guide last year, supported by enthusiastic regulars, and the entry is now endorsed: "Atmosphere very welcoming; good food and service; beautiful grounds, lovely surrounding countryside, and very reasonably priced." It's a 17th-century former tannery, still with a water-wheel, set in a peaceful location in a wooded combe at the heart of the Quantocks. It has large, well-tended grounds with an indoor swimming pool and sauna, a tennis court, and croquet. Public rooms, with beams and open fires, are not particularly large, and can be crowded in the evening; upstairs is "rather a rabbit warren of passages and corners" and bedrooms are small, but well appointed and comfortable. Some of the baths, too, are small but there's plenty of hot water. The owner is very much in evidence, the staff friendly and professional; the table d'hôte menu of straightforward dishes, with three or four choices for each course, changes daily. Cooking is "good, if not noteworthy". There is excellent walking from the front door, and the sea is not far. (*T and F Stratford; also G Latham*)

Open Mar–Nov.
Rooms 16 double, 6 single – 16 with bath and/or shower, all with telephone, TV, tea-making facilities; baby-listening on request. 3 in annexe across drive.
Facilities Lounge, smoking room, bar, restaurant. Indoor heated swimming pool, sauna. 3-acre grounds with tennis and croquet. Golf, riding nearby.
Location From A39 turn up lane between garage and *Plough Inn*. Follow signs through village.
Restrictions Not suitable for ♿. No smoking in main lounge and restaurant. Dogs in some bedrooms only; not in public rooms except bar.
Credit cards Access, Amex, Visa.
Terms B&B £28–£45; dinner, B&B £31.50–£52. Set dinner £13.50. Low-season rates. Reduced rates for children sharing parents' room; high tea on request.
Service/tipping: "Service included. If asked, we say there's no need to tip. If a guest insists, then the money is distributed to all staff."

HOPESAY Shropshire — Map 1

The Old Rectory BUDGET — *Tel* Little Brampton (058 87) 245
Hopesay, Craven Arms SY7 8HD

17th-century house adjacent to 12th-century parish church in tiny hamlet W of Craven Arms, off B4368 in lovely S Shropshire hills. Large drawing room with open fire, books, no TV. Large bedrooms, 1 with sitting room, with antiques and friendly touches. "Excellent" dinner at 7.15, with set main course, vegetables from the "magnificent" 2-acre garden. "Calmly efficient" hosts, Amy and Graham Spencer. Closed Christmas. 3 bedrooms, all with bath/shower. Not suitable for ♿. No children under 12. B&B double £50–£53. Set dinner £15.50. New nomination. More reports please.

HORTON Dorset — Map 2

Northill House BUDGET *Tel* Witchampton (0258) 840407
Horton, Wimborne BH21 7HL

"Everything you say. Rooms comfortable, excellent value." "Warm welcome. Large room, airy yet warm. Enormous bed, firm and very comfortable, with good bedside lamps and two hot-water bottles. The *en suite* bathroom, with daily change of towels, was large enough for us, but perhaps not for fat folk. Everything spotless, with fresh flowers in all rooms. Substantial breakfasts included freshly squeezed orange juice. No choice at dinner until the pudding stage, but nothing one could take exception to, and an excellent choice thereafter, the cheeseboard being exceptional. We believe this simple type of country hotel is what ordinary people would love to find in many locations. Alas there are not many Garnsworthy families around. Astonishing value." (*Mr and Mrs C Hatherall, R and M Farquhar; also RC Brown, and others*)

Courtney and Joy Garnsworthy's 19th-century redbrick former farmhouse stands in two-acre grounds adjoining a farm in an isolated situation. Bedrooms have views of the grounds, including pheasant and partridge, and fields beyond. There are good walks in the vicinity, as well as golf, fishing and riding, and the Dorset coast is not far away. Minor niggles: "No shelf to put the soap on while showering or bathing; and I burned my bottom on the towel rail, despite the warning notice!" "Some of the food a bit dry."

Open Mid-Feb–20 Dec.
Rooms 9 double – all with bath and/or shower, telephone, radio, TV, tea-making facilities. 4 in adjoining annexe. 1 equipped for ♿.
Facilities Lounge, bar, dining room, conservatory. 2-acre grounds.
Location 7 m N of Wimborne, ½ m from B3078.
Restrictions No smoking in dining room. No children under 8. No pets.
Credit cards Access, Amex, Visa.
Terms B&B: single £32, double £58; dinner, B&B: single £44.50, double £83. Snack lunches. Set dinner £12.50. 3- and 7-night breaks.
Service/tipping: "Tips not expected or solicited; but shared among staff if given."

HUDDERSFIELD West Yorkshire — Map 4

The Lodge *Tel* Huddersfield (0484) 431001
48 Birkby Lodge Road *Fax* (0484) 421950
Birkby, Huddersfield HD2 2BG

Our first entry for this "pleasant and prosperous city", in the residential suburb of Birkby, is owned by Garry and Kevin Birley. "It represents the kind of town hotel the Guide is looking for," writes our inspector. "Reasonably priced, personally managed and full of personality. It's a substantial, creeper-covered stone house, dating mostly from the turn of the century, in a street of solid Yorkshire houses, next to a factory converted into industrial units. A large garden with mature trees offers privacy and quiet. The house has beautifully preserved Art Nouveau interiors created by Edgar Wood, with many original features retained. Our room overlooking the front garden was decorated in a cheerful flowery style which complemented the stripped Edwardian wardrobe and dressing table. The bed was very comfortable, and sported, joy of joys, good quality cotton sheets. Good bedside lights, small modern bathroom, well supplied with toiletries, but, as with the bedroom, lacking surfaces on which to put things. Dinners are four-course set-price affairs with seasonal menus and sound cooking, much of it modern and imaginative. Wine list, covering the world, is well annotated. The restaurant does a brisk non-resident trade. Breakfasts are in need of some sharpening up. Toast is made from sliced bread, tea from teabags, but omelette Arnold Bennett was generous. Diners are subjected to taped ballads; worse, our breakfast was eaten to the accompaniment of the BBC's morning service, bringing back dismal childhood memories. But, niggles apart, any visitor to Huddersfield should be grateful to find accommodation of this standard for a modest outlay. The hotel has great character deriving from its architecture, the owners are friendly and unassuming but professional, and there is a palpable air of striving to achieve high standards."

Open All year except 26–29 Dec.
Rooms 1 suite, 6 double, 4 single – all with bath, shower, telephone, radio, TV, baby-listening. 1 double on ground floor with access for ♿.
Facilities Bar, lounge, library, billiard room, restaurant; private dining room, 2 conference rooms. 2-acre gardens.
Location Easy access from M62. Map on hotel tariff.
Restrictions No smoking in bedrooms. No dogs in public rooms.
Credit cards Access, Amex, Visa.
Terms B&B: single £55, double £65, suite £70. Set lunch £10.95, dinner £19.95, residents' dinner £14.95. Clay-pigeon shooting weekends. No accommodation charge for children under 12 in parents' room.
Service/tipping: "No service charge. We have no policy on tipping but leave it to guests."

HUNTSHAM Devon — Map 1

Huntsham Court
Huntsham Valley
Nr Tiverton EX16 7NA

Tel Clayhanger (039 86) 210
Fax (039 86) 456

César award in 1988: Utterly acceptable mild eccentricity

This choice example of high-Victorian architecture, with huge rooms, massive fireplaces, impressive panelling and marble pillars, in a secluded setting in rural Devon, is run by Mogens and Andrea Bolwig on house-party lines (and is often taken over by professional groups or private parties). The furniture is eclectic, with Victorian sideboards and outsize armchairs of the 1920s and 1930s. *Huntsham* is dedicated to music: there are pianos everywhere – a grand in the hall, uprights in the drawing room and bar, a pianola in the dining room – and a collection of over 6,000 records and cassettes, mostly classical with a leaning towards opera, which guests may play on a hi-fi. The bedrooms (no locks on doors, no TV or telephone) are named after composers; all have a pre-war radio set; two have an organ. Most have a huge bathroom *en suite*. Beethoven has a log fire, a seven-foot-wide bed, a baby grand piano, and two free-standing old bathtubs with silver claws side by side in the bathroom. Dinner is eaten communally, and there is no menu. Guests help themselves night and day to free tea and coffee in the butler's pantry. The bar can be help-yourself, too. Breakfast goes on most of the morning. There's a sauna, mini-gym, tennis, croquet and a lot of bicycles ("but they don't have good brakes"). Some visitors find the atmosphere altogether too laid-back, but to others it is highly enjoyable. "Staff attentive and pleasant." "Very good home-cooking, amazing wine cellar." "A truly unique experience." More reports please.

Open All year.
Rooms 3 suites, 11 double – all with bath, pre-war wireless; baby-listening possible.
Facilities Hall, drawing room, library with snooker, music room, bar, dining room; sauna, mini-gym, table-tennis. 8-acre garden with croquet, bicycles, tennis. Trout fishing in private lake, riding, golf nearby.
Location M5 to Taunton, then A361 towards Bampton; turn left at Huntsham signpost. Or exit 27 off M5, sharp right on bridge in Sampford Peverell; continue for 4 m.
Restrictions Not suitable for ♿. No smoking in dining room. No dogs (kennels 2 m away).
Credit cards Access, Amex, Visa.
Terms B&B: single £70, double £99, suite £109. Set lunch £15, dinner £25. House parties; midweek and weekend breaks; jazz, opera and special weekends; Christmas and New Year programmes. 1-night bookings sometimes refused for weekends. Reduced rates for children sharing parents' room.
Service/tipping: "Service included. We do not expect tips, but when a guest is happy with service and staff we accept a tip in the spirit in which it has been given. Not to do so would offend."

HURSTBOURNE TARRANT Hampshire — Map 2

Esseborne Manor
Hurstbourne Tarrant
Nr Andover SP11 0ER

Tel Hurstbourne Tarrant (0264) 76444
Fax (0264) 76473

Small late-Victorian manor, calling itself "an executive retreat", stylishly decorated, with new extension in "reasonably pretty" countryside between Newbury and Andover, well set back from A343. 2½-acre garden with tennis, croquet, golf. Owned by Michael and Frieda Yeo, formerly of the much larger and grander Ardanaiseig, *Kilchrenan, Scotland, and managed by Mrs Yeo's son Simon Richardson. Restaurant highly praised for modern cooking by Mark Greenfield; friendly service. 12 comfortable, well-equipped bedrooms, some with quite modern decor. No children under 12. No dogs. All major credit cards accepted. B&B: single £80, double £107–£124. Set lunch £15, dinner £31. Executive rates. New nomination last year, recently warmly endorsed, but there have been some criticisms of the accommodation. More reports please.*

IPSWICH Suffolk — Map 3

The Marlborough Hotel
Henley Road, Ipswich IP1 3SP

Tel Ipswich (0473) 257677
Fax (0473) 226927

Owned by the Gough family who also own the *Angel*, Bury St Edmunds (q.v.), and run by David Brooks, the *Marlborough* had an entry in earlier editions of the Guide, but was dropped for lack of feedback. It is now re-admitted following two warm recommendations: "We spent a fortnight here and were treated with kindness, thought and imagination. Meals were outstanding for their quality and choice, and reasonably priced." "Staff friendly and helpful, welcoming receptionist. Bedroom clean and comfortable, with fresh fruit, chocolates and lots of local information.

Newspapers and early morning tea included in the price. Breakfast offered an impressive choice." (*Prof. WR Niblett, Virginia and Charles Day*)

The hotel is a Victorian building quietly situated in a leafy suburb, overlooking Christchurch Park, and has a small, carefully tended garden, floodlit at night. The decor is traditional, with pastel colours, and antique or period furniture. Ipswich, the birthplace of Cardinal Wolsey, is well placed for exploring Suffolk, and the *Marlborough* offers many special-interest weekends, including sailing, flying, dry-skiing and riding, and theatre suppers in conjunction with the Wolsey Theatre.

Open All year. Restaurant closed for lunch Sat.
Rooms 1 suite, 15 double, 6 single – all with bath, shower, telephone, radio, TV, tea-making facilities, baby-listening. Some on ground floor.
Facilities Ramp. Lounge, bar, study, restaurant; conference facilities. ½-acre garden.
Location ½ m from A45 and A12, on N side of Christchurch park.
Restrictions Smoking in dining room discouraged. Very young children by arrangement.
Credit cards All major cards accepted.
Terms Rooms: single £70, double £90, suite £95. Breakfast: light £5.50, English £7.50. Set lunch £12, dinner £17.50; full alc £30. Weekend breaks, special-interest breaks. Christmas package.
Service/tipping: "We have never operated a service charge. My staff make it clear when asked that they don't expect tips. I wish our industry would make the obligatory service charge illegal."

JERVAULX North Yorkshire — Map 4

The Old Hall — *Tel* Bedale (0677) 60313
Jervaulx Abbey
Masham, Ripon HG4 4PH

Ian and Angela Close's home, formerly the servants' quarters of Jervaulx Hall, is a mellow stone house in almost four acres of ground with stabling and grazing sheep. Inside is an old pine staircase, a plaster frieze and tiles and stones from the abbey, and fresh flowers. Visitors enjoy the "private-party atmosphere – sherry in the lounge before dinner so that guests can be introduced, dinner with the hosts at a single large oak table, and conversation continuing over coffee in the lounge. Ian Close really knows the area and makes tourism much more than just a quick look round. His wife, Angela, is an excellent cook; food is mainly good roasts with all the trimmings, very well done and beautifully presented in a room full of antiques. Water comes from a private spring and tastes delicious. Bedrooms are particularly attractive – we have stayed in most of them; they all have good firm beds, well-equipped bathrooms, and some fine pieces of antique furniture. It is not a place for people who want a private weekend, but an excellent country house where conversation, good food and drink and lovely surroundings create a special atmosphere." (*Robert Swift*) More reports please.

Open All year.
Rooms 3 double – all with bath, shower, tea-making facilities. 2 self-catering cottages.
Facilities Drawing room, dining room. 4-acre grounds with access to Abbey grounds.
Location On A6108, 12 m N of Ripon, next to Jervaulx Abbey.

Restrictions Not suitable for ♿. No smoking in dining room. No dogs in public rooms.
Credit cards None accepted.
Terms B&B £32; set dinner £18.
Service/tipping: "Service included. Tipping should not be necessary. We pay staff properly."

KEMERTON Gloucestershire **Map 2**

Upper Court
Kemerton
Nr Tewkesbury GL20 7HY
Tel Overbury (038 689) 351

Not a real hotel, but a founding member of Wolsey Lodge group of homes taking paying guests, Georgian Cotswold manor house approached through lovely village 5 m NE of Tewkesbury on Bredon Hill. 15-acre grounds with pretty walled garden with swimming pool, tennis, croquet, lake with fishing and boating. The Herford family, "extremely welcoming and informal", have an antique and interior decorating business so "there is always something for sale". "Delicious" no-choice dinner with lots of home-grown vegetables. "Extremely good value." Closed Christmas. Antiques, chintzes, 4-poster or twin beds in the 5 bedrooms, all en suite. *Access, Visa accepted. 1991 rates: B&B: single £50, double £75. Set dinner £18. New nomination. More reports please.*

KESWICK Cumbria **Map 4**

Lodore Swiss Hotel
Keswick CA12 5UX
Tel Borrowdale (076 87) 77285
Fax (076 87) 77343

This large (for the Guide) hotel enjoys a splendid position just south of Keswick in forty-acre grounds, which include the Lodore Falls on Derwent Water which many rooms overlook. It is owned by the hotel chain Stakis PLC. Outwardly it is a stern Victorian Cumbrian pile, inside are large and comfortable public rooms, equally comfortable bedrooms of varying sizes, and many facilities for indoor and outdoor entertainment (see below). A visitor in late 1990 is highly enthusiastic: "We booked the Christmas package as we had heard that it had good children's facilities. This proved to be an understatement. Provision for young children is excellent, with friendly uniformed nursery nurses, their own menu, entertainer, swimming and personalised Christmas gifts. But they are dealt with so well and discreetly that they do not impinge on the enjoyment of those without children." Others have praised the management and the staff, many of whom have remained from the previous regime. (*Mrs E Stuart-Clarke*)

Open All year.
Rooms 2 suites, 63 double, 5 single – all with bath and/or shower, telephone, radio, TV, tea-making facilities, baby-listening.
Facilities Lift, ramp. Lounge, bar, restaurant, private dining room, functions room, library. Music on Sat. Indoor swimming pool, gym, squash court, games room, saunas, beauty salon, hairdresser, nursery with trained nurses. 40-acre grounds with swimming pool, tennis, children's play area.
Location 3½ m S of Keswick, on B5284 to Borrowdale.
Restrictions No smoking in restaurant. No dogs.
Credit cards All major cards accepted.

Terms [1991 rates] (Service at guests' discretion) B&B: single £61.50–£78, double from £108, suite from £184; dinner, B&B from £53 per person. Light lunches; set Sun lunch £12.50, dinner £22.50; full alc £32. Christmas and New Year packages. Reduced rates and special meals for children.

KING'S LYNN Norfolk — Map 3

The Tudor Rose BUDGET
St Nicholas Street
King's Lynn PE30 1LR

Tel King's Lynn (0553) 762824
Fax (0553) 764894

In town centre, "equally successful as pub, restaurant and hotel", part-medieval building carefully restored by Ian and Chris Carter. Recommended for "attentive and courteous" staff, "very adequate" bedrooms, good food in bars and restaurant; extensive vegetarian menu. Closed Christmas. 9 double, 5 single all with bath/shower. B&B double £50–£55. Set dinner £9.50; full alc £22. Recent nomination. More reports please.

KINGSTON BAGPUIZE Oxfordshire — Map 2

Fallowfields
Southmoor, Kingston Bagpuize
Nr Abingdon OX13 5BH

Tel Oxford (0865) 820416
Fax (0865) 820629

"Real value for money. When I lay in my four-poster in a large bedroom and realised I was paying only £34 I couldn't believe it. It would have been twice that anywhere else. Dinner, too, was very good at a most reasonable price. Mrs Crowther was a delightful hostess."

Once the home of the Begum Aga Khan, this is now a "private house taking in paying guests", and many Guide readers over the years have appreciated the "personal and kindly welcome" of its owner, Alison Crowther. It is full of good Victorian pictures, decent china and glass, and books. There is an immaculate garden with a small heated pool and a hard tennis court. The spacious bedrooms have good lighting, expensive chintzes, drapes and frills (a bit fussy for some tastes), deep-pile fitted carpets, and furniture is a mixture of antique and repro. Bathrooms are large, with instant hot water, masses of towels, and lots of extras. Some of the paintings are by Mrs Crowther (who also illustrates the dinner menus), others were collected by her late husband. Dinner, by candlelight, is at 8 pm; you are asked to choose from the menu by 6.30. The four courses are "plentiful and excellent", with lots of good vegetables grown on the premises, and a sweet trolley laden with high-cholesterol goodies. Staff are "exceptionally helpful without being obtrusive". (*Mrs EH Prodgers, and others*) In winter the house can be taken over for a weekend house party. A by-pass is due to open in 1992 which will reduce the traffic noise that can be heard on the north side of the house.

Open 1 Apr–30 Sep. Winter-weekend house parties for min 4 people except Christmas and New Year – advance booking only. Dinner not served Wed (snacks available).
Rooms 4 double – all with bath and/or shower, telephone, radio, TV, tea-making facilities.
Facilities Lounge, TV lounge, dining room. 2-acre garden, 10-acre paddock; tennis, table-tennis, croquet, heated swimming pool. Riding, golf, river and lake fishing, windsurfing and water-skiing at Stanton Harcourt Leisure Centre nearby.

Location On A420 8 m SW of Oxford, 6 m from Abingdon. Light sleepers may be disturbed by traffic on A420, in 1 north room.
Restrictions Not suitable for ♿. Smoking discouraged in dining room. No children under 10. Dogs at management's discretion, not in public rooms.
Credit cards Access, Visa.
Terms B&B: single £34, double £58; dinner, B&B: single £51, double £92. Set dinner £17. 5% discount to regular visitors.
Service/tipping: "We do not make a service charge, a fact made clear to clients. If they regard service as exceptional they may hand contributions to the proprietor for distribution to the staff."

KIRKBY FLEETHAM North Yorkshire — Map 4

Kirkby Fleetham Hall
Kirkby Fleetham
Nr Northallerton DL7 0SU
Tel Northallerton (0609) 748711
Fax (0609) 748747

This fine house, Elizabethan in parts but substantially remodelled 200 years ago to give it its present Georgian appearance, stands tranquilly in large grounds with a lake with ducks and swans and a well-preserved 12th-century Knights Templar church, but is only two miles from the A1. It is managed by Stephen Mannock, "who has extensive knowledge of places to see, walks to take, and fun things to do in the area". The decor is elegant country house in style; bedrooms, named after birds, are all different, with lovely views, comfortable and spacious, except for top ones which are smaller. Staff are helpful and courteous. English breakfast is "huge, with delicious coffee and lots to choose from – from black pudding to kippers". The wine list is extensive with some interesting and unusual wines. "We were made most welcome. Our bedroom was magnificent. Dinner was first-class. Not inexpensive, but we found it good value in every way." There is good accommodation for families and high teas are available for small children. (*Richard Lee, JA Lawrence*)

Open All year.
Rooms 22 double – all with bath and/or shower, telephone, radio, TV. Some on ground floor.
Facilities 2 lounges, dispense bar, restaurant; conference/functions facilities. 32-acre grounds with walled garden, lake with fishing, clay-pigeon shooting.
Location 1 m N of Kirkby Fleetham; follow signs to Kirkby Hall and church.
Restrictions Not suitable for ♿. Dogs in ground-floor bedrooms only; not in public rooms.
Credit cards All major cards accepted.
Terms [1991 rates] B&B: single £75, double £100–£170; dinner, B&B £79 per person. Set lunch £14, dinner £29. Reduced rates for children in family room; special meals.
Service/tipping: "No service charge. Tipping is optional; tips distributed to all staff."

KIRKOSWALD Cumbria — Map 4

Prospect Hill BUDGET
Kirkoswald
By Penrith CA10 1ER
Tel Lazonby (076 883) 500

"A find; fascinating, with wonderful views. Rooms comfortable and well equipped." "Well worth the detour; a delightful room with a substantial bed with a brass bedhead. A warm place to sleep and a good place to wake up in." (*J Kavanagh, R and C Phillips*)

This small hotel, owned and informally run by John and Isa Henderson, is a "pleasing conversion" of 18th-century farm buildings on an unclassified road in the Eden Valley, an untrippery area north of Penrith, easily reached from the M6. It has beams and open fires, some good old furniture and a collection of agricultural memorabilia. Bedrooms, not all *en suite*, vary in size; some are quite small. Inexpensive but "interesting and well-cooked" à la carte dinners are served "quietly and efficiently" in a fine old barn; the wine list is adventurous – "at last a pair of Chilean classics". There's a vegetarian menu, and a special one for small children needing an early meal. Generous breakfasts feature locally baked bread, "real" honey and marmalade. Two new bedrooms have been made in a coach house, one a family unit, the other a self-contained loft. A note of warning: "The hotel's water system is far from under control and provided lengthy and intrusive distraction at night and in the early morning." And an autumn visitor found his bedroom cold and poorly lit.

Open All year except 24–27 Dec.
Rooms 1 family, 8 double, 3 single – 6 with bath and/or shower (1 also with WC), 1all with tea-making facilities. 2 across courtyard.
Facilities TV lounge, reading room, bar lounge, bar, breakfast room, dining room. 1-acre grounds with croquet. Fishing nearby.
Location B6413 off A6 to Lazonby and Kirkoswald; $\frac{5}{8}$ m N of Kirkoswald on top of steep hill.
Restrictions Not suitable for ♿. Smoking in bedrooms strongly discouraged. No dogs.
Credit cards Access, Amex, Visa.
Terms [1991 rates] B&B: single £19–£42, double £41–£56, family suite (3 or 4 occupants) £71–£77; dinner, B&B £29–£31.50 per person approx. Packed lunches. Full alc dinner £18 (but no min charge). Surcharge for 1-night bookings over bank holiday weekends. Discounts for long stays and group bookings. Reduced rates for children by arrangement; special meals.
Service/tipping: "No service charge. When away we like to thank especially attentive staff with cash. Therefore our guests must be allowed to do the same. The guest/staff relationship is enhanced by such a gesture – when deserved."

LACOCK Wiltshire — Map 2

At the Sign of the Angel
Church Street, Lacock
Chippenham SN15 2LA

Tel Lacock (0249) 730230
Fax (0249) 73527

César award in 1989: Inn of the year

This 14th-century half-timbered inn at the heart of the ancient wool village of Lacock, now preserved by the National Trust, has been run by the Levis family for 38 years. It is quintessentially English with low doorways, oak panelling, polished brass and silverware, antique furniture, open fires, and comfortable sofas and easy chairs in the lounge; the atmosphere is "domestic and intimate"; service is "amiable *and* efficient". Most readers this year have endorsed earlier praise of the dinners served in the candle-lit dining room – "archetypal good honest English cooking using a wide range of high-quality ingredients". Much of the produce comes from local suppliers, and diners pay according to whether they take one, two or three courses in addition to the main one (invariably a roast, with a fish or vegetarian alternative). But one autumn visitor considered the dinner overpriced for what was offered and reported that at breakfast the home-made bread and marmalade mentioned in earlier Guide entries were not on offer. Another adds: "My wife could hear every word of my conversation in the lounge while she was in our bedroom next door."

Open All year except 22 Dec–6 Jan. Restaurant closed for Sat lunch; also Sun dinner to non-residents.
Rooms 10 double – all with bath, telephone, TV, tea-making facilities; 4 in cottage across garden. 1 on ground floor.
Facilities Lounge, 2 dining rooms. 1-acre garden with stream.
Location 7 m S of M4 (exit 17); E of A350 between Chippenham and Melksham. Limited off-street parking.
Restrictions Not suitable for ♿. No children under 8. No dogs in public rooms.
Credit cards Access, Amex, Visa.
Terms B&B: single £70, double £93. Set lunch £16, dinner from £22.50; full alc £32. Winter breaks, midweek summer breaks.
Service/tipping: "No service charge. We neither expect nor encourage tipping, but if it pleases a customer to leave something it will not be refused."

LANGHO Lancashire — Map 4

Northcote Manor
Northcote Road, Langho
Nr Blackburn BB6 8BE

Tel Blackburn (0254) 240555
Fax (0254) 246568

A restaurant-with-rooms set in pretty countryside on the edge of the Ribble Valley, with its back to the A59, 15 minutes from the M6. The manor, "all old world atmosphere" with beams, oak panelling, roaring fires and handsome staircase, is owned by Craig Bancroft and Nigel Haworth; the latter, Swiss trained, is also the chef. "It's a Victorian redbrick house," write our inspectors, "with later additions, and has an overwhelmingly Edwardian feel. On arrival we were offered tea in the sitting room, served promptly, for no charge. Our bedroom was spacious, with heavy Victorian/Edwardian furniture and pictures from the same period. Minus points were a lack of easy chairs, a central light fitting which threw a ghastly pallor over the room, and only one bedside light. The large bathroom was well equipped, with the original blue mosaic wall tiles. The sitting room where meals are ordered is crowded and often very smoky. Space was at a premium in the restaurant too. Food is ambitious modern cooking. Much of it succeeds though there is occasional coarseness and clumsiness in execution. Desserts were modern with the emphasis on fruit, sorbets and impressive pastry. There is a good range of interesting British cheeses and a small serving can be had cheaply, a praiseworthy policy. Service is all one could hope for – well trained, efficient, friendly and confident. The English breakfast was more than adequate, including freshly squeezed fruit juice, local yoghurt – and newspaper. No complaints either about the housekeeping, and we wholeheartedly endorse *Northcote Manor*'s entry in the Guide. It knows what it is about, delivers with style, attention and quality, and the owners and staff are exceedingly pleasant and unpretentious." More reports please.

Open All year except New Year's Day. Restaurant closed Sun, also lunchtime Mon (bar snacks available for residents only).
Rooms 6 double – 4 with bath, 2 with shower, all with telephone, radio, TV; baby-listening to be installed.
Facilities Bar, lounge, restaurant; private dining room. 2-acre grounds.
Location From M6, junction 31, take A59 towards Whalley. Hotel is on left at sign for Old Langho.
Restrictions Not suitable for ♿. No dogs in public rooms.
Credit cards Access, Visa.
Terms [1991 rates] B&B: single £60, double £70. Set lunch £12, full alc £20–£25. Weekend rates.
Service/tipping: "Optional 10% added to restaurant bills."

LANGLEY MARSH Somerset — Map 1

Langley House
Langley Marsh
Wiveliscombe TA4 2UF

Tel Wiveliscombe (0984) 23318
Fax (0984) 24573

Peter and Anne Wilson's 16th-century house with 18th-century additions and alterations stands in three acres of well-tended landscaped gardens in a rural corner of Somerset. It is "well decorated and immaculately clean, and has an elegant, well-proportioned drawing room with striking coral-coloured walls, fresh flowers and an open fire, and attractive bedrooms, of medium size, with some nice touches" (though one reader was surprised to find no dressing table in one). The small, slightly crowded dining room is drag-painted in a subtle green, with blending carpets and curtains – the effect is "charming and unusual". Dinner consists of four courses on weekdays and five at weekends, with no choice until dessert or cheese. Peter Wilson cooks (Mrs Wilson is front of house), and in 1991 earned a *Michelin* red "M" denoting a good meal, carefully cooked, if not up to rosette standards. "Food is on the *nouvelle* side, but portions are more generous, though far from huge. Everything looked and tasted good." "Very good ingredients. At last vegetables that taste of vegetables; at last a chef who doesn't overcook everything!" In the past readers have occasionally commented on Mr Wilson's fondness for the pepper pot; during a recent inspection visit this was not apparent until breakfast: "Just when my taste buds had relaxed – wham, the scrambled eggs hit back! But everything was very well cooked and presented, with freshly squeezed orange juice and particularly good toast; lovers of strong coffee need to state their preference." Service is "friendly, if uncoordinated at times". One reader complained of excessive extras on the bill. More reports please.

Open All year except Feb.
Rooms 1 family, 6 double, 1 single – all with bath (2 also have shower), telephone, radio, TV, baby-listening.
Facilities 2 drawing rooms, bar, restaurant, conservatory. 4-acre garden with croquet.
Location ½ m N of Wiveliscombe. Turn right at town centre.
Restrictions Not suitable for ♿. No smoking in restaurant. Children under 7 by arrangement. No dogs in public rooms.
Credit cards Access, Amex, Visa.
Terms [1991 rates] B&B £36.50–£59; dinner, B&B £59–£76.25. Set dinner £22.50 and £27.50. 2-day breaks all year. 1-night bookings sometimes refused weekends and bank holidays.

LASTINGHAM North Yorkshire — Map 4

Lastingham Grange — *Tel* Lastingham (075 15) 345 and 402
Lastingham YO6 6TH

César award in 1991: For preserving traditional virtues of country hospitality

This Guide favourite is a modest, well-run country hotel, thoroughly traditional in both decor and style of cooking, clean and comfortable, with helpful staff. It was opened as a hotel in 1946 by the father of the present proprietor, Dennis Wood, and has appeared in the Guide since the first edition. It is an old stone creeper-covered house that has a courtyard and large grounds with a carefully tended garden, fine old trees and fields, in a particularly tranquil setting in the heart of the North York Moors National Park. Newspapers, morning coffee and afternoon tea are included in the rates; shoes are cleaned if left outside the bedroom at night. "Continues to be our favourite country house hotel. Dennis Wood is the perfect host – helpful, friendly and welcoming without being intrusive. We particularly like the way they welcome children; not all hotels in this category do. The assault course is a great favourite. The meals are generally safe, occasionally excellent. Breakfasts are first-class." "Probably the quietest place I have ever stayed in, worthy of a whole row of *Michelin* rocking chairs. The large pink and yellow roses on our bedroom wallpaper were reminiscent of old-time French country hotels, but the room and bathroom were very comfortable. Dinner excellent – real home-cooking. And delightful proprietors." (*I West, Mrs RB Richards*)

Open Mar–Dec.
Rooms 10 double, 2 single – all with bath (7 also have shower), telephone, radio, TV, tea-making facilities, baby-listening.
Facilities Hall, lounge, dining room; laundry facilities. 10-acre grounds with garden, croquet, swings, slides, adventure playground. In National Park, near moors and dales; riding, golf, swimming nearby.
Location Off A170, 5 m N of Kirkbymoorside. Turn N towards Appleton-le-Moor 2 m E of Kirkbymoorside.
Restrictions Not suitable for ♿. No smoking in dining room. Dogs by arrangement only, not in public rooms.
Credit cards None accepted.
Terms [1991 rates] B&B: single £38–£51.25, double £76–£95.25; dinner, B&B: single £45.75–£66.50, double £91.50–£120.70. Set lunch £12.95, dinner £21.45. Light and picnic lunches available. Reduced rates for long stays and winter breaks. Children under 12 sharing parents' room free; special meals.
Service/tipping: "No service charge. Tipping is discouraged."

LAVENHAM Suffolk — Map 3

The Great House — *Tel* Lavenham (0787) 247431
Market Place, Lavenham
CO10 9QZ

Lavenham is said to be the finest surviving example of a medieval English town; it has ancient buildings, a fine church and timber-framed houses. How surprising therefore to find, inside *The Great House* in its market square, a "typical French restaurant-with-rooms" – with a Texan owner. The house is a well-preserved medieval building with a Georgian facade.

The poet Stephen Spender lived here in the 1950s, and one of the bedrooms is named after him. In the oak-beamed, candle-lit dining room with its original inglenook fireplace chef Régis Crépy produces "imaginative, beautifully presented" meals which he describes as "rural French and English"; the set menus are particularly good value. In summer meals can be served in the paved, flowery courtyard. There are only four bedrooms, all spacious, all with a sitting room or sitting area, bathroom (quite small), gas fire, TV, old beams; attractively decorated with floral fabrics and antiques. Windows may be on the small side and hard to shut tight; sloping floors with squeaking floorboards are another period feature. Some of the staff have so recently crossed the Channel that linguistic confusions can arise. Breakfast, however, is full English. Children are welcome at *The Great House.*

Open All year. Restaurant closed Sun night and Mon.
Rooms 3 suites, 1 double – all with bath and/or shower, telephone, radio, TV, tea-making facilities, baby-listening.
Facilities Bar/lounge, restaurant; courtyard. ½-acre grounds with swings.
Location Behind Market Cross. From High Street take Market Lane to Guildhall. Parking.
Restrictions Not suitable for ♿. No smoking in restaurant. No dogs in public rooms.
Credit cards Access, Visa.
Terms [1991 rates] B&B: single £50–£68, double £66–£78; dinner, B&B: single £63.95, double £93.90. Set lunch £9 and £14, dinner £14; full alc £25–£35. 2- and 3-night breaks. Reduced rates and special meals for children.
Service/tipping: "No service charge. Tips at guests' discretion, shared among staff."

LEAMINGTON SPA Warwickshire — Map 2

The Lansdowne
Clarendon Street
Leamington Spa CV32 4PF

Tel Leamington Spa (0926) 450505
Fax (0926) 420604

César award in 1989: Best townhouse hotel

David and Gillian Allen's Regency townhouse is near the centre of this once fashionable and still delightful watering place, convenient for Warwick Castle, the National Exhibition Centre (25 minutes by car) and the National Agricultural Centre (10 minutes). Public rooms are not large, but "delightfully done, with period pieces". Some bedrooms, too, are very small, but they are carefully furnished, spotless and attractive, with firm beds, though storage space can be limited if you are on a protracted visit. Breakfasts are good, dinner is "home-cooking in the best sense, with vegetables varied and interestingly done". The wine list is "unexpectedly large and well chosen by someone who knows what they are doing and takes pride in finding good wines at a reasonable price". (*Prof. Raymond Bell; also Philip Young, Robert Hartford, Mrs M Stanley-Smith*) The hotel is on a crossroads; front rooms are double-glazed, but if you like fresh air at night you should ask for a back one. Also there are more rooms with shower than bath, so if you want to wallow you should spell this out.

Open All year except 24–31 Dec.
Rooms 10 double, 5 single – 5 with bath and shower, 7 with shower, all with telephone, radio, TV, tea-making facilities, double-glazing; baby-listening by arrangement. 2 on ground floor.

Facilities Residents' lounge with TV, bar, restaurant. Small garden. Discounts for guests for many local attractions.
Location Central, on A425 (front rooms double-glazed). Small private carpark.
Restrictions No smoking in dining room. No children under 5. No dogs.
Credit cards Access, Visa.
Terms B&B £19.95–£43.95; dinner, B&B £33.65–£58.95. Set lunch £14.95, dinner £15.95; full alc £19.90. 2-night breaks; special deal for Warwick arts festival. Reduced rates for children sharing parents' room; special meals by arrangement. *Service/tipping: "No service charge. We have always felt this to be an unnecessary impost."*

LEDBURY Hereford and Worcester — Map 2

Hope End
Nr Ledbury HR8 1JQ

Tel Ledbury (0531) 3613
Fax (0531) 5697

César award: For resolute pursuit of a vision

"Few things in this world are perfection. This hotel is one of them. Those who have accused the Hegartys of being aloof miss the point; as everything is unobtrusively right (rooms spotlessly clean, beds made while you breakfast, for instance), there is no need for the hosts to smile continually. When anything is needed they are at hand, friendly and helpful. All that is missing is the twee extras one really can do without. The staff are just as efficient and attentive. The food is presented simply and with taste. At breakfast home-made bread, jams and marmalade are served; the eggs are laid by the hens which roam the garden." "Breathes peace and privacy. The grounds, rooms and meals all work in harmony to give the visitor a sense of well-being. Luxury in the traditional sense of a grand hotel may not apply, but there can be few places more beneficent in their effect. In the house peace reigns, with wood-burning stoves, polished floors, woven fabrics, pictures and books everywhere. The meals change and develop but are based on first-class materials fresh from the garden or local suppliers. They reflect the seasons imaginatively and satisfyingly. The grounds continue to develop. This year, for example, there is a huge new glasshouse/orangery in the walled garden." "Fascinating building. We very much like the combination of modern pine and textiles in a Regency frame. The setting is quite lovely; it has an unusual and slightly eccentric charm." (*Alan Blyth, N Williams; Sir Timothy Harford*)

Hope End is all that remains of Elizabeth Barrett Browning's childhood home in a beautiful hidden valley. Once a Moorish fantasy, most of the original was pulled down by later owners, leaving one lone minaret and huge stable gates. The hard-working owners tend a vast walled organic vegetable and fruit garden and continually improve the grounds; they are restoring the Georgian landscaped garden, and there are now "a Temple, Grotto, Belvedere and Gothic Island Ruin and other Surprises". Earlier readers have singled out for praise "the quality of silence – because it lies in a hollow, surrounded by high trees, there's no sound of traffic or wind"; the interior, "full of beautiful bare wood and autumn colours, with woven wool fabrics and unpretentious bedrooms, mostly pine-clad, pleasantly furnished, with woven covers on the beds"; and the food: "The style is Patricia Hegarty's own – modern British that has taken on board eclectic influences. Meals are healthy, avoiding salt and cholesterol where possible, and rely heavily on fresh produce, organically grown by the Hegartys. It is simple, almost purist." *Hope End* is now open seven days a week. The full five-course menu, which changes daily, has been expanded to offer three alternative main courses – meat, fish and a vegetarian dish; on Monday and Tuesday there is a shorter, lighter and cheaper supper for residents only.

As we have said in the past, the Hegarty style arouses strong feelings, not all of them positive; some readers find it altogether too austere, particularly as it is not inexpensive, and miss the trappings of a luxury hotel, and others are put off by "the emphasis on healthy eating". But the Hegartys say: "We have never pressed the point about 'healthy' food; it just seems natural to use the best ingredients available fresh from our garden. There is no pleasing everybody and we simply have to accept there are some who take against us. If you suppress your character and become like everyone else you are yet another bland hotel and are criticised for that." We repeat: those it pleases, are mightily pleased.

Open Mid-Feb–mid-Dec. Restaurant closed for lunch and to non-residents Mon and Tue (light meal for residents).
Rooms 1 suite, 8 double – all with bath, telephone, tea-making facilities; 1 in cottage 200 yds from main house, 1 in minaret.
Facilities 3 sitting rooms, dining room. Walled garden; 40 acres of parkland.
Location 2 m N of Ledbury, just beyond Wellington Heath. *Hope End* is signposted from just beyond railway station.
Restrictions Not suitable for ♿. No smoking in dining room. No children under 12. No pets.
Credit card Access.
Terms [1991 rates] B&B double £90–£135; £10 reduction for single occupancy. Set dinner £28.60 (Mon/Tue £15.50). Reduced rates for 2 or more nights; spring and autumn breaks.
Service/tipping: "No service charge. No tipping expected."

LEW Oxfordshire — Map 2

The Farmhouse Hotel and Restaurant BUDGET — *Tel* Bampton Castle (0993) 850297, *Telex* 83242
University Farm
Lew, Nr Bampton OX8 2AU

Modernised but unpretentious farmhouse with locally popular restaurant, 3 m SW of Witney, well set back from road and attached to 216-acre working farm in tiny village with fewer than 60 inhabitants. Run by Rouse family. Bedrooms (named after Oxford colleges) characterful, comfortable and well equipped; one adapted for ♿. Atmosphere too informal for some, we said last year, but jacket and tie are required for male diners. Endorsed this year for friendly and welcoming attitude and good service. Some criticisms of the food, and outside diners can overwhelm the place at times. Near Brize Norton airfield, but quiet at night. Restaurant closed Sun. No children under 5. No dogs. Access, Visa accepted. 6 double rooms, all with bath/shower. B&B: single £35, double £48. Set dinner £15.

We get less feedback from smaller and more remote hotels. But we need feedback on all hotels: big and small, far and near, famous and first-timers.

LIFTON Devon — Map 1

The Arundell Arms
Lifton PL16 0AA

Tel Lifton (0566) 84666
Fax (0566) 84494

This creeper-covered stone building, on the A30 (front rooms are sound-proofed and ventilated), formerly a coaching inn, has been owned by Ann Voss-Bark for over a quarter of a century and has had a Guide entry for many years. It is very much a sportsperson's hotel, "with the camaraderie that exists when people with a common interest are together", and is particularly popular with people who fish: it has twenty miles of salmon, trout and sea-trout fishing on the river Tamar and its tributaries, a three-acre stocked lake, and offers fishing courses of all kinds; there are two full-time fishing instructors. In winter there are shooting packages, and also bridge and golfing holidays, cookery courses and gourmet weekends; meetings and conferences, too, are catered for. The public rooms "are not at all slick but rather manage to look a bit shabby (in a very positive 'English' way) even with new curtain fabrics and extreme cleanliness". There is "wonderful" bar food; dinners, cooked by Philip Burgess, are "simple, unfussy and excellent; the same with breakfasts, especially if you have your own fresh trout to be steamed and served with bacon on toast. The rooms are simple, clean and adequate. Being here makes you want to forswear forever all those over-fussy hotels with choreographed dinners." "Wines also excellent – a wide selection at reasonable prices." "Nice, welcoming staff, happy to have our two young children; they gave us a separate bedroom for them at a nominal rate." (*DJ Fisher, and others*) Only micro-niggle: "Strangely, for such a hotel, no porridge for breakfast." But can we have more reports please?

Open All year except 4 days over Christmas.
Rooms 19 double, 10 single – all with bath and/or shower, telephone, TV, tea-making facilities; baby-listening in main building. 5 in annexe.
Facilities Lounge, cocktail bar, 2 restaurants; 3 conference rooms.
Location 3 m E of Launceston on A30 (front rooms sound-proofed).
Restrictions Not suitable for ♿. No smoking, no dogs in restaurant.
Credit cards All major cards accepted.
Terms B&B £40.50–£56. Set lunch £14.75, dinner £24.50; full alc £35. Fishing holidays Mar–Oct; shooting, bridge, bird watching, cookery holidays, gourmet weekends in off-season. Children under 16 free in parents' room; special meals on request.
Service/tipping: "This is a service industry; there should be no obligation, morally or otherwise, on guests to tip. Any gratuities given are pooled and distributed equally to all staff."

LINCOLN Lincolnshire — Map 3

D'Isney Place Hotel
Eastgate, Lincoln LN2 4AA

Tel Lincoln (0522) 538881
Fax (0522) 511321

Warm endorsements this year for David and Judy Payne's Georgian "B&B deluxe" with a garden, and some bedrooms overlooking the nearby cathedral. Back rooms are peaceful; those on the street side get some traffic noise, particularly on weekdays (but the windows are double-glazed). It has neither reception nor breakfast room; breakfast, continental or English, is served in the bedrooms which vary in size and style from quite simple singles to larger ones with a whirlpool bath. "Ours, at the back, was spacious and quiet with near-rural view of horses and jumps, good reading-in-bed lights, adequate storage space; the bathroom was a proper room with a window; there was fresh milk for tea- and coffee-making." "Very comfortable. Good English breakfast. Staff friendly and helpful. We heartily endorse the entry." "Housekeeping immaculate. What a bonus to see the cathedral floodlit on going to bed and again on waking." (*J and J Wyatt, PM Tattersall, Elizabeth and Stephen Wills*) The *Wig and Mitre* and *Harvey's*, both nearby, are recommended for meals. Parking can be a problem but the staff will help.

Open All year.
Rooms 1 suite, 14 double, 2 single – all with bath and/or shower (3 with jacuzzi), telephone, radio, TV, tea-making facilities; baby-listening by arrangement. Also 3 cottages, 100 yds away, each with 2 double bedrooms, lounge, dining room, kitchen.
Facilities Ramps by arrangement. No public rooms. 1-acre garden.
Location By cathedral. Rooms double-glazed. Carpark.
Restriction No smoking in 2 bedrooms.
Credit cards All major cards accepted.
Terms [1991 rates] B&B: single £39–£48, double £61–£69.50. Weekend breaks. No charge for very small children in parents' room. (No restaurant.)
Service/tipping: "No service charge. Tips not expected but guests often like to make personal gifts to staff."

LITTLE SINGLETON Lancashire — Map 4

Mains Hall
86 Mains Lane, Little Singleton
Nr Poulton-le-Fylde FY6 7LE

Tel Poulton-le-Fylde (0253) 885130
Fax (0253) 894132

This small old manor house, Grade II listed, full of character and history, "a peaceful and quiet place to stay", is near Blackpool but enjoys a pleasant pastoral setting in a garden overlooking meadows to the river Wyre. Inside are exposed beams, carved oak panelling and log fires, but lounge facilities are limited. Bedrooms, which vary in size, are well appointed; some have a four-poster. *Mains Hall* had an italicised entry in last year's Guide due to a change of owners. Readers have written warmly of the "most delightful" new proprietors, Roger and Pamela Yeomans, who arrived in early 1990: "They made us most welcome; staff helpful, bedrooms extremely comfortable, food excellent value." "It's now run in a more professional, commercial manner – the prices are higher – but the standard of comfort and warmth of welcome have improved." (*Gerald L Fox, CJ Wells, Richard Faulkner; also MJ Willmore*) Opinions of the food vary; we'd be glad of more reports.

Open All year. Restaurant closed Sun.
Rooms 9 double – all with bath and/or shower, telephone, radio, TV, tea-making facilities, baby-listening. 2 on ground floor.
Facilities Hall, library, bar, 2 dining rooms. 4-acre grounds with badminton, croquet, river frontage; fishing and sailing.
Location 7 miles NE of Blackpool. Leave M55 at exit 3; take A585 N to Fleetwood for 5 m. Hotel is on right, ½ m past 2nd set of traffic lights.
Restrictions No smoking in bedrooms. No dogs in public rooms.
Credit cards Access, Visa.
Terms B&B: single £45–£65, double £65–£130. Set dinner £22.50. Winter weekend breaks. Reduced rates and special meals for children.
Service/tipping: "Service included. Tipping not encouraged, but any tips are distributed among staff."

LIVERPOOL Merseyside — Map 4

The Grange
Holmefield Road, Aigburth
Liverpool L19 3PG

Tel Liverpool (051) 427 2950
Fax (051) 427 9055

Readers frequently complain about the dearth of Guide recommendations for many of Britain's major cities so we were particularly delighted to receive this warts-and-all recommendation for a hotel of character in a residential area about three and a half miles from the city centre: "Liverpool has few decent hotels and this is a welcome exception. The building is Victorian eccentric – weird and entertaining, and the decor of the public rooms, particularly the bar, is in questionable taste. Some bedrooms are in a modern wing, recently upgraded and very acceptable, with good beds and pleasant *en suite* facilities. The staff are welcoming and attentive. Breakfast is an honest, standard one. The restaurant serves good, even quite imaginative food which might not make *The Good Food Guide*, but is worth staying in for, especially in Liverpool. The carpark is locked at night and has closed circuit TV. The hotel tries very hard and succeeds most of the time. We will continue to use it if we can get in after you recommend it; how selfless can we be?" (*Antony Griew*) The hotel, which was built in 1842, is company-owned, and managed by Peter Wilson. It has a one-acre garden; some of its decorations – the scroll and gargoyles round the eaves, and the plaster work and marble which decorate the lounge and restaurant areas – were imported in the 19th century from Scandinavia and Italy. It is a mile and a half from the airport. More reports please.

Open All year. Restaurant closed for lunch except Sun.
Rooms 4 suites, 15 double, 10 single – 19 with bath and shower, 6 with shower, all with telephone, radio, TV, tea-making facilities, baby-listening.
Facilities Lounge, lounge/bar, TV room, restaurant; functions facilities. 1-acre garden with bar patio.
Location Off A561, 3½ m SE of centre. Detailed directions from hotel. Security-monitored parking at rear.
Restrictions Not suitable for ♿. No dogs.
Credit cards All major cards accepted.
Terms [1991 rates] B&B: single £31.35–£44.35, double £44.65–£59.35, suite from £65.20. Set Sun lunch £7.75, dinner £12.95; full alc £21.35. Weekend rates. Reduced rates and special meals for children.
Service/tipping: "No service charge. Gratuities at guests' discretion."

LONDON — Map 3

The Abbey Court
20 Pembridge Gardens, W2 4DU

Tel (071) 221 7518
Fax (071) 792 0858

A small, expensive, luxuriously equipped B&B in a relatively quiet street near Notting Hill Gate, convenient for transport to the West End and the City. Outside are window-boxes, bay trees and carriage lamps; inside are magnificent flower arrangements in the hall and reception, and antique and period furniture. Bedrooms are mostly medium in size, though at least one single is extremely small. They vary in style; some have grand four-posters, others are more cottagey. All have a marble bathroom with a whirlpool bath. The decor is pretty, not excessively lavish. Breakfast is generous, with freshly squeezed orange juice, home-made muesli, croissants and brioches. There is no restaurant, but light meals and tea are available, served in the bedroom. Not for the infirm, as the hotel is on five storeys and has no lift. Last year's entry is confirmed by *Richard Ponsford*: "Superb decor, extremely comfortable. Happy staff. Can't recommend too highly."

Open All year.
Rooms 16 double, 6 single – all with bath, shower, telephone, radio, TV.
Facilities Reception lounge. Small garden.
Location Central. Meter parking. (Underground Notting Hill Gate.)
Restrictions Not suitable for ♿. No children under 12. No dogs.
Credit cards All major cards accepted.
Terms Rooms: single £84, double £122–£150. Continental breakfast £8. (No restaurant, but light alc meals and teas served.)
Service/tipping: "We make no charge for service. This is a choice we leave to our guests."

The Academy — *Tel* (071) 631 4115
17–21 Gower Street, WC1E 6HG — *Fax* (071) 636 3442

This sympathetic conversion of two Grade II listed Georgian Bloomsbury houses, with some original features retained (and no lift), is handy for the British Museum and Law Courts. Its entry was dropped last year as a major refurbishment was underway. The result, we are told, is "very attractive". It has a patio garden where light lunches, tea and drinks are served, and which the quietest bedrooms overlook (front ones are double-glazed), and an agreeable library. Some bedrooms are studio suites with air-conditioning; beds "are built to American specifications". Fairly traditional but "delicious" food is served in the new restaurant where jazz pianists sometimes play, including our Contributing Editor, John Edington; pre-theatre meals and vegetarian dishes are available. The manager, Allan Agerholm, is Dutch. (*Mr and Mrs Bågstam; also Susan Welch*)

Open All year.
Rooms 2 suites, 23 double, 6 single – 4 with bath and shower, 20 with shower, all with telephone, radio, TV, tea-making facilities, baby-listening. 5 on ground floor.
Facilities Library, bar/restaurant. Patio.
Location Central. Patio rooms quietest. NCP carpark nearby. (Underground Tottenham Court Road, Goodge Street, Russell Square.)
Restriction No dogs.
Credit cards All major cards accepted.
Terms Rooms: single £58–£72, double £70–£85, suite £105–£120. Breakfast: continental £4.95, English £7.50. Set lunch £12.50, dinner £14.50; full alc £25. 2-night winter breaks.
Service/tipping: "Service included in accommodation bills. Mandatory 12½% added to restaurant bills. We don't believe in tipping except where customer considers service exemplary."

Athenaeum Hotel — *Tel* (071) 499 3464
116 Piccadilly, W1V 0BJ — *Fax* (071) 493 1860

The flagship hotel of the Rank chain has an enviable position overlooking Green Park (jogging maps and suits available for the energetic), and all the trimmings that one would expect from a deluxe West End hotel. There are two floors of no-smoking bedrooms, and all bedrooms are double-glazed and furnished "in the classic style"; the quietest ones are on the side, but they lack the view of the park. The large lounge is attractive in a "country-house style", the cocktail bar is mahogany-panelled. Food in the restaurant, with soft colours and alcoves, is excellent, if expensive; the menu is French. Light meals and teas are available round the clock in the lounge. Parking, shared with the adjacent hotel, costs £21.50 a day. For those who prefer to self-cater, the hotel rents apartments in an adjacent building on a quiet side street. Meetings and private functions are extensively catered for.

Open All year.
Rooms 22 suites, 80 double, 10 single – all with bath, shower, telephone (2 lines), radio, TV, in-house films; double-glazing, air-conditioning; 24-hour room service. 33 1- and 2-bedroom apartments in adjacent building. Baby-listening by arrangement.
Facilities Lifts. Lounge, cocktail bar, restaurant; conference and functions facilities.
Location Central; valet parking (£21.50 per day). (Underground Green Park.)
Restrictions No smoking in some bedrooms. Guide dogs only.
Credit cards All major cards accepted.
Terms [1991 rates] Rooms: single £178–£193, double £198–£213, suite £260–£330. Breakfast: continental £9.25, English £12.30. Set lunch £23, dinner £25–£31; full alc £35–£40. Weekend breaks. Special meals for children on request.
Service/tipping: "No service charge. Tips not expected, but guests who feel they have been well treated may wish to reward the staff."

Basil Street Hotel
8 Basil Street
Knightsbridge, SW3 1AH

Tel (071) 581 3311
Fax (071) 581 3693

Privately owned by the third generation of the family who founded it 80 years ago, this Edwardian building, in a small but busy road leading off Sloane Street, convenient for Hyde Park and Harrods, "offers modern comfort in an elegant old atmosphere" and has many regular visitors. It has numerous public rooms furnished with antiques, mirrors and paintings, a panelled restaurant serving French-oriented food, a coffee shop, a cellar wine bar and a ladies' club. The impressive room on the left of the entrance was once a booking hall for the London Underground. The 94 bedrooms include family rooms; most have a private bathroom. They are traditionally furnished and home-like, vary greatly in size, style and position and include a pleasant suite; some of them can be surprisingly quiet for central London. Others, however, do get traffic noise, "but there was a note offering earplugs"; there can also be disturbance from a nearby fire station or TV in neighbouring bedrooms. (*Diana Blake, Miss M Turpin, Richard Creed*) The hotel has a "Basilite" scheme whereby visitors who have stayed at least five times enjoy discounted tariffs and weekend concessions.

Open All year.
Rooms 1 suite, 44 double, 48 single – 73 with bath and shower, all with telephone, radio, TV.
Facilities Lounge bar, ladies' lounge, coffee shop, wine bar, dining room; facilities for conferences, functions, private meals.
Location Central; public carpark nearby. (Underground Knightsbridge.)
Restrictions Not suitable for ♿. No dogs in public rooms.
Credit cards All major cards accepted.
Terms [1991 rates] Rooms: single £56.25–£105.25, double £86–£141, family £197, suite £226.85. Breakfast: continental £4.90, English from £9.20. Set lunch £13.75–£15.75; full alc dinner £23. Weekend breaks. No charge for children under 16

sharing parents' room; special meals.
Service/tipping: "Service charge is non-existent, neither included nor excluded, and tipping is not encouraged though we recognise that most people when satisfied wish to show this by tipping."

The Beaufort
33 Beaufort Gardens, SW3 1PP

Tel (071) 584 5252
Fax (071) 589 2834

⊞ *César award in 1991: Most audacious city hotel*

Diana Wallis's small, pricy hotel which aims to provide "the atmosphere of an English country house in the heart of London" has an excellent position, on a quiet square just round the corner from Harrods. The atmosphere is "especially attractive and informal; with outstanding, friendly service". Much thought has been given to making the guest feel at home. On arrival you are given a front-door key. Bedrooms are stocked (but not cluttered) with numerous extras including fruit, chocolates, biscuits and bathroom goodies: "And they are of excellent quality," writes a visitor this year. "We enjoyed an elegant cognac from the decanter in our room before bed. The lemon curd at breakfast was the best I have tasted since my mother's home-made; and how nice to have butter that is not wrapped in horrid little tablets. The 'extras' now include personal laundry." It was the *Beaufort*'s pricing policy that led us to use the word "audacious" in last year's *César* citation. The room charge includes breakfast, full meals served in the bedroom (Roux brothers' *sous vide*), drinks from the 24-hour bar, membership of a nearby health club, videos – and much else besides. Apart from two porters all the staff are female, and women travelling on their own find this a particularly sympathetic place to stay. The decor is pretty, with pale colours, fresh flowers everywhere, original watercolours, and comfortable sofas and chairs. The staff are friendly and helpful, and once a month there is a champagne party for guests. *The Beaufort* is air-conditioned throughout. As is usual in buildings of this kind, some of the top rooms are quite small. (*Catrina Williams, and others*)

Open All year except Christmas and New Year.
Rooms 9 suites, 16 double, 3 single – all with bath and/or shower, telephone, radio, TV/video, tea-making facilities, baby-listening. Some on ground floor.
Facilities Lift. Lounge with honour bar. Free membership of nearby health club.
Location Central, near Harrods. Meter parking; public carpark nearby. (Underground Knightsbridge.)
Restrictions No children under 10 except for babies. Dogs by arrangement only.
Credit cards All major cards accepted.
Terms B&B: single from £150, double £160–£220, suite £250. Children free if sharing with parents. (No restaurant but light meals served in bedrooms 7–9 pm.)
Service/tipping: "We do not encourage tipping as the tariff is all-inclusive and staff well paid."

Blakes
33 Roland Gardens, SW7 3PF

Tel (071) 370 6701
Fax (071) 373 0442

"The bedroom was £295 a night, £70 more than the price quoted on the telephone," writes a visitor in late 1990, "but very pretty, predominantly white with a grisaille architectural *trompe l'oeil* frame of columns and pedestals given to every wall surface. This gave an impression of grandeur and size (the ceilings were high anyway). White painted floorboards, a few plain rugs, white sofa and chairs and a bowl of white roses and cabbage leaves. The bed was hung with yards of superior Christmas pudding material; it was comfortable with a firm mattress, good sheets that were changed after one night, and plenty of pillows. The room lacked books and good magazines but had a television hidden under one of the tables (awkwardly placed to watch – it was best to sit on the floor). The stereo and CD system was tastefully concealed in reproduction bookcases. The first night the room was not tidied while we were out, but on the second it was. The mini fridge had not been restocked before our arrival. Two of the lights had to stay on all night, dimmers turned down as much as possible, because the switches were too far behind substantial pieces of furniture. It was impossible to close the bathroom door without totally rearranging the rug. The combination of fridge and air-conditioning made the nights quite noisy, but we did not hear street sounds until an argument between delivery van and irate resident erupted just outside our window. Continental breakfast was delicious, on time, and £7.50 extra each. The staff, mostly foreign in the rooms, English at the front door and desk, were helpful and pleasant though perhaps overmindful of the prospect of a tip. The problem of parking was efficiently solved for us. The whole hotel smells of dried lavender and seems a place in its own right, quite unconnected to London and the street life outside. To get to our room we walked through a small courtyard reminiscent of a Japanese ryokan, with small pots of bay and privet and orange trees. It's nearly perfect – but the few irritating points ought, at that price, to be smoothed out."

Blakes' dark green exterior contrasts strikingly with its redbrick Victorian neighbours in a residential street a few minutes' walk from South Kensington underground. Its decor, theatrically stylish with a pronounced Oriental accent, is designed by the proprietor, Anouska Hempel, who is constantly refurbishing. Antiques, original paintings and rare silks abound; there is much black. All the bedrooms are different; some are opulent, with heavy drapes and dark colours, others are plainer and lighter but equally stunning. It is best to discuss the style of room you prefer when booking; none is particularly large. Reception is laid-back. In the darkly mirrored dining room in the basement, where tables have alternate black and white cloths, David Wilson's menus are cosmopolitan and pricy; food is lavishly decorated and generous in portion. There's lots of choice on the breakfast menu. The clientele is international and trendy.

Open All year. Restaurant closed 25/26 Dec.
Rooms 12 suites, 30 double, 10 single – all with bath and/or shower, telephone, TV, baby-listening; 12 with radio.
Facilities Lift. "Chinese Room" (lounge – light refreshments served), bar, restaurant.
Location Central; meter parking. (Underground South Kensington or Gloucester Road.)
Restrictions Not suitable for ♿. No dogs.
Credit cards All major cards accepted.
Terms [1991 rates] Rooms: single £120–£150, double £180–£300, suite £220–£550. Breakfast: continental £8.60, English £14. Full alc £80. Special meals for children on request.
Service/tipping: "We do not levy a service charge on accommodation; tips are at guests' discretion. We add a 15% charge to restaurant and room-service bills which is included in the waiting staff's wages."

The Capital *Tel* (071) 589 5171
22–24 Basil Street, SW3 1AT *Fax* (071) 225 0011

A smallish, sophisticated hotel, with a *fin de siècle* decor, owned by David Levin who also owns *L'Hotel* (below). It is in a narrow but busy side street near Harrods; parking is not easy, but the hotel has a small garage. The "very attractive" bedrooms, designed by Mrs Levin, have fabrics by the American designer, Ralph Lauren; they are double-glazed, air-conditioned and elegant in a country house sort of way, though with many urban extras, including full sound and vision service. Some are quite dark with patterned wallpaper and heavy drapes, others are lighter in style. Bathrooms are lavishly marbled, and comprehensively equipped. The restaurant, with its "gentle Nina Campbell interior" and imposing chandeliers, has long been a mecca for London gourmets; under chef Philip Britten it regained its *Michelin* rosette in 1990 for its fine French cooking; the "courteous and efficient service" is also appreciated. Full afternoon tea is served in the sitting room. Some of the bedrooms are quite small and one visitor reports this year: "The two rooms we had were almost entirely taken up by the bed and had very little room for the crib. To eat in the bedroom we had to sit at the desk or on the bed. We would have expected more flexibility from the room-service staff; only sandwiches were available after 7 pm." More reports please.

Open All year.
Rooms 8 suites, 28 double, 12 single – all with bath, shower, telephone, radio, TV; 24-hour room service.
Facilities Lift. Lounge, bar, restaurant; 2 private dining rooms. Business facilities.
Location Central. Rooms double-glazed; rear rooms quietest. Garage for 12 cars (£15 per night). (Underground Knightsbridge.)
Restriction Dogs at management's discretion, not in public rooms.
Credit cards All major cards accepted.
Terms [1991 rates] Rooms: single £150, double £175, suite £265. Breakfast: continental £7.50, English £10.50. Set lunch £20, dinner £46; full alc £50. Reduced rates and special meals for children.
Service/tipping: "Service included. No tipping expected."

The Connaught *Tel* (071) 499 7070
Carlos Place, W1Y 6AL *Fax* (071) 495 3262

"A matchless place: no other hotel has its style and confidence, no restaurant the sense of immutability that a long-standing, successful and select hotel background can confer." "On a chart of one to ten, I rate the *Connaught* as a ten." Typical comments on one of London's most exclusive hotels: it has no brochure, rates are "on application", guests' privacy is jealously guarded, the bedrooms are usually booked months in advance. Its unchangingness is beloved by its clientele. It is in the heart of Mayfair, in a relatively unbusy street. The decor is sophisticated, with comfortable furniture, antiques and luxurious fabrics; flowers abound. The restaurant, under *maître* chef Michel Bourdin, is *Michelin*-rosetted and formal, with gleaming panels, arched windows and glittering chandeliers, and solicitous service from staff in tailcoats or long white aprons; exquisite French dishes rub shoulders with steak and kidney pie and bread and butter pudding. "Eating there is sheer pleasure." Jacket and tie are *de rigueur – naturellement.*

Open All year.
Rooms 24 suites, 60 double, 30 single – all with bath, shower, telephone, TV; baby-sitting, 24-hour room service.
Facilities Lounge, cocktail bar, grill room, restaurant.
Location Central. No private parking. (Underground Bond Street.)
Restrictions Not suitable for severely ♿. No dogs.
Credit cards Access, Visa.
Terms On application.
Service/tipping: "15% added; shared among staff on 'points' basis."

The Draycott
24–26 Cadogan Gardens
SW3 2RP

Tel (071) 730 6466
Fax (071) 730 0236

This lush hotel, "offering style and comfort somewhere between an extremely upmarket B&B and the *Connaught*, in a country house atmosphere", was dropped from the 1990 Guide following a change of owner but now, little changed apart from some refurbishment, is readmitted following positive feedback. It consists of two large *fin-de-siècle* houses in a quiet street a stone's throw from Sloane Square, overlooking gardens at the back; the scent of apples in two huge urns greets you as you enter. There is a large drawing room looking on to the garden, and "a resolutely Pall-Mall-like smoking room, leathery and portrait-hung". Many bedrooms, too, are vast and luxuriously furnished, "with grandly draped beds, gas coal-fires, mini-bar, miscellaneous antiques and still more miscellaneous works of art"; bathrooms are "generously equipped with luxury soaps, shampoos, dressing gowns and things of that sort". There is no restaurant but there is a room-service menu; you breakfast in the bedroom or public rooms. "Friendly and helpful reception; room service efficient, food rather good," says one recent report. "Reception nice but confused," says another, "but otherwise it was heaven."

Note: "The *Draycott* is difficult to find thanks to the eccentric numbering system introduced by Victorian planners and the barely visible plaque that just whispers the hotel's name." Also one single room (No 21) is singularly small and faces the lift shaft.

Open All year.
Rooms 5 suites, 11 double, 8 single – all with bath, shower, telephone, radio, TV, baby-listening, mini-bar, 24-hour room service.
Facilities Drawing room, smoking room/bar, private dining/meeting room. ½-acre garden.
Location Between Pavilion Road and Draycott Avenue, behind Peter Jones. Meter Parking. (Underground Sloane Square.)
Restrictions Not suitable for ♿. No dogs.
Credit cards All major cards accepted.
Terms (Service at guests' discretion) Rooms: single £75–£130, double £165–£195, suite £225–£250. Breakfast £8–£10. (No restaurant; room-service meals.)

Durrants Hotel
George Street, W1H 6BJ

Tel (071) 935 8131
Fax (071) 487 3510

"Exceptionally good value for London. Our room, though small, was pleasantly decorated and equipped with all modern conveniences. Staff and owner extremely pleasant and helpful. Breakfast was plentiful, though not of exceptional quality. Despite its central location, it was extremely quiet at night." "We stay here once every couple of months when in London on business. For such a haven of tranquillity well worth the money. Some of the corridors could perhaps do with a coat of paint but this might spoil the air of timelessness in most of the downstairs areas (except for the foyer/hall which is fairly slick and very efficient). The bedrooms are small, verging on the poky in some cases, but clean and reasonably well furnished. The food isn't cheap but we feel it's quite good value for money. A little heavy, perhaps, but consistent – very much in keeping with the style of the hotel." (*Cathryn Bryck, MK Neill and KE Smith; also Ian Best*)

This traditional, well-bred and relatively inexpensive hotel encased in a late 18th-century shell has been added to over the years, creating a quaint, rambling effect. In summer, flowery window-boxes stretch along its facade. Formerly a coaching inn, it is one of the oldest privately owned hotels in London, and has been managed by the same family for over seventy years. It is convenient for Oxford Street, Harley Street, Marylebone Road and the Wallace Collection; the quietest bedrooms are in the rear. No recent report on the cooking, there are many good restaurants in the area. Reports suggest that some rooms need refurbishing, and one 1991 visitor was a disgruntled insomniac: "Asked for quiet room at back but noise from people and from lift, and light from corridor showing through ill-fitting door, made sleep difficult."

Open All year. Restaurant closed 25/26 Dec.
Rooms 6 suites, 70 double, 20 single – all with bath and/or shower, telephone, radio, TV. Some on ground floor.
Facilities 2 lifts. 4 lounges, bar, restaurant, breakfast room, tearoom; conference facilities.
Location Central (some front rooms could be noisy). Public carpark 5 mins' walk. (Underground Marble Arch.)
Restriction No dogs.
Credit cards Access, Amex, Visa.
Terms [1991 rates] Rooms: single £55–£75, double £85–£99, suite £140–£185. Breakfast: continental £5.25, English £8. Full alc from £25. Special rates for children by arrangement.
Service/tipping: "Service is included in all bills apart from the restaurant where an optional service charge of 12½% is added."

Ebury Court Hotel — *Tel* (071) 730 8147
24–32 Ebury Street, SW1W 0LU — *Fax* (071) 823 5966

This friendly, old-fashioned hostelry rambling through five adjoining houses conveniently near Victoria Station was run for over half a century by Diana and Romer Topham and was something of an institution – for the Guide and for many devotees. In July 1989 the Tophams retired, to be succeeded by their daughter and son-in-law, Marianne and Nicholas Kingsford, who were in the process of making considerable changes as we went to press last year, so it was given only an italicised entry. We were therefore delighted to hear from *RAL Ogston*, writing "at the risk of being thought a paid-up member of the *Ebury Court* Supporters' Club. Prices have gone up, but it's still good value by London standards. I wouldn't think of going anywhere else. It's still friendly and comfortable, but much less old-fashioned. Breakfast (full English, and good) is still served downstairs, but the ground floor, with a new lunch and dinner restaurant, has been glossified considerably. You are now welcomed by young ladies who use computers in a luxurious reception area." Food is traditional; the menu changes daily. The bedrooms are mostly small; not all have private facilities, but bathrobes are provided for the trip down the corridor to the public bathrooms, and more singles will be having a shower and loo installed during 1991. When possible at quiet periods, guests are "upgraded" to rooms with better facilities. More reports please.

Open Closed 2 weeks Christmas/New Year.
Rooms 1 triple, 26 double, 18 single – 21 with bath and shower, 1 with shower, all with telephone, radio, TV, tea-making facilities.
Facilities 2 lounges, 2 bars, 2 restaurants.
Location Central (front windows double-glazed), 3 mins' walk from Victoria Station. Parking difficult. (Underground Victoria.)
Restrictions Not suitable for ♿. No dogs in public rooms.
Credit cards Access, Diners, Visa.
Terms B&B: single £60–£65, double £100–£125, triple £150. Full alc from £18. 10% discount Dec–Feb.
Service/tipping: "Tipping at guests' discretion."

Egerton House *Tel* (071) 589 2412
17–19 Egerton Terrace, SW3 2BX *Fax* (071) 584 6540

"The latest small London hotel of the 'country house' concept. Thirty really comfortable and beautifully decorated rooms with *en suite* bathrooms, air-conditioning, satellite TV, mini-bar and 24-hour room service as well as a pleasant drawing room and honesty bar. Very friendly welcome, proper showers and proximity to Harrods make this a must. We would recommend to anyone except those with children (under-eights are not admitted)." (*Mrs AC Godfrey*) An inspector did indeed appreciate the country-house-in-South-Kensington qualities while finding a few weaknesses: "It's a pleasing redbrick period house in a quiet position. Good antiques and reproduction furniture in the public rooms, also pictures, dried and fresh flowers, but no magazines or books. Heavy fabrics are much used, with swagging and swathing so a feature is made of each window. The standard of housekeeping is high. There are some fine fireplaces, but sadly no evidence of use. Reception was cordial; our car was taken to a nearby carpark (£15 a day – they have three spaces) and our cases were carried to our room. The bedrooms are on four floors; most overlook the gardens. Ours was compact, mainly pink and blue, with draped curtains, heavily padded bedspread and bedhead, but quite ordinary furniture, and I would have liked two comfortable chairs instead of one pretty but hard one. Excellent wardrobe space. Lighting was poor. The bathroom was luxuriously appointed but sponge bags had to go on the floor. You can breakfast in the bedroom or the basement breakfast room, bright and fresh in blue and white. We thought £12.50 far too expensive for a cooked breakfast so took the £7 continental one with very cold, freshly squeezed orange juice, delicious fruit salad, a generous basket of toast, rolls and croissants, and good coffee. Staff were polite and friendly." The room-service menu offers anything from snacks to a three-course meal.

Open All year.
Rooms 1 suite, 17 double, 12 single – all with bath, shower, telephone, radio, TV.
Facilities Lifts. Drawing room, residents' bar, breakfast room.
Location Central. (Underground South Kensington.)

Restrictions Not suitable for ♿. No children under 8. No dogs.
Credit cards Access, Amex, Visa.
Terms [1991 rates] Rooms: single £98, double £130, suite £230. Breakfast: continental £7, English £12.50. (No restaurant, but 24-hour room service: light meals to full alc at about £30.)

The Fenja
69 Cadogan Gardens, SW3 2RB
Tel (071) 589 7333
Fax (071) 581 4958

This discreet and elegant small hotel in a residential street near Sloane Square, with some rooms overlooking Cadogan Gardens (to which guests have access), is "beautifully proportioned, and carefully decorated in Edwardian style, filled with antique and period furniture, original pictures and marble busts". Bedrooms, all different, are named after English artists and writers. Turner, a "superior double", is "remarkably quiet and impressively decorated in pale shades, with a magnificent four-poster, beautiful hexagonal table and Chippendale-style chairs"; Jane Austen is more feminine, with flowery fabrics. The bedrooms have fresh flowers and fruit; instead of a mini-bar there is a drinks tray with cut-glass decanters; you are charged for what you consume. "The excellent and very generous English breakfast set us up for the entire day." The *Fenja*, like its sister hotel *Cliveden* at Taplow (q.v.), goes in for cosseting service – cases carried, shoes polished, etc. "They even fed the parking meter for us." (*Francine and Ian Walsh*) There's no restaurant, but light meals can be served in the bedrooms.

Open All year.
Rooms 12 double, 1 single – all with bath and/or shower, telephone, radio, TV. 1 on ground floor.
Facilities Lift. Drawing room; conference room. Access to Cadogan Gardens.
Location Central, near Sloane Square. Meter parking. (Underground Sloane Square.)
Restrictions Not suitable for ♿. No dogs.
Credit cards Access, Visa.
Terms Rooms: single £105, double £138–£205. Breakfast: continental £6.50, English £9.75. (No restaurant, but light meals available.)

The Gore
189 Queen's Gate, SW7 5EX
Tel (071) 584 6601
Fax (071) 589 8127

Kensington hotel recently taken over and redecorated by Peter McKay of Hazlitt's (*q.v.*) *with the advantage of two good restaurants* – Bistrot 190 *in the building and* Restaurant 190 (*pricier*) *in the basement. Both run by fashionable, innovative chef Antony Worrall-Thompson. Victorian decor, with mahogany and walnut, oriental rugs, antique prints and furniture, but 20th-century comforts – direct-dial telephone, mini-bar, TV, etc, in the 58 rooms, most with bath/shower. Not suitable for ♿. All major credit cards accepted. B&B: single £79–£85, double £95–£99, suite £140. Breakfast: continental £5.45, English £9.45. Alc dinner in* Bistrot 190 *£20, set dinner in* Restaurant 190 *£38.50. New nomination. More reports please.*

We ask hotels to quote 1992 prices. Not all were able to predict them in the late spring of 1991. Some of our terms will be inaccurate. Do check latest tariffs at the time of booking.

The Goring
15 Beeston Place, SW1W 0JW

Tel (071) 834 8211
Fax (071) 834 4393

A dependably comfortable, well-kept hotel in a useful location near Victoria, Buckingham Palace and Westminster. It was built in 1910 by the grandfather of the present Mr Goring (who was born in Room 114), and claims to have been the first hotel in the world to have a bathroom and central heating in every bedroom. The atmosphere and decor are English traditional; bedrooms, in pastel colours, have good quality furniture and fabrics. Many guests are regulars, often on business. Staff are "friendly and very helpful"; many senior members have been at the hotel for years. There are "superb" public rooms including a large relaxing bar overlooking an inner courtyard garden and lawn (not, however, accessible to guests). The sedate and spacious restaurant offers quiet and professional service, traditional dishes, and a good choice for vegetarians. There is a new chef this year, John Elliott, who has seen service at two other Guide London hotels, the *Connaught* and the *Capital*. Best choices are said to be the dish of the day and fish specialities. (*Alfred Knopf, and others*) One reader considered both accommodation and restaurant overpriced.

Open All year.
Rooms 9 suites, 41 double, 34 single – all with bath, shower, telephone, radio, TV; some with air-conditioning. 24-hour room service.
Facilities Lift. Lounge, bar, restaurant; 5 functions rooms. 1-acre garden (no access for guests).
Location Central, by Buckingham Palace (front rooms are double-glazed). Garage and mews parking. (Underground Victoria.)
Restrictions Not suitable for ♿. No dogs.
Credit cards All major cards accepted.
Terms Rooms: single £135, double £185, suite £210. Breakfast: continental from £7, English from £10. Set lunch £19.50, dinner £25; full alc £40. Special meals for children on request.
Service/tipping: "No service charge for hotel but 10% added to restaurant bills. Guests are informed that tipping is not necessary or expected."

Hazlitt's
6 Frith Street, W1V 5TZ

Tel (071) 434 1771
Fax (071) 439 1524

Most visitors continue to enjoy this small hotel in the heart of Soho, well situated for West End theatres and restaurants. Back rooms are quietest. Formerly a nurses' home, it was created from three terrace houses built in 1718. It takes its name from the essayist, who died in one of the houses a century later; the 23 bedrooms are named after famous residents and visitors to the house. Rooms are generally light and airy; at the top of the house they are quite small, lower down they have high ceilings; all have agreeable prints and plants, firm beds (though the doubles are on the small side) and decent linen. Some of the bathrooms have a free-standing bath with brass taps, wooden towel rail and wooden loo seat. The hotel is furnished throughout with mahogany, oak and pine. Continental breakfast with fresh orange juice, "real" coffee, rolls and croissants is served in the bedrooms (there's no breakfast room); light refreshments and cream teas are available in a sitting room. "Clean and well cared for; staff conscientious and helpful, and they were wonderful to our young daughter." Not suitable for the infirm as there's no lift. (*Diana Cooper; also*

Mr and Mrs Bågstam) One visitor in late 1990, however, was comprehensively disappointed: "Our room, Sir Bentinck, was poky and dark. I had asked for a shower but we were given only a detachable rubber shower spray, rather perished, to jam on to the bathtaps. Heating was inadequate." More reports please. *Hazlitt*'s new sister hotel, the *Gore*, gets its first Guide entry this year.

Open All year except 21–26 Dec.
Rooms 1 suite, 17 double, 5 single – all with bath and/or shower, telephone, TV. 3 on ground floor.
Facility Lounge.
Location Central. NCP nearby. (Underground Tottenham Court Road.)
Restrictions Not suitable for ♿. No dogs.
Credit cards All major cards accepted.
Terms [1991 rates] (excluding VAT) Rooms: single £85, double £95, suite £140. Continental breakfast £5.50. (No restaurant, but teas and light refreshments available.)
Service/tipping: "We do not charge for service. Tips are pooled and distributed equally among staff."

Knightsbridge Green *Tel* (071) 584 6274
159 Knightsbridge, SW1X 7PD *Fax* (071) 225 1635

"Excellent in every way." "Courtesy and concern for your welfare." "One of the nicest things is that the staff are always the same and the welcome genuinely warm. They remember which suite I particularly like and deliver the right paper without asking. Refurbishment is complete and is most attractive. Prices have risen but are still very reasonable for this part of London. Breakfast still lovely and served at exactly the time requested." (*Mrs Alfred D Bell Jr, Mr and Mrs Alexander M Casey, Dr JR Backhurst; also Hugh and Pam Neil, Dr SB Bayly*)

This small family-owned hotel on Knightsbridge, close to Hyde Park, is unusual in having mostly suites, each with a double bedroom, sitting room and bathroom; they are simply and attractively decorated, well lit, comfortable, mostly spacious, and have good bathrooms; there are also double and single rooms. It does not offer the trappings of a luxurious hotel, and the only public room is the Club Room on the first floor where free tea and coffee are available all day. Continental or English breakfast is delivered to the room. Front rooms are double-glazed to keep out traffic noise; those at the back are quietest.

Open All year, except 4 days at Christmas.
Rooms 14 suites, 6 double, 4 single – all with bath, shower, telephone, TV, tea-making facilities.
Facilities Club Room with complimentary tea, coffee, cake.
Location Central (bedrooms overlooking Knightsbridge double-glazed). NCP in Pavilion Road nearby. (Underground Knightsbridge.)
Restrictions Not suitable for severely ♿. No dogs.
Credit cards Access, Amex, Visa.
Terms Rooms: single £85, double £100, suite £115. Breakfast: continental £6, English £8.50. (No restaurant.)
Service/tipping: "Our rates include a service charge; guests are discouraged from further tipping by a notice in the bedroom."

> If you think we have over-praised a hotel or done it an injustice, please let us know.

L'Hotel
28 Basil Street, SW3 1AT

Tel (071) 589 6286
Fax (071) 225 0011

A centrally located B&B owned by the Levins who also own the neighbouring *Capital* (q.v.). *L'Hotel* dispenses with such extras as porterage, hair-driers and bathroom accessories to maintain prices at a reasonable level for central London. Rooms, decorated in French country style, are all different, but each has fabric-lined walls, window blinds and curtains, a tiny but well-thought-out bathroom, pine chairs, chests and cupboards, efficient heating, attractive lighting, lots of hot water at all times and "good beds; and it was useful to have a kettle and crockery as well as a fridge with wine, soft drinks, etc. Pretty quiet for London." The staff are relaxed and pleasant, and there is a choice of eating arrangements for those not wishing to go far – the *Capital*'s rosetted restaurant next door or the good-value *Metro*, the busy wine bar in the basement, where French café food is accompanied by high-quality wines which can be bought by the glass. "Excellent" continental breakfasts, also served in the *Metro*, include fresh orange juice. Rooms vary: some are small and lack the cosy benefit of a gas coal-fire; those above the wine bar can be noisy until late into the night; the suite at the top is quietest. Parking is not easy. Much refurbishment has taken place in the last year. A regular writes: "As satisfactory as ever. We were given the suite at no extra charge as it was not taken that night. It's a pity more hotels don't do this. It costs them nothing, creates goodwill and often encourages the guest to book the better room on a return visit." (*Diana Blake, David Wooff; also JA Chesterfield*)

Open All year. Wine bar closed Sun and some public holidays, except for residents' breakfast.
Rooms 1 suite, 11 double – all with bath, shower, telephone, radio, TV, tea-making facilities, mini-bar. 1 on ground floor. (*Note:* No room service.)
Facilities Lift. Wine bar/brasserie.
Location Central. Rear bedrooms quietest. NCP opposite. (Underground Knightsbridge.)
Restriction Dogs at management's discretion.
Credit card Visa.
Terms B&B (double or single occupancy) £110, suite £145. Extra bed in room £20. Alc meal in wine bar £20.
Service/tipping: "Service included. Tipping at guests' discretion, divided among all staff."

Number Sixteen
16 Sumner Place, SW7 3EG

Tel (071) 589 5232
Fax (071) 584 8615

Last year's entry is endorsed with enthusiasm: "We found this a pleasant, comfortable and attractive base which we hope to use again." It is a conversion of four attractive late Victorian townhouses in a fairly quiet street only minutes from South Kensington tube station. It is filled with antique and period furniture and an interesting selection of paintings and prints. There is a comfortable lounge and bar, and a conservatory looking on to a very pretty garden. Bedrooms vary in size and price; quietest ones overlook the garden. (*Eithne Scallan, and others*) One caveat: "They could do with more staff at reception. The only person there seemed to be eternally on the phone."

Open All year.
Rooms 27 double, 9 single – 24 with bath and shower, 12 with shower, all with telephone, TV.
Facilities Lift. Reception, drawing room, bar, conservatory. Garden.
Location Central. Garden-facing rooms quietest. Parking 5 mins walk. (Underground South Kensington.)
Restrictions Not suitable for ♿. No children under 12. No dogs.
Credit cards All major cards accepted.
Terms [Until 1 Apr 1992] B&B: single £50–£95, double £110–£160, suite £175.
Service/tipping: "No service charge. No stated policy about tips, but staff are adequately paid; any tips given are shared equally."

The Portobello *Tel* (071) 727 2777
22 Stanley Gardens, W11 2NG *Fax* (071) 792 9641

This hotel celebrated its 21st anniversary in 1991 with an extensive refurbishment but – we hasten to reassure devotees of its wayward charm – no change of style. The hotel is in two six-floor Victorian terrace houses, on a quiet residential street within strolling distance of the Portobello Road market and not far from Kensington Gardens. The design, by Julie Hodgess, is an eclectic mix of styles, Victorian to Gothic, with gilt mirrors, marble fireplaces, four-posters, palms, Edwardiana, cane and wicker furniture. Some of the rooms, called cabins, are tiny, but they have essential elements of life-support such as colour TV, minute fridge and micro-bathroom. There are also, as you work downwards, normal-sized rooms and ritzy suites – the Bath Room has mirrors above the bed and painted clouds on the ceiling, the Round Room has a round bed and free-standing Edwardian bath. There is a small lift. The *Portobello* is "relaxed and discreet"; "eccentric and pleasantly surprising"; "staff most friendly and helpful". There is porterage and room service between 8 am and 4 pm, but reception are on duty day and night. For the benefit of international travellers, there is 24-hour bar-and-restaurant service in the garden-style basement where a simple menu is offered by owner Tim Herring's partner, chef Johnny Ekperigin, who is also chef at their trendy, similarly decorated bar and restaurant *Julie's*, in nearby Portland Road. Croissants are placed in each bedroom for do-it-yourself breakfasters, and English and continental breakfast is available round the clock in the restaurant. More reports badly needed. (Tim Herring reminds us that when the hotel opened the cabins cost £4 a night.)

Open 2 Jan–23 Dec.
Rooms 7 suites, 7 double, 11 single – 7 with bath and shower, 18 with shower, all with telephone, radio, TV, tea-making facilities, fridge.
Facilities Small lift. Lounge, bar, restaurant (open 24 hours to residents).
Location Central. Meter parking. (Underground Notting Hill Gate.)
Restrictions Not suitable for ♿. No dogs.
Credit card Access.
Terms Rooms: single £70, double £108, suite £165. Breakfast: continental £5.95, English £7.20. Full alc meals £25. Special meals for children.
Service/tipping: We believe that guests should not be denied the right to tip if they wish. We state clearly on the tariff that service is not included. But on bar and restaurant bills we include a 12½ percent service charge in the total. That money is passed on to the staff who worked the shift involved."

> We ask hotels to estimate their 1992 tariffs some time before publication so the rates given are often guesswork. Please always check terms with hotels when making bookings.

Swiss Cottage Hotel
4 Adamson Road, NW3 3HP

Tel (071) 722 2281
Fax (071) 483 4588

A conversion of terraced houses in a quiet residential street in north-west London, but conveniently placed for transport to the centre. It is a hotel of genuine character, mostly Edwardian and Victorian; there is a delightful Tea House suite in a cottage in the garden. Some studios and apartments are in nearby buildings. The hotel had an entry – often of an affectionate warts-and-all nature – in earlier editions of the Guide. Last year it returned, italicised, under new owners, and is now endorsed by a reader who knew it in its previous incarnation (and generally came with a do-it-yourself repair kit): "Perfect, I thought, as we were shown into one of its many large and delightful rooms. It used to have its faults – its quirky, aunt-like little ways – but now it's perfect: new plumbing, new wallpaper (sometimes less tasteful than before), thick white new towels, bowl of fruit on the marble coffee table by the velvet sofa. Just then we discovered a bedside light that was not working and a strange damp spot on the carpet. Oh dear! Same old lovable imperfections after all. But a phone call to the desk brought almost instant help, and we were looked after both by reception and in the dining room in the most courteous and cheerful way throughout our three-day stay. The new management is building on all the delights of the hotel – the antique furniture, individually decorated rooms, 'real' though sometimes strange paintings, oriental rugs – and adding excellent service and a very personal touch. Prices for all this are still reasonable." "Everything clean and tidy, very pleasant dining room; excellent English breakfast; good three-course dinner from a tempting à la carte menu. Parking comparatively easy." (*Margaret Farrell Clark, REL Pile*) We'd welcome more reports.

Open All year.
Rooms 7 suites, 48 double, 15 single – most with bath and/or shower, all with telephone, radio, TV. Also some self-catering apartments.
Facilities Lounge, bar, restaurant; functions/conference facilities. Patio.
Location From Swiss Cottage Underground take Eton Avenue exit; 2 mins' walk. Small carpark; street parking.
Restrictions Not suitable for ♿. Guide dogs only.
Credit cards All major cards accepted.
Terms (Service at guests' discretion) [1991 rates] B&B: single £66–£118, double £77–£128. Set lunch £14.95, dinner £16.95; full alc £22. Weekend rates. Children under 8 in parents' room free of charge.

Wilbraham Hotel
1 Wilbraham Place
Sloane Street, SW1X 9AE

Tel (071) 730 8296
Fax (071) 730 6815

A privately owned, traditional and moderately priced hotel near Sloane Square, which featured in earlier editions of the Guide, is restored to these pages by a regular visitor: "I know I can count on having a clean and comfortable room with a good bed (with old-fashioned cotton sheets), good lighting, and plenty of storage space. In cold weather it is well heated. Breakfast is delivered to the room at the time ordered and is perfectly adequate. I had delicious porridge today, and I like cold toast! Staff are friendly. Messages are taken. The Buttery Bar serves light meals, particularly nice if you are on your own. And of course the location is excellent. I never bother to take a room with a bathroom and have never had problems with using the public one. It's not at all fancy, which is precisely why I like it, and it's very good of its kind." (*Dr Suzanne Martin*)

Only niggle: "They quote a room rate and everything else is added – VAT, breakfast, etc." But that could be an advantage to some who may prefer to breakfast elsewhere in the area – the General Trading Company, or Peter Jones, for example.

Open All year.
Rooms 5 suites, 31 double, 16 single – 43 with bath and/or shower, all with telephone, TV on request.
Facilities 2 lifts, lounge, buttery.
Location Central. (Underground Sloane Square.)
Restriction No dogs.
Credit cards None accepted.
Terms (Excluding VAT) Rooms: single £42–£58, double £57–£72, suite £72–£90. Breakfast from £4. Set lunch £7, dinner £10.

LONG MELFORD Suffolk — Map 3

The Black Lion
The Green
Long Melford, CO10 9DN

Tel Sudbury (0787) 312356
Fax (0787) 74557

This old coaching inn, "informal, not luxurious, but extremely comfortable", overlooks the green in a picture-book village with many antique shops. In 1989 it was taken over and redecorated and refurbished by Stephen and Janet Errington who moved their *Countrymen Restaurant*, which they had run in Long Melford for six years, into the hotel. It is a truly family business: Stephen Errington, *Dorchester* trained, cooks, his wife "runs things extremely efficiently", her father acts as host behind the bar, and her mother covers the reception desk. Last year's entry is endorsed: "Superb location. Our room, No 1, looked over the green to the parkland of Long Melford Hall beyond. It was perfectly proportioned, spacious, nicely decorated and warm, with a good-sized bathroom. The atmosphere of the hotel was warm and friendly. Interesting books are available, and lots of local information. Food and wine were very good; of the two menus, the gourmet one is better and more interesting. Service with one exception was entirely satisfactory." In addition to the restaurant menus there are shorter, cheaper ones for residents. Quite a number of niggles: the bathroom had no shelf for sponge bag, a towel rail regularly collapsed and a shower malfunctioned. Breakfast orange juice was canned. Snack luncheon dishes were "tired" and there was noise from the bar until very late on Saturday night.

Open All year except Christmas/New Year. Restaurant closed Sun night, Mon lunch.
Rooms 2 suites (1 family), 7 double – all with bath, shower, telephone, radio, TV, tea-making facilities, baby-listening.
Facilities Lounge, bar, restaurant. Small walled garden.
Location On green of village 2 m N of Sudbury. Traffic might disturb light sleepers.
Restrictions Only restaurant suitable for ♿. "Well-behaved children welcome." No dogs in public rooms.
Credit cards Access, Visa.
Terms B&B: single £45–£55, double £65–£75, suite £85; dinner, B&B: single £60–£70, double £100–£110, suite £120. Set lunch £13–£17, dinner £20–£30 (light meals available to residents). Weekend breaks all year, winter breaks.

Reduced rates for children; special meals on request.
Service/tipping: "No service charge. Tipping discretionary but not encouraged. Tips distributed among staff."

LOWER BRAILES Oxfordshire — Map 2

Feldon House — *Tel* Brailes (060 885) 580
Lower Brailes
Nr Banbury OX15 5HW

Maggie and Allan Witherick's small, early 19th-century house, quiet, welcoming and furnished with taste and style, is in a walled garden in the heart of a village on the Shipston-on-Stour–Banbury road. It makes a good base for touring the Cotswolds and is convenient for Stratford-on-Avon. It has two dining rooms, one in a conservatory, and four bedrooms, two in a converted coach house where "the Chinese Room was perhaps the most attractively furnished and well-equipped hotel bedroom we have ever stayed in". All have a private bathroom, but those in the main house are not *en suite*, so a dressing gown might be worth packing. Allan Witherick cooks "very English meals, with good bespoke ingredients and no fancy tricks"; lots of fresh vegetables, very generous portions; no choice (likes and dislikes can be discussed in advance); three courses for lunch, four for dinner. Breakfast, a cooked, help-yourself affair, "perhaps even better than dinner", is served round a large Victorian table – "books are provided for the anti-social and the hung-over". "Not for anyone who dislikes church bells – the tower is right next door!" "Very reasonably priced; relaxed, family atmosphere. Service attentive, if slightly rushed at times." (*Gwen and Peter Andrews, Barbara Nicoll, and others*)

Open All year except 2 weeks in autumn. Restaurant closed Sun night.
Rooms 4 double – all with bath, shower, telephone, radio, TV, tea-making facilities. 2 in converted coach house.
Facilities 2 lounges, dining room, conservatory dining room. Small meeting facilities. Terrace. ⅔-acre garden with croquet.
Location In middle of village on B4035 between Shipston and Banbury. Near church. Parking.
Restrictions Not suitable for ♿. No smoking in conservatory. No children under 14. No dogs.
Credit cards Access, Visa.
Terms B&B: single £30–£44, double £42–£56; dinner, B&B: single £52.50–£66.50, double £87–£101. Set lunch £17.95, dinner £22.50. 3-day bargain breaks.
Service/tipping: "Service included. If anyone chooses to give more it is evenly distributed among all staff."

LOWER SWELL Gloucestershire — Map 2

Old Farmhouse — *Tel* Cotswold (0451) 30232
Lower Swell, Stow-on-the-Wold
Cheltenham GL54 1LF

There's some debate this year about this "very friendly, relaxed and unpretentious" hotel, which re-entered the Guide last year under new ownership. It is a Grade II listed 16th-century stone farmhouse in a secluded walled garden in a small and unspoiled Cotswold village near Stow-on-the-Wold. Part-owner, a young Dutchman, Erik Burger, is also the "very hardworking" manager; a new chef, Anthony Dunball, arrived in mid-1990. The hotel is informally run; staff are casually dressed (though Mr Burger tells us he now wears a tie *most* nights) and guests need not dress for dinner. Most bedrooms are in converted outbuildings, some a steepish walk up through the carpark. The bedrooms vary considerably, from "a large family room, comfortable and light", to "small, in a former pig house", but they are all well equipped, and even have direct-dial telephone and mini-safe. The residents' lounge was once a stable; there is a cosy bar with a log fire. Tables in the two small, beamed, low-ceilinged dining rooms are casually laid: "Cutlery often arrived after the food," writes one guest, "and when we asked for salt which would pour, rather than a salt mill, Mr Burger brought the chef's scoop full of salt which he poured in a heap on the tablecloth. Is this what is meant by informal?" Most readers have enjoyed the food on the fixed-price menu, offering five choices of each course, though some have found it unexceptional (but vegetables are praised). Some consider the desserts "unadventurous", while others have swooned over the treacle pudding; there's a very good choice of local cheeses. Families are welcomed. This year's niggles: "The stable bedrooms can get very hot in summer and walls between them are thin." "Our room needed a good dusting." "Tables in dining room cramped." More reports please.

Open All year. Restaurant closed for lunch Mon–Sat.
Rooms 1 suite, 13 double – 12 with bath (11 also have shower), all with telephone, radio, TV, tea-making facilities, baby-listening. 8 in annexes. 1 self-catering flat.
Facilities Lounge, bar, 2 dining rooms; conference facilities. 2-acre garden.
Location 1 m W of Stow-on-the-Wold by B4068. On right-hand side in village from Stow direction.
Restrictions Not suitable for ♿. No smoking in dining rooms. Dogs at management's discretion; in some bedrooms only (£1.50), not in public rooms.
Credit cards Access, Visa.
Terms B&B: double £40, suite £80; dinner, B&B: double £67, suite £107. Single occupancy rates by arrangement. Set Sun lunch £13.50, set dinner £13.50. Discounts for longer stays. 1-night bookings refused for Sat. Reduced rates and special meals for children.
Service/tipping: "Service included. When guests tip, staff (excluding manager) share it."

LUDLOW Shropshire — Map 2

The Feathers — *Tel* Ludlow (0584) 875261
Bull Ring, Ludlow SY8 1AA — *Fax* (0584) 876030

"A notable combination of antiquity and real comfort. Exceptionally well-appointed bedrooms and bathrooms, above-average food, good service and friendly reception co-exist with dark oak panelling, winding staircases, fine fireplaces and excellent plaster work. It all adds up to a rather special experience." (*Nancy Raphael*, endorsed by *Sarah Baird*)

The Feathers has been an inn since the 17th century. It has a spectacular half-timbered front elevation, carved mantelpieces and elaborately ornamented plaster ceilings, panelling and original fireplaces. Bedrooms are traditionally furnished but thoroughly modern in the comforts they offer; most are of a good size, and all have a private bathroom; some have fires and four-posters. Service is friendly and efficient, with "outstanding" porterage. The food is well served, and generally considered to be "of high quality". It is the premier hotel of a delightful town as well as a showpiece in its own right, and fills its rooms with the help of many special promotions, so be prepared for lots of passing trade, and conferences, banquets and coach parties. It is not ideal for the disabled – because of its venerable age, there are lots of steps. There is no garden, but a "very nice" patio off the dining room and a billiard room.

Open All year.
Rooms 28 double, 12 single – all with bath, shower, telephone, radio, TV, tea-making facilities, baby-listening.
Facilities Lift. 2 lounges, 2 bars, restaurant; billiard room. Conference/banqueting facilities.
Location In town centre. Carpark.
Restrictions Not suitable for ♿. No smoking in restaurant. No dogs in bedrooms.
Credit cards All major cards accepted.
Terms [1991 rates] B&B: single £62–£65, double £88–£104. Set lunch £12; full alc dinner £23. 2-night breaks. Christmas programme. Reduced rates and special meals for children.
Service/tipping: "No service charge. Tipping is a matter between staff and customer. It is not essential and service will not be affected."

LYNMOUTH Devon — Map 1

The Rising Sun
Lynmouth EX35 6EQ

Tel Lynton (0598) 53223
Fax (0598) 53480

An old smugglers' inn, now a hotel composed of a row of thatched cottages on the harbourside with, says its owner, Hugo Jeune, "crooked beamed ceilings, uneven creaky floors, leaded windows and spectacular sea views from most bedrooms". It is introduced thus by a female visitor: "Travelling on my own can be an ordeal, but not here. I had the warmest possible welcome. Bedrooms are small but very well equipped. The two evening meals I had were delightful – well-cooked food, beautifully presented, with excellent, friendly service. A good wine list offered quality wine in half-bottles, very welcome to the lone guest, and not often found." Other plaudits: "Comfortable, well managed, with much attention to detail." "Old-world charm combined with all modern amenities." The poet Shelley is said to have honeymooned in the hotel's cottage just up the hill, now its suite. "We particularly attract the romantics," adds Mr Jeune. (*Mrs Munro Glass, DR Tyler, NC Dickerson*)

Open All year except 2 weeks before Christmas.
Rooms 1 suite in cottage, 14 double, 1 single – all with bath and/or shower, telephone, radio, TV, tea-making facilities, baby-listening.
Facilities Small lounge, dining room, small terraced garden. Fishing rights on river Lyn.
Location On harbourside.
Restrictions Not suitable for ♿. Smoking forbidden in dining room, discouraged in bedrooms. No children under 5. Dogs by prior arrangement only.
Credit cards All major cards accepted.
Terms [1991 rates] B&B: single £35, double £79, suite £99. Bar lunches. Set dinner £16.95; full alc £25. Special breaks Feb–June, Oct–Dec. Reduced rates for children sharing parents' room; special meals by arrangement.
Service/tipping: "Service included; tips at guests' discretion."

> There are many expensive hotels in the Guide. We are keen to increase our coverage at the other end of the scale. If you know of a simple place giving simple satisfaction, please write and tell us.

MAIDEN NEWTON Dorset — Map 2

Maiden Newton House — *Tel* Maiden Newton (0300) 20336
Maiden Newton
Nr Dorchester DT2 0AA

"Utterly charming and professionally run. We stayed three nights and wished we could have stayed longer." "The room (spacious, airy and comfortable), the view and the hospitality were outstanding. Bryan Ferriss was there when needed and slipped away during coffee to let the guests get into lively conversation – a situation that had been set up by the seatings at dinner." (*D Quirk, Harold Johnson*)

Maiden Newton is in the heart of Hardy country – it is the Chalk Newton of *Tess of the D'Urbervilles* – and there is good walking in the area. *Maiden Newton House* is a honey-coloured antique-filled 15th-century Tudor mansion (rebuilt in the early 19th century) with mullioned windows, beautiful chimneys, high-ceilinged hall, elegant lounge and individually styled bedrooms. It is set in 11 acres of secluded parkland and gardens overlooking the river Frome, and is part hotel, part private house taking guests – log fires, warm bedrooms in winter, agreeable colour schemes, books and maps, dogs and cats, all adding to the home-like atmosphere. Bryan and Elizabeth Ferriss introduce guests to each other in the lounge, then sit down to dinner with them, one at each end of the table, an arrangement people find either fun or tiresome. No choice on the four-course dinner menu but you are given notice in case a dish is not to your liking, and special diets are happily catered for. It is "all real food, fresh vegetables and much variety and ingenuity"; fish dishes are a speciality. Bryan Ferriss is commended by readers for offering a glass of wine with each course from a carefully chosen selection.

Open Feb–Dec. Occasional closures during that time.
Rooms 5 double, 1 single – 5 with bath and shower, 1 with shower, all with TV.
Facilities Drawing room/bar, library/TV room, dining room; functions facilities. 11-acre grounds with stabling for visiting horses, croquet, $\frac{3}{4}$ m trout fishing on river Frome. Golf, sailing, riding, hunting, walking nearby.
Location From A356 in centre of village take road signposted Yeovil. Entrance gates 200 yds on left near church.
Restrictions Not suitable for ♿. No smoking in dining room and 2 bedrooms. No children under 12 in dining room at night (suppers by arrangement). Small dogs only; not in public rooms.
Credit cards Access, Visa.
Terms B&B £46–£95; dinner, B&B £80–£123. Set dinner £26.50. Lunches and packed lunches on request. 1-night bookings for weekends sometimes refused if made too far in advance. Weekly half-board rates; house-party rates.
Service/tipping: "We discourage tipping."

MALVERN WELLS Worcestershire — Map 2

The Cottage in the Wood — *Tel* Malvern (0684) 573487
Holywell Road — *Fax* (0684) 560662
Malvern Wells WR14 4LG

César award: For resurrecting a fitting home for one of the grandest hotel views in Britain

"The whaleback range of the Malvern Hills soars out of the flat Severn plain, a dramatic eastern outpost of the Welsh mountains, and rightly designated an area of outstanding natural beauty. *The Cottage in the Wood* is an eyrie perched high on wooded slopes at Malvern Wells with an eagle's-eye view over the vast Severn Valley and distant Cotswolds. It is a fairly grand cottage, being in fact a cosily elegant Georgian dower house, with additional bedrooms in a converted coach house, a hundred yards from the main building. The hotel has the air of a private home; fine period furniture and flowers abound. Bedrooms in the main building are pretty, stylishly individual; those in the Coach House are modern, with huge picture-windows and terrace or balcony. The hotel stands in seven acres of natural wood and shrubbery. On razor-trimmed lawns in front you can loll in a deckchair and contemplate the infinities of the view until your mind becomes a delicious blank. A soothing hideout of singular charm." (*Roger Smithells*)

That encomium comes from the first edition of the Guide. Subsequently standards slipped and the entry was dropped. We are glad to welcome it back under its new owners, John and Sue Pattin and their family, who have restored the hotel to its former excellence. Everything which Roger Smithells said in 1978 can stand in 1992, but there are now a further four cottagey bedrooms in adjoining Beech Cottage. The Coach House has the best views but its rooms tend to be smaller. The Pattins were new to hotelkeeping when they acquired the hotel four years ago, but they have taken to their new vocation with enthusiasm, zeal, professionalism – and personal warmth. The restaurant is an agreeable room to eat in. There is no set menu, but plenty of choice. Cooking is English in style; the wine list, though eclectic, also has an English bias. Furnishings are once again pretty and stylishly individual, flowers still abound. And, following a sign which reads simply "To the Hills", you can walk straight out from your rooms to a nine-mile range of the Malvern Hills and more than a hundred miles of tracks. (*HR, Avril Fishwick*)

Open All year.
Rooms 18 double, 2 single – all with bath (16 also have shower), telephone, radio, TV, tea-making facilities, baby-listening. 4 in Beech Cottage, 8 in Coach House.
Facilities Lounge, lounge bar, restaurant. 7-acre grounds leading to walks on 9 m of Malvern Hills.
Location 3 m W of Malvern. Take Ledbury road (A449). Turn right before Jet/Honda petrol station. Do not approach from southern end of Holywell road.
Restrictions Not suitable for ♿. No smoking in dining room. Dogs in outer buildings only; not in public rooms.
Credit cards Access, Amex, Visa.
Terms B&B: single £65, double £85–£120; dinner, B&B (2 nights min): single £50–£70, double £80–£118. Bar meals from £3; summer buffet lunch £7.50; full alc £26. Weekend and midweek breaks; Christmas and New Year packages; Cheltenham National Hunt Festival break. Reduced rates for children sharing parents' room; special meals by arrangement.
Service/Tipping: "Our prices are fully inclusive; there are no further additions, nor are they expected."

MATLOCK Derbyshire — Map 4

Riber Hall — *Tel* Matlock (0629) 582795
Matlock DE4 5JU — *Fax* (0629) 580475

Partly Elizabethan country manor 2 m S of town – turn off A615 at Tansley. In high, peaceful setting in 4-acre grounds with tennis, yet easily reached from

M1. Heavy oak beams, thick stone walls, public rooms in main building full of period furniture. Bedrooms – many with 4-posters and genuine antiques, and all with numerous extras – across a steep gravelled courtyard (awkward for disabled). Some criticisms of the welcome this year; some grumbles, too, about the cooking, though rich in ingredients and ambitious in style. Hence these italics. 11 double rooms, all with bath (some whirlpool), shower. No children under 10. No dogs. Access, Amex, Diners accepted. B&B: single £76–£90, double £90–£134. Set lunch £14; full alc dinner £33. Hideaway breaks in low season. More reports please.

MAWNAN SMITH Cornwall — Map 1

Meudon Hotel
Mawnan Smith
Nr Falmouth TR11 5HT

Tel Falmouth (0326) 250541
Fax (0326) 250543

"Despite the size of the hotel service is friendly, efficient and caring. Reception and bedrooms are comfortable. Excellent food on an extensive menu; good choice of wines." (*Mr and Mrs FD Santilhano*) One of this year's tributes to this old Cornish mansion, a mellow stone building with massive granite pillars and mullioned windows on to which has been grafted a modern bedroom wing. Its chief glories are its garden and its location in 200 acres of protected Cornish coastline between the Fal and Helford rivers, at the head of a lovely valley leading down to its own private beach. The garden – eight and a half acres of rare sub-tropical flowering shrubs and plants – was laid out in the 18th century by Capability Brown, and is still carefully maintained. The hotel has been run for many years by Harry Pilgrim and his family and offers old-fashioned service – beds turned down at night, shoes cleaned, early morning tea brought to the room (though there are tea-making facilities for those who prefer them) – of a kind which has long disappeared from many pricier establishments. The five-course dinner menu changes daily, with the emphasis on traditional dishes. Replying to last year's niggle – "There are always two or three items on the menu for which a large supplement has to be paid" – Mr Pilgrim writes: "The majority of *Meudon*'s guests are small eaters and our menus have evolved over many years to suit their requirements. The extra items are to satisfy those who prefer an element of à la carte and more generous portions. I do not think £8 is a large supplement." This year's niggle (continuing a debate in these pages): "The breakfast toast *was* made from plastic bread."

Open Feb–Dec.
Rooms 2 suites, 26 double, 4 single – all with bath, shower, telephone, radio, TV, tea-making facilities.
Facilities 3 lounges, bar, sun loggia, restaurant; laundry, hairdressing salon. 8½-acre grounds leading to private beach. Fishing, golf nearby. Lock-up garage £5.
Location 4 m S of Falmouth. From Truro take A39 for 7 m; then take A394 Helston road. Follow signs for Mabe/Mawnan Smith (4–5 m). In Mawnan Smith bear left at *Red Lion*. *Meudon* is on right after 1 m.
Restrictions Not suitable for ♿. No children under 5. Dogs by arrangement, not in public rooms.
Credit cards Access, Diners, Visa.
Terms [1991 rates] B&B £60–£88; dinner, B&B £55–£105. Set lunch £12.50, dinner £22.50; full alc £35. Reductions for long stays. 3-day spring and autumn breaks. Reduced rates for children; high teas.

Service/tipping: "No service charge; guests are not made to feel obliged to tip. Anything left is distributed evenly among all staff."

Nansidwell
Mawnan Smith
Nr Falmouth TR11 5HU

Tel Falmouth (0326) 250340
Fax (0326) 250440

This pretty Cornish country house, creeper-covered and mullion-windowed, enters the Guide warmly recommended. It is peacefully set in large grounds with beautiful sub-tropical gardens leading down to the sea, and is surrounded by National Trust coastland with excellent walks and small beaches. It has been owned for the last four years by Felicity and Jamie Robertson: "We run it as much as possible as though it was our own home – a comfortable, unfussy house by the sea." They have filled it with books, magazines, fresh flowers, chintzy fabrics, paintings and antiques. Public rooms are comfortable, with log fires in cool weather. Bedrooms, all different, are very attractively decorated. "Excellent" English cooking by Anthony Allcott makes much use of local ingredients, served in well-balanced portions. Herbs and much of the fruit are home-grown; breads, croissants, jams are home-made; home-smoked duck and pork sausages are a speciality. "Wholeheartedly recommended. The house, set among lovely gardens in miles of peaceful coastal scenery, is beautiful and unusual and exudes warmth and calm." (*Maggie Hunt*) There are no age-limits on children, but they are admitted only in limited numbers at any one time.

Open All year except Jan.
Rooms 12 double – all with bath, telephone, TV, tea-making facilities, baby-listening; radio on request. 2 on ground floor with access for ♿.
Facilities Drawing room, library, dining room. 9½-acre grounds with tennis, croquet; on sea with bathing, fishing.
Location From Truro take A39 for 7 m; then take A394 Helston road. Follow signs for Mabe/Mawnan Smith (4–5 m). In Mawnan Smith bear left at *Red Lion*. Hotel entrance on right.
Restriction No dogs in public rooms.
Credit cards Access, Visa.
Terms Dinner, B&B £60–£100. Set lunch £15, dinner £21; full alc £32. 10% discount Nov–Mar except 4-night Christmas package.
Service/tipping: "No service charge. Guests on long visits usually tip the staff and tips are distributed evenly. It does make the staff feel they are doing a good job."

MIDDLEHAM North Yorkshire — Map 4

Miller's House
Market Place
Middleham DL8 4NR

Tel Wensleydale (0969) 22630

Comfortable small hotel, Grade II listed, in cobbled market square of unspoilt historic village with fine ruined castle in heart of Yorkshire Dales. Well placed for touring Herriot country. Welcoming new owners, Judith and Crossley Sunderland, have extensively renovated with bright colours, and offer reasonably priced, good and quite adventurous food, excellent picnic hampers and also wine-tasting, racing, antique and "romantic" breaks. Closed Jan. 7 rooms, all with bath/shower. Not suitable for ♿. No children under 10. No dogs. Access, Visa accepted. 1991 rates: B&B double £59.90. Set dinner £17. Was in Guide under previous owners. More reports please.

MINCHINHAMPTON Gloucestershire — Map 2

Burleigh Court
Minchinhampton
Nr Stroud GL5 2PF

Tel Brimscombe (0453) 883804
Fax (0453) 886870

"What a lovely place! We thoroughly enjoyed the outdoor plunge pool, the putting green and golf net. Our room could not be faulted; the decor was much to our taste. The general atmosphere is light and bright. Our dinner was very good, not pretentious, and the sweet trolley was excellent; dining-room service was friendly yet professional, the wine list sound and reasonably priced." This 18th-century creeper-covered house in a well-kept garden, owned and run by the friendly Benson family, with managers Mrs Davies and Mrs Stewart, stands in an especially attractive five-acre garden designed by Clough Williams-Ellis on an extremely steep hillside; from the front there are magnificent views across the Stroud valley. The interior is pleasant and comfortable, rather than stylish, and "very English"; the public rooms have comfortable chairs and fires in winter. Dinners, served in the recently redecorated dining room, with French windows overlooking the grounds, offer "very good choice on the set menu", with "standard English hotel dishes offered alongside classic French provincial, modern British and vegetarian, as well as a 'health menu'"; vegetables are fresh and plentiful. Breakfasts are praised. Small children are welcomed. The bedrooms are all different in size and style; it is worth discussing your requirements when booking. As readers have said in the past *Burleigh Court* is "not for those in search of a luxury weekend with luggage-toting porters and 24-hour room service, but highly recommended for a restful and good-natured weekend". (*Dale and Krystna Vargas, and others*) Only criticism: "The Sunday cold buffet supper at 6 to 7.15 was a bit early for us."

Open All year except 24 Dec–4 Jan.
Rooms 2 suites, 15 double – all with bath and/or shower, telephone, radio, TV, tea-making facilities, baby-listening. 6 on ground floor in stable block adjoining main building.
Facilities 2 lounges, bar lounge, restaurant; private dining/conference room. 5-acre grounds with terrace, heated Victorian plunge pool, putting green. Golf, riding nearby.
Location ½ m S of A419 at Brimscombe; follow signs for Minchinhampton and *Burleigh Court.*
Restrictions No smoking in dining room. No dogs.
Credit cards All major cards accepted.
Terms [1991 rates] B&B £38–£64; dinner, B&B £54–£82. Set lunch £15.95 (bar lunches available Mon–Fri), dinner £22.95; on Sun set lunch £10.50, buffet supper from £10.95. Discounts for 3, 5, 7 nights and in quiet periods. 1-night bookings sometimes refused. Reduced rates for children sharing parents' room; special meals.
Service/tipping: "Tips not expected. There is, however, a box and money given is shared among the staff."

> If you have had recent experience of a good hotel that ought to be in the Guide, please write to us at once. Report forms are to be found at the back of the book. Procrastination is the thief of the next edition.

MITHIAN see ST AGNES — Map 1

Rose-in-Vale BUDGET

MORSTON Norfolk — Map 3

Morston Hall — *Tel* Cley (0263) 741041
Morston, Holt NR25 7AA — *Fax* (0263) 741034

Dennis and Jill Heaton's small hotel in Georgian house, quietly set in village 2 m W of Blakeney, in "delightful" wooded garden. Warmly recommended for friendly welcome, agreeable atmosphere and comfort. Attractive, thoughtfully equipped bedrooms. Good dinners, using fresh produce. Restaurant closed Thurs. 4 rooms, all with private facilities. Only restaurant suitable for ♿. No smoking in restaurant. Access, Amex, Visa accepted. Dinner, B&B £55–£70. Recent nomination. More reports please.

MOTCOMBE Dorset — Map 2

The Coppleridge — *Tel* Shaftesbury (0747) 51980
Motcombe — *Fax* (0747) 51858
Nr Shaftesbury SP7 9HW

Recently converted 18th-century farmhouse in 15 acres of meadow, woodland and gardens overlooking lovely Blackmore Vale, at N end of village 3 m NW of Shaftesbury. Lounge with flagstones and log fire; large and comfortable courtyard bedrooms. "Very good" à la carte meals in candle-lit restaurant; interesting bar meals. Guests offered membership of leisure centre in village; clay-pigeon shooting, riding, good walking nearby. 10 bedrooms, all with bath/shower. Access, Amex, Visa accepted. B&B double £45–£55. Full alc £19.95. New nomination. More reports please.

MOULSFORD-ON-THAMES Oxfordshire — Map 2

The Beetle and Wedge — *Tel* Cholsey (0491) 651381
Moulsford-on-Thames OX10 9JF — *Fax* (0491) 651376

"Delightful location, excellent food, friendly and helpful staff" begins one 1990 report on this old hotel on an attractive stretch of the Thames, with a riverside terrace. But many readers are critical and it is clear that during 1990/91 things went badly wrong, particularly at busy times and aggravated, no doubt, by the fact that the owners, Richard and Kate Smith, were dividing their time between the *Beetle and Wedge* and their other hotel, the *Royal Oak*, Yattendon. This has now been sold and they are devoting themselves fully to the Moulsford operation. They tell us that following criticisms in last year's Guide they have replaced old or damaged bedroom furniture and are improving standards of housekeeping, and the menu is now more balanced. "Our style of cooking does use lots of cream and butter," they write, "but some sauces contain no dairy products at all. We also attempt to give a good selection of grilled or poached items. And because our rooms are not quite what we hope they ultimately will be we compensate with good quality toiletries, coffees and teas, large towels. Our public rooms, too, have been redecorated." Such is the power of our readers, and we should be most grateful for up-to-date reports. Most critics of the accommodation have nevertheless enjoyed the à la carte meals which are served in the hotel restaurant and the *Boathouse*, though the latter includes a bar which can be crowded and noisy at times; there is meal service in the garden, too, in fine weather. Breakfasts are "first-rate", with fresh orange juice, fresh fruit, warm rolls and a choice of hot dishes.

Open All year except Christmas Day. Hotel restaurant closed Sun night. *Boathouse* open daily.
Rooms 10 double, 2 single – all with bath (6 also have shower), telephone, radio, TV, tea-making facilities, baby-listening. 4 in adjacent cottage. 2 on ground floor.
Facilities Lounge, 2 bars, 2 restaurants; private dining room; functions facilities on St John's College barge. ⅔-acre grounds on river with meal service, boating, fishing, overnight mooring.
Location On river, on edge of village 8 m NW of Reading.
Restrictions Not suitable for ♿. Dogs by arrangement, not in restaurant.
Credit cards All major cards accepted.
Terms B&B: single from £65, double from £75. Bar meals. Set Sun lunch £19.75; full alc in restaurant £30, in *Boathouse* £20. Champagne weekends; cooking tutorials. Reduced rates for children sharing parents' room; special meals on request.
Service/tipping: "No service charge. We leave tips to guests' discretion. They are distributed evenly among staff after deducting tax."

MULLION Cornwall — Map 1

Polurrian Hotel — *Tel* Mullion (0326) 240421
Mullion TR12 7EN — *Fax* (0326) 240083

"The warmth of the welcome, the care with which the chambermaid looks after our room, the smiles on the faces of all the staff – these are the features that make the *Polurrian* so special to us," write faithful regular visitors. One of the hotel's greatest assets is the way it caters for families, ensuring that a good time is had by parents and their children – from the very young to teenagers – in a "happy and informal" atmosphere; it has many facilities, both indoors and out (see below), for their entertainment. And it enjoys a "magnificent" position on cliffs on the Lizard peninsula, overlooking Polurrian cove. The National Trust owns most of the surrounding land and there are marvellous walks in both directions; even in August it is relatively quiet. Bedrooms are mostly furnished quite simply but they are comfortable. During the day the communal rooms are welcoming to all ages; high tea is served in the small dining room between 5.30 and 6.30 pm, and there is a daily choice of fresh foods as well as the ubiquitous hamburgers and sausages. In the evening things become formal: guests dress for dinner, "ties for the men, elegance for the women, gentle lighting". (*Gwen and Peter Andrews*) But even the most fervent admirers concede that the food (apart from "very good breakfasts") is not the hotel's strong point, being "too bland, especially when the head chef is away". One visitor this year was also troubled by a noisy cistern in a top-floor bedroom and found the staff "sometimes complacent" and the carpark inadequate. The *Polurrian*'s owner, Robert Francis, also owns the only hotel permitted on St Martin's in the Scillies (q.v.); he divides his time between the two. Special breaks on offer include bridge,

"Murder, mystery and mayhem", and snooker.

Open Mar–Nov.
Rooms 4 suites, 33 double, 3 single – all with bath, shower, telephone, radio, TV, baby-listening, 24-hour room service. Some ground-floor rooms; also self-catering apartments and bungalows.
Facilities 4 lounges (1 no-smoking), 4 bars, 2 restaurants; toddlers' playroom, laundry facilities. 12-acre grounds with outdoor swimming pool, tennis, croquet, toddlers' playground; Indoor Leisure Club with swimming pool, squash, sauna, solarium, snooker room, teenage centre with electronic games, etc (small charges made for some facilities). Beach at cliff bottom. Windsurfing, golf nearby.
Location ¼ m from Mullion village; go towards harbour, pass cricket field on left; turn for hotel is on right.
Restriction No dogs in public rooms; must be on lead in grounds (£4 a day plus £1 for meals).
Credit cards All major cards accepted.
Terms B&B £43–£78; dinner, B&B £50–£100. Set lunch £9.75, dinner £17. Special interest and activity breaks. Children under 6 free of charge in parents' room.
Service/tipping: "Service included; tips at guests' discretion."

MUNGRISDALE Cumbria — Map 4

The Mill Hotel — *Tel* Threlkeld (076 87) 79659
Mungrisdale, Penrith CA11 0XR

"Again, your description was spot on. The whole *Mill* experience makes many wish to return." "Richard Quinlan, because of his interest in his guests, catalyses communication between them so that after-dinner conversations provide an enjoyment one seldom encounters in a hotel. If anything, the *Mill* is even better than when we last stayed a year ago." "Warm, comfortable, well equipped. Location delightful." (*PE Carter, J Mandelstam, J Peck; also Elizabeth Sandham*)

Mungrisdale is only a dozen miles from the Penrith exit of the M6, but well away from the tourist pack, at the foot of the fells. *The Mill*, a simple but civilised cottage dating from the 17th century, has been owned and run by Richard and Eleanor Quinlan for the last nine years. It has a lovely setting with a millrace, waterfall and trout stream, and offers attractive accommodation, friendly service, and straightforward cooking using fresh local produce; bread is baked daily. Dinner is a set menu with some choice, served at 7 pm; there is a small, carefully selected wine list. Many guests are regulars. The furnishings are not lush; the style suits the surroundings and atmosphere. This is not a hotel for misanthropes; public rooms are small, and can be crowded at busy times. One niggle: "The food was served a bit fast."

Note: Not to be confused with a nearby pub with rooms, the *Mill Inn* at Mungrisdale.

Open Feb–Nov.
Rooms 9 double – 5 with bath and/or shower, all with TV, tea-making facilities; radio on request.
Facilities 3 lounges, dining room; games room; drying room. 2-acre grounds with millrace, waterfall and trout stream. Ullswater 5 m with fishing, sailing etc; hang-gliding, golf nearby.
Location 2 m N of A66. Leave M6 at Penrith (exit 40); turn off midway between Penrith and Keswick.
Restrictions Not suitable for ♿. No smoking in restaurant. Dogs at owners' discretion, not in public rooms.
Credit cards None accepted.

Terms B&B: single £30.50–£39, double £50–£69; dinner, B&B: single £41–£50, double £71–£90. Set dinner £17. Weekly rates. Reduced rates for children sharing parents' room; special meals.
Service/tipping: "No service charge. Tipping not required or expected."

NETTLETON Wiltshire — Map 2

Fosse Farmhouse — *Tel* (0249) 782286
Nettleton Shrub, Nettleton
Nr Chippenham SN14 7NJ

Standing alone in the middle of fields on the Roman Fosse Way, a short walk from Castle Combe, this old farmhouse, new to the Guide, has been imaginatively restored and decorated by Caron Cooper. She runs it with her mother June, who used to have an antique shop in London. Public rooms have flagged floors, a large black polished wood-burning stove, Victoriana, French antiques, and decorative items, many of which are for sale. Bedrooms are extremely pretty, with brass, chintz and lace, and bathrooms to match; some, with a small shower room, are in adjacent converted stables. There's a strong French accent about the food (three courses, with set main course) as well as the decor, though English breakfast is included in the rates and cream teas are a speciality; vegetarians are catered for. The enterprising Ms Cooper took the opportunity of the quiet spell during the Gulf War to visit Japan to woo the travel market, and as a result Japanese honeymooners now come to occupy the four-poster honeymoon suite, which also can be used as family accommodation. More reports please.

Open All year.
Rooms 1 honeymoon or family suite, 4 double, 1 single – 2 with bath and shower, 4 with shower, all with TV, tea-making facilities, baby-listening. 3 in converted stables.
Facilities Drawing room, dining room, tea shop/breakfast room; antique shop. 1½-acre orchard and lawn.
Location Just S of M4 between exits 17 and 18. From B4039, at village called The Gib, turn left opposite *Salutation Inn*. The farmhouse is 1st on right after approx 1 m.
Restrictions Only restaurant suitable for ♿. No dogs in public rooms.
Credit cards Access, Amex, Visa.
Terms B&B £30–£48.50; dinner, B&B £48–£66. Set lunch £15.50, dinner £18–£20. Christmas and New Year breaks. Reduced rates and special meals for children.
Service/tipping: "Service at guests' discretion."

NEW MILTON Hampshire — Map 2

Chewton Glen — *Tel* Highcliffe (0425) 275341
New Milton BH25 6QS — *Fax* (0425) 272310

Once the home of the writer, Captain Marryat, author of *The Children of the New Forest*, and now a sumptuous country hotel – one of the most expensive in Britain – with an international clientele, *Chewton Glen* celebrates its 25th anniversary this year. It is on the southern fringe of the New Forest, and is run by Martin Skan, named Hotelier of the Year by *Caterer and Hotelkeeper*, with an unusually large staff, some of whom have been with him for years. Decor is luxurious, with antiques and fine fabrics as well as modern comforts. The hotel has huge grounds with gardens, walking and jogging trails, a nine-hole golf course, swimming pool, tennis and croquet. A health club with indoor tennis courts, swimming pool, saunas, gymnasium and hairdressing salon opened at the end of 1990. Food, "modern French", under Pierre Chevillard, has earned the restaurant a *Michelin* rosette. There is a vegetarian menu.

"Faultless. Superb bargain break with the most welcoming service and excellent food," writes one 1990 visitor. "The pièce de résistance," says another, "is the charming sommelier who guides one through the wine album with understanding and care." "The best hotel of more than twenty-five rooms outside London," adds a third. (*Dr CS Shaw, JS Rutter, and others*) Other comments in this anniversary year are, sadly, less euphoric and include criticisms of slow service in the restaurant, and bills much higher than expected due to the number of extras. More reports please.

Open All year.
Rooms 13 suites, 49 double – all with bath, shower, telephone, radio, TV. 6 on ground floor. 1 suite in coach house, some suites in cottage in grounds.
Facilities Lounge, sun lounge, tearoom, bar, restaurant, 5 conference/banqueting rooms; pianist in lounge most evenings, snooker room; health club with indoor tennis courts, swimming pool, gymnasium, hairdressing salon. 70-acre grounds with lake, tennis, croquet lawn, putting, jogging course, heated swimming pool, helipad. 2–3 m walk through grounds to shingle beach; fishing, riding, sailing, golf nearby; chauffeur service.
Location Do not follow New Milton signs. From A35, take turning to Walkford and Highcliffe; go through Walkford, then left down Chewton Farm road. Entrance on right.
Restrictions Only restaurant suitable for ♿. No children under 7. No dogs; kennel facilities nearby.
Credit cards All major cards accepted.
Terms [1991 rates] Rooms (no single rate): double from £175, suite from £295. Breakfast: continental £9, English £14. Set lunch £22.50, dinner £40; full alc from £60. 2- and 5-night breaks; off-season rates; Christmas and Easter 4-day packages. 1-night bookings usually refused for Sat. Children's menu on request.
Service/tipping: "Our prices are fully inclusive; all our guests are made aware of this."

NEWLANDS Cumbria — Map 4

Swinside Lodge — *Tel* Keswick (076 87) 72948
Grange Road, Nr Newlands
Keswick CA12 5UE

This twin-fronted Victorian house, peacefully set at the foot of Catbells three miles from Keswick in an idyllically beautiful location, featured in the Guide under previous owners. It now returns, extensively refurbished and upgraded, and brought upmarket by "most obliging and very relaxed" Graham Taylor, formerly of another popular Guide hotel, *Breamish House*, Powburn (q.v.). "Excellent in every way. Every comfort in the bedrooms: fresh flowers, hair-drier, home-made biscuits, mineral water, etc, and they are tidied while you are at dinner." "Quiet, warm, clean and comfortable. Service sensitive and hospitable. High quality toiletries in the bathroom, lights good enough to read by in bedrooms and public rooms." "Breakfasts all one could ask for. No need for a packed lunch after such a meal! Dinners equally delicious, presented with care and forethought, never too much, but ample for all except perhaps the most hungry youthful types." (*Alan Taylor, TM Harvey, Patricia McCabe,*

Theo Schofield, and many others) The *Lodge* is unlicensed – bring your own wine; there are limited drying facilities for walkers' boots and clothes.

Open Feb–mid-Dec.
Rooms 9 double – 7 with bath and shower, 2 with shower, all with radio, TV, tea-making facilities.
Facilities 2 sitting rooms, dining room. ⅔-acre garden. Derwentwater 5 mins' walk with shingle beach and safe bathing.
Location 3 m SW of Keswick. Take A66 for Cockermouth; turn left at Portinscale; follow road to Grange.
Restrictions Not suitable for ♿. Smoking forbidden in dining room, discouraged in bedrooms. No children under 12. No dogs.
Credit cards None accepted.
Terms B&B: single £35–£42, double £54–£63; dinner, B&B: single £53–£60, double £90–£99. Packed lunches on request, set dinner £18. Reductions for longer stays; off-season mini-breaks.
Service/tipping: "No service charge. Tipping at guests' discretion."

NORTH HUISH Devon — Map 1

Brookdale House
North Huish
South Brent TQ10 9NR

Tel Gara Bridge (054 882) 402 and 415

"Very good value; fine food, well prepared, presented and served; outstanding hospitality. The proprietor was always unobtrusively there when needed. An excellent host." "Food astonishingly reliable, consistent and excellent. Charles Trevor-Roper is much more relaxed, and the atmosphere all the better for that. The gardens continue to improve." (*Harold J Johnson Jr, Richard Creed; also DA O'Brien*)

Charles and Carol Trevor-Roper's Victorian Gothic rectory, Grade II listed with fine moulded ceilings and marble fireplaces, stands at the head of a wooded valley in a secluded situation, in large wooded grounds with a waterfall, "a marvellous end to a gentle stroll". It is not far from the Plymouth–Exeter road (A38). There is plenty to do in the area – good walking, golf, riding and fishing. The bedrooms, sympathetically converted, vary considerably, and are priced according to size and position. The best are "large, well proportioned, thoughtfully equipped, with *en suite* bathroom positively stuffed with goodies"; the less good ones are considerably cheaper. The dining room, "repro-Regency with extravagant displays of real and artificial flowers", is in the hands of Terry Rich whose cooking, light in style, makes much use of local ingredients, many of them additive-free or organically produced; there's plenty of choice on the frequently changing set-price dinner menu. The rates include a generous English breakfast (served in the dining room). Mr Trevor-Roper writes: "We offer a friendly yet professional service. We do have some quirks – creaky floorboards, antiquated plumbing and a slightly faded decor – but the lack of glossy-magazine perfection helps our guests to relax."

Open All year except 3 weeks in Jan.
Rooms 8 double – all with bath, shower, telephone, radio, TV, tea-making facilities. 2 (cheaper) in cottage 25 yds from main building.
Facilities Lounge, bar, dining room. 4½-acre grounds with garden, stream, waterfall. Dartmoor 10 mins' drive, beaches 15 mins.
Location 7 m SW of Totnes. Off A38 take Avonwick, South Brent exit. In Avonwick turn right opposite *Avon Inn*, then first left to North Huish. Go up lane

to top of hill, turn right, signposted *Brookdale House*; at bottom of hill turn right, hotel is first on left.
Restrictions Not suitable for ♿. No smoking in dining room. No children under 10. No dogs.
Credit cards Access, Visa.
Terms [1991 rates] B&B: single £60–£90, double £75–£110; dinner, B&B £65–£117.50 per person. Set dinner £27.50. Bar lunches. Christmas, New Year, autumn and winter breaks. 1-night bookings sometimes refused at busy weekends.
Service/tipping: "No service charge added to bills, but if tips are offered they are not refused. We assume our customers are intelligent enough to decide whether to leave tips for staff. If they have made this decision it would be churlish to refuse."

OAKHAM Leicestershire — Map 4

The Whipper-In
Market Place
Oakham LE15 6DT
Tel Oakham (0572) 756971
Fax (0572) 757759

17th-century hotel in market square of former county seat of Rutland – fine hunt country; Rutland Water 2 m. "Very pleasing" decor, with antiques, old prints and pictures, log fires, but with some signs of wear especially in bar and bedrooms. Good English cooking, with emphasis on game and fish, in beamed dining room, "but service overstretched at breakfast". Courtyard and garden. Recommended with reservations, e.g. "no host figure". Closed 27–29 Dec. 24 rooms, all with bath/shower. Not suitable for ♿. All major credit cards accepted. 1991 rates: B&B double from £70. Set lunch £7.95–£10.95, dinner £18.95; full alc £29. New nomination. More reports please.

OTLEY Suffolk — Map 3

Otley House BUDGET
Otley, Ipswich IP6 9NR
Tel Helmingham (0473) 890253

"Superb value. Friendly, caring service. Food varied, tasteful and served beautifully." "Excellent in every way. Fine house, beautifully furnished with antiques. Large comfortable bedroom." "The croquet lawn is one of the best, and has the narrow hoops used by serious players of whom Mr Hilton is one. He is keen to give guests tips to improve their game." (*BA Orman, MW Atkinson, JP McCraken and E Goodison*) *Otley House*, owned and run by Mike Hilton and his Danish wife Lise, belongs to the Wolsey Lodge group of guest-taking private houses. It is a "fine, plain, square country house" in rural Suffolk, Grade II listed, with a Grade I staircase, in three acres of mature peaceful grounds with a small lake. Tea is served in the billiard room – there is an "excellent" billiard table – and guests gather for coffee and conversation in a Regency drawing room after dinner. The four-course dinners, taken communally with silver and crystal on the tables, are "delicious, varied, and well presented and served". There is no choice of menu; the owners like to be warned in advance of special diets or preferences; and Mrs Hilton is delighted to cook Scandinavian dishes for those who ask. The large light bedrooms, furnished with antiques, are "comfortable and sparkling clean with small extras such as pot-pourri, tissues, and a hair-drier".

Open 1 Mar–31 Oct. Dining room closed for lunch and on Sun except Easter and bank holidays.
Rooms 4 double – all with bath (3 also with shower), radio; 3 with TV; portable telephone available.
Facilities Hall, drawing room, TV/billiard room, dining room; tea terrace. 3-acre grounds with small lake, croquet. Golf, fishing, riding nearby.
Location In Otley village, 7 miles N of Ipswich, on B1079; opposite small road to Swilland.
Restrictions Not suitable for ♿. Smoking in billiard room only. No children under 12. No dogs.
Credit cards None accepted.
Terms B&B: single £32–£36, double £40–£48. Set dinner £14.50; vegetarian meals by arrangement. 1-night bookings sometimes refused for Sat.
Service/tipping: "Service included; any tips are given to the staff to share."

OXFORD Oxfordshire — Map 2

Bath Place Hotel
4 and 5 Bath Place
Oxford OX1 3SU
Tel Oxford (0865) 791812
Fax (0865) 791834

Restaurant-with-rooms, owned by Fawsitt family; tasteful renovation of group of 17th-century cottages with small rooms, narrow staircases, sloping floors, exposed beams and lots of character, in cobbled mews off Holywell Street. No vehicle access, some parking places (reserve in advance) quite close by. Though in historic centre, it's quiet at night. Inspectors in 1990 liked the decor and some of the cooking – "good ingredients, main course of Michelin *rosette standard"; others have found the portions as well as the style rather too* nouvelle. *"Service pleasant but amateurish, and prices high for what is offered." 10 double rooms, 6 with bath, 4 with shower. No dogs. All major credit cards accepted. 1991 rates: B&B: single £70–£85, double £84–£100. Set lunch £12.95, residents' dinner £19.50; full alc £26. More reports please.*

Cotswold House BUDGET
363 Banbury Road
Oxford OX2 7PL
Tel Oxford (0865) 310558

Jim and Anne O'Kane's no-smoking B&B in North Oxford continues to win favour: "Fully endorse the entry. The house was immaculate, my bedroom well equipped, the proprietors friendly and flexible. Good breakfast served promptly." "Choice of duvet or blankets. Nothing packaged at breakfast. Would there were something similar in Cambridge." "Bedroom warm and well lit; adequate in size, with excellent shower room. Thoughtful touches such as wine glasses, electric kettle, refrigerator. The owners are delightful and most welcoming." (*David AT Christy, Jean Carolin, PM Spence*)

Cotswold House has a small garden. It is two miles from the city centre; frequent buses stop almost at the door. Breakfast is traditional or vegetarian; there are plenty of pubs and restaurants nearby.

Open All year except Christmas.
Rooms 5 double, 1 single – all with shower, radio, TV, tea-making facilities.
Facilities Small lounge, dining room. Small garden.
Location Just off ring road on Oxford side of A423. Parking.
Restrictions Not suitable for ♿. No smoking. No children under 6. No dogs.
Credit cards None accepted.

Terms [1991 rates] B&B: single £30–£32, double £46–£52. Reduced rates for children sharing parents' room. (No restaurant.)

Old Parsonage
1 Banbury Road
Oxford OX2 6NN

Tel Oxford (0865) 310201
Fax (0865) 311262

Perfectly placed for University sightseeing at N end of St Giles, venerable creeper-clad 17th-century parsonage, once Oscar Wilde's residence, now resurrected after extensive renovations as sophisticated hotel – opened May 1991. No restaurant but Parsonage Bar serves light meals all day. Garden, roof terrace. First reports highly promising. If expectations fulfilled, will become Oxford's long-needed premier hotel for independent travellers. Closed Christmas. 30 rooms, all with bath, shower. Access, Amex, Visa accepted. B&B: single £95–£170, double £110–£150, suite £185–£220. Full alc £22. More reports eagerly awaited.

PADSTOW Cornwall — Map 1

Seafood Restaurant
Riverside, Padstow PL28 8BY

Tel Padstow (0841) 532485
Fax (0841) 533344

Rick and Jill Stein's popular restaurant-with-rooms with ringside views of Padstow and its harbour may lack public lounges and grounds but, as readers have said in the past, it "captures the best things of France and puts them into a lovely English setting". There are ten bedrooms, priced according to what they offer. Most are spacious – particularly room 4 which has a sitting room with a sofa bed and a view over the garden towards the estuary; 5 and 6 have a balcony and a view of Padstow. They are well equipped and simply decorated in light colours, with "pieces of old furniture and nice prints". Booking a room automatically entitles guests to a table at 7.30 or 9.30 pm in the busy restaurant, with similar decor: wicker chairs, plants, prints on white walls. "The food is superb. Staff are delightfully informal, but charming and attentive in their own way." The room price includes breakfast, either continental, with fresh orange juice and home-made croissants, or full English. The *Seafood* was omitted from the Guide last year because readers, while appreciating its restaurant, were critical of the accommodation. The Steins have responded by making many improvements – adding *en suite* facilities to the two smallest rooms and air-conditioning to one which tended to get hot, sound-proofing extractor fans, and: "We hope we have persuaded the council not to collect the rubbish before 8.30 am." A reader this year points out that if you stay more than a day or two you must be prepared for the fact that usually only one item out of three on the set menu changes each day. Another regrets the absence of a smoking ban in any part of the restaurant. More reports please.

Open Feb–16 Dec. Closed for lunch, on Sun night, and 1 May.
Rooms 10 double – all with bath, shower, telephone, radio, TV, tea-making facilities, mini-bar, baby-listening.
Facilities Restaurant. Bathing beaches ¼ m.
Location Central, overlooking harbour. Carpark.
Restrictions Not suitable for ♿. No dogs in public rooms.
Credit cards Access, Visa.

Terms B&B: single £31–£80, double £55–£105. Set dinner £26; full alc £38. 2-day break in low season. Reduced rates for children sharing parents' room.
Service/tipping: "Following a visit to France where service is compulsorily included in the price we feel we should follow suit. The problem is that to compensate staff for no longer receiving tips we would have to increase prices by about 10%. If inflation drops to below 5% we will do it."

PENCRAIG Hereford and Worcester — Map 2

Pencraig Court BUDGET — *Tel* Ross-on-Wye (098 984) 306
Pencraig
Nr Ross-on-Wye HR9 6HR

"The most important thing about this modest, inexpensive hotel," writes a late-1990 visitor, "is the friendliness of Mr and Mrs Sykes and their pleasant and cheerful staff. They were generous with those things necessary for a holiday – a good supply of light reading material, local guides and maps. The dinner menu is unambitious, but the English traditional breakfast was magnificent of its kind." *Pencraig* has been owned and run by the Sykes for nearly 20 years. It is an unassuming Georgian country house, comfortably modernised, overlooking the Wye just downstream from Ross, but front rooms get A40 traffic noise; those at the back overlooking the pleasant sloping garden with fine copper beeches are quiet. Rooms vary in size from "spacious and comfortable with a double and a single bed, sofa and two armchairs, more than adequate hanging and drawer space", to a small attic; they have well-appointed bathrooms. Decor is old-fashioned. (*Dr DH Clark, also G Roberts*) As in the past, however, some visitors have been critical of the food.

Open Apr–Oct inclusive.
Rooms 2 family, 7 double, 2 single – all with bath, TV, tea-making facilities.
Facilities 2 lounges, bar, restaurant. 4-acre grounds.
Location 3 m SW of Ross-on-Wye, on the A40. Garden-facing rooms quietest.
Restrictions Not suitable for ♿. No dogs.
Credit cards All major cards accepted.
Terms B&B: single £34–£41, double £46–£60; dinner, B&B: single £46–£53, double £70–£84. Bar lunches. Set dinner £13. Spring breaks. Reduced rates and special meals for children.
Service/tipping: "Our prices include tax and service. Gratuities not expected by our staff."

PENZANCE Cornwall — Map 1

The Abbey — *Tel* Penzance (0736) 66906
Abbey Street
Penzance TR18 4AR

César award in 1985: Utterly acceptable mild eccentricity

"Romantic" is the word for the Coxes' stylish but informally run 17th-century house in one of the narrow streets that run down from the centre of Penzance towards the harbour. There are magnificent views across Penzance Bay from the front; rear rooms look out over an attractive walled garden. It is eclectically decorated with flowers, magazines, books, curios, oriental rugs, paintings and photographs. There are open fires in the public rooms. Bedrooms, some large, are equally pretty and individual; some have a gas fire, one a pine bathroom with free-standing bath, but there is also "a shower and loo in a built-in wardrobe – a bit small for comfort".

"*Not* for everyone. It has an indefinable something – atmosphere, style, call it what you will," wrote a visitor last year. "I doubt that anyone would have mixed feelings; you fall in love with it, or it leaves you cold." English breakfast is "beautifully prepared, with good marmalade, crunchy toast, large dollops of butter unencumbered by wrappings". Dinners get a more mixed press: those in favour praise "the good meat and fish, fresh vegetables, fresh herbs on nearly everything, and not fussily *nouvelle*"; others are less enthusiastic. The hosts are laid-back, sometimes to a fault. And there's a niggle we have heard before: "Not sparkling clean."

Open All year.
Rooms 1 2-bedroomed suite in adjoining building, 6 double – 1 with bath and shower, 3 with bath, 3 with shower, all with TV, tea-making facilities, baby-listening.
Facilities Drawing room, dining room. Small walled garden.
Location Take road for seafront; after 300 yds, just before bridge, turn right, after 10 yds turn left. Hotel is at top of slipway. Courtyard parking for 6 cars.
Restrictions Not suitable for ♿. No children under 5. Small dogs allowed, not in public rooms.
Credit cards Access, Visa.
Terms [1991 rates] B&B: single £50–£65, double £70–£95, suite £105–£140. Set dinner £21.50; full alc £22.50. Winter breaks Nov–Mar; 3-day Christmas package. 1-night bookings sometimes refused over bank holidays. Reduced rates for children sharing parents' room; special meals.
Service/tipping: "No service charge. Tipping left to customers; there is no pressure. Anything given distributed to all staff."

POOL-IN-WHARFEDALE West Yorkshire — Map 4

Pool Court
Pool-in-Wharfedale
Otley LS21 1EH

Tel Leeds (0532) 842288
Fax (0532) 843115

Michael Gill's restaurant-with-rooms is a fine Georgian mansion with a "splendid interior, attractively decorated throughout". It is not in a particularly attractive setting (new houses and a busy trunk road impinge) but this does not deter visitors who enjoy its "excellent French food", cooked by David Watson, which has earned a *Michelin* red "M" (for cooking almost up to rosette standard), served in the elegant soft grey dining room, "sparkling with candle-light and beautiful crystal". On the main menu four-course meals are priced according to the main dish; some items are labelled "HE" for "healthy eating"; vegetarians are catered for; there is also a no-choice three-course dinner menu at £10 [1991]. There are no public rooms apart from the bar and the lounge that is used by diners in the evening; both are crowded at times. The six bedrooms are comfortable with masses of extras – fresh flowers, a fridge with wines and soft drinks, a tray with fruit, dates, raisins and nuts, books, even a little safe behind a picture on the wall; beds are turned down at night. Staff are "courteous, efficient and friendly". The continental breakfasts are "generous and delicious". Responding to last year's niggle, Michael Gill writes: "I know I am biased but I can't accept that the computerised push-button door entry is 'silly'. It cuts out many problems, such as the wife having the key while still in Harrogate and the husband therefore locked out of the room."

Open All year except 24 Dec–9 Jan, 2 weeks July/Aug. Closed Sun and Mon. Lunch served only to pre-arranged parties of 10 or more.
Rooms 5 double, 1 single – all with shower (5 also have bath), telephone, radio/alarm, TV, bar, fridge, wall-safe, double-glazing; baby-listening.
Facilities Bar, coffee lounge, 2 restaurants. ½-acre grounds.
Location 3 m N of Leeds airport on A658. Equidistant (9 m) from Leeds, Bradford and Harrogate.
Restrictions Not really suitable for ♿. No dogs; kennel facilities available.
Credit cards All major cards accepted.
Terms B&B [1991 rates]: single from £70, double £95–£120. Set dinner (3 courses, no choice) £10; main menu c. £29.50. Weekend rates. Cookery courses. 1-night bookings sometimes refused. Reduced rates and special meals for children by arrangement.
Service/tipping: "10% service charge for large private parties. Apart from that, tipping is entirely up to the guest. We don't ask for or expect it."

POOLE Dorset — Map 2

The Mansion House — *Tel* Poole (0202) 685666
Thames Street, Poole BH15 1JN — *Fax* (0202) 665709

A "really good" hotel in a handsome Georgian townhouse in a quiet cul-de-sac near the old parish church and Poole's bustling quay. It has a grand sweeping staircase leading up from the hall to a comfortable and stylish residents' lounge and well-equipped bedrooms with many extras – books, magazines, sherry and so on. A returning visitor recently enjoyed hers which was "big, beautifully furnished, with not too many gadgets so there was room for my things". The panelled restaurant is also a fashionable dining club, with lower prices for members (hotel residents are automatically made temporary members); chef Tony Parsons offers a long, traditional menu and also serves "unusually good" vegetarian dinners. Meals are also served in the less formal grill bar "at little tables with pretty lamps"; and there is a limited room service for meals. (*Mrs MD Prodgers*) More reports please.

Open All year.
Rooms 1 suite, 19 double, 8 single – all with bath, shower, telephone, radio, TV, baby-listening; tea-making facilities on request.
Facilities Lounge, bar, breakfast room, restaurant, grill bar; private dining room. Poole Quay 100 yds; fishing, boating, sailing.
Location Follow signs for Poole Quay. Thames St is off quay, between Fisheries Office and Maritime Museum – signposted to the parish church. 2 private carparks either side of hotel.
Restrictions Not suitable for ♿. No dogs.
Credit cards All major cards accepted.
Terms B&B: single £70–£78, double £104–£110, suite £150–£160; dinner, B&B £67–£93 per person. Full alc £25. Weekend rates. Special meals for children.
Service/tipping: "Service included; tips at customers' discretion."

****

Traveller's tale *It was before dinner that we met our host and concluded we wouldn't buy a used car from him. His hospitality and generally bonhomie were just too overpowering.*

****

PORT GAVERNE Cornwall — Map 1

Port Gaverne Hotel
Port Gaverne
Nr Port Isaac PL29 3SQ

Tel Bodmin (0208) 880244
Fax (0208) 880151

This unpretentious, reasonably priced 17th-century coastal inn enjoys a splendid position in a sheltered cove in an isolated village not far from Port Isaac. Just a small road separates it from a safe bay with sand, shingle and rock; there are good walks along the coast. Three rooms are in an annexe up a steep hill, and there are seven double-bedroomed cottages which can be let as suites or on a self-catering basis. It has been run by Frederick Ross and his wife for over twenty years and "manages to combine the atmosphere of an ancient inn with that of a comfortable small hotel". It is welcoming to families, many of whom have been visiting it for years. Most visitors praise it for the "courteous reception, friendly and prompt service at all times", and the well-appointed bedrooms (even the singles) with "comfortable beds, plenty of hanging space and an air of generosity – boiling hot water at all times, and lots of extras in the bathroom". This year there is praise for the food: "Very good dinners, including lobster, crab and fresh local fish." "Excellent, generous English breakfast, with fresh orange juice and home-made marmalade." It is popular with locals as well as residents at lunchtime. "Don't expect five-star facilities," we have said in the past, and one reader this year reports a lack of comfortable chairs in residents' lounge and bedroom, "and they hurry you in to dinner"; and two couples, despite booking well in advance, found themselves in "hot and noisy" rooms above the kitchen.

Open All year except 11 Jan–22 Feb.
Rooms 16 double, 3 single – 13 with bath and shower, 6 with bath, all with telephone, radio, TV, baby-listening. 3 in annexe, 15 in 7 cottages let as suites or on a self-catering basis.
Facilities Residents' lounge, TV lounge, 3 bars, dining room. Cottages have a courtyard, annexe has a garden.
Location Take B3314 from Delabole or Wadebridge, then B3267.
Restrictions Not suitable for ♿. Children under 7 who dine with parents served at 7 pm only. No smoking or dogs in dining room.
Credit cards All major cards accepted.
Terms B&B £40–£44; dinner, B&B (min 2 nights) £56.50–£60.50. Snack lunches, bar suppers; alc dinner £19.75. Weekly rates; golfing, honeymoon, Cornish Heritage, Christmas and New Year packages. Reduced rates and special meals for children.
Service/tipping: "Gratuities at guests' discretion, invested in a building society interest-bearing account and distributed to staff at Christmas and Easter."

PORTLOE Cornwall — Map 1

The Lugger Hotel
Portloe TR2 5RD

Tel Truro (0872) 501322
Fax (0872) 501691

Seaside hotel in fishing village on S Cornish coast not far from Truro. Run for three generations by the Powell family; recently totally refurbished. Recommended for lovely setting on water's edge and good food – traditional English, including very fresh fish; vegetarians catered for; smooth and efficient service. Open 7 Feb–7 Dec. 19 rooms (most spacious ones in annexe), all with bath and/or shower. Not suitable for ♿. No children under 12. No dogs. Dinner, B&B £40–£60. Set lunch £10.50, dinner £17.50. Re-nominated last year; entry endorsed but more reports please.

POSTBRIDGE Devon **Map 1**

Lydgate House BUDGET *Tel* Tavistock (0822) 88209
Postbridge
Yelverton PL20 6TJ

Hilary Townsend and Judy Gordon-Jones's "delightful" small hotel is in lovely and peaceful setting ¼ m off B3212 in centre of Dartmoor; river Dart, with bathing and fishing, runs through its 37-acre grounds. Recommended for clean, bright, welcoming but not effusive atmosphere. Food, with very limited choice, "good, simple but unusual", using local produce and home-reared meat; vegetarian dishes offered. Open early Mar–3 Jan. 8 rooms, 4 with bath, 2 with shower. No smoking in dining room. Access, Visa accepted. B&B £24. Set dinner £11.50. Re-entered Guide last year; entry endorsed this year but we'd like more reports.

POUGHILL Cornwall **Map 1**

Reeds *Tel* Bude (0288) 352841
Poughill, Bude EX23 9ELL

César award in 1990: Most cosseting guest house

"Our annual visit; everything still of the same high standard. Margaret Jackson bounds out within minutes of your tyres scrunching on the drive and gives the impression that your arrival is the event of her week, and your large suitcase is snatched by this frail enthusiast and whisked up the stairs ahead of you." "Comfort and peace are total. Mrs Jackson produced a delightful and original meal on each of the four nights." "Breakfast just as good as the rest of the cooking. Mrs Jackson remembers your likes and dislikes, and you know she has tried your room out to make sure that everything works." "One of the delights was afternoon tea on the veranda on a warm day, just this side of sleep as the bees, grasshoppers and buzzards made their presence known." As ever, praise from regulars and first-time visitors to this turn-of-the-century house quietly situated in a large garden in a little village (its name is pronounced poffil) close to the dramatic north Cornish coast. The National Trust owns much of the coastline and there are many fine walks in the area. The house is large, attractive and spotless. Bedrooms are spacious and restful, decorated in soft pastel colours, well equipped. Dinner at 8 pm is in private-household dinner-party style, with elegant linen, silver and candles. There are no choices, but your culinary preferences are discussed on booking and each morning. (*Jean Willson, T and H Mellor, Padi Howard, J Rochelle; also David N Ing, and others*) One correspondent feels it is quite expensive for what is on offer, but there are no hidden extras; coffee or tea is available at any time for no charge; and an inexpensive snack lunch of cheese and fruit is provided on request.

Open All year Fri pm–Tues am. Closed Christmas.
Rooms 3 double – all with bath, shower, tea-making facilities; radio on request.

Facilities Drawing room, hall with bar facilities, TV room. 4-acre grounds. Sea 1 m – sandy beaches and coastal walks. Fishing, golf nearby.
Location Take Poughill Road from Bude. Turn left at Post Office towards Northcott Mount. *Reeds* is about 400 yds on left.
Restrictions Not suitable for ♿. No smoking in dining room; smoking not encouraged in bedrooms. No children under 16. No pets.
Credit cards None accepted.
Terms B&B single £37.50, double £65. Light lunch (cheese and fruit) on request £3. Set dinner £19.50.
Service/tipping: "Service included. I am not in favour of tipping."

POWBURN Northumberland — Map 4

Breamish House — *Tel* Powburn (066 578) 266
Powburn, Alnwick NE66 4LL — *Fax* (066 578) 500

This unpretentious Georgian-style house, "furnished like a home, not a hotel", in a peaceful setting up a winding drive at the foot of the Cheviot hills, returned to the Guide last year under new owners, Alan and Doreen Johnson, and readers have been quick to endorse the entry: "A small hotel with a thoughtful and cheerful staff; just what we wanted on our journey to Scotland. We arrived on a stormy evening and were given a heart-warming welcome: we were immediately offered a cup of tea – just what we wanted – though it was after 6 pm. We had a very comfortable country-house-style bedroom and a carefully cooked five-course meal. It was like staying with well-heeled friends." Other visitors extol the "comforting and relaxing" atmosphere; the "pristine" bedrooms (all named after trees), with fruit, home-made shortbread, a pack of cards, bottled water, etc; the well-maintained gardens, and the breakfasts "which would meet the requirements of the hungriest and thirstiest person". (*Pam Rose, Mrs VM Williamson, Mr and Mrs BG Rose, Elizabeth Howey; also Mrs K Evans, Nancy Perkins Arata, and many others*) Not all bedrooms are large, however, and some visitors have disliked the muzak in the dining room.

Open Feb–Dec.
Rooms 10 double, 1 single – all with bath and/or shower, telephone, radio, TV, tea-making facilities, baby-listening. 1 over coach house.
Facilities 2 drawing rooms, dining room. 5½-acre grounds with woodland and stream.
Location In centre of village on A697, 22 m N of Morpeth.
Restrictions Only restaurant suitable for ♿. No smoking in dining room. Children under 12 by special arrangement only. Dogs by arrangement; not in public rooms.
Credit cards None accepted.
Terms [1991 rates] Dinner, B&B £47.50–£63. Special rates for long stays. Off-season breaks; Christmas package. Reduced rates and special meals for children.
Service/tipping: "We are against mandatory service charges. If guests insist on recognising exceptional service, tips are distributed among all staff according to hours worked."

****

Traveller's tale *An extraordinarily ugly calendar was hanging in the bathroom, issued by a manufacturing company of "Tube Manipulators" – and hung over the loo where gentlemen could read it. Could it have been a joke?*

****

PURTON Wiltshire — Map 2

The Pear Tree at Purton
Church End, Purton
Nr Swindon SN5 9ED

Tel Swindon (0793) 772100
Fax (0793) 772369

"A real find; difficult to commend it highly enough. Formerly an 'English Country Restaurant', now with a new wing with four bedrooms, the *Pear Tree* is a small, extremely comfortable, elegantly furnished and decorated hotel with an excellent restaurant in an attractive conservatory," write the nominators of the former rectory of the twin-towered parish church of St Mary's. "Francis and Anne Young have transformed the Cotswold stone building with impeccable taste and great skill. The large garden is by no means finished but has plenty of scope – and ample parking. Our room looked over the garden towards the unusual church and beautiful manor house. It had a welcoming decanter of sherry, bottled water, biscuits and a large bowl of peppermints. The *en suite* bathroom was ample, with every amenity including a jacuzzi. Afternoon tea was offered on arrival, at no charge. An imaginative gimmick: in the gents', the front page of the current *Financial Times* is pinned on a board above the urinals." (*Mr and Mrs RHW Bullock*) Cooking by Janet Pichel-Juan is "definitely English, while taking advantage of the best of traditional French methods". Each day there's a traditional pudding: Spotted Dick, jam roly-poly, bread and butter pudding, etc. Despite its quiet location the hotel is only four miles from the M4. Bedrooms are named after characters associated with the village. Jeans, shorts and portable telephones are prohibited in restaurant and lounges. More reports please.

Open All year except Christmas. Restaurant closed for lunch Sat.
Rooms 2 suites, 13 double, 3 single – all with bath, shower, telephone, radio, TV, baby-listening. Some on ground floor.
Facilities Ramps. Lounge, lounge bar, conservatory restaurant; functions facilities. 7½-acre grounds with croquet.
Location 5 m NW of Swindon. From M4 junction 16, follow signs to Purton; through village, turn right at Lloyds Bank.
Restriction No dogs in public rooms.
Credit cards All major cards accepted.
Terms B&B: single or double £87–£97, suite £114. Set lunch £16, dinner £25. Weekend breaks.
Service/tipping: "Our prices are fully inclusive. A tip is not expected, but if given is distributed among all staff."

RASKELF North Yorkshire — Map 4

Old Farmhouse BUDGET
Raskelf YO6 3LF

Tel Easingwold (0347) 21971

18th-century farmhouse off A19 NW of York, conveniently situated for touring in North Yorkshire. Run by the Frost family, and warmly recommended for comfortable bedrooms, with good storage space and modern bathrooms, and for particularly good home-cooking – 4-course dinners with plenty of choice; generous Yorkshire breakfasts. Emphasis on personal service rather than do-it-yourself. Open Feb–Dec. 10 double rooms, 6 with bath, 4 with shower. No credit cards accepted. Dinner, B&B £31.50–£41. Children under 2 free. Recent nomination, now endorsed but more reports welcome.

REDMILE Leicestershire Map 4

Peacock Farm BUDGET
Redmile, Nr Nottingham
NG13 0GQ

Tel Bottesford (0949) 42475

Nicki, Peter and Marjorie Need's informal and inexpensive guest house, with spacious bedrooms in converted outhouses; no longer a working farm, but still surrounded by farming activity and animals, and welcoming to families. 2½-acre grounds with small, unheated swimming pool, swings and seesaws; free use of bicycles. ½ m from village, near Belvoir Castle. Home-cooked meals in restaurant (old corn barn) decorated with agricultural memorabilia. 7 rooms, 1 with bath, 4 with shower. No smoking in dining room. Access, Amex accepted. Double room: B&B £32–£38.50; dinner, B&B £54–£67.50. Set lunch/dinner £11. New nomination. More reports please.

RICHMOND North Yorkshire Map 4

Howe Villa BUDGET
Whitcliffe Mill
Richmond DL10 4TJ

Tel Richmond (0748) 850055

César award in 1989: Perfection in the guest house division

"Our second visit to Anita Berry's lovely early 19th-century house with a beautiful garden; there will be many more. It is charmingly decorated, warm, comfortable and spotlessly clean, with flowers and plants everywhere. Bedrooms have all the oddments one could wish for. Cooking is superb and varied, and Anita serves it herself with speed and efficiency, and always with a smile and a brief chat. Breakfasts were excellent and generous. It would be hard to find a nicer small hotel with a more charming hostess." "In the entrance hall there's a wooden seat with several teddy bears, one of which wears an apron embroidered in small letters: 'Anita is tops'. That says it all." "You always meet charming, compatible people there – you have to fraternise, especially before dinner when you are given a drink on the house while you choose your starters and desserts." (*Moira Jarrett, NA Taplin, Eileen Broadbent, and many others*) Unanimous approval, as ever, for this reasonably priced Georgian house with only four bedrooms in a large garden, bounded by trees on one side and, on the other, a glorious stretch of the river Swale. The approach to *Howe Villa* is not particularly salubrious, but the house has large, elegantly proportioned rooms, and has been restored with taste and charm. Food is "English cooking at its very best, beautifully presented".

Open 1 Feb–1 Dec.
Rooms 4 double – all with bath and/or shower, radio, TV, tea-making facilities.
Facilities Drawing room, dining room. ½-acre garden on river Swale.
Location ½ m from centre of Richmond – take A6108 signposted Leyburn and Reeth; at the ATS tyre service station turn left, and keep left, following signs to *Howe Villa*.
Restrictions Not suitable for severely ♿. No smoking in restaurant and bedrooms. No children under 12. No dogs.
Credit cards None accepted.
Terms [1991 rates] Dinner, B&B double £84. Set dinner £18. Reductions for 2 days or more.

Service/tipping: "Guests like to say thank you, perhaps with a small gift. I accept, enjoying the pleasure it gives them, but do not like service charges."

ROSTHWAITE Cumbria — Map 4

Hazel Bank Hotel BUDGET
Rosthwaite
Nr Keswick CA12 5XB
Tel Borrowdale (076 87) 77248

Gwen and John Nuttall have carefully restored and modernised their 125-year-old house while preserving its Victorian atmosphere. It is quietly situated in large, beautifully landscaped grounds; each bedroom, attractively decorated and impeccably maintained, is named for the Fell it dramatically overlooks. The dining room is light and airy; dinner, cooked by John Nuttall and served at 7 pm, is wholesome and straightforward, with plenty of fresh vegetables; there's no choice except dessert. Visitors enjoy the friendly atmosphere: "Nothing is impersonal. When all are gathered for dinner, and in the bar and lounge afterwards, it is like a house party." The "friendly and helpful staff" are also praised. Prices are very reasonable. Many visitors to *Hazel Bank House* are returnees; it is often booked up months ahead. The Nuttalls cater for a large proportion of walkers, ramblers, etc; there is a drying room and packed lunches are provided. More reports please.

Open 21 Mar–1 Nov.
Rooms 8 double, 1 single – 3 with bath, 5 with shower, 4 with TV, all with tea-making facilities. 2 on ground floor.
Facilities Residents' lounge, bar lounge, dining room; drying room. 4-acre grounds. Derwent Water 4 m.
Location 7 m S of Keswick on B5289. Turn left up drive just before village.
Restrictions Not suitable for ♿. No smoking in dining room. No children under 6. Dogs by prior arrangement only (80p); not in public rooms.
Credit cards None accepted.
Terms Dinner, B&B £34–£36. Weekly rates. Reduced rates for children sharing parents' room. 1-night bookings refused if requested far in advance.
Service/tipping: "Tipping is not expected. If guests wish to show their appreciation the tips are distributed to all staff."

RUTLAND WATER Leicestershire — Map 4

Barnsdale Lodge
The Avenue, Rutland Water
Nr Oakham LE15 8AH
Tel Oakham (0572) 724678
Fax (0572) 724961

Recently restored 17th-century farmhouse 2 m from Oakham, overlooking Rutland Water. Edwardian style throughout from bedroom decor to frilly-white-aproned, black-dressed staff and traditional "Bill of Fare" in dining rooms – roast beef on a trolley always available. Good food also served less formally in buttery. Comfortable and friendly; aims to "combine the gracious living of yesteryear with standards of English service so often forgotten". 4-acre grounds. 17 rooms, all with bath/shower, some in converted barn. All major credit cards accepted. B&B: single £49.50, double £69.50. Light lunch from £3.95, dinner from £10; full alc £19. Enthusiastic new nomination. More reports please.

Don't trust out-of-date editions. Many hotels are dropped and new ones added every year.

RYE East Sussex **Map 3**

Jeake's House **BUDGET**
Mermaid Street
Rye TN31 7ET

Tel Rye (0797) 222828
Fax (0797) 222623

César award: Best budget B&B

"You say that gushing or bland reports are of little use to you, so we have thought hard about what fault we could find with *Jeake's House*; the answer is virtually none. Mrs Hadfield has the rare combination of perfectionism and personal warmth. Our bedroom, with sloping ceilings, was charming. The *en suite* bathroom was small but immaculately clean." "Mrs Hadfield's welcome could hardly have been bettered. Rooms had a very homely feeling; the furnishing, while not particularly expensive, was harmonious, and in keeping with the house." Many other visitors, too, have enjoyed this beautiful old listed building quietly located on one of Rye's cobbled streets. It has a Victorian parlour with upright piano, sheet music of the period and armchairs with antimacassars; there are shelves of old-fashioned books for guests to borrow. Bedrooms, some with brass or mahogany bedsteads, look over the old rooftops of Rye or face south across the marsh to the sea; most have private bath or shower. "My single didn't, but I didn't have to queue for the shower or bathroom – I just had to walk along the balcony above the breakfast room to reach them!" Breakfast is served to a background of soft piped classical music in the adjoining former Quaker meeting house: "A large, galleried, white-painted room with high windows and some good paintings; a welcoming fire, books, plants, small pieces of china, some very good; separate tables with white laundered linen and napkins." (*Stephen Harvey, DM and DE Livesley, and others*) Vegetarian as well as traditional breakfasts are on offer; the Hadfields help guests make dinner reservations in local restaurants. Only the breakfast orange juice and "fairly ordinary" toast are criticised. Parking can be a problem, but there is a carpark at the end of the road. *Jeake's House* now has a guests' sitting room and a residential licence.

Open All year.
Rooms 1 suite, 10 double, 1 single – 8 with bath, 2 with shower, all with telephone, radio, TV, tea-making facilities, baby-listening.
Facilities Sitting room, bar/sitting room, breakfast room.
Location In centre of Rye; carpark nearby.
Restrictions Not suitable for ♿. No smoking and no dogs in dining room.
Credit cards Access, Amex.
Terms B&B: single £21, double £38.50, suite £72. 1-night bookings sometimes refused for Sat in high season. Reductions for stays of 4 or more days. 10% reduction Nov–Mar Sun–Thu except Christmas and Easter. Reduced rates for children sharing parents' room. (No restaurant.)
Service/tipping: "We neither expect nor encourage tipping, but any gratuities are shared among staff."

****

Traveller's tale *The room was very small, the bathroom laughably so. There was a rathole by the toilet; the rat had probably left in search of a roomier apartment.*

****

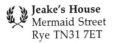

The Old Vicarage BUDGET *Tel* Rye (0797) 222119
66 Church Square
Rye TN31 7HF

Paul and Julia Masters's cosy pink vicarage, a listed building, where Henry James wrote *The Spoils of Poynton* before moving to nearby Lamb House, is approached along a footpath that leads between the church and a few cottages on either side. From the windows you can see the church tower (and hear the bell on the quarter hour). The small guests' lounge and breakfast room overlook the small walled garden. Pretty bedrooms, with Laura Ashley fabrics and wallpapers, have drinks tray, TV, hair-drier, magazines, information about local restaurants, etc. The atmosphere is friendly and relaxing; standards are high; English breakfasts are generous. A newspaper and a glass of sherry are included in the price. "Outstanding quality throughout." (*N Harmer*)

Note: Not to be confused with *The Old Vicarage Hotel*, a small hotel in East Street.

Open All year except Christmas.
Rooms 1 suite, 4 double – all with bath and/or shower, radio, TV, tea-making facilities.
Facilities Lounge, dining room. Walled garden.
Location Through Landgate Arch to High Street, first left East Street, left again to Church Square. Parking nearby.
Restrictions Not suitable for ♿. No smoking in bedrooms and breakfast room. No children under 10. No dogs.
Credit cards None accepted.
Terms B&B: single £24–£42, double £35–£50. Winter breaks Nov–Mar; weekly bookings Apr–Oct. 1-night bookings sometimes refused for Sat Apr–Oct. (No restaurant.)
Service/tipping: "No service charge. No tips expected – we enjoy what we do."

ST AGNES Cornwall **Map 1**

Rose-in-Vale BUDGET *Tel* St Agnes (087 255) 2202
Mithian, St Agnes TR5 0QD

Originally the winter home of a local mine captain, and peacefully set in a wooded valley close to the North Cornish coast, in large grounds with gardens, woodland and pasture, *Rose-in-Vine* entered the Guide last year in an italicised entry which is now promoted to full following this affectionate pen portrait: "By any standards a nice hotel; in terms of value unbeatable. The main part is an elegant Georgian country house. At the rear is a series of unattractive extensions, happily invisible from the front. Public rooms are pleasant and well furnished with a grand piano in one lounge, and plenty of books and games. The bedrooms have bath or shower (no bath goodies but at these prices one can't complain) and television. Housekeeping can be erratic in terms of replacing teabags and toilet rolls and unless you ask for extra soap you may have to leap out of the shower to fetch the one piece from the basin. But clean towels are provided daily. Avoid room 8 which overlooks the kitchen extractor. Tables in the dining room are divided into pairs by trellises, breaking down the length and narrowness of the so-called Trellis Room. The table d'hôte menus have three choices of starter. The main course is fish or meat and there are always five fresh vegetables, sometimes rather too *al dente*. Puddings are slightly nursery, but one is always home-made and (with the occasional exception) delicious – crumble, bread and butter pudding, etc. A cheeseboard follows and unlimited coffee in the lounge. The wine list is disappointing, and short on half-bottles. The cooked breakfasts are good save for the plastic marmalades which taste as nasty as they look. The hotel is set in 11 acres with the river Mithian running through. There is an open-air swimming pool and a games room with darts, table-tennis and bar billiards. The shortcomings do not stem from not caring and can be put right. Mr and Mrs Arthur deserve to succeed." Bar meals and packed lunches are available. More reports please.

Open Mar–Oct inclusive.
Rooms 17 rooms – all with bath and/or shower, telephone, TV, tea-making facilities, baby-listening. 3 on ground floor.
Facilities 3 lounges (1 with TV), bar, dining room; games room. 11-acre grounds with gardens, heated swimming pool, woodland, pasture, stream; sandy beach 1½ m.
Location NW of Truro off B3284 to Perranporth. Hotel is signposted.
Restrictions Suitable only for partially ♿. No smoking in restaurant. No children under 7 in public rooms after 7 pm (high tea at 6). No dogs in public rooms.
Credit cards Access, Visa.
Terms B&B £24.25–£29.75; dinner, B&B £30.25–£35.75. Set lunch £7.95, dinner £16; full alc £19.50. 2-, 5-, 7-day breaks off-season excluding bank holidays. Reduced rates and special meals for children.
Service/tipping: "No service charge made. Tipping entirely at customers' discretion."

ST AUSTELL Cornwall — Map 1

Boscundle Manor
Tregrehan
St Austell PL25 3RL

Tel St Austell (0726) 813557
Fax (0726) 814997

Andrew and Mary Flint's rambling old manor, part medieval with thick walls and beams but mainly 18th century, lies in a bosky setting about a mile from the sea at Carlyon Bay. It is furnished with a variety of assorted objects, some good antiques, some comfortable chairs, "but in no way *arranged* or set out to impress". Public rooms "are not opulent but have a country charm. Bedrooms are informal and comfortable, every piece of furniture and print chosen with loving care"; those in the main building have undergone a major refurbishment this year, with refrigerators being added to the doubles, and power showers to some bathrooms. Rooms in the cottages, with private patios, are popular; so is the Garden Room which has the best view. The conservatory is bright and inviting for breakfast. "The menu offers a wide choice of well-cooked food at a reasonable price" using fresh ingredients. There is a particularly attractive garden with a heated pool, and a golf practice area. *Boscundle Manor* has "mildly eccentric" characteristics, as we have said in the past; its informality was too much for one couple this year who minded the absence of formal reception, bedroom keys (though most rooms have a small safe) and staff and found the Flints "offhand", but those in favour appreciate "the combination of easy cordiality and comfort with understated luxury". (*JE Metcalfe*) More reports please.

Open Easter–end Oct. Restaurant closed for lunch, and Sun evening to non-residents.

Rooms 1 suite, 7 double, 2 single – all with bath and/or shower (5 with spa bath), telephone, radio, TV, some with tea-making facilities; baby-listening in main house. 3 in buildings in garden.
Facilities Sitting room, cocktail bar, dining room, private dining room, conservatory, games room. 9-acre grounds with 2-acre gardens, croquet, golf-practice area, heated swimming pool, lake, ponds, woodlands. Beaches 1 m and 6 m; riding, coastal walks, fishing nearby.
Location 2 m E of St Austell, 100 yds off A390 on road signposted Tregrehan.
Restrictions Not suitable for ♿. Dogs by arrangement; not in public rooms.
Credit cards Access, Visa.
Terms B&B: single £55.25–£65, double £93.50–£110, suite £127.50–£150. Set dinner £20. Special meals for children by arrangement.
Service/tipping: "All rates include service. We actively discourage anyone from leaving extra money."

ST BLAZEY Cornwall — Map 4

Nanscawen House — *Tel* Par (072 681) 4488
Prideaux Road, St Blazey
Nr Par PL24 2SR

This fine old country house, run by "kind and considerate" proprietors Janet and Keith Martin, entered the Guide last year and is now warmly endorsed: "Wonderful welcome. Only three bedrooms, beautifully equipped. Good home-cooked meals; breakfast, cooked to order, the best of our holiday." "Faultless service throughout, every effort made to please." *Nanscawen* enjoys a secluded location in five-acre grounds with a heated swimming pool and is convenient for touring in Cornwall, being only five miles from Fowey. Guests have their own entrance and a comfortable sitting room. There are log fires in winter; breakfast is served in a conservatory. All the bedrooms have private facilities including a spa bath. One has a four-poster. Mrs Martin cooks four-course, no-choice dinners using home-grown produce from her husband's extensive garden. Afternoon tea is now included in the tariff. *Nanscawen* is not licensed; bring your own wine. It is a no-smoking hotel. (*BE Carlick, Mrs M Daw*)

Open All year except 2 weeks at Christmas.
Rooms 3 double – all with bath, shower, telephone, radio, TV, tea-making facilities.
Facilities Drawing room, dining room, conservatory. 5-acre garden with swimming pool (heated until Sep). Golf, riding, beaches, sea- and river-fishing nearby.
Location After level-crossing in St Blazey, from Lostwithiel (A390), turn right opposite Texaco garage into Prideaux Road. *Nanscawen* is ¾ m on right.
Restrictions Not suitable for ♿. No smoking. No children under 12. No dogs.
Credit cards Access, Visa.
Terms B&B: single £45–£55, double £55–£60. Set dinner £17.
Service/tipping: "We do not expect tips, but some guests have been kind enough to buy us a plant for the conservatory."

****

Traveller's tale *A complimentary decanter with some sherry is becoming part of the normal expensive extras in country house hotels. In one hotel the decanter top seemed to have been secured with super glue, so I suppose this was a gesture rather than a proper offer.*

****

ST IVES Cambridgeshire — Map 3

Slepe Hall
Ramsey Road
St Ives PE17 4RB

Tel St Ives (0480) 63122
Fax (0480) 300706

A former girls' school, built in 1848, converted into a hotel in the 1960s, and now run by Jan and Colin Stapleton, is introduced to the Guide by a regular: "Some hotels are so much part of their locality that they afford guests a rather special sense of ease. Such is *Slepe Hall*. St Ives has been there for over a thousand years, an unpretentious gem on the banks of the Great Ouse, Oliver Cromwell's town on the edge of fen country. And the hotel is part of the fabric of St Ives. It is an elegant Victorian building with very comfortable rooms which, despite having been pushed around to meet a hotel's needs, are proper rooms rather than rationed rectilinear spaces. It has a large bar, a real one where local people come to drink beer or enjoy the excellent bar meals. The restaurant, elegant without need of gimmicks or trappings, looks on to an attractive garden. Its uncrowded tables are crisp with good linen and decorated with fresh flowers. The mainly English menu is excellent and the wine list chosen with intelligent understanding. And you would go a long way to find as helpful and unobtrusively friendly a head waiter as Luigi. We have stayed here in all seasons and have always felt the same sense of ease, of being in a very nice place. I hope others will seek it out, it is worth the effort." (*LS Powell*) The hotel's restaurant, *Rugeley's*, is named for the school's founder, the Revd John Rugeley. Each menu ends with a literary quotation. More reports please.

Open All year except 25/26 Dec.
Rooms 13 double, 2 single – all with bath, shower, telephone, radio, TV, tea-making facilities.
Facilities Lounge, bar, restaurant; conference/functions facilities. Small garden. 5 mins from river Great Ouse.
Location ¼ mile from centre.
Restrictions Not suitable for ♿. No dogs in public rooms.
Credit cards All major cards accepted.
Terms [1991 rates] B&B: single £52, double £65. Set lunch/dinner £13.95; full alc £23.75. Weekend breaks; champagne nights.

ST IVES Cornwall — Map 1

The Garrack
Burthallan Lane, Higher Ayr
St Ives TR26 3AA

Tel St Ives (0736) 796199
Fax (0736) 798955

"Exactly the sort of friendly, comfortable hotel that we would choose for a seaside holiday with our children," writes our inspector. "Warm welcome from the very competent and pleasant receptionist. Our room in the newer section was a fair size, with plain white walls with a very attractive watercolour, comfortable bed, and enough wardrobe and drawer space to accommodate clothes for at least a week's stay. The bathroom, though not very large, was well appointed. Michael Kilby, son of the owners, is behind the bar in the evenings. Many staff have been here some time; they are loyal, attentive and good in every department. The restaurant, with conservatory extension, attracts outside diners. We ate well at breakfast (every possible cereal and a dazzling array of marmalades, jams and honeys) and dinner. The house obviously had extensive gardens when it was built as the drive now leads between bungalows put up at different times, but there is still an attractive small area of well-planted flower garden and an extensive kitchen garden. The Garrack Club, open to locals, is a Swedish-style log cabin which houses the very small, very warm swimming spa/jet pool and a good all-day snack bar. It would be a haven on a wet day. For fine days there are lots of stupendous beaches within an easy drive. St Ives now tends to be tacky, and this offers a reliable retreat." "The cellar is one of the most comprehensive I have met," adds *JF Shuttleworth*, "with a delightful policy of a standard unit mark-up instead of rip-off prices."

This traditional seaside hotel, which the Kilby family have owned for twenty-five years, is run so that children and adults can enjoy themselves equally. It stands in two-acre grounds overlooking St Ives' spectacular surfing beach Porthmeor, well away from the hubbub of the town. Some of the rooms are in the creeper-covered older building, while more spacious ones are in a modern wing and enjoy a fine view over the bay. Books and games in the sitting room give it a lived-in feeling. Coffee is included in the reasonably priced table d'hôte dinner menu.

Open All year.
Rooms 17 double, 4 single – 15 with bath and shower, 2 with shower, all with telephone, radio, TV, baby-listening. Some in garden rooms.
Facilities Residents' lounge, TV lounge, bar lounge, dining room. Leisure centre with small swimming pool, sauna, whirlpool, solarium, coffee shop. 2-acre grounds.
Location ½ m from centre. From Penzance on B3311 turn right on B3306 towards St Ives. Hotel is off this, to left.
Restrictions Not suitable for severely ♿. Dogs by prior arrangement; in some rooms only, not in public rooms.
Credit cards All major cards accepted.
Terms B&B £28.50–£50; dinner, B&B £43–£64.50. Set dinner £14.50; full alc £18. Off-season breaks; Christmas programme. Reduced rates and special meals for children.
Service/tipping: "We believe the customer is entitled to good service and should not be charged for it. We have no objection if guests wish to show appreciation, but there is no obligation."

ST KEYNE Cornwall — Map 1

The Well House — *Tel* Liskeard (0579) 42001
St Keyne
Liskeard PL14 4RN

"We can't speak too highly of this most comfortable country house; Nick Wainford looked after us beautifully. There are few hotels where you find better cooking or more imaginative menus." "Every detail in the bedroom is thought out; fruit replenished daily, fresh sheets and towels. Returning after the finest meal imaginable – consistently first-class cooking, sauces out of this world – you find all the lights have been turned on in welcome. Excellent breakfast brought on a sensible tray. Service most attentive, without servility." "The entire establishment looked cared for. The room (spacious and airy, with large bathroom), the view, the hospitality were outstanding." Recent endorsements for this grey-stone Victorian house secluded in three and a half acres of grounds in a pretty, unspoilt spot in the Looe valley, five miles from the coast. The only changes since last year are the new chef, David Woolfall, whose cooking earns the plaudits above, and the sad demise of one of the two "dignified" King Charles spaniels – Leo survives. Public rooms, decorated in cool colours, have "a 1920s/1930s atmosphere". There is a cosy panelled bar and a lounge with log fire. The dining room is hung with pictures of food; its bay windows overlook the garden and swimming pool; the well-spaced tables are impeccably set. The wine list is "carefully selected, and wide-ranging in price". Breakfast includes exotic fruit salad, freshly baked croissants and brioches and home-made marmalade. Nick Wainford is a "perceptive and helpful" host; the atmosphere is courteous rather than easily convivial – and the prices are less high than those of many prestigious country house hotels. (*Juliet and David Sebag-Montefiore, Dr HR Dingle, Harold J Johnson Jr, JM Chandler*)

Open All year.
Rooms 7 double – all with bath, shower, telephone, radio, TV; baby-listening by arrangement.
Facilities Sitting room, bar, restaurant. 3½-acre grounds with tennis, croquet, heated swimming pool. Walking, fishing, riding, golf nearby.
Location 3 m S of Liskeard on B3254. At church take left fork to St Keyne Well; *Well House* is ½ m on left.
Restrictions Not suitable for ♿. No children under 8 in restaurant.
Credit cards Access, Amex, Visa.
Terms [1991 rates] B&B (continental): single £60, double £72–£105; dinner, B&B: single £85, double £97–£130. Cooked breakfast £7.50 extra. Full alc £32. 2-night bargain breaks Jan–Mar. 1-night bookings sometimes refused for bank holidays. *Service/tipping: "No service charge. Gratuities are not expected and are discretionary."*

ST MARTIN'S Isles of Scilly — Map 1

St Martin's Hotel
St Martin's, Isles of Scilly
Cornwall TR25 0QW

Tel Scillonia (0720) 22092
Fax (0720) 22298

César award in 1991: Island Hotel of the Year

Tucked into a hillside looking across a sandy beach towards Tresco, its cottage design blending into the coastline, this is the only hotel permitted on St Martin's, the third largest of the Scilly Islands. It was built to a design approved by the Duke of Cornwall (a.k.a. the Prince of Wales) and is owned by Robert Francis, also of the *Polurrian*, Mullion (q.v.) who divides his time between the two hotels. The setting, next to a sandy but never crowded beach, is "idyllic"; and "the use of stone and the light and airy interior with Laura Ashley fabrics create an atmosphere of quiet luxury devoid of pretentiousness". Public rooms "are spacious and comfortable; bedrooms are equally welcoming, with good beds and crisp bedding, and they are serviced while you dine". Like the *Polurrian*, this hotel welcomes children; accommodation and breakfast are free for under-16s sharing their parents' room, and there are high teas at 5.30 pm. A number of visitors have written in praise of the hotel but one who stayed in late 1990, while agreeing about the location, architecture and facilities, found the decor "bland in the extreme", was severely critical of the food and found the dining-room service "offhand and inconsistent". Since then a new chef has taken over, and we'd welcome reports on the cooking.

Open Mar–Oct, possibly Christmas/New Year.
Rooms 2 suites, 22 double – all with bath, shower, telephone, radio, TV, baby-listening.
Facilities Residents' lounge, lounge bar, restaurant; snooker room. 2½-acre grounds with indoor heated swimming pool. Sandy beaches 50 yds.
Location Only hotel on St Martin's. Helicopter from Penzance to Tresco, boat to St Martin's. Hotel will make transport arrangements.
Restrictions Not suitable for ♿. Smoking forbidden in residents' lounge, discouraged in restaurant and some bedrooms. Dogs in certain bedrooms only, not in public rooms.
Credit cards All major cards accepted.
Terms Dinner, B&B £75–£145. Set lunch £12.50, dinner £21.50; full alc £28. Single occupancy by arrangement. Sailing, diving, golfing breaks; off-season theme breaks. Free accommodation for children under 16 in parents' room; special meals.
Service/tipping: "Service included. We discourage tipping."

ST MARY'S Isles of Scilly — Map 1

Star Castle — *Tel* Scillonia (0720) 22317
St Mary's, Isles of Scilly
Cornwall TR21 0JA

St Mary's is easily reached by boat or helicopter from the mainland and is an excellent base for an island-hopping Scillonian holiday. This modest but welcoming hotel, owned and run by Mr and Mrs Reynolds, was originally an Elizabethan fortress with a dry moat and 18-foot-wide ramparts. It has a splendid position overlooking the town, harbour and neighbouring islands, and extensive grounds, with lawns enclosed by tall hedges forming welcoming sun traps. There is a covered heated swimming pool and a grass tennis court. Some of the bedrooms ("comfortable and well appointed") are in the old building; two singles, with shower, are in guardhouses on the ramparts. Other larger ones ("pleasant, though not luxurious") in two modern annexes in the garden are recommended for families, but they are not particularly well insulated. There is a dungeon bar where snack lunches are served; the dining room is the former officers' mess. Food has sometimes been criticised in the past but there's a new chef and visitors this year have been pleased: "It was of a high standard with interesting vegetables; local fresh fish especially delicious, lobster thermidor remarkable." "Food promptly served, and very hot. Staff friendly and helpful; we felt very welcome." (*Grace White, Mrs R English*)

Open Mar–Oct.
Rooms 22 double, 2 single – all with bath and/or shower, telephone, radio, TV, tea-making facilities. 16, with baby-listening, in 2 blocks in garden.
Facilities 2 lounges, games room, bar, restaurant. 4½-acre grounds with tennis, covered heated swimming pool. Sandy beaches, safe bathing and fishing nearby.
Location Central, overlooking town and harbour, but in large grounds so not noisy. Regular boats and helicopter flights to Scilly Islands from Penzance.
Restrictions Not suitable for ♿. Dogs in garden rooms only (£2 per day).
Credit cards None accepted.
Terms [1991 rates] Dinner, B&B £42.91–£57.22. Set dinner £16.50. Packed and bar lunches available; vegetarian meals on request. 5% reduction for 10 or more days. Reduced rates for children sharing parents' room; high tea.
Service/tipping: "No service charge. Tips are not expected – but gratefully received if given!"

SALCOMBE Devon — Map 1

Marine Hotel
Cliff Road
Salcombe TQ8 8JH

Tel Salcombe (054 884) 2251
Fax (054 884) 3109

A "pleasant, well-run, most civilised" hotel, with a ringside view of Salcombe's lovely estuary from the open-plan public rooms and most of the bedrooms. It returned to the Guide last year after another change of management, recommended "in spite of the odd hiccup", particularly for its position, which "is almost like being at sea". The pink and green decor throughout the hotel is "restful and charming". Bedrooms, many with balcony, are attractively decorated, with extra-large beds and balcony: "Not large but comfortable and well planned, with excellent storage and good lighting." Early morning tea and a newspaper, brought to the bedroom, are included in the rates. On the *nouvelle*-ish food there is dissent: the latest verdict is that it is "variable in the extreme". The sporting facilities are shared by the time-share apartments in the garden, so could be crowded at peak times. There is live music in the public rooms at dinner and Sunday lunch.

Open All year.
Rooms 1 suite, 41 double, 9 single – all with bath, shower, telephone, radio, TV, baby-listening; some with ramp.
Facilities Lift, ramps. Lounge, library, bar, restaurant, poolside brasserie, dinner-dance on Sat; indoor swimming pool, jacuzzi, sauna, solarium, gym, beauty salon. ¼-acre grounds with swimming pool, moorings, fishing.
Location 300 yds from centre; on water. Parking.
Restrictions No children under 7 in restaurant after 7 pm. No dogs.
Credit cards All major cards accepted.
Terms [1991 rates] B&B £58–£85; dinner, B&B £67–£95. Set lunch £10.50, dinner £22; full alc £39. Off-season breaks; Christmas and New Year breaks. Reduced rates and special meals for children.
Service/tipping: "Service included. We do not solicit gratuities, but any tips left are equally distributed among all staff except manager."

SALTFORD Avon — Map 2

Brunel's Tunnel House BUDGET
High Street, Saltford
Nr Bristol BS18 3BQ

Tel Saltford (0225) 873873

A "much cared for" guest house, "comfortable, clean and home-like, excellent value", with welcoming owners, Muriel Mitchell and her daughter Sarah Leighton, in a Grade II listed Georgian building, one of three tunnel houses in Britain, in a village between Bristol and Bath. It was bought by the famous 19th-century engineer, Isambard Kingdom Brunel, so that the Great Western Railway line he had designed could be excavated underneath. Trains still use the tunnel; there is a slight rumble when a train passes but it does not hinder conversation or sleep. The owners have decorated it with the aim of keeping its "honest, unprissy period appeal", and readers appreciate the prettily decorated bedrooms, with good hanging space, and the attractive sheltered garden. The no-choice dinner is "*very* acceptable, if not frightfully imaginative, and includes properly cooked vegetables"; there's "delicious toast" for breakfast. Last year an inspector said that the immediate surroundings lack appeal. Mrs Mitchell writes: "Saltford is very much a conservation village, a quiet rural backwater. It has a council estate, but it also has the oldest inhabited manor house in Somerset, a picturesque high street with many pretty cottages and period houses running down to the river, and it is an excellent touring departure point." More reports please.

Open All year except Christmas. Dining room closed for lunch.
Rooms 7 double – 1 with bath and shower, 6 with shower, all with telephone, radio, TV, tea-making facilities.
Facilities Lounge/bar, dining room. ½-acre garden. River Avon with marina 15 mins' walk; golf nearby.
Location Midway between Bath (5½ m) and Bristol (6½ m). At Saltford Motor Services on A4 turn up Beech Road; hotel faces bottom of Beech Road.
Restrictions Not suitable for ♿. No smoking in dining room. No dogs.
Credit cards Access, Amex, Visa.
Terms B&B: single £47, double £56.40; dinner, B&B double £74–£82.40. Set dinner £13. Weekend breaks. Reduced rates for children sharing parents' room; special meals by arrangement.
Service/tipping: "No service charge since courteous service is implicit in the way we work. Tipping left to the discretion of customers – it is neither expected nor encouraged, but if offered is not refused."

SANDY PARK Devon — Map 1

Mill End — *Tel* Chagford (0647) 432282
Sandy Park, Chagford TQ13 8JN — *Fax* (0647) 433106

This converted mill, whose wheel still turns in its quiet courtyard, is beautifully set in two-acre grounds in the Teign valley on the edge of Dartmoor. It has 12 miles of fishing on the river Teign; a ghillie is available by prior arrangement, and fishing tuition packages are offered in summer. There is also, we are pleased to hear, a singles offer from late June to mid-August, offering savings of about 20 percent for that long-suffering group. There are good walks from the gates of the hotel. "It's a wonderful place to relax, not at all fancy or pretentious, but if what you seek is comfort, relaxation and good food in a friendly atmosphere, this is it. Many of the guests are on return visits. The hotel's greatest assets are the hardworking owners Nicholas and Hazel Craddock who are much in evidence and always have time to chat; in the evening when they are tending the bar or refilling your coffee they make you feel like guests rather than patrons. Dinners are not too rich or overly sauced; the vegetables are fairly ordinary but everything else is above average. The sweet cart is a treat in itself." "What impressed us was the courteous and attentive staff." The decor is homely rather than elegant; some bedrooms are modern, some old and chintzy; they are not overlarge. There is plenty of choice (of traditional English cooking) on the menu. (*Kary and Grayson Kabler, Dr AJ Rose*)

Open All year except 1 week before Christmas.
Rooms 15 double, 2 single – 14 with bath and shower, 3 with bath, all with telephone, radio, TV, tea-making facilities, baby-listening. Some on ground floor.
Facilities 2 lounges, bar, restaurant. 2-acre grounds. River frontage with fishing; clay-pigeon shooting, game shooting available.
Location Take A30 to Whiddon Down; turn S on A382 (do not go into Chagford). Hotel is at Dog Marsh Bridge near hamlet of Sandy Park.

Restrictions No smoking in dining room. No dogs in public rooms.
Credit cards All major cards accepted.
Terms Rooms: single £28–£55, double £45–£75. Breakfast £5–£8. Dinner, B&B: single £50–£80, double £110–£135. Set lunch from £15, dinner from £20. Winter wine and food weekends; fishing tuition packages in summer. Special singles offer end June–mid-Aug. Reduced rates and special meals for children sharing parents' room. 1-night bookings refused at Christmas.
Service/tipping: "No service charge. In general we discourage tipping but some people like to leave quite large sums of money and it seems churlish to prevent them as hotel staff are not highly paid. What is received is distributed by a committee on a pro rata basis."

SEAHOUSES Northumberland — Map 4

Beach House BUDGET
Sea Front, St Aidans
Seahouses NE68 7SR

Tel Seahouses (0665) 720337
Fax (0665) 720103

Mr and Mrs Craigs's modest hotel is on the edge of the fishing village, between the beach and the busy harbour, and has panoramic views of the sea and Farne Island. Seahouses is in a designated area of outstanding natural beauty and is well placed for exploring the Northumbrian coast and countryside and the Border area. The hotel entered the Guide in italics last year, and many visitors, some of them regulars, have since written to praise the welcoming proprietors, the comfortable bedrooms, and the "varied and excellent" six-course dinner: "There are three choices of every course. Mrs Craigs selects the best local fish every day; all vegetables are fresh. The main dishes range from traditional roasts or game in season to cordon bleu offerings, and are followed by delicious desserts or regional tarts and puddings and a good cheeseboard. The staff are without exception efficient and helpful at all times." There's a good choice of inexpensive wines. The breakfast menu "is comprehensive; the bread rolls baked freshly each morning by Mr Craigs are very popular." (*MH Yates-Mercer; also Mrs Helen Anthony, A and BM Massam, and others*) One reader found some of the decor a bit fussy, "but it is always in first-class condition, and spotlessly clean".

Open End Mar–early Nov.
Rooms 2 suites, 10 double, 2 single – all with bath and/or shower, telephone, radio, TV, tea-making facilities. 1 on ground floor.
Facilities Ramp. Hall lounge with bar, 2 lounges (1 with TV and snooker table). Small garden; sandy beach 500 yds.
Location On seafront. 500 yds from village centre.
Restrictions No smoking in dining room. No dogs in public rooms.
Credit cards Access, Visa.
Terms Dinner, B&B £39–£44. Set dinner £15.50. Reduced rates 1 Oct–end May. Reduced rates for children sharing parents' room.
Service/tipping: "Service at guests' discretion; tips shared among all staff."

****

Traveller's tale *The new owners have all the hallmarks of that terrifying breed, the 'professional caterer'. Portion control abounds in the form of little butter pats, little cream pots, little coffee sachets. There are no books, no flowers, no fresh fruit in the bedrooms. In fact there are no books anywhere, not even in the oak-panelled library. Perhaps they are worried that someone might steal them.*

****

SEAVIEW Isle of Wight — Map 1

Seaview Hotel
High Street, Seaview PO34 5EX

Tel Seaview (0983) 612711
Fax (0983) 613729

"A delightful small Victorian hotel." "Staff all helpful and informative. Early morning tea came on the dot at 7.15 am each day. First-class plumbing and splendid towels in the smart new bathroom." Nicholas and Nicola Hayward's seaside hotel – public areas extensively redecorated this year – is an unassuming three-storey bay-windowed Edwardian house with a symmetrical facade, at the foot of the High Street and near a beach in an old-fashioned and picturesque sailing village, normally a peaceful place, but buzzing with activity in July and August. The house has something of the atmosphere of a maritime museum, with fine paintings and artefacts of ships everywhere; the main bar, "the most delightful I know", is a naval wardroom, the public bar has old oars, masts and ship wheels. The attractively decorated bedrooms vary in size; front rooms have a view of the sea and coast, back ones are perhaps quieter. The restaurant is popular with non-residents and can be very busy; at certain times of year there are two sittings. "The cooking is imaginative and unpretentious. As a near non-carnivore I particularly appreciated the generous helpings of fresh vegetables. It is typical of the Haywards' management that as a bar snack one can order anything from a hot crab ramekin to a simple plate of chips." Last year one guest felt there was a limited choice of main dish on the half-board menu. Mrs Hayward replies: "We believe we offer a good selection: two vegetarian dishes, two meat, two fish and a daily dish. We are always prepared to do something special but I will not have a huge menu and start producing dishes from the freezer." Children are welcome, though the very young are not allowed in the restaurant after 7.30 pm; high tea is served for them at 5.45 pm or they are served in a special room if dining later. (*Philip Norman, WL Hewlett*) More reports please.

Open All year except Christmas Day.
Rooms 2 suites, 14 double – 14 with bath, 2 with shower, all with telephone, radio, TV, baby-listening. 2 with patio on ground floor.
Facilities 2 lounges, 2 bars, restaurant. Patio and courtyard. Sea and sandy beaches 50 yds, with sailing, fishing, windsurfing, etc.
Location In centre of village, near sea. Follow signs for seafront. Parking.
Restrictions No smoking in 1 lounge; smoking discouraged in dining room. No small children in dining room after 7.30 pm. No dogs in public rooms.
Credit cards Access, Amex, Visa.
Terms B&B: single from £45, double from £70; dinner, B&B: single from £56.50, double from £90. Full alc £15–£20. Breakaway, weekend, weekly tariffs. Reduced rates and special meals for children.
Service/tipping: "We do not make a service charge, nor expect tips."

SHENINGTON Oxfordshire — Map 2

Sugarswell Farm BUDGET
Shenington, Nr Banbury
OX15 6HW

Tel Tysoe (029 588) 512

Rosemary Nunneley is the "delightful host" on this working dairy farm in rural Oxfordshire, in a "quite new" house, built of stones from a demolished cottage. There is a cosy lounge with a log fire and comfortable sofas. The three bedrooms enjoy rural views and have good beds, ample drawer space, large and well-equipped bathroom. In the dining room, papered in dark red with white paintwork, visitors (never more than six) eat round a large table in dinner-party style. Food is "excellent"; there's no choice, but vegetables and so on are served in individual tureens. *Sugarswell* is a good holiday centre: Stratford, Warwick and the Cotswold villages are in easy reach. It's a mostly no-smoking establishment, but there is one room where the desperate can go for a puff. No licence; bring your own wine. One possible snag: "Dinner is at 6.30 pm."

Open All year.
Rooms 3 double – all with bath, tea-making facilities.
Facilities Drawing room, dining room. 360-acre farm.
Location 8 m NW of Banbury W of A422 to Stratford-on-Avon.
Restrictions Not suitable for ♿. Almost entirely no-smoking. No children under 15. No pets.
Credit card Amex.
Terms B&B: single £26–£30, double £38–£45; dinner, B&B: single £41–£43, double £68–£75. Set dinner £16. Unlicensed.
Service/tipping: "No service charge. Tips at guests' discretion; shared among staff."

SHEPTON MALLET Somerset — Map 2

Bowlish House BUDGET — *Tel* Shepton Mallet (0749) 342022
Wells Road
Shepton Mallet BA4 5JD

"We warmly endorse your entry," writes *Corinna Haward*. "Charming welcome, warm and comfortable bedroom and *outstandingly* delicious dinner. We were a bit demanding – my husband wanted two starters and no pudding – but this was no problem. The little touches were exceptional, such as the home-made walnut and almond bread, and the rose petals among the crisp salad garnish of the hot mushroom soufflée." Linda and Bob Morley's "delightful" restaurant with only four bedrooms, "not grand, but elegant and comfortable", is in a beautiful Palladian house, scheduled Grade II, in a National Conservancy area. Last year readers wrote in praise of the "extraordinary personal attention of Mr Morley", the "comfortable bedroom with nice personal touches, not the usual commercial guest packs" and the "home" rather than "restaurant" cooking of Mrs Morley who is self-taught – "not unsophisticated, just not over-elaborate". The reasonably priced menu has plenty of choice including a vegetarian main course; the wine list is extensive and not pricy. Public rooms are on an intimate scale, with some good antique furniture. There's a cosy bar, and an agreeable conservatory for after-dinner coffee. It is a good place to stay if sightseeing in Bath, Wells, Glastonbury, Stourhead. In reply to last year's niggles the Morleys write: "Rooms 4 and 5 now have new beds. The slight traffic noise from the nearby road is not too much of a problem – but the very quiet room at the back is subject to a dawn chorus!" The generous continental breakfast includes freshly squeezed orange juice, Greek yoghurt and American peanut muffins; eggs and bacon or a kipper cost extra.

Open All year except 26–28 Dec.
Rooms 4 double – all with bath, radio, TV, tea-making facilities.
Facilities Lounge, bar, dining room, conservatory. ¼-acre garden.

Location ¼ m outside Shepton Mallet, on A371 to Wells.
Restrictions Not suitable for ♿. No smoking in dining room while other guests are eating. No dogs in public rooms.
Credit cards Access, Visa.
Terms [1991 rates] (No service charge) B&B (continental) double £46; dinner, B&B double £83. English breakfast £3.50. Set dinner £18.95.

SIX MILE BOTTOM Cambridgeshire Map 3

Swynford Paddocks
Six Mile Bottom
Nr Newmarket CB8 0UE

Tel Six Mile Bottom (063 870) 234
Fax (063 870) 283

A mansion in large grounds, six miles from Newmarket, nine from Cambridge, where Byron allegedly carried on an incestuous affair with his half-sister, Augusta Leigh, returns to the Guide after an interval of some years, nominated by two regular correspondents, one writing *in situ*: "Lovely country house, easy to find, nice garden set in fields with horses; from my bedroom I can see mares and foals playing. My room is well decorated, well lit and heated, supplied with what one needs, but no chi-chi extras. It was cleaned properly while I was out. No resident owner, but the young foreign staff are friendly and caring and not overwhelming. The menu offers three vegetarian choices, not the best I have eaten, but acceptable; perfect salads, lots of half-bottles on a very good wine list." "Very comfortable, a warm welcome, a nice bar, *huge* bedrooms and bathrooms, lovely grounds and only mild traffic noise from the nearby road. Much used by the horsey fraternity during race meetings, and probably best out of season, but a useful base for exploring the area." (*Mrs EH Prodgers, Dr and Mrs A Winterbourne*) More reports please.

Open All year.
Rooms 12 double, 3 single – all with bath, shower, telephone, radio, TV, tea-making facilities, baby-listening.
Facilities Lounge bar, dining room, functions room. 5-acre grounds with tennis, croquet, putting, giant chess.
Location On A1304, 6 m SW of Newmarket.
Restrictions Not suitable for ♿. No smoking in dining room. No dogs in public rooms.
Credit cards All major cards accepted.
Terms [1991 rates] B&B: single £66.50–£71.50, double £102.50–£143. Full alc £30. Weekend breaks; anniversary breaks. Christmas package. Reduced rates and special meals for children.
Service/tipping: "All our prices include service. Gratuities are not expected. If guests wish to reward staff for exceptional service they are free to do so."

SLAIDBURN Lancashire Map 4

Parrock Head Hotel
Slaidburn, Clitheroe BB7 3AH

Tel Slaidburn (020 06) 614

Richard and Vicky Umbers, "friendly and welcoming in the nicest possible way, without being pushy", own and run this former farmhouse in a remote and beautiful location at the foot of Bowland Fells, on the Lancashire–Yorkshire border, with dales on one side, majestic moorland on the other. Three bedrooms, "spacious and comfortable", are in the main building; six are in two blocks of garden cottages. *Parrock Head* is "spotlessly clean", and warm even in the depths of winter; there are log fires in the large sitting room on the first floor and a library filled with books and magazines, maps and tourist information. Guests are introduced to each other before dinner. In the spacious dining room, which also caters to non-residents, the Umbers offer a reasonably priced à la carte menu. There was a change of head chef in early 1991 and recent visitors report: "Dinners attractively served, beautifully cooked. Vegetables are a speciality, though we thought it a little unnecessary to stuff courgettes with carrots. Breakfasts the best we've had anywhere." "Excellent food and service; the house wine was much superior to some offered as such." Packed lunches too have been praised. (*Donald and Joan Tranter, Richard O Whiting; also Rebecca Boulos, April Young, and others*) Rooms in the annexe may be quieter than those in the main house which are directly off the bar and lounge. One visitor this year was dismayed to return drenched from a walk and find that there was no hot water in the middle of the day.

Open All year except Christmas week.
Rooms 9 double – all with bath, shower, telephone, radio, TV, tea-making facilities, baby-listening. 6 in garden cottages. 3 on ground floor.
Facilities 2 lounges, bar lounge, restaurant. 1½-acre grounds; reservoir fishing 2 m; bird watching.
Location 9 m N of Clitheroe. 1 m NW of Slaidburn village up Woodhouse Lane.
Restrictions Not really suitable for ♿. No smoking in dining room. Dogs in garden cottages only; not in public rooms.
Credit cards Access, Amex, Visa.
Terms [1991 rates] Dinner, B&B: single £36–£38.50, double £53.50–£59. Set Sun lunch £11.50; full alc £18.50. Light and packed lunches available. Weekend and midweek breaks. 1-night bookings refused for Sat June–Oct. Reduced rates for children sharing parents' room; special meals.
Service/tipping: "No service charge. Tips not requested but accepted if offered and distributed monthly to all staff."

SOAR MILL COVE Devon — Map 1

Soar Mill Cove Hotel
Soar Mill Cove
Nr Salcombe TQ7 3DS

Tel Kingsbridge (0548) 561566
Fax (0548) 561223

This small hotel, not far from Salcombe in the South Hams, is owned and run by Norma and Keith Makepeace and their son, also Keith, and entered the Guide last year, nominated by two readers. It is "beautifully situated at the head of an isolated cove, surrounded by National Trust land, with splendid cliff walks starting from its grounds. Our bedroom with floral decor was comfortable and well furnished, with a large sitting area and a patio. The proprietors and staff are friendly and helpful." "About half the rooms have a wonderful sea view, the others overlook a sheltered garden; it has five-acre grounds with putting green, grass tennis court and indoor and outdoor swimming pools. The hotel is ideal for a holiday with young children. Ours were made very welcome right from the beginning. Plus points are the lack of steps (it is all on ground level); the fact that you can listen in to the children after their bedtime on a telephone handset; the very good laundry facilities, and the freshly cooked food for their supper at 5:30 pm. It was such a relief to know that here was a hotel that wasn't going to serve a fortnight's supply of beefburgers, fish fingers, chips and ice-cream." Adult meals also come in for praise, with plenty of choice including fresh local fish, lobster, meat and garden produce, and an especially appreciated sweet trolley. The dining room and lounge have large windows overlooking the bay. More reports please.

Open 15 Feb–28 Dec.
Rooms 1 suite, 13 double, 2 single – all with bath, telephone, radio, TV, tea-making facilities, baby-listening.
Facilities Lounge, bar lounge, 2 restaurants. 5-acre grounds with indoor and outdoor swimming pools, tennis, table-tennis, donkeys. Sandy bay across meadow.
Location Approx 5 m SW of Kingsbridge by A381. Turn sharp right at Malborough; follow signs for Soar.
Restrictions Suitable for only partially ♿. No smoking in restaurant. Dogs by arrangement, not unaccompanied in bedrooms, not in public rooms.
Credit cards Access, Visa.
Terms B&B £50–£76; dinner, B&B £55–£80. Set lunch £15, dinner £28. Special breaks all year. Christmas house party. Reduced rates and special meals for children.
Service/tipping: "No service charge. Tipping entirely at guests' discretion."

SOUTH MOLTON Devon — Map 1

Whitechapel Manor — *Tel* South Molton (076 95) 3377
South Molton EX36 3EG — *Fax* (076 95) 3797

John and Patricia Shapland's "friendly, relatively informal" but upmarket country house hotel, in a fine Grade I listed Elizabethan manor, stands in large grounds in an isolated setting near Exmoor National Park. The interior is "simple, light and pleasant, warm and welcoming", with much of its original charm. The entrance hall is dominated by a magnificent carved oak Jacobean screen. The rooms have high ceilings, some with intricate plaster carvings and mouldings, and deep recessed windows. Furnishings and fabrics throughout are of the highest quality. "Spotless" bedrooms, in various shapes and sizes, "have all the essentials"; bathrooms are "adequate" or large, "with constantly replenished large towels". The Shaplands' talented young chef, Thierry Lepretre-Granet, is awarded a *Michelin* rosette for his "modern, sophisticated" cooking on a four-course menu, though some readers have found portions too *nouvelle*. "Breakfast is excellent, and the morning tea and newspapers, included in the charge, were accompanied by very good chef-made biscuits." (*Mattye B Silverman, Adam Moliver, Ben and Juliet Browne, and others*) A few niggles: little change on the menu during a three-day visit; one visitor was critical of the continental breakfast served in the bedroom; the room named Peverel is said to be poorly insulated. And: "It is not for the fainthearted or those who have problems walking – you must climb twenty wide steps to reach the front door, and the carpark is a hundred yards away down a hill."

Open All year.
Rooms 1 suite, 7 double, 2 single – all with bath, shower, telephone, radio, TV, baby-listening.
Facilities Lounge, bar, restaurant. 15-acre grounds with garden, croquet. Fishing, golf, riding nearby. Exmoor 2 m. Sea 18 m.
Location Leaving M5 motorway at junction 27, follow signs to Barnstaple and South Molton. At South Molton turn right at 2nd roundabout.

Restrictions Not suitable for ♿. No smoking in dining room. No dogs.
Credit cards Access, Visa.
Terms [1991 rates] B&B: single £65–£75, double £90–£170. Set lunch £30, dinner £40. Packed lunch available. Winter rates. Christmas, New Year, Easter packages. Special meals for children.
Service/tipping: "Service included. Tipping not expected, but we would not cause offence by refusing."

SOUTH PETHERTON Somerset — Map 2

Oaklands House — *Tel* South Petherton (0460) 40272
8 Palmer Street
South Petherton TA13 5DB

"One of the most delightful hotels we have ever visited," write the nominators of "this recent branching-out from the long-established restaurant downstairs, *Le Tire Bouchon*. Madame Merlozzi met us as we drove up, saw to the luggage and showed us to our room. Like the four other bedrooms it was pretty, airy, and roomy, but they are all quite individual. It was spotlessly clean and very comfortable, like a room in a private house in the best possible sense. There's a pretty garden and outdoor heated swimming pool. No bar, but drinks are available at all times. M. Merlozzi is the chef. He is Corsican, hence the many pictures of Napoleon (his wife comes from Burgundy). The food is as good as we have had anywhere; the quite short wine list is fine. A delicious continental breakfast was brought to our room. South Petherton is a picturesque village about seven miles from Yeovil, ideally situated for Wells, Bath, Montacute and the towns and villages of Hardy country." (*Evangeline and Tenniel Evans*) Front rooms can be noisy from early-morning tractors. The Merlozzis offer very reasonable two-day and weekly breaks. When the restaurant is closed light suppers can be provided in the bedrooms.

Open 6 Feb–15 Dec. Restaurant open Tue–Sat evening, Sun lunch. Light suppers available to residents Sun, Mon.
Rooms 1 suite, 4 double – 3 with bath, 2 with shower, all with telephone, tea-making facilities; TV on request.
Facilities 3 drawing rooms, dining room. Functions facilities. ¾-acre grounds with heated swimming pool.
Location Just N of A303, between Yeovil and Ilminster.
Restrictions Not suitable for ♿. No dogs in public rooms.
Credit cards Access, Visa.
Terms B&B: single £40–£50, double £50–£60, suite £75. Set dinner £19.50. Half-board rates 2 nights min; weekly rates.
Service/tipping: "Our guests are presented with a net account and reminded, if they enquire about service, that our terms are inclusive."

SOUTHWOLD Suffolk — Map 3

The Swan — *Tel* Southwold (0502) 722186
Market Place — *Fax* (0502) 724800
Southwold IP18 6EG

Southwold is a charming, unspoiled seaside town, neither trippery nor twee, built round a series of greens, with a fine church, a lighthouse and a shingle beach. Much of it is owned by Adnams, the brewers and wine merchants, including the *Swan*, a stately building, with white-framed windows, iron balconies, and union flag flying, rather more imposing than the town hall next door in the little market place. It was recently restored at vast expense "and is now a hotel of fine standing with an authentic ambience and few fripperies", extremely well managed by Dudley Clarke. It entered the Guide last year with an enthusiastic report from a regular visitor, which is now warmly endorsed: "For a hardly excessive amount of money we enjoyed very friendly service and an exceptionally good meal. Everything spotless, good crisp sheets, blankets and coverlets of sensible weight, bath big enough to stretch out in and a shower that really worked." "Staff are welcoming and anxious to please. Reception rooms are spacious, full of light and comfortably furnished." Traditionally furnished bedrooms in the main building have a view over the square, the new ones quietly situated in the back garden are smaller (and cheaper), and rather exposed, having large glass windows. The dining room is stylish, but unstuffy (no jackets-and-tie rule), with white linen, candles, sparkling glasses, lots of space. Three menus are proposed for each meal, but you are allowed to mix your choices; coffee with friandises is included. There was a new chef in January 1991; first reports suggest a fall-off from previous high standards, but we'd be grateful for more. The wine list, not surprisingly, is comprehensive. English breakfast included good, freshly brewed coffee and wholemeal toast. There are cots, high chairs and special meals for children. (*Fiona Dick; also DW Tate, Martin Lipson, William A Howard, CR*) The same niggle as last year: "No bathroom shelf." One winter visitor found the bedroom too hot even after she'd turned off the radiator. And a casual visitor, hoping for tea, was surprised to find that for a non-resident a simple "cuppa" was not available; she had to order a full cream tea which cost, for two, £11. Mr Clarke defends this saying that the rights of residents are the hotel's priority and the £11 fully justified: "Scones are baked daily in our own bakery, the jam is hand-made; there's a selection of up to six teas, bone china, silver teapot and cutlery, a blazing fire, newspapers and magazines."

Open All year.
Rooms 2 suites, 37 double, 6 single – 43 with bath and shower, 2 with shower, all with telephone, radio, TV; baby-listening if requested in advance. 18 in garden. Some on ground floor.
Facilities Lift, ramps, wheelchair etc for ♿. Drawing room, reading room, bar, dining room; conference facilities. Garden. Sea 150 yds.
Location Central, on market square, by town hall.
Restrictions No smoking in dining room. Dogs by arrangement, in garden rooms only.
Credit cards Access, Amex, Visa.
Terms [1991 rates] B&B: single £41–£62, double £75–£99, suite £118–£128. Bar lunch from £2.50, set lunch £13.50–£19.50, dinner £16.95–£27. Midweek winter breaks. Christmas and New Year programmes. Reduced rates for children sharing parents' room; high teas 5.30–6 pm.
Service/tipping: "No service charge. Gratuities at customers' discretion."

"Budget" labels indicate hotels offering accommodation at up to about £40 for dinner, bed and breakfast or £25 for B&B and £15 for an evening meal. But we would emphasise that this is a rough guide only, and does not always apply to single rooms.

SPARK BRIDGE Cumbria — Map 4

Bridgefield House
Spark Bridge
Nr Ulverston LA12 8DA

Tel Lowick Bridge (022 985) 239
Fax (022 985) 379

Spark Bridge is on the banks of the river Crake, a short drive to the fells and the lakes; the scenery is beautiful if less dramatic than further north, and it is well away from the tourist hordes. David and Rosemary Glister's late 19th-century gentleman's residence on a quiet country lane has again delighted two regulars. "It is beautifully decorated and furnished in Victorian style, and very warm at all times thanks to excellent central heating. The sitting room is charming and comfortable, with a log fire, and plenty of chairs in groups so one can sit and read in peace. None of this awful introduction of guests to one another, where the names are anyway instantly forgotten. The dining room is spacious; one cannot overhear other people's conversation." "Rosemary Glister's cooking at dinner is marvellous, breakfasts are always good and include home-produced honey and marmalade." Dinner is at 7.30 for 8 sharp. While having a drink guests choose starters and desserts – there is only one main course, accompanied by "interesting" vegetables. (*Moira Jarrett, PE Carter*) The hardworking Glisters' generosity and ungrasping attitude towards people who often get second-class-citizen treatment in hotels deserves a mention: no supplementary charges for singles or one-night stays; children are welcome – no charge for high-chairs, cots, high teas or the laundering of babies' clothes.

There is, however, a sharply dissenting view this year, from a visitor who was cold on a chilly weekend, criticised the housekeeping, was disappointed with the dining room decor and the dinner, minded the lack of choice for breakfast, and warns that water can run out in a very dry spell as the house has its own water supply. It should perhaps be emphasised that *Bridgefield House* does not offer the services of a fully fledged hotel. More reports please.

Open All year, but for lunch only on 25 Dec.
Rooms 5 double – all with bath, shower, telephone, radio, baby-listening; tea-making facilities on request.
Facilities Drawing room, bar, dining room. 3-acre garden.
Location Off A5092 on back road from Spark Bridge to Lowick Bridge.
Restrictions Not suitable for ♿. No smoking in dining room. "Well-disciplined dogs only", not in public rooms.
Credit cards Access, Visa.
Terms [1991 rates] B&B £38; dinner, B&B £57. Packed lunches on request; set dinner £22.50 to non-residents. Spring and autumn breaks. Children 3 and under free, under 12 50% reduction; high teas; free laundry service for babies' clothes. *Service/tipping: "The inclusion of a service charge should be banned by law; it is only an increase in the tariff."*

SPREYTON Devon — Map 1

Downhayes BUDGET
Spreyton, Crediton EX17 5AR

Tel Bow (0363) 82378

This traditional Devon farmhouse, dating from the 16th century, is only twenty miles west of Exeter, but it's in deep countryside high in the mid-Devon hills. A car is essential. It can accommodate no more than six guests at a time; guests have their own pretty lounge with log fire, books, parlour games and TV. Dinner, by candle-light, is served between 7 pm and 9.30, at a time agreed with guests (four courses, with two choices of starter and dessert, ending with cheese and coffee). No licence but guests' wine is decanted for them. There is a large barn with a games area and studio. "You couldn't find anywhere better for a holiday on Dartmoor," a reader wrote last year. "The personal touch is everywhere; Mrs Hines works very hard to make sure you have a good time." This is warmly endorsed: "A kind and generous welcome; food very good. We were exceptionally lucky with our fellow guests, but were not expected to sit at the same table." "Mrs Hines enquired immediately about any food dislikes I might have – a good start. I was welcomed with a pot of tea in front of the fire. There were fresh flowers everywhere; lighting was soft, but good enough to read by in lounge and bedroom. Everything was spotless, bedroom warm and comfortable. My dinner was excellent and generous, with enough vegetables for two hearty eaters. Fresh orange juice and coffee for breakfast, home-made jam and marmalade." (*Dorothy Whittington, Theo Schofield, also Mrs J James*) This is a working farm; there can occasionally be a whiff of agriculture.

Open 1 Jan–20 Dec.
Rooms 3 double – 2 with bath, all with radio. 1 on ground floor.
Facilities Lounge with TV, dining room. 15-acre grounds with games room, studio; garden, pasture.
Location 9 m SW of Crediton. Leave A30 at Whiddon Down (Merrymeet roundabout), follow signs to Spreyton. *Downhayes* is on left 1½ m N of Spreyton on Bow Road.
Restrictions Not suitable for wheelchairs. No smoking in bedrooms. No children under 12. No pets.
Credit cards Access, Visa.
Terms (Not VAT-rated) B&B £18.50–£32. Light lunch on request £6. Set dinner £12.50. Weekly half-board rate. 5-day embroidery course in June and Sep. Unlicensed – bring your own drink.
Service/tipping: "We do not impose a service charge, nor do we expect tips."

STADDLEBRIDGE North Yorkshire — Map 4

McCoy's
The Tontine, Staddlebridge
Nr Northallerton DL6 3JB

Tel East Harlsey (060 982) 671

César award in 1989: Utterly acceptable mild eccentricity

A stone Victorian house at the Cleveland Tontine, where two busy main roads converge but effective double-glazing keeps the bedrooms "surprisingly quiet", is run by the three McCoy brothers with a friendly staff. It has no grounds to speak of, but good views. The decor is "a successful mixture of comfort and flamboyance". Bedrooms are large, with bright wallpaper and curtains and comfortable beds; there are bold flowered fabrics and large squashy sofas in the lounges; furniture is "a mix of antiques, bamboo and junk"; there are lots of potted plants and flowers. Peter McCoy is in charge of the accommodation. Tom is the chef in the restaurant, which is small and furnished in 1930s style. His cooking is generally praised: "delicious", "eclectic", "confident", "occasionally reckless". Eugene cooks "straightforward but stylish meals" with "strong sauces and flavours", served in generous portions, in the busy bistro downstairs which is more simply furnished and cheaper, with close-packed tables, blackboard menus and loud rock music. Breakfast is served until lunchtime and is "a long, leisurely meal including exotic fruits, excellent coffee, and newspapers". Not everyone considers that the restaurant dinners justify their high prices. The McCoys have bought an eight-acre field at the back of the restaurant and hope to build a small hotel, but so far have failed to get planning permission. Meanwhile the "awfulness of stairs, corridors and entrances", reported last year, is the McCoys cheerfully tell us "just the same as ever . . .".

Open All year except 25/26 Dec and 1 Jan. Restaurant closed Sun and Mon. (Bistro open.)
Rooms 6 double – all with bath, shower, telephone, radio.
Facilities 2 lounges, breakfast room, bistro with bar, restaurant. Small grounds.
Location Junction of A19/A172 (rooms double-glazed). 6 m NE of Northallerton.
Restriction Not suitable for ♿.
Credit cards All major cards accepted.
Terms (Service at guests' discretion) B&B: single £75, double £95. Full alc in bistro £30, in restaurant £50.

STAMFORD Lincolnshire — Map 3

The George
71 St Martin's
Stamford PE9 2LB

Tel Stamford (0780) 55171
Fax (0780) 57070

César award in 1986: Finest old coaching inn

Stamford is a remarkably unspoilt medieval town, and *The George* is its historic coaching inn, preserving plenty of innish features such as a flower-tubbed cobbled courtyard, but neither prettified nor self-conscious. Bedrooms are "beautifully decorated" and comfortable with well-appointed bathrooms and towels that are changed daily. Comfortable sofas abound in the public rooms, and the oak-panelled dining room is "very fine"; it offers traditional roasts as well as more modern cooking. In the garden lounge, filled with exotic plants, cheaper and simpler food is available. Reports this year are in the main favourable: "We had what must have been one of their nicest rooms (No 29). It was spacious, panelled, furnished with antiques. The atmosphere was welcoming, service friendly. We enjoyed lunchtime on Monday (market day) when the bar was full of local farmers. Breakfast and lunch were very good." "Room exceptionally comfortable with many thoughtful touches. Food excellent, staff exceptional – friendly, courteous, but not obsequious." (*Mary Fagan, Mrs JM Simpson*) One visitor, however, was less lucky: "Radiator turned off, so bedroom was freezing. Dracula-style creaking bathroom door which no one had noticed. No residents' lounge so on a busy Saturday there was nowhere to sit. Saturday dinner is in two shifts; we had to eat at 9.30 and were still waiting for coffee at midnight."

Open All year.
Rooms 1 suite, 34 double, 12 single – all with bath and/or shower, telephone, radio, TV, baby-listening; 24-hour room service.
Facilities 2 lounges, 2 bars, restaurant; 4 private dining rooms, business centre. 1-acre grounds with patio and monastery garden. Golf ½ m; fly fishing and sailing at Rutland Water 5 m.

Location In town centre (front rooms double-glazed; rooms overlooking courtyard are quietest). Parking for 100 cars.
Restrictions Only restaurant suitable for ♿. No dogs in restaurant.
Credit cards All major cards accepted.
Terms B&B: single from £75, double from £97.50, suite from £108. Light lunches from £12.50; full alc from £30. Weekend breaks, Christmas package. Reduced rates for children sharing parents' room; special meals.
Service/tipping: "Service included. Gratuities are at guests' discretion and distributed between all staff on a points basis."

STAPLEFORD Leicestershire — Map 4

Stapleford Park — *Tel* Wymondham (057 284) 522
Stapleford, Melton Mowbray — *Fax* (057 284) 651
LE14 2EF

César award in 1989: Most exciting newcomer of the year

"19th-century hospitality, backed up by 20th-century technology" is the aim of *Stapleford Park Country House Hotel and Sporting Estate,* to give it its full title. Owned by ebullient Chicagoan Bob Payton (he of deep-pan pizza fame) and his wife Wendy, it is a luxurious country house with elements of an American resort hotel; many outdoor pursuits are on offer in the 500 acres of woods and parkland (see below), and there's an equestrian centre in an impressive stable block. The house is a fine building of beautiful ivory-coloured stone in a mixture of periods and styles, in a lovely lakeside setting. Inside are stone arches, lots of mahogany, magnificent wood carvings attributed to Grinling Gibbons, a "clubby" library, and a 19th-century Elizabethan-style wing. Cooking on a wide-ranging menu with a distinctly transatlantic accent is by a husband-and-wife team, Rick Tramonto and Gale Gand, also from Chicago. Breakfast with fresh orange juice, blueberry muffins and good coffee is served on Peter Rabbit china in the vaulted 16th-century refectory. The "signature bedrooms", each completely different, have been designed by "famous names" – Lady Jane Churchill, Lindka Cierach, Liberty, Tiffany, etc. Despite the "off-beat jokiness of the brochure" visitors have reported that "the welcome by Bob Payton and his entire staff is warm, friendly and relaxed". "Not a cheap night out," writes a 1991 correspondent, "but the rooms are worth the money. Large, very well decorated and luxurious. The bathroom could best be described as lush – we felt rather like Liberace without the piano. Service was smooth, courteous and unobtrusive. Our only complaint (not a minor one in view of the price) was the food, which was very average. However, the meal was enjoyable despite this because the service in the dining room (and at breakfast next day) was so good." Perhaps the Tramonto/Gand duo are best with the least sophisticated dishes: a noted restaurant critic warmly praised a lunch of cheeseburger, Caesar salad and superb home-made ice-cream. One winter visitor found her top-floor bedroom dark and cold, and service outside the dining room "amateurish". The Paytons have been granted planning permission to add a forty-bedroom extension and 18-hole and 9-hole golf courses, but work on these is not expected to start in the near future. More reports please.

> Please write and confirm an entry when it is deserved. If you think that a hotel is not as good as we say, write and tell us.

Open All year.
Rooms 2 suites, 33 double – all with bath, shower, telephone, radio, TV, baby-listening.
Facilities Lift. Drawing room, salon, 3 sitting rooms, library, dining room, breakfast room; functions facilities. 500-acre parkland with church, lake with fishing, tennis, mini-golf, basketball, croquet, clay-pigeon shooting, jogging track, equestrian centre.
Location 4 m E of Melton Mowbray. From A1 turn off at Colsterworth; take B676 for 9 m, turn to Stapleford.
Restrictions No smoking in dining room. Children under 10 by prior arrangement only.
Credit cards All major cards accepted.
Terms [1991 rates] (Service at guests' discretion) B&B (continental): single or double from £120, suite from £230. English breakfast £8.50. Full alc £30. 2 night min stay at weekends. Winter weekend breaks. Christmas programme. Special meals for children on request.

STOKE GABRIEL Devon — Map 1

Gabriel Court Hotel
Stoke Gabriel
Nr Totnes TQ9 6SF

Tel Stoke Gabriel (080 428) 206

"Haven of peace and comfort" in delightful village SE of Totnes on river Dart. The Beacom family's old white-painted manor house in 3-acre terraced Elizabethan garden with heated swimming pool, tennis, croquet is recommended for warm welcome, excellent home-cooking using local salmon, meat and game, and home-grown vegetables. "Children welcomed and treated most kindly"; dogs also welcome. Closed Feb. 17 double rooms, 3 single, all with bath/shower. Not suitable for ♿. All major credit cards accepted. B&B double £70–£80; dinner, B&B (min 4 days) double £110–£120. New nomination. More reports please.

STON EASTON Somerset — Map 2

Ston Easton Park
Ston Easton, Nr Bath BA3 4DF

Tel Chewton Mendip (0761) 241631
Fax (0761) 241377

César award in 1987: Comprehensive excellence in a luxury country house hotel

Peter and Christine Smedley's "country house hotel on the grand scale", an immense Palladian mansion of Bath stone, immaculately restored, stands in 26 acres of parkland with gardens designed by Humphry Repton in the 18th century. The river Norr flows over Repton's flight of shallow cascades in the gardens, which are still being restored; there is now a tennis court. The sitting rooms and library are grand, furnished in 18th-century style with antiques and pictures, comfortable sofas and elegant flower arrangements. The dining room by contrast is modern in style, its panelling painted white; tables, with bamboo chairs, are set with long tablecloths, flowers and candles. Bedrooms, individually designed by Jean Monro, an expert on 18th-century decoration, are elegant, with antiques, good lighting, luxurious fabrics. Those on the first floor have the huge windows and fine proportions of the original master bedrooms, while those on the floor above are smaller. "Grand hotels can be unsympathetic and formal, but the reverse is true here. Everyone goes out of their way to put guests at their ease and to help with advice about local sights, walks, etc. The receptionists are totally unsnooty and natural, the young manager most obliging and informative. Everyone takes time to chat with guests. There are one or two regulations: no portable phones to be used; men must wear jacket and tie for dinner; guests are asked not to smoke in the bedrooms but unfortunately are allowed to in the dining room. The dining room is supplied with fruit, vegetables and herbs from an impressive kitchen garden. The food, though not over-ambitious, doesn't quite make it, though the style is commendably light. Cooked breakfast is excellent, continental not quite as good because of the quality of the bread. But the whole is such an enticing package that the occasional shortcomings at mealtimes become insignificant." "*Tout confort,* plus real luxury; no muzak. Everything one could possibly want in the bedroom and bathroom, but what is outstanding is the friendliness, combined with sheer professionalism of the staff. Mrs Smedley is constantly around and seems to enjoy being a very good, seemingly casual, hostess." (*David Wooff, Lady Davenport-Handley*) Visitors' accommodation is upgraded at no extra cost when the rooms are available. Dogs are not allowed in the house but are kennelled in a heated basement and are fed and exercised by staff first thing in the morning. Shoes are cleaned, cars are valeted.

Open All year.
Rooms 2 suites in garden with tea-making facilities, 19 double – all with bath, shower, telephone, radio, TV.
Facilities Drawing room, salon, library, 2 restaurants; private dining room; billiard room, museum kitchen, servants' room for chauffeurs etc. Terrace. 26-acre grounds with tennis, river, fishing.
Location On A37 from Bristol to Shepton Mallet.
Restrictions Only restaurant suitable for ♿. Smoking in bedrooms discouraged. No children under 12. No dogs in building (free kennelling on premises by prior arrangement).
Credit cards All major cards accepted.
Terms [1991 rates] B&B (continental): single from £75, double £135–£320. English breakfast £8. Set lunch £24, dinner £35. Vegetarian and low-fat meals on request. 4-day Christmas programme; midweek summer breaks, winter tariff. 1-night bookings refused for bank holidays.
Service/tipping: "No service charge included nor gratuity expected."

STONOR Oxfordshire — Map 1

The Stonor Arms — *Tel* Turville Heath (049 163) 345
Stonor — *Fax* (049 163) 8863
Nr Henley-on-Thames RG9 6HE

A restaurant to which *Michelin* awards the near-rosette accolade of a red "M" now has nine bedrooms in a purpose-built new wing, and we sent along an inspector who reports enthusiastically: "It's very much a Guide hotel, small enough for the guests to matter, with very nice staff indeed. Stonor is a tranquil hamlet in the Thames valley with a mellow Tudor manor house set in a wooded park where you can walk. The inn has been lovingly and beautifully renovated and is managed by a young couple, Stephen and Anne Frost, who came from *Cromlix House*, Kinbuck, in Scotland (q.v.). Our bedroom was large, airy and thoughtfully planned, with good lighting and storage, fresh flowers, TV, books etc, and a pristine but cosy bathroom. It was serviced during dinner. Afternoon tea, with warm fingers of home-baked shortbread was brought to the room for no extra charge. There is a sumptuous suite upstairs, with a well-furnished drawing room, superb hand-printed paper and a gas log-fire. The main dining room is beautifully formal, with a light and spacious conservatory extension. Cooking is imaginative but not intimidating; each dish has its own variation of vegetables, a nice change from the usual uniform side dish of vegetables served whatever the main course. The staff were all charming, friendly and efficient. Breakfast, in the bright and pretty bar conservatory overlooking the gardens, was one of the best I've had in this country – generous continental is included in the room price, cooked is £5.50 extra. A good selection of newspapers was put out – and we were told to take away any we wanted; we were not rushed." The main restaurant serves fixed-price dinners Monday to Saturday and a traditional Sunday lunch; there is also an informal bar restaurant serving lunch and dinner seven days a week from an à la carte menu. "Though we categorise ourselves as a restaurant-with-rooms," say the Frosts, "we do provide room service between 8 am and 11 pm." More reports please.

Open All year. Main restaurant closed for lunch weekdays, dinner on Sun.
Rooms 2 suites, 7 double – all with bath, shower, telephone, radio, TV, tea-making facilities. 1 suitable for ♿.
Facilities Ramps. Small sitting room, bar, bar restaurant, main restaurant. ½-acre garden. River Thames 4 m.
Location NW of Henley off A423 to Oxford. 1 m from Henley turn on to B480 to Stonor and Assendon. Hotel is 3 m further.
Restriction Guide dogs only.
Credit cards Access, Visa.
Terms [1991 rates] B&B (continental): single £82.50, double £92.50, suite £137.50. Cooked breakfast £5.50 extra. Set Sun lunch £19.95, dinner £28.50; full alc bar lunch/dinner £20.50. Special breaks all year; activity breaks. Reduced rates and special meals for children.
Service/tipping: "No service charge. Gratuities at guests' discretion; they should only tip if they really want to, for exceptional service. Tips are divided among all members of staff."

STRATFORD-ON-AVON Warwickshire — Map 2

Stratford House
Sheep Street
Stratford-on-Avon CV37 6EF

Tel Stratford-on-Avon (0789) 268288
Fax (0789) 295580

"Quite expensive, but good value, with a relaxed, unfussy atmosphere" – our inspector's verdict last year on this small Georgian house, owned by Sylvia Adcock, in one of the town's prettiest old streets, very near the theatre. "You enter through a paved passage/patio – very pretty with exuberant plants, hanging baskets, stoneware and statues. Inside it is pleasant understated English, with rosy Sanderson's soft furnishings and moss-green carpets." Bedrooms are not large, but clean and well lit, with a good bathroom. The restaurant, also open to non-residents, is "well thought out, with splendid well-framed prints and attractive tableware; half of it is a large conservatory jutting out into the patio". There is a new chef this year and a visitor in March 1991 reports: "It is not easy to satisfy each member of a party aged from ten upwards, eating at 7 pm. They did so with ease. And though that night they had to accommodate two large dinner parties, one of which lasted until after 3 am, by 8 am our host and a somewhat sleepy waiter were dispensing a delicious if excessive breakfast to admiring clients in an immaculately fresh dining room. The culinary high spot, however, was the home-made chocolates – worth crossing England for." (*Jeremy P Carver*) Another visitor was less enthusiastic: his lamb was tough, the service mediocre. And he could have done without a Vivaldi tape constantly replaying, not to mention Beethoven's Ninth at breakfast. "Oh, for silence!" More reports please.

Open All year. Restaurant closed Sun and Mon, but light meal provided for residents.
Rooms 1 family, 9 double – 7 with bath and shower, 3 with shower, all with telephone, radio, TV, tea-making facilities, baby-listening.
Facilities Lounge, bar, restaurant; conference/functions facilities. Patio, garden with dining facilities.
Location Central. 100 yds from theatre. Hotel has parking arrangements.
Restrictions Not suitable for ♿. No dogs.
Credit cards All major cards accepted.
Terms (Service at guests' discretion) B&B: single £51–£66, double £55–£69, family £87. Set lunch £10–£12, dinner £10–£18; full alc £18–£22. 2-day breaks Tue–Sat; winter rates. Reduced rates and special meals for children.

STRETTON Leicestershire — Map 4

Ram Jam Inn
Great North Road
Stretton LE15 7QX

Tel Stamford (0780) 410776
Fax Oakham (0572) 724721

This old coaching inn on the Great North Road is a motel with a difference, owned by Tim Hart of nearby *Hambleton Hall* (q.v.). It is an open-plan pub with two snack bars and a restaurant serving wholesome food, and a small but comfortable sitting area; it does a thriving lunch trade. The bedrooms are large, with large bathrooms, and quiet because they face away from the A1. "If only there were more hotels like this – near the road, easy to find, offering comfort but not luxury. Delightful bedroom, well furnished and decorated with no unnecessary frills. Good simple dinner, without flummery. The owner of *Hambleton Hall* was acting as manager and I was well served. My bill was so reasonable that I queried it because I thought they must have forgotten something." "Very good stopover. Bed very comfortable. All in good taste. Good value breakfast." "Huge double bed. Excellent service." (*Mrs MD Prodgers, John and Carol Riddick, E Blakeley*) In deference to the drink–driving laws, the *Ram Jam* offers all-day tea and coffee and has a breath-tester at the door.

Open All year except 25 Dec.
Rooms 7 double, 1 single – all with bath, shower, telephone, radio, TV, tea-making facilities.
Facilities Ramps. Bar, restaurant, 2 snack bars; meeting rooms. 2-acre grounds.
Location On W side of A1, 9 m N of Stamford. Travelling S take B668 exit for Oakham; travelling N turn off through Texaco garage just past B668 turnoff.
Restrictions Only restaurant suitable for ♿. No smoking in 1 snack bar.
Credit cards Access, Amex, Visa.
Terms [1991 rates] Rooms: single £39, double £49, family £61.50. Breakfast: continental from £1.50, English from £3.25. Set lunch £10, dinner £15.20; full alc £15–£20.
Service/tipping: "Service included in room rates; tips at guests' discretion; waiters keep their tips."

Don't keep your favourite hotel to yourself. The Guide supports; it doesn't spoil.

STURMINSTER NEWTON Dorset — Map 2

Plumber Manor
Sturminster Newton DT10 2AF

Tel Sturminster Newton (0258) 72507
Fax (0258) 73370

César award in 1987: Sustained excellence in a middle-price country hotel

Again this year there's warm praise for this Guide favourite, a handsome Jacobean house in the heart of Hardy countryside which has been the home of the Prideaux-Brunes since the early 17th century and for the past 19 years has been run as a restaurant-with-rooms by brothers Richard and Brian Prideaux-Brune. The atmosphere is very much family rather than country house hotel; labradors lie around on the lawn and in front of the fire, and accompany you on walks. "It's so peaceful and relaxing – absolute freedom to do your own thing." But despite the casual air, everything has been carefully thought out. The jovial (and hardworking) Richard is much in evidence – he waits and does reception and bar. "His hospitality was exceptional; he helped us deal with a problem regarding lost luggage in a way which went well beyond the bounds of duty." There are six bedrooms, "comfortable, spacious and uncluttered", in the house, opening off a gallery hung with family portraits, and ten, particularly well appointed, in a converted stable block 50 yards away – "ours was one of the nicest we encountered on our British holiday". Dinner, cooked by Brian Prideaux-Brune, is served in the spacious dining room. There are two set menus; the more expensive one has more choice. "While showing a distinct preoccupation with the traditional – loin of venison, rack of lamb, etc – the food succeeds in pleasing where more elaborate country house fare sometimes fails by going over the top in fussiness. Breakfast, often the acid test, passed with flying colours." *Plumber Manor* styles itself as a restaurant-with-rooms; those in search of lavish public rooms and comprehensive cosseting would probably be happier elsewhere, but the consistency of its standards and the comfort of the bedrooms make it a far more attractive hotel than many that boast that name. (*Mrs J Cookson, Harold J Johnson Jr, Hugh and Moira Aldersey-Williams; also Catherine Borley, RF Fernsby*)

Open 1 Mar–end Jan. Restaurant closed for lunch.
Rooms 16 double – all with bath, shower, telephone, TV, tea-making facilities. 10 (6 on ground floor) in stable block 50 yds from main building.
Facilities Lounge/bar, gallery, restaurant in main house; sitting/meeting room in converted barn. 4-acre gardens with tennis, croquet, trout stream.
Location 2 m SW of Sturminster Newton; on A357 to Hazelbury Bryan.
Restrictions No children under 12. No dogs.
Credit cards All major cards accepted.
Terms [1991 rates] (Service charge included) B&B: single £55–£70, double £77–£104. Set dinner £19 and £24. 10% reduction for 2 or more nights; winter bargain breaks.

> The success of this guide in North America has led to sister publications on American and Canadian hotels based on the same principles. Readers with recent experience of good hotels in North America are urged to send their nominations to Sandra W Soule, America's Wonderful Little Hotels and Inns, PO Box 150, Riverside Avenue, Riverside, Conn. 06878, USA.

SWAFFHAM Norfolk — Map 3

Strattons
Ash Close
Swaffham PE37 7NH

Tel Swaffham (0760) 23845
Fax (0760) 23845

An unusual venture which came into being only in 1990 enters the Guide; it's a Grade II listed house (18th century with Victorian additions) which, though only a few yards from Swaffham's famous marketplace, approached by a narrow lane, enjoys an almost country setting in an acre of garden with a croquet lawn, old trees and a view of the church. The owners, Leslie and Vanessa Scott, met at art school, and their taste is reflected in the decor; there are antique furniture, *objets d'art* and paintings (many for sale; the Scotts actively promote local artists) in the public rooms. The bedrooms are in country-house style with modern bathrooms, each completely different (and described in detail in the tariff to help you make your choice). Each has a name: Venetian, Louis, Palladian, etc. Contrasting with the elegance of the decor, the Scotts' style is informal; they pride themselves on the "hurry-free" atmosphere. "Dinner," they say, "can take four hours; breakfast, too, is a pleasure to be savoured. We have miniature game birds, guinea fowl, rabbits, cats and dogs which adore people and create a feeling of homeliness. A large collection of books, reflecting our interest in architecture, is at guests' disposal." Mrs Scott is a self-taught cook, English in style, offering at least three choices at each stage of the menu and using fresh local ingredients. "A totally new experience. I felt I was staying with friends, so warm and friendly was the atmosphere." (*Jacqueline Scott*)

Open All year.
Rooms 1 suite, 4 double, 2 single – 3 with bath and shower, 4 with shower, all with telephone, TV, tea-making facilities, baby-listening.
Facilities Drawing room, dining room; conference facilities. 1-acre garden with patio.
Location Central; just off Market Place. Ample parking.
Restrictions Not suitable for ♿. No smoking in dining room and bedrooms.
Credit cards Access, Amex.
Terms B&B: single from £49.50, double from £66, suite from £74.80; dinner, B&B: single from £66, double from £99. Lunch from £2, set dinner £16.50. Christmas package. 10% discount for 2 nights or more.
Service/tipping: "No service charge added. Tipping actively discouraged."

TALLAND-BY-LOOE Cornwall — Map 1

Talland Bay Hotel
Talland-by-Looe PL13 2JB

Tel Polperro (0503) 72667
Fax (0503) 72940

"Probably the best hotel we have visited in this price range; very comfortable, with a friendly feel." "Anywhere that can integrate and please 5 to 85-year-olds in harmony deserves praise. As a travel writer, it's almost my favourite place in the UK." Two of this year's endorsements for this family holiday hotel in a peaceful coastal setting. "The proprietor's presence (often oppressive in privately owned hotels) was just right. He appeared in the bar before dinner, chatted with the customers in an amiable fashion and was not seen again until the following evening. Yes, the bar was full before dinner, but so it should be; there's a no-smoking overflow lounge next door. The food was excellent throughout; significantly the dining room was full each night, and some diners were locals." "Rooms with sea view are large, with plenty of storage space, bathrooms large and well equipped. Breakfast excellent, service very efficient. Dinner great value; lovely wines at extremely reasonable prices." (*Dale and Krystina Vargas, Ian Hume and Ros Granger, Neil and Ros Macmillan; also A Eisinger, and others*)

This 16th-century Cornish country house, with an unpretentious decor, in two and a half acres of carefully tended sub-tropical gardens, with an "impeccably maintained" swimming pool, overlooks an unspoilt bay. Most bedrooms are agreeably furnished in traditional style, but some are less satisfactory. You should discuss your requirements on booking. Breakfast is a generous affair, with carefully prepared cooked dishes. A buffet lunch is offered by the pool in summer. Out of season the owners, Major and Mrs Ian Mayman, fill the hotel with bridge, bird-watching, painting, archaeology, geology and yoga holidays.

Open Mid-Feb–end Dec, Christmas and New Year.
Rooms 1 suite, 18 double, 5 single – all with bath and/or shower, telephone, radio, TV, baby-listening. 2 in hotel grounds, 1 across lane. 2 on ground floor adapted for ♿.
Facilities Lounge, no-smoking lounge, bar, dining room. 2½-acre grounds with swimming pool, putting, croquet. 5 mins' walk to beach with safe swimming.
Location 2½ m SW of Looe, turn left at hotel sign on Looe–Polperro road.
Restrictions No children under 5 in dining room at night. Dogs in certain rooms only (£3); not in public rooms.
Credit cards All major cards accepted.
Terms Dinner, B&B £44–£83. Set lunch £9, dinner £18; full alc £30. 1-night bookings refused in high season. Bridge, bird watching, painting, archaeology, geology, yoga, honeymoon, Christmas and New Year packages. Reduced rates for children sharing parents' room; high teas.
Service/tipping: "No service charge. We do not encourage tipping; it is left entirely to guests' discretion."

TAPLOW Buckinghamshire — Map 1

Cliveden
Taplow SL6 0JF
Tel Burnham (0628) 668561
Fax (0628) 661837

This magnificent Grade I listed stately home, meticulously restored and elegantly furnished, in large and lovely National Trust grounds on the Thames, "offers a delightful escape from reality where you can enjoy being cosseted with old-world charm". It entered the Guide last year, warmly nominated: "Certainly one of the best hotels we have stayed at in Britain. What is extraordinary is that in such grand surroundings there is real human warmth. The care is what one would expect: everything from offering to unpack to unflinchingly catering for the personal – sometimes eccentric – whims of the customers. The public rooms are spectacular, with breathtaking views. The bedrooms are all quite different – those I have seen are marvellous. The ones on the second floor have the best views. The dining room must be one of the finest in Britain; food is serious and interesting and there is an extraordinary wine list for customers with deep pockets; breakfast, taken round a huge table, is friendly and unstuffy. The hotel manager is there on weekdays, and there are two assistant managers whose personal qualities and ability are of the highest order. Children are accepted, and the baby-sitting is most professional. The facilities are marvellous; the pavilion with heated swimming pool, jacuzzi, gymnasium, etc is a lovely place to relax, and its staff are welcoming, intelligent and delightful. The only possible disadvantage is that at weekends the grounds are full of National Trust visitors, but even then it is possible to escape to the pavilion area which is totally private. *Cliveden* is, of course, very expensive but to my mind offers good value for money." (*Dr Alan Lucas*) There are two restaurants: the *Terrace*, and *Waldo's* which is more intimate. In addition to the bedrooms in the main house there are others, less spectacular but very well decorated and equipped, in the garden wing a short distance away – service can take a while to reach them. One niggle: "The muzak in the pavilion was strangely out of character; silence or Mozart would have been more appropriate."

Open All year.
Rooms 8 suites, 20 double, 3 single – 30 with bath and shower, 1 with shower, all with telephone, radio, TV; baby-listening on request. 9 on ground floor.
Facilities Lift. 4 sitting rooms, 2 dining rooms, bar, grill room, billiard room, conference room. 375-acre grounds. Indoor and outdoor swimming pools, tennis, sauna, jacuzzi, gymnasium, health and beauty treatments, massage, squash, horses, practice golf, jogging routes, fishing, 3 boats for river trips.
Location 10 m NW of Windsor. Exit 7 from M4.
Restriction Not suitable for ♿.
Credit cards All major cards accepted.
Terms (Excluding National Trust entrance fee: £3.80 per person) B&B (continental): single £185, double £205–£298, suite £355–£465. English breakfast £9.10. Set lunch £28, dinner £45; full alc £50. Summer, fitness, Christmas and New Year packages, music weekends. 1-night bookings sometimes refused for weekends. Reduced rates and special meals for children sharing parents' room. *Service/tipping: "No service charge. Tips not expected."*

TAUNTON Somerset — Map 1

The Castle
Castle Green
Taunton TA1 1NF

Tel Taunton (0823) 272671
Fax (0823) 336066

César award in 1987: Best town hotel

This luxurious 300-year-old hostelry, owned by the Chapman family (Kit Chapman, known to ITV viewers as presenter of "Simply the Best – a Celebration of British Food", is managing director), stands wisteria-covered and castellated in the centre of the town, though in a quiet oasis of high ground on the site of the old castle, with pleasant moated gardens at the back. It has had a Guide entry since our first edition, but was dropped last year when it was put up for sale. Kit Chapman wished to spend more time on books and television, and his parents, Peter and Etty, were planning to retire after 40 years in harness. The Chapmans subsequently changed their minds, and withdrew the *Castle* from the market. Kit Chapman is now firmly back in control. The kitchens lost their *Michelin* rosette when chef Gary Rhodes departed in September 1990, but the large kitchen staff, now headed by Philip Vickery, is reported to be turning out excellent cooking, based on British traditional themes. The hotel's public rooms are attractive and elegant, with old oak furniture, tapestries and paintings and a fine wrought-iron staircase. Bedrooms are variable in both size and style; the best ones are the garden ones. Housekeeping has been described as "exemplary". Service, often praised as "friendly and keen", has at times also been considered patchy, but visitors have liked the lack of pretension, as well as the surroundings. We look forward to reports on the re-established Chapman regime. In winter and spring there are weekends of fine wine and music. The *Castle* offers special rates for honeymooners, and parents and old boys of local schools.

Open All year.
Rooms 1 suite, 21 double, 13 single – all with bath, shower, telephone, radio, TV, baby-listening.
Facilities Lift. Lounge, lounge/bar, restaurant; private dining/meeting rooms. ½-acre grounds. Trout fishing and clay-pigeon shooting nearby.
Location Central (follow signs for castle), but quietly situated. Garages and parking.
Restrictions No smoking in dining room while meals are being served. No dogs in public rooms.
Credit cards All major cards accepted.
Terms [1991 rates] B&B: single £70, double £95–£135, suite £180–£250. Set lunch from £13.50, dinner £22.50; full alc £42.50. West country breaks; Christmas package; wine and musical weekends. Reduced rates and special meals for children.
Service/tipping: "No service charge. Service at guests' discretion."

TAYNTON Oxfordshire — Map 2

Manor Farm Barn BUDGET — *Tel* Burford (099 382) 2069
Taynton, Burford OX8 4UH

César award in 1987: Best rural B&B

"It would be impossible to praise this establishment too highly. A beautiful, well-thought-out barn conversion, with large, elegant reception rooms, and spacious bedroom and bathroom. All very prettily furnished, with a large bowl of fruit, seductive piles of magazines, and every possible grooming requirement in large pots, not tiny packets. Breakfast was perfect too, with as many choices of cereal as a supermarket, bowls of fruit, delicious bacon, eggs, etc. All this in acres of beautifully cared-for garden, with very friendly owners. Amazing prices too. We've been twice now and will keep on going." Mr and Mrs Florey's welcoming, comfortably modernised Cotswold stone farmhouse enjoys a rural setting in a "delightful" unspoilt hamlet near Burford, which has a lovely old church, but no shop, pub or post office. Tranquillity is guaranteed by the extensive grounds and adjoining pastures down to the river Windrush. It has only three bedrooms, all with beamed ceiling and private bathroom. Breakfast – the only meal served – is taken communally at an elegant mahogany table. It's an excellent base for touring the Cotswolds, but you will need a car. (*Angela and Ray Evans; also Martin L Dodd, and others*)

Open Feb–Dec except Christmas.
Rooms 3 double – all with bath, shower, radio, TV, tea-making facilities.
Facilities 2 lounges, dining room. 8-acre grounds with garden and paddocks.
Location 1½ m NW of Burford; A361 then A424. Turn off to village. Entrance is by church gate.
Restrictions Not suitable for ♿. No smoking in dining room. No children under 10. No dogs.
Credit cards None accepted.
Terms B&B double from £45.50. 1-night bookings refused Sat. (No restaurant.)
Service/tipping: "Service included. Tips not required or looked for."

TEIGNMOUTH Devon — Map 1

Thomas Luny House BUDGET
Teign Street
Teignmouth TQ14 8EG

Tel Teignmouth (0626) 772976

This beautifully proportioned Georgian house, near the fish quay in the old quarter of Teignmouth, was built by the marine artist Thomas Luny, and has been turned into an informal, very small, reasonably priced hotel by John and Alison Allan. You approach through an archway into a courtyard where there is ample parking. The lounge and dining room, both with open fires, lead through French windows into a walled garden. There are only four bedrooms, all different; three are generous in size, the fourth "might not be suitable for a long stay", but all are well supplied with Malvern water, books and magazines. So many readers have written in unqualified praise of *Thomas Luny* that we suspect a little gentle nudging has gone on. But the consensus is summed up by these two reports: "House warm, spacious and beautifully decorated. The Allans made us comfortable from the moment of arrival to the moment of departure. Breakfasts and dinner are excellent, being varied and simple with imaginative use of fresh local ingredients. All the bread is home-made – and delicious." "Dinner, three-course, no choice, but very good. If your object is peace and quiet and reading this might not be for you since much time is spent making conversation. If you don't mind that, you would have to search far and wide for better value." (*Nancy Drucker, JFL Bowes; also Charles Janson, and many others*)

Open Mid-Jan–mid-Dec.
Rooms 4 double – 3 with bath and shower, 1 with shower, all with telephone, radio, TV.
Facilities 2 lounges, dining room. Walled garden. 5 mins' walk to sea with sandy beach.
Location Central. Follow signs to quay, then Teign Street. Courtyard parking.
Restrictions Not suitable for ♿. No smoking in dining room. No children under 12. No dogs.
Credit cards None accepted.
Terms (Not VAT rated) B&B £27.50; dinner, B&B £41. Set dinner £13.50.
Service/tipping: "No service charge levied, nor tips expected."

TETBURY Gloucestershire — Map 2

Calcot Manor
Tetbury GL8 8YJ

Tel Leighterton (0666) 890391
Fax (0666) 890394

Endorsements, but also criticisms this year for this "handsome Cotswold manor in rather dull farmland a few miles west of Tetbury", with a *Michelin* rosetted restaurant. Owned and run by Brian and Barbara Ball, with son Richard, it has a range of venerable outbuildings, including a fine 14th-century tithe barn and a heated outdoor swimming pool. Bedrooms, which vary in size, have been cleverly fitted into the old house and there are newer ones in a converted stable block. Some have a large and luxurious bathroom. "The *Manor* has a domestic feel, with an emphasis on quality in spite of the un-designerish approach. Furnishing fabrics are not skimped; some very desirable pieces of pottery are dotted about. Bedrooms are bright, modern, and furnished in a style not uncommon in prosperous suburbs throughout the land. Ours, with a small bathroom (which lacked shelf space), had a large, comfortable bed with crisp cotton sheets, good lighting, lots of pink and blue in the decor. The Ball family run the place highly professionally but with an emphasis on a family-run operation. Reception is informal, Mr Ball and his manager carry bags and explain local places of interest. Ramon Farthing is a chef of uncommon talent; the cooking is confident and classy; dishes are complex but light. There's a set-price menu with four choices on each of three courses plus cheese, and a simpler and cheaper daily menu with less choice priced according to the number of courses taken, but neither menu changed from night to night. Prices are high. Drinks before and after the meal are served in two pleasant, bright sitting rooms scented with wood smoke. A greedy Labrador puts on a heart-rending pantomime as it begs for *petits fours*. Breakfast, apart from the coffee, is first-class." (*David Wooff; also Mr and Mrs R Doak, T and R Rose*) The criticisms – service can be patchy, and: "Little was given away: a bowl of fruit left at the top of the stairs for guests to help themselves was rather a sorry collection; there was no question of rooms being traded up though the hotel was underoccupied." More reports please.

Open All year. Restaurant closed to non-residents Sun night.
Rooms 16 double – all with bath, shower (4 have whirlpool bath), telephone, radio, TV. 9 on ground floor in courtyard.
Facilities Ramps. Lounge with dispense bar, drawing room, restaurant (pianist on Sat night); private dining room, conference facilities. 4-acre grounds with croquet lawn, outdoor swimming pool (heated May–Sep). Fishing, golf, riding nearby.
Location 3 m W of Tetbury on A4135. Parking.
Restrictions No smoking in dining room. No children under 12 as residents. No dogs.
Credit cards All major cards accepted.
Terms B&B: single £80–£125, double £100–£145; dinner, B&B: single £104–£160, double £158–£220. Set lunch £13–£18, dinner £29–£38. Weekend and midweek breaks; off-season breaks; Christmas package; gourmet and wine weekends in autumn. 1-night bookings refused during Badminton, Gold Cup week, Gatcombe horse trials, some bank holidays.
Service/tipping: "We do not make a service charge and tips are not expected."

THORNBURY Avon — Map 2

Thornbury Castle
Thornbury
Bristol BS12 1HH

Tel Thornbury (0454) 418511
Fax (0454) 416188

An imposing building, owned by Maurice Taylor, on the edge of an attractive and well-heeled village, peacefully set in vast grounds with well-tended gardens and a vineyard. The castle was never finished, but the remains, mostly dating from the early 16th century, have been luxuriously renovated and make an impressive hotel. Many of the guests are American. Baronial public rooms have huge fireplaces, mullioned windows, antique furniture and tapestries. The restaurant, popular with local diners, is in two dining rooms and is variously considered "sombre" or "magnificently baronial". Last year opinions of the cooking were mixed, but now, under Derek Hamlen, the cuisine is worthy of its setting. There is an extensive wine list including good-value wines from all over the world. Bedrooms vary considerably in size; all have a well-appointed bathroom and lavish extras. Some are as impressive as the public rooms, "with stone walls, ornate plasterwork ceiling, fireplaces, oriental rugs, tapestries and antiques". Verdicts on the hotel are generally positive: "One of our favourite hotels, it runs like clockwork most of the time; relaxing yet smart." "Staff mainly young and friendly; they take a lot of trouble." "Breakfast, served in the bedroom, was first-class." (*Mr and Mrs A Daniels; also David Morris, and others*) But some readers have felt there's a slightly impersonal, international feeling to the castle, and there are a few niggles: "Mean bath towels." "The muzak is classical, but it's still muzak."

Open All year except 2–11 Jan.
Rooms 1 suite, 15 double, 2 single – all with bath, shower, telephone, radio, TV; tea-making facilities on request. 5 across small courtyard.
Facilities 2 lounges, 2 dining rooms. 12-acre grounds with walled garden, vineyard, farm. Clay-pigeon shooting. Fishing nearby.
Location 12 m N of Bristol, at N edge of Thornbury, just off B4061; lodge gate beside St Mary's parish church.
Restrictions Not suitable for ♿. No smoking in dining rooms. No children under 12. No dogs.
Credit cards All major cards accepted.
Terms B&B: single £75–£80, double £95–£190, suite £165–£190. Set lunch £18, dinner £30.50. Winter breaks. Christmas programme. 2-night min stay for weekends.
Service/tipping: "Our guests are entitled to good service. Gratuities are not expected."

TOWERSEY Oxfordshire — Map 1

Upper Green Farm BUDGET — *Tel* Thame (084 421) 2496
Manor Road
Towersey OX9 3QR

We long to have more rural retreats within a fifty-mile radius of London, especially those in the budget category. Euan and Marjorie Aitken's B&B farmhouse, which makes its Guide debut this year, is thatched and 15th-century, with an adjoining 18th-century barn called Paradise across the lawned yard. Its position off a cul-de-sac lane is a chocolate-box artist's dream, with an enchanting garden, lots of flowers in tubs, a duck pond and views towards the Chilterns. Three of the bedrooms are in the farmhouse, where bathrooms may have to be shared; the six rooms in Paradise all have *en suite* facilities. Marjorie Aitken was formerly in the antique business, and a picker-up of unconsidered trifles. Her rooms are filled, but not disagreeably cluttered, with lovely and amusing things – country antiques, lace and patchwork – and have TV, central heating and the like. Breakfasts, served in the barn's old stables, include home-grown fruit and home-made jams, as well as a richer diet for those who want the full works. The village pub, a short walk away, offers evening meals, and there are many good restaurants nearby. Heathrow airport is only three-quarters of an hour's drive away, Oxford is 30 minutes. (*HR*)

Open All year.
Rooms 7 double, 2 single – 7 with bath and/or shower, all with TV, tea-making facilities. 6 in converted barn across farmyard. 2 on ground floor.
Facilities Lounge, breakfast room. 7-acre grounds.
Location 1½ m E of Thame off A4129.
Restrictions Not suitable for severely ♿. No smoking. No children under 13. No pets.
Credit cards None accepted.

Terms B&B: single £17.28, double £33.50. 1-night bookings refused for Christmas and bank holidays. (No restaurant.)

TREBARWITH STRAND Cornwall — Map 1

The Old Millfloor BUDGET — *Tel* Camelford (0840) 770234
Trebarwith Strand
Tintagel PL34 0HA

Janice Whaddon-Martyn's small secluded guest house is set in a fern-filled glen by a millstream, with old beams, gleaming wood, fresh flowers and clever use of fabrics, light and colour. Bedrooms have "an old-fashioned feel, with white walls, pure white linen, lots of lace, big feather pillows". Dinner, with limited choice and "an emphasis on flavour not richness", is by candle-light in the small beamed dining room; menus tend to feature home-made soups and ice-creams, fresh vegetables, clotted cream. No licence, bring your own wine. "Very tranquil," writes a recent visitor, "with wonderful Aga-cooked food. No charge for early morning and cream teas. Freshly cooked rolls and scones, *lovely* breakfast." Not for the disabled or infirm, since there is a steep path down from the road (best to take the minimum of luggage), but perfect for families: lots of pets, ten acres of grounds and the beach ten minutes' walk away; and the prices are ridiculously modest. (*K Armstrong*) More reports please.

Open Easter–Nov.
Rooms 3 doubles with H&C, TV.
Facilities Restaurant with lounge. 10-acre grounds with garden, orchard, paddocks, stream. Beach 10 mins' walk. Riding centre 2½ m.
Location 2 m S of Tintagel.
Restrictions Not suitable for ♿. No dogs.
Credit cards None accepted.
Terms (No VAT) B&B £15. Dinner £11.50 (unlicensed – bring your own wine). 1 child in parents' room free; special meals.
Service/tipping: "No service charge. Tips not expected."

TREGONY Cornwall — Map 1

Tregony House BUDGET — *Tel* Tregony (087 253) 671
Tregony, Truro TR2 5RN

This village house, part 17th century, part Victorian, in a peaceful and charming inland Cornish village at the entrance to the Roseland Peninsula, about six miles from the sea, was dropped from the Guide last year when it changed hands. After the arrival of the new owners, Barry and Judy Sullivan, we were inundated with reports urging its reinstatement. "The Sullivans have continued the previous owners' high standards. Food is similar, simpler to some extent, and to our taste more pleasing. The whole place is immaculate." "Comfortable and tastefully decorated. Our hosts thoroughly spoiled us. Meals not rushed; everything fresh or home-made. First-class wine cellar." "Delicious four-course meal. Portions not too huge, so you did not end up feeling bloated." "Good value all round. Pot of tea on arrival most welcome; breakfast especially good." "Bedroom, with soft colours and Victorian bedspread, most pleasing. We were introduced to our fellow guests at pre-dinner drinks, which were served in a cosy corner of the beamed, stone-floored dining room with oriental rugs." (*Stephen R Holman, Elaine A Layfield, Mrs J Ernst, G and M Rees, Mrs RD Anderson; also Andrew Daugulis, Mrs EM Atkinson, Sir John Holland, and many others*) Vegetarians are catered for, given advance warning. The Sullivans say they will not increase their prices in 1992. There is a self-contained cottage suite, up a separate staircase, where children from seven to twelve can stay at half price. The house is on the village's main street, but it is quiet, and front rooms are double-glazed.

Open Mar–Oct inclusive.
Rooms 5 doubles (2, in cottage, can form family suite), 1 single – 1 with bath and shower, 1 with bath, all with tea-making facilities.
Facilities Lounge with TV, dining room with bar and sitting area. ½-acre garden. Sandy beaches, Cornish coastal path within 6 m.
Location A390 St Austell–Truro. After Sticker and Hewas Water fork left on B3287; follow signs for St Mawes and Tregony.
Restrictions Not suitable for ♿. No smoking in dining room. No children under 7.
Credit cards None accepted.
Terms (Not VAT rated) Dinner, B&B £27.50. Reductions for 7 or more days. Children 7–12 half price in cottage suite.
Service/tipping: "No service charge added. Tipping neither expected nor encouraged."

TRESCO Isles of Scilly — Map 1

The New Inn — *Tel* Scillonia (0720) 22844
Tresco, Isles of Scilly
Cornwall TR24 0QQ

Tresco is a private island, two miles by one, renowned for the Abbey Gardens, with exotic plants from all over the world. No cars are allowed – there are bicycles for hire – so Tresco (day trippers apart) is exceptionally peaceful. "If you want an island holiday away from it all with very good food, very reasonably priced, go to the *New Inn*. Better value for money you will not find." Chris and Lesley Hopkins's welcoming inn does not have impressive public rooms and facilities, just two bars, a lounge, a small garden with a swimming pool, and it's near a sandy beach. Bedrooms are small but adequate, with pretty floral decor and good lighting; many enjoy a sea view; bathrooms have good fluffy towels but lack "freebies". The food, on a simple but imaginative set menu with plenty of choice, is "of a high standard, combining fresh ingredients, skilful cooking and excellent presentation". Fish dishes are particularly good; so are breakfasts and bar lunches. The staff are friendly and helpful. (*Ken and Mildred Edwards*) This year the Hopkins have introduced an early sitting for dinner, with a reasonably priced children's menu for guests with young families who want to dine *en famille*. More reports please.

Open All year.
Rooms 10 double, 2 single – all with bath, shower, telephone, radio, TV, tea-making facilities, baby-listening.
Facilities Lounge, lounge bar, public bar, restaurant. Garden with swimming pool. Sandy beaches with safe bathing, fishing.
Location Scheduled helicopter flight or boat from Penzance except Sun. Hotel will make travel arrangements.
Restrictions Not suitable for ♿. No dogs allowed on Tresco.

Credit cards None accepted.
Terms Dinner, B&B £35–£55. Bar lunches. Set dinner £17. 3- and 4-day breaks including helicopter fare. Christmas and New Year packages. Reduced rates and special meals for children.
Service/tipping: "It is time to face up to the truth. Pay and conditions in the industry mean that tips are a necessary evil. I have yet to visit an average hotel or restaurant in any country that was pompous enough to say they didn't accept gratuities, so why should British hotels be expected to refuse what is often one of the best reflections of the standards offered by a hotel? My staff do very well for tips, which are pooled and shared equally among them."

The Island Hotel
Tresco, Isles of Scilly
Cornwall TR24 0PU

Tel Scillonia (0720) 22883
Fax (0720) 23008

Longtime Guide favourite, modern building by sea in 5-acre grounds with swimming pool, private beach, dramatic views of rocky coast and other islands. Now with new manager, recently enlarged and with public rooms modernised. Visitors who knew it under earlier regime lament changes from the old regime and more casual atmosphere, but food on large menu still good, dining room service friendly, bedrooms comfortable and it is "making a conscious effort to appeal to families with young children". Open Feb–Nov. 40 rooms, all with bath/shower. Not suitable for ♿. Access, Amex, Visa accepted. Dinner, B&B £61–£115. More reports please.

TROUTBECK Cumbria — Map 4

Mortal Man
Troutbeck, Nr Windermere
LA23 1PL

Tel Ambleside (053 94) 33193

"As good as ever," writes a regular. "A warm, comfortable inn. The bedrooms have been upgraded and even have trouser presses. Delightful view from all rooms." "Endorse all your comments, particularly about the meals which are outstanding in choice, quality and quantity. Different menu daily, all beautifully presented and served." (*IC Dewey; DJ Logan*) Annette and Christopher Poulsom's white-painted Lakeland inn, peacefully set on a hilltop above the Troutbeck valley, is over 300 years old, though its name derives from an early 19th-century sign showing two dalesmen, one jolly and rubicund, the other lank and lean: "O mortal man that lives by bread/What is it makes thy nose so red?/Thou silly fool that look so pale/Tis drinking Sally Birkett's ale." It has oak beams, thick walls and a simple but comfortable decor. The residents' lounge has an open fire in winter, old hunting prints on the walls, comfortable easy chairs, gleaming brass-topped tables. In the adjoining bar good pub food is served. Visitors enjoy the friendly, relaxed atmosphere presided over by the Poulsoms; the English breakfasts and the packed lunches are praised and the overall verdict is "excellent value for money".

Open Mid-Feb–mid-Nov.
Rooms 10 double, 2 single – all with bath, shower, telephone, radio, TV, tea-making facilities.
Facilities Lounge, lounge bar, public bar, restaurant. ½-acre grounds.
Location 3 m N of Windermere on A592.
Restrictions Not suitable for ♿. No children under 5.

Credit cards None accepted.
Terms Dinner, B&B £41–£47. Set Sun lunch £11, dinner £17.50. Bar meals. Reductions for longer stays.
Service/tipping: "Service included. The rates quoted above are what I like to get – no more, no less."

TROWBRIDGE Wiltshire — Map 2

The Old Manor
Trowle, Trowbridge BA14 9BL
Tel Trowbridge (0225) 777393
Telex (0225) 765443

Barry and Diane Humphreys's fine listed house, part medieval with Queen Anne alterations, in 4-acre grounds on A363 to Bradford on Avon, ½ m from the handsome market town of Trowbridge. Comfortable, well-equipped bedrooms, varying in size, furnished in pine, in recently converted barns and cowsheds. Good plain cooking with fresh ingredients; limited choice; meals for residents only. No hidden charges. Closed 1 week in winter. 14 rooms, all with private facilities. No dogs. All major credit cards accepted. B&B double £52–£59.50; full alc £20. Recent nomination. More reports please.

ULLINGSWICK Hereford and Worcester — Map 2

The Steppes
Ullingswick
Nr Hereford HR1 3JG
Tel Hereford (0432) 820424

Ullingswick is a tiny Domesday-old hamlet quietly situated in the Wye valley, well placed for exploring the county of Hereford and the Welsh Marches. The *Steppes* is a pretty Grade II listed 17th-century country house, rich in exposed beams, inglenook fireplaces and other period features, and furnished with antiques; there is a cellar bar, with flagged floor and rough stone walls; two bedrooms are in converted stables, with vaulted ceilings. It is run in a highly personal style by Henry and Tricia Howland; visitors appreciate the comfortable and spacious bedrooms, with good beds and reading lights and large bathrooms, and the four-course dinners (no choice except by prior arrangement), which are served at 7.30 pm by candle-light. (There is also an à la carte menu offering "less adventurous" food, and vegetarian dishes, but you must order from this by 10 am.) A substantial continental breakfast, available from 7.30 am, can be served in the bedroom (£2 extra). English, from 9 am, in the dining room, must be ordered the night before. Mr Howland is defensive about the music that is played "even at breakfast": "It is from our classical record collection built up over many years, and is very much part of the atmosphere of the *Steppes*; what we play is carefully chosen to be conducive to the consumption of a meal – it is never rousing or stirring. But the speaker complained of last year has been moved to a more suitable position." (*KG Mather, BRA Blaxall*)

Open All year except 2 weeks before Christmas and 2 weeks after New Year.
Rooms 6 double – all with bath, shower, telephone, radio, TV, mini-bar, tea-making facilities. 1 on ground floor. 2 in courtyard cottage.
Facilities Lounge, bar, dining room. 1½-acre garden with duck pond, sheep, rabbits, chickens; riding, fishing nearby.
Location 7 m NE of Hereford off A417 Gloucester to Leominster road.

Restrictions ♿ by prior arrangement. No smoking in bar and dining room. No children under 12. No dogs in public rooms.
Credit cards Access, Amex, Visa.
Terms B&B: single £30–£35, double £55–£65; dinner, B&B: single £36–£48, double £70–£90. Bargain breaks all year; Christmas and New Year 3-day house parties.
Service/tipping: "Service included. Tips neither expected nor asked for; nonetheless often given."

ULLSWATER Cumbria — Map 4

Howtown Hotel BUDGET — *Tel* Pooley Bridge (076 84) 86514
Ullswater, Penrith CA10 2ND

César award in 1991: Best budget hotel of the year

"A wonderful oasis and a reminder of what a good middle-class hotel must have been like at the turn of the century. Everything spick and span. Service outstandingly good. Food impeccable and just as described in your Guide. Wine list good, with wines from many regions, and astonishingly reasonable." "Confirm what I wrote after our fifth visit: it is such a pleasure to have the bed turned down during dinner, and early morning tea brought to the room rather than to have to make it yourself. The whole place is spotless, comfortable and welcoming, with Mrs Baldry keeping a discreet eye on everything to see that her guests are well looked after. We shall return again and again." This comfortable farmhouse on the unspoilt southern shore of Ullswater has long been a favourite of Guide readers, particularly walkers and climbers, and is run by Jacquie Baldry and her son David – the fourth generation of the family to be involved. It is a long low building set back from the road. Few of the bedrooms have private facilities; furnishings are comfortable and homely. The food is generous rather than sophisticated – dinner, with limited choice, is at 7 pm; cold and packed lunches are available. The atmosphere is relaxed and the tariff astoundingly low. The hotel has its own private foreshore on Ullswater. (*Mr and Mrs C Moncreiffe, Sally Saysell*) *Howtown* is not easy to get into, due to the very high return rate.

Open End Mar–1 Nov.
Rooms 13 double, 3 single – 3 with bath, 1 with shower, 4 in 2 annexes in grounds. 4 self-catering cottages.
Facilities 4 lounges, 2 bars, TV room, dining room. 2-acre grounds. 300 yds from lake with private foreshore; walking, climbing, riding, golf nearby.
Location On E shore of lake 4 m S of Pooley Bridge.
Restrictions Not suitable for ♿. No children under 7. Dogs at management's discretion (£1 a day); not in public rooms.
Credit cards None accepted.
Terms [1991 rates] Dinner, B&B £29.15. Lunch: cold on weekdays from £6.40, table d'hôte on Sun from £7.70; set dinner £9.75; cold supper on Sun from £7. Reductions for 4 or more nights. 1-night bookings sometimes refused. Reduced rates for children sharing parents' room.
Service/tipping: "No service charge. Any gratuities offered are distributed equally among the staff."

> We ask hotels to estimate their 1992 tariffs, but many prefer not to think so far ahead and give their 1991 tariffs. Many hotels on the continent do not return our questionnaire. So the prices we quote should be checked on booking.

Sharrow Bay
Ullswater, Penrith CA10 2LZ

Tel Pooley Bridge (076 84) 86301 and 86483
Fax (076 84) 86349

César award in 1985: For distinguished long service

"There is no hotel in Europe that one can return to with so much pleasure as this. Brian and Francis, two gentlemen of the old school, courteous, warm, welcoming and still directing their staff, masterfully ensure that their guests are comfortable, sated and happy. They give everyone individual attention and that most precious commodity – time. A well-trained band of men and women support them and the standards of cooking are maintained. They never leaped on the *nouvelle cuisine* bandwagon but our meals showed flair, and accurate cooking and seasoning. We came here twenty-five years ago on our first wedding anniversary and have returned many times since, never to be disappointed." "What service! A tiny remark on our first visit long ago has resulted in the waiter appearing at my shoulder after the main course on every subsequent visit. 'We have prepared a little of your favourite toffee pudding for you if you would like it.' Heaven!" "Staff so highly trained that nothing suffers in the owners' absence. Mr Lawrence, the charming manager, keeps tight control yet manages to go far beyond the call of duty in caring for guests. The food defies description; breakfast and afternoon tea being almost as sumptuous as dinner, after which one only has the energy to walk to the lodge and climb into a bed as comfortable as one's own."

Once again readers are moved to literary heights on visiting Brian Sack and Francis Coulson's celebrated hotel on the beautiful, less crowded eastern shore of Ullswater. Forty-four years ago they created the concept of the country house hotel. It has spawned many imitators, but there is only one *Sharrow Bay*, renowned for the prodigal generosity of the meals and a similar prodigality in the furnishings in the bedrooms, filled with innumerable cosseting extras. Throughout the house, too, there is a profusion of *objets d'art*, collected over the years. Some of the bedrooms, particularly those in the main house, are small; those in the annexe, *Bank House*, a mile away, are larger (you need a car). An unusually large staff, many of whom have been there for years, cope with the residents and the casual diners; such is *Sharrow Bay*'s fame that public rooms can get crowded when the restaurant is busy. One reader last year thought things were regimented; the proprietors reply: "We do *not* insist on people going into the dining room at a set time; in fact we prefer them not to do so. But they seem to decide of their own free will to go in together and as they are shown the sweet trolley before they sit down, a queue does form from time to time." (*Francine and Ian Walsh, Richard Gollin, Jackie Jackson; also Pat and Jeremy Temple, Heather Sharland, and many others*) Only niggle: "The wine list is a trifle dull; this is often the case where really interesting food is served."

Open Mar–early Dec.
Rooms 6 suites, 17 double, 7 single – 26 with bath and/or shower, all with telephone, radio, TV; 4 with tea-making facilities. 17 in cottages, Lodge annexe and Bank House, at varying distances from main building. 5 on ground floor.
Facilities 4 lounges, conservatory, breakfast room, 2 dining rooms. 12-acre grounds at Sharrow, 5 acres at Bank House; garden, woodlands; ½ m of lake shore with safe bathing, private jetty and boathouse; fishing, boating, walking, climbing.

Location On E shore of Ullswater, 2 m S of Pooley Bridge. Turn by small church in Pooley Bridge and take Howtown Lane. (M6 exit 40.)
Restrictions Not suitable for ♿. No smoking in dining room. No children under about 13. No dogs.
Credit cards None accepted.
Terms [1991 rates] Dinner, B&B: single £82–£113, double £148–£170, suite £196–£236. Set lunch from £23.50 (light lunches also available weekdays), dinner from £38.50. 10% midweek reductions Mar, Nov. 1-night bookings sometimes refused, especially weekends.
Service/tipping: "No service charge. We and our staff give our services freely and do not expect to be rewarded by clients directly. If a particularly persistent client wishes to impose his will upon us we say (we hope without causing offence) that tipping is a feudal system and degrades both giver and receiver."

UPPINGHAM Leicestershire — Map 1

The Lake Isle
16 High Street East
Uppingham, Rutland LE15 9PZ

Tel (0572) 822951
Fax (0572) 822951

Claire and David Whitfield's restaurant-with-rooms is in the main street of this attractive small market town in an 18th-century building which has had many uses in its time: it was last known as "Sweeney Todd's", the hairdressers – Uppingham School boys had their hair cut in what is now the "warm and welcoming" bar. Bedrooms (and a lounge) are in a building at the rear and an adjacent cottage; they vary in size and character, from first-floor rooms with large windows to cottage-style ones on the second floor; some are very small. Mrs Whitfield ("no smoothie, but a dedicated hotel professional") is front of house, her husband cooks. Last year the entry was italicised due to criticisms of the welcome and some bedrooms. The Whitfields tell us they are happier with their staff this year, and: "We try to compensate for the smallness of some of the rooms with all the little extras we supply and we give guests information about the size and location of rooms when they book so there will be no disappointments." Most visitors this year have been pleased both with the accommodation ("sophisticated fabrics . . . top-class goodies in the bathroom") and the meals (set prices for three or five courses) in the attractively panelled and beamed dining room. "We ate three dinners and enjoyed them all; not brilliant, but on the whole well cooked and presented, with generous portions. Breakfasts simply wonderful. Service deft, courteous, mostly very friendly and without any 'enjoy your meal' claptrap. Cleaning staff very superior; their pride in their work and the hotel was a delight." Rutland Water is six miles away; there are many stately homes worth a visit in the area, such as Belvoir Castle, Burghley House and Belton House. (*Charles Gorer; also Dr and Mrs Frank, John Wright*) A couple with a baby and dog "could hardly move" in a small ("though comfortable") bedroom with an odd-shaped bathroom, and found "little variety on the menu – a lot of the starters and main courses were very spicy". More reports please.

Open All year.
Rooms 1 suite in adjacent cottage, 9 double, 1 single – all with bath and/or shower (1 with whirlpool), telephone, radio, TV, tea-making facilities.
Facilities Lounge, bar, restaurant; private dining room, meeting room. Walled garden. Rutland Water with fishing, bird watching, sailing, windsurfing 6 m.

Location Entrance at rear on foot via Reeves Yard. By car Queen Street and 2 right turns to rear.
Restrictions Not suitable for ♿. No dogs in public rooms.
Credit cards All major cards accepted.
Terms B&B: single £39–£45, double £58–£66, suite £70–£74. Set lunch £12, dinner £23. Wine evenings; weekend reductions; Christmas package.
Service/tipping: "We do not add a service charge; if a customer wishes to leave a tip it is shared among all staff."

VERYAN Cornwall **Map 1**

The Nare Hotel *Tel* Truro (0872) 501279
Carne Beach, Veryan TR2 5PF *Fax* (0872) 501856

"A very dependable seaside hotel in a superb location. Food first-class, good choice, as much or as little as you want and take as long as you wish. Service cheerful and efficient by young Cornish staff. By the second evening everyone knew us by name. The hotel is relaxed, but efficiently run by owners who live on the premises and dine in the restaurant each night." "The new owners, Mr and Mrs Gray, have improved both accommodation and service to such an extent that this has now become my favourite hotel in the UK." "Food of a high standard. Packed lunches more than adequate. Beds turned down at night and hot-water bottles provided. A log fire in March added to the homely atmosphere." These and other warm endorsements of last year's italicised entry promote to a full entry this seaside hotel in a particularly agreeable situation on the Roseland peninsula, surrounded by National Trust land and with direct access to a safe, sandy beach which it overlooks. It stands in sub-tropical gardens, with swimming pool, tennis court and secluded corners for sunbathing. Inside are numerous public rooms attractively furnished with antiques, oriental rugs and comfortable sofas, and filled with flowers. Bedrooms, many spacious, but some quite small, are well equipped; many have sea view and balcony or patio. In the dining room, which also enjoys the sea view, local produce is used (and male guests are expected to wear jacket and tie for dinner); good light lunches and cream teas are also served, outdoors in fine weather. Free golf is offered to the hotel's guests at Truro Golf Club. Families are catered for: there's a children's play area, and an early supper is provided for under-7s. (*Ken and Mildred Edwards, Clive Newman, LB Pinnell; also Charles Foden and George Atkinson, and others*)

Open All year.
Rooms 34 double, 6 single – all with bath and/or shower, telephone, radio, TV, tea-making facilities; 34 with baby-listening. 7 on ground floor, 2 with access for ♿.
Facilities Drawing room, writing room, bar with terrace, restaurant, luncheon room, conservatory, games room, children's play area. 4-acre grounds, with gardens, swimming pool (heated Easter–Oct), tennis, on safe sandy beach with boat, sailboards, sea fishing.
Location 13 m SE of Truro. S of Veryan on Gerrans Bay.
Restrictions Smoking discouraged in dining room. No children under 7 in dining room at night. No dogs in public rooms.
Credit cards Access, Visa.
Terms B&B: single £40–£95, double £80–£160. Set dinner £22; full alc £28. Half-board rates (3 days min); weekly rates. Reduced rates and special meals for children.
Service/tipping: "Service included. Tips at guests' discretion."

WALKINGTON Humberside — Map 4

The Manor House
Northlands, Walkington
Hull HU17 8RT

Tel Hull (0482) 881645
Fax (0482) 866501

Derek and Lee Baugh's imposing, luxuriously appointed yellow-brick 19th-century manor house with mock-Tudor black and white gabling is quietly situated in three-acre grounds with mature trees, manicured lawns and rolling fields beyond, but is not far from Kingston-upon-Hull. Public rooms are large, comfortable and lavishly decorated; so are bedrooms, with kingsize beds, huge windows overlooking the gardens, plenty of sitting and storage space, and smart furniture of the gilt-knobs-with-everything style; bathrooms are fitted in, sometimes slightly awkwardly, but are well equipped. The blue candle-lit restaurant with conservatory extension is popular locally; the menu is extremely flowery. Chef/*patron* Derek Baugh's "fairly flamboyant style of cooking – *nouvelle* in Yorkshire-sized portions" is in character with everything else. Service is "helpful and willing". But one 1991 visitor's stay was spoilt by a "paltry" breakfast with carton juice and £1.50 extra for cereal. More reports needed please.

Open All year except 25/26 Dec and New Year's Day. Restaurant closed lunchtime and Sun evening.
Rooms 5 double – all with bath, shower, telephone, radio, TV, tea-making facilities.
Facilities Drawing room, restaurant, conservatory. 3-acre grounds.
Location 3 m SW of Beverley. Take Newbald Road off Beverley Westwood York Road.
Restrictions Not suitable for ♿. No children under 12.
Credit cards Access, Visa.
Terms B&B: single £71.50, double £88. Set dinner £25. 2-night half-board package.
Service/tipping: "No service charge. Service at guests' discretion, shared among staff on basis of hours worked."

WAREHAM Dorset — Map 2

The Priory
Church Green
Wareham BH20 4ND

Tel Wareham (0929) 551666
and 552772
Fax (0929) 554519

Last year's entry for the former Priory of Lady St Mary is enthusiastically endorsed by readers after a three-week visit: "We have now stayed four times. Mr and Mrs Turner are always on the spot ensuring that the highest standards are maintained. The staff remain mostly the same; they greeted us with genuine warmth. The grounds are beautiful, and so peaceful you don't realise you are only a couple of minutes from Wareham high street. The food is excellent; the menu changes daily and there is a wide choice of wines. There are lovely flower arrangements by Mrs Turner. The best bedrooms are in the converted boathouse, with private patio, and in the parts of the hotel that overlook the river, the Purbeck hills and the gardens. There's no extra charge for meals served in your room and you can have a snack lunch on the lawn, lazing on your sunbed."

The medieval cluster of buildings is sandwiched between the river Frome and the town church in an unspoilt Dorset town. "Its transformation from priory to hotel," a reader wrote last year, "has been handled with taste and care. Every bedroom is furnished and decorated individually and includes the best available towels and bathrobes, an extensive mini-bar and practically every convenience you could wish for. The staff are professional and cheerful. Dinner in the converted abbot's cellar was of a high standard, English in style, with four delicious courses; a full breakfast is served until 10.30 am in the bedrooms or dining room. There are two beautifully furnished lounges. Thank God there is no piped music; the Turners obviously prefer the real thing, and a wonderful pianist entertained us on Saturday evening; loudspeakers in the restaurant enabled diners to enjoy the performance." (*Ralph and Betty Smith; also Debby Jellett, and others*)

Open All year.
Rooms 2 suites, 16 double, 3 single – all with bath and/or shower, telephone, radio, TV; tea-making facilities on request. 2 suites, 2 doubles in riverside boathouse. Some on ground floor.
Facilities 2 lounges, bar, restaurant; pianist on Sat and holiday nights. 4½-acre grounds with river frontage; mooring, fishing.
Location By town church and river.
Restrictions No smoking in dining room. No dogs.
Credit cards All major cards accepted.
Terms [1991 rates] B&B: single £60–£80, double £75–£170, suite £175. Set lunch: weekdays £9.95–£11.95, Sun £14.95. Dinner £22.50 (£26.50 on Sat); full alc from £30. Off-season breaks; Christmas package.
Service/tipping: "Service at guests' discretion."

WARMINSTER Wiltshire — Map 2

Bishopstrow House
Boreham Road
Warminster BA12 9HH

Tel Warminster (0985) 212312
Fax (0985) 216769

"This is the weekend of blizzards," writes a visitor *in situ* in December 1990. "And we might be holed up for a few days. But why worry? You couldn't find a better place. There is indoor tennis and swimming pool (outdoor ones too), which must be exceptional in this type of place, and various other activities. Six of us are here on a winter break which is pretty cheap bearing in mind the quality of the hotel, service and food. The public rooms are comfortable and not over-formal; there are log fires which is necessary as the central heating is not perfect. Our bedroom is large and well furnished and the bathroom has all the usual toys plus hair-drier and dressing gowns. As the heating was not sufficient (it's freezing outside) we have been given convector heaters. Fruit and biscuits are supplied in the bedroom. Service is efficient and friendly. The chef, Chris Suter, was recently named Young Chef of the Year. The menu has plenty of choice and we have all enjoyed the food; he is imaginative, with new ideas based on both classical and *nouvelle* cuisine. Good wine list with varieties from many countries." "Expensive, but memorable for the utter courtesy and friendliness of the staff. Even a snack lunch was served with style. Most comfortable rooms, furnished period style. Civilised calm." (*David Morris, Brian MacArthur*) This late Georgian country house in large grounds bordering the river Wylye (with fishing) is now owned by the Blandy brothers who also own *Reid's*, Madeira, and *Charingworth Manor* in the Cotswolds (qq.v.); it's managed by David Dowden. It re-entered the Guide last year in italics and is now upgraded to a full entry. Public rooms have English and French antiques, Persian carpets and 19th-century paintings. Suites have luxurious bedrooms and bathrooms with large circular bath, some with whirlpool. Children are welcome, and there is good family accommodation.

Open All year.
Rooms 3 suites, 27 double, 2 single – all with bath, shower, telephone, radio, TV, baby-listening.
Facilities 3 lounges, restaurant, breakfast room, conference room. 27-acre grounds. Indoor and outdoor tennis and swimming pool, sauna, solarium; fishing, clay-pigeon shooting, golf available.
Location E of Warminster (10 mins by car), on B3413.
Restriction No dogs in public rooms.
Credit cards All major cards accepted.
Terms B&B: single £63.45, double £126.90, suite £276.45; dinner, B&B £87.50–£153.50. Set lunch £15.50, dinner £33; full alc £39.50. Summer and winter breaks. Reduced rates for children; special meals 5.30–6.30 pm.
Service/tipping: "No service charge. Tipping left to guests' discretion; distributed by tronc *system."*

WASDALE HEAD Cumbria — Map 4

Wasdale Head Inn
Wasdale Head, Nr Gosforth
CA20 1EX

Tel Wasdale (094 67) 26229
Fax (094 67) 26334

This unsophisticated but efficiently run inn, in an isolated and magnificent setting not far from Wastwater, is famous in the annals of British mountaineering, and popular among walkers and climbers. It has a panelled and comfortably old-fashioned residents' bar and lounge. The main bar is named after the inn's first landlord, Will Ritson, reputed to be the world's biggest liar; in his memory liar competitions are held once a year. The pine-panelled bedrooms are simple and not large, but clean, comfortable and well lit, all with private facilities, plenty of hot water and lovely views. "Telephone, but no TV, praise be!" There is a jolly snug bar serving "good home-made food" and "a splendid selection of beers". Visitors enjoy the warm welcome, the substantial breakfast, announced by a gong at 8 am, and the "interesting" packed lunches. The five-course dinners, served "on the dot at 7.30 pm" in the dining room with its authentic old furnishings, have limited choice, and are "mostly very good, and adequate in quantity. Puddings very 'moreish'." The atmosphere is relaxed; there are no dress rules. There is a large drying room and a simple laundry service. (*H Way, DA Cash*) More reports please.

Open Mid-Mar–mid-Nov, 28 Dec–13 Jan.
Rooms 8 double, 2 single – 8 with bath, 2 with shower, all with telephone, tea-making facilities, baby-listening. Self-catering units and apartments nearby.
Facilities Residents' lounge, residents' bar, public bar, restaurant; drying room. 3-acre grounds.
Location 10 m up Wasdale Head from Gosforth or Santon Bridge. Follow signs from A595.
Restrictions Not suitable for ♿. No children under 7 in dining room at night (high tea available). No dogs in public rooms.
Credit cards Access, Visa.

Terms [1991 rates] Dinner, B&B: single £51.50, double £99. Bar lunches. Set dinner £16. £3 reduction for 4 nights or more.
Service/tipping: "No service charge. We do not accept tips."

WATERHOUSES Staffordshire — Map 4

The Old Beams — *Tel* Waterhouses (0538) 308254
Waterhouses ST10 3HW

"The standard of accommodation and cooking was perfect. Warm welcome from Ann Wallis. Extremely well-fitted bathroom with towelling dressing gown, shampoo, hangover remedies. Dinner was faultless. Breakfast, too, was a model. What I particularly liked, apart from the warm atmosphere and decor, was that it was excellence without pretension; no hushed tones, no unnecessary fussiness; good service without servility." Nigel and Ann Wallis's small, 18th-century, heavily beamed (as its name implies) restaurant-with-rooms is on the edge of the Peak District National Park on the Ashbourne to Leek road (all rooms are double-glazed). The bedrooms, of varying sizes, are comfortable, immaculately kept, kitted out with numerous extras, with top-quality furnishings and fabrics. All but one are in the annexe opposite. In the beamed restaurant with a conservatory extension where a grand piano is sometimes played, Nigel Wallis's cooking – "*nouvelle*-ish, but with generous portions, using excellent, fresh ingredients" – gets a *Michelin* red "M", halfway to a rosette. His wife, Ann, efficiently and exuberantly looks after front of house and makes the desserts. Very good house wines. There is a lovely garden, floodlit at night. (*John Edington, and others*)

Open All year except 2 weeks Jan. Restaurant closed Mon, Sat lunch, Sun evening.
Rooms 6 double – all with bath, telephone, radio, TV, baby-listening. 5 in annexe opposite. 3 on ground floor.
Facilities Reception lounge/bar, restaurant with conservatory, private dining room. ½-acre garden.
Location On A523 between Ashbourne and Leek. All rooms double-glazed.
Restrictions Smoking forbidden in restaurant, discouraged in bedrooms. No children under 8. No dogs.
Credit cards All major cards accepted.
Terms [1991 rates] B&B: single £52–£72.50, double £67.50–£87. Set lunch £15.50, dinner £28.
Service/tipping: "No service charge. We advise against tipping."

WATERMILLOCK Cumbria — Map 4

Leeming House — *Tel* Pooley Bridge (076 84) 86622
Watermillock — *Fax* (076 84) 86443
Penrith CA11 0JJ

Still the only Guide hotel belonging to the ubiquitous Forte chain, this is an early Victorian house in magnificent, well-kept grounds with mature trees running down to Ullswater. The views, particularly from the first-floor bedrooms, are superb. Readers praise the comfortable public rooms, the professionalism of the manager, Christopher Curry, the well-trained and friendly staff and the high standard of housekeeping. Bedrooms are serviced during dinner and the generous bath towels changed twice a day. The restaurant, with garden views, is elegant and quite formal (jacket and tie *de rigueur* for men). "The six-course dinners were imaginative and attractively presented, with high quality ingredients – but tables for two rather small. We appreciated fresh orange juice for breakfast and excellent scrambled egg." Bedrooms in the main building, though not large, are well decorated but one reader this year reports: "Our peace was marred by the fact that our neighbours' bath seemed to be just behind our bedhead; we could hear them squeaking and slipping in the bath – before 6 am one day; and the shower fitting in our bath was unsatisfactory." A new wing, carefully designed to blend with the main building, opened in October 1990, adding twenty-six bedrooms, which one of the first occupants pronounces "excellent and luxuriously appointed". There are also a new library and conservatory. We'd be glad to know what effect these additions, inevitably bringing more residents and diners, have had on the atmosphere, described to us in the past as "calm and relaxed though dignified". (*Ann Webber, Margaret Richmond*)

Open All year.
Rooms 39 double, 1 single – all with bath and/or shower, telephone, radio, TV, tea-making facilities, baby-listening. 10 on ground floor, 1 equipped for ♿.
Facilities Drawing room, sitting room, library, cocktail bar, dining room, conservatory; conference facilities. 20-acre grounds with lake frontage (fishing, sailing, etc), arboretum and helipad.
Location On W shore of Ullswater on A592.
Restrictions No smoking in dining room and 9 bedrooms. No dogs in public rooms.
Credit cards All major cards accepted.
Terms B&B: single £68.70–£113.70, double £97.40–£162.40. Set dinner £32.50; full alc lunch £22. Half-board rates (2 day min). Christmas and New Year packages. Small shooting parties. 1-night bookings sometimes refused for weekends and bank holidays. Reduced rates for children sharing parents' room; special meals by arrangement.
Service/tipping: "All prices include service; any gratuities are collected and distributed to all staff."

The Old Church Hotel
Watermillock
Penrith CA11 0JN

Tel Pooley Bridge (076 84) 86204
Fax (076 84) 86368

"Staff and service excellent; comfortable room." "Owners very obliging. Food imaginative." *HLF, and WR Rowland* write to endorse the entry for Kevin and Maureen Whitemore's small hotel in a lovely lakeside position with fine views. It is an 18th-century house reached by a long private drive off the A592. The comfortable lounges are decorated in soft colours and there is plenty of evidence throughout of Mrs Whitemore's enthusiasm for soft furnishings – she runs upholstery courses in the hotel twice a year in low season. Guests gather in the bar at 7.30 for the 8 pm dinner – English cooking with plenty of choice, served in a pretty dining room with old wooden tables and fresh flowers; teas are also a feature of *The Old Church Hotel*. Rooms vary in size and style, so it is worth discussing the accommodation you want when booking. There are very good facilities for babies and small children. Some readers, however, feel it is quite expensive for what is on offer, and one considered the decor "severe".

If you are nominating a hotel, we'd be grateful if you could send us the brochure.

Open Mar–Nov inclusive. Closed for lunch Mon.
Rooms 10 double – all with bath, telephone; 5 with TV, tea-making facilities; baby-listening on request.
Facilities Hall, 2 lounges, bar, dining room. 1-acre grounds on lake with mooring and fishing; windsurfers and rowing boat available.
Location 3 m S of Pooley Bridge; 5 m from junction 40 on the M6.
Restrictions Not suitable for ♿. No smoking in dining room. No dogs.
Credit cards Access, Visa.
Terms [1991 rates] B&B: single £85–£140, double £120–£165; dinner, B&B: single £110–£165, double £150–£210. Full alc lunch £12.50; set dinner £29.50. Weekly rates. 1-night bookings sometimes refused for weekends and bank holidays. Soft furnishing courses Mar and Nov. Reduced rates and special meals for children. *Service/tipping: "We hope service charge and tipping will disappear. We normally suggest that money offered should be spent on the guests' next visit."*

WATERROW Somerset — Map 1

Hurstone — *Tel* Wiveliscombe (0984) 23441
Waterrow, Wiveliscombe TA4 2AT

Unanimity this year about this "unpretentious, relaxing" Georgian farmhouse in a tranquil rural setting, which now formally dubs itself a country hotel rather than a farmhouse hotel. "The atmosphere is just right; John Bone is a very pleasant, friendly, helpful man. Though the weather was appalling, we were always warm and comfortable; the hotel was efficiently centrally heated and there was a log fire in the sitting room, and loads of hot water at all times. The bedroom, newly decorated, was most attractive. At our request we were given conventional bedding rather than duvets. We particularly liked breakfast being served until 10 am." "The manager/chef has departed and John Bone is once again in day-to-day charge, supported by a corps of genuinely friendly people including a really good cook, Linda Featherstone. On arrival I was welcomed by name and offered tea and biscuits for which I was not charged. All the bedrooms, the dining room and sitting rooms face south, and all have splendid views. One doesn't have to worry that the last in or the single person gets the worst room. It is beautifully quiet at night, apart from owls and sometimes the ducks squabbling in their shed. There are lots of books and magazines, nice art on the walls and antique bits and pieces dotted about. Lovely food, plenty of half-bottles of wine and perfectly palatable house wines available in any quantity from a glass upwards." Bedrooms are not large, but "really well thought out. Good beds with lights you could read by. Extra special welcome for dogs [but no dogs in public rooms]; very important to us." The hotel does a busy restaurant trade; there is plenty of choice on the menu; cheese and cider are home produced. Children are welcome, and discounts for families offered. (*Moira Jarrett, Robin Houston, Mrs A Phillips; also Patricia Pells, CRG Quick*)

Open All year.
Rooms 1 family suite (1 double, 1 single), 4 double – all with bath, shower, telephone, TV, tea-making facilities, baby-listening.
Facilities Lounge, TV lounge, dining room. Terrace and gardens; 65-acre farmland with small trout river; fishing rights. Riding, tennis, golf nearby.
Location ¼ m off B3227 at Waterrow (signposted); 3 m SW of Wiveliscombe.
Restrictions Not suitable for ♿. Smoking discouraged in restaurant. No dogs in public rooms.
Credit cards Access, Amex, Visa.

Terms B&B: single £47.50–£52, double £75–£82.50, suite £95–£104.50. Set Sun lunch £8.75, set dinner from £17.50. Weekend and midweek breaks all year except public holidays; 5% discount for long stays; Christmas and New Year programmes. Reduced rates and special meals for children.
Service/tipping: "No service charge. Tips are not expected, but if anything is left it is shared by the staff."

WELLAND Hereford and Worcester — Map 2

Holdfast Cottage — *Tel* Hanley Swan (0684) 310288
Welland, Nr Malvern WR13 6NA

Small hotel, with quite small rooms; 17th century at heart, now mostly Victorian. In quietly situated 2-acre garden, 4 m SE of Malvern, facing Little Malvern Priory and Malvern hills on one side and Bredon hill and the Cotswolds on the other. Agreeable terrace for sitting in warm weather. Owned and run by Dennis and Diana Beetlestone. 8 bedrooms, simple but comfortable, all with bath and/or shower. Not suitable for ♿. Access, Visa accepted. B&B double £64–£72. Set dinner £14–£18.50. Entry recently endorsed, but some reservations about the dinners. More reports please.

WEST CLIFFE Kent — Map 3

Wallett's Court — *Tel* Dover (0304) 852424
West Cliffe, St Margaret's-at-Cliffe — *Fax* (0304) 853430
Dover CT15 6EW

Chris Oakley's manor house, dating in parts to Domesday, in 3-acre grounds in rural setting near Dover, handy for ferry. Antiques, exposed brickwork, fine fireplaces, black wood-burning stoves. Bedrooms in main building traditional, comfortable, mostly quite large; the four in annexe are basic (though insulation has been improved this year). Locally popular restaurant serves 3-course dinner at £17.50 on weekdays, gourmet meal on Sat for £25. Mixed reports this year: many regulars still enthusiastic, but there are also criticisms of welcome, housekeeping, decor and food. Hence these italics. Closed 1 week Nov, 1 week Christmas/New Year; restaurant closed for lunch and on Sun. 7 rooms – all with bath, shower. Not suitable for ♿. No dogs. Access, Visa accepted. B&B: single £35–£50, double £45–£65. More reports please.

WESTON UNDER PENYARD Hereford and Worcester — Map 2

Wharton Lodge — *Tel* Ross-on-Wye (0989) 81795
Weston under Penyard — *Fax* (0989) 81700
Nr Ross-on-Wye HR9 7JX

Handsome Georgian country house off A40 SE of Ross-on-Wye in 15-acre park, recently converted into a hotel by the Goughs whose family home it has been for four generations. Elegant designer decor – antiques, ornaments, fine fabrics. Very good dinner cooked by Hamish Deas ("outstanding suppliers, distinctive flavours") in "romantic" dining room; courteous service. Recommended by our inspector with qualifications: "No comfortable seating in bedroom or drawing room, breakfast poorly served, no contact with owner." 9 rooms, all with bath/shower. Not suitable for ♿. No children under 8. No dogs. All major credit cards accepted. Rooms: single £90, double £115–£130. Set dinner £25. More reports please.

WHIMPLE Devon — Map 1

Woodhayes *Tel* Whimple (0404) 822237
Whimple, Nr Exeter EX5 2TD

This large white Georgian country house, in a peaceful apple-orchard village off the A30, re-entered the Guide last year under new owners, Frank and Katherine Rendle. The entry is enthusiastically endorsed: "A lovely warm home, with cosy fires burning, and truly a family concern – Mrs Rendle cooks, Mr Rendle serves; the evening meal was a seven-course masterpiece. We were pampered lovingly and we hated to leave." "Mrs Rendle discusses the menu with you each day and caters for every whim. Fish comes from Brixham; vegetables and meat are chosen with care. Rolls, petits fours, biscuits and cakes are all home-baked. Portions are just right. There are *no* extras except wine and aperitifs." "Mrs Rendle mother-henned us and made us feel welcome. We had one of the nicest hotel rooms we have ever stayed in – spacious, beautifully furnished with antiques, sparkling clean and supremely comfortable. The large airy bathroom was equally inviting, and equipped with big bottles of toiletries and high-quality soap." "The most relaxing place we've stayed at in years. Caring hosts, garden perfect for sitting and reading, lounges full of soft-cushioned furniture, more-than-ample meals. All too much for normal life-style, but wonderful for a few days." (*Mr and Mrs Anthony Edwards, FK Poulton, Mary Woods, Bill and Ellen Bentsen*) Mrs Rendle writes: "Though we have a set menu we can offer an alternative at every course. I try to cook what you'd have at a dinner party at home, keeping each course light and colourful. We tell our visitors they have only to pick up the phone if they want anything at *any* time; a number are elderly, and they find this reassuring, particularly at night." Some minor "nits to pick": only one bedside light in a double room; "strange music at dinner, but fortunately not loud".

Open All year.
Rooms 6 double – all with bath with shower attachment, telephone, radio, TV; tea-making facilities on request.
Facilities 2 lounges, bar, restaurant. 4-acre grounds with tennis and croquet.
Location 8 m E of Exeter, ¾ m off A30; on right just before Whimple village.
Restrictions Not suitable for ♿. No children under 12. No dogs.
Credit cards All major cards accepted.
Terms B&B: single £55, double £75; dinner, B&B: single £68, double £98. Set lunch £14, dinner £22.50. Reduced rates for children sharing parents' room; special meals on request.
Service/tipping: "Service is included. We actively discourage tipping."

WILLINGTON Cheshire — Map 4

Willington Hall *Tel* Kelsall (0829) 52321
Willington *Fax* (0829) 52596
Nr Tarporley CW6 0NB

Hidden away in tiny village just off A54 E of Chester, interesting old house, with "dramatic" grey and red brick patterned frontage, in 17-acre park with tennis. Warm and comfortable; old-fashioned decor and "air of slightly faded gentility". Bar snacks. Restaurant popular locally; straightforward, adequate English cooking, service can be "Fawlty-esque"; breakfast so-so. Closed 25 Dec. 10 rooms, all with bath/shower. Only restaurant suitable for ♿. Access, Diners, Visa accepted. B&B: single £54, double £80. Set lunch £12.50; full alc dinner from £20. New nomination. More reports please.

WILLITON Somerset — Map 1

The White House — *Tel* Williton (0984) 32306
Williton TA4 4QW

César award in 1988: For combining the best of two worlds – French flair with English dependability

Owner/chefs Dick and Kay Smith have been over 23 years at this symmetrical white house with louvred shutters which stands on the main road of the small town, separated from it by a semi-circle of lawn with a couple of tall palms. It is well placed for exploring Somerset, particularly the Quantocks, and has had a Guide entry almost continually since our first edition in 1978. The building is full of good paintings and prints and attractive objects; furniture is a mixture of antique and modern, chosen with taste. Public rooms and areas are peaceful and well kept. The hotel is personally run, and the owners very much in evidence; it does not offer a house-party atmosphere or sybaritic luxury, but the atmosphere is "relaxed, friendly and civilised", and the bedrooms – some in the main building, others in converted stables and coach house in the courtyard – are thoughtfully equipped. The restaurant is the focus of the hotel; *Michelin* awards it a red "M" for the quality of the cooking, a combination of French Provincial, traditional English and modern; vegetables are particularly good. The wine list is extensive and interesting. English breakfasts, too, are highly praised. More reports please.

Open Mid-May–early Nov. Restaurant closed for lunch.
Rooms 1 family suite, 11 double, 1 single – 10 with private facilities (1 not *en suite*), all with telephone, radio, TV; tea-making facilities on request. 4 in courtyard annexe, some on ground floor.
Facilities Lounge, bar, restaurant. 2 m from coast; shingle beach 2 m, sandy beach 8 m.
Location On A39 in centre of village; courtyard rooms quietest. Parking.
Restrictions No smoking in dining room. Dogs by arrangement, not in public rooms.
Credit cards None accepted.
Terms [1991 rates] B&B £26–£41; dinner, B&B £52–£68. Set dinner £25. Bargain breaks all year. Reduced rates for children in family suite.
Service/tipping: "We do not make a service charge. If guests add anything to the bill it is given to the staff involved."

****

Traveller's tale *There were 18 pictures and plates on the bedroom walls, dotted among the lath and plaster and beams. The bathroom (15 plates and pictures) had every bit and bob imaginable but I couldn't find the soap for ten minutes because it was disguised in a little cotton bag tied up with ribbon.*

****

WINDERMERE Cumbria **Map 4**

The Archway **BUDGET** *Tel* Windermere (096 62) 5613
13 College Road
Windermere LA23 1BY

Anthony and Aurea Greenhalgh's small no-smoking guest house is enthusiastically nominated by two readers: "Strongly recommended for comfort, good value and excellent food. It's a slate Victorian terraced house in a quiet road but very near shops, station, bus, etc. There's a nice open view of green field and trees opposite. You can see the lake only from some top rooms (my single overlooked a carpark). Bedrooms are Laura Ashley style, with Victorian quilts and duvets and pine-y furniture, magazines, home-made biscuits, and hot-water bottles for cold nights. The lounge/dining room is pink, with antiques, 'real' books, chintz settee, log fire; at the rear is the dining area with separate pine tables and a big dresser. Evening meals are at 6.45 with no choice – three courses in winter, two in summer. Menus are imaginative; everything is fresh and organically grown, ending with help-yourself desserts (only complaint – no cheese platter available). Presentation is good, with nice china and silver. Breakfast is chosen from a full-page printed menu which included orange juice freshly squeezed (much offstage whirring!), home-made wholemeal bread, muesli and yoghurt, free-range eggs, superb locally cured bacon, Cumberland sausages. The proprietors are welcoming and helpful. Guests speak but aren't forced to mingle." (*Mrs Kate Kelly; also Linda Goldberg*)

Open All year. Dinner not served Sun in summer.
Rooms 4 double, 1 single – all with shower, telephone, radio, TV, tea-making facilities.
Facilities Lounge/dining room. Small garden. Lake Windermere 15 mins.
Location 3 mins' walk from centre. W of Main Road.
Restrictions Not suitable for ♿. No children under 12. No smoking. No dogs.
Credit cards None accepted.
Terms B&B £20–£23; dinner, B&B £30.50–£33.50. Set dinner: 2-course in summer £10.50, 3-course in winter £13.50. Winter midweek bargain breaks. Christmas package. 1-night bookings sometimes refused at weekends in high summer.
Service/tipping: "Service included. Tipping not encouraged or expected. If it does happen we accept and buy a new touring map!"

Holbeck Ghyll *Tel* Ambleside (053 94) 32375
Holbeck Lane *Fax* (053 94) 34743
Windermere LA23 1LU

This large late-Victorian house, with Art Nouveau features such as stained glass in the style of Charles Rennie Macintosh, enjoys a secluded setting in the hills with fine views of Lake Windermere and Langdale Fells, and was once the hunting lodge of the Earl of Lonsdale who bequeathed the famous Lonsdale Belt to boxing. It is introduced to the Guide by an inspector. "It stands in well-established, well-kept and delightful landscaped gardens up a steep drive off the road to Ambleside, its peaceful setting contrasting with the tourist activity close by. In the public areas are high ceilings, wood panelling, large pieces of antique furniture, mirrors, good quality floral-patterned curtains and thick, richly coloured carpets. Our bedroom was similar in style. The atmosphere is one of formality and good taste, but unpretentious. Dinner was delicious, and beautifully presented; the wine list is extensive, with a good half-bottle range, and reasonably priced. Breakfast, too, was good, and service throughout was efficient, from pleasant and attentive staff. The hotel is not cheap (our children's fairly standard high tea, for example, cost £17.88 each), but it was hard to fault. The owners, David and Patricia Nicholson, who acquired the hotel in 1988 and have refurbished extensively, are a young, energetic couple and in charge of a team that clearly works well." Endorsed by *Mrs M Harris*: "For a few days one feels like an 'Upstairs' person from 'Upstairs, Downstairs'." More reports please.

Open 1 Feb–31 Dec.
Rooms 14 double – 12 with bath and shower (1 with bath only, 1 with shower only), all with telephone, radio, TV, tea-making facilities, baby-listening.
Facilities Large hall, 2 lounges, bar area, restaurant, billiard room. 2-acre gardens with putting green; also woods leading to lakeshore. Free leisure facilities ½ m: swimming, squash, gym, etc.
Location 3 m N of Windermere off road to Ambleside. Past Brockhole Visitor Centre on left, take right turn (Holbeck Lane) to Troutbeck. Drive ½ m on left.
Restrictions Not suitable for ♿. No smoking in restaurant. No dogs in public rooms.
Credit cards Access, Visa.
Terms Dinner, B&B £45–£90. Set lunch (Sun only) £14, dinner £25; full alc £30. Off-season breaks. 10% reduction for 5 or more nights. Christmas and New Year packages.
Service/tipping: "Service included. We neither encourage nor expect tips but we do find guests tend to feel that they have received exceptional service, and most of them leave something as a tip, which is divided among all the staff."

WINTERINGHAM South Humberside — Map 4

Winteringham Fields
Winteringham DN15 9PF
Tel Scunthorpe (0724) 733096
Fax (0724) 733898

Germain and Annie Schwab's small manor house – "really excellent in the restaurant-with-rooms category" – is quietly situated in the centre of an old village dating back to Roman times on the south bank of the Humber estuary. Most of the rooms have views of the river and the Humber Bridge. Inside it is heavily beamed – "those over five foot eight should be careful" – and quite dark, with narrow corridors and staircase, heavy Victorian furniture and interesting *objets d'art*. "The wind can come whistling off the water in winter but there are roaring fires in bar and sitting room. The bedrooms are small but very comfortable, nicely decorated, and equipped with fruit, flowers, biscuits, etc. Bathrooms are immaculate, with plenty of hot water and warm towels; housekeeping is generally exemplary. The Schwabs are good hosts. Mr Schwab, who is Swiss, cooks – and extremely well; his wife runs front of house and restaurant, helped by a pleasant and proficient young staff. The restaurant, which is popular locally, has exceptionally large, comfortable chairs at well-spaced tables. The menu is short, with daily fish specialities from nearby Grimsby. The wine list is keenly priced, with interesting regional French and Swiss varieties. Breakfast was excellent, served at a large well-set table with a huge selection of home-made jam and marmalade and cold meats, and Mr Schwab to ask what you would like cooked. All in all, a very pleasant, relaxing place." "As near perfection as anything has a right to be. Compares favourably with London hotels at four times the price and French restaurants with two rosettes." (*Pat and Jeremy Temple, HA Johnson; also S Beresford*)

Open All year except Sun, first 2 weeks Jan, first week Aug, Christmas, New Year.
Rooms 6 double – all with bath, shower, telephone, TV. 2 in courtyard. 2 on ground floor.
Facilities Lounge, bar, conservatory, restaurant, private dining room. ¼-acre grounds.
Location In centre of village, 4 m from Humber Bridge.
Restrictions Not suitable for ♿. No smoking in restaurant or bedrooms. No dogs.
Credit cards Access, Visa.
Terms B&B (continental): single £58, double £75–£90. English breakfast £6. Set lunch £15.50; full alc dinner £38.
Service/tipping: "Service included; but tips always accepted with as much pleasure as they are given."

WITHERSLACK Cumbria — Map 4

The Old Vicarage
Witherslack
Grange-over-Sands LA11 6RS
Tel Witherslack (044 852) 381
Fax (044 852) 373

César award in 1990: Outstanding hospitality – Lakeland style

This small Georgian hotel is in the less dramatic but still attractive walking country south of Lake Windermere, and though only 15 minutes from the M6, it is quiet and secluded, away from the heart of the village, and well kept, clean and comfortable. It is run by Roger and Jill Burrington-Brown and Stanley and Irene Reeve with, this year, a "very pleasant and helpful" manager, David Moses, and chef, Stuart Harrison. There are William Morris curtains, Heal's lampshades, lots of pine and cane in the bedrooms, ample reading lights. Duvets on the beds, but you can ask for traditional bedding. The five "lovely" deluxe rooms in the Orchard House have "an excellent, enormous bathroom" and many extras including a CD player. One visitor returning after a three-year gap reports: "The brochures are more polished, new rooms and a tennis court have been built and prices have gone up but the character has not changed; the staff are friendly and helpful." "Welcome fabulous, dinners out of this world. Accommodation extremely comfortable," adds another. The five-course set dinner ("at 7.30 for 8") offers no choice except for hot or cold desserts. Cooking is English; portions very generous. Breakfasts are "excellent, everything freshly cooked – delicious home-made brioche, toast made from home-made bread". But while many readers endorse the above sentiments there are also criticisms: "We'd have preferred fewer courses for less money." "Food rather bland. Dinner a ritual; everyone is served each course at the same time so it goes at the pace of the slowest eater. Chef does the rounds *every* evening, after the main course; most embarrassing." "Our room was very small and had a less-than-private *en suite* arrangement." "Who wants a CD player in the Lake District?"

Open All year. Restaurant closed for lunch.
Rooms 12 double, 1 single – all with bath and/or shower, telephone, radio, TV, tea-making facilities. 5 in Orchard House, 1 suitable for ♿.

Facilities 2 lounges, restaurant, breakfast room, private dining room. 5-acre grounds with tennis, lawns, woodlands. Sea 3 m, Lake Windermere 8 m, river fishing 5 m. Fell walking.
Location From M6 take exit 36; follow route to Barrow-in-Furness. Turn off A590 signposted Witherslack and take first turn left past phonebox. Hotel is ½ m along this lane on left.
Restrictions No smoking in restaurant. Dogs by arrangement only; not in public rooms.
Credit cards All major cards accepted.
Terms [1991 rates] B&B £32–£61.50; dinner, B&B £58–£87.50. Set dinner £26. 2-day midweek breaks. Reduced rates for children; high tea.
Service/tipping: "Service included. We do not imply that tips are required, but naturally we are pleased and grateful if guests choose to show that they are perhaps more than satisfied. Tips are shared among staff twice yearly."

WOODSTOCK Oxfordshire — Map 2

The Feathers
Market Street
Woodstock OX7 1SX

Tel Woodstock (0993) 812291
Fax (0993) 813158

A former coaching inn in the centre of the showplace town, a few minutes' stroll from Blenheim Palace – you can walk round the lake before breakfast. It has expanded over the years into neighbouring buildings, which gives it a meandering nature, and gone upmarket, though it still serves the functions of a town hotel: there is a courtyard where drinks and tea are served, and its bar lunches are popular with locals. It has low beamed ceilings and small but comfortable lounges with log fires, interesting furniture, books and flowers, and an old-fashioned, comfortable bar. Bedrooms vary in size; the best ones have high ceilings and are well furnished with a modern bathroom. The *Feathers* was omitted from the Guide last year after a change of ownership, but is brought back by praise from recent visitors. "Very pleasant, warm and welcoming." In the partly panelled dining room, with starched white linen tablecloths, crystal, candles and fresh flowers, the cooking by young chef David Lewis is "superb; very expensive, but worth it". "A most wonderful meal . . . Service great, surroundings lovely – not too grand, but comfortably smart. We were given a nice picnic next day." "Breakfast also very good." (*D Whittington, C Citrozi, Norma Kessler; also RO Marshall*) One reader was surprised to find that a "suggested gratuity" of 15% had been added to his dinner bill; the hotel says, "No one need pay it."

Open All year.
Rooms 3 suites, 13 double, 1 single – all with bath and/or shower, telephone, radio, TV, baby-listening, 24-hour room service; tea-making facilities on request.
Facilities 2 lounges, bar, restaurant. Courtyard for drinks and lunches.
Location In town centre, but quiet at night. Street parking; public carpark nearby.
Restrictions Not suitable for ♿. Dogs by prior arrangement; not in public rooms.
Credit cards All major cards accepted.
Terms B&B: single £75–£85, double £90–£125, suite £145. Set lunch £16.50 (£17.50 on Sun), dinner £19.50 (£29.50 on Sat); full alc £30. Winter and spring breaks.
Service/tipping: "15% suggested gratuity added to restaurant bills but guests don't need to pay it."

> If you find location details inadequate, please don't fail to let us know.

WOOLER Northumberland — Map 4

The Ryecroft *Tel* Wooler (0668) 81459
Wooler NE71 6AB

David and Patricia McKechnie's hotel of character in market town at foot of Cheviot Hills, with one wing on A697 (rooms double-glazed). Redbrick exterior, 1930s decor; well-proportioned reception lounge with welcoming fires; spotlessly clean; well-trained, efficient and experienced staff. "Dinner in restaurant with conservatory extension consistently good; breakfast outstanding." ½-acre grounds. Closed 2 weeks Nov, Christmas. 11 rooms, 9 with bath or shower. Dinner, B&B £43–£51. Was in earlier editions. Now warmly re-nominated: "Excellent of its kind." More reports please.

YORK North Yorkshire — Map 4

The Grange *Tel* York (0904) 644744
Clifton, York YO3 6AA *Fax* (0904) 612453

This sophisticated hotel, five minutes' walk from the Minster, entered the Guide in italics last year, and the entry has now been warmly endorsed: "Everything about it is impressive. It is elegantly designed and furnished, and managed with meticulous care and attention. We were especially impressed by the bathrooms. The restaurant is outstanding. The chef, Cara Baird, was trained by the Roux brothers, and they should be proud of her." "Comfortable, with a spacious atmosphere. Lovely quiet bedrooms with good-sized beds. Food so delicious and reasonable we ate in on both nights. Really friendly, helpful people, but not intrusive. A classy joint." Our inspector, too, appreciated the *Grange*: the good reading lights, the large drawing room with open fire, magazines and newspapers, the tranquil restaurant, the good fresh orange juice for breakfast. But she had a few criticisms: limited storage space, some lapses in the decor, a disappointing wine list, poor breakfast toast. The hotel is on a busy road though quiet at night, and front rooms are double-glazed. There's a spacious carpark at the rear. In addition to the Ivy Restaurant there is a brasserie in a converted cellar, open from 10 am, serving lighter meals including after-theatre suppers. (*Judy Cracknell, Colin and Susan Prescot; also Maria Hobson, C Whitehead*)

Open All year.
Rooms 26 double, 3 single – all with bath and/or shower, telephone, radio, TV, baby-listening; tea-making facilities on request. Some on ground floor.
Facilities Drawing room, morning room, library, restaurant, brasserie; conference facilities.
Location On A19 N to Thirsk (front rooms double-glazed). 400 yds from Bootham Gate. Parking.
Restriction No dogs in public rooms.
Credit cards All major cards accepted.
Terms B&B: single £80, double £95–£125. Set lunch £13, dinner £21; full alc £28. 2-day breaks including entry to York museums and attractions; Christmas break. Reduced rates and special meals for children by arrangement.
Service/tipping: "Prices include service and tips are not expected. If a tip is left, it is shared out among all the staff."

We need feedback on all entries. Often people fail to report on the best-known hotels, assuming that "someone else is sure to".

Hobbits **BUDGET** *Tel* York (0904) 624538
9 St Peter's Grove
Clifton, York YO3 6AQ

Rosemary Miller's "comfortable, reasonably priced and friendly hotel", a handsome late-Victorian building "with some very nice features" and spacious rooms, is "a haven of calm" in a leafy street a good ten minutes' walk or an easy bus-ride from the centre of York. Decor and furnishing are stylish and attractive, and the house is full of jugs, which Mrs Miller collects. There are five "beautifully decorated and stylish" bedrooms, some up a winding staircase in an attic "which adds to their charm". *Hobbits* is warmly praised again this year for the "friendly and helpful hostess, who is a mine of information on York", and the breakfast, communally served at a long table with white tablecloth and shining silver, though there is a separate small table for those wanting more privacy. There is an "excellent" cooked breakfast as well as "healthy options of fruit, very good gooseberry yoghurt, decent bread and toast". *Hobbits* is Mrs Miller's family home; it includes two children, a cat, a dog and canaries. She now offers off-season breaks including an evening meal – "English and vegetarian dishes mainly". (*HNC Saunders, Steve and Helene Charles, Mirit Ehrenstein; also Charles Gorer, Roisel Hodgson, Giles and Kate Dove, and others*) Only niggle: "The guests' lounge is not up to the standards of the rest of the house."

Open All year except Christmas week.
Rooms 4 double, 1 single – all with shower (1 also with bath), radio, TV, tea-making facilities, fridge.
Facilities Lounge, TV lounge, dining room. Small garden with patio. River Ouse 5 minutes with fishing, boating.
Location Just off A19 from N. Private parking.
Restrictions Not suitable for ♿. No smoking in dining room and 2 bedrooms.
Credit cards Access, Visa.
Terms B&B: single £22.50–£25, double £45–£50. Reduced rates for children. Off-season breaks including evening meal.
Service/tipping: "No service charge. Tips not expected but if given are courteously received and shared among staff."

Middlethorpe Hall *Tel* York (0904) 641241
Bishopthorpe Road *Fax* (0904) 620176
York YO2 1QB

This noble house with imposing facades stands in large grounds near York racecourse. It was rescued from decay by Historic House Hotels Ltd, who also restored *Bodysgallen Hall*, Llandudno, and, more recently, *Hartwell House* at Aylesbury (qq.v.). Built in the reign of William III and subsequently the home of the diarist Lady Mary Wortley Montagu, *Middlethorpe Hall*, with gardens and parkland appropriate to its grandeur, has been immaculately restored in keeping with its period. The interior decoration is "in excellent taste; public and private rooms comfortable and quiet" (but a few bedrooms are small and one, in the stables, adjacent to the maids' closet, is not recommended). Most reports this year are positive, and the food, about which there has been debate in the past, is considered much improved: "The best country house hotel we've stayed at in England; everything – rooms, service, food – was excellent." "First-rate, worth the high price." "Wonderful building, full of history." (*C and J Kenaston, David P Sykes, Mr and Mrs Bågstam*) But one reader felt its joys were somewhat diminished by the situation – "uncomfortably close to a very busy main road", and autumn visitors found their room in the converted stable block a bit chilly. More reports please.

Open All year.
Rooms 6 suites, 20 double, 4 single – all with bath, shower, telephone, radio, TV; 2 suites with tea-making facilities in cottages; 18 courtyard rooms.
Facilities Lift. Drawing room, library, bar, 2 restaurants; private dining facilities. 26-acre grounds with croquet, walled garden, lake. Racecourse, golf nearby.
Location 1½ m S of city, by racecourse.
Restrictions Not suitable for ♿. No children under 8. No dogs.
Credit cards Access, Amex, Visa.
Terms [1991 rates] Rooms: single £83–£99, double £115–£129, suite £165–£189. Breakfast: continental £6.50, English £9.50. Set lunch £16.90, dinner £29.25; full alc £43.80. Champagne breaks Nov–Apr; 2-day summer breaks; Christmas package.

Mount Royale *Tel* York (0904) 628856
The Mount, York YO2 2DA *Fax* (0904) 611171

Richard and Christine Oxtoby's hotel, Gothic in appearance but mainly William IV with modern extensions, has long been the final English entry in the Guide, appreciated by readers for its un-hotel-like atmosphere, with long-serving friendly staff – and dogs and cats. The second generation of Oxtobys – their son, and daughter and daughter-in-law, both confusingly called Sarah – are now playing an increasing part in its running. It is near the racecourse, a few minutes' walk from Micklegate Bar and three-quarters of a mile from the Minster. Front rooms get traffic noise though this is mitigated by double-glazing; back ones overlook the attractive garden with a swimming pool and are quiet; the spacious ones in the garden annexe, connected to the main building by a covered walkway, are "charming, with many little extras". Returning regulars report: "The staff are always helpful and there is plenty of local information available. The food has improved this year; portions are slightly smaller, cooking a little lighter, and a few more adventurous dishes are offered. The wine list has altered a lot; there is a wide variety of bottles from all over the world." "Well-cooked, *al dente* vegetables," adds another visitor. "My husband remembers his cooked breakfasts, especially the poached smoked haddock, with a watering mouth." (*Pat and Jeremy Temple, S Wakely, also MP Franklin*) One niggle: "The housekeeping could be improved – but it is one of the nicest places to stay in York."

Open All year except 24–30 Dec.
Rooms 6 suites, 16 double, 1 single – all with bath, shower, telephone, radio, TV, tea-making facilities, baby-listening. 4 in garden annexe with covered walkway to main building. Some on ground floor.
Facilities 2 lounges (pianist 6 nights a week), bar, restaurant with conservatory; meeting room. 1½-acre grounds with swimming pool heated May–Oct.
Location On A64 from Tadcaster (front rooms double-glazed). On right just before traffic lights at junction with Albemarle Road, opposite sign to Harrogate (A59). Parking for 20 cars.
Restrictions Not suitable for ♿. Dogs by arrangement; not in public rooms.
Credit cards All major cards accepted.
Terms [1991 rates] B&B: single £62.50–£80, double £70–£90, suite £95. Set dinner £21.95. 2-day breaks (excluding bank holidays). 1-night bookings refused for some bank holidays. Reduced rates for children sharing parents' room; special meals by arrangement.
Service/tipping: "No service charge except in restaurant when 10% is added for parties of 6 or over. Tips optional."

Wales

Plas Bodegroes, Pwllheli

ABERDOVEY Gwynedd **Map 1**

Penhelig Arms
Aberdovey LL35 0LT

Tel Aberdovey (0654) 767215
Fax (0654) 767690

Harbourside inn since 1700s, with fine views across estuary, owned since 1989 by Robert and Sally Hughes, who have carried out major refurbishments. On main road, so not ideal for families with small children. But warmly recommended for friendly owners and courteous reception, well-maintained accommodation, "flowers everywhere", excellent bathrooms filled with extras, and serious ambitious cooking by Sally Hughes. Bar and restaurant open all year, hotel closed 25/26 Dec. 11 bedrooms, all with bath/shower. Not suitable for ♿. Smoking discouraged in restaurant. Access, Visa accepted. B&B £31–£39. Bar meals from £1.60, Sun lunch £9.50, set dinner £15.75. New nomination. More reports please.

ABERSOCH Gwynedd Map 4

Porth Tocyn *Tel* Abersoch (075 881) 3303
Abersoch LL53 7BU *Fax* (075 881) 3538

César award in 1984: Best family hotel

A long-time favourite of Guide readers, and a particularly good hotel for a holiday with children – though it's not exclusively a family hotel – the *Porth Tocyn* stands in a choice position on a headland overlooking Cardigan Bay and Snowdonia. "The most pleasant hotel of its kind that I have ever stayed at. The Fletcher-Brewer family work extremely hard and really seem to enjoy what they are doing." (*RAL Ogston*) That unreserved eulogy echoes much similar praise in previous years: "Truly excellent, well run, with most comfortable bedrooms, helpful and extremely willing service, and plenty of room (not just one lounge, but several, all well appointed and with lovely views). Food most enjoyable. Any small complaints (a broken bedside light, a jammed wardrobe) were dealt with *at once*. One of the nicest hotels I've ever stayed in." Readers in the past have also praised the two-course dinner (including coffee and *petits fours*) offered as an alternative to those unable to cope with five courses, the impressive Welsh cheeseboard, the "old-fashioned 'nursery' puds", the lack of music in the dining room, the imaginative self-service buffet lunch on Sunday, and "fresh flowers everywhere; the atmosphere of a family home but a professional standard of service". "This hotel must rank as one of the best for families in the whole UK." (*EAO Whiteman, S Parsons, and others*)

Open 1 week before Easter–mid-Nov.
Rooms 14 double, 3 single – all with bath, shower, telephone, TV; radio, tea-making facilities, baby-listening on request. 3 on ground floor.
Facilities 6 sitting rooms, restaurant, bar, TV room. Garden with tennis, swimming pool (heated May–end Sep). Set in hotel's 25-acre farm; sea a few mins' walk, safe bathing. Heritage coastal walk, water sports, fishing, golf, riding nearby.
Location 2½ m S of Abersoch, through hamlets of Sarn-bach and Bwlchtocyn; follow signs marked Gwesty/Hotel.
Restrictions Smoking discouraged in restaurant. No children under 7 in dining room at night (high teas available until 6.15 pm). No dogs in public rooms.
Credit card Access.
Terms B&B £31–£52.50. Buffet lunch Sun £14. Set dinner £17.30 (2 courses), £23 (5 courses). Bargain breaks out of season. 1-night bookings sometimes refused in high season. Reduced rates and special meals for children.
Service/tipping: "No service charge. Tipping is fast dying out here. It is irrelevant to a proper modern hotel bill. We do not promote tipping, but if someone wants to leave something by way of appreciation that is fine."

Riverside *Tel* Abersoch (075 881) 2419
Abersoch LL53 7HW

John and Wendy Bakewell's family hotel, agreeably situated between harbour and river Soch, recommended for comfortable accommodation, welcoming atmosphere, pleasant small garden and indoor swimming pool and, above all, "excellent, sophisticated home-cooking with French bias"; breakfasts "up to same standard". Beach, safe bathing 5 mins. Children warmly welcomed. Open 1 Mar–5 Nov. 12 bedrooms, all with bath/shower. Not suitable for ♿. No smoking in restaurant. No dogs. All major credit cards accepted. 1991 rates: B&B from £35; dinner, B&B from £52.50. Bar lunches. New nomination. More reports please.

BRECHFA Dyfed — Map 1

Tŷ Mawr
Brechfa
Nr Carmarthen SA32 7RA

Tel Brechfa (0267) 202332
Fax (0267) 202437

16th-century house in small village "out of this world" on edge of Brechfa forest. Exposed beams and stonework on ground floor, with "warm and comfortable lounge (no television!), and pretty two-level dining room". French windows lead to garden and stream. In earlier editions under previous owners, now re-nominated with "charming, helpful and friendly" new owners, Beryl and Dick Tudhope, unostentatious accommodation, good, quite ambitious cooking, excellent bread from own bakery, reasonably priced wine and warm welcome. Safe sandy beaches nearby; fishing arranged. 5 bedrooms, all with bath and shower. Not suitable for ♿. No dogs in public rooms. Access, Amex, Visa accepted. B&B £29–£38; dinner, B&B £42–£52.50. Endorsed this year, but more reports would be welcome.

CRICKHOWELL Powys — Map 1

Gliffaes
Crickhowell NP8 1RH

Tel Bwlch (0874) 730371
Fax (0874) 730463

"The position is extraordinarily peaceful, beautiful and, above all, quiet. The Brabner family are friendly, low-key, laid-back – and guaranteed never to ask, 'Is everything to your satisfaction?' The hotel is comfortable, with some nice antiques that look as though they've always been there. No hint of interior design, so children are happy there. The plumbing is interesting. We had a pre-war bath and the water was barely tepid at 7 pm." "There is nowhere quite like it. In perfect weather its remoteness makes it a wonderful source of refreshment. In the evening, all one can hear is the song of birds and the sound of the river. The hotel is as hotels were fifty years ago. Guests are looked after but not pandered to." As in previous years, bouquets and brickbats fly around the campaniles of this imposing Italianate mansion with its magnificent gardens in the valley of the Usk, midway between the Brecon Beacons and the Black Mountains. It's an unashamedly traditional country hotel, run for more than forty years by the Brabner family. Lots of fishing tackle everywhere – the hotel has two stretches on the Usk and there are eight fishable reservoirs in the vicinity – and lots of polished Victorian furniture. Criticisms are often delivered in good spirit: "We've got used to the *Gliffaes* way of doing (or not doing) things and consider the pluses outweigh the minuses; but others, used to more conventional ideas of service, find the whole system rather irritating. I remember feeling exactly the same thirty years ago." "The service at mealtimes was haphazard and unprofessional, but willing." "The staff, mostly young Australians, are pretty casual. It is unusual perhaps, on choosing a Burgundy, to be told, 'That will put some colour in your cheeks.' However, I would return as often as I could."

"Beds were untidy, and the towels ghastly colours. But this delightful hotel feels like home." (*RAL Ogston, Robert Vigars, and others*)

Open Mid-Mar–end Dec.
Rooms 22 double (6 can be let as singles) – 17 with bath, 5 with shower, all with telephone, radio, tea-making facilities, baby-listening. 3 (with TV) in lodge ¾ m away.
Facilities 2 sitting rooms, bar, billiards room, conservatory, dining room. 29-acre grounds with gardens, tennis, croquet, putting; brown trout and salmon fishing in river Usk.
Location 2½ m W of Crickhowell. Turn left off the A40 at *Gliffaes* sign; 1 m to hotel gates.
Restrictions Not suitable for ♿. No smoking in dining room. No dogs in hotel (kennels available).
Credit cards All major cards accepted.
Terms B&B £30.50–£41.50; dinner, B&B £47–£58; full board £54.50–£66. Set lunch £10.25, dinner £16.50; full alc £28.50. Reduced rates and special meals for children.
Service/tipping: "Our total charges are for food, facilities and service."

CWMYSTWYTH Dyfed — Map 1

Hafod Lodge BUDGET — *Tel* Pontrhydygroes (097 422) 247
Cwmystwyth
Aberystwyth SY23 4AD

This small and remote guest house, which first appeared in the Guide last year, is again warmly recommended for its setting in some of Wales's most wild and spectacular scenery, its comfort, and the hospitality of the owners, Colin and Jenny Beard. "Quite excellent; one is treated more like a family friend." "The ideal place of retreat for a three-day break. The food is cooked by Mrs Beard and is of a very high standard." "An added attraction is the lack of canned music; and the service is efficient, considerate and friendly." "Marvellous value for money." (*DS Yerburgh, Dr George H Guest, Mr and Mrs CH Diamond, and others*)

Open All year.
Rooms 3 double – all with bath and/or shower, radio, baby-listening.
Facilities 2 lounges, restaurant, garden.
Location On B4343 between Devil's Bridge and Rhayader (14 m E of Aberystwyth).
Restrictions No smoking; no dogs in restaurant.
Credit cards None accepted.
Terms B&B £24; dinner, B&B £40. Set dinner for non-residents (by reservation only) £19. Reduced rates and special meals for children.
Service/tipping: "We do not expect tips, but should a guest wish to, the money is shared by the staff."

EGLWYSFACH Powys — Map 1

Ynyshir Hall — *Tel* Glandyfi (0654) 781209
Eglwysfach
Nr Machynlleth SY20 8TA

Twelve acres of landscaped gardens surrounded by the 365 acres of the Ynyshir bird reserve provide the idyllic wooded setting, on the southern shore of the Dovey estuary, of Rob and Joan Reen's 16th-century manor house with Georgian and Victorian additions. Recently refurbished, it is an interesting mix of Victorian pieces, oriental rugs and contemporary paintings by Rob Reen, a professional painter and former art teacher. A light and airy atmosphere is achieved through the use of pastel colours. Bedrooms are named after famous painters. "The Reens are a delightful couple who made us feel very much at home. All the finishing touches quietly executed. A fabulous chinchilla cat completed the scene – not officially allowed in public rooms, but sightings made. Dinner mostly excellent; vegetables (many from the walled garden) good. Breakfast huge." "What impressed us most was the degree of personal service and attention by the owners." (*Diana Blake, James Harkness, and others*) Short breaks on offer include painting courses, bridge and music weekends. One gripe: "Lighting for make-up insufficient, as usual!"

Open All year except possibly 2 weeks in Jan.
Rooms 2 suites, 6 double, 1 single – 8 with bath and shower, 1 with shower, all with telephone, radio, TV.
Facilities Lounge, bar, restaurant. 12-acre landscaped gardens. Near Dovey estuary and beaches; sailing, fishing, riding, golf nearby.
Location Just W of A487, 6 m SW of Machynlleth, 11 m NE of Aberystwyth.
Restrictions No children under 9. No smoking in restaurant. Dogs by arrangement only.
Credit cards Access, Amex.
Terms [1991 rates] B&B £30–£60; dinner, B&B £49.50–£79.50. Set lunch/dinner £19.50–£21. Special breaks; music, bridge weekends; painting courses. Reduced rates for children sharing parents' room.
Service/tipping: "Gratuities not encouraged or expected but when given are shared out equally among staff."

GANLLWYD Gwynedd — Map 1

Dolmelynllyn Hall — *Tel* Dolgellau (0341) 40273
Ganllwyd LL40 2HP

New to the Guide, and part 15th-century with later additions, this hotel was completely refurbished and redecorated in 1988 when the present owners, Jon and Joanna Barkwith, arrived. Father and daughter (she is the "excellent" cook), they are "interesting people with a fund of local knowledge". Our inspector was enthusiastic: "Old-fashioned, in a lovely situation; heavenly garden with a lake at the bottom, surrounded by National Trust country and walks in fields full of sheep. The house is large and ugly from the outside but inside has a good feeling with big rooms furnished in an individual and higgledy-piggledy way. My room had a good double bed and overhead reading light and a bathroom with lots of little extras. Downstairs there is a large reception/entrance hall, with flowers everywhere. The bar is a fairly large conservatory full of well-tended plants, including a mimosa tree. It's very much a family enterprise; the five-course dinner, using mostly home-grown produce and not relying on 'disguising' sauces, with a good choice for each course, was pleasantly served with Mr Barkwith very much in evidence." More reports welcome.

Open 1 Mar–30 Nov.
Rooms 1 suite, 7 double, 3 single – 10 with bath and shower, 1 with shower only, all with telephone, radio, TV, tea-making facilities.
Facilities Sitting room, library, bar, dining room, meeting room. 5-acre grounds. River fishing ¼ m.
Location On A470, 5 m N of Dolgellau.

Restrictions Not suitable for ♿. No smoking in dining room, sitting room or 3 bedrooms. No children under 8. No dogs in public rooms.
Credit cards Access, Amex, Visa.
Terms B&B £35–£40; dinner, B&B £51.50–£62.50. Lunch (by arrangement) £15; set dinner £18.75. Reduced rates for 6 days or more. Low-season breaks.
Service/tipping: "Service included. Tipping not encouraged, but to refuse, when insisted upon, is churlish. Anything given is distributed to staff monthly in proportion to hours worked."

LLANDRILLO Clwyd — Map 4

Tyddyn Llan *Tel* Llandrillo (049 084) 264
Llandrillo, Nr Corwen LL21 0ST *Fax* (049 084) 264

César award in 1989: Welsh hotel of the year

Once again, readers have written in comprehensive praise of Peter and Bridget Kindred's "beautifully restored, cleverly and sympathetically extended" 18th-century, grey-stone country house hotel. Standing in tranquil countryside in the Vale of Edeyrnion, it offers restful views of the surrounding Berwyn mountains. Guests can enjoy fishing on the hotel's private one-and-a-half mile beat; guides are available for walking through the local forests and along old droving roads. The house is comfortable and "furnished with good furniture and taste". French windows lead on to a pillared veranda where guests can enjoy afternoon tea and watch croquet. "Attention to detail was excellent – even to the point of re-icing our wine cooler in the bedroom prior to our return later in the day." (*Jean Willson, R Barnett, Heather Sharland, Robert Greenstock, BA Orman, and others*) David Barratt, who took over the kitchen last year, left in June 1991. First reports are favourable, but we'd be glad of more.

Open All year.
Rooms 10 double – all with bath and/or shower, telephone, radio, tea-making facilities, baby-listening.
Facilities 2 lounges, 2 dining rooms, 1 TV lounge, bar. Occasional musical evenings. 3-acre grounds with water garden, croquet. Private fishing in river Dee behind hotel, ghillie available; guided walks.
Location Through Corwen on A5 take B4401 to Llandrillo.
Restrictions Not suitable for ♿. No dogs in public rooms.
Credit cards Access, Visa.
Terms B&B: single £45–£48.50, double £70–£78; dinner, B&B: single £62.50–£67, double £107–£117. Set lunch £12–£15, dinner £18.50–£22.50. Special interest weekends; mini-breaks (2 or more nights); Christmas and New Year house parties. Reduced rates and special meals for children.
Service/tipping: "Service left to customers' discretion."

LLANDUDNO Gwynedd — Map 4

Bodysgallen Hall *Tel* Deganwy (0492) 584466
Llandudno LL30 1RS *Fax* (0492) 582519

César award in 1988: For a notable contribution to architectural conservation and first-rate hotel management

"Arguably my favourite hotel anywhere in the world." (*Sir Timothy Harford*) That was unarguably the warmest of the many compliments received in 1990/91 for this Grade I listed house standing in its own parkland on a hillside about a mile away from the Victorian seaside resort of Llandudno. The house is mainly 17th century with skilful later additions, including nine cottages grouped around a secluded courtyard bright with flowers. Among its delights are a 17th-century knot garden and an 18th-century walled rose garden. Two of its finest rooms are the large entrance hall and first-floor drawing room, both with oak panelling, splendid fireplaces and stone-mullioned windows. The bedrooms are spacious and elegant, with extras such as bottled Welsh spring water and home-made biscuits; bathrooms are Edwardian-style with handsome fittings. The hotel is run by a private company, Historic House Hotels Ltd (see also *Middlethorpe Hall*, York, and *Hartwell House*, Aylesbury, in England), dedicated to restoring and bringing to life buildings of architectural merit. The food, under the direction of chef Martin James – modern in style with impeccable ingredients – pleases readers once again. "By any standards an upmarket country house hotel but I liked its total lack of pretension." "You certainly get what you pay for. The value is excellent." "Super-romantic." (*Dr Keith Hotten, DW Tate, Ed Hobson and Judy Seabridge, and many others*) A few niggles: impersonal reception; being charged for mineral water in the bedroom; inadequate heating in the bedroom.

Open All year.
Rooms 9 cottage suites, 15 double, 3 single – 27 with bath and shower, 1 with shower, all with telephone, radio, TV; tea-making facilities in cottages.
Facilities Hall, drawing room, cocktail bar, library, dining room; conference centre. 247-acre parkland with gardens, tennis and croquet. Sandy beaches 2 m. Riding, shooting, fishing nearby.
Location SE of Llandudno on A470; 1 m on right.
Restrictions No children under 8. No smoking in dining room. Dogs in cottages and grounds only.
Credit cards All major cards accepted.
Terms Rooms: single £80–£118, double £112–£158, suite £141–£162. Breakfast: continental £6, Welsh £8.95. Set lunch £15, dinner £30. Off-season winter and spring champagne breaks.
Service/tipping: "Our prices include a mandatory service charge. It is given to all staff at the end of each month according to length of service, tax being deducted at source."

The St Tudno
North Parade, Llandudno
LL30 2LP

Tel Llandudno (0492) 874411
Fax (0492) 860407

César award in 1987: Best seaside resort hotel

An enterprising, stylishly decorated hotel on the seafront of this Victorian resort, run by Martin and Janette Bland, which receives much praise for its friendly welcome, caring and attentive staff, accommodation (though some rooms are small) and food. Readers particularly appreciate the provision of an empty fridge in the rooms "to fill up with your own things", and trouser-presses, thermos jugs of iced water and home-made biscuits are now extra bedroom enticements. "We ate two excellent dinners, prepared with flair and imagination, and very much appreciated the freshly prepared cooked English breakfast – but 'healthy' items such as home-made muesli are also available." The pretty decor of the dining room is liked: "Its green and white trellis wallpaper and plants make you feel you are eating in a garden." "Nice to see standards being maintained. Very good food, outstanding wine list." "A superb welcome, room tastefully done up (a little twee), highly recommended." (*Richard O Whiting, AJ Garrett, Barbara and William Mason, Mr and Mrs FPA Wood, and others*)

Open All year.
Rooms 1 suite, 19 double, 1 single – all with bath and/or shower, telephone, radio, TV, tea-making facilities, fridge, baby-listening. 1 double with shower on ground floor.
Facilities Lift. Sitting room, coffee lounge, lounge bar, restaurant; indoor heated swimming pool. 2 patios. Safe sandy beaches, fishing, sailing, windsurfing; golf nearby.
Location Central, opposite pier. Promenade parking, carpark, garage.
Restrictions No smoking in dining room and sitting room. No children under 5 at dinner. "Small and well-behaved dogs only"; not in public rooms.
Credit cards Access, Amex, Visa.
Terms B&B £37.50–£79.50; dinner, B&B £55–£102. Bar lunches. Sun lunch £12.95, dinner £17.50–£22.50. Half-board breaks all year; Sun night reductions. 1-night bookings often refused for bank holidays and Sat. Reductions for children sharing parents' room; high tea.
Service/tipping: "If customers enjoy personalised service and feel inclined to tip they should be allowed to do so. As hoteliers, we would never dream of adding a service charge automatically."

LLANFACHRETH Gwynedd — Map 4

Tŷ Isaf BUDGET
Llanfachreth
Nr Dolgellau LL40 2EA

Tel Dolgellau (0341) 423261

Traditional Welsh longhouse, dating from 1624, in 3-acre garden in secluded hamlet in Snowdonia National Park. Was in an earlier edition, now re-nominated under "warmly hospitable" new owners Graham and Diana Silverton, recommended for "well-furnished, comfortable and warm rooms with many extras" and 4-course dinner with plenty of choices, all prepared from fresh produce, and with pre-prandial complimentary drink. Closed Christmas, New Year, 3 weeks Oct, 3 weeks Nov. 3 bedrooms, all with bath/shower. Not suitable for ♿. No children under 13. No smoking in restaurant or bedrooms. 1991 rates: B&B £20–£30; dinner, B&B £29–£39. Set dinner £9. More reports please.

LLANGAMMARCH WELLS Powys — Map 1

The Lake
Llangammarch Wells LD4 4BS

Tel Llangammarch Wells (059 12) 202
Fax (059 12) 457

A half-timbered Welsh manor house, exceptionally well endowed with suites, in fifty acres of woodland bordered by the river Irfon, with a well-stocked lake and with several fine fishing rivers close by, "an excellent hotel in a beautiful area devoid of good hotels". A reader this year wrote of her "most lovely suite with faultless fabrics, mellowness and style – with views to the river and the marvellous lake". Another recent view: "Jean-Pierre Mifsud and his wife are extremely friendly hosts and their staff provide a relaxed, courteous and helpful service. The bedrooms are large, comfortable and well equipped, as are the bathrooms. The reception rooms are impressive, and the airy dining room is a delight. Dinners are good (the presentation occasionally over-elaborate). There's a splendid cheeseboard, and the breakfasts are excellent. Prices extremely reasonable." The extensive wine list has around 300 offerings, including fifty clarets. (*Erica Wallace, Amy and Stephen Pratt, also Mrs KJ Milligan, and others*)

Open All year.
Rooms 9 suites, 10 double – all with bath, shower, telephone, TV. 2 on ground floor.
Facilities 2 lounges, small cocktail bar, dining room. 50-acre grounds with lake, practice golf course, tennis. 4½ m of river fishing (tuition available).
Location 8 m W of Builth Wells, S of A483 to Garth; follow signs to hotel.
Restrictions No smoking in dining room. No children under 8 in dining room. No dogs in public rooms.
Credit cards Access, Visa.
Terms Dinner, B&B £65–£75. Set lunch £13.50, dinner £22.50. 2-night breaks. Christmas and New Year packages. Reduced rates for children; special meals on request.
Service/tipping: "Prices fully inclusive. Tips not expected. If guests insist, money is shared equally by staff."

LLANSANFFRAID GLAN CONWY Gwynedd — Map 4

The Old Rectory
Llanrwst Road
Llansanffraid Glan Conwy
LL28 5LF

Tel Aberconwy (0492) 580611
Fax (0492) 584555

"By far the nicest accommodation and best food experienced in seven weeks in Britain!" writes a Californian enthusiast this year in praise of Michael and Wendy Vaughan's sophisticated guest house. Georgian in origin, the *Old Rectory* stands in secluded grounds up a steep drive, with views over the river Conwy estuary to Conwy Castle and Snowdonia. Other recent comments: "The Vaughans were most welcoming, and saw to our needs immediately." "The bedrooms are extremely well kept and the public rooms, furnished with pictures, family photos and beautiful flowers, are a delight." "Our room was as well furnished and equipped as a country-house bedroom should be. Plenty of hot water, gloriously comfortable (and dramatic-looking) bed, two armchairs set to look out over the small garden to the estuary and mountains in the distance – what more could one want? Dinner is, in effect, a dinner party, with guests introduced to each other over cocktails before sitting down together at a large table in the dining room. Michael Vaughan serves unobtrusively and Wendy Vaughan's food is outstanding." There is a fixed menu, using local produce, with a choice of puddings or Welsh cheeses. "Our companions were very good company and no one went to bed before midnight." Breakfasts too are warmly commended: "The full range on offer including freshly squeezed orange juice and the best Welsh Rarebit we've ever tasted, made with Guinness – delicious!"

The village is a convenient stop on the way to the Holyhead crossing to Ireland; and for a longer stay, this part of North Wales offers a lovely landscape for walking, historic castles, and the beautiful north-west coast.

The Vaughans know the area well and are happy to suggest places to visit. Theirs is a no-smoking establishment. (*Mrs AE Wolfe, RW Bathurst, Betty Barnfield, and others*)

Open 1 Feb–7 Dec. Dining room closed for lunch and occasionally for dinner (guests warned when booking).
Rooms 4 double – all with bath and/or shower, telephone, radio, TV, tea-making facilities.
Facilities Sitting room, morning room, dining room. 2½-acre grounds. Sea with safe bathing 3 m; fishing, golf, riding, sailing, dry ski-slope nearby.
Location On A470, ½ m S of junction with A55.
Restrictions Not suitable for ♿. No smoking. No children under 10. No dogs.
Credit cards Access, Visa.
Terms Dinner, B&B: single £79.50–£89.50, double £120–£135. Set dinner £24.50. 2-day breaks. 1-night bookings refused for bank holidays. Reduction for children sharing parents' room (£15 B&B).
Service/tipping: "No service charge. If guests leave anything, it's divided among the staff."

LLANWDDYN Powys — Map 4

Lake Vyrnwy
Llanwddyn
Montgomeryshire SY10 0LY

Tel Llanwddyn (069 173) 692
Fax (069 173) 259

A substantial turn-of-the-century Tudor mansion standing 150 feet above the lake with a notable view down its four-and-a-half-mile length, and set in 24,000 acres of meadow and forest. Under previous owners it won a César in 1986 "for preserving traditional values in a sporting hotel". Sporting activities, especially fishing, are still a major draw, but the deliberately cultivated old-fashioned air has vanished. A recent inspector's report: "The public rooms are elegant in a club-like way: really comfortable leather chairs, fishing and sporting prints, and a gun book. The drawing room is pale yellow and blue with window-seats along a wall and a wonderful view. There are masses of beautifully upholstered chairs, and a log fire in the early evening. Our bedroom had some of the prettiest curtains I have seen. Service in the main dining room is by nice Welsh ladies and lasses. Children are welcome – there is masses of room for them to run in, and things to climb on. But make sure you book a room overlooking the lake; the ones at the rear have a scruffy view. If tranquillity is what you are seeking, avoid bank holiday weekends and the summer holidays." Reports this year endorse this commendation and speak well of the range and dependable quality of the cooking (a vegetarian dish is always on offer), and the good value of the wine list. "Most important, however," concludes one reader, "the staff were thoughtful, courteous, and anxious to please. The setting and the ambience inside the building do much to convey a sense of warmth, but it is the staff who give the hotel that special, indefinable human quality." (*Brian MacLeod Rogers, John Bird, and others*)

Open All year.
Rooms 2 suites, 24 double, 4 single – all with bath and/or shower, telephone, radio, TV, baby-listening.
Facilities Drawing room, cocktail bar, public bar, restaurant. 33-acre grounds; sporting rights on 24,000 acres meadow, moorland and forest; 1,100-acre lake for fishing, sailing.

Location At SE corner Lake Vyrnwy, well signed from Shrewsbury, Chester and Welshpool.
Restrictions Only restaurant suitable for ♿. No-smoking area in conservatory. No dogs in public rooms; kennels available.
Credit cards All major cards accepted.
Terms B&B: single £45.50, double £54.50–£82, suite £105. Dinner, B&B (2 day min): single £53.95, double £79.50–£107, suite £130. Set lunch £9.45 (Sun £10.45), dinner £19.25. 1-night bookings refused bank holidays and peak weekends. Reduced rates and special meals for children.
Service/tipping: "Entirely at guests' discretion. Collected in tronc *and distributed to all."*

LLYSWEN Powys — Map 1

Llangoed Hall — *Tel* Llyswen (0874) 754525
Llyswen, Brecon LD3 0YP — *Fax* (0874) 754545

César award in 1990: Most auspicious newcomer

One of the finest country houses in Wales, built by Clough Williams-Ellis (of *Portmeirion* fame – q.v.), opened its doors as a luxury hotel in May 1990. A connoisseur of hotel excellence sent us this report soon after its opening: "*Llangoed Hall* has the instant makings of a very splendid country hotel. The building itself might have been *designed* for conversion with fine big public rooms overlooking a croquet lawn and tennis court, and a meadow running down to the Wye, while its bedrooms are cheerful and airy and have been turned into delightful *en suite* bedrooms and suites – furnished half in antiques (I think) and half in Laura Ashley, whose widower Sir Bernard is the financial angel behind it all. The setting is perfectly lovely – wooded hills behind, river meadow in front, and a brilliant young gardener, Chris Frank, is bringing the formal and vegetable gardens of the old house back to glory (and has added a maze); indeed part of the pleasure of the place is the experience of seeing a great country house brought to life more or less from scratch, the hall having been uninhabited for years, and sadly neglected for longer still. As for the service, though it was a bit rough, perhaps, during the night I was there, it shows signs of being very professional. Breakfast included Welsh exotica like laver bread and grilled smoked salmon with poached eggs, while on the dinner menu there was red mullet with pea and coriander mousse, breast of chicken filled with wild mushrooms, poached fruits served with prune and armagnac ice-cream. I thought (as a sneerer at excessively grand hotels) that *Llangoed* had got just about the right balance between poshness and informality. If all goes well, *Llangoed* will almost certainly become the No 1 hotel in Wales. Expensive, but worth it as an extremely comfortable base in the middle of an exquisite and mercifully little-developed countryside." (*Jan Morris*) Recent visitors fully endorse Jan Morris's critique: "A hotel in the *Inverlochy* (q.v.) league. Superb food. Service not as bad as 'rough' suggests, but as yet more enthusiastic than professional. But everything will come right." (*Robert Fairweather; also Pat and Jeremy Temple*)

Open All year.
Rooms 5 suites, 16 double, 2 single – all with bath, shower, telephone, radio, TV, baby-listening.
Facilities 2 drawing rooms, library, dining room; 2 private dining rooms. 11 acre grounds with tennis court, croquet. Salmon and trout fishing, riding nearby.
Location 11 m SE of Builth Wells and 11 m NE of Brecon on A470.

Restrictions Not suitable for ♿. No smoking in dining room. No children under 8. Dogs in kennels in grounds only.
Credit cards All major cards accepted.
Terms [1991 rates] B&B: single from £95, double £125–£185, suite £175–£215. Set lunch £17.50, dinner £35.50. Special meals for children on request.
Service/tipping: "We do not expect a tip nor do we charge service. Should a client tip we put it in a bank account and, when there is a worthwhile amount, we share it among the staff."

NANTGWYNANT Gwynedd — Map 4

Pen-y-Gwryd BUDGET — *Tel* Llanberis (0286) 870211
Nantgwynant
Llanberis LL55 4NT

An inn since the early 1800s, in the heart of the Snowdonia National Park, and famous in the annals of mountaineering. It is run by Chris and Jo Briggs with their daughter Jane and her husband, Brian Pullee. "The hotel has a timeless quality; the furnishings and decor are much as I remember them on my first visit in 1938. There is no chromium plate and no unnecessary frills. It caters for all types, but its greatest appeal is to climbers, walkers and fishermen. There has been a great climbing tradition here for over one hundred years and, in 1953, Hunt and Hillary and most of the Everest team stayed here before flying out to Nepal. Not all the bedrooms have *en suite* bathrooms but there is always lashings of hot water for tired climbers. The breakfasts and dinners are excellent, and there are packed lunches for those who spend the day on the hills. The heart of the hotel is the bar-cum-smoke room, with its old, high-backed oak settles; on the wall are displayed boots, goggles and other mementos donated by members of the Everest team. It is to this room that so many guests repair after dinner for coffee and the lost art of conversation. The unique ambience of this hotel must appear as a very welcome haven for all those people who seek a break from the stress of modern life." (*Dr JRF Innes*) One couple, old habitués, felt that the inn had lost some of its former atmosphere and were critical both of the cooking and the packed lunch. More reports please.

Open Mar–early Nov, New Year, weekends only Jan and Feb.
Rooms 17 double, 3 single – 1, with bath, on ground floor across courtyard.
Facilities Lounge, residents' bar, smoke room, games room, restaurant. 2-acre grounds; natural swimming pool. River fishing nearby.
Location From Nantgwynant signposted *Pen-y-Gwryd.*
Restriction No smoking at breakfast.
Credit cards None accepted.
Terms B&B £18.50; dinner, B&B £29. Bar and packed lunches £3, set dinner £10.50. Reduced rates and special meals for children.
Service/tipping: "We have a staff gratuity box. If people wish to leave something they can. They usually do!"

"Budget" labels indicate hotels offering accommodation at up to about £40 for dinner, bed and breakfast or £25 for B&B and £15 for an evening meal. But we would emphasise that this is a rough guide only, and does not always apply to single rooms.

NEWPORT Dyfed Map 1

Cnapan BUDGET *Tel* Newport (0239) 820575
East Street, Newport
Pembrokeshire SA42 0WF

Newport, Dyfed – not to be confused with the one in Gwent – is an attractive small town, with a good bookshop, a couple of art galleries and nice little houses on hilly streets. In the centre stands this "charming guest house", run by John and Eluned Lloyd and their daughter and son-in-law, Judith and Michael Cooper. Mother and daughter cook a wide choice of home-prepared food, including vegetarian and other dishes for special diets. "Excellent food, and huge portions, even for those hungry after walking all day!" Breakfasts are serve-yourself-as-much-as-you-like, with home-made bread. "We were welcomed by all four owners, given a delicious sandwich lunch, and helped with advice on places to visit. Our rooms were full of useful guidebooks, other interesting books and magazines, and beautiful decorations." "The drawing room and 'bar' were lovely and well supplied with board games and other such trivial pursuits to make any guest feel completely relaxed and happy." Much entices near the village as well: you can be exploring the rock pools on Parrog beach after a ten-minute walk, or picking up the spectacular coastal path towards Cwm-yr-Eglwys in fifteen. (*Mirit and Michael Ehrenstein, and others*) More reports please.

Open All year except 25/26 Dec and Feb. Restaurant closed Tue Apr–Oct, and to non-residents Mon–Fri Nov–Jan.
Rooms 5 double – all with shower, radio, TV, tea-making facilities, baby-listening; telephone by arrangement.
Facilities Lounge, bar, restaurant. Small garden. 10 mins' walk to estuary and sea; fishing, bird watching, pony trekking, golf, boating nearby.
Location In centre of small town (but quiet at night). Parking.
Restrictions Not suitable for ♿. No smoking in dining room; discouraged in bedrooms. No dogs.
Credit cards Access, Visa.
Terms B&B £22–£27; dinner, B&B £36–£41. Full alc £19. 1-night bookings refused for bank holidays and high-season weekends. Reduced rates for children sharing parents' room; nursery teas.
Service/tipping: "We dislike service charges and equally the idea of 'building them in'. However, if customers wish to show extra appreciation, we accept the tips which we then distribute among the staff."

NEWPORT Gwent Map 1

West Usk Lighthouse BUDGET *Tel* Newport (0633) 810126
St Brides *Fax* (0633) 815582
Nr Newport NP1 9SF

Our first lighthouse hotel or guest house, built 1821, on estuaries of rivers Usk and Severn, with extensive views over Bristol Channel, run by New Age couple Frank and Danielle Sheahan. Recommended for "super accommodation, friendly hosts and great service". Special feature is the flotation room, "where guests can float away the stress in their lives"; there's also a seminar room equipped with personal computers. Vegan and vegetarian restaurant. 1-acre grounds with fishing. 6 bedrooms, 3 with shower. Not suitable for ♿. No smoking. No dogs.

Access accepted. B&B: single £20, double £44 (with water bed £48). Set dinner £15. New nomination. More reports please.

PORTMEIRION Gwynedd — Map 4

Hotel Portmeirion
Portmeirion LL48 6ET

Tel Porthmadog (0766) 770228
Fax (0766) 771331

César award in 1990: Brilliant restoration of a great hotel to former glory

"If the real world has become too much for you, what you need is a few days at the *Portmeirion,*" begins a recent report on this unique hotel which stands on the edge of an estuary in Tremadog Bay, surrounded by a spectacular Italianate village complete with piazza, campanile, pavilions and colonnade. In summer as many as 3,000 visitors come to the village daily, but the hotel is protected against this invasion. "This is the folly-village built by the late Sir Clough Williams-Ellis," says an earlier report, "on a private wooded peninsula above Traeth Bach. Cottages in the village can be rented separately; but the hotel itself is a new persona of truly phoenix-like burnish. The exterior remains that of a comfortable and unpretentious early Victorian Welsh *plas;* the interior has been refurbished in an exuberant mixture of oriental dazzle and overblown *World of Interiors.* No expense has been spared – even the fire doors are elegant – and there is any amount of ruching and draping and gilding and silking. Set against the heightened exotica of Portmeirion village, and contrasted with its incomparable setting above a wide sandy estuary, where herons stalk and cormorants dive immediately outside the hotel windows, the building triumphantly brings off its decor. While some clients may find its taste suspect, others will enjoy it for its very extravagance." Many other readers, too, wax lyrical about the hotel. One, who first visited the place in the 1950s, judges it: "Magical. Lovely views – breathtaking to see a huge, yellow moon rising over the water." (*Dr R Wise, Erica Wallace, S and W Beresford, Dr Ian Anderson*) Dinner is generally appreciated – both the wide choice and the dishes – but the breakfasts, the service at meals and the reception receive, as last year, more brickbats than bouquets: "mass catering style", "horribly weak coffee", "definitely not fresh orange juice", "hopeless reception, with no one in charge" – and more in the same vein. We hope for improvements next year. Please keep us posted.

Open All year except 5–31 Jan.
Rooms 1 suite, 13 double in hotel; 5 suites, 15 double in village – all with bath, shower, telephone, radio, TV; tea-making facilities in village rooms.
Facilities 3 lounges, 2 bars (harpist or pianist most nights), dining room, children's supper room; functions room. 70-acre grounds with lakes, swimming pool (heated early May–end Sep), tennis; free golf at Porthmadog Golf Club. Sandy beaches.
Location SW of Penrhyndeudraeth, SE of Porthmadog, off A487 at Minffordd.
Restrictions Not suitable for ♿ (but 3 village rooms have no steps and are accessible by car). No smoking in dining room and 2 lounges. No dogs.
Credit cards All major cards accepted.
Terms [1991 rates] B&B: single £48.50–£99.50, double £65–£117, suite £76–£148. Dinner, B&B: single £71.50–£122.50, double £111–£163, suite £122–£194. Set lunch £13.50, dinner £24.50; full alc £29.50. Christmas, New Year and off-season breaks. Min 2-night bookings at weekend in high season. Reduced rates and special meals for children.

Service/tipping: "Tips are not expected. Any received are shared equally among the staff involved."

PWLLHELI Gwynedd — Map 4

Plas Bodegroes
Nefyn Road, Pwllheli
LL53 5TH

Tel Pwllheli (0758) 612363
Fax (0758) 701247

César award: Outstanding restaurant-with-rooms

This Grade II listed Georgian manor house, in a peaceful setting in the Lleyn Peninsula, converted by Welsh-born Chris Chown and his Faroese wife Gunna á Trødni into a comfortable restaurant-with-rooms, has now won the accolade of a *Michelin* rosette. The style of cooking is modern with inspired sauces and the flavour of real food; only the best local produce is used. "It's amazing," wrote our inspector, "to find cooking of this calibre in such an out-of-the-way spot. The house is stylish without being grand, soothing in layout and well proportioned; with pleasing views of lawns and beeches, and utter silence except for rookery noises and other more melodious birdsong." There's a pleasant, old-fashioned veranda – the perfect spot for a quick snooze. Though Chris Chown calls this a restaurant-with-rooms, bedrooms are well equipped and clean (front ones are the larger, with four-posters and the best views). Breakfast in a small, east-facing room in the sunshine included "freshly squeezed orange juice, real porridge, perfectly poached eggs. Worth a long detour from anywhere." Pwllheli is a quiet seaside resort; there is golf nearby, and lots of interesting sightseeing. (*Tom and Rosemary Rose, Dr Claire Sillince*)

Open Mar–31 Oct. Closed Mon.
Rooms 8 double – all with bath, shower, telephone, radio, TV, 2 with mini-bar, 1 with jacuzzi.
Facilities Bar, lounge, 2 dining rooms, breakfast room. 6-acre grounds. Safe, sandy beach 1 m. Golf nearby.
Location On left on Nefyn road (A497) 1 m W of Pwllheli.
Restrictions Only restaurant suitable for ♿. No smoking in main dining room and 1 bedroom. Dogs by arrangement; not in public rooms.
Credit cards Access, Visa.
Terms Dinner, B&B £55–£90. Set dinner £25. 1-night bookings refused bank holidays and Sat in season.
Service/tipping: "Service included, tipping discouraged, but we accept a tip if a guest insists, and the money is split equally among the staff."

REYNOLDSTON West Glamorgan — Map 1

Fairyhill
Reynoldston, Gower
Nr Swansea SA3 1BS

Tel Gower (0792) 390139
Fax (0792) 391358

18th-century mansion, restored by owners, John and Midge Frayne, in 24 acres of park and woodland with trout stream, in heart of Gower peninsula. Country house atmosphere – books, magazines, etc. Restaurant highly praised. Fraynes said to run hotel "with charm and zest". John Frayne says he enjoys seeing twitchy businessmen leaving revitalised and smiling. Closed 25/26 Dec and

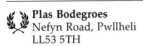

Jan. 13 bedrooms, 11 with bath/shower. Not suitable for ♿. No smoking in restaurant. Access, Visa accepted. B&B: single £65–£75, double £75–£85. Full alc £28. Omitted from earlier editions after criticisms of accommodation. Now warmly re-nominated. More reports please.

TALSARNAU Gwynedd — Map 4

Maes-y-Neuadd
Talsarnau LL47 6YA

Tel Harlech (0766) 780200
Fax (0766) 780211

Dating originally from the 14th century, and enlarged in the 16th and 17th, *Maes-y-Neuadd* (pronounced Mice-er-Neyath, meaning the Meadow of the Mansion) is tucked into a wooded hillside smothered in rhododendrons, looking out across Snowdonia National Park and reached by a narrow lane which climbs a one-in-five hill. There are oak beams, decorated plasterwork and an inglenook fireplace. Eight acres of lawns, orchards and paddocks surround it; the renowned Royal St David's golf course is only three miles away, and Portmeirion and Harlech castle are nearby. The two couples who own it, the Horsfalls and the Slatters, have completely restored this attractive, grey, granite-and-slate mansion, furnishing it with good antique and modern furniture. Last year a conservatory lounge was added, and three new bedrooms in the coach house, designed by architect co-owner Michael Slatter. "The Slatters and Horsfalls are just as friendly and welcoming as ever, taking a real interest in chatting to their guests and helping them in any way." (*EH and RF Warner, and others*) Andrew Taylor, chef since October 1989, gets a better press this year than last though still mixed; some readers would prefer a simpler alternative to the five-course menus. The prices of wines and spirits are on the high side. Some criticisms, too, of service and housekeeping. More reports please.

Open All year except 8–16 Dec. Lunch by reservation only Mon–Sat.
Rooms 4 suites, 11 double, 1 single – all with bath and/or shower, telephone, TV, baby-listening. 4 in coach house 10 yds from main building. 3 on ground floor suitable for ♿.
Facilities Lounge, conservatory, bar, dining room; small conference room/private dining room. 8-acre grounds with helipad, sun terraces, croquet, orchard and paddock. Sea, golf, riding, sailing, fishing, climbing nearby.
Location Off B4573, 3 m NE of Harlech. Hotel sign at junction.
Restrictions No smoking in dining room. Children under 7 at management's discretion, not in dining room for dinner. No dogs in public rooms.
Credit cards All major cards accepted.
Terms B&B: single £41–£45, double £92–£136, suite £160–£175; dinner, B&B (2 nights min): single £55–£60, double £110–£182, suite £110–£195. Set lunch £14, dinner £24. 3-day Christmas house party. Special breaks. 1-night bookings refused New Year, Easter, Christmas. Reduced rates for children sharing parents' room; special meals on request.
Service/tipping: "No service charge. Tipping entirely at guests' discretion; tips shared among staff."

Do you know of a good hotel or country inn in the United States or Canada? Nominations please to our sibling publication, America's Wonderful Little Hotels and Inns, PO Box 150, Riverside Avenue, Riverside, Conn. 06878, USA.

TALYLLYN Gwynedd — Map 4

Minffordd *Tel* Corris (0654) 761665
Talyllyn, Tywyn LL36 9AJ

César award in 1985: Outstanding value in a country hotel

"Peace, tranquillity and unobtrusive personal service make this better than a 'home from home'." The *Minffordd* is an exemplary small family hotel in the medium-price range, at the head of one of the most peaceful and little-known valleys in Wales, the Dysynni valley. The footpath to the top of Cader Idris starts by the front gate, Talyllyn lake is half a mile away, and some of Wales's most beautiful scenery lies all round this former coaching inn (its name means "roadside"). Bernard and Jessica Pickles have owned the hotel for fourteen years, and their son Jonathan is the excellent chef. They have preserved the old-world atmosphere of the rambling building while comfortably modernising it. Everything is spick and span. It is not a hotel for the misanthrope: guests are introduced to each other and the smallness of the public rooms makes socialising inevitable, though tables in the dining room are well spaced. Some recent tributes: "Excellent packed lunches, a table where children could play draughts and backgammon, splendid food." Another enthusiast writes: "Can I add anything to all the gentle praises that have appeared in the Guide? Only this: when you go, stay at least three days. Any less would be cheating yourself." Warning: half board only. "Bed-and-breakfast guests," says Bernard Pickles, "are as ships that pass in the night, never to enjoy what we have to offer them." (*Mrs M Green, Mrs Lesley Brown, MH Williams, and others*)

Open Mid-Mar–end Oct, weekends Nov–Dec, 3 days at Christmas. Closed 1st week July. Restaurant closed to non-residents Sun and Mon.
Rooms 6 double – 5 with bath and shower, 1 with shower, all with telephone, radio, tea-making facilities.
Facilities Sun room, lounge bar, parlour, dining room; laundry facilities. 3-acre garden; paddock and river. Talyllyn lake ½ m – fishing by arrangement.
Location 8 m SW of Dolgellau; at junction of A487 and B4405.
Restrictions Not suitable for ♿. No smoking in dining room, parlour, sun room or bedrooms. No children 3–12. No dogs.
Credit cards Access, Diners, Visa.
Terms Dinner, B&B: single £50–£59, double £80–£98. Set dinner £15.50; packed lunches on request. Off-season breaks; reductions for long stays; Christmas package. 1-night bookings refused at peak times. Reduced rates and special meals for children.
Service/tipping: "Service is free and part of the caring family atmosphere. Tips are not part of our arrangements."

THREE COCKS Powys — Map 1

Three Cocks Hotel *Tel* Glasbury (0497) 847215
Three Cocks, Nr Brecon LD3 0SL

"One of the bright spots on our tour through England and Wales" – an American visitor's tribute this year to this 15th-century inn with a cobbled forecourt, ivy-clad walls, worn steps and great oak beams. It stands in grounds of one and a half acres in the Brecon Beacons National Park, half a mile from the river Wye. It is owned by Michael Winstone and his Belgian wife Marie-Jeanne; he is the chef, and the cooking has French and Belgian overtones. "The owners are delightful, friendly but professional in their relationship with their guests. The food is extremely good, vegetarians are well catered for if their requirements are made known in advance, and the wine selection is worth drinking. There's a lovely wood-panelled lounge." Breakfasts are also praised. Last year's report referred to bedrooms and bathrooms being separated only by curtains. Mrs Winstone tells us that doors have now been fitted. (*Monte Dale Witte, David and Lynn McGarvey, Dr and Mrs RJ Davies, and others*) Bedrooms vary in size. One couple, who had a poky double, also complained that there was no heating on a chilly night and that the towels were flimsy. More reports please.

Open Mid-Feb–end Nov. Restaurant closed Sun lunch, Tue.
Rooms 7 double – all with bath, shower; radio, baby-listening on request.
Facilities Reception lounge, lounge, TV lounge, breakfast room, dining room. ¼-acre grounds.
Location 5 m SW of Hay-on-Wye on A438 Brecon–Hereford road. Rear rooms quietest. Parking.
Restrictions Not suitable for ♿. No dogs.
Credit cards Access, Visa.
Terms B&B: single £36–£54, double £54; dinner, B&B double (min 2 nights) £84. Set lunch/dinner £21; full alc £29. Reduced rates and special meals for children. *Service/tipping: "Left to the customers' discretion."*

TREFRIW Gwynedd — Map 4

Hafod House — *Tel* Llanrwst (0492) 640029
Trefriw, Gwynedd LL27 0RQ — *Fax* (0492) 641351

Converted 17th-century farmhouse, with barn restaurant, on bank of Conwy valley, overlooking Denbigh moors. Well placed for touring North Wales; golf, climbing, pony trekking, lake and river fishing nearby. "Offers quality accommodation without losing the original farmhouse atmosphere." 1-acre garden. 7 well-appointed bedrooms, all with bath/shower, balcony; 2 have 4-poster and jacuzzi. Not suitable for ♿. No children under 11. No dogs. All major credit cards accepted. B&B £30; dinner, B&B £45. Set dinner £15. Recent nomination. More reports please.

WHITEBROOK Gwent — Map 2

The Crown at Whitebrook — *Tel* Monmouth (0600) 860254
Whitebrook, Nr Monmouth — *Fax* (0600) 860607
NP5 4TX

Again, this year, many favourable reports on Sandra and Roger Bates's extended and modernised 17th-century inn, in a steeply wooded valley a mile from the river Wye. "Perhaps the description 'restaurant-with-rooms' implies a certain lack of facilities, but this is not so. The bar-cum-sitting room is comfortable to sit in as well as to drink in." Much praise for the food: "The style is French, but not too *nouvelle*; admirable, original but not pretentious and literally cooked to order"; and for the "sensible wine list, with outstanding and reasonable house claret". "Relaxed, informal, but very professional service." Rooms are small but well equipped, with plenty of wardrobe space. "At night there was only the susurration of the breeze in the trees and the softly running Wye. In the morning we woke to the sound of robins and more wrens than I've seen in years." (*RAL Ogston, RC Petherick, Jill Marshall, DG Randall, PLB Mynors, and others*)

Open All year except Christmas, 3 weeks Jan. Restaurant closed to non-residents Sun night, Mon lunch.
Rooms 12 double – all with bath, shower, telephone, radio, TV, tea-making facilities, baby-listening by arrangement. 1 on ground floor.
Facilities Lounge bar, restaurant, breakfast room. 3-acre garden with terrace.
Location 5 m S of Monmouth; W of A466 at Bigsweir Bridge, 2 m up narrow lane.
Restrictions Suitable for only partially ♿. Smoking discouraged in restaurant. No dogs in restaurant.
Credit cards All major cards accepted.
Terms B&B £38–£48; dinner, B&B (min 2 nights) £55–£65. Set lunch £14.25, dinner £24.50. Children free if sharing adults' room; special meals by arrangement.
Service/tipping: "If someone wishes to reward staff for their efforts, the gratuity is accepted and shared among them."

Scotland

Knockinaam Lodge, Portpatrick

ABERFELDY Tayside **Map 5**

Farleyer House
Aberfeldy
Perthshire PH15 2JE

Tel Aberfeldy (0887) 20332
Fax (0887) 29430

"The most comfortable, beautiful, charming place we have stayed in anywhere in the world" – a Californian visitor's unqualified appreciation of the 16th-century former dower house of Castle Menzies, run by Frances and Bill Atkins, which opened its doors as a hotel two years ago. Nestling on a hillside overlooking the Tay valley, it's an hour or so's drive from Edinburgh or Glasgow and already a fixture on many a gourmet tourist circuit. Decorated in a welcoming country-house style, well endowed with antiques, it is praised for its solid comfort: "Reception rooms very good indeed, service most adequate, tea excellent, the sheets divine." Other writers have appreciated "the fresh flowers in every room, the elf-like maid service that magically straightened one's rooms during breakfast, the unfailing good humour and courtesy of the staff". But for many visitors it is the innovative British cooking of Frances Atkins that draws them to *Farleyer*: "Rates 3 in the *Good Food Guide* and deserves it." The wine list and the selection of malt whiskies are as extensive as you would expect. (*Prof. VA Fronkin, Paul Schachter, Michael Firth, RS McNeill*) Some grumbles may be heard in the general chorus of praise: room heating has been found inadequate by several reporters, prices are said to be "south of England" but bedrooms aren't always up to the tariff, and then there are the extras on the bill: "£10 for a pot of tea and a handful of biscuits was a bit much."

Open All year except end Nov/1st week Dec (hotel); restaurant also closed Feb.
Rooms 2 suites, 8 double, 1 single – all with bath, shower, telephone, radio, TV.
Facilities Drawing room, 2 libraries (1 with drinks dispensary), restaurant. 70-acre grounds with garden, croquet, golf, woods; shooting, riding arranged; salmon/trout fishing ½ m.
Location In Aberfeldy take B846 across Wade Bridge to Kinloch Rannoch.
Restrictions No smoking in dining room. No children under 10. Dogs by prior arrangement; not in bedrooms or public rooms.
Credit cards Access, Amex, Visa.
Terms Dinner, B&B £80–£125. Set lunch £20, dinner £30. "Theme breaks."
Service/tipping: "Left to guests' discretion." [But bills say "Service is not included".]

ACHILTIBUIE Highland — Map 5

Summer Isles Hotel — *Tel* Achiltibuie (085 482) 282
Achiltibuie, by Ullapool
Ross and Cromarty IV26 2YG

Unequivocal praise for Mark and Geraldine Irvine's individual and sophisticated hotel, in a remote and beautiful setting north-west of Ullapool. Reached by a 15-mile single-track road, it is a splendid base for bird-watchers, walkers and fishermen (it holds fishing rights in the area), and has spectacular views over the sea and a great scattering of little islands. The owners advise guests to bring wellingtons, binoculars, paint-boxes, comfortable old clothes – their dogs if they like (so long as they don't appear in the dining room or lounge). The gulf stream is at the foot of the croft, but the weather can change from Arctic to Aegean inside a week. "It is no exaggeration to say that this hotel pleased us in every way. Its size, fabric, furnishing, equipment and management match perfectly its Highland coastal-village environment and are first-rate in quality. The Irvines and their staff do not intrude, but they are always available to ensure that needs are met," said one reader. Another said, succinctly: "Very comfortable. Food sensational. Convivial atmosphere. Excellent packed lunch. Lovely beach." Most guests change for dinner, served promptly at 8 pm. It is a sophisticated five-course meal and practically everything is home-produced or locally caught. "We know of nowhere that first-class food is so simply and subtly cooked; and the menu was not repeated at all during our ten nights' stay." "Guests are encouraged to try as many puddings as they like; some have sampled them all." "The most satisfying food that we have encountered in thirty years of travelling." Bedrooms are comfortable though not lavishly appointed; some are quite small. The Loghouse Suite is recommended for families: "Fresh milk in the fridge and top-ups of fruit during the week." (*JE Thornton, Margaret H Box, J and M Cole, Barbara Wooldridge, Roger Bland, Virginia and Charles Day, and others*)

Open Easter–mid-Oct.
Rooms 2-roomed suite (sleeps 2–5; available for self-catering Oct–May), 10 double – 8 with bath and shower, 3 with bath. Suite and 7 rooms in Loghouse annexe 3 yds from main building. Some on ground floor.
Facilities Sun lounge, cocktail bar, public bar, dining room, café for teas and light lunches. Sea and beaches nearby; fishing, walking, bird watching.
Location 10 m N of Ullapool; take twisting single-track road skirting lochs Lurgain, Badagyle and Oscaig for 15 m. Hotel is just past post office.
Restrictions Not suitable for ♿. No smoking in dining room. No children under 8. No dogs in public rooms.
Credit cards None accepted.
Terms B&B: single £41–£55.50, double £59–£83, suite £107. Set dinner £29.
Service/tipping: "Service included in all prices; we do not expect our customers to tip. If guests insist on showing special appreciation, the money is divided evenly among all staff."

ARDUAINE Strathclyde — Map 5

Loch Melfort Hotel
Arduaine, by Oban
Argyllshire PA34 4XG

Tel Kilmelford (085 22) 233
Fax (085 22) 214

"Its situation must afford one of the most superb views from any hotel, not just in Scotland, but in the entire world," writes one reader of this characteristic loch-side house converted into a small modern hotel with a motel-like extension, which lies on the coast road between Oban and Crinan, with views towards the islands of Jura and Scarba. All rooms have large picture-windows facing the sea. Philip and Rosalind Lewis, fresh to the hotel business – he a refugee from the motor trade, she from publishing – took over last year and most visitors during the first twelve months of their regime have warmly approved: "Philip Lewis, who does all the cooking, has a very good touch and is keen to use local fresh products. The wine list has been revamped and is reasonably priced and interesting." "Food first-rate, service friendly and competent." Children are welcomed. (*MH Hibbert, SDC Vargas, AJD Simmons, Anne Laurence, and others*) One reader described his room as "comfortable, but certainly not luxurious". Another complained of "a rather tatty room with malfunctioning lavatory not cured during stay".

Open 1 Mar–3 Jan.
Rooms 1 suite, 25 double – all with bath and/or shower, telephone, radio, tea-making facilities, baby-listening. 20, with balcony/patio, in separate wing. 10 on ground floor.
Facilities Portable ramp. 2 lounges, library, restaurant. 26-acre grounds; on loch; safe bathing (cold), windsurfing, fishing, moorings for yachts.
Location 19 m S of Oban on A816.
Restrictions Smoking discouraged in dining room. No dogs in main house.
Credit cards Access, Visa.
Terms B&B £25–£57.50; dinner, B&B £42–£69.50. Bar meals; picnic lunches. Set dinner £20–£22. Christmas and New Year packages. Reduced rates for children sharing parents' room; special meals on request.
Service/tipping: "No service charge. Tipping at guests' discretion. Tips distributed among all staff."

> Inevitably some hotels change hands or close after we have gone to press. You should always check on this when booking, particularly in the case of small establishments.

ARDVASAR Skye, Highland — Map 5

Ardvasar Hotel BUDGET — *Tel* Ardvasar (047 14) 223
Ardvasar, Sleat, Isle of Skye
Inverness-shire IV45 8RS

A white-washed stone former coaching inn, a mile from the Armadale Ferry, which was built as a hostelry in the 18th century and still serves the needs of visitors from over the water as well as locals. "First impressions are misleading; decor and furnishings in seaside-bedsit style were an inauspicious start. But all is soon forgiven; the bustling bar serving meals to passers-by has a lovely atmosphere and the food is superb. Fresh, locally caught fish are the stars of the menu but it is all varied and imaginative with a suitable Scottish style." "It is a very comfortable, relaxing place where no one minds if you turn up soaking wet in old walking clothes (they have a big boiler room for drying clothes and boots). Mrs Fowler looks after her guests very well and is always most cheerful and obliging." "No dried flowers and Laura Ashley, or freebies in the bathroom, but everywhere is sparkling clean, and there is a generous supply of goodies for making drinks, and loads of hot water." (*SDC Vargas, Margaret Wall; also Mr and Mrs Turner, I and JW Bennion*)

Open Mar–Nov.
Rooms 8 double, 2 single – all with bath and/or shower, tea-making facilities; 4 with TV; baby-listening on request.
Facilities Lounge, TV lounge, cocktail bar, public bar, dining room. Small garden. Safe but rocky bathing ½ m.
Location In tiny village. 2 ferries to island, Kyle of Lochalsh–Kyleakin and Mallaig–Armadale, operate all year round but latter takes vehicles only in summer. Also car ferry Glenelg–Kylerhea in summer.
Restrictions Not suitable for ♿. Smoking discouraged in dining room and bedrooms. Dogs at management's discretion.
Credit cards Access, Visa.
Terms B&B £25–£30; dinner, B&B £41–£46. Set dinner £17; picnic lunches and bar meals available. Children sharing parents' room charged for meals only; special meals on request.
Service/tipping: "No service charge. Tipping not expected but if anyone is pleased enough to want to tip, we are pleased to thank them personally!"

AUCHENCAIRN Dumfries and Galloway — Map 4

Balcary Bay Hotel — *Tel* Auchencairn (055 664) 217 and 311
Auchencairn
Nr Castle Douglas DG7 1QZ

Two correspondents admonish us for failing to do justice, in last year's Guide, to the "idyllic" location of this modernised 17th-century smuggler's inn. "It is so lovely facing Balcary Bay and the island and hills beyond," begins one reader. "We would sit fascinated by the light and the sky and the way the sea seemed hardly to move. The only sound was of birds." This unpretentious and reasonably priced inn, which retains much of its old character and atmosphere, is owned and run by Ron and Joan Lamb and their son Graeme, and is quietly situated on the shore road just outside the village of Auchencairn. "The spacious, well-furnished, decorated and equipped bedrooms, giving on to the ever-changing view of the bay, are delightful." "Delicious dinners; the fish was fresh and nicely cooked, the soups were home-made, and there was a good selection of desserts. Efficient service by pleasant local women." There is a limited-choice set menu using local produce, and an extensive à la carte menu and wine list. The hotel has central heating throughout, with comfortable public rooms, and stands in well-tended mature gardens with extensive views. Sporting interests are well catered for in the area, and there are numerous good walks. (*Ruth West, JE Thornton, and others*)

Open Early Mar–Christmas.
Rooms 14 double, 3 single – all with bath and/or shower, telephone, radio, TV, tea-making facilities.
Facilities 2 lounges, cocktail bar, restaurant, snooker room. 3½-acre grounds on bay with sand/rock beach. Safe bathing, fishing, sailing, golf, riding, shooting nearby.
Location Off A711 Dumfries–Kircudbright road, 2 m S of Auchencairn on shore road.
Restrictions Not suitable for ♿. No dogs in public rooms.
Credit cards Access, Visa.
Terms Dinner, B&B £43–£60. Set lunch/dinner £17; full alc £23. Bar meals available. Early and late season rates; reductions for 3- and 7-night stays. Children up to 12, sharing parents' room, ½ price; special meals.
Service/tipping: "Payment for service is not expected or encouraged. Gratuities are shared among all staff."

BALLATER Grampian — Map 5

Darroch Learg — *Tel* Ballater (033 97) 55443
Ballater, Aberdeenshire AB35 5UX — *Fax* (033 97) 55443

In four-acre grounds on the side of a wooded mountain, ten minutes' walk from Ballater, the *Darroch Learg* offers a quiet setting and lovely scenery. It is two pink-and-grey granite country houses, overlooking the Dee Valley and the Grampians, and makes a good centre for a golfing or fishing holiday. Readers have written enthusiastically this year about this hotel that has been in the Franks family for twenty-seven years. "Very attractive rooms, comfortably and charmingly furnished, with pleasing extra touches (such as current *Vogue* on the bedside table). Public rooms are also very comfortable and in a cold, wet July the log fire and central heating were most welcome." "The restaurant offers an attractive choice of mainly traditional dishes, and this is a house where breakfast kippers come in pairs; there is undyed smoked haddock too." "The proprietor and staff are friendly and attentive without being obtrusive." "Good value for money." (*Miss SJ Rogers, Angus and Ann Sibley, Harry and Miriam Cooper, and others*)

Open Feb–Nov.
Rooms 18 double, 3 single (5 in separate building) – all with bath and/or shower, telephone, radio, TV, tea-making facilities, baby-listening. 1 on ground floor.
Facilities 3 lounges (1 no-smoking), restaurant, 4-acre grounds, ¼ m from river Dee.
Location On A93, ¼ m NE of Ballater.
Restrictions Not suitable for ♿. No smoking in drawing room and 4 bedrooms. No dogs in public rooms.
Credit cards Access, Visa accepted.
Terms (Service included) B&B £25–£40; dinner, B&B £42–£57. Set Sunday lunch £8.50–£10.50, set dinner £17. Reduced rates and special meals for children. Special rates for stays of 3 days or more; low-season rates Nov, Feb–Apr.

BANCHORY Grampian **Map 5**

Banchory Lodge
Banchory, Kincardineshire
AB31 3HS

Tel Banchory (033 02) 2625
Fax (033 02) 5019

"We have nothing but praise for this hotel after more than twenty years of annual visits at many seasons." "High standards all round – beautiful public rooms and bedrooms, exceptionally well decorated and maintained. Food consistently good and well cooked; immaculate dining-room service." "The owners really understand the art of running a hotel. You could even see to shave in the bathroom!" "We had one of the most luxurious family rooms encountered in our travels. If only there were more hotels like this in Scotland." Just some of this year's encomia for this white-painted Georgian building, filled with Victorian and Edwardian furniture and bric-à-brac lovingly collected over the years by the resident owners for over twenty-five years, Mr and Mrs Jaffray. It enjoys a "majestic location", with the river Dee running through its wooded grounds, and has many loyal returnees, including fishing folk and golfers (there are three courses close by). (*CI and CA Phillips, Neil Phillips, TD Stephens, and others*) One reader's pleasure in his "excellent" dinner and breakfast was diminished by chain-smokers.

Open 1 Feb–13 Dec.
Rooms 10 suites, 12 double, 1 single – all with bath, shower, telephone, radio, TV, tea-making facilities, baby-listening.
Facilities 2 lounges, cocktail bar, dining room, private dining room. 12-acre grounds; river with salmon and trout fishing (book well in advance). Golf nearby.
Location 10 mins' walk from centre.
Restrictions Not suitable for ♿. Dogs at management's discretion; not in public rooms or unattended in bedrooms.
Credit cards All major cards accepted.
Terms [1991 rates] (Excluding VAT) B&B: single £60, double £85–£100; dinner, B&B: single £80, double £125–£140. Reduced rates for children; special meals.
Service/tipping: "Service included. Central pool in office for tips."

Invery House
Bridge of Feugh, Banchory
Kincardineshire AB3 3NJ

Tel Banchory (033 02) 4782
Fax (033 02) 4712

"A truly superb hotel, outstanding in every way. Beautiful bedrooms and bathrooms. Impeccable service. Incredible setting." So began a recent report on this pale pink mansion, purchased in 1985 by Stewart and Sheila Spence and carefully transformed into a highly sophisticated country house hotel. "As you approach from the south you pass over the rushing river Feugh. White boulders guide you to the house. The flagstoned porch is liberally filled with antiques, flowers and stuffed birds, as is the main hall, which is warm underfoot, mostly peach with green velvet, and has dark Edwardian furniture. Our bedroom, Rokeby (all the bedrooms are called after novels by Sir Walter Scott who is said to have visited the house) was a riot of designer chintz. The bathroom had everything, even a telephone (though the bath was awkward to use, approached up two steps, and with the taps in the middle). Drinks were served in the drawing room where we chose our dinner and consulted the vast wine list. In the sage-green dining room we sat in huge upholstered armchairs, so enormous we were miles away from each other across the table." (*Jane Kaminski, Lt Col SJ Furness, Pat and Jeremy Temple*) More reports would be welcome.

Open All year.
Rooms 2 suites, 11 double, 1 single – all with bath, shower, telephone, radio, TV.
Facilities Bar, 2 lounges, 2 restaurants; 2 private dining/conference rooms. 60-acre grounds with 1 mile private fishing, croquet, putting, helipad. Chauffeur-driven car available for guests' use. Golf nearby.
Location 18 m W of Aberdeen. Take A93 to Banchory then B974 S to Fettercairn for 1 m. Look for sign.
Restrictions Only restaurant suitable for ♿ (ramp). No smoking in restaurant. Children under 8 by arrangement. Dogs in kennels only.
Credit cards All major cards accepted.
Terms B&B: single £80–£140, double £90–£170, suite £180–£280. Set lunch £18.50, dinner £34.50. Autumn, winter and spring breaks. Reduced rates for children sharing parents' room; special meals on request.
Service/tipping: "Service included; tips at guests' discretion and distributed quarterly to everyone."

BEATTOCK Dumfries and Galloway — Map 5

Auchen Castle
Beattock, Moffat
Dumfriesshire DG10 9SH

Tel Beattock (068 33) 407
Fax (068 33) 667

Hazel and Robert Beckh's traditional hotel, just north of Beattock village in the Scottish borders and a useful overnight stop, has attracted plenty of favourable comment again this year. This grey sandstone mid-19th-century mansion, former home of the William Younger family, sits imposingly in a fifty-acre woodland garden complete with trout lake. "We had a big room, decorated in muted tartan, looking over the large and varied garden. The staff were outstandingly pleasant. An excellent dinner, and a huge choice at breakfast including liver and bacon and Arbroath smokies, to the bewilderment of some American guests. We were particularly impressed by the upkeep of the extensive grounds and, above all, by the forward planning – new planting of trees that would not reach maturity for a couple of generations. A real hand of love looks after this place." Another reader adds: "The hotel deserves glowing tributes. We were greeted by the owner who had no difficulty with our late arrival for dinner. The standard of furnishings was exceptional and dinner a masterpiece of achievement. The atmosphere at the 'disco dinner' on Saturday was so relaxing that no one in the restaurant could resist becoming involved." "Lovely setting, nice rooms, good food, first-class." (*Mrs RB Richards, RP Williams; also W Long, David Turner, David Sebag-Montefiore*)

Open All year except 3 weeks over Christmas and New Year.
Rooms 22 double, 3 single – 13 with bath, 12 with shower, all with telephone, radio, TV, tea-making facilities, baby-listening. 10 in Cedar Lodge annexe.
Facilities Lounge, bar, dining room; 2 conference rooms. Sat dinner-dance mid-Oct–end Mar. 50-acre grounds with trout loch; boat. Fishing on river Annan; golf, riding, tennis, sailing nearby.
Location 1 m N of Beattock village with signed access from A74.
Restrictions Not suitable for ♿. No dogs in dining room.
Credit cards All major cards accepted.

Terms [1991 rates] B&B: single £43, double £53–£64; dinner, B&B: single £45.25, double £72.50–£94. Bar lunches. Set dinner £11.50–£15. Special breaks; golf holidays. Reduced rates and special meals for children on request.
Service/tipping: "Service included. Tips not expected and this is stated on room card, but any received are distributed in full to staff."

BLAIRGOWRIE Tayside — Map 5

Kinloch House
By Blairgowrie
Perthshire PH10 6SG

Tel Essendy (025 084) 237
Fax (025 084) 333

César award in 1991: The embodiment of Scottish hospitality

"A recent visit has confirmed my first impressions of this well-run country house hotel. *Kinloch House* has maintained its high standard of housekeeping, good food and comfortable accommodation." So writes a regular reader this year about David and Sarah Shentall's ivy-covered hotel, with oak-panelled hall and bar and a magnificent gallery, in a 25-acre estate complete with highland cattle. It is popular with shooting parties, having a game larder, drying facilities and kennels for the gun-dogs, and also with fishermen and golfers (there are forty golf courses within an hour's drive). It has one of the best restaurants in the area (on the formal side, jackets and ties expected). "A place of real warmth and character where one immediately feels welcome and relaxed. The presence of family portraits, *objets d'art*, fresh flowers and books adds to the impression of staying in a very comfortable home rather than a hotel. Housekeeping standards are high." There is also praise for the views from the bedrooms, and for the peaceful setting – "often the only sounds to be heard are the cries of wild geese and ducks". The bedrooms are well appointed; several small double rooms have recently been converted to single, answering criticism that some rooms were cramped; lighting may be unsatisfactory in some bathrooms. "The restaurant was a delight, the service first-class, the food beyond criticism, and reasonably priced." (*Rosamund V Hebdon, Mr and Mrs JE Rednall, Mrs L Morley, and others*) Opinions differ about the proprietor: "a genial host", "friendly and courteous" to some, but others complain of a "headmasterly" or "condescending" manner.

Open All year, except 20–30 Dec.
Rooms 2 suites, 14 double, 5 single – all with bath and/or shower, telephone, radio, TV, tea-making facilities, baby-listening. 4 on ground floor.
Facilities Ramp. Lounge, TV lounge, cocktail bar, conservatory, dining room. 25-acre grounds with highland cattle and croquet lawn. River and loch fishing, shooting, stalking, golf nearby.
Location 3½ m W of Blairgowrie on A923 Dunkeld road.
Restrictions No smoking in dining room. Dogs in certain bedrooms only, not in public rooms. No children under 7 in dining room.
Credit cards All major cards accepted.
Terms Dinner, B&B £66–£82.50. Bar lunches. Set lunch £13.50, dinner £20.75. Reductions for stays of 3 or more nights. 1-night bookings occasionally refused in peak season. Reduced rates and special meals for children by arrangement.
Service/tipping: "Tipping not encouraged. If guests insist the money is distributed to appropriate staff."

Please never tell a hotel you intend to send a report to the Guide. Anonymity is essential for objectivity.

BRIDGE OF MARNOCH Grampian — Map 5

The Old Manse of Marnoch BUDGET *Tel* Aberchirder (0466) 780873
Bridge of Marnoch
By Huntly, Aberdeenshire AB54 5RS

On the banks of the river Deveron, this 19th-century guest house is again warmly recommended for its "friendliness, cleanliness, food – all superb; and the attention to detail in the bedrooms was excellent. Everything you would have at home was supplied." It is much used by the fishing fraternity; and shooting and stalking can also be arranged. There are wooded walks down to the river, and five-acre grounds with old-fashioned roses, a formal herb parterre, and a walled kitchen garden. The decor reflects the many years the proprietors, Patrick and Keren Carter, spent in the Middle East. Bold colours predominate in the public rooms; the dining room, where dinner is served family-style, is dark red with nautical prints. "The *Old Manse* lifts itself effortlessly from the guest-house/B&B level by virtue of its food. It's a well-run and friendly small hotel in an interesting part of Scotland." (*Mrs E Jones, Sally Saysell; and others*)

Open All year, except 2 weeks Nov and occasional winter days.
Rooms 5 double – 3 *en suite,* 2 sharing bath and shower, all with radio, tea-making facilities.
Facilities Lounge with TV, lounge/writing room, dining room. 5-acre garden with herb parterre, stream and walks to river. Fishing, stalking, and shooting arranged. Cookery workshops off-season.
Location On B9117 less than 1 m W of A97 Huntly–Banff route.
Restrictions Not suitable for ♿. No smoking in dining or writing room. No dogs in dining room.
Credit cards None accepted.
Terms [1991 rates] B&B: single £28–£40, double £38–£50; dinner, B&B: single £43–£53, double £64–£80. Set dinner £15 (£17 to non-residents). Reduced rates for children sharing parents' room; special meals on request.
Service/tipping: "Guests are not expected to tip their hosts."

BUNCHREW Highland — Map 5

Bunchrew House *Tel* Inverness (0463) 234917
Bunchrew, by Inverness-shire IV3 6TA *Fax* (0463) 710620

Alan and Patsy Wilson's pink sandstone Scottish baronial concoction, set around a 15th-century tower, stands in 18 acres of wooded grounds on the shores of Beauly Firth. Close enough to Inverness for convenience, yet far enough for peace and tranquillity, its major attraction may be the beautiful glens that stretch to the south and west – Affric, Strathglass and Strathconon. Inside, there is dark panelling, thick carpets and open fires. From the dining room, you can see the waves breaking on the shore. Field glasses are provided for bird-watching diners. Food is "really outstanding" according to one 1991 visitor. Others have found the menu decidedly over-ambitious, but the accommodation and the welcome of owners and staff have again been praised, endorsing this recent report: "The place became home within hours. When we arrived, tea and shortbread appeared by magic. It's one of the few hotels that still bring you early morning tea and turn down beds. And the redoubtable head waiter even donned waders to help me out of the hotel's boat after a late-night sail in search of seals." There are five new bedrooms this year. (*G and E Townend, CJ Uncles, P and S Hawkins, Mrs Rita D Darwin*) More views, please, on the food.

Open All year.
Rooms 11 double – all with bath, shower, telephone, radio, TV, baby-listening.
Facilities 2 lounges, cocktail lounge, 2 restaurants. Rolls-Royce with chauffeur, helicopter available for sightseeing. 18-acre grounds. Free salmon fishing, boat, rods.
Location 3 m from centre of Inverness on A862 towards Beauly.
Restrictions No smoking in restaurants or bedrooms. Guide dogs only.
Credit cards Access, Amex, Visa.
Terms B&B: single £50–£82, double £75–£115. Set lunch £9.75, dinner £21.00. 3-day breaks all year. Reduced rates and special meals for children.
Service/tipping: "Service included. Tipping totally at guests' discretion for exceptional service."

BUSTA Shetland — Map 5

Busta House
Busta, Brae
Shetland ZE2 9QN

Tel Brae (080 622) 506
Fax (080 622) 588

Said to be the oldest continuously inhabited building in Shetland, Peter and Judith Jones's country house hotel is situated in rural, if windswept, surroundings overlooking the sea with its own small harbour. It is friendly and personal, with a locally recruited staff who know and love Shetland. The house has a history, about which a novel and a radio play have been written, involving the drowning of all the sons of the then Laird of Gifford who owned Busta, the birth of a love child, and a subsequent law suit which lasted over 100 years, bankrupting the Busta estates. There is also a ghost, seen, we're told, by perfectly rational (and sober) guests. More to the point for 20th-century travellers, the food is good, local produce where possible, especially fish, lamb, Orkney beef and cheese. There is always a stock of at least 120 malt whiskies, and a full and sensibly priced wine list. There is a good and frequently replenished stock of books and magazines; and the owner has a spinning wheel in the drawing room – lessons given on rainy days. "A most pleasant surprise in such a remote place. It will certainly lure us back." (*Ruth and Paul Haigh*)

Open 3 Jan–22 Dec.
Rooms 18 double, 2 single – all with bath and/or shower, telephone, radio, TV, tea-making facilities; baby-listening by phone.
Facilities Lounge, library, bar, restaurant. 4-acre grounds; own small harbour, with cabin cruiser for guests' use. Loch and sea fishing; sailing, diving from nearby sailing club – guests become automatic members.
Location A970, N from Lerwick, 27 m SW of Brae.
Restrictions Not suitable for ♿. No smoking in restaurant and library. No dogs in public rooms.
Credit cards All major cards accepted.
Terms [1991 rates] B&B £36.25–£51; dinner, B&B £42–£68.75. Bar lunches. Set dinner £19.50. Weekend breaks, holiday packages inclusive of travel. Reduced rates and special meals for children.
Service/tipping: "No service charge. Tips not encouraged; if given they are distributed pro rata to all staff."

Please make a habit of sending a report if you stay at a Guide hotel.

CALLANDER Central — Map 5

Brook Linn BUDGET — *Tel* Callander (0877) 30103
Leny Feus, Callander
Perthshire FK17 8AU

Small elegant Victorian country house in elevated position 10 mins' walk from town centre with fine views over Trossachs. Spectacular scenery, wonderful for hill walkers. Proprietors Fiona and Derek House – "sociable without interfering" – have created a relaxed and informal atmosphere where the guests still get personal attention. Children welcome. "Imaginative" home-cooking; vegetarians catered for; desserts specially recommended. Fixed mealtimes: 8.30 am breakfast, 7 pm dinner. Packed lunches available. Open Easter–Nov. 7 bedrooms, all with shower. 2-acre garden. No smoking. Credit cards not accepted. Dinner, B&B £28–£30. New nomination. More reports please.

CANONBIE Dumfries and Galloway — Map 5

Riverside Inn — *Tel* Canonbie (038 73) 71512
Canonbie, Dumfriesshire DG14 0UX

César award in 1985: Best inn of the year

"One of our all-time favourites," says a regular reader. And so it is for many others who write every year in praise of Robert and Susan Phillips's small inn or restaurant-with-rooms, a 17th-century fisherman's retreat on the banks of the Esk, well placed for touring Hadrian's Wall and the Solway coast, and as a staging post on long-haul journeys. There are six pleasantly decorated bedrooms, two in a garden cottage overlooking the river; they vary in size (it is wise to discuss your requirements on booking) and have "everything that a good hostess would put there from fruit to needle and thread, and books". But it is the food which attracts the highest praise – "excellent and most imaginative, served in a delightfully appointed dining room". "Not the sort of food one expects in a country pub, more like a first-class five-star hotel." "We particularly liked the bar meals in such attractive cosy rooms. Open log fires and a feeling of warmth and welcome throughout, though quite understated." (*Christopher Davy, Moira and John Cole, Stephanie Sowerby, Caroline McIntosh; also RV Hebdon, and many others*) Mrs Phillips tells us she has now introduced a supper menu as an alternative to the full dinner.

Open All year except Christmas, 2 weeks Feb, 2 weeks Nov.
Rooms 6 double – 4 with bath, 2 with shower, all with radio, TV, tea-making facilities. 2 in cottage in garden. 1 on ground floor.
Facilities Reception/coffee lounge, lounge bar, residents' lounge, dining room. Small garden. Park opposite with children's play area. River Esk 100 yds; salmon and sea-trout fishing (permits from hotel).
Location M6 exit 44. 14 m N on A7; turn off into Canonbie. Inn is at bottom of hill by river Esk bridge.
Restrictions No smoking in dining room and some other public rooms. No children under 6. No dogs.
Credit cards Access, Visa.
Terms B&B double £67. Bar lunches; supper menu £15–£18, set dinner £19.50. 2-day breaks Nov–May. Weekly rates. Reduced rates and special meals for children.
Service/tipping: "Tipping is not encouraged."

COLONSAY Strathclyde — Map 5

Isle of Colonsay Hotel *Tel* Colonsay (095 12) 316
Argyllshire PA61 7YP *Fax* (095 12) 353

César award in 1988: Island hotel in a class of its own

Visitors come to Colonsay to enjoy its remote setting and its golden beaches. There are dramatic rocky cliffs, woods, heathland and lochs, and good terrain for cycling. Infrequent ferry schedules will maroon visitors on the island for at least two days, but many choose to stay longer. At the centre of its life is the 250-year-old *Isle of Colonsay Hotel*, overlooking Scalasaig harbour and run by Kevin Byrne, a man of formidable energy, with his wife Christa. Last year he told us he had opened his own bookshop specialising in "the rather arcane subject of Colonsay and Oronsay". This year he announces wildlife boat trips, guided walks to sites of archaeological interest that visitors would not normally find, and the purchase of a microlight aircraft for use in aerial survey. "Our aim," he says, "is to try to enhance tranquillity; we actually want our guests to leave feeling at least a little better than when they arrived. It isn't easy." Bedrooms vary in size, are conventional in decor and some have views; all have central heating and electric blankets. We badly need more reports.

Open 1 Mar–5 Nov and 2 weeks New Year.
Rooms 8 double with shower, 3 single – all with radio, tea-making facilities; TV, telephone, baby-listening on request. 1 garden bungalow with shower for family accommodation.
Facilities Residents' lounge, sun room, cocktail bar, public bar, Seafood Bar (May–Sep), restaurant. 1-acre grounds with garden, burn, sandpit, vegetable gardens. ½ m to sandy beach and lochs.
Location 400 yds W of harbour. Car/passenger ferry from Oban Mon, Wed, Fri (37 m crossing, 2¼ hours); additional ferries in high season; hotel courtesy car to/from all sailings.
Restrictions "Disabled guests welcome but facilities not perfect." No smoking in dining room. No dogs in public rooms.
Credit cards All major cards accepted.
Terms Dinner, B&B £30–£60. Set dinner £17. Because of ferry, min stay has to be 2 nights. Reductions for long stays; off-season breaks. Children sharing parents' room charged only for meals, except in high season.
Service/tipping: "No service charge; our staff are properly paid. Gratuities are shared by our domestic staff among themselves."

CREETOWN Wigtownshire — Map 5

Hill of Burns *Tel* Creetown (067 182) 487
Creetown DG8 7HF

New to the Guide this year, *Hill of Burns* is a small mansion, extended in the early 19th century, now converted into a traditional country house hotel. It is set in three acres of wooded grounds and gardens, in an elevated position overlooking the river Cree estuary and Wigtown bay. "A really splendid hotel run by an enthusiastic young couple, Mr and Mrs Stephen Moore. The appointments are excellent – a side table for one's newspapers at breakfast, thick towels, rich curtains; the whole atmosphere is tranquil and relaxing." "Generous portions of local fresh smoked salmon and lobster, excellent Galloway beef and lamb, and we particularly appreciated the fresh vegetable soup and the wide range of desserts." Well-furnished and exceptionally spacious bedrooms with "real wardrobes, plenty of dressing table space and enough room for a settee, table and chairs". "Service is unobtrusive and invariably helpful, towels are changed every day, and fresh flowers were placed in our room along with flowering plants and some excellent pot-pourris." "Anyone who likes the Lake District but is weary of the crowds would find the area congenial." (*Mr and Mrs C Borland, John Ingman; also David Wood*)

Open Feb–Dec.
Rooms 1 suite, 5 double – 4 with bath, shower; all with telephone, radio, TV, tea-making facilities, baby-listening.
Facilities Drawing room, dining room, billiard room. 3-acre grounds with croquet lawn. 5 m from safe, sandy beach. Free golf on local courses.
Location Take road opposite clock tower in village and continue up hill; hotel gates on right.
Restrictions No smoking in restaurant. "Not really suitable for very young children." No dogs in public rooms.
Credit cards Access, Visa accepted.
Terms [1991 rates] B&B £23–£35; dinner, B&B £38–£50. Set dinner £17.50. 2-day breaks, weekly terms. Reduced rates for children under 12 sharing parents' room. *Service/tipping: "No service charge; tipping is not encouraged."*

CRINAN Strathclyde — Map 5

Crinan Hotel
Crinan, Argyllshire PA31 8SR
Tel Crinan (054 683) 261
Fax (054 683) 292

Re-nominated after an absence, a hotel famous for its incomparable location: it lies at the seaward end of the eight-mile Crinan Canal, connecting Loch Fyne to the Atlantic, and looks across to the mountains of Mull and the Isle of Jura. It has been welcoming yachtsmen, fishermen and travellers for over 200 years; and has been owned by the Ryan family for twenty-one of them. "Our room was palatial with a panorama of the sea from the main window and a wonderful view of the end of the canal from the bathroom; it was warm, spotless and welcoming. Staff were efficient and courteous." Because of its unique position, all rooms have sea views, and a number of bedrooms have a private balcony. The hotel has recently been refurbished and furnishings have been chosen with care; paintings by Mrs Ryan (the artist Frances Macdonald) hang in the public rooms. Lock 16, on the roof of the hotel, is an esteemed (though expensive) seafood restaurant, dubbed by Ronay the best fish restaurant in the UK, 1991; from the rooftop bar you can watch your dinner of jumbo prawns, clams, lobsters, mussels and oysters being landed. On the ground floor is the Telford Room, less spectacular views, more modest in price. (*Dr RA Houston*)

Open All year, except 5 days at Christmas. Lock 16 restaurant closed Sun, Mon and Oct–Apr.
Rooms 1 suite, 18 double, 2 single – all with bath and/or shower, telephone, radio, TV; tea-making facilities on request.
Facilities Lift. 2 lounges, 3 bars, 2 restaurants; pianist in rooftop bar before dinner. Garden. Safe, sandy beaches nearby; fishing available.
Location At Lochgilphead follow A83 over small roundabout by town centre; right at next roundabout; follow A816 Oban sign. After 2 m turn left to Crinan through Cairnbaan on A841.

Restriction No dogs in restaurant.
Credit cards Access, Visa.
Terms [1991 rates] B&B: single £60–£65, double £95–£110, suite £150–£220. Set dinner £25; full alc in Lock 16 £35. Winter half-board rates. Reduced rates for children sharing parents' room; special meals on request.
Service/tipping: "No service charge. Tips at guests' discretion, distributed by tronc *system."*

CULNAKNOCK Skye, Highland — Map 5

Glenview
Culnaknock, Portree
Isle of Skye IV51 9JH

Tel Staffin (047 062) 248

In lovely island setting, 13 m N of Portree, small inn owned and run by Linda Thomson. Warmly recommended for pristine rooms full of extras and exceptional home-cooking including breakfasts, teas, bar snacks. Restricted opening Oct–Easter. 5 rooms, 3 with shower. Not suitable for ♿. Access, Visa accepted. B&B double £56. Set dinner £20. New nomination. More reports welcome.

DRUMNADROCHIT Highland — Map 5

Polmaily House
Drumnadrochit
Inverness-shire IV3 6XT

Tel Drumnadrochit (045 62) 343

This rambling Edwardian mansion in 18-acre grounds is a few miles west of Loch Ness. It has pleased readers for many years, being wonderfully positioned for visiting the dramatic scenery of the glens nearby, and offering a tranquil rural setting. Its ambience is more like a private house than a hotel. The bedrooms are individually decorated and furnished: "Comfortable beds and carpets that were ecstasy to the feet; the bathroom was also well equipped." "A relaxed atmosphere, not at all stuffy. We had a small sofa and window-seat, so it was a nice place to sit and read. The food was excellent, the packed lunches outstanding in quantity and quality." "We learned to take one lunch for the two of us because of their generosity." Alison Parsons's menus combine enterprising starters (cream of prawn, sweet pepper and ginger soup, savoury walnut roulade with asparagus and quail's eggs) with more traditional local fare (wild salmon with sorrel sauce, fillet of Aberdeen Angus beef). "Her exquisite cooking puts the hotel in a class of its own." (*Edith and David Holt, J Coats, Clare Fletcher; and others*) More than one reader complained of inadequate heating. One couple had a shabby room and thought their breakfast poor.

Open Easter–end Oct.
Rooms 7 double, 2 single – doubles with bath, all with radio.
Facilities Drawing room, reading room with TV (residents only), restaurant with bar. 18-acre grounds with tennis, croquet, unheated swimming pool; fishing, shooting, stalking, pony trekking nearby.
Location 2 m W of Drumnadrochit on A831 Cannich road.
Restrictions Not suitable for ♿. No smoking in dining room. Dogs in grounds only.
Credit cards Access, Visa.

Terms B&B £45–£50. Set dinner £20–£28. Discounts for long stays. Redu
for children sharing parents' room; high teas at 6 pm on request.
Service/tipping: "Tips are neither expected nor solicited – but nor are they refused."

DUNKELD Tayside — Map 5

Kinnaird — *Tel* Ballinluig (079 682) 440
Kinnaird Estate — *Fax* (079 682) 289
By Dunkeld, Perthshire PH8 0LB

A welcome newcomer to the ranks of the Scottish country house hotels, luxury division, this fine, Grade B listed 18th-century house is on a privately owned estate of 9,000 acres, with magnificent views over the Tay valley and "soothing Scottish scenery as far as the eye can see". It has been restored to its former grandeur by its owner, Mrs Constance Ward, grand-daughter of a distinguished American innkeeper, and its manager and chef is Mosimann-trained John Webber, formerly at *Cliveden* and *Gidleigh Park* (qq.v.). "We stayed in the Balmacneil Suite, which is enormous and must be one of the best-appointed hotel rooms in Britain. The sitting room is old-fashioned and comfortable, the dining room is panelled by interesting painted murals (provenance unknown, but they look French). We naturally enjoyed John Webber's cooking." "The house is delightful, in that it has not been refurbished to death, and has the great atmosphere of a proper, lived-in house that no interior designer has yet imitated satisfactorily." A wide variety of sporting facilities is available for guests, from fishing for salmon and trout, to shooting for pheasant, grouse and duck, and roe stalking; there's excellent walking and bird watching. (*GAS Beale, John and Padi Howard, and others*)

Open All year, except Feb.
Rooms 1 suite, 8 double – all with bath, shower, telephone, radio, TV, baby-listening. 1 on ground floor.
Facilities Ramp. Lounge, study, 2 dining rooms; billiard room. 9,000-acre estate, with gardens, tennis, croquet, shooting; salmon and trout fishing on river Tay ½ m.
Location 6¾ m N of Dunkeld on B898, just off A9 to Pitlochry.
Restrictions No children under 12. No smoking in restaurant. No dogs in house (kennels available).
Credit cards Access, Amex, Visa.
Terms [1991 rates] B&B single £85–£150, double £120–£165, suite £210. Set lunch from £17.50, dinner from £34. Winter breaks.
Service/tipping: "Service not charged and tips not expected."

DUNOON Strathclyde — Map 5

Enmore — *Tel* Dunoon (0369) 2230
Marine Parade, Kirn — *Fax* (0369) 2148
Dunoon, Argyllshire PA23 8HH

"Fit for royalty. My favourite hotel for relaxing, comfort and value for money," writes a reader after a return visit to this small, far from expensive but pampering hotel in a Victorian villa, owned by David and Angela Wilson. Dunoon, a popular seaside resort a century ago, makes a convenient base for exploring the isles of Arran and Bute and the Mull of Kintyre. The *Enmore* overlooks the Clyde estuary a mile out of town. The bedrooms are filled with creature comforts: well-chosen books, electric dressing gowns; many have views of the sea, garden, ...e distance. The Wilsons are keen on beds – there are ...nd a water-bed, and two bathrooms have a jacuzzi. ... popular and include flowers, champagne, chocolates ...ed. But the hotel also gets high marks for its restaurant: "Each meal was a joy – fresh vegetables, fresh local salmon, shellfish, venison." "Good, nicely balanced starters and main courses and interesting soups." "A different dinner menu on each of the thirteen nights." "Scrupulously clean and well appointed, relaxed and cheerful service, varied and flavoursome food, reasonable cost. What a joy it was to come away feeling proud to be British and not ashamed of what we offer." The staff are unruffled by children. (*JC Ford, JH Whitehead; also Dr R and Mrs A Littlewood, A Taylor, and others*)

Open All year.
Rooms 1 suite, 8 double, 2 single – all with bath and/or shower, telephone, radio, TV, baby-listening; 1 with water-bed, 2 with whirlpool bath; tea-making facilities on request. 2 on ground floor.
Facilities 2 lounges, games room, bar, dining room, shop; 2 squash courts. 1-acre grounds with private shingle beach across road; safe but cold bathing, boating. Golf, swimming pool, tennis, pony trekking nearby.
Location On Marine Parade between 2 ferries, 1 m N of Dunoon.
Restrictions Not suitable for ♿. No smoking, no dogs in dining room.
Credit cards Access, Diners, Visa accepted.
Terms [1991 rates] B&B: single £35–£38.50, double £75, suite £110; dinner, B&B: single £57.50, double £113, suite £146. Bar lunches. Set dinner £19; full alc from £13.50. Squash coaching weekends; special interest breaks. Reduced rates and special meals for children.
Service/tipping: "If tips are given, they are fairly shared out among staff."

DUNVEGAN Skye, Highland — Map 5

Harlosh House — *Tel* Dunvegan (047 022) 367
By Dunvegan, Isle of Skye
IV55 8ZG

On shores of Loch Caroy, part of Loch Bracadale, and close to Dunvegan Castle, "small and cosy" croft-style house, recommended for magnificent views, homely atmosphere and the cooking of owner Peter Elford, who makes his own bread, pasta, "the best haggis ever", also ice-cream and sorbets. Restaurant open evenings only; seafood a speciality. Wide range of malt whiskies. A perfect spot for walking or observing wildlife, with fishing, sailing, pony trekking and shooting close by. Open Easter–mid-Oct. 6 double rooms, 5 with bath/shower. Not suitable for ♿. No smoking in restaurant. No dogs. Access, Visa accepted. Dinner, B&B £55. New nomination. More reports please.

EDINBURGH Lothian — Map 5

28 Northumberland Street BUDGET — *Tel* Edinburgh (031) 557 8036
Edinburgh EH3 6LS

Recently opened in Grade A listed Georgian house, furnished with antiques, in heart of city close to Princes Street (guests get own key). Recommended for friendly welcome from "charming" owner, barrister Mrs Eirlys Smith. Well-appointed, attractively decorated bedrooms and bathrooms. Scottish breakfast served in elegant dining room. 3 bedrooms, all with bath/shower. Not suitable for ♿. No smoking in public rooms. No dogs. 1991 rates: B&B £22.50–£25. Dinner available by arrangement; plenty of restaurants close by. New nomination. More reports please.

Sibbet House
26 Northumberland Street
Edinburgh EH3 6LS

Tel (031) 556 1078
Fax (031) 557 9445

Elegant Georgian stone-built family home in New Town, 5 mins' walk from city centre, owned by Jim and Aurora Sibbet. He is a former antique dealer, so the house is sympathetically furnished with antiques, as well as 20th-century conveniences: central heating, electric blankets, colour TV, tea- and coffee-making facilities, hair-driers. Recommended for spotlessly clean rooms, copious (communal) breakfast, and friendly, but not overpowering, hosts. Bagpipe-loving owner will play on request. Many restaurants, pubs nearby. Open Feb–Nov. 3 double rooms, all with bath/shower. B&B: single £40, double £46. Recent nomination, now enthusiastically endorsed. More reports please.

ELGIN Grampian — Map 5

The Mansion House
The Haugh, Elgin
Moray IV30 1AW

Tel Elgin (0343) 548811
Fax (0343) 547916

An imposing 19th-century Scots baronial mansion, complete with castellated tower and stair turret, standing in five acres of grounds with many fine trees, overlooking the river Lossie, a quarter of a mile from the town centre. It is owned and run by Fernando Oliveira, who comes from Portugal, and his Scottish wife. Our inspector recently gave the hotel a general seal of approval: she noted the warm reception, her comfortable room ("a symphony of blue and white"), the dining room softened by pretty pink tablecloths and tulip-shaped wine glasses, and the fairly priced set-menu dinner. The wine list, with nearly 100 wines, included many bottles under £10, and 20 half-bottles. A reader cites the "varied and delicious table d'hôte menus, beautifully presented". Another found the atmosphere "relaxed and friendly" throughout his stay, and "the breakfast delicious: porridge and cream, Arbroath smokies and fresh rolls". The hotel is popular with visitors on business and "discerning fishing and shooting parties". (*Stephen J Wheeler, R Plumb, and others*) Some rooms may be subject to noise from the adjoining country club.

Open All year.
Rooms 19 double, 4 single – all with bath, shower, telephone, radio, TV, tea-making facilities, baby-listening.
Facilities Residents' lounge, bar, bistro, dining room; functions room. Heated indoor pool, sauna, jacuzzi, Turkish bath. Gymnasium. 5-acre grounds with children's play area. River with fishing nearby.
Location From A96 turn off Elgin High St into Alexandra Rd; take turning into Haugh Rd, then first turning on left. Parking.
Restrictions Not suitable for ♿. Smoking discouraged in restaurant. No dogs.
Credit cards All major cards accepted.
Terms B&B: single £60–£65, double £90–£100; dinner, B&B: single £70–£75, double £100–£130. Set lunch £10, dinner £20; full alc £25. Reduced rates for

children; special meals. 2- and 3-night weekend breaks.
Service/tipping: "Service included. Tipping not expected."

ERISKA Strathclyde **Map 5**

Isle of Eriska
Eriska, Ledaig, by Oban
Argyllshire PA37 1SD

Tel Ledaig (063 172) 371
Fax (063 172) 531

"Perhaps its outstanding feature is its magnificent isolation," writes an enthusiastic American visitor about this imposing Victorian mansion on a tiny private island off the west coast, linked by a bridge to the mainland. There are magnificent views down the Lynn of Lorne to Mull, and the island is rich in flora and fauna. "A charming place, with attentive staff and owners and the willingness to please that is the hallmark of a well-run establishment. Every day there was a fresh vase of wild flowers on the dressing table, and a plate of fruit on the dresser." The hotel is owned by Robin Buchanan-Smith, a minister of the Church of Scotland, and his wife Sheena, and run on country-house lines. For many years it has had a devoted following of those who love its old-fashioned, fairly formal (jacket and tie at dinner) style of hospitality. "They are totally committed to the guest." "One of the more endearing features is we never signed a chit – the staff kept track of the drinks we ordered and the laundry we had done, so we felt like guests in a private home." Food is good, and plentiful. "My husband, a vegetarian, had his own menu printed daily and the fear that he would fare less well than the rest of us turned out to be groundless." (*Elizabeth Lutz, Jamie Berry; also MGB Scott, CJ Uncles*) Serve-yourself breakfasts "under silver covers" continue to be an Achilles heel.

Open Mar–Oct.
Rooms 1 suite, 15 double – all with bath, shower, telephone, radio, TV, tea-making facilities, baby-listening. 2 on ground floor with access for ♿.
Facilities Ramp. 2 halls, drawing room, library, dining room. 320-acre grounds with tennis, croquet, putting green, water sports, ponies. Loch 5 mins.
Location 12 m N of Oban. 4 m W of A828.
Restrictions No children under 10 in dining room at night (high tea at 6 pm). No dogs in public rooms.
Credit cards Access, Visa.
Terms [1991 rates] B&B: single £73–£110, double £125–£140. Set dinner £33. Off-season rates. Children sharing parents' room charged only for meals.
Service/tipping: "No service charge. No tipping."

FORSS Highland **Map 5**

Forss House
Forss, by Thurso
Caithness KW14 7XY

Tel Forss (084 786) 201

Small hotel in under-represented corner of Scotland, converted from listed Victorian home, in attractive 20-acre wooded setting with salmon stream. Abundant wildlife including herons, owls and often otters. Recommended for tasteful furnishings, comfortable beds, undisturbed quiet. Good dinner and wine list, outstanding breakfast ("crispy bacon with soft and creamy scrambled eggs"). 7 double rooms, all with private bath/shower (2 in sportsman's lodge overlooking river). Access, Amex, Visa accepted. 1991 rates: B&B £... Reduced rates and special meals for children. Recent nomination. More re... please.

FORT WILLIAM Highland — Map 5

The Factor's House
Torlundy, Fort William
Inverness-shire PH33 6SN

Tel Fort William (0397) 705767
Fax (0397) 702953

Built in the early part of the century for the factor (estate manager) of what is now *Inverlochy Castle* (see below), the *Factor's House* is owned and run by the convivial Peter Hobbs, son of *Inverlochy*'s owner, Grete Hobbs, as an entirely independent enterprise and at half the prices of the *Castle*. It stands on the lower slope of Ben Nevis in the heart of the West Highlands. The house is modern and has a fresh, light, airy feeling. Bedrooms are furnished in white-painted bamboo with cool Designers Guild wallpaper, but are on the small side and somewhat austere; some have poor insulation ("I was woken up by snores from the room next door!"). The lounges, too, are small which makes private conversation difficult. However, the simplicity of the decor has not diminished readers' praise for the hotel. "Full marks; quite the most friendly hotel I have stayed at. Every member of staff seemed genuinely interested in the guests." The food has also been a high spot but the hotel has a new chef this year. Most, but not all reports of the new regime are encouraging: "Menus have changed in content, style remains much as before – i.e. good quality and well cooked but with a fairly limited choice. The wine list has been heavily pruned." There is a new manager, too; Ranald Duff has departed for new pastures. More reports on these changes welcome. (*Paula Leigh, April Young, Iain Baillie, VF Ferguson, M and M Firth*)

Open Mid-Mar–mid-Nov. Restaurant closed Sun and Mon.
Rooms 7 double – all with bath and/or shower, telephone, TV.
Facilities 2 lounges, dining room. Small garden but guests have access to *Inverlochy*'s 500-acre grounds and tennis court. Sailing, fishing, pony trekking, golf, clay-pigeon shooting available.
Location 3 m NE of Fort William on A82, just after turning to *Inverlochy Castle*.
Restrictions Not suitable for ♿. No children under 6 in dining room. No dogs.
Credit cards Access, Visa accepted.
Terms B&B: single £58.75–£65, double £65–£85. Set dinner £20. Special meals for children on request.
Service/tipping: "We do not expect tips but it's one sure way of knowing if people have enjoyed themselves!"

Inverlochy Castle
Torlundy, Fort William
Inverness-shire PH33 6SN

Tel Fort William (0397) 702177
Fax (0397) 702953

César award in 1984: For incomparable grandeur

"Superb and faultless", "exquisite and stylish" are recent accolades for this spectacular Scottish baronial house in 500 acres of grounds, rich in rhododendrons, which won its César in our first year of those awards. Its fame and impressive advance booking owe much to its châtelaine, Grete Hobbs, who twenty-three years ago turned her husband's family home ountry house hotel. Earlier praise: "It is in a class of its for its 'incomparable grandeur' as for its exceedingly d the remarkable friendliness of those who run it. The d the drawing room are warm with blazing fires and sofas and armchairs." "Flowers everywhere. Spacious, decorated bedroom." "Room service and service at dinner were smooth, swift and courteous. The key to the hotel's success is its manager, Michael Leonard; he has been there many years yet his perfectionist eye and his enthusiasm are as keen as ever." "After dinner our first night, we had a game of chess. The next night, we left the dining room and were delighted to find coffee, delicious *petits fours* and the chess set ready and waiting for us by the fire." (*Peter Hutchinson, and others*)

Note: In 1991 we warned that the hotel was for sale. Happily, it has now been withdrawn from the market.

Open 1 Mar–mid-Nov.
Rooms 1 suite, 14 double, 1 single – all with bath, shower, telephone, radio, TV, baby-listening; 24-hour room service.
Facilities Great hall, drawing room, 2 dining rooms, billiard room; facilities for small conferences out of season. 500-acre grounds with gardens, tennis; trout fishing, golf, pony trekking nearby. Chauffeur-driven limousines for hire.
Location Take turning to NW off A82 3 m N of Fort William just past golf club. Guests met by arrangement at station or airports.
Restrictions Not suitable for ♿. No smoking in dining room. Children under 12 accepted only if sharing parents' room. No dogs in hotel (kennels available).
Credit cards Access, Visa.
Terms B&B: single £121, double £165–£180, suite £220–£275. Set lunch £25–£30, dinner £39–£43. Reduced rates and special meals for children.
Service/tipping: "No service charge; tipping is not expected."

GLASGOW Strathclyde — Map 5

One Devonshire Gardens
1 Devonshire Gardens
G12 0UX

Tel Glasgow (041) 339 2001
and 334 9494
Fax (041) 337 1663

A trendy, opulent hotel, "furnished with magisterial confidence", in the fashionable West End suburb a short distance from the city centre. "You ring the bell each time to enter what looks like a very elegant private house." "We had the most amazing room, huge and in a decadent/Victorian style which managed to remain tasteful and unintimidating. Fresh fruit and magazines, numerous pillows on the vast four-poster, a bath in which a six-foot rugby player could lie flat out, and many big towels, all combined to make an extremely comfortable, nay, sensuous, place to stay." Another reader called the hotel "sumptuous and stunning". The restaurant, oppressively grand to some ("black 'fleurs du mal' wallpaper"), achieves high scores: "First-rate and not overpriced considering its excellence." But several niggles again: no contact from owner or management; uneven housekeeping; and disappointing breakfasts. More reports, please.

Open All year.
Rooms 2 suites, 25 double – 24 with bath and shower, 3 with shower, all with telephone, radio, TV. 1 on ground floor.
Facilities 2 drawing rooms, study, clubroom/bar, restaurant. Boardroom and private dining room. Walled garden and patio.

Location 2 m from city centre at intersection of Great Western and Hyndland roads. Back rooms quietest.
Restriction No dogs in public rooms.
Credit cards All major cards accepted.
Terms [1991 rates] B&B: single £95–£110, double £125–£140; suite £165. Set lunch £18, set dinner £30. Special meals for children on request.
Service/tipping: "No charge for service. Tipping entirely up to guests. All tips divided among staff."

GLEN CANNICH Highland — Map 5

Cozac Lodge
Glen Cannich by Beauly
Inverness-shire IV4 7LX
Tel Cannich (045 65) 263

Returned to Guide last year under new owners Brian and Enid Butler, attractive 1912 hunting lodge in scenic, remote setting overlooking loch SW of Inverness. Fishing, pony trekking, stalking available. Mahogany-panelled hall, large dining room, sitting room with comfortable chairs, log fires. Recommended for warm hospitality, relaxed atmosphere, "spacious bedroom and bathroom with boiling hot water", "delicious" 5-course fixed-menu dinner, and value for money. 7 rooms, all with bath/shower. No smoking in restaurant. Access, Amex, Visa accepted. Dinner, B&B £42–£59. Recent nomination, but we'd like more reports please.

GLENCRIPESDALE Highland — Map 5

Glencripesdale House
Glencripesdale, Loch Sunart
Acharacle, Argyllshire PH36 4JH
Tel Salen (096 785) 263

César award in 1989: Non-pareil *hotel for those who want to get even further away from it all*

Favourable reports continue for Bill and Susan Hemmings' civilised guest house, one of the most remote hostelries in Britain. It stands on the south side of Loch Sunart and at the end of an eight-mile rough forestry track that takes an hour to drive. Guests arriving by train will be met by Bill Hemmings at Fort William, the railhead. Deer graze on the front lawn. There's excellent beachcombing: "Great varieties of shells from across the Atlantic and amazing examples of stones positively riddled with quartz and other bright metals, dazzling in the sunshine." *Glencripesdale* is a modernised 18th-century farmhouse; bedrooms are caringly furnished and comfortable. The book-lined sitting room is equally welcoming. In such a remote setting, "you *have* to get on with your fellow guests". During the day, however, readers report walking for hours without encountering another soul. "A trip in the boat with Dr Hemmings, seeing seals, otters, etc, is a must, and a delight." "Mrs Hemmings's meals are delicious, imaginative, and never repetitive – a miracle here." "Especially memorable were the coddled eggs and fresh baked bread at breakfast." Packed lunches, which change daily, are also highly commended. Two warnings about the terrain: "Much of the walking from the house involves an initial hike through dense woods, and even when you get out into the open, the going can be *exceedingly* rough if there has been much rain." "Low ground clearance may make the track unsuitable for certain cars." (*Alan Greenwood, JMT Ford, AG Saunders, G Frew, J Sandeman-Allen, S Beresford, and others*)

Important note: Acharacle is only a postal address; it is a two-hour drive from the house. If you arrive by car, the Hemmings appreciate an offer to pick up supplies on the way.

Open 1 Mar–31 Oct. Christmas and New Year.
Rooms 4 double – 2 with bath, 2 with shower.
Facilities Library/lounge, dining room, children's playroom. 2-acre grounds; nature reserve ¼ m; rock and shingle beaches, fishing nearby; windsurfer and inflatable boat with outboard motor for hire.
Location *Do not* go to Acharacle. Hotel is on S side of Loch Sunart. Take A861 towards Strontian; fork left on A884. *Glencripesdale* is through Laudale estate. (Hotel will send detailed directions.)
Restrictions Not suitable for ♿. No smoking in dining room. Dogs by arrangement, but not indoors.
Credit cards None accepted.
Terms Dinner, B&B (including packed lunch) £63. Bar lunch £3.50–£6, set dinner £16.50. Reduced rates for children; special meals on request.
Service/tipping: "Service included. Any gratuities left go to the Cancer Research Campaign which has now received £3,000 since we opened in 1984."

GLENLIVET Grampian — Map 5

Minmore House BUDGET
Glenlivet
Banffshire AB3 9DB

Tel Glenlivet (080 73) 378
Fax (080 73) 472

This recently refurbished Victorian country house, owned and run by Belinda Luxmoore, is in the heart of whisky country and was formerly the home of George Smith, founder of Glenlivet, whose distillery is just next door. It stands in four acres of secluded garden above the river Livet on which it has fishing rights, and fishing is also available on the Avon and Spey. The area, beautiful and untouristy, has lots of good walks, and also castles and gardens and almost a score of golf courses. Reports this year continue to praise the well-appointed accommodation and Mrs Luxmoore's "caring concern for the well-being of her guests". "It would be difficult to find better value for money. Mrs Luxmoore's cooking was superb. Three months later, her roast duck is still a vivid memory." "And," says a grateful fisherwoman, "you know they will cheerfully dry your sodden clothes and offer you a warming cup of tea." (*Hon. Mrs Monica Parish, JFL Bowes, Patricia Trew, and others*) Afternoon tea with cakes in the drawing room is included in the rates, as well as a miniature whisky, fresh fruit, flowers and home-made shortbread in the bedroom.

Open 1 May–31 Oct. Dining room closed for lunch.
Rooms 1 suite, 7 double, 2 single – all with bath, radio, tea-making facilities, baby-listening.
Facilities Hall, drawing room, bar, dining room. 4-acre grounds with terraced garden, croquet, tennis, unheated swimming pool. Fishing on rivers Livet, Avon and Spey by arrangement.
Location From Grantown-on-Spey take A95 towards Ballindalloch; turn right on to B9008 at *Delnashaugh Inn*. Follow signs to Glenlivet.
Restrictions Only restaurant suitable for ♿. No smoking in dining room. No dogs in public rooms.
Credit cards Access, Visa.

Terms [1991 rates] B&B £28; dinner, B&B £40–£42. Set dinner £16. Special rates for retired service men and women. Weekly rates. 1-night bookings occasionally refused. Reduced rates for children; special meals.
Service/tipping: "Service is included and this is explained if a tip is offered. If, however, a guest insists, the tip is evenly distributed among staff."

HARRAY LOCH Orkney — Map 5

Merkister BUDGET
Harray Loch, Dounby
Orkney KW17 2LF

Tel Harray (085 677) 366
Fax (085 677) 515

In own grounds on edge of Loch Harray, considered by many the best trout-fishing loch in Orkney, modest hotel owned and run by keen fisherman Angus MacDonald and his family. Good reports of service and food. Elma MacDonald will cook your catch for breakfast. 100 yds to loch; boats, own bird hide; horse riding. Open Apr–Oct. 18 rooms – 12 with bath/shower. Not suitable for ♿. Access, Amex accepted. 1991 rates: B&B £28–£36; dinner, B&B £40–£45. Recent nomination. More reports please.

INVERNESS Highland — Map 5

Dunain Park
Inverness
Inverness-shire IV3 6JN

Tel Inverness (0463) 230512
Fax (0463) 224532

"This most charming and elegant country house epitomises the Scottish welcome we have come to love; and without the stuffiness one sometimes experiences in an hotel of this quality." Readers continue to give high praise to this Italianate early 19th-century country house near Inverness, owned by Ann and Edward Nicoll. Bedrooms are individually decorated "in the most delightful fashion". There are books everywhere, also stereo and tapes. The lounges have log fires and there are pleasing views from the windows; the hotel sits in six acres of gardens and woodlands overlooking the Caledonian Canal. "There was complete peace and no traffic noise." "Our room was large and airy, with superb views. Every comfort was provided, from bath gels and flannels to recent issues of Scottish magazines, and the staff were all friendly and helpful." "There were fresh flowers everywhere and everything was spotless." Reports on Ann Nicoll's cooking have mostly been equally enthusiastic: "Sends even middle-aged stomachs happily to sleep." This year, they are offering only an à la carte menu. There is a heated indoor pool and sauna where guests can work off the splendid food (though it is not large enough to satisfy really athletic swimmers). We appreciate a note on *Dunain Park*'s menus: "Guests are asked not to smoke in the dining room. If you wish to withdraw to a lounge, please let us know and we will be happy to delay your next course." (*Jennifer Nelson, Louise Lamb, Anna Kaposi and Gary Bullock, JD Spencely, and many others*)

Open All year. Restricted meal service during owners' holidays – probably 2 weeks Feb, 2 weeks Nov.
Rooms 8 suites, 6 double – all with bath (8 also have shower), telephone, radio, TV; tea-making facilities by arrangement. 2 suites, both with kitchenette, in converted coach house, 100 yds from hotel. Some suites at ground level.

Facilities 2 lounges, dining room. Indoor heated swimming pool, sauna. 6-acre grounds with garden, badminton, croquet. Fishing, shooting, golf, tennis nearby.
Location 2½ m S of centre of Inverness, off A82 to Fort William. Turn left shortly after Craig Dunain hospital which is on right.
Restrictions No smoking in dining room. "Children must be well behaved." No dogs in public rooms, nor in certain bedrooms.
Credit cards All major cards accepted.
Terms [1991 rates] B&B £46.50–£65. Alc lunch £15, dinner £22.50. Reduced rates 3- and 7-day stays. Reduced rates for children sharing with two adults; special meals on request.
Service/tipping: "Gratuities at guests' discretion, distributed to all staff."

IONA Strathclyde — Map 5

Argyll Hotel BUDGET — *Tel* Iona (068 17) 334
Isle of Iona
Argyllshire PA76 6SJ

"The rooms are plain, even spartan, but that is appropriate for the magical island, and the house is full of delightful books, among which I found a Ph.D. thesis on the geology of the island by none other than our hostess." On the tiny pilgrim island of Iona (three and a half miles long and one and a half wide), reached by a five-minute ferry journey from the Isle of Mull, Mrs Fiona Menzies's hotel stands in the village street facing the sea; it is just a few minutes' walk from the ferry landing. The bedrooms are smallish, beds are said to creak, and the "private facilities a wee cubbyhole", but all agree about "the magic of the island, the hotel's wonderful location, and the interesting people one meets there". An earlier visitor described "the drawbridge-up pleasure of seeing the last ferry leave in the evening bearing the day's visitors away", and the sound of the sea, lulling her to sleep at night. There are two sitting rooms with open fires (and no TV), full of local history and bird books, and a built-on sun lounge. "The dining room is lovely with a fantastic view, and staff are helpful", but recent reports on the food have been uneven, though walkers appreciate setting out with Mrs Menzies's substantial packed lunch. (*Dr DH Clark, Mrs Dowell, and others*)

Open Easter–mid-Oct.
Rooms 9 double, 10 single – 2 with bath and shower, 8 with bath, all with tea-making facilities; baby-listening on request.
Facilities 2 lounges, sun lounge, dining room. Sea and loch fishing.
Location In village, near jetty. Iona reached by car or bus across Mull to Fionnphort, then passenger ferry. No cars on Iona. Carparks at Oban and Fionnphort.
Restrictions Not suitable for ♿. No smoking in dining room and 1 lounge. No dogs in dining room.
Credit cards Access, Visa.
Terms B&B £22–£31; dinner, B&B £36–£45. Set dinner £14; snacks and light lunches from £3. 1-night bookings occasionally refused weekends. Reduced rates and special meals for children.
Service/tipping: "No service charge. Tips not expected; any given are divided equally among all employees."

Please don't be shy of writing again about old favourites. Too many people feel that if they have written once, years ago, there is no need to report on a revisit.

KENMORE Tayside — Map 5

Kenmore Hotel
The Square, Kenmore
Perthshire PH15 2NU

Tel Kenmore (088 73) 205
Fax (088 73) 262

In centre of one of Scotland's prettiest villages, overlooking river Tay, Scotland's oldest inn, built 1572, in two buildings on opposite sides of the square. Robert Burns stopped over in 1758. Recommended for friendly, helpful staff, good restaurant, comfortable lounge/bar with blazing log fire, relaxed atmosphere. Excellent base for walks by river or in surrounding mountains. Own golf course; river and loch fishing for salmon and trout, boats available. 38 rooms – all with bath/shower. No smoking in restaurant. Dogs in lodge only. B&B £24.50–£48. Set dinner £18.25. Endorsed this year but we'd welcome more reports.

KENTALLEN Highland — Map 5

Holly Tree
Kentallen, by Appin
Argyllshire PA38 4BY

Tel Duror (063 174) 292
Fax (063 174) 345

Kentallen's former railway station, enlarged and extensively renovated, right on the shore of Loch Linnhe, is now a hotel owned and run by Alasdair and Jane Robertson. "It still retains Edwardian features – the Glasgow Art Nouveau ticket office is intact; the Railway Bar was formerly the station's tearoom. But the bedrooms are distinctly of the present, spacious and delightfully furnished in a combination of traditional (lots of pine) and modish (peach chintz etc), with expensive, specially designed carpets throughout." There are extensive views over the loch; the hotel has a mile of private waterside grounds. "Excellent breakfasts include porridge with Drambuie and cream." An earlier report: "You will not get the grandeur or the superior deference of *Claridge's*, but you will get charming, efficient service, and delightful food." Again, this year, readers appreciate the relaxed attitude towards children: "Jane Robertson fed our baby, while we had breakfast, and Alasdair was happy to heat his meals or prepare special food." "The Robertsons' young daughter served part of our breakfast, which gave the place an air of informality we liked very much." "They took our children out in their fishing boat in the morning, not charging for their accommodation or meals despite our protests." (*Mrs Maureen Simpson, Mr and Mrs G Turner, N Wood, and others*) One reader found the housekeeping and food more "erratic" than on previous visits.

Open All year.
Rooms 11 double – all with bath (10 also have shower), telephone, TV, tea-making facilities, baby-listening. 2 on ground floor.
Facilities Residents' lounge, lounge bar, restaurant. 5-acre grounds with slipway, boats for residents' use, fishing, safe bathing in loch. Riding, windsurfing, skiing nearby.
Location On A828, 3 m S of Ballachulish Bridge.
Restriction No smoking in dining room. Dogs by arrangement, not in public rooms.
Credit cards Access, Amex, Visa.
Terms Dinner, B&B: single £65, double £122. Set dinner £26. Autumn/winter breaks; Christmas and New Year packages. Reduced rates for children; special meals.
Service/tipping: "No service charge. Tipping left to each customer's discretion."

KILDRUMMY Grampian — Map 5

Kildrummy Castle
Kildrummy, by Alford
Aberdeenshire AB3 8RA

Tel Kildrummy (097 55) 71288
Fax (097 55) 71345

One of those great Scottish baronial houses built around the turn of the century, *Kildrummy Castle* has been a hotel for the past twenty-six years. It is in the heart of the Donside, about an hour's drive from Aberdeen in fifteen acres of fine gardens overlooking the ruins of a 13th-century castle. There have been many appreciative correspondents. The appeal for anglers is its 3½-mile private stretch of the Don for trout and salmon fishing. Further attraction for some is the library, "a fascinating fabric-covered room full of character, with a crackling log fire". Lunch and four-course dinner menus offer more than a dozen choices including hearty Scottish soups, North Sea prawns, venison and pheasant, as well as lighter dishes – "nothing too extravagant, but good-sized portions and well cooked". Readers praise the unobtrusive, "courteous and friendly" service, and the "well-equipped bedrooms (hair-drier, electric blankets, TV, radio) *and* early morning tea". (*April Young, and others*)

Open All year, except Jan.
Rooms 15 double, 1 single – all with bath and/or shower, telephone, radio, TV, tea-making facilities.
Facilities Drawing room, library, cocktail lounge, dining room, billiard room. 15-acre garden; 3½ m private fishing on river Don. Golf nearby.
Location NE of Ballater on A97 Ballater–Huntly road.
Restrictions Not suitable for ♿. No smoking in dining room. No dogs in public rooms.
Credit cards Access, Amex, Visa.
Terms B&B £47–£55; dinner, B&B £53–£77. Set lunch £13, dinner £22.50; full alc £30. Children free if sharing with 2 adults; special meals.
Service/tipping: "Tipping at guests' discretion. All staff share."

KILFINAN Strathclyde — Map 5

Kilfinan Hotel
Kilfinan, Nr Tighnabruaich
Argyllshire PA21 2EP

Tel Kilfinan (070 082) 201
Fax (070 082) 205

This old coaching inn in the tiny clachan of Kilfinan has been providing food and shelter for travellers for over a hundred years. It is run by kilted Tony Wignell and his wife Gina and is popular as a base for hunting, shooting and fishing, but has also been recommended as "a most restful place to spend a few days, and ideal for bird-watchers, painters, photographers and walkers". "A truly remote setting, with only a handful of houses, including this pub – and food worthy of a *Michelin* star." "The welcome was as warm as the log fire, and the service was excellent." "Our bedroom was large and airy with fine views of the tombstones in the churchyard next door." The bathrooms are well stocked with extras. "Never saw any domestic staff or heard a vacuum cleaner but clearly they were about as our room was kept spotless." "Service in the dining room is first-class and, after a superb dinner, we made use of the Alka Seltzer provided in our bathroom." (*D Carswell, Rosanne Porter, Gillian Cave, Letitia Sinker, Prof. IB Houston, PH Williams, and others*)

Open All year.
Rooms 11 double – 10 with bath, 1 with shower, all with telephone, radio, TV, baby-listening.
Facilities Public bar, bar lounge, 2 dining rooms; functions room. 1-acre grounds. Private sandy beach on Loch Fyne 1 m. Fishing on Kilfinan Burn; sea angling, golf, deer stalking, clay-pigeon shooting nearby.
Location In tiny village, next to church. On B8000 9 m NW of Tighnabruaich.
Restriction Not suitable for ♿.
Credit cards Access, Amex, Visa.
Terms (Service not included) B&B: single £45, double £69; dinner, B&B: single £67, double £113. Set lunch £12. Full alc dinner £27.50. Reduced rates for children sharing parents' room; special meals.

KILLIECRANKIE Tayside — Map 5

Killiecrankie Hotel
Pass of Killiecrankie
By Pitlochry
Perthshire PH16 5LG

Tel Pitlochry (0796) 3220
from early 1992 (0796) 473220
Fax (0796) 2451
from early 1992 (0796) 472451

At the northern entrance to the pass of Killiecrankie, three miles from Pitlochry, a pleasant small hotel in a beautiful wooded setting, overlooking the river Garry. The bedrooms are individually decorated using furniture in natural pine made by local craftsmen. It re-entered the Guide last year, with many favourable reports, under the new ownership of Colin and Carole Anderson, and these have been endorsed this year. "The Andersons are a wonderful couple who immediately make you feel at home." "Staff and owners friendly and helpful; everywhere spotlessly clean", "very comfortable beds", "good house wine", "food better than before, astoundingly imaginative, beautifully cooked". In addition to the formal menu in the main restaurant they now offer a wide choice of bar snacks. There are four acres of grounds, with putting and croquet; golf, fishing and hill walking are nearby. (*David Thibodeau, AJD Simmons; also Mrs SE Fry, Mrs MH Box, and others*) Since last year, all rooms have had *en suite* facilities, telephone, TV and a new heating system. One reader, while praising the breakfasts, felt dinner menu was decidedly over-ambitious.

Open 1 Mar–3 Jan.
Rooms 9 double, 2 single – all with bath and/or shower, telephone, radio, TV, tea-making facilities, baby-listening. 4 on ground floor.
Facilities Lounge, cocktail bar, dining room. 4-acre grounds with putting, croquet. Killiecrankie RSPB reserve just across river.
Location 3 m N of Pitlochry, just off A9, signposted Killiecrankie.
Restrictions No smoking, children under 5, or dogs in dining room.
Credit cards Access, Amex, Visa accepted.
Terms B&B £34.75–£43.85; dinner, B&B £57.50–£63.95. Reduced rates and special meals for children. 1-night bookings sometimes refused. Spring, autumn breaks.
Service/tipping: "We do not make a service charge; however, any gratuities that are offered are distributed to all staff."

> "Set meals" refers to fixed-price meals, which may have ample, limited or no choice on the menu. "Full alc" is the hotel's own estimated price per person of a three-course meal taken à la carte, with a half-bottle of house wine. "Alc meals" are as full alc but do not include the cost of wine.

KILMORE Strathclyde — Map 5

Glenfeochan House — *Tel* Kilmore (063 177) 273
Kilmore, by Oban
Argyllshire PA34 4QR

"Mrs Baber really is a genius and her smoked salmon alone is worth the journey. Breakfasts were much the best we had in Scotland, with eggs at least five minutes old." This latest report is typical of the compliments offered to this sophisticated guest house in a turreted Victorian building, former baronial home of the Clan Campbell. It stands at the head of Loch Feochan in a 350-acre estate which includes a six-acre garden – one of the Great Gardens of the Scottish Highlands – and is run by Patricia Baber, a former Cordon Bleu teacher, her husband, David, and her son, James Petley. There are only three bedrooms; meals (taken communally) are for residents only – guests are consulted about the menu in the morning, and much of the food is produced by the estate. Some other tributes: "The soft warm lighting of the entrance hall and the magnificent staircase with its beautifully pargeted canopy tell you at once that you've made the right choice. A most excellent dinner in the elegant dining room, cooked by our hostess, followed by coffee in an equally elegant drawing room. The setting is splendid: trees, loch and mountain changing all the time as sun and cloud chase over the landscape. At the right time of year you will be stunned by the colour – great carpets of daffodils and snowdrops so thick you cannot see the grass, and mountainous masses of rhododendrons, many species not to be seen elsewhere in Britain." "An exquisite private home." "Fresh flowers and fruit every day in the bedroom." "We were treated as though our every whim was important." (*David G Felce, Diana Birchall, John and Shirley Kitchen, and others*)

Open 1 Mar–31 Oct.
Rooms 3 double – all with bath, radio, TV, tea-making facilities. 3-bedroom cottage for letting.
Facilities Drawing room, dining room, TV room. 350-acre estate with 6-acre garden and 1½-acre walled garden, open to public; croquet, boules. Salmon and sea-trout fishing free to guests, clay-pigeon shooting, hill walking, loch bathing.
Location 5 m S of Oban on A816 at head of Loch Feochan.
Restrictions Not suitable for ♿. No smoking in dining room or in bedrooms. No children under 10. Dogs by arrangement only; not in bedrooms or public rooms.
Credit cards None accepted.
Terms B&B double £112. Packed lunch £5, set dinner £27. 4-day breaks, and discount for RHS members in low season.
Service/tipping: "Our service is given freely. If any tips are received, the money is shared among all the staff."

KINBUCK Central — Map 5

Cromlix House — *Tel* Dunblane (0786) 822125
Kinbuck, Dunblane — *Fax* (0786) 825450
Perthshire FK15 9JT

The Hon Ronald Eden, whose family have owned the 5,000 acres of *Cromlix* for four centuries, turned his massive Victorian house into a luxury hotel in 1980. There is one fishing loch within strolling distance – and others nearby – plus a grouse moor and lovely wooded grounds where deer, sheep, pheasants, wild duck and rabbits abound. The house itself is grand in a formal way: there is a Victorian conservatory, a good library and a chapel; the large entrance hall is panelled, the morning room has comfortable chintz chairs and a giant log basket beside the elegant fireplace, and the dining room is candle-lit at night, with stiffly starched white tablecloths. "This hotel is absolutely superb. A beautiful house, expert hotelkeeping and exquisite food. Service is immaculate." "Good welcome, grand house but friendly; excellent food and service. Large suites, with huge bedroom, lounge and bathroom. The staff are well drilled and human. An ideal combination of luxury and friendly service." Prices are "what one would expect to pay for such a high standard". (*Stephen J Wheeler, S Beresford, Heather Sharland, Anna Kaposi and Gary Bullock, WH Davidson*) Ian Corkhill replaced Simon Burns as chef in December 1990. Reports on the restaurant would be welcome.

Open All year except Christmas.
Rooms 8 suites, 6 double – all with bath, shower, telephone, radio, TV.
Facilities Sitting room, library, 2 dining rooms, conservatory. 5,000-acre grounds with croquet, clay-pigeon shooting, trout fishing, tennis, riding and shooting (advance booking advisable).
Location ¼ m N of Kinbuck, 4 m S of Braco. Take A9 out of Dunblane; turn left on to B8033; go through Kinbuck village, take second left after a small bridge.
Restrictions Not suitable for ♿. No smoking in dining rooms. No dogs in public rooms.
Credit cards All major cards accepted.
Terms B&B: single £75–£115, double £100–£140, suite £125–£210. Dinner, B&B: single £107–£147, double £164–£204, suite £189–£274. Set lunch £22, dinner £32. Winter breaks. 4-day Christmas and New Year packages. Reduced rates for children sharing parents' room; special meals.
Service/tipping: "Service included. If guests wish to leave tips in addition it is left to their discretion."

KINGUSSIE Highland — Map 5

Columba House — *Tel* Kingussie (0540) 661402
Manse Road, Kingussie
Inverness-shire PH21 1JF

On outskirts of Kingussie, on knoll among pine trees, once manse of nearby St Columba church. Ian and Myra Shearer provide "home-like" atmosphere; antiques, fine carpets, welcoming fire in lounge; spacious, comfortable bedrooms. Food in pink and white dining room mainly traditional using "things that are as naturally grown as possible": home-produced vegetables and eggs, local meat, fish and game. Vegetarians well catered for, with "rather more interesting dishes than the usual". 2-acre grounds with pretty garden, putting and croquet. 7 bedrooms, all with bath/shower. No smoking in restaurant. Credit cards not accepted. Dinner, B&B £35–£44. New nomination. More reports please.

Note: The *Ospreys*, long a Guide favourite in Kingussie, has been sold.

****

Traveller's tale *The "soup of the day" was the same three nights running, and the proprietress was not particularly amused when I suggested that it was really the soup of the day before yesterday.*

****

KNIPOCH Strathclyde — Map 5

Knipoch Hotel
Knipoch, by Oban
Argyllshire PA34 4QT

Tel Kilninver (085 26) 251
Fax (085 26) 249

The original house was first mentioned in 16th-century records of feuds and rivalry between Scottish clans; it is now a fairly formal and pricy country house hotel, owned and run by the Craig family. Most readers continue to write in favour, particularly of the tranquil setting in beautiful surroundings overlooking Loch Feochan, an arm of the sea stretching four miles inland just south of Oban. Inside are welcoming log fires, attractive flower arrangements, lots of highly polished wood surfaces, Persian rugs on stripped-pine floors, deep leather armchairs. "We were welcomed by the owner in a hall with a real log fire, brought tea, and our sons fed promptly and efficiently. Our rooms were comfortable. Quality does not come cheap, but it was worth it." "The pièce de résistance was undoubtedly the marvellous food on the set menu; all the meals we had were excellent." "If one is eating grandly for six nights, there has to be a lightness of touch – and there is." "We left feeling refreshed and relaxed, if a little short of money." (*Paul Trevisan, Prof. DV Lindley, Mr and Mrs R Partridge, David Lea-Wilson*) But there have again been grumbles about some of the rooms: "Dreary, like a commercial hotel, and although overlooking the very beautiful loch, also took in the fairly busy main road."

Open Mid-Feb–mid-Nov. Lunch by arrangement only.
Rooms 18 double – all with bath, shower, telephone, radio, TV, baby-listening; tea-making facilities on request.
Facilities Reception hall, lounge, bar, 3 dining rooms. 3-acre grounds. On sea loch; fishing, sailing, golf, tennis, hill walking, pony trekking nearby.
Location 6 m S of Oban on A816.
Restrictions Not really suitable for ♿. No smoking in dining room. No young children in dining room. No dogs.
Credit cards All major cards accepted.
Terms [1991 rates] B&B £56; dinner, B&B £89. Set dinner £36. Reduced rates for 4 days or more. Children under 5 half price; special meals.
Service/tipping: "No service charge. If tips are offered they are accepted, since to refuse can offend. They are never *solicited."*

MOFFAT Dumfries and Galloway — Map 5

Beechwood
Harthope Place, Moffat
Dumfriesshire DG10 9RS

Tel Moffat (0683) 20210
Fax (0683) 20889

"A friendly and welcoming atmosphere pervades the whole house, and the bedrooms, with *en suite* bathrooms, have many generous extras. Carl Shaw, the chef under the previous owners, has happily decided to remain, and his cooking leaves nothing to be desired, in quality or presentation. Real orange juice for breakfast; three choices in each of five courses for dinner – and good value!" Another report calls the cooking "just about the best in our tour of Scotland". A warm endorsement for this grey-stone Victorian house, once a girls' school, standing in a twelve-acre beech wood just outside Moffat, which re-entered our pages last year with new owners Lynda and Jeffrey Rogers. Rooms are comfortable and quiet. Decor tends towards the floral – a little too frilly for some. Moffat is about three-quarters of an hour north of Carlisle, an hour or so from Glasgow and Edinburgh – a useful stopover going north or south or a centre from which to tour the region. (*Isobel D Dalling, Prof. James Joll, GB Townend, and others*)

Open Feb–Dec.
Rooms 7 double – all with bath and/or shower, telephone, radio, TV, tea-making facilities, baby-listening.
Facilities Lounge, cocktail bar and library, restaurant, conservatory. Small garden.
Location Proceed along High Street. Turn into Harthope Place between church and school.
Restrictions Only restaurant suitable for ♿. No smoking, no dogs in restaurant.
Credit cards Access, Amex, Visa.
Terms [1991 rates] B&B: single £44.70, double £63.66; dinner, B&B: single £56.45, double £93.80. Set lunch £12, dinner £17.50. Reduced rates for stays of 3 or more nights. Reduced rates and special meals for children.
Service/tipping: "At discretion of customer. Distributed among all staff."

MUIR OF ORD Highland — Map 5

The Dower House
Highfield, Muir of Ord
Ross-shire IV6 7XN
Tel Inverness (0463) 870090
Fax (0463) 870090

"Another little gem", this slightly Gothic one-storey series of linked 19th-century cottages was originally built for the dowager of the MacKenzie-Gillander family and is now a welcoming small country hotel owned by Robyn and Mena Aitchison. They formerly ran a restaurant, *Le Chardon*, in nearby Cromarty, but decided to expand so that their family could have more space. Our inspector's report: "The furnishings are a mixture of Victorian, pine and loose-covered comfortable chairs and sofas. We loved the decor – a riot of patterns, borders and bows done with huge flair and a vibrant colour sense. But it is very feminine and very much to the taste of American travellers, on whose itinerary the hotel already is. The lounge is small, with a bar; the dining room warm and welcoming with polished tables, chairs upholstered in green, likewise green napkins tied with green tartan ribbons. Dinner was very good: marinaded fish salad, chicory soup, hare with juniper berries, butterscotch pudding with rum sauce, Scottish cheeses, then good coffee by the fire with home-made truffles. We slept well in utter peace and quiet. We thought it all very good value." (Warmly endorsed in 1991 by *Ms JC Shillaker and NJ Burt*)

Open All year except 3rd week Oct, 2 weeks Feb/Mar. Group booking only at New Year.
Rooms 1 suite, 4 double – all with bath or shower, telephone, radio, TV.
Facilities Lounge, dining room. 3-acre grounds with trees and lawn, small formal garden, swings, tree house.
Location 11 m NW of Inverness. 1 m N of Muir of Ord, at double bend, signal left; go through green and white lodge gates. Follow private drive 300 yds.
Restrictions No smoking in dining room. No dogs in public rooms.
Credit cards Access accepted.
Terms [1991 rates] Dinner, B&B £67–£87. Set lunch £12.50, dinner £23.50. Reduced rates for children sharing parents' room; special meals.
Service/tipping: "Service at guests' discretion. Money is shared among all staff."

Report forms (Freepost in UK) will be found at the end of the Guide.

NAIRN Highland **Map 5**

Clifton House
Viewfield Street
Nairn IV12 4HW

Tel Nairn (0667) 53119
Fax (0667) 52836

César award in 1987: Utterly acceptable mild eccentricity

"We were quite enraptured," begins one of many reports, praising Gordon Macintyre's individualistic old family hotel, looking over the Moray Firth and stuffed with paintings, sculptures, bas-reliefs, *objets trouvés* and books galore. "Gordon Macintyre is a collector of everything and the rooms offer much to explore. The dining room is theatrical." "Such high standards of proprietor, food, wine and other guests in an hotel with a very unpretentious facade; and near other hotels of awful mediocrity." Some years ago, a reader found "the clutter on every available surface neither fascinating nor interesting, just plain irritating, everything contrived for effect". Mr Macintyre rose to the defence: "Of course it's done for effect!! Masses of flowers, all over the place, are put there for effect; the curtains are lined and interlined for effect, the linen table napkins are starched for effect; the pictures are hung for effect. In the winter, when we have recitals, we have musicians who play for effect; and I love it. It is, in effect, my life." The cooking is French in style, generally appreciated though one reader commented on a limited choice if you were staying more than a couple of nights. Lots of Scottish cheeses and an excellent, eclectic selection of wines and whiskies. (No compulsion to pay if the taste of the wine you ordered is incompatible with the food.) The hotel uses its own hens, ducks and geese, the fish is fresh and the salmon wild, and the bread, oatcakes, muesli, marmalade and jams are all made in the kitchen. Breakfast is served from 8 am onwards, without time limit, and the hotel is happy to provide picnic lunches. (*Dr JB Wylie, Martha Prince, and others*)

Open Feb–Nov.
Rooms 10 double, 6 single – 15 with bath, 1 with shower; beds have continental quilts, but conventional bedding available on request.
Facilities 2 lounges, TV room, 2 restaurants. 1-acre grounds. Fishing, shooting, riding, beach, golf, tennis, swimming pool nearby. Plays, concerts, recitals Oct–Mar.
Location 500 yds from town centre; coming from Inverness turn left at roundabout on A96. Parking for 20 cars.
Restrictions Not suitable for ♿. No dogs in dining room. No smoking in 1 restaurant.
Credit cards All major cards accepted.
Terms [1991 rates] B&B: single £46–£51, double £88–£96. Dinner, B&B £62 per person (min 4 days). Weekly rates. Full alc £25.
Service/tipping: "A service charge is not imposed; nor is tipping expected."

NEWTON STEWART Dumfries and Galloway **Map 5**

Creebridge House BUDGET
Minnigaff, Newton Stewart
Wigtownshire DG8 6NP

Tel Newton Stewart (0671) 2121

Attractive grey-stone Scottish country house, once owned by Earls of Galloway, in 3 acres of garden and woodland short walk from town centre. Comfortable drawing room, informal bar featuring 30 malt whiskies and selection of real ales, dining room with menu based on fresh, local produce. Cooking, by chef and co-owner Chris Walker, specially recommended. Croquet; fishing arranged on rivers Cree and Bladnoch. 18 rooms – all with bath/shower (1 on ground floor with ramp). B&B: single £25–£33, double £46–£60. Set dinner £14.95; full alc £20. Briefly but warmly endorsed this year, but we would still welcome more and fuller reports.

NEWTONMORE Highland — Map 5

Ard-Na-Coille
Kingussie Road, Newtonmore
Inverness-shire PH20 1AY
Tel Newtonmore (0540) 673214
Fax (0540) 673453

This small Edwardian shooting lodge set high above the road in two acres of pine trees, with magnificent views over Strathspey towards the Cairngorms, continues to elicit praise, following the programme of upgrading. Readers commend the owners, Nancy Ferrier and Barry Cottam, for their welcome and their evident desire to please; and for Barry's "fresh, original and beautiful" cooking. New beds and newly decorated bedrooms and bathrooms have all been appreciated. So has the wine list: "First rate, and at bargain-basement prices." A representative verdict: "The food and service were outstandingly good and the terms very reasonable." (*Gerald L Fox, Dr and Mrs J Stewart, GK Moffat*)

Open 29 Dec–mid-Nov except 1 week Apr, 1 week Sep.
Rooms 6 double, 1 single – all with bath and/or shower, telephone, radio, baby-listening.
Facilities Lounge, TV lounge, dining room; drying room; terrace. 2-acre grounds. Fishing, golf, riding, shooting, hill walking nearby; skiing at Aviemore 15 m.
Location Leave A9 at Newtonmore/Kingussie signs. Hotel is at northernmost edge of Newtonmore, just outside speed restriction signs.
Restrictions Not suitable for ♿. No smoking in restaurant. Dogs in 2 bedrooms only, not in public rooms.
Credit cards Access, Visa accepted.
Terms Dinner, B&B £55–£65. Set dinner £25. Off-season breaks. 1-night bookings possibly refused bank holidays. Reduced rates for children sharing parents' room; high teas.
Service/tipping: "Service charges should be abolished by law. Tipping is an iniquitous anachronism. We do not expect gratuities from our customers, but if any are left staff receive an equal share and the remainder is used to support a community charity."

ONICH Highland — Map 5

Allt-nan-Ros
Onich, by Fort William
Inverness-shire PH33 6RY
Tel Onich (085 53) 210 and 250
Fax (085 53) 462

The name of this hotel is Gaelic for the burn of the roses. It is on the north shore of Loch Linnhe, on the Fort William–Glasgow road, and enjoys panoramic views of the surrounding mountains and lochs. Originally built as a Victorian shooting lodge, it has been attractively converted by its owners, Lachlan, Fiona and James MacLeod. Correspondents continue to write in praise of the friendly staff and the warm welcome on arrival by the young kilted James MacLeod. "It is a warm-hearted, very Scottish house/hotel, with excellent service. All rooms are spotless and comfortable. There's a country-house atmosphere (definitely *no* TV in the lounge!) with friendly chat in the evening." (*John and Ann Holt, Mrs RB Richards, and others*) One reader found the staff a bit overstretched, when busy. A new chef arrived Easter 1991. First report speaks well of his cooking, but we'd welcome further comments. Warning: the hotel is close to the busy A82. Some rooms are double-glazed.

Open Mar–early Nov.
Rooms 18 double with bath and shower, 3 single with shower – all with telephone, radio, TV, tea-making facilities, baby-listening. 2 in converted stable. 5 on ground floor.
Facilities Ramps, WC for ♿. Hall, lounge, lounge bar, dining room. 4-acre grounds. Terraced lawn overlooking road and loch. Fishing from shoreline; shingle beach; boat available.
Location On A82 10 m SW of Fort William. Some rooms double-glazed.
Restriction No smoking in dining room. No dogs in public rooms.
Credit cards All major cards accepted.
Terms B&B £38.50–£43; dinner, B&B £54.50–£60.50. Alc lunch £12; set dinner £21. 3-, 5- and 7-day breaks. Reduced rates and special meals for children.
Service/tipping: "If people tip, we distribute the sum equally among the staff."

PEAT INN Fife — Map 5

The Peat Inn
Peat Inn by Cupar
Fifeshire KY15 5LH
Tel Peat Inn (033 484) 206
Fax (033 484) 530

César award in 1990: Newcomer of the year, restaurant-with-rooms division

"About the closest I can imagine to staying in a top-class French restaurant-with-rooms, without having to cross the Channel", is how one reader described her visit to *The Residence*, the recently built annexe to David and Patricia Wilson's long-renowned *Peat Inn.* Set at a country crossroads six miles from St Andrews, the inn offers some of the finest food in Scotland and, since 1987, eight luxurious mini-suites in the new block adjoining the restaurant, sympathetically built to blend with the environment. "The view from the bedroom window is of Fife fields," wrote a recent visitor. "Open the window and the smell of peat smoke drifts by." The bedrooms have been individually decorated, some in bold patterns, with a separate sitting area, marble bathrooms, TV with teletext, a desk, slippers and bathrobes ("changed along with the towels when we went to dinner!"); even Scrabble and playing cards. "It was pure Hollywood. We really enjoyed it." But the real reason one comes here is the restaurant, one of only six Scottish establishments to win a *Michelin* rosette in 1991. David Wilson's cooking has earned him many awards; there is also an outstanding wine list. "Breakfast of fresh orange juice and fruit, wonderful coffee, fresh croissants and masses of wonderful toast, butter and preserve." (*J and K Lodge, J McCracken and E Goodison, Mr and Mrs Colin Estaugh, Judith Camp, and others*) Regrettably, complaints recur about the lack of welcome, and the standard of housekeeping: cold rooms, plumbing defects, lights not working. More reports please.

Open *Residence* open all year except 2 weeks Nov, 2 weeks Jan. Restaurant closed Sun and Mon.
Rooms 8 suites – all with bath, shower, telephone, radio, TV. 1 suitable for ♿.

Facilities Ramp. 2 lounges (1 in *Residence*), restaurant. ¾-acre grounds.
Location At junction of B940/B941 6 miles S of St Andrews.
Restrictions No smoking in restaurant. No children under 12. No dogs.
Credit cards All major cards accepted.
Terms B&B £115–£125 per suite. Set lunch £17.50, dinner £28–£38; full alc £36.
Service/tipping: "We add nothing to the bill and staff do not expect extras."

PEEBLES Borders — Map 5

Cringletie House — *Tel* Eddleston (072 13) 233
Peebles EH45 8PL — *Fax* (072 13) 244

"Excellent in every way. Friendly, efficient service and outstanding food. Probably the best country house hotel we have visited during the past five years." One of many enthusiastic reports received this year for this pink-stone mansion built in the Scottish baronial manner with turrets and dormers, surrounded by garden, woodland and an estate of twenty-eight acres. A truly magnificent setting, with extensive views over the surrounding hills. Stanley and Aileen Maguire, the resident owners for twenty years, are now ably assisted by the next generation. "Quite the most pleasant hoteliers we have come across. We were welcomed with home-made scones and tea, lent maps for our walks, and made to feel completely at home." "The garden was beautifully maintained with well-kept lawns and flowerbeds; the walled vegetable garden must make many visitors envious." "The service is beyond reproach." "The food was excellent. Plentiful helpings, wonderfully cooked fresh vegetables, super sticky desserts, and the best breakfasts we've had anywhere." Many of the bedrooms have high ceilings; they are prettily furnished, with an absence of fussiness. "A very peaceful place; the only noise is the sheep and the birds." (*GJ Bennett, Val F Ferguson, MR Farley, John Freebairn, Mrs KJ Milligan, David Angwin; also S Sowerby, Tony and Avril Reynolds, and others*)

Open Mar–1 Jan.
Rooms 12 double, 1 single – all with bath, shower, telephone, radio, TV, baby-listening.
Facilities 2 lounges (1 no-smoking), lounge bar, dining room. 28-acre grounds with tennis, 9-hole putting green, croquet, children's play area. Golf, fishing nearby.
Location 2½ m N of Peebles on A703.
Restrictions Not suitable for ♿. No smoking in dining room and 1 lounge. No dogs in public rooms.
Credit cards Access, Visa.
Terms (Service at guests' discretion) B&B: single £44, double £80. Lunch from £5 (Sun £13.50), set dinner £22.50. Off-season rates. Reduced rates for children sharing parents' room; high teas.

PLOCKTON Highland — Map 5

The Haven — *Tel* Plockton (059 984) 223
Innes Street, Plockton
Ross and Cromarty IV52 8TW

Converted merchant's house 50 yds from seafront in delightful West Highland village with white-washed cottages along shore road. Easy access for boats; good sailing, trout fishing nearby. Recommended as "cosy, with books in most spare spaces, welcoming reception, staff friendly and efficient, wholesome food, good choice of wine. Excellent value for money." Open 1 Feb–20 Dec. 13 rooms, all with bath/shower. Not suitable for ♿. No children under 7. No smoking in restaurant and 2 sitting rooms. B&B £28–£31.50; dinner, B&B £42–£48. Set dinner £18. Endorsed this year, but more reports would be useful.

PORT APPIN Strathclyde **Map 5**

Airds
Port Appin, Appin
Argyllshire PA38 4DF

Tel Appin (063 173) 236
Fax (063 173) 535

"A lovely experience. Throughout, we felt there was a real commitment to providing a fine service. All the staff were unusually friendly – when we came in soaking wet one of them immediately offered to hang our clothes to dry in the boiler room. The food was wonderful." An enthusiastic American visitor expresses the feelings of many about the hospitality and high standards of hotelkeeping offered by Eric and Betty Allen at their early 18th-century ferry inn with a lovely view towards Loch Linnhe, the islands of Lismore and the mountains of Morvern. Across a small road there is a lawn where you can take tea or drinks and admire the view. "From the outside the building is disconcertingly modest, giving no hint at all of the sophistication, comfort and space within; the atmosphere is proudly Scottish from the red thistle design on the carpet to the plaid ribbons around the starched linen napkins in the dining room. The tartan-skirted waitresses have quiet lilting West Coast voices; the atmosphere exudes peace and quiet." The dining room is elegant, and Betty Allen's cooking, rewarded in 1991 by a *Michelin* rosette, is a major draw. "The wine list is exceptional, and the wine service serious; if you ask Eric Allen's advice you won't go far wrong." The drawing room has deep, softly cushioned sofas and chairs. Flower arrangements abound. Bedrooms, which vary in size, are stylish and comfortable; fluffy thick white towels are changed twice a day. (*Carol W Garvin, J and P Howard, Robert Ribeiro, PL Aston, and others*)

Open Mid-Mar–early Jan.
Rooms 1 suite, 12 double, 1 single – all with bath and/or shower, telephone, radio, TV, baby-listening. 2 in garden annexe.
Facilities 2 lounges, small residents' bar, dining room. Small garden; near loch with shingle beach, bathing, fishing, boating; pony trekking, forest walks.
Location 2 m off A828, 25 m from Fort William and Oban. Parking for 30 cars.
Restrictions Not suitable for ♿. No smoking in dining room. No children under 5. No dogs.
Credit cards None accepted.
Terms Dinner, B&B £90–£122. Set dinner £36. Christmas/New Year breaks. Reduced rates for children sharing parents' room; special meals.
Service/tipping: "No service charge; we do not expect tips. When guests insist, the money is distributed to all members of staff."

Do you know of a good hotel or country inn in the United States or Canada? Nominations please to our sibling publication, America's Wonderful Little Hotels and Inns, PO Box 150, Riverside Avenue, Riverside, Conn. 06878, USA.

PORTPATRICK Dumfries and Galloway — Map 5

Knockinaam Lodge
Portpatrick, Wigtownshire
DG9 9AD

Tel Portpatrick (077 681) 471
Fax (077 681) 435

César award: Country house hotel of the year

"Within 24 hours at the hotel, we were so impressed that we decided to return for Christmas," writes a reader this year, of this much-praised luxury hotel, which nestles in a wooded glen with steep cliffs on three sides. On the fourth side it faces the sea, looking towards the coast of Ireland: a magnificently wild, remote setting. There are superb cliff walks and, in spring, carpets of bluebells and primroses in the woods. A second correspondent dubbed it "Just about the perfect small hotel". A third offered more sustained praise: "The decor is country house in the best sense of the term: pretty pastel chintzes; squashy sofas in impeccable upholstery; immaculate white paint; excellent housekeeping. The bathroom was completely covered in a flower- sprigged wallpaper; there were fluffy white towels and bath robes. All very cosseting – but that is the essence of *Knockinaam*." The restaurant, too, which wins the accolade of a *Michelin* rosette, this year also comes in for readers' acclaim: "On a par with some of the more famous restaurants in London." Set menus change daily and guests who find the choice limited, or prefer something less exotic are offered "a highly satisfactory alternative". The hotel is owned and run by Marcel Frichot, who is French, and his English wife, Corinna, and the hospitality that they offer their guests is said to be "way above normal standards". (*DG Felce, Mrs Jean Dundas, William Rankin, AJB Vernon, WR Rowland, and others*)

Open 15 Mar–4 Jan.
Rooms 9 double, 1 single – all with bath/shower, telephone, radio, TV; baby-listening by arrangement.
Facilities Lounge, residents' lounge, bar, restaurant. 30-acre grounds, with garden and croquet. Private beach 100 yds, swimming "for the brave"; sea fishing. Wildlife, walks, golf nearby.
Location 9 m SW of Stranraer. 3 m before Portpatrick on the A77 there is a left turn, well signposted.
Restrictions Bedrooms not suitable for ♿. No smoking in restaurant. No young children at dinner. No dogs in public rooms.
Credit cards All major cards accepted.
Terms Dinner, B&B: single £92.50, double £152. Set lunch £18. Set dinner £32. 1-night bookings refused for public holidays. Reduced rates for children under 12 sharing parents' room; high teas. Special winter rates, except Christmas and New Year.
Service/tipping: "Service included. Tipping not encouraged; any money left is distributed among the staff."

PORTREE Skye, Highland — Map 5

Viewfield House BUDGET
Portree, Isle of Skye
IV51 9EU

Tel Portree (0478) 2217

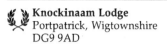

"An absolute delight! Quirky but great. A step back in time." "This is in no way a typical hotel or boarding house – it is an experience of a previous way of life." So begin two recent reports about this very individual guest house, set in twenty acres of lovely grounds. "The shabby splendours are altogether appealing, but the visitor needs to be prepared for the threadbare carpets. We saw no evidence of any *en suite* facilities, nor did we hear any such plans; but hot water was plentiful." Food is "excellent, home-cooking, all done on a 1957 Aga, and served communally at a candelabra'd table". Service is warm and friendly. "Hugh Macdonald was a charming and attentive host; we would recommend the hotel to our more discriminating friends." *Viewfield House* entered the Guide three years ago, nominated for its "lack of commercial imperatives". Bedrooms have no telephone, no TV; they have hand basins and electric fires. It was the home for many years of Colonel 'Jock' Macdonald and his wife Evelyn, who ran the place as an extended house party. Family traditions are maintained by Colonel Jock's grandson Hugh and his wife Linda, and guests are still expected to contribute to the enhancement of life after dinner. (*J Hyams, Moira and John Cole, Nancy and Denis Elliott, AM Henley*)

Open Easter–mid-Oct.
Rooms 9 double, 5 single – all with H&C, tea-making facilities; baby-listening available.
Facilities Drawing room, TV room, dining room. 20-acre grounds with croquet, swings, woodland walks (and midges).
Location On S side of Portree, 10 mins' walk from centre; driving towards Broadford turn right just after BP petrol station on left.
Restrictions Not suitable for ♿. No smoking in dining room. No dogs in public rooms.
Credit cards Access, Visa accepted.
Terms B&B £18.50–£22. Dinner, B&B £30.50–£34. Set dinner £12 (£15 to non residents). Reduced rates for children; special meals on request.
Service/tipping: "No stated policy. We don't expect people to tip unless they want to because they feel they have received outstanding service."

QUOTHQUAN Strathclyde — Map 5

Shieldhill
Quothquan, Biggar
Lanarkshire ML12 6NA

Tel Biggar (0899) 20035
Fax (0899) 21092

"Exceptionally well-restored country house, and totally unlike any in which I have stayed." Owned by two Californians, Christine Dunstan and Jack Greenwald (she is originally from Cheshire), this elegantly refurbished grey-stone manor house, with parts dating from the 13th century, is set in the rolling hills of Lanarkshire, overlooking the river Clyde. It has an oak-panelled lounge, formal drawing room, library and a bar. The bedrooms vary in size. Some have fireplaces, four-posters, jacuzzi. Second-floor bedrooms may be very small, with only a shower. All, however, have been given the Laura Ashley treatment. *Shieldhill*, which opened in 1988, now receives praise not only for its accommodation but also for "the professionalism and friendliness of the staff", and particularly for its "outstanding" food which "has put this little-known corner of Lanarkshire right on the culinary map". (*John Borron, RN Adamson, David A Donald, and others*)

> If you are recommending a bed-and-breakfast hotel and know of a good restaurant nearby, do mention it in your report.

Open All year.
Rooms 1 suite, 10 double – all with bath and/or shower, telephone, radio, TV, baby-listening; tea-making facilities on request.
Facilities 2 lounges, dining room, bar, library. 7-acre grounds, croquet. River fishing 10 mins' walk.
Location 5 m NW of Biggar, off B7016, signposted.
Restrictions Not suitable for ♿. No smoking in dining room or bedrooms. No children under 12. No dogs.
Credit cards All major cards accepted.
Terms B&B: single £88–£120, double £98–£130, suite £150. Full alc dinner £29. Off-season breaks. Reduced rates for children; special meals on request.
Service/tipping: "Any tips are distributed to all members of staff based on hours worked."

RHUM Highland — Map 5

Kinloch Castle — *Tel* Mallaig (0687) 2037
Isle of Rhum
Inverness-shire PH43 4RR

An exotic pink sandstone shooting lodge with towers and crenellations, unchanged since it was built in 1901 for the millionaire textile magnate Sir George Bullough, now a small hotel and self-catering hostel for visitors to this unique island wildlife reserve. "Nowadays most of the population is furred or feathered: red deer, which are studied by resident naturalists, wild goats and eagles. Sir George found this wilderness of rock and loch, heather, scree and waterfalls so romantic that he built a holiday home there; today *Kinloch Castle* is a monument to Edwardian self-indulgence, where guests can recover from hill walking in exotic bathrooms, enter the dining room to the Grand March from *Aida* performed by his mechanical organ, and play billiards in a room from which the cigar-smoke is sucked by his prototype air-conditioner." "Visitors can use all rooms. The bathrooms (none *en suite*) are original and amazing, the forerunners of today's whirlpool/spa baths. Not exactly comfortable bedrooms (though some are better than others), because everything is original and a bit past its prime. It really is like staying in a museum. Dinner and breakfast are taken at the vast dining table in the formal dining room overlooking the bay; the food is okay; the whole experience of staying in the hotel makes up for inadequacies. It's probably best not to stay too long." The castle's bistro serves lunch, and meals for the hostel residents and locals. (*TP, LH*) More reports please.

Open Mar–Oct.
Rooms 7 double, 2 single in castle, 13 in hostel in former servants' quarters (blankets, pillows and pillowslips provided).
Facilities Great hall, drawing rooms, smoking/billiard room, library, ballroom, dining room, bistro. Occasional ceilidhs. 26,000-acre nature reserve; trout fishing (sea and loch).
Location Off coast opposite Mallaig (West Highland rail terminus for trains from Glasgow). No cars allowed. Take Caledonian MacBrayne ferry (Mallaig 0687 2403) or arrange charter with Bruce Watt Cruises (Mallaig 0687 2320) or Murdo Grant (Arisaig 068 75 224). Journey approx 1 hr.
Restrictions No children under 7 in castle. No pets.
Credit cards None accepted.
Terms (Service at guests' discretion) Dinner, B&B £65. Self-catering in hostel £8. Packed lunches £3.59. Set dinner £22. Reduced rates for children.
Service/tipping: "We do not believe in an automatic service charge but most guests insist on contributing something to the staff; this is divided equally among them."

SCARISTA Western Isles — Map 5

Scarista House — *Tel* Scarista (085 985) 238
Scarista, Isle of Harris PA85 3HX

Georgian manse – one of few listed buildings in Western Isles – in 2-acre grounds on magnificent Atlantic coast of Harris, overlooking 3-m stretch of beach. Cherished by Guide readers under previous owners, now owned by Ian and Jane Callaghan. Reports, many from admirers of old regime, give general approval to hospitality of new management and praise breakfasts but otherwise offer mixed reports on the food. But "nothing can detract from the location, which is unsurpassed". Open Apr–Oct. No smoking in restaurant. No children under 8. No credit cards. 7 double rooms with bath/shower. B&B £39–£55. Set dinner £23. More reports please.

SCONE Tayside — Map 5

Murrayshall — *Tel* Perth (0738) 51171
Scone, By Perth — *Fax* (0738) 52595
Perthshire PH2 7PH

New to the Guide, this refurbished Victorian mansion, now a country house hotel and restaurant at the smarter end of the range, stands in 300 acres of parkland with its own golf course. Our inspector reports: "A haven of country house chic. A friendly welcome from reception; a porter who grabbed our bags before we were over the threshold. Our bedroom was on the small side, curtained with red roses, with fruit, bottled water and, a Japanese touch, two carnations floating in a saucer of water. The bed had real sheets and blankets – very comfortable. The bathroom was similarly small but had a good-sized bath, hot water galore and a rather strange blue alcove behind, which should have housed Venus de Milo. The decor in the *Old Masters Restaurant* was bland, even cold, and guests were paying serious food homage; somewhere a pianist was playing 'Unchained Melody'. Waitresses fluttered about silently with white-draped trolleys on hushed wheels. The *nouvelle*-style four-course meal was quite an experience; the minute portions were all delicious, though sometimes with too many flavours. The wine list went on for ever, with nearly 200 wines from all over the world, from £8.75 to £185 a bottle. Next morning, an excellent breakfast." Her verdict: "A comfortable, luxury country house hotel. But beware, it's very leisured. Come down to dinner early – it takes three-quarters of an hour before you go in. Have a light lunch; the portions of food, though small, are quite exotic and there are a lot of them. The staff were unfailingly polite. A pleasant, if impersonal, stay – an owner in evidence would help – ideal for rich golfers, fishers, corporate entertainers." More reports please.

Open All year, except 1st 2 weeks Jan.
Rooms 3 suites, 16 double – all with bath, shower, telephone, radio, TV, baby-listening.
Facilities Lounge, bar, restaurant, clubhouse; meeting rooms. 300 acre grounds; golf, tennis, bowls, croquet, clay-pigeon shooting; river Tay 5 mins; pre-bookable fishing.
Location 4 m N of Perth off A94, signposted.
Restrictions Not suitable for ♿. No children under 10. No dogs in public rooms.
Credit cards All major cards accepted.

Terms B&B: single £70–£95, double £105–£130, suite £125–£240; dinner, B&B £82.50–£90 per person. Set lunch (Sun) £14, dinner £32.50. Golf breaks, cookery workshops. Reduced rates for children; special meals on request.
Service/tipping: "The price is for the room and all that goes with it including the service from the staff. Any 'gifts' left by customers are such and are not left under obligation."

SELKIRK Borders — Map 5

Philipburn House — *Tel* Selkirk (0750) 20747
Selkirk TD7 5LS — *Fax* (0750) 21690

This hotel "prefers the friendly Austrian *gemütlich* atmosphere to the often vacant grandeur and opulence of other baronial-style hotels". So says its brochure, and, from our readers' reports, many share this view. Now in its 20th year under the ownership of Anne and Jim Hill, it returned to the Guide last year with high praise for its combination of sophisticated meals for parents and supervised activities for children. The house, built in 1751, has a wooded setting in Border country where there is splendid walking and fishing. It has been much extended over the years; the interior is Tyrolean in style, with hand-carved wooden furniture, floral cushions and flower baskets on the walls. "Our children were in heaven from the moment we arrived. They were able to fish, horseback-ride, and play in the hotel grounds under the supervision of the staff, completely independently of us. We were able to walk with the local guide who had wonderful stories of the history of the area." "They are adept at making the adults feel special too, which is refreshing for a mother of small children. It is a lovely place to relax and enjoy excellent food and wine." The menu, changing daily, offers three or four starters and main courses (many suitable for vegetarians), and puddings such as "sticky toffee pudding with custard, farmhouse blackcherry pie warm from the stove, spotted dick with rum and cream, chocolate Calvados crunch". The wine list is comprehensive. (*N and D Mulliken, Alison Masson*)

Open All year.
Rooms 2 suites, 14 double – all with bath and/or shower, telephone, radio, TV, tea-making facilities, baby-listening. 2 cottages, 2 poolside apartments, lodge separate from main building. 1 bedroom on ground floor.
Facilities Ramps. Residents' lounge, bar, coffee room, 2 restaurants; conference facilities, games room; laundry. Dinner dancing in poolside restaurant Sat. 5-acre grounds with heated swimming pool, children's play area. Riding, golf, hill walking, fishing nearby.
Location ¾ m W of Selkirk.
Restrictions No smoking in restaurant. Dogs by arrangement only, not in public rooms.
Credit cards All major cards accepted.
Terms [1991 rates] Dinner, B&B £55–£78. Set lunch £12.50. Full alc £25. Reduced rates for children; high tea at 5 pm.
Service/tipping: "Entirely at guests' discretion, and divided among all staff; staff do not expect tips and they do refuse them for any helpful extras they find themselves doing."

> "Budget" labels indicate hotels offering accommodation at up to about £40 for dinner, bed and breakfast or £25 for B&B and £15 for an evening meal. But we would emphasise that this is a rough guide only, and does not always apply to single rooms.

SHIELDAIG Highland — Map 5

Tigh An Eilean
Shieldaig, Strathcarron
Ross-shire IV54 8XN

Tel Shieldaig (052 05) 251
Fax (052 05) 321

"A splendid little hotel in a more than splendid setting" was one reader's verdict on this attractively decorated inn on the edge of the sea in an unspoilt fishing village in the Torridon hills of Wester Ross. It entered the Guide last year and has since been warmly endorsed. "Bedrooms are comfortable, but not large. The food is excellent; the wine list offers outstanding value. Above all, the hotel is most efficiently run and spotlessly clean, with a friendly atmosphere maintained by a staff who achieve it without appearing to be rushed off their feet." Another writes: "The best small hotel I have stayed in for a long time. The food should make many others blush. All rooms are beautifully warm and it is evident that considerable money has been spent on modernising the bedrooms and public rooms. Drinks are help-yourself on an honesty basis. Oh for more *Tigh an Eileans.*" (*I and JW Bennion, IC Dewey*)

Open Easter–late Oct.
Rooms 9 double, 3 single – 5 with bath and shower, all with tea-making facilities.
Facilities 2 lounges, residents' bar, public bar, TV room, dining room; drying room. Private fishing on river Balgy and Loch Damh. Sea trips arranged.
Location In centre of village off A896.
Restrictions Not suitable for ♿. No dogs in public rooms.
Credit card Access accepted.
Terms B&B £27.35–£28.50; dinner, B&B £42.95–£44.25. Set dinner £15.95. Reduced rates and special meals for children.
Service/tipping: "At customers' discretion."

STRONTIAN Highland — Map 5

Kilcamb Lodge
Strontian, Argyllshire
PH36 4HY

Tel Strontian (0967) 2257

"We have travelled to many parts of the British Isles; never have we been treated with such kindness and consideration as at *Kilcamb Lodge,*" writes a visitor from Ohio about this small, secluded, hospitable hostelry on lovely Loch Sunart. Set in thirty acres of grounds, and with a third of a mile of private beach, it is a haven for wildlife. Fishing on Loch Shiel and Loch Doilet, boating and pony trekking can be arranged. "One of the finest small hotels we have stayed in – for the friendly atmosphere produced by John and Suzanne Bradbury. They say it is an extension of their home, and what a beautiful one too." "The food was superb; quality, choice and presentation all of a high standard. Sue Bradbury sets a standard that numerous other hotels should take note of." "The hospitality was outstanding, with help over places to visit, maps to borrow, and the owners' wide knowledge of the area to dip into. Being in the hotel business, I can especially appreciate the hard work that goes into providing such high standards." (*Dr Daniel and Linda Farrell, Dr and Mrs JD Owen, S Liddington; also James Kavanagh*)

Open Easter–20 Oct.
Rooms 8 double, 2 single – 5 with bath, 5 with shower, all with TV, baby-listening.
Facilities Lounge, bar, dining room. 30-acre grounds, ⅓ m private beach, fishing, boating, pony trekking nearby.
Location From A82 S of Fort William take Corran ferry, then A861 to Strontian.
Restrictions Not suitable for ♿. No smoking in dining room or bedrooms. No dogs allowed.
Credit cards None accepted.
Terms B&B £38; dinner, B&B £50. Set dinner £21; full alc £25. Reduced rates and special meals for children.
Service/tipping: "No service charge. Tipping not encouraged. If a customer leaves a tip it is distributed to all staff – not *to management."*

TANGUSDALE BEACH Barra, Outer Hebrides — Map 5

Isle of Barra Hotel
Tangusdale Beach, Castlebay
Isle of Barra PA80 5XW

Tel Castlebay (087 14) 383
Fax (087 14) 385

Built about thirteen years ago by the Highlands and Islands Development Board, at a cost of £300,000, the *Isle of Barra* was, at first, considered a folly. Indeed, it proved hard to fill and the English manager and his wife, "in her ankle-length tartan skirt", headed back south, and the hotel was sold to George and Maureen Macleod, who were born on the island. This enterprising couple now run a thriving hotel concern, filled six nights a week by coach parties which "do not intrude, as they dine earlier and we are seldom up in time to see them at breakfast". Situated on the beach, with a marvellous outlook, similar to *Baile-na-Cille* at Timsgarry (q.v.). It's a good place for beachcombing, bird watching and hill walking, with one or two extremely safe beaches; there are also places where seals and otters can be seen without lengthy or difficult walks. "The staff are charming; the food is good – fish dishes excellent." "We produced a lobster one morning and told them exactly how we wanted it for dinner that evening, and they made an excellent job of it." "If you want modern comfort in a newish hotel on this lovely island, this is the place for you. A rare find on an island which is five hours on the boat from Oban." (*W Ian Stewart, RS McNeill*) There is a five-hour ferry four times a week from Oban, and a daily flight from Glasgow. Watching the scheduled air service landing on the enormous cockle-shell beach is "unfailing entertainment".

Open Apr–Oct.
Rooms 35 double – all with bath, shower, radio, TV, tea-making facilities, baby-listening. Also 2 self-catering houses.
Facilities Residents' lounge, 2 bars, dining room. Occasional ceilidhs. Beach nearby.
Location 2 m W of Castlebay. From ferry turn left; keep on main road. If without car, advise hotel; they will meet you.
Restrictions Not suitable for ♿. No smoking in restaurant. No dogs in public rooms.
Credit cards Access, Visa.
Terms B&B £25–£40. Set dinner £16.50. Reductions for 4 days or more. Special air package. Reduced rates for children sharing parents' room; special meals.
Service/tipping: "No service charge. Any tips given are distributed to staff."

We are particularly keen to have reports on italicised entries.

TIMSGARRY Lewis, Outer Hebrides Map 5

Baile-na-Cille **BUDGET**
Timsgarry, Uig
Isle of Lewis PA86 9JD

Tel Timsgarry (085 175) 242
Fax (085 175) 241

César award in 1990: Shangri-La of the Outer Hebrides

"We mainly offer peace, quiet and spiritual recovery for those who work hard or live in urban areas," writes Joanna Gollin of the 18th-century manse on the wild west coast of Lewis that she and her husband, Richard, have converted into a welcoming hotel. It sits on the edge of a sandy bay "at the end of a 15-mile single-track road across a soggy landscape of peat interspersed with tiny lochs. When you reach Timsgarry, however, the scenery changes to soft, springy turf, hazy blue hills, and long white sands." It is appreciated for "the marvellous collection of tapes, records and books (for rainy days!), the comfortable furnishings . . . but more important than all this is the atmosphere. The owners *genuinely* enjoy having guests, and Joanna is a lovely cook." Most bedrooms, which are described by readers as "basic", have sea views; some are a little small (three-quarters are in converted stables and cowsheds) and with "limited" cupboard and drawer space. The food is praised even by those who dislike the communal eating arrangements. Richard Gollin travels almost daily to Stornaway to collect supplies, and guests without transport can be deposited at various points for walking and climbing. It is a wonderful area for naturalists. "This remote area would not suit people looking for sophisticated five-star treatment, but for anyone wanting to get away from it all it is an ideal hideaway." (*CB Jones, Dr JCH Kelnar, and others*)

Open 25 Mar–15 Oct.
Rooms 2 family suites, 10 double, 2 single – 8 with bath, all with tea-making facilities, baby-listening. 9 in 3 converted stable blocks by main entrance. Some on ground floor.
Facilities 3 lounges (1 with TV, 1 with music), dining room; drying room. 3-acre grounds with walled garden, children's play area, cricket pitch, direct access to beach (dinghy, windsurfer and fishing rods available). Near 7 sandy beaches with safe bathing; fishing, sailing.
Location 34 m W of Stornoway. Take A858 from Stornoway or Tarbert to Garynahine, B8011 towards Uig; at Timsgarry shop turn right down to shore. *Note*: All road signs are now in Gaelic only.
Restrictions Not really suitable for ♿. No smoking in dining room and certain sitting areas. No dogs in dining room.
Credit cards None accepted.
Terms Dinner, B&B: single £34–£47, double £68–£94, suite £89–£128. Set lunch/dinner £16–£18 (lobster dinner extra); packed lunches. Weekly packages for walkers, bird-watchers, fishermen. Reduced rates and special meals for children.
Service/tipping: "We are one hundred percent against compulsory service charges and are getting militant with it. I have noticed that service is added where it is so bad that you wouldn't leave a tip!"

The length of an entry need not reflect the merit of a hotel. The more interesting the report or the more unusual or controversial the hotel, the longer the entry.

TIRORAN Mull, Strathclyde — Map 5

Tiroran House — *Tel* Tiroran (068 15) 232
Tiroran, Isle of Mull
Argyllshire PA69 6ES

"For situation, comfort, welcome and cuisine, this place is our standard for comparison," writes a well-travelled reader about this enchanting and comfortable former shooting lodge owned by Robin and Sue Blockey. It sits above Loch Scridain, with fifteen acres of gardens and woodland sweeping down to the water, and is well situated for visiting all parts of Mull. The drive from the ferry is forested, barren, mountainous, gently undulating and coastal in turn; much of it is single track. *Tiroran* by contrast is an oasis of sophistication and civilisation. The two drawing rooms are decorated in pretty fabrics and have many antiques; small arrangements of flowers are everywhere. The larger bedrooms are just as thoughtfully furnished, with comfortable beds, small sofas, "bath towels so big they can wrap round you twice". Some bedrooms are quite small. One of the two dining rooms is a flower-filled conservatory with a view of the water, the other a warm soft red room with bookcases, a fireplace and oak tables. The table settings are "a delight". The packed lunches are "marvellous". Guests are often out walking or touring during the day; most enjoy having a drink together before dinner to share their sightseeing experiences. "For a few the service may seem slow," one correspondent told us, "but that is an expected drawback when the guests are being served like friends at a private dinner." "A gem," said another. Said a third: "I doubt, after years of using the Guide, that I have ever stayed anywhere that I enjoyed so much." "The Blockeys clearly live up to the motto 'service before self'." (*James AS Dickson, April Young, Dr E Gerver, Paul and Christine Butler, Gillian Smith*)

Open 30 May–30 Sep.
Rooms 8 double, 1 single – all with bath, radio, tea-making facilities. 3 in cottage 40 yds away.
Facilities 2 drawing rooms, 2 dining rooms. 15-acre grounds with woodland, lawn, stream; croquet. On sea loch safe for bathing, sailing, canoeing.
Location Oban–Craignure ferry (45 mins) bookable with Caledonian McBrayne, The Pier, Gourock PA19 1QP. (Lochaline–Fishnish ferry, not bookable, but much cheaper, necessitates a longish but superb drive through Morvern.) From Craignure take A849 to Fionnphort. At head of Loch Scridain (17 m) turn right on to B8035; after 5 m turn left to Tiroran (1 m). Entrance through stone gate marked *Tiroran* and *Bungalow*.
Restrictions Not suitable for ♿. No smoking in dining room. No children under 10. Dogs by arrangement, not in public rooms.
Credit cards None accepted.
Terms [1991 rates] Dinner, B&B £85–£100. Packed lunch £6. Set lunch £12.50, dinner £29. Reductions for stays of 3 nights or more.
Service/tipping: "There is no service charge and no gratuities are expected."

****

Traveller's tale *After dinner we were pleased to note that the beds had been turned down – but to our surprise, one pillow was covered in large crumbs and bits of burnt toast, presumably the previous occupants' continental breakfast, left in the bedcover.*

****

ULLAPOOL Highland — Map 5

Altnaharrie — *Tel* Dundonnell (085 483) 230
Ullapool, Wester Ross IV26 2SS

César award in 1987: Away-from-it-all delight in the featherweight class

"A rare gem. Dinners well up to its *Michelin* rating, exceptionally comfortable, friendly and helpful." "Not a hotel, an experience." This former drover's inn, idyllically set on the shore of loch Broom and firmly established as one of Britain's finest restaurants-with-rooms, is one of only six restaurants in Scotland to earn a *Michelin* rosette. "Every serious patron of unique hotels should visit it so as to set a standard against which to judge all the others." It is owned and run "with a unique, creative vision" by Fred Brown and his Norwegian wife Gunn Eriksen (she is the cook), and its decor is described as Scottish–Scandinavian. "The whole thing is a bit precious but not pretentious, and to achieve this in such a remote spot must have required great logistic planning." There is no road, so guests are ferried in the hotel's launch from Ullapool harbour – a ten-minute ride. There are six scheduled ferries a day, and additional trips can be arranged. It helps if you enjoy your fellow guests: "One is obliged to be in close contact with others, both pre- and post-prandially, because only one small lounge is available – but this is not offered as a criticism." Much of the food is grown or caught locally, but cheeses come from France and Norway as well as Ireland, Scotland and England; and there are three desserts every night. As one reader said: "You must try them all, or Gunn will be upset!" Dinners are fixed, five courses, so guests are asked when booking to say if they have any allergies. Take wellington boots. (*David N Ing, W Ian Stewart, Carol W Garvin, Marjory and Michael Thrusfield; also Rev AG Mursell, Mrs M Wall, Dr James Mair, Elizabeth Lutz*) *Altnaharrie* is a no-smoking hotel.

Open End Mar–early Nov. Occasional closures in summer; please telephone.
Rooms 8 double – all with bath and/or shower. 2 in cottage close to house.
Facilities Hall, 2 lounges, dining room. 15-acre grounds with gardens, on loch; pebbled beach, safe (but cold) bathing; trout and salmon fishing by arrangement; hill walking.
Location On S shore of Loch Broom. Access by launch from Ullapool harbour (normal collection times 10.15, 11.00, 12.30, 14.45, 16.45, 18.00). Private parking in Ullapool. Guests requested to telephone on arrival in Ullapool.
Restrictions Not suitable for ♿. No smoking. Children "only if old enough to enjoy our dinner which usually lasts over 2 hours". Dogs by arrangement, not in public rooms.
Credit cards None accepted.
Terms Dinner, B&B £100–£125. 1-night bookings occasionally refused. Reduced rates for children sharing parents' room.
Service/tipping: "Tipping is discouraged. Staff are asked politely to refuse any tips offered."

The Ceilidh Place — *Tel* Ullapool (0854) 2103
14 West Argyle Street — *Fax* (0854) 2886
Ullapool, Wester Ross IV26 2TY

César award in 1986: Utterly acceptable mild eccentricity

"Where else would one find an exhibition of children's paintings in the dining room and a couple rehearsing in the lounge on concertina and hurdy-gurdy?" This singularly individual establishment attracts comments, as always, from both ends of the spectrum, though the ayes prevail. Those in favour like it because it is "above all, so relaxed and relaxing, like being invited into someone's home"; others feel that this informality is well over the top. The hotel – also clubhouse, restaurant, coffee shop, bookshop – near the centre of Ullapool is run by Jean and Robert Urquhart (he a TV actor when not a hotelier) as a new-world establishment with genuine verve. Its attractions are the reasonably priced accommodation and the myriad activities: sea angling, water skiing, loch fishing and pony trekking, as well as more leisurely pursuits such as listening to music and poetry reading. There is a "good lounge with an honesty bar and free fresh coffee and tea". The wine list is a "rack of bottles" on a dresser at the end of the room. The place can be very busy at times; service, by "an interesting and friendly staff", is generally thought to be enthusiastic and helpful. Reports on the food vary from "absolutely excellent", the majority, to "mediocre". "The ageing hippy atmosphere" reported a few years back is now said to have totally disappeared. (*JAS Dickson, J Hyams, Paul Trevisan, RLA Gollin*) Several readers have commented on the slow and erratic service in the restaurant, and found the annexe bedrooms uninviting.

Open All year except 2 weeks mid-Jan.
Rooms 12 double, 3 single – 8 with bath, all with telephone. Guest's pantry for tea-making. 10 extra rooms (simpler, with bunk beds, etc.) in Clubhouse annexe.
Facilities Lounge, Clubhouse bar with live music, coffee shop, games room, bookshop, dining room; ceilidhs, jazz, classical, folk-music evenings once a week winter, 3–4 nights summer. Garden. Rocky beach.
Location First right after pier at W end of Main Street. Large carpark.
Restrictions Not suitable for ♿. No smoking in restaurant. No dogs in public rooms.
Credit cards All major cards accepted.
Terms B&B £23–£40; bed in Clubhouse £8.50–£10. Packed lunches available. Set dinner £18; full alc £28. Special rates for 6 days or more; occasional courses; activity holidays. 1-night bookings sometimes refused. Reduced rates for children sharing parents' room; children's portions in restaurant.
Service/tipping: "We do not look for tips. Wages should be paid that people can live on and prices charged must cover this. However, some people do leave tips and they are shared by everyone."

WALLS Shetland Islands — Map 5

Burrastow House — *Tel* Walls (059 571) 307
Walls, Shetland ZE2 9PB

On the remote west side of Shetland, in a peaceful setting where you may see otters and seals, stands this "fine, small Georgian house, 'Scottish-plain'", with views across to the island of Vaila. Inside, it is "warm, comfortable and furnished with good pictures and *objets d'art*"; there are peat fires, a cosy library, and a dining room where guests can enjoy excellent food. Warm praise, again this year, for "the delightfully relaxed but efficient hostesses, Bo Simmons and Ann Prior", who are knowledgeable about Shetland and genuinely welcoming of children and pets. "They are also splendid cooks, taking it in turns; marvellous local salmon, lobsters, lamb and beautifully fresh vegetables." "Dinner has a nice balance of local and more exotic dishes. Fish, soups, puddings – even scrambled eggs – particularly recommended. Good (organic) house wines and a nice and catholic collection of other wine at welcoming, modest prices." "The house is decorated in a very sympathetic and relaxing way. The furniture is a well-worn miscellany picked up from local sales, which gives the hotel a very lived-in appearance. It is like staying in a house rather than a hotel as both the owners are so welcoming. The style may not suit everyone, but if you do not mind occasional pop music it is charming." (*RT Clement, Dr and Mrs J Stewart, S Stanley, Mrs N Patrick*)

Open Mar–end Oct, Dec.
Rooms 3 – all with bath, tea-making facilities; telephone, radio, TV, baby-listening on request.
Facilities Sitting room, dining room, library with TV/video. ¾-acre grounds. Own pier and boat for residents; access to sandy beach; safe swimming. Fishing, riding, windsurfing locally.
Location 27 m W of Lerwick, 2 m SW of Walls. From Lerwick to Walls, up hill; on brow turn left, proceed 2 m to dead end.
Restrictions Not suitable for ♿. No smoking in dining room or bedrooms. No dogs in dining room.
Credit cards None accepted.
Terms B&B from £41; dinner, B&B from £51. Set dinner £18.50. Special breaks 1 Oct–31 Mar.
Service/tipping: "Service included. Tips given only if people feel that they want to; then the money is shared among all the staff."

WEST LINTON Borders — Map 5

Medwyn House — *Tel* West Linton (0968) 60542
Medwyn Road, West Linton
Peeblesshire EH46 7HB

Many an "emphatic yes" this year for Anne and Mike Waterston's former coaching inn, converted to a Victorian country house in 1864, now a small hotel, with a panelled hall with open fire, large drawing room, just three spacious, elegant bedrooms and thirty-acre grounds with gardens and woodland. "The hotel and grounds are maintained to an immaculate standard. The operation is conducted in a delightfully informal manner but the efficiency of all they undertake is total." Readers talk of the "exceptional welcome"; "Anne Waterston's food cooked to perfection"; "five-star treatment with no formality". "Mike Waterston cleans your car windows while you eat breakfast – that's luxury!" A recent visitor writes: "A super quiet place to stay if you want to explore Edinburgh (eighteen miles away) or the surrounding countryside." No licence but a glass of sherry is offered free before dinner and you're welcome to bring your own wine (no corkage). (*JEM Ruffer, VJ Shaw, April Young, Sue Hemmings, Angela Jacques, Margaret R Wall, Norma Kessler, and others*)

Open 1 Mar–7 Jan.
Rooms 3 double – all with bath, telephone, radio, tea-making facilities, baby-listening; TV on request. 3-bedroomed cottage sometimes available.
Facilities Lounge/hall, drawing room, dining room. 30-acre grounds, croquet, stabling; 18-hole golf course next door (50% reduction on greens fees).
Location Medwyn road is off A702; signposted Baddinsgill.
Restrictions Not suitable for ♿. No smoking in dining room or bedrooms. Children under 12 by special arrangement only. No dogs in public rooms.
Credit cards None accepted.
Terms B&B £30–£40; dinner, B&B £48–£58. Set dinner £18. Reduced rates and special meals for children by arrangement.
Service/tipping: "Tipping not encouraged but received gratefully from insistent guests and distributed to staff at end of main season."

Channel Islands

Château La Chaire, Rozel Bay

HERM **Map 1**

The White House *Tel* Guernsey (0481) 722159
Herm, via Guernsey *Fax* (0481) 710066

ꕤ *César award in 1987: Best family hotel away from it all*

Herm, three miles from Guernsey, is one and a half miles long and one mile wide, with one church, one pub – and one hotel, the *White House*. It has a population of approximately 40 including children (though it has to meet an invasion of 1,000 or more day visitors from Guernsey in the summer). It is also a unique fief, now run by Adrian and Penny Heyworth, the son-in-law and daughter of the Tenants of Herm, Peter and Jenny Wood. "Herm is still a haven of peace," writes a reader, "particularly when the last trip boat has returned to Guernsey and the island is left to the oystercatchers and the hotel residents." In the hotel "there is a total absence of canned music and not one television set. If you want to keep up with events in the mad world outside you can order a paper which arrives, weather permitting, in time for lunch." It is praised for its wonderful sea views, its "kindly, efficient staff", good value, and the "excellent" food prepared by head chef Chris Walder. "The selection of seafood dishes was, by any standard, ambitious." The hotel has a solar-heated swimming pool and there are isolated beaches within a few minutes' stroll; day trippers have their own restaurant and rarely intrude. Residents change for dinner, but the *White House* welcomes children and "the high teas at 5 pm are quite an institution". Lots of board games and jigsaws for rainy days. (*Nigel and Jennifer Jee, Michael Hubbard, and others*) There have been niggles about the bedroom furniture ("MFI type"), the hot-water system ("not very hot at 7 am"), and about the peremptory demands for down payment from a travel agent in Guernsey who looks after the hotel's bookings.

Open Mar–Oct.
Rooms 30 double, 2 single – all with bath, radio, tea-making facilities, baby-listening. 22 in 3 cottages in grounds. 7 on ground floor.
Facilities 3 lounges, 2 restaurants. 2-acre garden with solar-heated swimming pool, tennis. Sandy beaches with safe bathing; private harbour and mooring facilities; fishing.
Location 3 m from Guernsey via hourly ferry service from St Peter Port (15–20 minutes). Hotel meets guests at airport or ferry. (No cars on Herm.)
Restrictions Herm not really suitable for ♿ (those wishing to visit must land at high tide). No smoking in 1 restaurant. No dogs.
Credit cards Access, Visa.
Terms Dinner, B&B £32.50–£44.50. Set lunch £9.25, dinner £14.25. Reduced rates for children, special meals.
Service/tipping: "Gratuities are at guests' discretion. When given, they are shared equally among the staff."

ROZEL BAY Jersey — Map 1

Château La Chaire
Rozel Bay, St Martins

Tel Jersey (0534) 63354
Fax (0534) 65137

"If you are looking for a small luxury hotel with absolute peace in Jersey, I do not believe this can be beaten. From the moment we checked in, receiving a welcoming glass of sherry or port, the manager and his staff could not have been more helpful. The general character, decor and furnishings are excellent." Built in 1843, *La Chaire* nestles on the slope of the Rozel valley on the north-eastern tip of Jersey, six miles from St Helier, "off the beaten track even by Jersey standards", in an "idyllic" position. It has panelled public rooms, handsomely decorated bedrooms, and a sophisticated restaurant whose seafood is specially commended: "The choice and quality of the food was first-class, always beautifully presented, nearly *Good Food Guide* standard." "The main reason why this hotel is such a pleasure to stay at is the efficiency and friendliness of the management and staff." The hotel is surrounded by a somewhat neglected terraced garden and there is a sandy beach with safe bathing nearby. (*RM Everett, Dr JR Backhurst, RA McSweeney, and others*) One complaint: loud pop music in the rather gloomy bar.

Open All year.
Rooms 13 double – all with bath, shower, telephone, radio, TV.
Facilities Lounge, bar, 2 restaurants, conservatory. 7 acre garden with rare shrubs and trees. Sandy beach with safe bathing nearby, also harbour with fishing from pier head.

Location 6 m NE of St Helier. Follow signs for St Martin's church, then signs for Rozel. First turning on left in village; hotel carpark 200 yds on left.
Restrictions Not suitable for ♿. No children under 7. No dogs in bedrooms or restaurant.
Credit cards All major cards accepted.
Terms (10% service charge added to non-resident diners' bills) B&B: single £52–£100, double £74–£115; dinner, B&B: single £67.50–£116.50, double £105–£148. Set lunch £10.25, dinner £21.95; full alc £28.50. Winter and Christmas breaks. Reduced rates for children sharing parents' room.
Service/tipping: "No service charge to residents. Tips at guests' discretion; shared evenly among all staff."

Le Couperon de Rozel *Tel* Jersey (0534) 65522
Rozel Bay, St Martins *Fax* (0534) 65332

A converted Napoleonic fortress, now "a most elegant and pretty hotel, superbly run and staffed, with excellent food and a well-chosen and reasonable wine list". It enters the Guide with warm praise from a regular reader, who first saw it twenty-five years ago and happily reports that it has changed only for the better. "Under the superb management of Pasquale Silvestri, a perfectionist who will turn his hand to anything, including cleaning the swimming pool, this is as well run an establishment as we have found anywhere. The public rooms are comfortable and stylish, with Italianate overtones; from the lounge you can see the Normandy coast, some thirteen miles away; and there is a well-stocked and efficient bar. Our bedroom was very good indeed, beautifully furnished and well equipped, and with an exquisite little bathroom. The two dining rooms are the prettiest imaginable; both look out on to a rose-decked courtyard. The table d'hôte menu was so good that we didn't bother with the à la carte being devoured by the well-heeled Jersey residents who eat here. When we left, the delightful Australian receptionist embraced us both. Signor Silvestri and the head waiter said how much they had enjoyed looking after us and hoped we would go again. Most of the other guests book from year to year." (*Stephanie Sowerby*) New nomination. We look forward eagerly to more reports.

Open Mid-Apr–mid-Oct.
Rooms 1 suite, 35 double – all with bath, shower, telephone, radio, TV, baby-listening.
Facilities Lounge, bar, 2 restaurants. Terrace with heated outdoor swimming pool; sand/rock beach, safe bathing.
Location On Rozel bay.
Restriction No dogs.
Credit cards All major cards accepted.
Terms B&B double £68–£88; dinner, B&B double £80–£100. Set lunch £7.50, dinner £15; full alc £27. Reduced rates and special meals for children.

ST PETER PORT Guernsey Map 1

La Frégate *Tel* Guernsey (0481) 724624
Les Côtils *Fax* (0481) 720443

Once an 18th-century manor house (though the facade has been much altered since), now a hotel which pleases many readers, with a "stunning position" in its own terraced garden high on a hill above St Peter Port's bustling harbour, about five minutes' walk from the old markets with their striped awnings and locally caught seafood. Bedrooms are spacious and well furnished in a functional but comfortable style; some have double-glazed patio windows and private balcony; most enjoy "the spectacular view right across the St Peter Port harbour to Herm in the distance". Staff are "gracious and helpful". The restaurant receives particular praise: "It is excellent, the staff courteous, attentive and well trained." The style is fairly formal – tie and jacket essential – with a busy local following attracted by the ambitious and comprehensive menu (French with a good selection of seafood). The table d'hôte menu (for residents only) is served between 7 and 7.30 pm, full à la carte from 7 to 9.30 pm. (*Paul and Christine Butler, and others*) There have, however, been reports about lapses in housekeeping and service, poor heating and "meagre breakfasts".

Open All year.
Rooms 9 double, 4 single – all with bath, shower, telephone, TV, tea-making facilities; 6 with balcony.
Facilities Residents' lounge, cocktail bar, restaurant. 2-acre grounds with terraced gardens. 3 mins' walk to harbour with fishing, 10 mins to indoor leisure centre; beaches nearby.
Location Near Candie Gardens. 5 mins' walk from town centre. Difficult to find: request map in advance, or telephone for directions on arrival on the island. Private carpark.
Restrictions Not suitable for ♿. No children under 14. No dogs.
Credit cards All major cards accepted.
Terms [1991 rates] Rooms: single £48, double £88–£95. Breakfast: continental £4, English £7. Set lunch £12, dinner (residents only) £18; full alc from £25. 1-night bookings refused Apr–Sep.
Service/tipping: "Service included. Tipping entirely at guests' discretion."

Midhurst House **BUDGET** *Tel* Guernsey (0481) 724391
Candie Road

"We felt very much at home here," writes a recent visitor to Brian and Jan Goodenough's "modest but immaculate hotel" in an elegant Regency townhouse quietly located ten minutes' walk up from the harbour. "Our bedroom had been decorated since our visit the year before, not because it needed doing but because the owners are forward-looking in all they do to make *Midhurst* the best." "Jan is an efficient and unobtrusive host" and is happy to discuss guests' dinner preferences before they set off for the day. "The meal Brian prepared was marvellous." Dinners are four-course (two choices per course) made only from fresh ingredients bought daily at the market. "Drinks in the sitting room at 6.30 pm help to create a friendly atmosphere." A drawback for some is the early dinnertime but for others, Jan Goodenough explains, it is an attraction: the majority of guests are "over 50s" who enjoy a gentle stroll after dinner while it is still light; and many attend concerts, theatres, and so on starting at 8 pm, and this way they are not rushed. Prices are very reasonable. "If Brian is in a good mood, he will take you for a walk and show you some breathtaking views of Guernsey." From all accounts, he usually is. (*HA Ralph, FM Rothwell; also B and E Hoyle, Georgina Woolley, and others*)

Open Easter–mid-Oct.
Rooms 7 double – 2 with bath, 5 with shower, all with telephone, radio, TV, tea-making facilities. 3 in cottage annexe. 4 on ground floor.
Facilities Lounge, dining room. Small garden. Sea 10 mins' walk.

Location 5 mins' walk from town centre, near Candie Museum and Cambridge Park. Limited free lock-up garaging; free public parking nearby.
Restrictions Not suitable for ♿. No smoking in dining room. No children under 8. No dogs.
Credit cards None accepted.
Terms B&B: single £29, double £44–£56. Set meals £7.50. "Taste of Guernsey" breaks in low season. Reduced rates and special meals for children. Doubles let as singles low season only.
Service/tipping: "No service charge. Tipping is not expected. If guests insist this is distributed among staff in proportion to hours worked."

ST SAVIOUR Guernsey — Map 1

La Hougue Fouque Farm BUDGET — *Tel* Guernsey (0481) 64181
Route du Bas Courtil

Readers continue to enjoy this quiet, comfortable family hotel in a converted farmhouse in the centre of Guernsey, surrounded mainly by green fields. It is set in spacious grounds and has a well-maintained pool with tables and umbrellas (sometimes – especially on Friday and Saturday evenings and Sundays – overrun by non-residents). Service is friendly; a few housekeeping lapses were swiftly resolved. Traditional English cooking is generally appreciated; bar lunches come in for special commendation: "The quantity of food was exceptional and the quality very good; we did not exercise enough restraint." Transport from airport or harbour can be arranged. (*Martyn Smith*) More reports please.

Open All year.
Rooms 2 suites, 14 double – all with bath, telephone, radio, TV, tea-making facilities, baby-listening. 2 on ground floor.
Facilities Lounge, bar, restaurant. Pianist Fri and Sat. 4-acre grounds; garden, solar-heated pool. Sandy beach 1 m.
Location In countryside, near small chapel (a famous attraction).
Restriction No dogs.
Credit cards Access, Visa.
Terms [1991 rates] B&B £20–£34; dinner, B&B £28–£42. Set lunch £8.50, dinner £12.00; full alc from £15. Reduced rates for children; special meals.
Service/tipping: "At customers' discretion."

ST SAVIOUR Jersey — Map 1

Longueville Manor — *Tel* Jersey (0534) 25501
Fax (0534) 31613

César award in 1986: The pearl in the Jersey oyster

"Simon Dufty is the most gracious host. I left overfed and cosseted." (*Stephen Holman*) A tribute this year to this mecca among country house hotels in the Channel Islands which stands in large grounds at the foot of its own private wooded valley, one and a half miles inland from Jersey's capital, St Helier. It is well away from the tourist hubbub, and – a plus for golfers – only two and a half miles from the Royal Jersey Golf Club. The setting is sophisticated. The hotel has comfortable sitting-around places including a small, well-chosen library; outside there is a large heated swimming pool where lunch may be taken in fine weather. The bedrooms, individually decorated, are "lovely" and "lavish and comfortable".

The hotel has been run by the Lewis and Dufty families for the past forty years. Its restaurant has enjoyed wide acclaim, and the wine waiters have been praised for being "exceptionally helpful without the snobbery so many seem to affect". Andy Baird, late of *Hambleton Hall* (q.v.), took over as chef last year. Most early reports have been favourable, though one reader thought the food pretentious and overpriced. More reports please.

Open All year.
Rooms 2 suites, 30 double – all with bath (7 also have shower), telephone, radio, TV. 8 on ground floor.
Facilities Lift. 2 lounges, bar, restaurant, library; conference facilities. 16-acre grounds with tennis, swimming pool (heated in season), putting green. Golf, bowls, squash, within easy reach. 1 m from sea with sandy beaches.
Location 1½ m E of St Helier; bus stop near main gates. From airport, take main road to St Helier; near harbour follow sign A17 to Georgetown. Then take A3 for 1 m; hotel is on left.
Restrictions No children under 7. No smoking in part of dining room. No dogs in public rooms.
Credit cards All major cards accepted.
Terms B&B: single £75–£90, double £110–£185, suite £215–£255; dinner, B&B: single £100–£115, double £160–£235, suite £265–£305. Set lunch £19, dinner £27.50; full alc £38. Winter weekend breaks; Christmas/New Year package. Reductions for children sharing parents' room.
Service/tipping: "All prices are inclusive of service."

SARK — Map 1

Petit Champ BUDGET — *Tel* Sark (0481) 832046
Sark, via Guernsey

Pleasant, late 19th-century granite house, owned by Terry Scott and wife, in secluded part of the 3½ m-long, car-less island, well away from day trippers' tracks. Bedrooms centrally heated, most with sea view, but "fairly spartan"; no radio or TV. *Well-tended, sheltered 1-acre garden with solar-heated swimming pool in disused quarry. 10 mins' walk down to bay with sand at low tide – a half-hour climb back. Bring shoes for rock scrambling, torch for exploring caves, binoculars for bird watching, smart evening attire. Open mid-Apr–early Oct. 16 bedrooms, all with bath/shower. Sark unsuitable for ♿. No smoking in dining room and lounge/library. Children must be old enough to sit with parents at dinner. No dogs. All major credit cards accepted. Dinner, B&B £40–£45. New chef appointed as we go to press. Can we have more reports, please?*

Stocks BUDGET — *Tel* Sark (048 183) 2001
Sark, via Guernsey — *Fax* (048 183) 2130

"Extremely friendly and comfortable" old-established hotel in characteristic Sark granite. In centre of island, in Dixcart valley, so ideally placed for exploring. Run by Armorgie family, and praised this year for service by "friendly and helpful staff", and for Paul Armorgie's "exceptionally good" food. Informal style but ties expected in restaurant at dinner. 1-acre grounds with swimming pool, sun terrace; 500 yds from beach. Open Mar–Oct. 24 rooms, all with bath/shower. Sark unsuitable for ♿. No dogs. Access, Visa accepted. Dinner, B&B £30–£40. Reduced rates and special meals for children. Inclusive holiday packages. Was in earlier editions, now re-nominated. More reports please.

Northern Ireland

Glassdrumman House, Annalong

ANNALONG Co Down **Map 6**

Glassdrumman Lodge
85 Mill Road
Annalong BT34 4QN

Tel Annalong (039 67) 68585
Fax (039 67) 67041

Annalong nestles in the shadow of Slieve Binian, one of the most spectacular peaks in the mountains of Mourne – magnificent walking terrain. In the early 1980s Graeme and Joan Hall moved from Belfast to Glassdrumman House and started a farm in this lovely pastoral setting. They learned to cook and bake and tend their herd of Aberdeen Angus cattle. A surplus of produce and an enterprising spirit led to their opening restaurants, a farm shop, a delicatessen and a boutique. Later they bought the *Lodge*, a farmhouse a mile and a half down the road, which they converted to provide accommodation. Bedrooms vary in size, but all have a good view of mountains or sea. "Ours was beautifully furnished to a very high standard with bathroom to match," says a report this year. "A most enjoyable stay, and imagine our delight when we came to leave the next morning and found the car had been washed." There is a library with hundreds of books. Two three-course set dinners, one English, one French, are served at the *Lodge* from Monday to Friday (there are patios for outdoor dining in summer); on Saturday a seven-course set menu, with limited choices, is on offer at the *House*. Meals are eaten communally. One visitor was surprised to find herself sitting down – admittedly at a vast refectory table – with the Revd Ian Paisley and bodyguards. (*Mrs JC Smye*)

Open All year.
Rooms 8 double – all with bath, shower, telephone, TV; nanny available.
Facilities Drawing room, library, 2 dining rooms; conference and office facilities. 8-acre gardens, 35-acre farm, duck pond, tennis court. Reciprocal rights to health and country club, 6 m away. Rocky beach 1 m, safe bathing, sandy beach 8 m.
Location Off A2, 6 m S of Newcastle, 1 m N of Annalong.
Restrictions Not suitable for ♿. No dogs in bedrooms or public rooms (in barns only).
Credit cards Access, Visa.
Terms [1991 rates] B&B: single £45, double £65–£75. Dinner, B&B: single £62.50, double £82.50–£92.50. Set lunch £10, dinner £17.50.
Service/tipping: "At customers' discretion."

COLERAINE Co Londonderry — Map 6

Blackheath House — *Tel* Aghadowey (0265) 868433
112 Killeague Road
Blackhill, Coleraine BT51 4HH

Joe and Margaret Erwin own this late Georgian rectory, set in two acres of landscaped gardens in the midst of a prosperous farming area – "a very peaceful location". *Blackheath House* started life as *Macduff's* restaurant, which continues to have a strong local following; Margaret Erwin has run the kitchen since 1974. The building stands four-square and solid, in a large mature garden with a lily pond. The interior is comfortably cluttered with old furniture, and has the general ambience of restfulness and old-world gentility. Rooms are spacious and well maintained, with flowers, fruit, books, and so on. Dinner is à la carte with plenty of choice and considered excellent value for money. Breakfast is a hearty affair; those not worried about cholesterol can indulge in a monster Ulster Fry. The Causeway coast is just ten miles away (beaches and cliff walks), and there are eight 18-hole and two 9-hole golf courses within twenty minutes' drive. (*Mrs JC Smye*) More reports please.

Open All year except Christmas, New Year. Restaurant closed Sun and Mon.
Rooms 6 double – 2 with bath and shower, 4 with shower, all with telephone, radio, TV, tea-making facilities.
Facilities Residents' lounge and dining room, restaurant with lounge. Indoor swimming pool (heated May–Sep). 2-acre garden. Fishing, shooting, riding, golf nearby; sea 11 m.
Location 4 m N of Garvagh on A29 Killeague road, signposted to left.
Restrictions Not suitable for ♿. No children under 12. No dogs.
Credit cards Access, Visa.
Terms B&B £30. Full alc dinner £20–£22.
Service/tipping: "Tips should not be expected; it is left entirely to the customer. If anyone does tip the money is divided between those who have contributed to the service of that customer."

> In your own interest, always check latest tariffs with hotels when you make your bookings.

DUNADRY Co Antrim **Map 6**

The Dunadry Inn
Dunadry BT41 2HA

Tel Templepatrick (084 94) 32474
Fax (084 94) 33389

Recommended by airline pilot whose job normally confines him to "modern, air-conditioned boxes" of hotels, converted cotton-bleaching factory in large grounds with beautiful gardens, on edge of the Six Mile Water, a good trout and salmon river. Popular venue for functions and conferences. Country Club nearby with heated indoor swimming pool. Bedrooms have pleasant outlook. There's a decent restaurant, a wide variety of bar meals and an excellent afternoon tea: "The Ritz *Northern Ireland style." Very friendly service. Closed Christmas and Boxing Day. 67 rooms, all with bath and shower. No dogs. All major credit cards accepted. 1991 rates: B&B £24–£60. Set lunch £10.75; full alc £20–£25. Children up to 12 free; special meals on request. More reports please.*

Republic of Ireland

Currarevagh House, Oughterard

ADARE Co Limerick — Map 6

Dunraven Arms
Main Street

Tel Limerick (061) 396209
Fax (061) 396541

Warm endorsements for this attractive old inn in a picture-postcard village ten miles from Limerick. "The rooms are fine and the service as ever delightfully Irish. We turned up with a kitten we had adopted and, while they demurred at letting us keep her in our room, they made genuine efforts to solve the problem and she spent two nights in a garage at the home of a waitress." "A delight to stay in. The Irish have the extraordinary ability to welcome you as though it were the hotel's opening day and you their first guest. Only when you get to Ireland do you realise how genuine and (apparently) unforced it is. We were welcomed and waited on with the utmost kindness and warmth. We had a huge, luxurious bedroom with a bathroom to rival that in the Budapest *Hilton.* Most bedrooms look out on to the most beautiful garden." There are lots of outdoor pursuits nearby, particularly golf, fishing and equestrian activities. The hotel has been described as "half the price of

…ers, and twice the fun". (*Tony Price and Angela Lambert, and others*) Reports on the food have been less unanimous.

Open All year; closed to non-residents Good Friday.
Rooms 3 suites, 41 double, 3 single – all with bath and/or shower, telephone, radio, TV. 11 on ground floor.
Facilities Lounge, TV room, library, 2 bars. 3-acre garden; fishing, riding, golf nearby.
Location In village; opposite entrance to Adare Manor.
Restriction Dogs by arrangement.
Credit cards All major cards accepted.
Terms [1991 rates] (Excluding service) Rooms: single IR£35–IR£50, double IR£50–IR£77, suite IR£125. Breakfast: continental IR£4.75, Irish IR£6.75. Set lunch IR£9.50, dinner IR£19.50; full alc IR£24. Christmas and Easter breaks. Reduced rates and special meals for children.
Service/tipping: "Mandatory 12½% service charge added and distributed to all staff."

AGLISH Co Tipperary — Map 6

Ballycormac House **BUDGET**
Aglish, Nr Borrisokane

Tel Nenagh (067) 21129
Fax (0509) 20040

A 300-year-old farmhouse surrounded by gardens and paddocks in peaceful countryside four miles from Lough Derg, *Ballycormac* might be described as a country cottage hotel. It has a small living room, prettily furnished bedrooms that are "comfortably big by contrast", and welcoming open turf fires (also central heating). There is sailing and fishing on the Lough, but the hotel will appeal especially to readers who enjoy riding. The owners, John and Rosetta-Anne Paxman, specialise in half-bred Irish hunting horses and will arrange morning rides or five-star riding packages, from Monday to Friday: two days riding, and full accommodation. A "very good tea is served each afternoon. At 8 pm the guests reassemble for drinks in the same room. The food is cordon bleu, the bread and cakes home-made"; vegetables come out of the organic garden, eggs are free range. In winter, guests come for fox hunting and rough shooting. "The cost is reasonable, and the service good provided guests don't expect it all hours of the day." More reports please.

Open All year except Christmas. Dining room closed for lunch.
Rooms 1 suite, 3 double, 1 single – all with bath, 1 with TV.
Facilities 2 sitting rooms, dining room. 20-acre grounds with garden, paddocks. Sailing, boating, fishing, bird watching nearby; hunting and shooting in winter.
Location 3 m N of Borrisokane: just after Borrisokane take first right turn off Portumna Road, then after 3 m turn left into Aglish village; follow red hotel signs.
Restrictions Not suitable for ♿. Smoking forbidden in bedrooms, discouraged in public rooms. Dogs by arrangement.
Credit cards All major cards accepted.
Terms [1991 rates] B&B IR£19–IR£23. Set dinner IR£16. 50% reduction for children under 12; special meals.
Service/tipping: "We leave it entirely up to our guests. Whatever is left by them, we distribute evenly to all staff."

> Our italicised entries indicate hotels which are worth considering, but which, for various reasons – inadequate information, lack of feedback, ambivalent reports – do not at the moment warrant a full entry. We should particularly welcome comments on these hotels.

BALLINA Co Mayo — Map 6

Mount Falcon Castle — *Tel* Ballina (096) 21172
Fax (096) 21172

"I loved its uniqueness. I wasn't asked to sign in. I didn't get a room key. The delightfully furnished room was the size of a small bungalow. Everything was home-produced, including butter, jam and marmalade. Cora, the wolfhound, takes a little getting used to, but once she has her chair by the fire in the lounge she is very relaxed. Anytime I am in the area, I will stay again." This grey-stone mansion, dating from 1876, lies just south of Ballina in the beautiful wild countryside of County Mayo. It is excellent for fishing, being set in a large estate on the banks of the river Moy, on which it has eight miles of rights. The castle was bought in 1932 by Constance Aldridge and her husband, Major Robert, to entertain their fishing friends and has been run ever since as a country house hotel, grand yet informal. Log fires and fresh flowers greet you in the reception rooms; bedrooms are large and comfortable. In country-house style, dinner is at a fixed time; guests are seated at the long mahogany table with the hostess, now in her eighties, at its head. Menus make use of the best local produce, straightforwardly cooked; there's plenty of local salmon (*Mount Falcon* produces its own excellent gravad lax), local meat and game and vegetables grown on the estate farm. (*Michael Kenefick*) More reports please.

Open 1 Apr–31 Jan. Closed Christmas.
Rooms 9 double, 1 single – all with bath, shower.
Facilities Drawing room, sitting room, dining room. 100-acre grounds with tennis, woodland, pasture, river frontage with fishing; shooting in winter. Riding nearby; golf 10 m.
Location 4 m S of Ballina on Foxford road.
Restrictions Not suitable for ♿. No smoking in dining room.
Credit cards All major cards accepted.
Terms B&B IR£40; half board IR£52.50; full board IR£60. Set dinner IR£16.50. 3 nights min stay June–Oct. Weekly rates; family holidays; reduced rates for children; special meals.
Service/tipping: "10% added to bill."

BALLINDERRY Co Tipperary — Map 6

Gurthalougha House — *Tel* Borrisokane (067) 22080
Ballinderry, Nenagh — *Fax* (067) 22154

"It is decorated with a lot of taste and a little money," was the nominator's verdict in 1986. This is a 19th-century house on the shores of Lough Derg at the end of an avenue which winds for a mile through 150 acres of forest, with woodland walks and a great variety of wildlife: squirrels, badgers, otters, hawks, jays and kingfishers. In the distance are lovely views to the mountains of Clare and Galway. The gentle informality of Michael and Bessie Wilkinson (he the cook, she front of house) has appealed to many readers. Dinners are entirely by candle-light, in a room furnished in the simple elegance of a bygone age; there is a small, daily-changing menu. Bedrooms, some "a bit scruffy at the edges, part of their aristocratic charm", have been described as the sort Lord Peter Wimsey might easily have occupied. "The bathroom (and bath) were easily the largest we've seen anywhere." "The Wilkinsons and their hotel form a slightly idiosyncratic combination, one to which I shall certainly return." (*Esler Crawford, S and W Beresford, and others*)

Open Mar–Nov, New Year.
Rooms 8 double – 6 with bath, 2 with shower, all with telephone.
Facilities Sitting room, library, dining room. 150-acre grounds with forest walks, gardens; ¼ m lakeshore with private quay, safe bathing, boats, ghillie available; windsurfing, pony trekking.
Location On shores of Lough Derg, W of Ballinderry village, which is 16 m N of Nenagh. (Signposted from Borrisokane.)
Restrictions Not suitable for ♿. No small children or dogs in dining room.
Credit cards Access, Amex, Visa.
Terms B&B IR£29–IR£35. Set dinner IR£21. Weekend breaks. 33% reduction for children under 10; high teas.
Service/tipping: "Service included. Tipping at guests' discretion."

BALLYLICKEY Co Cork — Map 6

Ballylickey Manor House — *Tel* Bantry (027) 50071
Ballylickey, Bantry Bay — *Fax* (027) 50124

Built some 300 years ago by Lord Kenmare as a shooting lodge, and the home of the Franco-Irish Graves family for four generations, the *Manor House* retains many picturesque old features, despite having been gutted by fire ten years ago, and is furnished with lovely antiques and paintings. There is a sea view from the first floor. The gardens are well tended, with mature trees, hedges, dahlia and rose beds; and there is a croquet lawn. Reception rooms in the main building are "splendid, with log fires and handsome draperies". "Mrs Graves is French and has brought with her a lot of French touches, which are reflected in everything from the patchwork murals to embroidered sheets in the bedrooms." "Our bedroom was enchanting with clever use of fabrics, and plenty of magazines." In winter, meals are taken in the "gorgeous green dining room"; in summer, "guests have to scrunch their way down the drive to the poolside restaurant, which is somewhat Mediterranean in feel, with Limoges plates which are totally in keeping with the French atmosphere". Food is "good and interesting, using local produce, and with great attention to detail". The wine list is "strong on French wines, and expensive". "Staff were most helpful; we arrived unwell, and a simple dinner was prepared and served in our room." (*Francine Walsh, Martin King*) Breakfast, however, was said to be "not particularly generous, with *ordinary* orange juice, overcooked scrambled egg and undercooked toast; but with good jam and marmalade, and coffee". Readmitted after a seven-year interval.

Open End Mar–Nov.
Rooms 5 suites, 6 double – all with bath, shower, telephone, TV, baby-listening. 7 in garden cottages. Some on ground floor.
Facilities 3 drawing rooms, bar, 2 dining rooms. 10 acre garden; heated outdoor swimming pool; private salmon and trout fishing. Sea 500 yds (unsuitable for swimming).
Location On main road between Bantry and Glengariff.
Restrictions Dogs by arrangement, "if they don't fight with owners' dogs"; not in public rooms.
Credit cards Access, Visa accepted.
Terms (Excluding 10% service charge) B&B: single IR£73, double IR£77, suite IR£110–IR£130. Set dinner IR£20.50; full alc IR£25–IR£28. Reduced rates for

children on application; special meals.
Service/tipping: "We prefer to have a service charge so that those behind the scene receive their part."

Sea View House *Tel* Bantry (027) 50073 and 50462
Ballylickey, Bantry Bay *Fax* (027) 51555

"The hotel has been transformed from, effectively, a very superior guest house with good food to a 'proper' hotel with aspirations to 'grand' food. Usually extensions mean disaster, but here more has *not* meant worse. All the redecoration is in excellent taste. Everything gleams." One endorsement among many for Kathleen O'Sullivan's friendly, unpretentious, comfortable hotel set in five-acre grounds near Bantry, with good views over Bantry Bay and distant mountains. It is a very personal establishment; readers comment on the "efficiency, skill and personality" of the hostess, as well as the "unfailingly courteous and helpful staff", the value for money and the food. "Excellent soups; fresh and juicy fish and shellfish dishes; vegetables *al dente*; delicious tarts and Pavlovas; good value wine." Buffet breakfasts are generous with an endless list of hot and cold choices. Packed lunches are available, and tea and cakes in the afternoon. (*R Creed, John and Helen Wright, Francine Walsh, and others*) A couple of gripes: one reader felt that the menu had become over-ambitious, with too free a hand with the cream; and a new ground-floor bedroom was somewhat exposed to public view.

Open Mid-Mar–mid-Nov.
Rooms 17 double – all with bath and/or shower, telephone, baby-listening; TV, tea-making facilities on request. Some in cottage in garden. 1 on ground floor.
Facilities Lounge, TV room, cocktail bar, 2 dining rooms. 5-acre grounds. Fishing, boating, beaches, golf nearby.
Location 3 m N of Bantry towards Glengarriff, 70 yds off main road.
Restriction No dogs in public rooms.
Credit cards Access, Amex, Visa.
Terms (Excluding 10% service charge) B&B IR£27.50–IR£35; dinner, B&B IR£40–IR£50. Set lunch IR£12, dinner IR£19. Midweek and weekend breaks. Reduced rates and special meals for children.
Service/tipping: "10% service charge is added in lieu of gratuities; our clients prefer this as it ensures a more equitable distribution."

BALLYMOTE Co Sligo — Map 6

Temple House *Tel* Sligo (071) 83329
Ballymote

A Georgian mansion in 1,000 acres of farmland and woods overlooking Temple House lake (excellent for coarse fishing) and the ruins of the castle built by the Knights Templar in 1200 AD; it has been the home of the Percevals for more than three centuries. There are two sitting rooms with open fires; and five bedrooms, all with central heating and electric blankets. "The bedrooms and public rooms are magnificent – far better than any top London hotel; but don't expect London service. Mrs Perceval cooks and serves the food. Only 12 persons can stay at one time, and everyone sits around one large dining table. It was like being invited to a dinner party each night, never knowing who the other guests would be. Boats are available for hire on the lake, and children's rods may be borrowed. It remained light until 11 pm, so fishing was possible after dinner – a wonderful way to relax. The most beautiful place I have stayed at for years." (*ML Dodd*) The garden is run organically with particular attention to conservation; on Tuesdays there are "special treats for serious music lovers". More reports welcome.

Open Easter–30 Nov.
Rooms 4 double, 1 single – all with bath and/or shower.
Facilities 2 sitting rooms, dining room. Formal terraced garden. 1,000-acre farm and woodlands, lake; coarse fishing, boating.
Location Ballymote is 14 m S of Sligo; once there, ask for directions to hotel at Esso Garage.
Restrictions Not suitable for ♿. No dogs.
Credit cards Amex, Visa.
Terms B&B IR£30–IR£34; dinner, B&B IR£46–IR£50. Set dinner IR£16. Midweek and weekend breaks. Reductions for long stays. Reduced rates for children sharing parents' room; special meals on request.
Service/tipping: "Service charge not added. Tips not expected, but occasionally offered, and much appreciated."

BALLYVAUGHAN Co Clare — Map 6

Gregans Castle

Tel Ennis (065) 77005
Fax (065) 77111

"The setting is stunning, particularly if you have one of the rooms with a view towards Galway Bay (well worth asking for)." "Most helpful hosts, most relaxing decor; our suite with its own patio was delightful." Peter and Moira Haden's country house hotel is in the heart of the Burren, an area roughly halfway between Galway and Shannon airport, full of rare flowers and plants (alpine and arctic), and a paradise for botanists and ornithologists. It is also rich in historic and prehistoric remains, and Yeats and Lady Gregory lived nearby. A new wing of bedrooms and suites was added last year. Visitors appreciate the comfortable accommodation, the "well-tended garden with most pleasing planting", the good service and friendly staff. The beds are firm, the bathrooms spotless, and "there are plenty of places to sit in after dinner". In the library there is "an interesting selection of books including a history of the Papacy in umpteen volumes, Chekhov short stories, and books about millionaires". Most readers appreciate the cooking, with occasional reservations. (*Richard Creed, Lord Evans of Claughton, Mrs L Hill; also John and Helen Wright, Mrs G Dundas*)

Open Apr–late Oct.
Rooms 4 suites, 18 double – all with bath (21 also have shower), telephone. 7 on ground floor.
Facilities Hall, lounge, library, bar, dining room. 12-acre grounds with parkland, gardens, ornamental lake, croquet. Safe, sandy beach 4½ m; harbour with swimming and boating 3½ m.
Location On N67 between Ballyvaughan and Lisdoonvarna, 3½ m SW of village, at foot of Corkscrew Hill.
Restriction No smoking in restaurant. No dogs.
Credit cards Access, Visa.
Terms [1991 rates] (Excluding 12½% service charge) B&B: single IR£65, double IR£84–IR£110, suite IR£140. Set dinner IR£22. Half-board rates for 3 or more nights. Reduced rates for children; special meals on request.

BANTRY Co Cork — Map 6

Bantry House

Tel Bantry (027) 50047
Fax (027) 51417

César award in 1991: Best bed-and-breakfast – Irish style

In a spectacular setting overlooking Bantry Bay and the Caha mountains is a grand classical Irish country house, open to the public but offering accommodation in two newly decorated wings. It is owned by Mr and Mrs Shelswell-White; he is a direct descendant of Richard White, first Earl of Bantry, and in between answering the door to visitors, he rushes off to a quiet corner to play his trombone. It entered our pages with an inspector's high praise: "The house is magnificently situated overlooking the water. Dark blue gates set into a high stone wall flanked by lodges are all that can be seen from the road. When one arrives there is not a great deal of available service or 'human contact', but one is constantly aware of the thought and care behind the operation." Guests have the use of a separate sitting room, billiard room, dining room and television room, and also free access to the main rooms of the house, including its library with fine period furniture, tapestries and family portraits. "The bedrooms are pretty, warm and comfortable. Requests are dealt with promptly and kindly. There's a lovely new breakfast room." The countryside surrounding Bantry is delightful, and nearby are small cheese-makers, good little restaurants, and the studios and workshops of artists and potters. It is a great area for sailing and water sports, "a trifle more chilly than the Mediterranean, but much cleaner". *Bantry House* now provides dinners to residents by arrangement at 7 pm on weekdays in the summer months. We would welcome reports on these.

Open All year except Christmas day.
Rooms 1 suite, 8 double – all with bath/shower, telephone, tea-making facilities.
Facilities Sitting room, billiard room, dining room, TV room. Occasional concerts in library. 20-acre grounds, near sea. Sandy beach ½ m.
Location ½ m from centre, towards Cork; signposted on Inner Harbour wall.
Restrictions Not suitable for ♿. Dogs in grounds only.
Credit cards Access, Amex, Visa.
Terms [1991 rates] B&B IR£35–IR£45. Set dinner IR£18–IR£20. Wine licence only. Reductions for 5 days or more and for groups booking all rooms. Reduced rates and special meals for children.
Service/tipping: "Bills state that service is not included."

BIRR Co Offaly — Map 6

Tullanisk
Birr

Tel Birr (0509) 20572
Fax (0509) 20572

Promising new enterprise in 18th-century dower house in wooded grounds of Earl of Rosse's Birr Castle estate whose famous gardens guests can visit without charge. "Friendly and convivial" hosts Susan and George Gossip have installed their own antique furniture, china and pictures in the elegant rooms. 4/5-course dinners, warmly recommended, taken communally at 8 pm; no menu and no choice, but preferences discussed when booking. Good choice of wines. 5-acre gardens with croquet; shooting, hunting, riding, fishing on estate. Children welcome. Closed 22–27 Dec, 2–13 Feb. 7 bedrooms, 5 with bath. Smoking forbidden in restaurant, discouraged in bedrooms. No dogs. Access, Visa accepted. 1991 rates: B&B: single IR£37, double IR£60; dinner, B&B: single IR£53.50, double IR£93. Set dinner IR£17.50. New nomination. More reports please.

CASTLEBALDWIN Co Sligo — Map 6

Cromleach Lodge
Castlebaldwin, Nr Boyle

Tel Sligo (071) 65155
Fax (071) 65455

Admired for its superb setting on a hillside above lovely Lough Arrow, this country house hotel offers spreading vistas with hardly a house in sight – rural Ireland at its best. Here an ambitious local couple, Christy and Moira Tighe, have enlarged their own home into a sophisticated guest house. The welcome is warm; service is friendly and efficient; cooking is serious and professional. Good-sized bedrooms, all with south-facing views. "Excellent quality breakfast", served on unusual Rosenthal china, includes good home-made wheaten bread and preserves. "Unbelievable value." (*Rosemary Reeves, Mr and Mrs RL Jackson*) Some find the decor in the bar/lounge and bedrooms over-ornate, and the piped mealtime music irritating.

Open All year except 24/25 Dec.
Rooms 10 double, 2 single (suitable only for children) – all with bath and/or shower, telephone, tea-making facilities.
Facilities 2 lounges, dining room, private dining room, conservatory. 1-acre garden. Private access to Lough Arrow; boating, surfing. Hotel can arrange fishing, walking, hill climbing and archaeology trips.
Location 10 m N of Boyle, off N4 Dublin–Sligo road. Turn E at Castlebaldwin.
Restrictions Not suitable for ♿. No smoking in dining room, 1 lounge, 5 bedrooms. No dogs.
Credit cards Access, Amex, Visa.
Terms [1991 rates] B&B IR£52–IR£62; dinner, B&B IR£73–IR£83. Set dinner IR£23–IR£28. Reduced rates for children sharing parents' room; special meals before 7 pm.
Service/tipping: "No service charge. Tipping at guests' discretion. All tips are shared among staff."

CASTLEKNOCK Co Dublin — Map 6

Avondale House
Scribblestown, Castleknock
Dublin 15

Tel Dublin (01) 386545
Fax (01) 539099

New to the Guide, on the banks of the river Tolka, an early 18th-century former hunting and fishing lodge on the Earl of Granard's estate, now offering country house accommodation, set in parkland, but only three miles from the centre of Dublin, overlooking Phoenix Park. "An utter joy. Nicely idiosyncratic in that it has just three rooms, but what rooms! Frank and Josie Carroll have installed real and semi-real antiques in this gorgeous Georgian house, with a wonderful sense of colour and humour. The bedroom was spectacular – ecclesiastical with Gothic touches, plus a king-sized bed of supreme comfort; the bathroom was piled high with soft towels. The food at dinner and breakfast was excellent." (*Angela Lambert and Tony Price*)

Open 5 Jan–22 Dec.
Rooms 2 double, 1 single – all with shower.
Facilities Drawing room, dining room. In park; river with fishing, 18-hole pitch and putt.
Location 3½ m N of Dublin. From Phoenix Park by Ashdown Gate, cross N3 (Navan Road) and River Road, then go through first set of gates (lodge on right).
Restrictions Not suitable for ♿. No dogs.
Credit cards None accepted.
Terms B&B: single IR£40, double IR£56. Set dinner IR£18. Reduced rates and special meals for children.

CLONES Co Monaghan — Map 6

Hilton Park — *Tel* Monaghan (047) 56007
Scothouse, Clones — *Fax* (047) 56033

Set in 600 acres of parkland, including a golf course, three lakes and many lovely views, this mansion, the family home of eight generations of the Madden family, was dropped from the Guide last year because of lack of feedback. Comments this year, however, confirm earlier reports of Johnny and Lucy Madden's stylishly informal hospitality, house-party style. They serve traditional Irish cooking and the quality of the food, many of the ingredients for which come from their own organic gardens, "alone warrants a visit". Accommodation "is gracious to the point of being unforgettable, although they may not have spent millions of pounds doing it up". One American reader was so taken with what he describes as his "all-time favorite accommodation in Ireland", that he is planning a return trip, in order to pick up a cotton robe that he inadvertently left behind. (*B Scott-McCarthy, and others*) More reports please.

Open Easter–30 Sep.
Rooms 3 suites, 2 doubles – all with bath, tea-making facilities.
Facilities 3 drawing rooms, restaurant, TV room. 600 acres of parkland, 3 lakes, golf course. Tennis, fishing and riding available.
Location 3 m S of Clones, on Ballyhaise Road; gates ¼ m before golf club.
Restrictions Not suitable for ♿. No dogs.
Credit cards Amex, Visa accepted.
Terms B&B IR£35–IR£42. Set dinner IR£18.50. 1 dressing room that could accommodate a child (IR£25); special meals for children by request. Shooting parties in winter, by arrangement.
Service/tipping: "We leave it to our guests' discretion and hope for the best."

CORK Co Cork — Map 6

Arbutus Lodge — *Tel* Cork (021) 501237
Montenotte — *Fax* (021) 502893

"Beautiful views, a wonderful restaurant, and the true hospitality of a warm Irish family." One reader's recent commendation of *Arbutus Lodge*, once the home of the Lord Mayor of Cork, and now run by the Ryan family: father, mother, two sons and their wives. It is named for the arbutus tree in its prize-winning garden, which has many rare trees and shrubs. The house is in the posh suburb of Montenotte, fifteen minutes' walk or five minutes' drive from the centre of town. It was built about 1800, a master cooper's house, and some rooms still reflect the solid virtues of its origins. Others, in the modern extension grafted on either side of the main building, are "more functional than beautiful". There was criticism, last year, both of decor and room maintenance, but the owners tell us that redecoration and renovation has been undertaken. The candle-lit restaurant is spacious, with starched white tablecloths and fresh flowers; it has a large bay window giving a view of the city and river below. Michael Ryan serves fine Irish meat and seafood, and offers a "tasting menu" (six courses *plus* sorbet and coffee) as well.

Open All year except 24–30 Dec. Restaurant closed Sun (bar meals available).
Rooms 11 double, 9 single – all with bath and/or shower, telephone, radio, TV, tea-making facilities, baby-listening.
Facilities 2 lounges, bar, restaurant. ½-acre garden with patio and croquet.
Location 1½ m up hill from town centre. Parking.
Restrictions Not suitable for ♿. No dogs.
Credit cards All major cards accepted.
Terms [1991 rates] B&B: single IR£30–IR£75, double IR£60–IR£105. Set lunch IR£15.75, dinner IR£19.75; full alc IR£30. Weekend rates; gourmet weekends. Reduced rates and special meals for children.
Service/tipping: "At guests' discretion, only if service is special."

DINGLE Co Kerry — Map 6

Doyle's Townhouse — *Tel* Tralee (066) 51174
John Street — *Fax* (066) 51816

The little fishing port of Dingle, in the far Gaelic-speaking south-west, is a natural centre for exploring the beautiful Dingle peninsula, with its fine local crafts, and the nearby Blasket islands. Up till now, however, it has lacked a Guide-worthy place to stay, though it has had, in Doyle's Seafood Bar, a long-established and admirable restaurant, one of only a dozen in Ireland to win a *Michelin* red "M". Now, John and Stella Doyle have opened the house next door as a small hotel, and it makes its Guide debut with early visitors all speaking warmly of its character and hospitality. There's a downstairs sitting room, furnished nostalgically in the style of a traditional Irish small-town hotel, and eight attractive bedrooms with brass bedsteads, antique furniture and good fabrics, with marble-tiled bathrooms *en suite*. (*Helen Anthony, and others*)

Open Mid-Mar–mid-Nov. Restaurant closed Sun.
Rooms 8 double – all with bath, shower, telephone, radio, TV. 2 on ground floor.
Facilities Sitting room, small public bar, restaurant. Sea angling, golf, horse riding, windsurfing nearby.
Location Town centre.
Restrictions No smoking in restaurant. No dogs.
Credit cards Access, Diners, Visa.
Terms [1991 rates] (Excluding service charge) B&B IR£27.50–IR£35. Full alc IR£22.50. Special rates for children sharing parents' room; "small portions for little people".
Service/tipping: "Mandatory 10% service charge added. No tips expected."

> The success of this guide in North America has led to sister publications on American and Canadian hotels based on the same principles. Readers with recent experience of good hotels in North America are urged to send their nominations to Sandra W Soule, America's Wonderful Little Hotels and Inns, PO Box 150, Riverside Avenue, Riverside, Conn. 06878, USA.

DUBLIN — Map 6

Kilronan House
70 Adelaide Road
Dublin 2

Tel Dublin (01) 755266
and 751562
Fax (01) 782841

Recommended as "excellent little guest house in an expensive city. Well run, immaculate housekeeping and peaceful ambience." Extensively refurbished in 1991. Within walking distance of Dublin's most famous landmarks. Closed 24 Dec–1 Jan. Not suitable for ♿. Smoking in top-floor bedrooms only. 11 bedrooms, 4 with bath/shower. Access, Visa accepted. B&B: single IR£30–IR£38, double IR£50–IR£60. Only breakfast served. Was in earlier editions, now re-nominated. More reports please.

DUNLAVIN Co Wicklow — Map 6

Rathsallagh House

Tel Naas (045) 53112
Fax (045) 53343

"We adored it. It is grand without being fancy, and as near as I have ever been to staying in someone's gracious, pleasant home without the nuisance that this can cause." (*Paul Palmer*) The latest encomium for Kay and Joe O'Flynn's "very grand" country house in huge grounds 35 miles from Dublin in the heart of racing country – "a betting-slip toss from three leading racecourses". "It's a long block of converted Queen Anne stable buildings surrounded by untold acres of lawns, croquet, golf, with a gurgling brook somewhere nearby, and sheep and horses everywhere, close enough to see, far enough not to disturb. Kay O'Flynn cooks, wonderfully; Joe runs the large farm and co-hosts at night." There are twelve guest rooms, "warm and of extreme luxury", each with a "generous bathroom with a huge tub and bath sheets rather than towels; cupboards galore, tea trays, bookshelves – with the right books. Dinner, after pour-yourself drinks in the drawing room, was four courses of delicate joy. At night the beds were made ready and, as we seemed in need of coddling, hot-water bottles inserted to help us sleep. In the morning, after a dip in the indoor solar-heated swimming pool, an Irish breakfast awaits – freshly baked breads, rolls, toast, home-made jams, eggs, black pudding, sausages and perfect bacon." The atmosphere is said to be welcoming and "tranquil except perhaps on the nights of the local hunt meeting" – *Rathsallagh* is a good base for hunting with some of Ireland's leading packs, and horses may be hired.

Open All year.
Rooms 8 double, 4 single – all with bath (7 also have shower), telephone, tea-making facilities; TV on request. 4 in courtyard. 2 on ground floor.
Facilities Drawing room, sitting room, dining room, bar, conference room; billiard room, indoor heated swimming pool. 500-acre grounds with tennis, croquet, golf academy, pheasant and clay-pigeon shooting, hunting.
Location 2 m SW of Dunlavin.
Restrictions No smoking in sitting room. No children under 12. No dogs in bedrooms or public rooms.
Credit cards Access, Diners, Visa.
Terms B&B IR£65–IR£85; dinner, B&B IR£90–IR£110. Set dinner IR£25. Weekend and midweek breaks; house-party rates.
Service/tipping: "No service charge; we feel it should be up to the guest. If he feels he has been taken care of in a special way, his tip is distributed among all staff."

GOREY Co Wexford — Map 6

Marlfield House — *Tel* Gorey (055) 21124
Courtown Road — *Fax* (055) 21572

"Lovely, lovely house in gorgeous grounds. Absolutely dazzling entrance hall with exceptionally smart antique furniture, pillars, spectacular flower displays, water singing in the gold fishponds on either side of the front door." The former dower house of the Courtown estate, a noble three-storey Regency house in large grounds with a lovely garden, tennis and croquet, is now Ray and Mary Bowe's sophisticated country house hotel. "The bedrooms are superb, with antiques, dramatic wallpapers and curtains, hand-embroidered sheets and real lace pillows; lovely bathrooms with an abundance of towels, bathrobes, generous toiletries, potted plants." Six sumptuous suites, each with a different theme – Irish, Georgian, French, etc – and a marble fireplace and large marble bathroom, are in a new wing "which blends in perfectly". Breakfasts are "good, plentiful and very fresh". *Michelin* awards a red "M" for the quality of the "modern French" cooking, using local produce and home-grown vegetables and herbs, served in the dining conservatory which is "pure fantasy, full of greenery and mirrors, with enormous hanging baskets of geraniums". Service, by a "welcoming and highly competent" staff, is fast and efficient. And *Marlfield House* is in a choice position, a mile from the sea with sandy beaches, close to a golf course, and with plenty of the beauty spots of County Wicklow at hand. (*Francine Walsh*) Next year the Bowes promise a lake and wildfowl reserve.

Open All year except Dec.
Rooms 7 suites, 12 double – all with bath, shower, telephone, TV; tea-making facilities, baby-listening on request. Some on ground floor.
Facilities Reception hall, drawing room, library/bar, conservatory/restaurant. 36-acre grounds with tennis, croquet. Sea with sandy beaches, safe bathing 1 m.
Location 1 m from Gorey on the Courtown road.
Restrictions Smoking discouraged in dining room and some public rooms, forbidden in bedrooms. No dogs.
Credit cards All major cards accepted.
Terms [1991 rates] B&B: single IR£65–IR£120, double IR£115–IR£125, suite IR£165–IR£375. Set lunch IR£17, dinner IR£28. Weekend and midweek reductions off-season. Reduced rates and high teas for children on request. *Service/tipping: "10% service included; tipping discouraged."*

KANTURK Co Cork — Map 6

Assolas Country House — *Tel* Kanturk (029) 50015
Fax (029) 50795

"The exterior of the house, with its little river, weir and mini-island (on which a fellow guest took refuge to practise her vocal scales), is enchanting and photogenic. The interior is homely, rather than plush, and original, but not artistic; things are there because the owners like them." So reads a 1991 report on this small, elegant 17th-century manor house, set in beautiful grounds, which has been the home of the Bourke family for more than seventy years, and a hotel for the past quarter century. "A truly beautiful and peaceful hotel. You are welcomed into the family home and you feel like an old friend." Bedrooms and bathrooms are basic and old-world, but there is ample wardrobe space. Dinner is simple but well cooked; there are some fine wines. "Service in the dining room was perfect and effortless." Joe Bourke has taken over the day-to-day running of the hotel from his parents; his wife, Hazel, is the chef. Everything denotes care and good housekeeping – from the raked gravel *outside* the gate, to the polished furniture in the public rooms, and the sparkling glass and damask napkins in the dining room. The house is well proportioned, with white paint and green creepers. (*Francine Walsh, Martin King, Nichola Arditti*)

Open Mid-Mar–1 Nov.
Rooms 9 double – all with bath, shower (3 have whirlpool), telephone, radio. 3 in courtyard building.
Facilities Hall, drawing room, dining room, private dining room. 10-acre grounds with gardens, tennis, croquet; river with boating and trout fishing. Salmon fishing and golf nearby.
Location 3½ m NE of Kanturk; turn off road towards Buttevant.
Restrictions Not suitable for ♿. No dogs in bedrooms or public rooms.
Credit cards Diners, Visa.
Terms B&B: single IR£50–IR£60, double IR£80–IR£140; dinner, B&B: single IR£76–IR£83, double IR£135–IR£195. Set dinner IR£26. 1-night bookings refused for high season if made in advance. Reduced rates for children sharing parents' room; special meals by prior arrangement.
Service/tipping: "Our prices are fully inclusive and tipping is actively discouraged; but if guests insist on showing appreciation in this way the money is shared by all staff."

KENMARE Co Kerry — Map 6

Hawthorn House BUDGET — *Tel* Killarney (064) 41035
Shelbourne Street

"If you wish to eat the best breakfast in the land, if you wish to be treated with kindness and consideration in surroundings of spotless cleanliness, and all for a very modest outlay, *Hawthorn House* is the place for you." Ann Browne's reasonably priced B&B has frilly decor, but "it is run superbly. Enormous thought has gone into the rooms. Fruit and chocolate biscuits await you; there are nice magazines, paperbacks and books on the birds and flora of Ireland. We had drinks in the little sitting room where everyone was introduced. A party of young Dutchmen were directed to a good 'singing pub'; others went to a restaurant. I'm glad we chose the small breakfast plate: a regular one consisted of six rashers of bacon, three sausages and an egg, all of good quality and perfectly cooked. It is a wonderful base in a charming little town, with magnificent scenery all around." The restaurant has been closed, but there is a good choice of eating places in town. (*Dr Law Bellamy, and others*)

Open All year except Feb, and 3 days Christmas.
Rooms 7 double, 1 single – 2 with bath, 6 with shower.
Facilities Lounge, breakfast room.
Location In town centre (opposite PO), but quiet. Parking.
Restrictions Not suitable for ♿. No dogs.
Credit cards None accepted.
Terms B&B: single IR£20–IR£35, double IR£34–IR£40. (No restaurant.)
Service/tipping: "Service included. Tips not expected."

Park Hotel Kenmare *Tel* Killarney (064) 41200
Fax (064) 41402

One of Ireland's grandest country house hotels set in immaculate parkland and with beautiful views of the Kenmare estuary and the mountains of west Cork. A report this year gives the hotel the thumbs-up, though with two reservations. "Our room, on the fourth floor, was gorgeous: elevated bed, instant ancestors above, smart antiques, display cabinets with lovely china, plenty of lights, totally quiet – the highlight of our tour. Bathrooms, also with interesting prints, are large and modern, with marble floor, luxurious towels, bathrobes and generous toiletries, which are renewed evening and morning. Chambermaids are pleasant and chatty. The dining room is huge and noisy. Service is prompt and considerate, but waiters fly in and out of swing doors, and the parquet floor does not help to muffle their footsteps. Dinner was accompanied by music from a noisy, thumpy harpist one night, a classical guitarist the other. A lady plays the piano and sings in the bar – anything from *Molly Malone* to *Je ne regrette rien*. A lot of cheerful Irish singing ensues. Cooking is fair to good; there is a tendency to cook things 'well done'. Nice salmon, competent sweets, cheese comes ready plated, mostly French. Satisfactory wine list, with bottles from all over the world, and the recommendations from the maître were knowledgeable and good. Breakfast was a mixed pleasure with wishy-washy porridge, genuine orange juice, good scrambled egg with salmon and an excellent selection of breads and rolls. Management is pleasant and courteous; porters carry; information is readily given. We would thoroughly recommend the place. Pity about the noisy dining room." (*Francine and Ian Walsh*)

Open 23 Dec–3 Jan, Easter–mid-Nov.
Rooms 9 suites, 37 double, 3 single – all with bath, shower, telephone, radio, TV, baby-listening. Some on ground floor.
Facilities Ramps, lift. Drawing room, cocktail lounge, TV room, restaurant. 11-acre grounds with tennis, golf, croquet. Rock beach, safe bathing, fishing 5 mins' walk.
Location 60 m west of Cork, adjacent to village. Signposted.
Restriction No dogs.
Credit cards Access, Visa.
Terms B&B: single IR£105–IR£120, double IR£190–IR£240; dinner, B&B: single IR£140–IR£155, double IR£260–IR£310, suite IR£360–IR£430. Set lunch IR£17.50, dinner IR£38; full alc IR£49–IR£55. Christmas and New Year programmes. Reduced rates for children sharing parents' room; special meals.
Service/tipping: "Tips at guests' discretion."

KILLEAGH Co Cork Map 6

Ballymakeigh House **BUDGET** *Tel* Youghal (024) 95184
Killeagh

250-year-old family farmhouse/guest house in rich farmlands of E Cork, run by Margaret Browne, voted Ireland's "Housewife of the Year 1990". Nominator writes: "Everything shows signs of care, from Friesian herd, to pretty house, tennis court and conservatory. Food very good, too." Traditional Irish breakfasts, freshly baked soda bread and home-made jams. Golf, horse riding, sea angling nearby. Restaurant open weekends only off-season. 6 bedrooms, all with bath/shower. Not suitable for ♿. No smoking in bedrooms. No dogs in house. No credit cards accepted. B&B IR£16–IR£24; dinner, B&B IR£30–

IR£38. 50% reduction for children sharing parents' room. Cooking courses in winter. New nomination. More reports please.

LETTERFRACK Co Galway **Map 6**

Rosleague Manor *Tel* Letterfrack (095) 41101
Letterfrack, Connemara *Fax* (095) 41168

A Regency house in twenty-acre grounds seven miles north of Clifden, overlooking a sheltered bay surrounded by mountains and forests. Visitors this year warmly endorse this recent report: "A five-star recommendation: I came for three days away from urban, pre-packaged supermarket living. It could not have answered the demand better – about the only thing that comes from a package here is cornflakes. The food is virtually one hundred percent home-grown or locally caught, with fish at the top of the bill. The wines are notably cheaper than in other Irish hotels of this standard. But the real quality of *Rosleague* lies in the atmosphere. The first thing you notice is that there is not a TV to be seen; the second is that there is not a clock in sight: no one is reminded of the passing of time, the Marschallin in *Rosenkavalier* would have loved it. She might even have gone into the bar and met the locals." Well situated for walks in Connemara National Park, the hotel is also recommended for the view: "I could see eleven mountains from my bedroom without craning my neck." Patrick and Anne Foyle, brother and sister, are warm and friendly hosts: "They welcomed my 70-year-old parents, who had arrived chilled to the bone and luggage-less from a delayed flight. Patrick turned up the heat in the room with the canopied bed, offered whiskies, and laid on sandwiches next to the fire in the lounge an hour later – smoked salmon and smoked chicken. A beautiful 'old house' feel about the place." A visitor from France writes: "L'attention de Madame Anne Foyle et de Monsieur Paddy Foyle mérite une citation particulière." (*John Higgins, MM Marlowe, M. and Mme Fournel, and others*) One reader mentioned "rather geriatric flowers" and suggested that more frequent opening of windows might help release the smell of stale tobacco.

Open Easter–Nov.
Rooms 20 rooms – all with bath and/or shower, telephone. 2 on ground floor.
Facilities Drawing room, sitting room, conservatory, dining room; billiard room/library. 20-acre grounds, tennis, path to water's edge (no beach).
Location 7 m N of Clifden, on the road to Leenaun/Westport.
Restrictions No smoking in dining room. Dogs by arrangement in bedrooms, not in public rooms.
Credit cards Access, Visa.
Terms [1991 rates] B&B IR£30–IR£75; dinner, B&B IR£51.50–IR£81.50. Set dinner IR£21.50; full alc IR£20. Off-season weekend breaks. Reduced rates and special meals for children.
Service/tipping: "Strictly at discretion of guests."

****

Traveller's tale *The plates for the steaks were cold. On being told this the waitress (one of the owners) said, "Chefs simply won't heat plates this damp," and walked off.*

****

MOUNTRATH Co Laois — Map 6

Roundwood House *Tel* Portlaoise (0502) 32120
Fax (0502) 32711

César award in 1990: Outstanding Irish hospitality

Readers continue to pull out all the stops in praise of Frank and Rosemarie Kennan's fine Palladian house – "an architectural gem" – which stands in large grounds in the shadow of the unspoilt and beautiful Slieve Bloom mountains. "Everything was quite delightful and almost without fault. Warm welcome; all very relaxed; wandered among the budding trees and the daffodils; had a word with the St Bernard and the cock, who does his bit at dawn. Had the most delicious dinner and, after lazy rising, a breakfast of home cereals, fresh juice, porridge, super tasty fry, fresh brown griddle-scones and assorted home-made preserves. Left and thought all day how nice it had been, and returned pleading to be taken in again at 6 pm." "Frank Kennan gets the prize for the most congenial host and his wife deserves a prize for being a most wonderful cook, with that rare quality, flair." "I was bowled over. A great sense of effortless hospitality overwhelms you as soon as you set foot in the place." (*Eithne Scallan, Anne Hilb; also John and Jan Sparrow, Sir Andrew Armstrong*)

Open All year.
Rooms 2 suites, 6 double – 6 with bath, 2 with shower, all with baby-listening. 2 in old house attached to main building.
Facilities Drawing room, library, dining room. 18-acre grounds with croquet, swings, stables. Golf, river fishing nearby.
Location N7 from Dublin to Limerick. At Mountrath turn right at T-junction, then left on to Kinnitty Road. Proceed 3 m exactly.
Restrictions Not suitable for ♿. No dogs in bedrooms or public rooms.
Credit cards All major cards accepted.
Terms B&B: single IR£29–IR£35, double IR£58, suite IR£110. Dinner, B&B IR£47–IR£53 per person. Set Sun lunch IR£10, dinner IR£18. Reduced rates for children sharing parents' room; special meals.
Service/tipping: "No service charge. Full profit-sharing system in operation so no tipping necessary."

MOYARD Co Galway — Map 6

Crocnaraw *Tel* Clifden (095) 41068
Moyard, Connemara

Lucy Fretwell's Georgian country house on the shores of Ballinakill Bay is set in twenty acres of prize-winning gardens and fields with fine views: "Among the most restful and therapeutic I know." There are good beaches, fishing and golf nearby. *Crocnaraw* is "not a hotel in the accepted sense. It is slightly frayed around the edges, and full of character, all odd shapes, nooks and crannies. The decor has not changed for years; it is a relaxed combination of old and new chairs, different colours, woven rugs, etc, creating a sense of individual taste far removed from the interior designer. The dining room is simple and airy with plain wooden floor and wooden furnishings." Most bedrooms overlook the garden and the mountains beyond and are large and light, with a spacious bathroom. Readers have liked the whole effect, but refurbishment is now said to be overdue in some areas, food is variable, and the grounds less well maintained. "But it is still a very special oasis, and good value for the price." More reports please.

Open Apr–Oct.
Rooms 6 double, 2 single – 6 with bath (1 also has shower). 1 on ground floor.
Facilities Dawing room, sitting room, dining room. 20-acre grounds with gardens, lake, woodland. Golf, fishing, sandy beaches nearby.
Location 6 m N of Clifden on road to Westport.
Restrictions No dogs in public rooms. No children under 10.
Credit cards Access, Diners, Visa.
Terms [1991 rates] B&B IR£27–IR£35; dinner, B&B IR£45–IR£53. Set lunch IR£12, dinner IR£20. Reduced rates for children sharing parents' room.
Service/tipping: "Service at guests' discretion."

OUGHTERARD Co Galway — Map 6

Currarevagh House

Tel Galway (091) 82312
Fax (091) 82313

César award: The quintessence of Irish hospitality

"'Punctuality will be appreciated', says a notice in the bedroom and, sure enough, a gong sounds and everyone troops in to dinner on the stroke of 8 pm. If that sounds like regimentation, it is nothing of the kind. It is a unique cocktail of slightly quaint formality and obliging and cheerful hospitality, in which everything works admirably." With the atmosphere of a bygone age, this mid-Victorian country house is in a "blissfully quiet setting" in huge grounds on the banks of Lough Corrib and offers some of the best scenery and fishing in Ireland. Readers continue to praise the capacious beds, splendid bathroom fittings, Edwardian furniture and good home-cooking, including a lavish help-yourself breakfast. *Currarevagh* (pronounced curra-reeva) has been in the Hodgson family for five generations; it is now run by Harry Hodgson and his wife, June, who, writes a regular, "are friendly and helpful, and a mine of information about the locality". "Because it lacks formal elegance and designer stylishness, it is comfortable and relaxing. The no-choice country-house-style menu may disappoint some, but for us not to have to make decisions except about wine, and to know what to expect on a Friday, is a relief. Dinner is generally a roast with all the trimmings and second helpings are always available. Gradually over the years the meat has got rarer (when appropriate) and the vegetables crisper and more imaginative. The starters and desserts are light in touch." Another reader felt the dinners were slightly uninteresting "but this was forgiven as the breakfasts and afternoon teas were *so* good". (*A O'Dowd, Valerie Watson, Sara A Price; also HF King, Clare Fletcher*)

Open Apr–Oct. By arrangement other times for parties of 8 or more (except Christmas and New Year). Lunch by arrangement, for residents only.
Rooms 13 double, 2 single – 13 with bath, 2 with shower. 3 on ground floor in mews.
Facilities Drawing room, sitting room, library, bar, dining room. 150-acre grounds with lakeshore fishing (ghillie available), boating, swimming, tennis, croquet. Golf, riding nearby.
Location 4 m NW of Oughterard on Lakeshore road.
Restrictions Not ideal for ♿. No smoking in dining room. Children under 12 by arrangement. Dogs by arrangement, only on lead in public rooms.

Credit cards None accepted.
Terms B&B: single IR£37–IR£52, double IR£74. Set dinner IR£16.80. Full-board rates (min 3 days); weekly rates. 1-night bookings sometimes refused for high season if booked too far ahead. Reduced rates for children sharing parents' room; special meals by arrangement.
Service/tipping: "10% added for service and divided among all staff. Our problem used to be that front staff received tips (some quite large) and kitchen staff received nothing. Guests are asked not to tip individual members of staff."

RATHMULLAN Co Donegal — Map 6

Rathmullan House — *Tel* Letterkenny (074) 58188
Rathmullan, Letterkenny — *Fax* (074) 58200

Early 19th-century country house in dramatic setting by Lough Swilly. Wheeler family offers well-furnished accommodation, "100% cotton sheets" in bedrooms, friendly and attentive service and "excellent food, well cooked, with much variety"; buffet-style breakfasts especially praised. "Particularly attractive pavilion-style dining room, with silk-draped ceiling and lovely views. Indoor heated saltwater swimming pool, sauna, steamroom. 4-acre grounds with flower gardens, tennis. 50 metres from sandy beach. Open 15 Mar–22 Oct. 23 bedrooms, 21 with bath/shower. Not suitable for ♿. No smoking in restaurant. No dogs. All major credit cards accepted. B&B from IR£32.50; dinner, B&B IR£52. Set lunch IR£11.50, dinner IR£18.50. Was in earlier editions, now re-nominated. More reports please.

RATHNEW Co Wicklow — Map 6

Hunter's BUDGET — *Tel* Wicklow (0404) 40106
Newrathbridge — *Fax* (0404) 40338

One of Ireland's oldest coaching inns, of "exquisite simplicity", has been in the Gelletlie family since 1825 and is now owned and run by Maureen Gelletlie. "Little has changed in the last quarter century except that a few more of the rooms have 'facilities' and the window frames rattle less than they did. Outside is a rambling garden with appropriately rambling roses, running down to a stream. Tea and whiskey are served throughout the day, usually jointly. A coal fire always burns in the diminutive bar. Food is copious – no hint of the *nouvelle* here – and fish is especially good. Don't expect a key to your bedroom. The old, honest style rules here." "Excellent; polite staff, perfect food and service, very clean." (*John Higgins, Jan Morris, Andrew Reeves*) One reader was less enthusiastic about the hotel's bygone charms, complaining of poor heating and imperfect housekeeping in his room.

Open All year. House guests only over Christmas/New Year.
Rooms 13 double, 4 single – 10 with bath and shower, all with telephone, tea-making facilities. 1 on ground floor.
Facilities Lounge, TV room, bar, dining room. 5-acre gardens by river; fishing. Golf, tennis, riding, sea fishing nearby.
Location 28 m S of Dublin. Turn off N11 Dublin–Wexford at Ashford.
Restriction Dogs by arrangement; not in public rooms.
Credit cards All major cards accepted.
Terms [1991 rates] B&B IR£30–IR£35. Set lunch IR£12, dinner IR£18.50. Reduced rates and special meals for children by arrangement. 1-night bookings refused for some bank holiday weekends.
Service/tipping: "No service charge; tipping at guests' discretion."

Tinakilly House *Tel* Wicklow (0404) 69274
Rathnew *Fax* (0404) 67806

"This stately home stands in delightful wooded grounds and as you enter the hall you immediately sense a warmth of welcome, enhanced by the lovely furnishings," writes one reader about this grey-stone mansion of monumental splendour, with views to the sea a quarter-mile away. It offers old-fashioned opulence – golden chandeliers and sconces, polished dark wood, rococo fireplaces, softly upholstered formal sofas and chairs, red carpets, potted plants, and a magpie miscellany of glittering bric-à-brac. The rooms, including the bedrooms, some of which have four-poster beds of imperial dimensions, are large and high-ceilinged with tall windows. The splendour originated with Captain Robert Halpin, one-time commander of Brunel's *Great Eastern* who, in his retirement, constructed this remarkable building and its bosky pleasure gardens. The present owner, William Power, is a knowledgeable hotelier and "controls a happy team". "The staff, without exception, were most cheerful and willing. The food and the imaginative menus were quite exceptional." (*Capt. R Hart, AE Jeckel*)

Open All year.
Rooms 16 suites, 13 double – all with bath and/or shower (4 have whirlpool bath), telephone, radio, TV, tea-making facilities. 5 on ground floor.
Facilities Hall, bar, residents' lounge, 3 dining rooms; conference facilities. 7-acre grounds, tennis court. Golf and bird sanctuary nearby.
Location From Dublin on N11, go through Rathnew village on R750. House signposted on left after about ¼ m.
Restrictions No smoking in restaurant. No dogs.
Credit cards All major cards accepted.
Terms B&B: single IR£70–IR£80, double IR£90–IR£140, suite IR£120–IR£200. Set lunch IR£17.50, dinner IR£27. Off-season breaks, Christmas programme. 1-night bookings refused Sat, Christmas, New Year. Reduced rates and special meals for children.
Service/tipping: "From 1 January 1992, there will be no service charge and tips will not be expected."

RIVERSTOWN Co Sligo Map 6

Coopershill *Tel* Sligo (071) 65108
Riverstown *Fax* (071) 65466

César award in 1987: Outstanding Irish hospitality

"I have stayed in country houses amateurishly trying to be hotels and in hotels professionally trying to be country houses. This is a real country house, tranquil and unspoiled but with nothing amateurish about the way it is run. Both bedrooms and public rooms are capacious and give the small number of guests space to feel at home." "Upon driving up to the house, we were entertained by the working sheepdogs who were moving a herd of sheep from one pasture to another. It was truly a sight to behold. Lindy and Brian O'Hara are wonderful hosts, and greeted us with warmth and charm. Dinner was excellent and the rooms spacious and well appointed." So begin two reports this year on this grey-stone family mansion in the heart of Yeats country. It stands in a spectacular position, with the Bricklieve mountains and vast peat bogs to the south, and the town of Sligo and the sea to the north. Many readers have endorsed an earlier report: "One of the grand houses built by the landed Anglo-Irish families in the 18th century. It is situated in a huge estate and in complete silence. The rooms are tall and gracious and the furniture old-fashioned (five bedrooms have four-poster or canopied beds). Do not expect a smart hotel – this is the home of an old Irish family in which you are a welcome guest." The O'Haras "are unobtrusive yet totally attentive to everyone's needs". "Their hospitality was just right, and I wish we had stayed longer." For those who do, there are many delightful walks and wildlife is abundant. (*A O'Dowd, Tatiana Maxwell; also Prof. L Rees, and others*)

Open Mid-Mar–31 Oct. Out-of-season house parties by arrangement.
Rooms 7 double – all with bath and/or shower, telephone, tea-making facilities.
Facilities 2 halls, drawing room with TV and piano, dining room; table-tennis room. 500-acre grounds with garden, woods, farmland, river with coarse fishing. Trout fishing, sandy beach, championship golf course nearby.
Location At Drumfin crossroads, 11 m S of Sligo on N4, turn to Riverstown. *Coopershill* signposted from Drumfin.
Restrictions Not suitable for ♿. Smoking in drawing room only. No dogs in house.
Credit cards All major cards accepted.
Terms B&B IR£38–IR£45; dinner, B&B IR£56–IR£64. Light lunch IR£5; set dinner IR£19. Reductions for stays of 3 nights or more. 50–75% reduction for children under 12 sharing parents' room; special meals on request.
Service/tipping: "If guests wish to leave a tip, the money is distributed among the staff."

ROSEMOUNT Co Westmeath — Map 6

Coolatore House BUDGET — *Tel* Athlone (0902) 36102
Rosemount, Moate

On slopes of Knochastia, reputed centre of Ireland, rambling Victorian home offering "private rather than hotel-style accommodation" in centre of 12-acre arboretum. Drawing room and library with antiques and family heirlooms. Recommended for beautiful furnishings, "simple but decent dinner" (no choice, taken with other guests), modest terms. Fox hunting and lake fishing (coarse and game) arranged. Advance bookings only. 4 rooms (1 en suite, others with bathrooms nearby). Not suitable for ♿. No children. No dogs in public rooms. Credit cards not accepted. B&B: IR£25–IR£30. Set dinner IR£18. Recent nomination. More reports please.

SCHULL Co Cork — Map 6

Ard na Greine — *Tel* Skibbereen (028) 28181
Fax (028) 28573

1 m W of village, Frank and Rhona O'Sullivan's country house, with Ireland's first Elektro wind generator for heating and hot water, overlooking Fastnet Rock lighthouse, sea and mountains. Was in earlier Guide editions, now re-nominated for "comfortable accommodation, superlative food – seafood at its best and tender steaks – efficient and cheerful service". Open Easter–1 Nov. 6 bedrooms, all with bath/shower. No children under 12. No dogs. All major cards accepted. Dinner, B&B IR£37.50–IR£62.50. Pub lunch; set dinner IR£18.50. Can we have more reports please?

> If you think we have over-praised a hotel or done it an injustice, please let us know.

SHANAGARRY Co Cork — Map

Ballymaloe House
Shanagarry, Nr Midleton

Tel Cork (021) 652531
Fax (021) 652021

César award in 1984: For generating house-party conviviality

"Our expectations were high and we were not disappointed. A truly delightful place, very un-hotel-like; the lack of plushness was refreshing." "As good as ever; restful, excellent food; Sunday supper is out of this world." Two of many similar reports, received this year, about *Ballymaloe*'s hospitality, its comfortable if a bit shabby rooms, the "admirable amalgam of friendliness and formality", the wonderful meals – "the selection of hors d'oeuvre such as I have never seen before, and the most perfect ice-cream I have ever eaten", "the very distinguished wine list", etc, etc. Visitors return, year after year, to Myrtle and Ivan Allen's gracious, rambling hotel, more Georgian than anything else, with a Norman keep on one side and relatively modern pink-washed cottages on the other. Decor is restrained and unfrilly, but the walls are full of Ivan Allen's "modern, vivid and very covetable" picture collection. The bedrooms vary in size; most are quite large. "My room was more a suite than a bedroom: large bathroom with fresh large warm towels each day, six-foot bed large enough for three and supplied in expectation with six pillows, large sofa, ample drawer and cupboard space." Close to the house lies a 400-acre farm; and three miles beyond is the charming little fishing port of Ballycotton. Virtually everything you eat, apart from the fish, is home-grown or raised on the Allens' farm. "The grounds are delightful, complete with small lake and canoe, and flower-bordered stream with bridges crossing it which are perfect for playing 'Pooh sticks'. Children of all ages seem to pop up everywhere from nowhere." *Ballymaloe* is an exceptionally convivial house, with nearly all the extended Allen family contributing to the special quality of its hospitality. (*NM Mackintosh, Sir Andrew Armstrong, IT Glendinning, Mrs Jean Dundas, John Higgins, Mrs JC Smye, Mel Calman*)

Open All year except Christmas.
Rooms 28 double, 2 single – all with bath and/or shower, telephone, baby-listening by arrangement. 12 in courtyard, 4 on ground floor suitable for ♿.
Facilities 3 sitting rooms, 5 inter-connecting dining rooms, TV room. 500-acre farm and grounds with tennis, heated swimming pool, 6-hole golf course, croquet, children's play area; craft shop. Ballymaloe Cookery School and herb garden nearby. Sea 3 m, with safe sand and rock beaches; fishing, riding by arrangement.
Location 20 m E of Cork; 2 m E of Cloyne on Ballycotton road, L35.
Restriction No dogs in public rooms, nor in some bedrooms.
Credit cards All major cards accepted.
Terms B&B IR£44–IR£74; dinner, B&B IR£77–IR£104. Set lunch IR£15, dinner IR£30. Winter bargain breaks. Reduced rates for children sharing parents' room; special meals.
Service/tipping: "We have dropped the mandatory service charge. If guests wish they may leave a tip with the receptionist to go into the kitty for all the staff."

> Always let a hotel know if you have to cancel a booking, whether you have paid a deposit or not. Hotels lose thousands of pounds and dollars from "no-shows".

Co Wexford **Map 6**

Newbay Country House *Tel* (053) 22779
Wexford *Fax* (053) 24318

No hotel but a family-run house, 2 m W of Wexford, owned by Paul and Mientje Drum, incorporating 14th-century castle and 17th-century farmhouse, "furnished with hand-me-downs and some excellent antiques". Recommended for "originality of decor", warm welcome, good food, "quaffable" house wine. Communal dinner served to residents only. Breakfast highly commended: eggs from their hens, good soda bread, first-class home-made jams; Mrs Drum makes a delicious Dutch pancake. Extensive grounds with farmyard animals and peacocks. Handy for Rosslare ferry (9 m). Open 17 Mar–15 Nov. Dining room closed Sun and Mon. 6 bedrooms, all with bath/shower. Not suitable for ♿. No children 2–10. No dogs. Access, Visa accepted. B&B IR£24–IR£30. Set dinner IR£16. New nomination. More reports please.

WICKLOW Co Wicklow **Map 6**

Knockrobin Country House *Tel* Wicklow (0404) 69421
Fax (0404) 69420

1830s country house, ½ m N of town, approached by rhododendron-lined avenue, secluded in woods and next to bird reserve along marshes. Personal possessions and pictures give it family home atmosphere. Visitors from Colorado were taken with the "lovingly and individually decorated bedrooms" and the cooking: seasonal game, freshly caught fish; specialities include 19th-century recipes from owner Alison Andrew's grandmother. Vegetarians catered for. 10-acre grounds, clay-pigeon shooting, croquet; fishing nearby. Open Mar–31 Jan. Restaurant closed to non-residents Mon. 2 suites, 3 doubles, all with bath/shower. Not suitable for ♿. No dogs in house. Access, Diners, Visa accepted. 1991 rates: B&B IR£35–IR£40. Set lunch IR£12.50, dinner IR£19. New nomination. More reports please.

The Old Rectory *Tel* Wicklow (0404) 67048
Fax (0404) 69181

Paul and Linda Saunders's Victorian house in one-acre landscaped grounds is in the heart of the beautiful Wicklow countryside, close to many showplace houses. It was in earlier editions of the Guide but was dropped due to lack of feedback. It is restored following enthusiastic reports from recent visitors. "A delightful house. An outstanding dinner cooked by Linda Saunders, immaculate housekeeping." Bedrooms, which vary in size, are individually designed, "a bit fussy and overly Victorian" for some, but "well furnished with many useful extras, very comfortable". The table d'hôte menu changes daily; there is always a vegetarian choice. "Dinners were quite an experience; no-choice menus but each well balanced, interesting and beautifully presented. We were impressed by Linda's imaginative use of ingredients, and their freshness and their novelty – and we liked the general atmosphere of relaxed informality." (*Tatiana Maxwell, John and Helen Wright, and others*)

Open Easter–mid-Oct.
Rooms 5 double – all with bath and/or shower, telephone, radio, TV, tea-making facilities.
Facilities Lounge, cocktail lounge, restaurant. 1-acre grounds.
Location Just off route N11, ⅓ m from centre of Wicklow town on Dublin side.
Restrictions Not suitable for ♿. No smoking in restaurant. Guide dogs only.
Credit cards All major cards accepted.
Terms B&B: single IR£55, double IR£78; dinner, B&B: single IR£78, double IR£124. Set dinner IR£23. Heritage gardens, hill-walking packages. Reduced rates and special meals for children.
Service/tipping: "Service is an integral part of your visit. Tips are not expected, but if guests feel that they have received above-average attention and wish to leave something, they are welcome to."

Alphabetical list of hotels

England

Abbey Penzance 142
Abbey Court London 109
Academy London 110
Alston Hall Holbeton 91
Amerdale House Arncliffe 5
Angel Bury St Edmunds 42
Archway Windermere 202
Arundell Arms Lifton 107
Ashfield House Grassington 75
Ashwick House Dulverton 63
At the Sign of the Angel Lacock 100
Athenaeum London 110
Audley House Bath 13
Austins Aldeburgh 2
Aynsome Manor Cartmel 46
Barnsdale Lodge Rutland Water 150
Basil Street London 111
Bath Place Oxford 140
Beach House Seahouses 161
Beamish House Alnwick 149
Beaufort London 112
Beetle and Wedge Moulsford-on-Thames 133
Bel Alp House Haytor 87
Bell Inn Aston Clinton 7
Bibury Court Bibury 22
Bishopstrow House Warminster 194
Black Lion Long Melford 124
Blakeney Blakeney 24
Blakes London 112
Bond's Hotel and Restaurant Castle Cary 48
Boscundle Manor St Austell 153
Bourne Eau House Bourne 30
Bovey House Beer 20
Bowlish House Shepton Mallet 163
Bradford Old Windmill Bradford-on-Avon 31
Breamish House Powburn 147
Bridgefield House Spark Bridge 169
Brockencote Hall Chaddesley Corbett 48
Brookdale House North Huish 138
Brunel's Tunnel House Saltford 159
Budock Vean Budock Vean 41
Bulstone Branscombe 34
Burgh Island Bigbury-on-Sea 23
Burleigh Court Minchinhampton 132
Calcot Manor Tetbury 182
Callow Hall Ashbourne 6
Capital London 114
Casterbridge Dorchester 61
Castle Taunton 180
Cavendish Baslow 11
Chapel House Atherstone 8
Charingworth Manor Charingworth 51
Chedington Court Chedington 52
Chelwood House Chelwood 53
Chewton Glen New Milton 136
Chilvester Hill House Calne 43
Church House Grittleton 79
Cliveden Taplow 179
Clos du Roy Box 31
Collin House Broadway 38
Combe House Holford 92
Congham Hall Grimston 78
Connaught London 114
Coppleridge Motcombe 133
Cotswold House Chipping Campden 55
Cotswold House Oxford 140
Cottage in the Wood Malvern Wells 128
Crantock Bay Crantock 58
Crosby Lodge Crosby-on-Eden 59
Crouchers Bottom Chichester 53
Crown Blockley 26
Crudwell Court Crudwell 60
D'Isney Place Lincoln 107
Danescombe Valley Calstock 44
Devonshire Arms Bolton Abbey 26
Dove Brighton 37
Downhayes Spreyton 169
Draycott London 115
Durrants London 115
Eagle House Bathford 17
Ebury Court London 116
Egerton House London 117

Elms Abberley 1
Esseborne Manor Hurstbourne Tarrant 95
Evesham Evesham 68
Fallowfields Kingston Bagpuize 98
Farlam Hall Brampton 34
Farmhouse Lew 106
Farthings Hatch Beauchamp 83
Feathers Ludlow 126
Feathers Woodstock 205
Feldon House Lower Brailes 125
Fenja London 118
Fischer's at Baslow Hall Baslow 12
Flitwick Manor Flitwick 70
Fosse Farmhouse Nettleton 136
Frog Street Farm Beercrocombe 21
Gabriel Court Stoke Gabriel 173
Garrack St Ives 155
George Dorchester-upon-Thames 62
George Stamford 171
Gidleigh Park Chagford 49
Glebe Farm Diddlebury 61
Gonville Cambridge 44
Gore London 118
Goring London 119
Grafton Manor Bromsgrove 39
Grange Liverpool 109
Grange York 206
Gravetye Manor East Grinstead 65
Great House Lavenham 103
Grinkle Park Easington 64
Hambleton Hall Hambleton 79
Harrop Fold Bolton-by-Bowland 26
Hartwell House Aylesbury 9
Hassop Hall Hassop 81
Hawnby Hawnby 86
Haydon House Bath 14
Hazel Bank Rosthwaite 150
Hazlitt's London 119
Heddon's Gate Heddon's Mouth 88
Hell Bay Bryher 40
Highbullen Chittlehamholt 56
Highfield House Hawkshead 85
Hintlesham Hall Hintlesham 89
Hobbits York 207
Holbeck Ghyll Windermere 202
Holdfast Cottage Welland 199
Holne Chase Ashburton 7
Hope End Ledbury 105
Horn of Plenty Gulworthy 79
Howe Villa Richmond 149
Howtown Ullswater 189
Hunts Tor House Drewsteignton 62
Huntsham Court Huntsham 94
Hurstone Waterrow 198
Island Tresco 187
Ivy House Braithwaite 33
Jeake's House Rye 151
Kirkby Fleetham Hall Kirkby Fleetham 99
Knightsbridge Green London 120
L'Hotel London 121
La Belle Alliance Blandford Forum 25
Lake Isle Uppingham 191
Langley House Langley Marsh 102
Lansdowne Leamington Spa 104
Lastingham Grange Lastingham 103
Le Manoir aux Quat'Saisons Great Milton 76
Leeming House Watermillock 196
Lindeth Fell Bowness-on-Windermere 30
Little Barwick House Barwick 10
Little Hemingfold Farmhouse Battle 19
Little Hodgeham Bethersden 21
Lodge Huddersfield 93
Lodore Swiss Keswick 97
Long House Great Langdale 76
Look Out Branscombe 35
Lord Crewe Arms Blanchland 24
Lovelady Shield Alston 3
Lower Pitt Restaurant East Buckland 65
Lugger Portloe 145
Lydgate House Postbridge 146
Lynton House Holdenby 91
Maiden Newton House Maiden Newton 128
Mains Hall Little Singleton 108
Mallory Court Bishop's Tachbrook 23
Manor Farm Barn Taynton 181
Manor House Walkington 193
Mansion House Poole 144
Marina Fowey 71
Marine Salcombe 159
Marlborough Ipswich 95
McCoy's Staddlebridge 170
Meudon Mawnan Smith 130
Middlethorpe Hall York 207
Milford House Bakewell 10
Mill Mungrisdale 135
Mill End Sandy Park 160
Miller's House Middleham 131
Millstream Bosham 29
Monkey Island Bray-on-Thames 36
Morston Hall Morston 133
Mortal Man Troutbeck 187
Mount Royale York 208

Museum Farnham 70
Nanscawen House St Blazey 154
Nansidwell Mawnan Smith 131
Nare Veryan 192
Netherfield Place Battle 20
New Inn Tresco 186
Northcote Manor Langho 101
Northill House Horton 93
Northleigh House Hatton 83
Number Sixteen London 121
Nuthurst Grange Hockley Heath 90
Oaklands House South Petherton 167
Old Beams Waterhouses 196
Old Church Watermillock 197
Old Cloth Hall Cranbrook 58
Old Farmhouse Lower Swell 125
Old Farmhouse Raskelf 148
Old Hall Jervaulx 96
Old Manor Trowbridge 188
Old Millfloor Trebarwith Strand 185
Old Parsonage Oxford 141
Old Rectory Campsea Ashe 45
Old Rectory Great Snoring 77
Old Rectory Hopesay 92
Old Vicarage Rye 152
Old Vicarage Witherslack 204
Orchard Bathford 18
Otley House Otley 139
Ounce House Bury St Edmunds 42
Paradise House Bath 15
Parrock Head Slaidburn 164
Peacock Farm Redmile 149
Pear Tree at Purton Purton 148
Pencraig Court Pencraig 142
Penmere Manor Falmouth 69
Pheasant Harome 80
Pheasant Inn Bassenthwaite Lake 13
Plumber Manor Sturminster Newton 177
Polurrian Mullion 134
Pool Court Pool-in-Wharfedale 143
Port Gaverne Port Gaverne 145
Portobello London 122
Priory Wareham 193
Prospect Hill Kirkoswald 99
Queensberry Bath 15
Ram Jam Inn Stretton 176
Reeds Poughill 146
Riber Hall Matlock 129
Rising Sun Lynmouth 127
Rose-in-Vale St Agnes 152
Rothay Manor Ambleside 3
Rough Close Hawkshead 86
Ruskin Harrogate 81
Ryecroft Wooler 206
St Martin's St Martin's 157
Seafood Restaurant Padstow 141
Seatoller House Borrowdale 28
Seaview Seaview 162
Sharrow Bay Ullswater 190
Simonstone Hall Hawes 84
Slepe Hall St Ives 155
Soar Mill Cove Soar Mill Cove 165
Somerset House Bath 16
Stapleford Park Stapleford 172
Star Castle St Mary's 158
Starr Great Dunmow 75
Steppes Ullingswick 188
Stock Hill House Gillingham 73
Ston Easton Park Ston Easton 173
Stonor Arms Stonor 174
Stratford House Stratford-on-Avon 175
Strattons Swaffham 178
Suffolk House Chichester 54
Sugarswell Farm Shenington 162
Summer Lodge Evershot 67
Swan Southwold 167
Swinside Lodge Newlands 137
Swiss Cottage London 123
Swynford Paddocks Six Mile Bottom 164
Sydney Gardens Bath 17
Talland Bay Talland-by-Looe 178
Tanyard Boughton Monchelsea 29
Tarr Steps Hawkridge 84
Thomas Luny House Teignmouth 182
Thornbury Castle Thornbury 183
Thornworthy House Chagford 50
Thruxted Oast Canterbury 46
Topps Brighton 38
Tregildry Gillan 72
Treglos Constantine Bay 57
Tregony House Tregony 185
Tudor Rose King's Lynn 98
Uplands Cartmel 47
Upper Court Kemerton 97
Upper Green Farm Towersey 184
Wallett's Court West Cliffe 199
Wasdale Head Inn Wasdale Head 195
Wateredge Ambleside 4
Weaver's Haworth 87
Well House St Keyne 156
Wharton Lodge Weston under Penyard 199
Whatley Manor Easton Grey 67
Whipper-In Oakham 139
White House Williton 201

White Moss House Grasmere 74
Whitechapel Manor South Molton 166
Whiteleaf at Croyde Croyde 59
Whitfield House Goathland 74
Wilbraham London 123
Willington Hall Willington 200
Winterbourne Bonchurch 27
Winteringham Fields Winteringham 203
Woodhayes Whimple 200
Woodmans Arms Auberge Hastingleigh 82
Woolley Grange Bradford-on-Avon 32

Wales

Bodysgallen Hall Llandudno 214
Cnapan Newport 221
Crown at Whitebrook Whitebrook 226
Dolmelynllyn Hall Ganllwyd 213
Fairyhill Reynoldston 223
Gliffaes Crickhowell 211
Hafod House Trefriw 226
Hafod Lodge Cwmystwyth 212
Lake Llangammarch Wells 216
Lake Vyrnwy Llanwddyn 218
Llangoed Hall Llyswen 219
Maes-y-Neuadd Talsarnau 224
Minffordd Talyllyn 225
Old Rectory Llansanffraid Glan Conwy 217
Pen-y-Gwryd Nantgwynant 220
Penhelig Arms Aberdovey 209
Plas Bodegroes Pwllheli 223
Porth Tocyn Riverside Abersoch 210
Portmeirion Portmeirion 222
St Tudno Llandudno 215
Three Cocks Three Cocks 225
Tyddyn Llan Llandrillo 214
Tŷ Isaf Llanfachreth 216
Tŷ Mawr Brechfa 211
West Usk Lighthouse Newport 221
Ynyshir Hall Eglwysfach 212

Scotland

Airds Port Appin 264
Allt-nan-Ros Onich 261
Altnaharrie Ullapool 274
Ard-Na-Coille Newtonmore 261
Ardvasar Ardvasar 232
Argyll Iona 252
Auchen Castle Beattock 235
Baile-na-Cille Timsgarry 272
Balcary Bay Auchencairn 232
Banchory Lodge Banchory 234
Beechwood Moffat 258
Brook Linn Callander 239
Bunchrew House Bunchrew 237
Burrastow House Walls 275
Busta House Busta 238
Ceilidh Place Ullapool 274
Clifton House Nairn 260
Columba House Kingussie 257
Cozac Lodge Glen Cannich 249
Creebridge House Newton Stewart 260
Crinan Crinan 241
Cringletie House Peebles 263
Cromlix House Kinbuck 256
Darroch Learg Ballater 233
Dower House Muir of Ord 259
Dunain Park Inverness 251
Enmore Dunoon 243
Factor's House Fort William 247
Farleyer House Aberfeldy 229
Forss House Forss 246
Glencripesdale House Glencripesdale 249
Glenfeochan House Kilmore 256
Glenview Culnaknock 242
Harlosh House Dunvegan 244
Haven Plockton 263
Hill of Burns Creetown 240
Holly Tree Kentallen 253
Inverlochy Castle Fort William 247
Invery House Banchory 234
Isle of Barra Tangusdale Beach 271
Isle of Colonsay Colonsay 240
Isle of Eriska Eriska 246
Kenmore Kenmore 253
Kilcamb Lodge Strontian 270
Kildrummy Castle Kildrummy 254
Kilfinan Kilfinan 254
Killiecrankie Killiecrankie 255
Kinloch Castle Rhum 267
Kinloch House Blairgowrie 236
Kinnaird Dunkeld 243
Knipoch Knipoch 258
Knockinaam Lodge Portpatrick 265
Loch Melfort Arduaine 231
Mansion House Elgin 245
Medwyn House West Linton 276
Merkister Harray Loch 251
Minmore House Glenlivet 250
Murrayshall Scone 268
28 Northumberland Street Edinburgh 244

Old Manse of Marnoch Bridge of Marnoch 237
One Devonshire Gardens Glasgow 248
Peat Inn Peat Inn 262
Philipburn House Selkirk 269
Polmaily House Drumnadrochit 242
Riverside Inn Canonbie 239
Scarista House Scarista 268
Shieldhill Quothquan 266
Sibbet House Edinburgh 245
Summer Isles Achiltibuie 230
Tigh An Eilean Shieldaig 270
Tiroran House Tiroran 273
Viewfield House Portree 265

Channel Islands

Château La Chaire Rozel Bay 278
La Frégate St Peter Port 279
La Hougue Fouque Farm St Saviour 281
Le Couperon de Rozel Rozel Bay 279
Longueville Manor St Saviour 281
Midhurst House St Peter Port 280
Petit Champ Sark 282
Stocks Sark 282
White House Herm 277

Northern Ireland

Blackheath House Coleraine 284
Dunadry Inn Dunadry 285
Glassdrumman Lodge Annalong 283

Republic of Ireland

Arbutus Lodge Cork 295
Ard na Greine Schull 306
Assolas Country House Kanturk 298
Avondale House Castleknock 294
Ballycormac House Aglish 288
Ballylickey Manor House Ballylickey 290
Ballymakeigh House Killeagh 300
Ballymaloe House Shanagarry 307
Bantry House Bantry 293
Coolatore House Rosemount 306
Coopershill Riverstown 305
Crocnaraw Moyard 302
Cromleach Lodge Castlebaldwin 294
Currarevagh House Oughterard 303
Doyle's Townhouse Dingle 296
Dunraven Arms Adare 287
Gregans Castle Ballyvaughan 292
Gurthalougha House Ballinderry 289
Hawthorn House Kenmare 299
Hilton Park Clones 295
Hunter's Rathnew 304
Kilronan House Dublin 297
Knockrobin Country House Wicklow 308
Marlfield House Gorey 298
Mount Falcon Castle Ballina 289
Newbay Country House Wexford 308
Old Rectory Wicklow 308
Park Kenmare Kenmare 300
Rathmullan House Rathmullan 304
Rathsallagh House Dunlavin 297
Rosleague Manor Letterfrack 301
Roundwood House Mountrath 302
Sea View House Ballylickey 291
Temple House Ballymote 291
Tinakilly House Rathnew 305
Tullanisk Birr 293

Maps

1 South-West England and South Wales
2 Wessex and the Cotswolds
3 South-East England
4 North Wales, the Midlands and the North of England
5 Scotland
6 Ireland

British Isles Maps

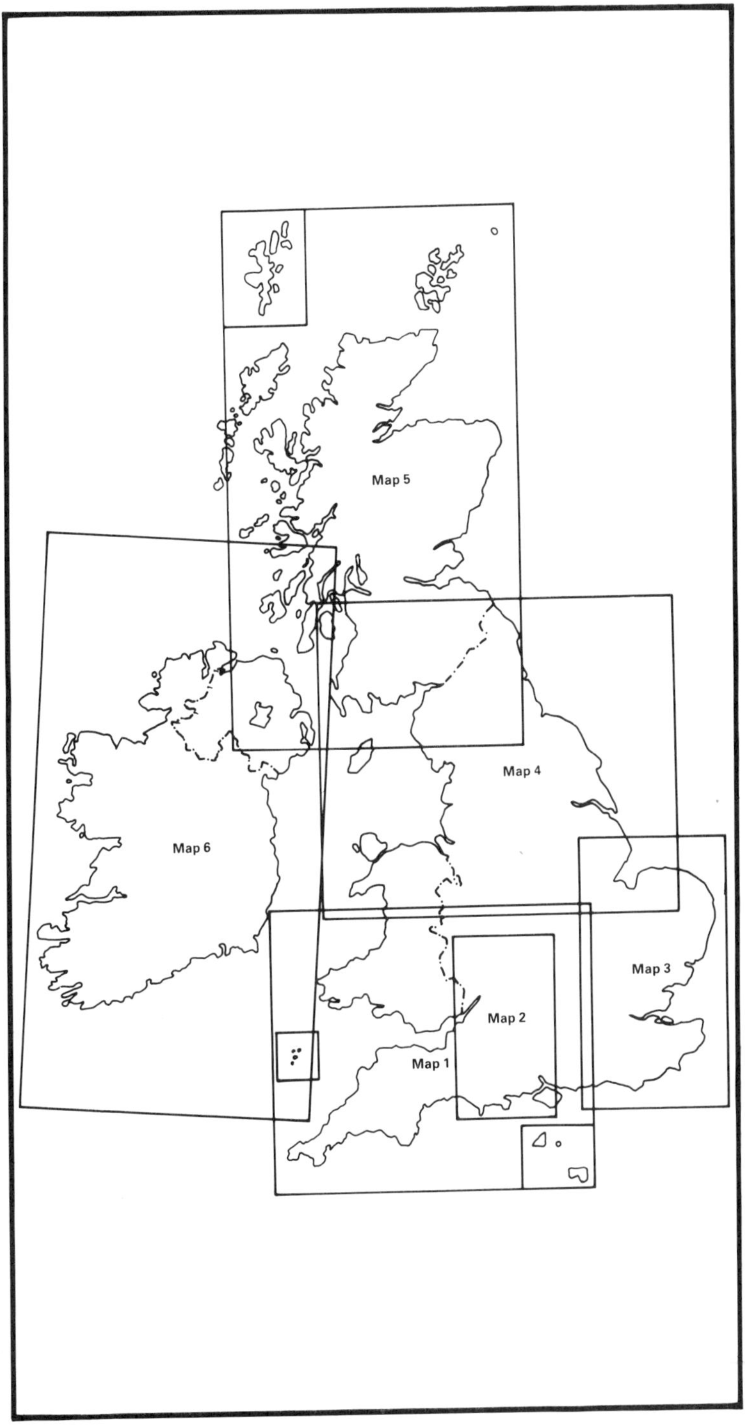

Map 1 South-West England and South Wales

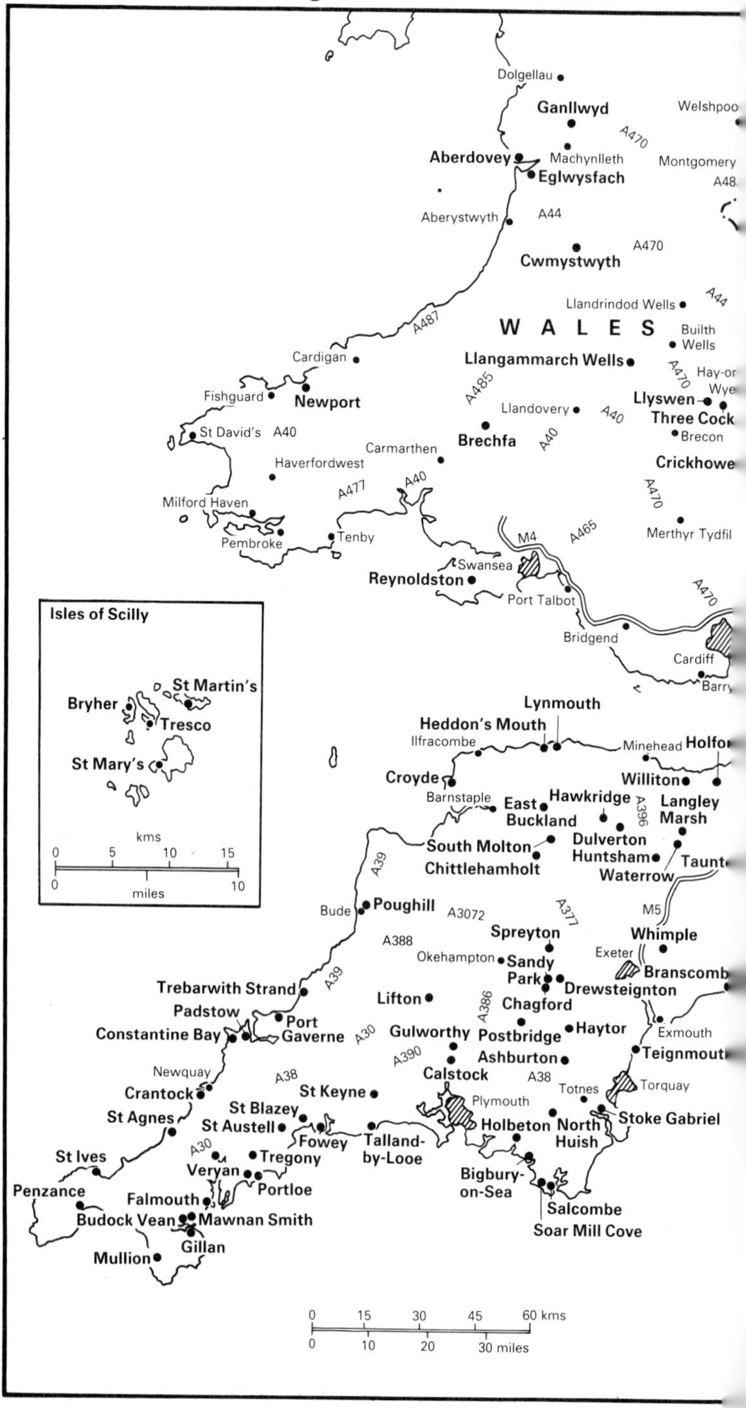

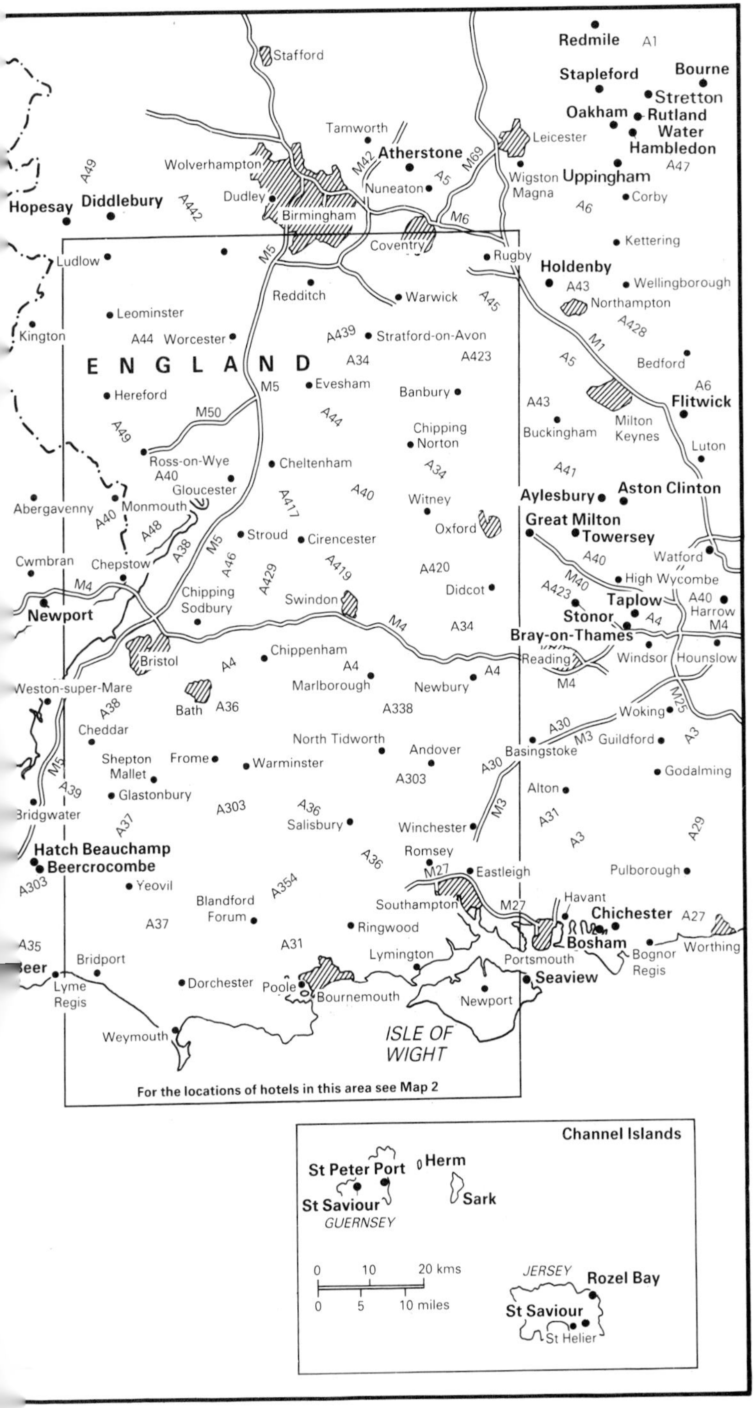
ENGLAND
Redmile
Stapleford
Bourne
Stretton
Oakham
Rutland Water
Hambledon
Uppingham
Holdenby
Atherstone
Hopesay
Diddlebury
Stafford
Tamworth
Leicester
Wolverhampton
Dudley
Birmingham
Nuneaton
Coventry
Wigston Magna
Corby
Kettering
Rugby
Wellingborough
Northampton
Ludlow
Redditch
Warwick
Leominster
Kington
Worcester
Stratford-on-Avon
Bedford
Hereford
Evesham
Banbury
Flitwick
Milton Keynes
Buckingham
Luton
Chipping Norton
Ross-on-Wye
Cheltenham
Gloucester
Aylesbury
Aston Clinton
Abergavenny
Monmouth
Witney
Oxford
Great Milton
Towersey
Stroud
Cirencester
Watford
Cwmbran
Chepstow
High Wycombe
Didcot
Taplow
Harrow
Chipping Sodbury
Stonor
Newport
Swindon
Bray-on-Thames
Windsor
Hounslow
Reading
Bristol
Chippenham
Marlborough
Newbury
Weston-super-Mare
Bath
Woking
Cheddar
North Tidworth
Basingstoke
Guildford
Andover
Shepton Mallet
Frome
Warminster
Godalming
Alton
Glastonbury
Bridgwater
Salisbury
Winchester
Hatch Beauchamp
Beercrocombe
Romsey
Eastleigh
Pulborough
Yeovil
Havant
Blandford Forum
Southampton
Chichester
Ringwood
Bosham
Worthing
Portsmouth
Bognor Regis
Bridport
Lymington
Seaview
Beer
Lyme Regis
Dorchester
Poole
Bournemouth
Newport
Weymouth
ISLE OF WIGHT
A1
A47
A6
A5
A43
A45
A428
M1
M6
M69
M42
M5
A49
A442
A44
A439
A34
A423
M50
A40
A41
A417
A48
A38
A46
A429
A419
A420
M40
M4
A4
A36
A338
A30
M3
M25
A3
A303
A39
A37
A31
A354
M27
A27
A29
A35
For the locations of hotels in this area see Map 2
Channel Islands
St Peter Port
Herm
Sark
St Saviour
GUERNSEY
0
10
20 kms
0
5
10 miles
JERSEY
Rozel Bay
St Saviour
St Helier

Map 2 Wessex and the Cotswolds

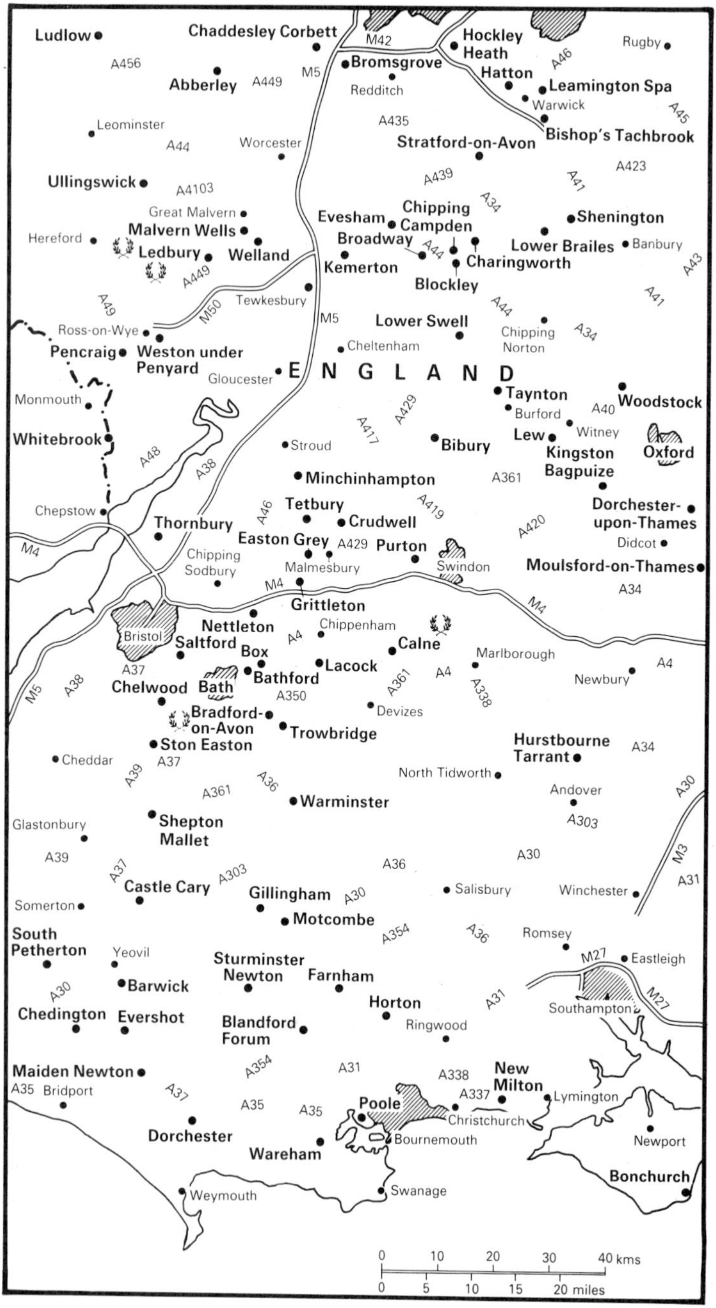

Map 3 South-East England

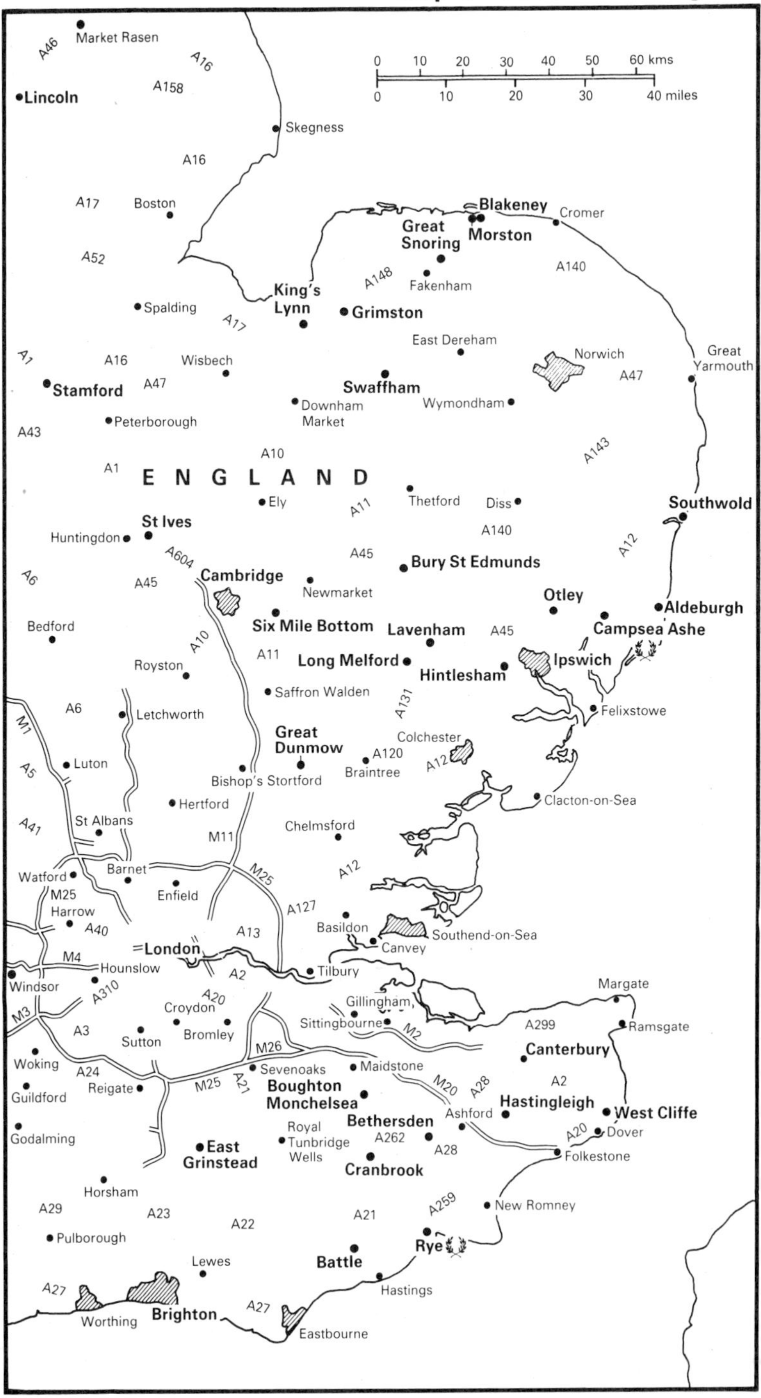

Map 4 North Wales, the Midlands and the North of England

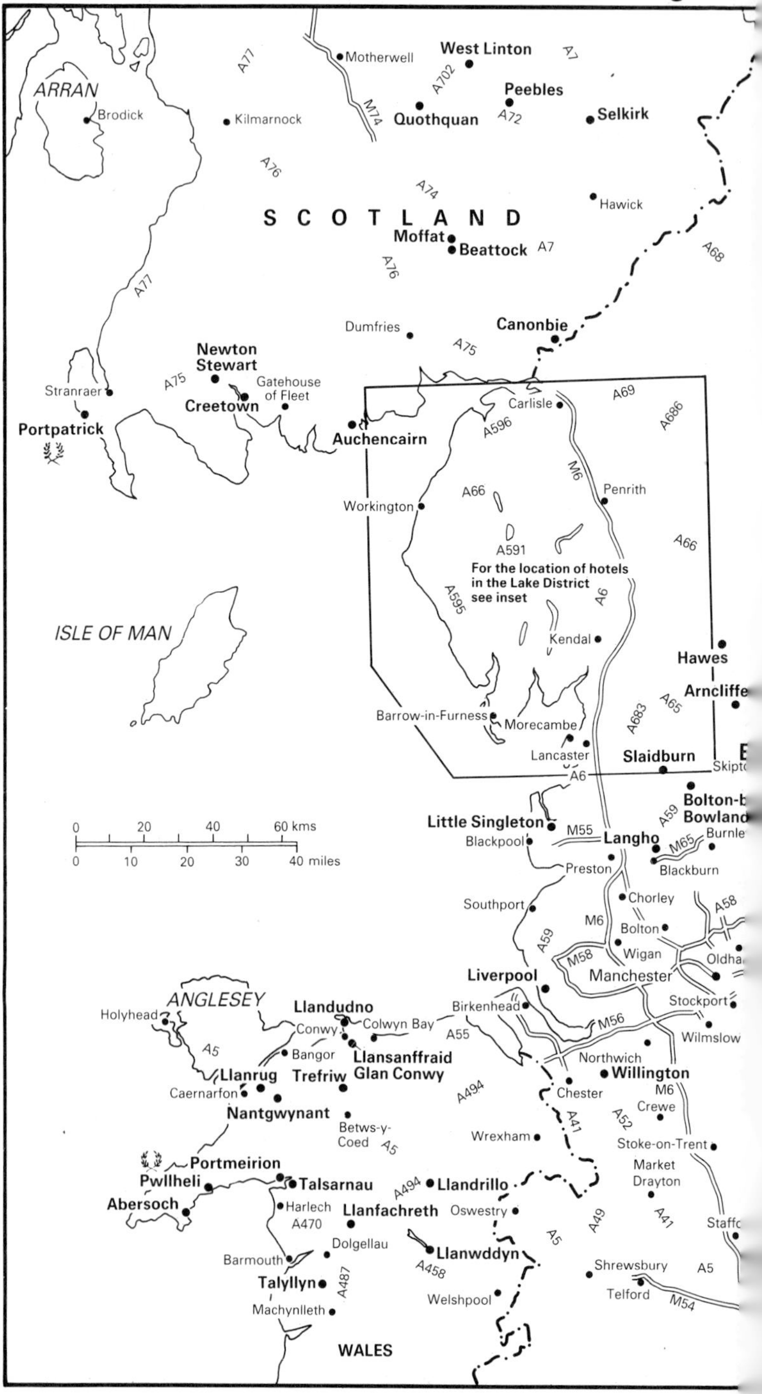

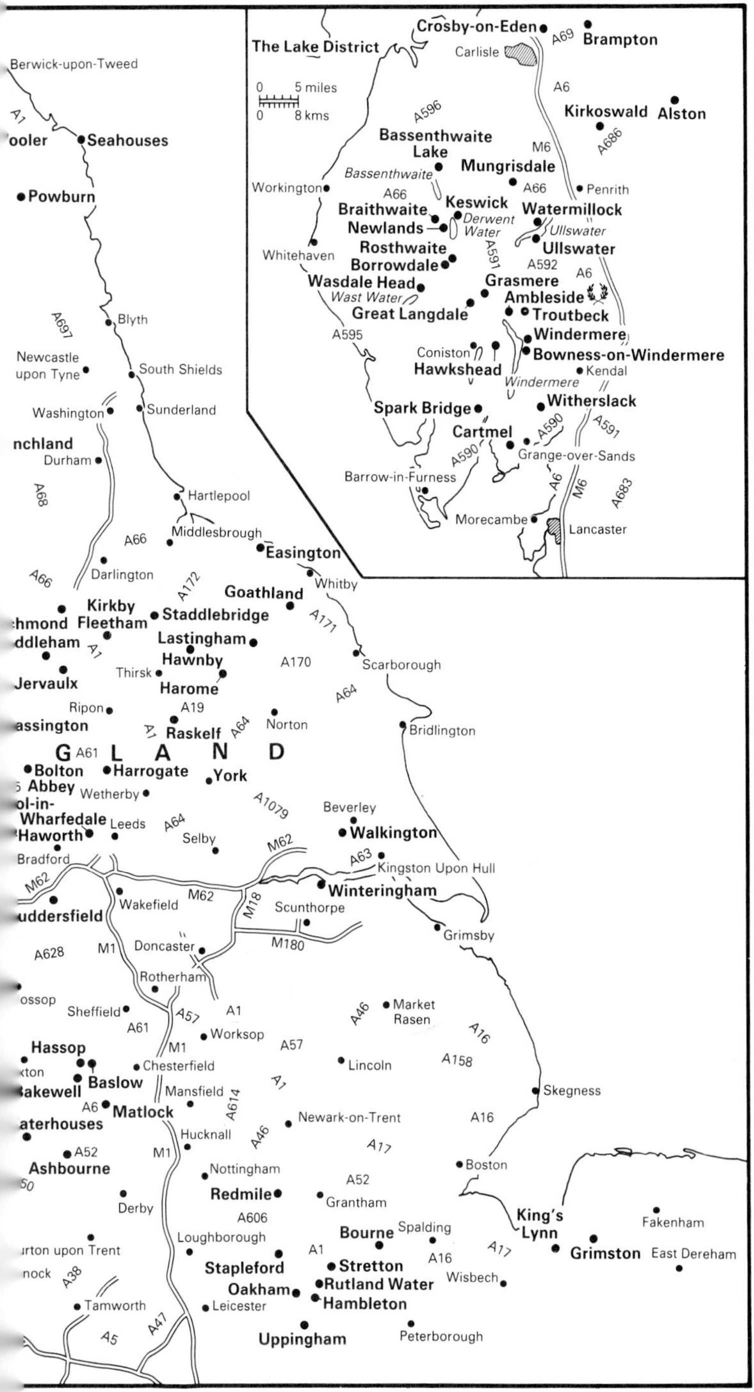

The Lake District

```
0        5 miles
|‑‑|‑|‑|‑|‑|
0        8 kms
```

Crosby-on-Eden
Carlisle
Brampton
A69
Kirkoswald
Alston
A6
M6
A686
Bassenthwaite Lake
Workington
Bassenthwaite
A66
Mungrisdale
A66
Penrith
Braithwaite
Keswick
Watermillock
Newlands
Derwent Water
Ullswater
Whitehaven
Rosthwaite
Ullswater
Borrowdale
A591
A592
A6
Wasdale Head
Grasmere
Wast Water
Ambleside
Great Langdale
Troutbeck
A595
Windermere
Coniston
Bowness-on-Windermere
Hawkshead
Kendal
Windermere
Spark Bridge
Witherslack
Cartmel
A590
A591
Barrow-in-Furness
A590
Grange-over-Sands
A6
M6
A683
Morecambe
Lancaster

Berwick-upon-Tweed
A1
ooler
Seahouses
Powburn
A697
Blyth
Newcastle upon Tyne
South Shields
Washington
Sunderland
nchland
Durham
A68
Hartlepool
A66
Middlesbrough
Easington
A66
Darlington
Whitby
Goathland
Kirkby
Staddlebridge
A172
A171
hmond
Fleetham
Lastingham
Scarborough
ddleham
A1
Hawnby
A170
Thirsk
Jervaulx
Harome
Ripon
A19
assington
A1
Raskelf
Norton
A64
Bridlington
G A61 L A N D
Bolton
Harrogate
York
Abbey
Wetherby
ol-in-
Beverley
Wharfedale
Leeds
A64
Walkington
Haworth
Selby
M62
A63
Bradford
Kingston Upon Hull
M62
Winteringham
uddersfield
Wakefield
M62
M118
Scunthorpe
Grimsby
A628
M1
Doncaster
M180
ossop
Rotherham
Sheffield
A57
A1
A46
Market Rasen
Hassop
A61
Worksop
A16
xton
Chesterfield
A57
A158
akewell
Baslow
M1
Lincoln
Skegness
A6
Matlock
Mansfield
A1
A614
aterhouses
Hucknall
A46
Newark-on-Trent
A16
Ashbourne
M1
A17
A52
Boston
Derby
Nottingham
Redmile
A52
Fakenham
urton upon Trent
Loughborough
Grantham
King's Lynn
nock
A38
A606
Bourne
Spalding
Grimston
East Dereham
Tamworth
A1
Stapleford
Stretton
A16
A17
A5
A47
Oakham
Rutland Water
Wisbech
Leicester
Hambleton
Uppingham
Peterborough
```

# Map 5 Scotland

# Map 6 Ireland

# Hotel reports

The report forms on the following pages may be used to endorse or criticise an existing entry or to nominate a hotel that you feel deserves inclusion in next year's guide. Either way, there is no need to use our forms or, if you do, to restrict yourself to the space available. All nominations (each on a separate piece of paper, please) should include your name and address, the name and location of the hotel, when you stayed there and for how long. Please nominate only hotels you have visited in the past twelve months unless you are sure from friends that standards have not fallen since your stay. And please be as specific as possible, and critical where appropriate, about the character of the building, the public rooms and the bedrooms, the meals, the service, the nightlife, the grounds. We should be glad if you would give some impression of the location as well as of the hotel itself, particularly in less familiar regions. And any comments about worthwhile places to visit in the neighbourhood and – in the case of bed-and-breakfast hotels – recommendable restaurants in the area, would also be much appreciated.

You should not feel embarrassed about writing at length. More than anything else, we want the guide to convey the special flavour of its hotels; so the more time and trouble you can take in providing those small details which will help to make a description come alive, the more valuable to others will be the final published result. Many nominations just don't tell us enough. We mind having to pass up a potentially attractive hotel because the report is inadequate. There is no need to bother with prices or with routine information about number of rooms and facilities. We obtain such details direct from the hotels selected. What we are anxious to get from readers is information that is not accessible elsewhere. And we should be extremely grateful, in the case of foreign hotels and new nominations, to be sent brochures if you have them available. Nominations for the 1993 edition, which will be printed in the UK in autumn 1992, should reach us not later than 25 May 1992. The latest date for comments on existing entries is 5 June 1992. Our address is Europe's Wonderful Little Hotels and Inns, 61 Clarendon Road, London W11 4JE, England or, if posted in the UK, Freepost, London W11 4BR (no stamp needed).

We would ask you please never to let on to a hotel your intention to file a report. Anonymity is essential to objectivity. We would not have thought it necessary to say this, but we have heard that some readers have made a habit of telling hotel managers or owners that they would be reporting to us.

Please let us know if you would like more report forms, which may also be used, if you wish, to recommend good hotels and inns in North America to our equivalent publication in the US, America's Wonderful Little Hotels and Inns. Its address is PO Box 150, Riverside, Conn. 06878, USA.

*Champagne winners*

As usual we have awarded a dozen bottles of champagne for the best reports of the year, and a bottle apiece will go to the following generous and eloquent readers: Mr Alan Blyth, Miss Amanda Craig, Mr Robin Houston and Mr Felix Singer, all of London; Mrs Moira Jarrett of Welwyn, Herts; Mr ATW Liddell of Middleton Stoney, Oxfordshire; Mr RAL Ogston of Ludlow, Shropshire; Mr Denis E O'Mulloy of Cambridge; Mr Dave Watts of Theydon Bois, Essex; Dr and Mrs A Winterbourne of Mouguerre, France, and Mr John Stege of Macon, Georgia, USA.

A further case will be on offer for 1993. No special entry form is required; everything we receive in the course of the year will qualify. A winner may be someone who nominates a new hotel or comments on an existing one. We award champagne to those whose reports are consistently useful as well as to individually brilliant examples of the art of hotel criticism.

[1992]

To: *The Good Hotel Guide,* Freepost, London W11 4BR

NOTE: No stamps needed in UK, but letters posted outside the UK should be addressed to 61 Clarendon Road, London W11 4JE and stamped normally. Unless asked not to, we shall assume that we may publish your name if you are recommending a new hotel or supporting an existing entry. If you would like more report forms please tick ☐

Name of Hotel ______________________________

Address ______________________________

______________________________

Date of most recent visit

☐ New recommendation

Duration of visit

☐ Comment on existing entry

Report:

*I am not connected directly or indirectly with the management or proprietors*

Signed ______________________________

Name and address (capitals please) ______________________________

______________________________